JOCELYN BAINES

Joseph Conrad

A Critical Biography

PENGUIN BOOKS

Penguin Books Ltd, Harmondsworth, Middlesex, England
Viking Penguin Inc., 40 West 23rd Street, New York, New York 10010, U.S.A.
Penguin Books Australia Ltd, Ringwood, Victoria, Australia
Penguin Books Canada Limited, 2801 John Street, Markham, Ontario, Canada L3R 1B4
Penguin Books (N.Z.) Ltd, 182–190 Wairau Road, Auckland 10, New Zealand

—

First published by Weidenfeld and Nicolson 1960
Published in Pelican Books 1971
Reprinted in this edition 1986

—

—

Printed and bound in Great Britain by
Cox & Wyman Ltd, Reading
Set in Intertype Baskerville

To Claire

Contents

Acknowledgements and Note on the Text

It is impossible to mention all those who have helped me in the writing of this book with acts of kindness and I hope that they will accept my thanks expressed in a general form; I hope also that I shall be forgiven by anyone whose name has been inadvertently left out of the list that follows.

Among those to whom I am particularly indebted are: Miss Róża Jabłkowska for supplying me with a typescript of most of the Polish material, Professor Kwiatkowski, who helped me with the Polish background, Mr Zdzislaw Najder who generously put his valuable original research at my disposal and Dr Wit Tarnawski for numerous kindnesses; Mrs Ilsa Barea, Count Melgar, and Mr Xavier de Salas, who helped me with the Spanish material; Mlle Forget, Professor Marcel Clavel, and M. Charles Salvi who gave me information connected with Conrad's stay in Marseilles; Mr James Graham, Mr F. Harold Gray, and Ir. R. Haverschmidt for their help over Conrad's period in the East Indies; Mr J. Vinson for supplying material connected with Conrad's stay in Mauritius; Mr Frank MacShane and Mr Edgar Wright, who helped me in many ways and allowed me to read their theses on the work of Ford Madox Hueffer and Conrad respectively; Professor Albert Guerard, who allowed me to read the galley-proofs of his *Conrad the Novelist* (unfortunately my manuscript was already finished and so I have only been able to make brief, inadequate reference to this profound study); Mr John Halverson and Professor Ian Watt for allowing me to use the typescript of their article, 'The Original Nostromo', before it was published; Dr John D. Gordan, Mrs Katherine Lamb, and Mr R. H. Sauter for letting me read and quote from the originals or copies of unpublished letters from Conrad to James B. Pinker, Ford Madox Hueffer, and John Galsworthy and for doing everything possible to enable me to get the text of these letters correct; Professor William Blackburn, who allowed me to read the galley-proofs of his *Joseph Conrad; Letters to William Blackwood and David S. Meldrum* and the typescript of a number of unpublished letters written by Conrad; Sir Harold Nicolson for help in many ways; Dr Robert F. Metzdorf and Miss Marjorie G. Wynne, who have done everything possible to make the magnificent Yale collection of Conradiana easily available to me; Messrs Borys and John Conrad and Richard Curle for countless acts of kindness and for an apparently inexhaustible patience in the face of endless questions and requests; Mrs Danilewicz, Mr Benedict Nicolson, Mr Oliver Warner, Dr I. Wieniewski, and Mr Angus Wilson, who read parts or the whole of the manuscript: they have made many suggestions that I have adopted and have enabled me to correct many mistakes.

I want particularly to thank Mr Adam Truscoe for translating or summarizing all the Polish material that I have used and Miss Ann Grubb for typing a very messy manuscript.

Among my biographical predecessors I acknowledge my debts to G. J. Aubry whose 'official' *Joseph Conrad; Life and Letters*, compiled with assiduous respect, has greatly eased my task. I want also to pay particular tribute to John D. Gordan on whose outstandingly fine work of scholarship, *Joseph Conrad; the Making of a Novelist*, I have much depended when covering Conrad's period in the East and his beginnings as a writer.

It is even more difficult to acknowledge indebtedness to Conrad's critics, particularly as I have tended only to mention them when I have disagreed with them. I hope that they will accept a general acknowledgement and will forgive me if I appear to have plagiarized them. I must confine myself to mentioning that I have found the critical writings of Mr Edward Crankshaw, Professor Albert J. Guerard, Mr Douglas Hewitt, Mr F. R. Leavis, and Professor Morton D. Zabel particularly stimulating.

Numbered references to the sources on which this book has been based are given on pp. 555–593; when, however, a reference leads to a comment of substantial relevance to the text it is incorporated in a footnote. I have always tried to use original sources, but sometimes, particularly in the case of published letters, this has not been possible. For convenience reference is made to the printed text of all published letters regardless of whether the originals have been consulted, but discrepancies between my version and the source referred to are, at least in intention, reversions to the original. The text of the letters printed in Aubry's 'official' *Joseph Conrad; Life and Letters* (here abbreviated as *L.L.*) is unfortunately unreliable. There are numerous small and several important mistakes, while the punctuation has been arbitrarily 'corrected' throughout. It would have been unsatisfactory, because inconsistent, to print some letters exactly as they were written and others in Aubry's style. I have therefore compromised to the extent of adopting a standard punctuation and spelling out in full all insignificant abbreviations. The only exception is in the case of Conrad's letters to Mme Poradowska, which are printed, again in intention, substantially as they were written. The reason is that they provide a unique opportunity to see how Conrad wrote French – a subject on which much nonsense has been spread and believed.

Thaddeus Bobrowski's letters to Conrad are in the National Library of Warsaw; Apollo Korzeniowski's letters to Casimir Kaszewski, the Buszczyński letters, and the 'Bobrówski Document' are in the Jagellon Library, Cracow. Conrad's letters to William Blackwood and David Meldrum are quoted from Professor Blackburn's edition, mentioned above; his letters to Richard Curle are quoted from *Conrad to a Friend; 150 Selected Letters from Joseph Conrad to Richard Curle*, his letters to Edward Garnett from *Letters from Conrad, 1895–1924*. The whereabouts of other letters, etc., is given, as far as possible, after the relevant quotation, in the notes or in the list of acknowledgements.

Since this book was published Mr Zdzislaw Najder has published much important material on Conrad, above all, *Conrad's Polish Background* (Oxford, 1964). I have only been able to make a handful of corrections to this printing as a result of his work but I would like to refer readers to this book for the finely edited, full text of the Conrad/Bobrowski material.

All quotations from Conrad's writings are made from the Uniform Edition (the Medallion Edition has the same pagination). I am grateful to the Conrad Estate and to Messrs J. M. Dent for permission to quote from Conrad's works and from those letters of which they own the copyright.

[I]

Polish Years

APOLLO and Evelina Nałęcz Korzeniowski had been married for eighteen months when, on 3 December 1857, their first and only child was born.[1] He was christened Józef Teodor after his respective grandfathers and Konrad presumably after the hero of Mickiewicz's epic patriotic poem, *Konrad Wallenrod*. And he was a Nałęcz Korzeniowski, Nałęcz being the heraldic name of the family coat-of-arms.

There had been strong and protracted opposition to the marriage from Evelina's parents, the Bobrowskis, for although the Korzeniowskis were an old and respected family of landed gentry the Bobrowskis justifiably feared an unreliable strain in them. We owe most of our knowledge of the character of the two families to Evelina's brother Thaddeus, who, after the death of Conrad's parents, was to become his self-appointed guardian. Thaddeus's picture of the Korzeniowskis is doubtless biased, because he was temperamentally the antithesis of all that they seemed to represent; but he was also a very fair-minded man. He seems to have had the mentality of a genial family lawyer; to have been a kind, sympathetic, indulgent but cautious, precise, and practical man with a touch of complacency and self-righteousness.

He caustically describes Apollo's father, Theodor, as a brave if narrow-minded soldier who was firmly convinced that he was 'the first warrior in Europe, an excellent estate administrator, and a man whose services to the country were unequalled; but, in point of fact, he was nothing but a utopian'.[2] In support of this Thaddeus says that Theodor was so incompetent that he lost the estate and village given as his wife's dowry together with 'the rest of their money in his mismanagement of the Korytna estate'. Thaddeus also says that 'he considered himself a great politician and a supreme patriot; without listening to common sense he was always ready to saddle a horse and chase the enemy out of the country'.[3] Conrad has added to the portrait of his grandfather the information that he 'wrote a tragedy in 5 Acts, verse, privately printed, and so extremely dull that no one was ever known to have read it through'.[4] He was apparently very proud of his three sons, Robert, Hilary, and Apollo, although, according to Thaddeus, Robert 'was an inveterate card-player and drunkard, who, having contributed largely to the ruin of his own family, was killed in 1863', in the insurrection. Hilary does not come off much better. He was, writes Thaddeus, a utopian like his father; he was full of impractical schemes, of whose soundness he was able to convince others as well as himself. Just before the insurrection of 1863 he was exiled to Tomsk, where 'he again tried his hand at farming . . . and engaged in various speculations until he died in 1878, leaving nothing but debts – just as he had in the Ukraine'.[5]

Apollo, too, shared several of his father's characteristics, but here Thaddeus's censure is tempered by strong affection and some respect, although there is always a tinge of condescension and it is unlikely that any of Apollo's faults would have escaped him. Thaddeus and Apollo had been to school together in Żytomierz (Zitomir), but there was too big a difference between their ages – Apollo was nine years older – for any close friendship at that time. They both went to St Petersburg University, where Thaddeus read law and Apollo, who apparently went down without graduating, read Oriental languages and Law;[6] but it was only later, in the provinces, that they became close friends. Thaddeus says that Apollo was the only man in the whole district whom he could 'get together with and like'.[7] The friendly feelings were mutual, and Apollo evidently admired Thaddeus's balance and sanity. There is an early letter from Apollo to Thaddeus which strikingly illustrates the difference between the two men's characters, and incidentally shows elements of the same temperament with which Thaddeus had to contend in the case of the young Conrad:

After reading your letter, I was simultaneously sad and content. Sad, because I read of a truth both sad and impossible for me to fulfil; content because I feel that what you wrote is the expression of your conviction, the norm of your life, which in such wise can provide few disappointments; even those it does provide are first foreseen and hence less painful. But what is evident truth for some, for others in view of their spiritual disposition, owing to a tangle of circumstances, and the exhaustion of moral force, becomes a good impossible to be attained. Nevertheless, it is necessary to strive for it; and when the brow is covered with sweat, when inspiration fails in one's breast, when the wounded foot steps ever more slowly and painfully – it is still necessary to pay heed to the voice that calls to us: Go on – go on further! It is necessary to exert every effort and all one's strength to reach – what? The Lord only knows.

It all seems to be a *romance*, but, believe me, it's real. What can we call the essence of life? The efforts, serious and petty troubles of everyday life aimed at gaining an existence independent in the sense of pecuniary and material matters? Or, else, a bent for material pleasures, becoming a vicious habit, which is transformed into second nature, where the animal prevails over the man? Or, as you state, an honest life, with the purpose of spreading good, to the best of one's ability, around oneself?

I am floundering in these everyday troubles and sinking – hopelessly. In self-justification I shall only say: that it is not for my own sake. The second I used to apply formerly, as a medicine against the disease of dreaming – but it is not omnipotent. It often sufficed to experience one word, one glance of a superior being, to make me disgusted with such a life, and I again fell into that half-angelic, half-human state, so unbearable yet at the same time as intoxicating as opium.

The third I regard as the poetry of life, the most beautiful poetry – for in it I see beauty, truth, and good, ennobling the soul which has given itself to me alone [*sic*].

I am as if on the eve of some great solemn festivity: I know that the next day will be a holiday with every pleasure and delight, but in the meantime, for me, there are only fasts and mortifications.

It is not my wont to complain of fate. The few careless words in my previous letter gave you reason to draw up that noble proclamation which I can at least feel and comprehend. I thank you for it. I needed to make a partial confession; for it to be complete would require too much space and time; so I release you from it.

Though, if I entered into the details of my life, I would perhaps convince you that it is not my fault that I am what I am!

Let us speak of you. I don't believe much in my future – but I have blind confidence in the future of people whom I love. [11 May 1849]

He then goes on to tear to shreds with witty malice the provincial family whose estate he is supposed to be helping to manage.

Thaddeus has given in his memoirs his opinion of Apollo's character at this time:

He had established the reputation in the country of being very ugly and excessively sarcastic. In actual fact he was certainly not beautiful, bah! not even handsome but the expression of his eyes was very pleasant, and his malice was only verbal – of the drawing-room type; for neither in his feelings nor in his actions did I ever perceive it. Violent in emotions, unreservedly and sincerely loving people; unpractical in his deeds, often helpless and unresourceful. In speech and writing often implacable, in everyday life he was frequently far too indulgent – evidently for the sake of balance, as I demonstrated to him many times; last but not least, he had what I call two sets of weights and measures – for the very little and silly, and for the mighty of this world . . .

He was very pleasant in the drawing-rooms; he attracted women by his ugliness, his originality and his talents – we know how great is their interest in all they are ignorant of. Men liked him for his ease in conversation and his unfailing courtesy, his traditional old Polish attention to his elders and his delicacy towards those younger than he. . . . When he chose to practice what may be called his 'public' malice he chose his victims from among those who had in some way harmed him or who were in general puffed up in wealth or rank, and here he usually had the laughter on his side.[8]

Thaddeus liked to think that the Bobrowskis, in contrast, exemplified the qualities of sanity and reliability. But not all the Bobrowskis were staid and balanced. Thaddeus's Uncle Nicholas, who of all Conrad's relations seems most to have captured his imagination, apparently had some qualities at least in common with Theodor Korzeniowski. He had gone into the army at the age of sixteen, which had restricted his education and outlook. He had served under Napoleon in the Russian campaign and for the rest of his life Napoleon remained his god. Although he had a melancholy temperament and lived the life of a recluse he could at times be impulsive; he was fundamentally a weak and vacillating character, but fortunately was very ready to submit to his brother's opinions with regard to his own affairs. This perhaps was why, unlike Theodor Korzeniowski, he did not squander his wife's fortune. He was a brave and honest man, but very egotistical, although he never liked to talk about his military exploits.[9] Thaddeus's brother, Stanislas, was a gay and likeable guards officer with the Korzeniowski habit of getting into debt;[10] while another brother, Stephen, whom Thaddeus describes with enthusiasm and respect, played a leading part in the preparations for the 1863 insurrection. He was killed, or rather, in view of his nearsightedness, murdered, in a duel in 1863, probably for political reasons, but the cause of the quarrel was apparently never known for certain.[11]

(2)

Apollo Korzeniowski's courting of Evelina Bobrowski brought to a head the difference of attitude in the two families. The Bobrowskis cannot be blamed for their opposition to the marriage and the future was to confirm their worst fears. Thaddeus writes:

> My parents were by no means anxious to have him as a son-in-law. My mother liked his company and his mode of life, but could not perceive in him any qualifications for a good husband; she agreed with my father that, having no profession, – for he lived at his father's home, occupying himself with nothing and owning nothing – he was an undesirable suitor in spite of his pleasant society manners.[12]

Later in his memoirs Thaddeus uses much the same words, amplifying the opinion of his father, who 'considered that he [Apollo] lacked practical acumen and resourcefulness, that he was by nature idle, for, though in theory managing his father's estate, he read, wrote and rode more than he worked'.[13]

Joseph Bobrowski made it clear to Apollo that he did not want him to marry Evelina and dangled various eligible girls in front of him, but Apollo refused to be tempted. Even after Joseph Bobrowski died his wife continued to oppose the marriage out of respect for his wishes.

In despair Apollo retired to his home province of Podolia, where he took the post of an estate manager.* Some time later, however, he heard that Evelina and her mother were staying nearby, at Terekov, with Mrs Bobrowska's brother, Adolf Pilchowski, who was reputed to enjoy furthering the love-affairs of the young. With revived hope, Apollo went over to Terekov. It was now five years after Joseph Bobrowski's death and eight since Apollo and Evelina had first met. The situation had been putting a strain on Evelina's health, which was never very good, and it is probable that Mrs Bobrowska had taken her daughter to Terekov with the aim of getting the matter settled. At any rate, with the help of Adolf Pilchowski, Apollo was able to persuade Mrs Bobrowska to let him become engaged to Evelina, and on 8 May 1856 they were married in the parish church of Oratov;[14] Apollo was then thirty-six and Evelina twenty-three.

Thaddeus had an intense love and admiration for his sister, Evelina. Many years later Conrad told Garnett:

> There was an extraordinary Sister-Cult in that family from which I profited when left an orphan at the age of ten. And my mother was certainly no ordinary woman. Her correspondence with my father and with her brothers which in the year 1890 I have read and afterwards destroyed was a revelation to me; I shall never forget my delight, admiration and unutterable regret at my loss (before I could appreciate her), which only then I fully understood.[15]

Evelina died in 1865, when Conrad was seven, and he writes

* Bobrowski, *Pamiętniki*, II, 67. Podolia was a Little Russian province of the Tsar, which had been part of the Polish Commonwealth from 1385 until the Partition of 1793; the Poles formed a minority of about twelve per cent but most of the land was in Polish ownership.

in *A Personal Record* that 'this is . . . the year in which I first begin to remember my mother with more distinctness than a mere loving, wide-browed, silent, protecting presence, whose eyes had a sort of commanding sweetness'.[16] He fills out his portrait of Evelina with a passage taken almost verbatim from Thaddeus's memoirs, which he turns into a conversation between Thaddeus and himself during one of his visits to Poland. Thaddeus had written:

> My elder sister possessed the fine outer appearance of a woman of the world and with a higher level of education than was usual among women of our class. She was capable of soaring flights of intellect and heart and had a less easygoing nature, making far greater demands and, at that period, requiring more attention from others than she was ready or able to give them. Being of rather feeble health and struggling between love for her future husband and the expressed will of her father, whose memory and judgment she respected, she was unable to maintain her moral balance. Dissatisfied with herself, she could not give others that inner contentment which she lacked. It was only after her union with the man she loved that she developed in later life those rare qualities of intellect and emotion, mind and heart, which distinguished her. Amidst the most unpleasant upheavals in her personal life, in which all the national and social hardships appeared, she always succeeded in fulfilling the role imposed by the duties of a wife, a mother and citizen, sharing her husband's exile and worthily representing the ideal of Polish womanhood. She thus gained the respect and veneration of her own people and of others.[17]

As Thaddeus says, Evelina's short married life was not easy. The Korzeniowskis spent the first year at Łuczyniec, where Apollo had taken a post of estate manager while they were waiting for the Bobrowski estate of Oratov to be sold so that the dowry could be paid. Apollo seems to have been concerned less with managing the estate than with his writing and he liked to take refuge in a wood on the land of his friend and neighbour Stephen Buszczyński.[18] When the dowry was paid, the Korzeniowskis, with the additional help of Evelina's mother, took the lease of Derebczynka Manor, near Berdichev in the Ukraine,* in order to farm the estate, and it was here that Conrad was born. Like other Korzeniowskis, Apollo had no aptitude for practical affairs and the family was forced to leave Derebczynka after three years, having lost nearly all the money invested in it.[19]

After the failure of this venture Apollo seems to have decided to devote himself exclusively to his real interests: literature, and political activity aiming at the liberation of the Poles from foreign rule. He had already got a small body of work to his credit. He had written a couple of comedies, *Komedia* (*Comedy*) and *Dla miłego grosza* (*For the Love of Money*), as well as a number of poems, mostly of a mystically religious and patriotic nature; he had also translated Vigny's *Chatterton* and contributed a preface extolling Vigny's philosophy of life.[20] Now he went to Żytomierz, the seat of a Catholic bishopric, and a lively intellectual centre presided over by J. I. Kraszewski, Poland's most prominent and prolific novelist of the period. There he joined a group engaged in publishing popular literature to educate the peasants. He also began a translation of Hugo's *Légende des Siècles* in collaboration with the novelist Adam Plug, and the two men planned to do a complete translation of Hugo's works; the first part of the *Légende* was published in 1860, followed by *Hernani* in 1862 and *Marion Delorme* in 1863.[21] Kraszewski was at this time directing the theatre at Żytomierz, and put on Apollo's *Dla miłego grosza.*[22]

As to political activity, it was almost inevitable for any patriotic Pole to become involved in this as long as the nation was forcibly divided and dominated by foreign powers. There were of course Poles who appeared to have reconciled themselves to the situation. But the majority seem to have differed merely as to the best means of freeing themselves from foreign domination and once again becoming an independent nation.

* This Little Russian area had, like Podolia, formed part of the Polish Commonwealth from 1385 until the Partition of 1793, but the Polish element was much sparser, consisting of about three per cent, mostly landowners.

Thaddeus has described Apollo's political attitude:

Though he considered himself a sincere democrat and others even considered him 'extremist' and 'red' he had a hundredfold more traits of the gentry in him (as I often told him) than I had in myself, though I was not suspected, either by him or by others, of being a democrat. In point of fact, he had an exceedingly tender and soft heart – hence his great sympathy for the poor and oppressed; and this was why he and others thought he was a democrat. But these were only impulses of the heart and mind inherent in a member of a good family of the gentry; they were not truly democratic convictions. I could never establish the real composition of his political and social ideas, apart from a hazy inclination towards a republican form of state incorporating some equally hazy agglomeration of human rights as set out by the Constitution of May the Third – which for our times was not far-reaching enough.[23]

After the failure of the Polish insurrection of 1830 the greater part of the élite of the nation had gone into exile, to France, Belgium, or Britain. Cut off from their own country, they became increasingly remote from practicality. Many of them were infected by strange fantasies about Poland's messianic role and, under the influence of Towianski, there developed a cult of Napoleon and the House of Bonaparte.

Meanwhile, in Poland two groups were prominent. The larger maintained a dogged, if passive, resistance to foreign oppression, while the other, headed by the progressive-minded Count Wielopolski, realized the futility, at least for the present, of opposition and decided to see whether cooperation could not wheedle some valuable concessions from the Russians.

The outbreak of the Crimean War again raised Polish hopes, which had been dormant since the failure of the 1830 uprising. Among those stirred was Apollo who set about planning a revolt. He suggested that Thaddeus should join the conspiracy, but he, practical as ever, advised against a resort to force, recommending that the Polish landowners should grant land to the peasants and so win them over to the national cause;[24] it has, however, been suggested that Thaddeus was the author of an audaciously imaginative plan to cut off the Russian troops in the Crimea from their supply bases in Central Russia.[25] There was indeed a spontaneous uprising among the peasants of Podolia and the Ukraine and, according to Buszczyński, Apollo hurried there to try to provide some leadership, but the revolt was not supported by the gentry and was quickly and ruthlessly suppressed.[26]

The allies had let it be known that they had no intention of supporting any revolt against Russian imperialism; thus, despite the Russian defeat in the Crimea, the death of the hated Nicholas I, and Anglo-French support for Italian unity, the Poles gained nothing from the Treaty of Paris. Count Orlov, Alexander II's representative at the peace conference, was able to close his report to his chief, Nesselrode, with the words: 'I am completely gratified by the fact that I have not heard the name Poland pronounced at the sessions in the presence of the representatives of the great European powers.'[27] The Poles considered that they had been deceived and betrayed again; Thaddeus thought that they had only deceived themselves.[28]

The new Tsar did, however, inaugurate a far more liberal policy towards the Poles. He appointed the kindly Gorchakov Viceroy of Poland and proclaimed a general amnesty, promising to restore, upon good behaviour, full civil rights to political prisoners and exiles. An Academy of Medicine which the Poles hoped would be the forerunner of a national university was established in Warsaw; as was an Agricultural Society which, under the presidency of Andrew Zamoyski, became one of the centres of Polish national aspiration.[29]

But these were not the sort of developments to satisfy the extremists, among them Apollo Korzeniowski; for Polish national freedom seemed as far off as ever. Moreover, the extremists' influence had been strengthened by the failure of Poland to gain any national recognition by diplomatic methods at the peace conference and by the return of most of the exiles and political prisoners. The situation became increasingly tense, and in the summer of 1860 the funeral of

Mrs Sowińska, widow of the Polish general who died defending Warsaw in the 1830 uprising, was made the occasion of a mass demonstration. Thenceforth nearly every public occasion and national anniversary became the pretext for some sort of demonstration or disorder. In the new year some of the most hotheaded patriots and groups of students began to arrive in Warsaw. On 27 February a gigantic demonstration was charged by Russian troops and at least five people were killed. The Tsar was petitioned and did in fact grant certain reforms, as well as giving extensive powers over economic and cultural affairs to Wielopolski.[30] But important sections of the community were in no mood for gradual reform.

Apollo Korzeniowski had been in the forefront of the intense clandestine political activity in Żytomierz and in May he went to Warsaw ostensibly to found a new literary monthly of the same type as the *Revue des Deux Mondes*, to be called the *Dwutygodnik* (*Fortnightly*), but actually to be at the centre of political developments.[31] He had left his family in Żytomierz, but kept in close touch with Evelina, whose letters were full of rhapsodies on the sweetness and goodness of their three-year-old son. One letter, dated 23 May, is distinguished by the first piece of writing from Conrad's hand, though guided by his mother:

> Daddy, I like it here, I run about the garden, but I don't like it when the mosquitoes sting. I will come to Daddy when it stops raining. Olutek sent me a fine little whip, dear Daddy, lend me a groat and buy something for Olutek in Warsaw. Were you at that Barbara's where Grannie? Conrad

Another letter to Apollo from Żytomierz, from Conrad's grandmother, rounds off the impression of Conrad as a model child:

> Words cannot describe the sweetness of this child. He is very friendly with the poor, telling them family news and asking them to pray for the return of his father from Warsaw. I discovered this from the beggars at the church.[32]

In Warsaw there were two conflicting groups of Polish

patriots: the 'Whites' or conservatives revolving round Zamoyski and the Agricultural Society, who, at least at this time, were in favour of peaceful pressure on the Russians to grant the Polish national demands, and the Reds, composed chiefly of students and intellectuals who were agitating in favour of open opposition. It was to the 'Reds' that Apollo attached himself; one of those who took part in the troubles refers to him as the only influential person among the Reds.[33] He is described as 'an honourable but too ardent patriot'[34] and apparently 'went about Warsaw dressed in peasant fashion, in a peasant smock, frightful cap and knee-boots, attracting universal attention and exerting quite an influence on the youths gathered around him, by his intelligence, education, talent as a writer, and by his eloquence'.[35] He was one of the leaders of the demonstration in Warsaw on 12 August, the anniversary of the Union of Lublin (between Poland and Lithuania in 1569), and was reputedly the author of the leaflet calling on the populace to demonstrate.[36] Despite the mounting tension in Warsaw, Apollo was anxious to have his family with him. He had found rooms at 45 Nowy Świat, one of Warsaw's main streets, and in August or September was joined by his wife and child.[37] Evelina evidently knew about his political activities, in part at least, and must have realized the danger, but she was as ardent a patriot as her husband.

Apollo continued his political agitation and led the Red attempt to persuade the people not to vote in the municipal elections of 23 September, which produced accusations of treachery and broken promises from the Whites. He immediately set about organizing another mass demonstration to take place at Horodło on 10 October, the anniversary of the Union of Horodło (between Poland and Lithuania in 1413). Four days after the demonstration martial law was proclaimed and the Reds had to change their tactics; what had been legal was now illegal. On Apollo's initiative a clandestine City Committee was formed in Warsaw on 17 October, the day after Russian troops had ejected demonstrators from the Cathedral and churches. This committee subsequently developed into the Central National Committee and virtually controlled Polish opposition to Russia until the crushing of the 1863 insurrection. This was Apollo's last political action as a free man, because a few days later, on 21 October 1861, he was arrested and imprisoned in the citadel.[38]

According to Aubry, who was able to have the court records examined (they were burned during the last war), Apollo was accused of action against Wielopolski, of being the author of a pamphlet *Unia Litwy z Polska* (*Lithuania's Union with Poland*), and inciting people to sing the hymn *Boże coś Polske* ('God that hast Poland . . .') in church on the feast-day of the Tsarina. To this was added a further charge that he had wished to escape and had given his wife a plan of his cell.[39]

But a record of the proceedings of the Permanent Investigation Commission has survived, and that contains a different indictment. Apollo is accused of (i) organizing a secret committee with the name of 'Mierosławski's Reds', which was to oppose the elections to the Warsaw Municipal Council; (ii) having caused, with others, the disturbances in Miodowa Street and in Wedel's cake and coffee shop; (iii) being the author of the demand that Lithuania be united with Central Poland and of the pamphlet entitled *Narodzie! Baczność!* (*Nation! Attention!*); (iv) organizing in Żytomierz a requiem mass for those killed during the Warsaw demonstrations in 1861, when his wife was said to have pinned on mourning cockades.

The record states that the defendant did not admit his guilt, but that evidence against him was provided by his wife's letters and those of 'a certain Czarniecka of Żytomierz', which 'illustrated his inimical intentions' and warned him of the danger of arrest.*

* Record of the Permanent Investigation Commission, Part II, no. 4091. This was discovered by Najder in A.G.A.D. (Public Record Office of Ancient Documents). Presumably the discrepancy between the two versions of the indictment is explained by changes made during the various stages of the investigation.

The examining commission before which he had appeared over a period of six months handed him over to a military tribunal to be sentenced as a politically dangerous person. The president of the tribunal was a Colonel Roznow, a former colleague of Stanislas Bobrowski in the Grodno Hussars, and, perhaps for this reason, Apollo was sentenced to what was considered the rather mild punishment of exile to a distant Russian province.[40] Buszczyński says that the judges became so bored with the reading of the long verdict that they stopped it before the end and told Apollo to sign the document. Apollo replied that he would sign where the reading had been stopped, and the judges agreed. The record of the case states that Evelina was sentenced as well as Apollo, but Buszczyński claims that she volunteered to join her husband in exile and was allowed to do so provided she submitted to the same conditions as he; the court record is not conclusive evidence because the Russians had no desire to draw attention to people ready to become martyrs. On 8 May 1862 the Korzeniowskis left for their exile with an escort of two policemen, one for each of the adults. Again according to Buszczyński, preparations had been made to rescue Apollo before he left Warsaw, but he had refused, answering: 'I understand every sacrifice for the country; but you should not risk yourselves for an individual, and I have not such merits that you should sacrifice yourselves for me.'[41] Whether or not this is true it is in character and should not be dismissed as a piece of posturing; in other, less dramatic ways, Apollo showed himself to be a truly modest man.

What followed was a typical example of the unsystematic mixture of brutality and kindness which the monstrously incompetent Russian autocracy engendered. Apollo had asked for himself and his family to be sent to Perm, where the governor, Lashkarev, was a former schoolmate. Apparently Lashkarev heard about this and felt that he might be put in an embarrassing position, because the Korzeniowskis were turned back just before reaching Perm. They were then taken to Vologda, but on the way, outside Moscow, Conrad, who was now four years old, became dangerously ill. The escort was unwilling to stop, but the parents refused to go on with their son in this condition. A passer-by offered to find them a doctor from Moscow, and Apollo, remembering that Professor Dr Młodzianowski was at the University, sent him a note. Młodzianowski soon arrived and saved Conrad, who was suffering from pneumonia; but the local authorities refused to allow the journey to be further delayed. Apollo later caustically described the episode:

> The doctor applied leeches and medicine. Just at this point they started harnessing the horses. Naturally, I protested against continuing the journey particularly as the doctor expressed the opinion that the child might die if this were done. My passive resistance postponed the departure but caused my guard to report to the local tyrants. Most civilized; the report was noted and the decision was taken that, as a child is born only ultimately to die, the journey was to proceed at once.[42]

Then, when the party was near Nizhni Novgorod, Evelina became so weak that the escort had to carry her from post to post. But they refused to allow a halt. A passing guards officer saw what was happening and went back to Nizhni Novgorod to tell the local governor and chief-of-police of the escort's callous behaviour. The police chief at once rode off and ordered the journey to be interrupted. And when he found out that Evelina was the sister of the ubiquitous Stanislas, whose wild oats seem to have sprouted into a remarkable crop of goodwill, he took the family to a comfortable house in the town.

At last they arrived in Vologda, where they were treated with the greatest consideration by the governor, a very humane White Ruthenian named Chominsky. But this could not transform the climate or situation. Apollo described the place to his Zagórski cousins:

> What is Vologda? A Christian is not bound to know this. Vologda is a great three-verst marsh on which logs and trees are placed parallel to each other in crooked lines; everything rotting and shifting under one's feet; this is the only means of communication available to the natives. Alongside these logs, piles have been driven in at intervals and on these Italian villas have

been erected by the nobility of the province, all of whom live here. The climate consists of two seasons of the year: a white winter and a green winter. The white winter lasts nine-and-a-half months and the green one two-and-a-half. We are now on the onset of the green winter: it has already been raining ceaselessly for twenty-one days and that's how it will be to the end.

During the whole winter the frost remains at 25–30° [Réaumur] while the wind from the White Sea, held up by nothing, brings constant news from the polar bears. . . . The population is a nightmare: disease-ridden corpses. [16 June 1862, Vologda, *Tygodnik Illustrowany*, No. 4, 1920]

There has been preserved a charming memento from this period, a photograph of Conrad aged five with the inscription on the back: 'To my dear grandmother who helped me send cakes to my poor father in prison. Pole, Catholic, Gentleman. 6 July 1863. Conrad.'[43]

On 16 January 1863, while the exiles were at Vologda, the Central National Committee in Warsaw called the Polish people to arms to throw off the Russian oppressors. It was an irresponsible action, as there was no coordinated plan and the various groups of potential opponents of the Tsar, not forgetting the discontented or liberal Russians, were hopelessly divided from each other. Nonetheless, the rebels achieved considerable success at the start, and if the Poles had had any help from other nations they might have succeeded in freeing themselves from Russia. As it was, the Russians put down the rising with their customary ruthlessness, although some rebels were still fighting into 1865, and there followed the inevitable period of repression.[44] Two of Apollo Korzeniowski's brothers were involved in the insurrection; Robert was killed and Hilary exiled to Tomsk. As has been said, Evelina's brilliant brother Stephen, who had become one of the most prominent members of the Central National Committee, was killed in a duel with a political opponent. Thaddeus had refused to join the insurrection, from wisdom and certainly not from lack of courage, because he had not hesitated earlier to go and help Stephen escape when he was being pursued by the Russian police.[45]

(3)

Because of the murderous climate at Vologda, both Evelina and her son steadily lost strength. But then Chominsky and the police chief successfully recommended that the family should be transferred to a milder climate; thus, in the summer of 1863, the Korzeniowskis arrived without an escort and under parole in Chernikhov, a hundred and twenty-five miles north-east of Kiev, to the immense surprise of Prince Golitsin, the governor and another humane man. Golitsin then even allowed Evelina to go with Conrad to spend some months with Thaddeus on his estate at Novofastov, between Berdichev and Kiev.[46]

Thaddeus immediately realized that Evelina was very ill; she was in an advanced stage of tuberculosis, and the only hope was a long rest with careful nursing. However, the governor, Bezak, decided that when her permit was up she must return to Chernikhov or be sent to the prison hospital at Kiev. The local police chief told Thaddeus of this confidentially and, in consequence, Evelina returned to Chernikhov in the autumn, accompanied by her mother.[47]

Conrad has recalled the departure from Thaddeus's house in *A Personal Record*:

> I remember well the day of our departure back to exile. The elongated, bizarre, shabby travelling-carriage with four post-horses, standing before the long front of the house with its eight columns, four on each side of the broad flight of stairs. On the steps, groups of servants, a few relations, one or two friends from the nearest neighbourhood, a perfect silence, on all the faces an air of sober concentration; my grandmother all in black gazing stoically, my uncle giving his arm to my mother down to the carriage in which I had been placed already; at the top of the flight my little cousin in a short skirt of a tartan pattern with a deal of red in it, and like a small princess attended by the women of her own household: the head *gouvernante*, our dear, corpulent Francesca (who had been for thirty years in the service of the B. family), the former nurse, now outdoor attendant, a handsome peasant face wearing a com-

passionate expression, and the good, ugly Mlle Durand, the governess, with her black eyebrows meeting over a short thick nose, and a complexion like pale brown paper. Of all the eyes turned towards the carriage, her good-natured eyes only were dropping tears, and it was her sobbing voice alone that broke the silence with an appeal to me: '*N'oublie pas ton français, mon chéri.*' In three months, simply by playing with us, she had taught me not only to speak French but to read it as well. She was indeed an excellent playmate. In the distance, halfway down to the great gates, a light, open trap, harnessed with three horses in Russian fashion, stood drawn up on one side with the police captain of the district sitting in it, the vizor of his flat cap with a red band pulled down over his eyes.[48]

In Chernikhov Evelina's health declined rapidly. Just over a year after her return, on New Year's Day of 1865, Thaddeus visited her, taking with him a doctor who held out some hope that she could be saved. But a month later he realized that she was doomed.[49]

The failure of the 1863 insurrection and the illness of his wife had crushed Apollo's spirit; the sardonic combativeness of his early letters from exile gave way to a despairing mysticism. He wrote to his friend Casimir Kaszewski:

> My poor wife has been dying, for several years, from her sickness and from the repeated blows which have been falling on our family. During the last four months she has been cruelly ill, confined to her bed, with barely enough strength to glance at me, to speak with muted voice. The lack of everything here to support body and soul – the lack of doctors and medical facilities have brought her to this condition. . . . May God be with us – for people can do little for us now. I am everything in the house – both master and servant. I do not complain of this as a burden; but how often has it been impossible for me to help the poor, unhappy woman or bring her relief! Our little Conrad is inevitably neglected in the midst of all this. [26 February 1865]

and two days later:

> I believe, best of friends, that two or three days ago I sent you a letter. . . . I think I did, as I don't know what I am doing – what I feel – and I remember nothing. You will understand when I tell you: my wife is very, very ill – there is hope only in God. . . . Homesickness like rust has slowly eaten away my wife's strength.

For the last eighteen months she put it all down to nerves; the doctors here – are they really doctors? – persisted in declaring: 'It's nothing – nothing – it'll pass.' In my anxiety I, who would never do anything for myself, have begged and prayed that we might be moved from this place so as to find doctors worthy of the name. Constantly misled and put off I lost this hope. Then, some months ago she had a sudden burning fever, a chest complaint and an internal tumour, the result of bad circulation which calls for an operation. . . . Her mind alone remains unshaken. I ask myself, is this courage or does she not know how ill she really is? Who could read the answer in her eyes, if I, to whom they have ever been an open book, cannot see what is written there? And yet, I cannot read her eyes. Only, sometimes, a stronger pressure of her hand in mine, or in little Conrad's, testifies to her courage. . . . We are wretched and unhappy indeed, but thank God that we have been allowed to bear this fate together. We pray that God remove the chalice of bitterness from our lips – for we have drunk from it overmuch, more than enough. But we thank him that our lips jointly drink up that potion. We should not change it for nectar if each of us had to drink separately.

Just over a month later, on 18 April 1865, Evelina died at the age of thirty-two.

Apollo was thus left with the full responsibility of bringing up his seven-year-old son, and it would be hard to imagine a person less fit to undertake this task. Not only was he spiritually lacerated by the succession of misfortunes, but he was a sick man and financially destitute. Unknown to all but himself, his family had been supported during much of their exile by Evelina's brother Casimir. But Casimir had three children of his own, and when Thaddeus discovered what had been going on he took over the burden of supporting Apollo and Conrad. He made an arrangement whereby he himself administered a fund set up for Conrad; because, as he explained later, Apollo, 'with all his uprightness of character, could never keep a groat'.[50]

Moreover, now that his wife was dead, it seems that the only thread attaching Apollo to life was anxiety about Conrad's future; his desire was to ensure this as far as possible and then cut the thread. He wrote to Kaszewski:

Do you remember saying to me at the sad moment of our parting, while you were looking at our little Conrad: 'If you do not come back soon, send him to me and I shall take care of him as I do of my little Bronek?' Now that she will never return and I too may never come back, and little Conrad will probably have to grow up without me, fulfil your promise. He is all that remains of her on this earth and I want him to be a worthy witness of her to those hearts that will not forget her. And who, better than you, best and most noble of souls, could clothe him in that immaterial raiment? .... I should like to be tranquil on this point. Her heart and soul were so set upon this child that I cannot leave him, I cannot separate myself from him, unless I feel certain that he will fulfil her hopes; and to take no steps to that end would be, it seems to me, to be false to my poor wife. I have arranged that Conrad should have a little patrimony sufficient for the needs of life and learning; and after that some crumbs will remain. I have made every sacrifice already to secure his future. He may add to your cares but, at least, he will not be an expense to you. Tell me, dear friend, if you will do this for me, so that I may know what instructions I ought to give those into whose hands, when the time comes, the little orphaned Conrad will fall. [10 June 1865]

But this was for the future. Meanwhile Apollo himself had to do something about giving his son the rudiments of an education. He wrote pathetically to Kaszewski:

How can I thank you for all your kindness to my poor little orphan. What you have promised him was our dream in the days of our deepest distress and an encouragement for the ominous future. ... Your promise to send me school books and syllabuses fills me with joy. I await its fulfilment with impatience. Sell my writing table to buy these books. It was a favourite of hers but she will never see me working at it again. [18 September 1865]

Some weeks later he again returned to the vital need for school books – and also gave an insight into Conrad's character:

I remind you again to send school books and syllabuses for my little Conrad. I want to prepare him according to the school syllabuses. Since the autumn my health has considerably declined and my little one has had to take care of me. We are alone on this earth. ... He has inherited his talents from his mother's family, but on the practical side he is not to be envied because he takes after me. [31 October 1865]

More important for Conrad than the presumably rather meagre conventional instruction that Apollo was able to provide must have been the influence of Apollo's own intellectual occupations. Living in sombre isolation from everyday life, he had become increasingly absorbed in literature; he did not feel capable of original work, but concentrated on doing translations, particularly of Shakespeare and Hugo, in the hope that these would bring in some money. Conrad has described how Apollo drew him into his work; he recalled how his father one day came upon him looking at some manuscript sheets of a translation of *Two Gentlemen of Verona*:

> I was greatly confused, expecting to get into trouble. He stood in the doorway looking at me with some surprise, but the only thing he said after a moment of silence was: 'Read the page aloud.'
>
> Luckily the page lying before me was not over blotted with erasures and corrections, and my father's handwriting was otherwise extremely legible. When I got to the end he nodded and I flew out of doors thinking myself lucky to have escaped reproof for that piece of impulsive audacity.[51]

He also remembered being asked to read the proofs of his father's translation of *Les Travailleurs de la Mer*.[52] It is easy to understand how this prodigiously boring book would have struck a responsive chord in both father and son; in the portrait of Gilliat's position, in isolation amid a hostile society, they would have seen a reflection of their own fate:

> Les volcans lancent des pierres et les révolutions des hommes. Des familles sont ainsi envoyées à de grandes distances, des destinées sont ainsi dépaysées, des groupes sont dispersés et s'émiettent; des gens tombent des nues. . . . Ils étonnent les naturels du pays. D'où viennent ces inconnus? c'est ce vésuve qui fume labas qui les a expectorés. On donne des noms à ces aérolithes, à ces individus expulsés et perdus, à ces éliminés du sort; on les appelle émigrés, réfugiés, aventuriers. S'ils restent, on les tolère;

s'ils s'en vont, on est content.... J'ai vu une pauvre touffe d'herbe lancée éperdument en l'air par une explosion de mine...

La femme qu'à Guernsey on appelait *la Gilliat* était peut-être cette touffe d'herbe-là.

La femme vieillit, l'enfant grandit. Ils vivaient seuls et évités.[53]

Life with his father must have been unbearably oppressive for Conrad, but Apollo did at least realize this and told Kaszewski:

The poor child does not know what it is to have a playmate of his own age; he looks at my wizened sorrow and who knows whether this sight does not cover his youthful heart with wrinkles and his awakening soul with hoar frost. That is one of the important reasons forcing me to tear this poor child from my gloomy heart.[54]

Like his father, Conrad turned to books to help him through the long, lonely days.[55] In *A Personal Record* he wrote that he had been 'a great reader' since the age of five[56] and recalled having read as a child history, voyages, novels, in Polish and French; among them Fenimore Cooper, Captain Marryat, Dickens; and *Gil Blas* and *Don Quixote* in abridged editions.[57]

But no book could have provided an adequate escape from the morbid religiosity which Apollo displayed in a letter to his cousins, John and Gabriela Zagórski:

I have passed through heavy and even terrible days of brooding on God's blessings, and if I survive, it will be thanks not to my own, but to God's strength. I know I have not suffered and never could suffer like our Saviour, but then I am only a human being. I have kept my eyes fixed on the Cross and by that means fortified my fainting soul and reeling brain. The sacred days of agony have passed, and I resume my ordinary life, a little more broken but with breath still in me, still alive. But the little orphan is always at my side, and I never forget my anxiety for him. And so, my friends, I am still alive, and still love what is left me, and still love as fervently as ever, though I can no longer give anything to the object of my affections. Whatever remains for me to do in life, I cannot either sacrifice or give anything, for I have nothing to sacrifice or offer up. It is sad indeed for a man to see the two doors through which alone he can approach the presence of God shut against him, but such is the will of Providence. When my bitterness chokes me, I read your second dear letter and the pride of despair changes into divine sadness. My tears flow, but their fount is reason. Then, my composure recovered, I take up my life again, which is entirely centred upon my little Conrad. I teach him what I know, but that, unfortunately, is little. I shield him from the atmosphere of this place, and he grows up as though in a monastic cell. For the *memento mori* we have the grave of our dear one, and every letter which reaches us is the equivalent of a day of fasting, a hair shirt or a discipline. We shiver with cold, we die of hunger. We are overwhelmed by the destitution of our fellow men, our brothers, but prayer remains to us, and in our prayers, I call God to witness, there is scarce a word about ourselves. Should I describe this place I would say that on one side it is bounded by locked doors behind which the being dearest to me breathed her last, without my being able to wipe even the death sweat from her brow, while on the other, though there the doors are open, I may not cross the threshold, and I see what Dante did *not* describe, for his soul, appalled though it was with terror, was too Christian to harbour inhuman visions. Such is our life. [18 January 1866, *L.L.*, I, p. 16]

Other letters, to Kaszewski, show all too plainly the melancholy atmosphere in which father and son were engulfed:

When your letter arrived I was in such a state of prostration that I had to ask Conrad to write to you that your letter was the only drop of sweetness in this useless, used-up life of a sick man that I lead. [31 January 1866]

And:

My little Conrad is well and we are working: although oppressed by many, many things. Ah! if I could describe all that; what an interesting article that would make. [18 February 1866]

He was making headway teaching Conrad French, but still needed a geometry textbook; and again his most urgent wish was to find a satisfactory place to send Conrad.[58]

In May, just over a year after Evelina's death, Apollo did send Conrad away, to spend the summer with Thaddeus at

Novofastov, where he was able to have the company of Thaddeus's daughter, Josephine, and other children of his own age. During this summer Conrad apparently had his first sight of the sea; Thaddeus is said to have taken him for a couple of months to the seaside at Odessa in the hope of restoring his health.[59]

It was probably also during this stay at Novofastov that Conrad met Prince Roman Sanguszko, the distinguished Polish patriot about whom he wrote in his story 'Prince Roman'. Conrad was mooching about the house alone when he suddenly came upon Thaddeus and his guest. Prince Roman had taken part in the insurrection of 1830 and had been sentenced to the Siberian mines; he was now old and stone-deaf and had to be communicated with by means of a pencil and pad. After discovering Conrad's name he asked:

> 'And how old is this shy little boy?'
>
> Before I could answer my uncle wrote down my age on the pad. I was deeply impressed. What was this ceremony? Was this personage too great to be spoken to? Again he glanced at the pad, and again gave a nod, and again that impersonal, mechanical voice was heard: 'He resembles his grandfather. . . .' The unrelated, inexpressive voice said: 'Give me your hand'.
>
> Acutely conscious of inky fingers I put it out timidly. I had never seen a deaf person before and was rather startled. He pressed it firmly and then gave me a final pat on the head.
>
> My uncle addressed me weightily: 'You have shaken hands with Prince Roman S—. It's something for you to remember when you grow up.'[60]

Apollo missed his son intensely and, in spite of the more carefree life at his uncle's, Conrad seems to have been 'homesick'.[61]

His grandmother therefore took him back to Apollo at Chernikhov in October, but his health, which had never been robust, then broke down and his grandmother took him to Kiev for medical treatment; after a month in Kiev he spent the rest of the winter at Novofastov.[62] Apollo described his complaint as grave.[63]

Apollo himself was becoming increasingly ill with tuberculosis and at the beginning of December 1867 was granted a passport, valid for one year, to go with Conrad to Algiers and Madeira.[64] But he had neither the money nor the health to travel so far. However, he was at least able, in January of the new year, to go with Conrad to Lwów in Galicia, which under Austrian rule was the most liberally governed province in Poland. From there he visited his friends the Mniszeks on their estate near Przemyśl and then went to Topolnica,[65] whence he wrote a letter to Kaszewski which showed a gleam of his former spirit:

> I have given up Galicia and have limited my efforts to improving my state and caring for Conrad's health. Both wandering exiles, we need each other; he needs me as his miserable guardian and I him as the only power that keeps me alive. I am now in a little mountain resort at Topolnica and for the last ten days have been drinking sheep's milk with such enthusiasm that when the Imperial and Royal Police came to ask me how I was spending my time in Galicia, I could in all conscience answer: 'drinking sheep's milk'. If there is any improvement in my health I haven't noticed it; but as I drink from this source of health without disgust and feel no ill-effects, experienced people state that this signifies the healthy action of sheep's milk. . . . My boy is again suffering from his old complaint. . . . It is difficult to order him to learn while in such a state of health: but he is already eleven and has done virtually no work for the last two years. [Undated, Jagellon Library, MS 3057 K pp. 53–4)

They returned to Lwów in October, but Apollo continued to give Conrad lessons at home because he objected to the impure Polish spoken at the gymnasium.[66] This had to be abandoned when Apollo's health became worse, and Conrad was put under a tutor from the gymnasium.[67] At the end of the year he wrote to Kaszewski:

> My little Conrad is well and that cheers me up most, because his nerves were in a very bad state. He is going through the formal syllabus of the local schools though he will not go to his class this year. He is fairly able but so far has no love of study and there is nothing definite in him yet. Of course he is only eleven. But I

should be glad, before I close my eyes, to foresee the general direction of his future path in life. He likes to criticise all, but unmaliciously. He is sensitive in his attitude and good beyond words. [24 December 1868]

One interesting piece of information has been preserved from Conrad's stay in Lwów. Apparently he had taken to writing plays, perhaps in emulation of his father, which were acted among his friends. They had patriotic themes, with the Russians always coming off worst; one of them was called *The Eyes of John Sobieski.** He proclaimed that he had great talent and would become a great writer.[68] A delightful anecdote, related a few years later, suggests that the young Conrad had a high opinion of his own importance; it is said that he once interrupted the discussion of a group of venerable gentlemen with the unexpected question: 'And what do you think of me?' To which the reply was: 'You're a young fool who interrupts when his elders are talking.'[69]

In February 1869 Apollo moved to rooms in Poselska Street in Cracow.[70] He had found the atmosphere in Lwów oppressively Austrian and doubtless hoped that Cracow, as an ancient seat of Polish culture, would be more congenial. Apparently he had also been offered a post on the editorial staff of *Kraj* (*Country*),[71] but he was far too ill by then to do any work. Conrad was sent to a day school, and every evening came back to do his homework in an atmosphere of immanent death, which must have put an intense strain on the highly-strung boy. Not only was Apollo himself dying, but he had become absorbed in a cult of his dead wife. A visitor to the Korzeniowski establishment at this time relates how he arrived one day to find Apollo

sitting motionless in front of his wife's portrait; he did not move

* Roman Dybowski quoting Mrs Jadwiga Kałuska (née Tokarska), who knew Conrad at this time: 'Zmłodiści Józefa Conrad!', *Czas*, 25 December 1927. Supporting evidence comes from Zygmunt Radziczynski, who states that Conrad had at this time 'written a little comedy which he wanted us to act, but somehow nothing came of it' (Czosnowski, loc. sit.) Leon Syroczyński told Aniela Zagórska that Conrad used to write comedies and act them with the Syroczyńska girls.

and little Conrad, who was coming in behind me, put his fingers on his lips and said: 'Let's go quietly through the room, because father always looks intently at Mother's portrait on the anniversary of her death – all day, saying nothing and eating nothing.'[72]

Many years later Conrad looked back on these months:

There, in a large drawing-room, panelled and bare, with heavy cornices and a lofty ceiling, in a little oasis of light made by two candles in a desert of dusk I sat at a little table to worry and ink myself all over till the task of my preparation was done. The table of my toil faced a tall white door, which was kept closed; now and then it would come ajar and a nun in a white coif would squeeze herself through the crack, gliding across the room, and disappear. There were two of these noiseless nursing nuns. Their voices were seldom heard. For, indeed, what could they have had to say? When they did speak to me it was with their lips hardly moving, in a claustral clear whisper. Our domestic matters were ordered by the elderly housekeeper of our neighbour on the second floor, a Canon of the Cathedral, lent for the emergency. She, too, spoke but seldom. She wore a black dress with a cross hanging by a chain on her ample bosom. And though when she spoke she moved her lips more than the nuns, she never let her voice rise above a peacefully murmuring note. The air around me was all piety, resignation, and silence.

I don't know what would have become of me if I had not been a reading boy. My prep finished I would have had nothing to do but sit and watch the awful stillness of the sick room flow out through the closed door and coldly enfold my sacred heart. I suppose that in a futile childish way I would have gone crazy. But I was a reading boy. There were many books about, lying on consoles, on tables, and even on the floor, for we had not had time to settle down. I read! What did I not read! Sometimes the elder nun, gliding up and casting a mistrustful look on the open pages, would lay her hand lightly on my head and suggest in a doubtful whisper, 'Perhaps it is not very good for you to read these books.' I would raise my eyes to her face mutely, and with a vague gesture of giving it up she would glide away.

Later in the evening, but not always, I would be permitted to tip-toe into the sick room to say good-night to the figure prone on the bed, which often could not acknowledge my presence but by a slow movement of the eyes, put my lips dutifully to the nerveless hand lying on the coverlet, and tip-toe out again. Then I would go to bed, in a room at the end of the corridor, and often, not always, cry myself into a good sound sleep.[73]

On 23 May Apollo died;[74] Conrad's grandmother described how, 'with bitter tears, he prayed for the soul of his father kneeling between the priest and the nuns, until at length Mr Buszczyński took him away and pressed him to his heart'.[75] The funeral was made the occasion of a tribute by the people of Cracow to a man who had sacrificed his life to his conception of patriotic duty; Conrad walked at the head of the enormous procession.* The ghost of this tragic figure was to haunt Conrad throughout his life.

Many years afterwards he described his father as:

> A man of great sensibilities; of exalted and dreamy temperament; with a terrible gift of irony and of gloomy disposition; withal of strong religious feeling degenerating after the loss of his wife into mysticism touched with despair. His aspect was distinguished; his conversation very fascinating; his face, in repose sombre, lighted all over when he smiled.[76]

This characterization is borne out by those of Apollo's letters which have survived. Apollo had evidently always had a volatile disposition, but with a strong undercurrent of pessimism. After his exile he showed in a morbidly accentuated form qualities which, according to Herzen, were typical of Poles of this period:

* After describing the funeral in the Author's Note to *A Personal Record* Conrad said: 'What had impressed me much more intimately was the burning of his manuscripts a fornight or so before his death' and went on to describe how he himself witnessed the scene. This memory is mangled by his having told Garnett some years earlier that his father's piles of MSS were 'burnt after his death according to his last will' (letter of 20 January 1900). But Conrad was mistaken in both versions. A letter from Stephen Buszczyński to (?) Joseph Kraszewski, of 19 January 1870 reads: 'The late Apollo Korzeniowski . . . left with me all his unpublished manuscripts. If the publication of poetry (in exceptional circumstances) enters within the scope of *Tygodnik*, I am always at your service. That is why I inform you of this.

'There are among them some very beautiful things, *inter alia*, apart from original poems, translations of Shakespeare's plays and of V. Hugo.

'My deceased friend entrusted his works to me. I should like to find a publisher. . .'

In the depths of their souls there is an element of mediaevalism alien to us, and a crucifix before which they can pray at moments of grief and fatigue. In Krasiński's poetry the *Stabat Mater* drowns the national hymns, and draws us not to the triumph of life, but to the triumph of death, to the day of Judgment.[77]

It might be suggested that the political situation in Poland was to blame for Apollo's tragic life. But, whereas it was obviously responsible for the form that his misfortunes took and aggravated his material suffering, it is unlikely that his tortured nature would have fitted contentedly into any human society.

He was evidently unsuited for any sort of practical activity, whereas his intellectual capacity was not of a kind to bring him much satisfaction. His literary work was not very impressive and he gained little recognition during his life; his translations of Hugo and Heine are well thought of by competent judges; two of his plays, *Komedia* and *Dla miłego grosza*, were, according to Bobrowski, very well received, but are not apparently outstanding; and, again in the opinion of competent judges, his poetry is derivative from Krasiński and not of great merit. In his poetry, like Mickiewicz and Słowacki when they came under Towiański's influence, he expressed a mystical belief in Poland's messianic role to redeem other nations through sacrifice. In his life he exemplified this belief and seems to have had a noble, selfless character able to inspire love and respect.

(4)

Conrad was now an orphan at the age of eleven. He was put under the guardianship of his doting grandmother, Theophilia Bobrowska, and of Count Ladislaw Mniszek.[78] But it was his Uncle Thaddeus who quickly took upon himself the full responsibility for Conrad's welfare; he had, according to Apollo, transferred all the love which he had felt for his sister to his nephew.*

* Letter to Kaszewski, 22 November 1866. Bobrowski had suffered, and was to suffer more, from the loss of those close to him. As well as

Shortly after Apollo's death Mrs Bobrowska took Conrad for a cure to Wartenberg in Bohemia, and he was then, in accordance with his father's wishes, placed in the educational establishment of a Mr Louis Georgeon,[79] Florianska Street, Cracow, where Mrs Georgeon and her two elderly daughters looked after a small group of pupils; he could not be sent to the gymnasium because he did not know Latin or German.

He was soon to feel the novel influence of Bobrowski's sternly practical approach to life; his uncle wrote him a letter setting out the principles on which he would be brought up:

Conrad, my dear,

It has pleased God to afflict you with the greatest misfortune that can affect a child – the loss of parents. Yet, God has in his goodness graciously permitted your best of grandmothers and me to guard over you, over your health, education and future fate. You know how we love you and that all the affection we had for your late parents has been transferred to you. You know also that your parents were always worthy of our affection – so you, as their son, should be doubly worthy as their son and become worthy of our love. That is why you should try to profit by the teachings given you as also by the advice given you by friends chosen by your late father and by us, by such friends as Messrs. Stephen Buszczyński and A. [*sic*] Georgeon, accepting in all matters their views and instructions.

Without a thorough education you can never become anybody worthwhile in this world, you will never be able to support yourself – a thorough education is gained by thoroughly mastering the first notions of every subject essential for every educated man – such as I expect you want to be and as we desire to see you in the future. Apply yourself therefore, my child, to a thorough mastering of beginnings. I know that beginnings often seem boring to children – but it is necessary to try to overcome this by working and the determination to endure. Desiring to become an engineer or a tech-

Evelina, his other sister, Theophila, and two of his brothers, Stephen and Stanislas, had died young. His wife died after giving birth to his only child, who herself died in 1871. There was thus a large gap in Bobrowski's affections for Conrad to fill.

nician it is necessary to begin with arithmetic and geometry; desiring to become a doctor or lawyer, with learning languages, geography, etc. In short, one arises from the other, one is built upon another. Thus, you must favour not what is easy and interesting but what is useful even though sometimes difficult; for, a man who can do nothing thoroughly has no strength of character and endurance, cannot work by himself and direct himself, and is no longer a man but becomes a doll serviceable in nothing. So my child, do your best not to be or become a doll but a useful, industrious and skilful man, hence a worthy one, and so reward us for our pains and anxieties during the course of your upbringing.

Your education has been thought out and your needs supplied – all you have to do is to learn and look after your health until even in this, though chiefly dependent on the will of God, by taking the advice of your elders you will be able to recover your health fully, not yielding unnecessarily to impressions, feelings and thoughts inappropriate to one of your age!

Write to us, my child, at least once a month, write what you think and feel. You know that news of you is always welcome, particularly for the peace of mind of your best of grandmothers, and is eagerly awaited by me and Josie – so be punctilious in this.

You are beginning your schooldays with the desire to become a useful and decent man by following the advice of decent people – with the help of God – on this new road. I give you my heartfelt blessing, as your loving uncle.

T. Bobrowski.

Josie embraces you, Emily and Frania too. [20 September 1869]

Thaddeus arranged for a young man named Adam Pulman to tutor Conrad, and it was he who took him to the watering-place of Krynica during the summer of 1870 for the sake of his health.[80] Then, probably later in this year, Conrad was sent to the gymnasium, apparently not St Anne's, as had been supposed,[81] but the less well known St Jacek's nearer his home, on Sienna Street.*

* Najder's research has shown that Conrad's name does not figure on the list of the pupils of St Anne's printed in the *Memorial Book Celebrating the Three Hundredth Anniversary of the Founding of St Anne's Gymnasium in Cracow* (Cracow, 1888), nor do those of Constantine Buszczyński or the

Conrad seems to have disliked school-life,[82] and it is not surprising, in view of his unorthodox upbringing, that he should have found the unaccustomed discipline of regular work irksome. It is probable, too, that academically he was by temperament lazy;[83] although his grandmother had been able to report that he was industrious,[84] this was just after his father's death, which had doubtless chastened him, and Apollo had earlier found that he 'showed no love of study'.[85] Apparently he liked always to be untrammelled, and at school or at home preferred to lounge rather than sit.[86]

He became increasingly bored and restless under the restrictions of this new regime and, according to his uncle, began some time in 1872 to press to be allowed to go to sea. In May of the following year, on doctor's advice, he was sent with Pulman for a six weeks' tour of Switzerland, which in fact was prolonged to nearly twice this time because of an outbreak of cholera in Cracow.[87] In *A Personal Record* Conrad says that Pulman was charged by Thaddeus with the task of dissuading him from his desire to go to sea; he tells of endless argument during this holiday, of how an encounter with one of a group of British engineers working on the St Gothard tunnel gave strength to his purpose and led to Pulman's capitulation with the words: 'You are an incorrigible, hopeless Don Quixote. That's what you are.'[88]

When they arrived back in Cracow it was decided – chiefly, it seems, for financial reasons – that Conrad should be put under the care of a distant cousin, Antony Syroczyński, who lived at Lwów.[89] There he was lodged in a boarding-house for orphans of the 1863 insurrection which had been founded by Ambrose Syroczyński. Antony Syroczyński had a daughter named Tekla, with whom Conrad appears to have fallen in love.[90]

Taube boys, mentioned as Conrad's school friends. There is also no trace of his name in the records of the school in the Voivodship Record Office in Cracow. St Jacek's was the other gymnasium in Cracow, but there is no confirmation that Conrad went there, because its records have been destroyed.

Conrad's allusions to his childhood love-life are contradictory. In the Author's Note to *Nostromo* he says that Antonia Avellanos was modelled on his 'first love':

How we, a band of tallish schoolboys, the chums of her two brothers, how we used to look up to that girl just out of the schoolroom herself, as a standard-bearer of the faith to which we all were born but which she alone knew how to hold aloft with an unflinching hope!. . . . I was not the only one in love with her; but it was I who had to hear oftenest her scathing criticism of my levities . . . or stand the brunt of her austere, unanswerable invective.[91]

The claim that Antonia was modelled on his first love must be treated with circumspection because she corresponds so closely to the Antonia Ribera described in Eastwick's *Venezuela,* a book on which Conrad drew for *Nostromo.*[92] None the less it is possible that he did have some such relationship with a girl named Janina Taube, although his characterization of her as 'une toute petite personne avec des cheveux bouclés et d'une gentillesse exquise'[93] resembles Mrs Gould more than Antonia Avellanos. While he was under the care of Louis Georgeon the establishment was moved from Florianska Street to a large house at 43 Franciszkanska Street. The Taube family lived in the same building, and Conrad became friendly with the three boys of his own age and with Janina. She wrote to Conrad at the address of his publisher after his first two novels had appeared and in his reply he said: '. . . La vue de votre signature a reveillé toutes les images du passé dont les plus heureux moments ont été dus à la bont é de Madame votre Mère, et à ces amitiés d'enfance dont on comprend mieux le charme à mesure qu'on s'en éloigne dans le dur pélerinage de la vie.'[94] In his next letter to her he recalled in more detail these childhood memories and asked to be remembered warmly to her brothers, 'mes seuls – à vrai dire – camarades d'enfance'.[95]

In a cancelled opening to *The Arrow of Gold* Conrad elaborated on his early loves; and the novel was originally to take the form of a series of letters to a woman whom the hero had not seen 'for something like five and thirty years':

> When they last saw each other they were not only very young but I may say youthful.
>
> A great austerity of feelings and convictions is not an uncommon phenomenon in youth. But that young girl seems to have been an uncommon personality, the moral centre of a group of young people on the threshold of life. Her own education appears to have been not finished at the time. But she had the power of an exalted character.
>
> Of that time he reminds her at great length. And no wonder. He was in love with her. But he never betrayed this sentiment to her, to anybody. He rather affected resistance to her influence. He even tried to cheat his own self in that respect.
>
> The secret of this resistance is that she was not his first love. That experience had come to him the year before in the late summer of his last school holiday . . .
>
> From the nature of things first love can never be a wholly happy experience. But this man seems to have been exceptionally unlucky. His conviction is that – in colloquial phrase – he had struck there something particularly wicked and even devilish. . . . If she was really devilish then she may count it for an amazing success. My opinion, however, is that the girl was simply very ordinarily stupid. . . . I imagine that at first he amused her, then he bored her, (perhaps was in the way of some more serious flirtation) and then discovering that she could make him suffer she let herself go to her heart's content. She amused herself again and again by tormenting him privately and publicly with great zest and method and finally 'executed' him in circumstances of peculiar atrocity – which don't matter here.
>
> Perhaps he was unduly sensitive. At any rate he came out of it seamed, scarred, almost flayed and with a complete mistrust of himself, an abiding fear.[96]

Although occurring as a prelude to a novel, it is likely that this passage is close to the truth because it would otherwise be pointless, as it has no bearing on the rest of the novel. It is clear that the girl described as his second love here is the same as that described as his first love in the Author's Note to *Nostromo* (the significant leave-taking pressure of the hand occurs in both accounts[97]). Tekla Syroczyńska apparently bore no resemblance to this austere girl,[98] but it is not known how like she was to the stupid girl. As Conrad remained with the Syroczyńskis until just before leaving for Marseilles, the reconstruction that fits the facts most easily is that he first experienced a romantic hero-worship of Janina Taube, then had a turbulent love-affair with Tekla Syroczyńska, and, finally, when he went to say good-bye to the Taubes before leaving Poland, was given the encouraging squeeze of the hand by Janina Taube.

By September 1874 Conrad had convinced his uncle that he should be allowed to join the French merchant navy and he left the Syroczyńskis for Cracow, where he spent a little over three weeks preparing for his departure.[99] In October* his uncle, and his grandmother, who was in tears, saw him off on the train, alone, for Marseilles.

(5)

Conrad has given his explanation of how the desire to go to sea was formed in him and how he doggedly persisted in it until he had overcome all opposition and had his way. Looking back to this time more than thirty years later, he concluded that his imagination had been captured by his reading about the sea, in fiction such as Hugo's *Travailleurs de la Mer*[100] and the tales of Fenimore Cooper and Captain Marryat,[101] and in other books, such as Garneray's *Récits, Aventures et Combats*[102] or the accounts of famous voyages of exploration like McClintock's *Voyage of the 'Fox' in the Arctic Seas.*[103] Then there were books of travel which, though not connected with the sea, stimulated a general wanderlust in him; he mentioned Mungo Park's, James Bruce's, and Livingstone's travels of exploration of the African continent.[104] Of McClintock's book he wrote: 'The great spirit of the realities of the story sent me off on the romantic explorations of my inner self; to the discovery

* Probably on 15 October, as this was the day from which Bobrowski dated Conrad's first half-yearly allowance (Bobrowski Document). cf., *L.L.*, I, p. 27.

of the taste of poring over maps; and revealed to me the existence of a latent devotion to geography which interfered with my devotion (such as it was) to my other schoolwork'. This, admittedly, was in an essay on 'Geography and Some Explorers'[105] which he had been asked to write, but there are other testimonies to his enthusiasm for geography. In the same essay he repeats a story illustrating his wanderlust, which, apocryphal or not, he had told twice before: looking at a map as a child, he had put his finger 'on a spot in the very middle of the then white heart of Africa' and said that some day he would go there.[106]

This apparently was the stuff out of which Conrad wove daydreams of a kind common to most boys; and although some of the details may not be true, there is no reason to doubt the general truth of this explanation as far as it goes. But it would be a mistake to stop here. Most boyhood fantasies are as insubstantial as thistledown, and Conrad's would not have withstood the hostile blasts of disapproval to which they were evidently subjected, unless there had been other factors, whose influence neither he nor anyone else could fully know, leading him to demand ceaselessly for two years to be allowed to go to sea,[107] and finally to triumph.

One reason that has been persuasively advanced for Conrad's desire to go to sea or, in its negative form, to leave Poland, is his position as the son of a Polish patriot who had been imprisoned by the Russians for revolutionary activities. Would he not always remain a marked man, like Razumov, without enough freedom to lead a satisfactory life?[108] This argument would be more convincing if Conrad had been a few years older when his desire was first formulated or if he had not been living in Austrian Poland. When he was still at school, and before he had thought of a career, he would have been unconscious of suffering under any disadvantage; while, at least since her defeat at Sadowa in 1866, the Austro-Hungarian Empire had been following a liberal policy towards her Polish subjects, and the persecution of Conrad's father by the Russians would not have stood against the son. Moreover, Conrad's subsequent attitude towards Austria was markedly friendly[109] and in sharp contrast to his feelings about Russia and Germany.

The most plausible explanation seems to be that temperamentally and because of his upbringing Conrad disliked the conventional, disciplined school life to which he had been forced to submit and that he therefore longed primarily to escape to freedom and adventure, a form of psychological rather than political claustrophobia. But his uncle would never have allowed this, and so Conrad had to dress up his desire respectably. His romantic notion of the sea, created by his reading, and the fact that the sea was the one object for which it was necessary to leave Poland, supplied the perfect answer.

When an action, decided upon at leisure, has such far-reaching consequences as Conrad's, one is apt to assume that it must have been the result of the most careful deliberation, but there is no reason to suppose that Conrad had any idea of the momentousness of his decision. He was too young for the future to assume much importance in his mind and too ignorant of the world and himself to judge what his decision might entail. In retrospect he claimed that he had, even in Poland, resolved 'if a seaman, then an English seaman',[110] but there is nothing to support this assertion, and it conflicts with the known facts. Another statement of Conrad's, that what he 'had in view was not a naval career, but the sea',[111] is, in its vagueness, much closer to the truth.*

There remains the less important problem of why Bobrowski acquiesced in an action which violated all his notions of a sound preparation for life. He must have doubted whether he was justified in opposing a wish expressed so keenly and for so long, but this in itself was probably not

* It should be noted in this connection, as Mr Tymon Terlecki has recently pointed out ('Conrad w Kulturze Polskiej', *Conrad Żywy*, 1957, pp. 100–113), that there was a general restlessness and desire to escape actuality among the younger generation of Poles which later expressed itself in the oriental exoticism of the literary movement known as 'Young Poland'.

enough; Conrad was after all only sixteen. It may well be, as Najder suggests, that Bobrowski was rather thankful to be rid, at least temporarily, of his troublesome nephew.[112] Conrad had shown little inclination to adapt himself to a regular, disciplined life; moreover he had upset the Syroczyński household through his romance with Tekla, and Bobrowski may well have thought it best that he should be allowed to sow his wild oats on foreign soil. He would no doubt return chastened in six months or so.*

* I am grateful to Mrs Danilewicz for an additional explanation. She points out that, being a Russian citizen and the son of a political convict, Conrad was liable to Russian military service: and moreover, not as an officer, the status to which his social class would have entitled him, but in the ranks, and perhaps for as long as twenty-five years. Although there is no reason to suppose that Conrad himself was at all concerned about this danger, Bobrowski most probably felt that the further Conrad was away from the Russians the better. He had already tried unsuccessfully to obtain Austrian naturalization for Conrad (see Document) and was continuously to impress on him the need to become the citizen of some country other than Russia.

[II]

French Experience

BEFORE sending Conrad off to Marseilles his Uncle Thaddeus had arranged that he should be paid the 'modest but sufficient' allowance of 2,000 francs a year in monthly instalments.[1] He had also asked a Pole named Victor Chodźko, who was in the French merchant navy, and another man named Baptistin Solary to keep an eye on Conrad.[2] Conrad describes his first meeting with Solary in *A Personal Record*:

This Solary (Baptistin), when I beheld him in the flesh, turned out a quite young man, very good-looking, with a fine black, short beard, a fresh complexion, and soft, merry black eyes. He was as jovial and good-natured as any boy could desire. I was still asleep in my room in a modest hotel near the quays of the old port, after the fatigues of the journey *via* Vienna, Zurich, Lyons, when he burst in flinging the shutters open to the sun of Provence and chiding me boisterously for lying abed. How pleasantly he startled me by his noisy objurgations to be up and off instantly for a 'three years' campaign in the South Seas'.[3]

Apparently Solary introduced Conrad to life among the pilots in the Vieux Port. Again, Conrad gives an account of his activities:

The very first whole day I ever spent on salt water was by invitation, in a big half-decked pilot-boat, cruising under close reefs on the lookout, in misty, blowing weather, for the sails of ships and the smoke of steamers rising out there, beyond the slim and tall Planier lighthouse cutting the line of the windswept horizon with a white perpendicular stroke. They were hospitable souls, these sturdy Provençal seamen. Under the general designation of *le petit ami de Baptistin* I was made the guest of the Corporation of Pilots, and had the freedom of their boats night or day. And many a day and a night too did I spend cruising with these rough, kindly men, under whose auspices my intimacy with the sea began. Many a time 'the little friend of Baptistin' had the hooded cloak of the Mediterranean sailor thrown over him by their honest hands while dodging at night under the lee of Chateau d'If on the watch for the lights of ships. Their sea-tanned faces, whiskered or shaved, lean or full, with the intent wrinkled sea-eyes of the pilot-breed, and here and there a thin gold loop at the lobe of a hairy ear, bend over my sea-infancy. . . . And I have been invited to sit in more than one tall, dark house of the old town at their hospitable board, had the bouillabaisse ladled out into a thick plate by their high-voiced, broad-browed wives, talked to their daughters – thickset girls, with pure profiles, glorious masses of black hair arranged with complicated art, dark eyes, and dazzlingly white teeth.[4]

Bobrowski may also have come to some arrangement with the ship-owning firm of Delestang as to Conrad's employment. At all events it was always on one or other of their ships that he sailed while he was based on Marseilles. He made his first voyage two months after his arrival, as a passenger on the *Mont Blanc*, an old sailing-ship belonging to this firm; she was commanded by Captain Ournier and sailed for Martinique on 11 December 1874.[5] One of the essays in *The Mirror of the Sea* contains a passage which presumably refers to this voyage:

The very first Christmas night I ever spent away from land was employed in running before a Gulf of Lions gale, which made the old ship groan in every timber as she skipped before it over the short seas until we brought her to, battered and out of breath, under the lee of Majorca, where the smooth water was torn by fierce cat's-paws under a very stormy sky.

We – or, rather, they, for I had hardly had two glimpses of salt water in my life till then – kept her standing off and on all that day, while I listened for the first time with the curiosity of my tender years to the song of the wind in a ship's rigging. . . . The wind was fair, but that day we ran no more.

The thing (I will not call her a ship twice in the same half-hour) leaked. She leaked fully, generously, over-flowingly, all over – like a basket. I took an enthusiastic part in the excitement caused by that last infirmity of noble ships, without concerning myself much with the why or wherefore.[6]

The *Mont Blanc* arrived back at Marseilles on 23 May

1875[7] and sailed again for the West Indies on 25 June under a Captain Duteil;[8] this time Conrad was listed as an apprentice.[9] On the return voyage the ship ran into some very rough weather and much of the sail was carried away.[10] She made Le Havre on 23 December, where she had to stay for repairs. Conrad had decided to leave the ship here,[11] and he returned to Marseilles, spending a few days in Paris on the way.[12] He apparently lost his trunk at Le Havre, for which he later received a stern rebuke from his uncle.

He remained based on Marseilles for the next six months, but nothing precise is known about how he occupied himself. He probably became a visitor to the Delestangs, whom he describes in *A Personal Record*. M. Delestang was

> such an ardent – no, such a frozen-up, mummified Royalist that he used in current conversation turns of speech contemporary, I should say, with the good Henri Quatre; and when talking of money matters reckoned not in francs, like the common, godless herd of post-Revolutionary Frenchmen, but in obsolete and forgotten *écus**

From hints which Conrad dropped it appears that M. Delestang was deeply involved in the Carlist venture.[13] Madame Delestang was 'an imperious, handsome lady in a statuesque style' who reminded him of Lady Dedlock and who would sometimes take him to the Prado in her carriage.[14]

Conrad also apparently savoured the café and bohemian society of Marseilles. Aubry mentions that among those he knew were a sculptor named Frétigny who appears as Prax in *The Arrow of Gold* and Clovis Hugues, a journalist, poet, and politician whom he knew very slightly.[15] Hugues, six years older than Conrad, had gone into journalism and had been sent to prison in 1871 for an article that he had written

* *A Personal Record* pp. 124–6. Conrad here states that M. Delestang was a banker and that it was through him that he received his allowance. Aubry accepts this, but Delestang et Cie were not bankers and it does not seem from the Bobrowski Document that Conrad's allowance was paid through them.

in *Fraternité*. After his release in 1875 he worked for the left-wing Marseilles newspaper *L'Égalité* and in November 1876 became chief editor of *La Jeune République*. On 3 December 1877 he fought a duel with Joseph Daime, a journalist on the Bonapartist *L'Aigle*, and killed him. He was tried and acquitted on 22 February 1878,[16] just at the time when Conrad's own troubles reached their climax.

In *The Arrow of Gold* there are several allusions to the bohemian set of Marseilles and also to the restaurants, smart or bohemian, at which 'M. George' would eat. Aubry says that Conrad, 'even towards the end of his life, still pronounced with some emotion' the name of the Café Bodoul[17] which was a fashionable haunt of royalists in the rue Saint Ferréol. No doubt he also visited the theatre and the opera;* Marseilles had a lively intellectual life at this period; there was the flourishing 'Cercle Artistique' which a group of young men had founded in 1866 for the popularization of the arts, and there was the distinguished school of Provençal poets, the Félibrige, over which Mistral and Roumanille presided.†

(2)

Whatever Conrad did during this period ashore he managed to run through a lot of money, thus upsetting his uncle, who noted:

> I learned from a letter written by Victor Chodźko on 5 April that, having withdrawn from the Banker the whole of your allowance for the eight months from January to October this year, i.e. 1200 francs, you lent this money (or perhaps simply lost it), and that you were in want.

* It was presumably in Marseilles that he saw the plays of Scribe and Sardou to which he referred in later life (letter to Garnett of Sunday [12 March 1811], *Letters from Conrad*, 243). He also enjoyed opera, confessing a particular fondness for Meyerbeer (letter to Galsworthy, 18 June 1910, *L.L.*, II, p. 110), and again this taste was probably acquired in Marseilles.

† For a pedestrian account of intellectual life in Marseilles during this period see J. Charles-Roux, *Souvenirs du Passé; le Cercle Artistique de Marseille*, Paris etc., 1906.

Then in May you wrote to me about this, apologising but not explaining things. Finally on 22 May you telegraphed, asking for 700 francs, which were paid to you. On 2 July, again on your telegraphic request, I had 400 francs paid to you, and when you were leaving Marseilles, you wrote asking me to pay 165 francs to Mr. Bonnard, your acquaintance, who lent you the last-named sum – and this I did.

In such manner, during three months, you expended over and above your allowance, 1265 francs or 664 Gulden. As it is but fair that everyone pay for his stupidities from his own pocket, and as I have no extraordinary income to cover the extraordinary expenditure of my Nephew, I have therefore used for this purpose *your own 500 Gulden* (the gift of Miss Korzeniowska) which had been deposited with the Galician Bank; the balance of 166 Gulden has been assumed by me. This comes to – 150 roubles. As an outcome of your youthful escapade there thus remains of your own money, now, only Gulden 1000.00.[18]

It was just as well that, on 8 July 1876, Conrad sailed again to the West Indies, this time on M. Delestang's other, new ship, the *Saint-Antoine*: the list of the crew gives his nominal rating as steward, with a salary of 35 francs a month.[19] The first mate of the *Saint-Antoine* was Dominic Cervoni, a Corsican of forty-two[20] who was to figure colourfully in Conrad's life and his work. He is described in *The Mirror of the Sea*:

His thick black moustaches, curled every morning with hot tongs by the barber at the corner of the quay, seemed to hide a perpetual smile. But nobody, I believe, had ever seen the true shape of his lips. From the slow, imperturbable gravity of that broad-chested man you would think he had never smiled in his life. In his eyes lurked a look of perfectly remorseless irony, as though he had been provided with an extremely experienced soul; and the slightest distension of his nostrils would give to his bronzed face a look of extraordinary boldness. This was the only play of feature of which he seemed capable, being a Southerner of a concentrated, deliberate type. His ebony hair curled slightly on the temples. He may have been forty years old, and he was a great voyager on the inland sea.[21]

This 'modern and unlawful wanderer with his own legend

of loves, dangers, and bloodshed'[22] who was yet 'the embodiment of fidelity, resource and courage'[23] was the model for Nostromo[24] and, presumably, also for Peyrol in *The Rover* and Attilio in *Suspense*. Also among the crew, as apprentice, was Dominic's nephew, César Cervoni, a young man a month older than Conrad[25] who was to figure so basely in Conrad's account of the wrecking of the *Tremolino*.

From various hints which Conrad dropped it seems that he took part in some nefarious activities, perhaps with Dominic, while the *Saint-Antoine* was based on the West Indies. In *The Arrow of Gold* appears:

> I had just returned from my second West Indies voyage. My eyes were still full of tropical splendour, my memory of my experiences, lawful and lawless, which had their charm and their thrill; for they had startled me a little and amused me considerably.[26]

In a letter to Richard Curle he mentions having been ashore at various places on the coast of Venezuela;[27] then in the Author's Note to *Victory* he says that Ricardo 'was a fellow passenger of mine on board an extremely small and extremely dirty little schooner, during a four days' passage between two places in the Gulf of Mexico whose names don't matter'.[28] He adds that he 'had some of my own very pressing business to attend to, which in the end got mixed up with an earthquake and so I had no time to give to Ricardo'.[29] Unfortunately, what really happened in the West Indies remains a mystery.

While he was in the West Indies Conrad's irresponsible behaviour in France caught up with him in the form of a stern rebuke from his uncle:

> You will . . . find a long letter for you at M. Delestang's in Marseilles in which I recapitulate your activities during the last two years and give my advice and desires for the future – and I expect you to adjust yourself to them not only in thought and words but also in actions!!!!!
>
> You have always, my dear fellow, annoyed me with your lack of order and your carefree treatment of things – in which you remind

me of the Korzeniowski family – always wasting everything – and not of my dear sister, your mother, so painstaking in everything. Last year, you lost your trunk with your things: what else was there to have in mind during a journey except yourself and your things? Do you need a nurse, and why should I be one? Now, again you have lost your family photographs and Polish books, and you want me to make up a set of one and the other! What for? So that you may again lose them at the first opportunity!! Whoever values a thing, takes care of it. I have to this day a *paper picture* given me by my mother when I was journeying to school for the first time, in 1839. It has been with me everywhere and I still have it in the same state as when I was given it – and why? Because I looked after this souvenir with all my heart. And this my worthy sir *n'y met pas de coeur*. So, if you don't care for cherished souvenirs (for there's no accounting for tastes, and such do exist), why clamour for them and cause others trouble? However, whatever family photographs I can get together, I'll send you once again – but, if you lose them, please don't speak to me about them any more, because I won't believe that you care for them . . .

Well, there's your scolding for your lack of order in preserving your property. You really deserve a second one; for your untidy way of writing letters – I've written about this several times. Is it impossible to have a supply of paper with you and to write decently? I sincerely wish my nephew to be a decent maan and that's why I scold him – though this doesn't prevent me from loving you and blessing you, my dear boy – and this I do.

Embracing you heartily, your uncle

T. Bobrowski

P.S. Did your personal papers also get lost together with your trunk? If so, it would be very troublesome. Write the truth, so that I could start getting at least your birth-certificate. Don't forget to write to me about this. [9 October 1876]

When Conrad arrived back at Marseilles on the *Saint-Antoine* on 15 February of the new year,[30] his uncle's immensely long letter was waiting for him:

. . . Two years ago, I with constricted heart, Grandmother with tears, both of us with a blessing, submitted to your desire and let you go free into the world – to fly on your own – though with our advice and help – and when you read this letter you'll have completed your nineteenth year. An age at which one is a finished young man, often even earning one's living and sometimes supporting a family, – in any case, an age at which one is quite responsible before God and before people, and before oneself for one's own deeds.

After we parted, I assumed the obligation of supplying you with means for your support until you were in a state to secure them yourself. The means are, it is true, modest but sufficient, and appropriate to my capabilities, perhaps stretched somewhat – but voluntarily determined after securing the opinion of Mr. Chodźko. You, on your part, bound yourself to benefit by these means most prudently for your education and personal good!!

Let us then, after the lapse of two years, make a recapitulation of the past to ascertain to what extent each of us has fulfilled his duties: and this recapitulation, answering our questions, will enable us to correct any shortcomings that we find in our behaviour – and will require each of us to think of corrective measures so that these can be avoided in future!!

You had allotted for yourself fr. 150 monthly, i.e. fr. 1800 allowance and fr. 200 for extraordinary expenses. – fr. 2000 per annum; fr. 4000 for two years. With the reservation that this is help doubly and strictly restricted, and that exceeding it in your favour must: either deprive me of certain comforts or force me to reduce the help given to your uncle, my brother, to whom with five children I can give barely one and a half times more (i.e. 10,000 roubles per annum) than I give you as a single person.

I don't know whether you have ever, with pencil in hand, recapitulated what you have received during the last two years undemanded and on demand? I surmise that you haven't gone deep into these accounts – for, if it were so – what has happened, wouldn't have been. – To remind you, here you have our account for two years:

				Extra
in 1874	5/17th October, for a/c allowance		fr. 150	
	4/16th November	ditto	fr. 150	
	6/18th December	ditto	fr. 900 &	fr. 300
in 1875	4/ January – stolen			fr. 250
	3/15th June – one payment		fr. 200	
	9/21st June, a/c allowance		fr. 1000	
	15/27th July – to Mr. Chodźko			fr. 200
	19th November to Havre			fr. 300
in 1876	2/14th January – a/c allowance		fr. 1200	
	12/24th April	ditto	fr. 200	
	8th June			fr. 700

			Extra
in 1876	4th July		fr. 400
	20th July		fr. 165
Telegrams and forwarding (16 rbs, 37 gulden)			fr. 104
	Total a/c allowance	fr. 3800	Extra fr. 2,419
Deducting 300 fr. for initial kit and 200 additional for the second year, making together during two years, apart from allowance		fr. 4000	Extra fr. 1919

In short: during two years
you have by your transgressions
engulfed maintenance for the
whole third year!!!

Thus you have the bare facts – based on figures, which you will certainly not deny – for every expense was either for you or caused by you. And now, *Panie Bracie* [literally 'Mister Brother'], let us reflect together whether such expenditure by you is and was possible, fair and worthy??? As regards possibility, perhaps it seems to you that I can afford such extraordinary expenditure out of devotion for a 'most dearly-beloved nephew'? Nothing of the kind ... Is it fair that I should have to repair your thoughtlessness at the cost of my own comfort, I should say even, of essential needs? Would it be a worthy thing for me, because of your thoughtlessness, to reduce the help I give to my brother and nephews, who have, if not a greater (for there are six persons), then certainly not a smaller right than you to my heart and help?

I am but too sure that the threefold reply to the threefold questions of mine would be: And impossible! And unfair! And unworthy! That would be the answer of your heart – but I want an answer from your will – not words, which I have had more than once – but deeds, i.e. the strictest adaptation in expenditure to the means that I have allotted you – and if these do not suffice, according to you – earn [some more] – and you'll have it. If, however, you can't earn it, then content yourself with what you have from the work of others, – until you are able to supplant it with your own and gratify your desires.

Apart from the fact of expenditure itself, I can state frankly that I was not pleased with the tone in which you speak about what happened. *Vous passez condamnation trop complaisante sur les sottises, – que vous avez faites!* Certainly, there's no reason to commit suicide or to retreat to the Carthusians because some silliness has been done – even though it very acutely affects someone very near to you – but a little more contrition would not be amiss – and particularly a more thoughtful mode of behaviour which would prove that after a temporary imprudence thoughtfulness and commonsense have prevailed! But these last-named, *Panie Bracie*, in spite of the greatest desire, I have not observed – unfortunately! First of all you maintain stubborn silence for two whole months – you are silent while, you must know, this silence disquieted me! Then, you write me a long letter admitting your fault, but do not write how much you need for the repair of the absurdities committed, while the plainest commonsense would have bid you connect one with the other and not expose me to uncertainty and the disquiet of surmises. Further still, knowing how I detest telegrams, and how much trouble and cost they entail (for I live 28 miles from the Station), you telegraph for 700 francs in June. Finally, having a whole month to inform me that you still need 400 francs, you wait again and as late as July 4th telegraph again. In conclusion, departing, you require me to pay a debt of 165 francs, this time, thank God, by letter! Where is there thought, prudence, deliberation??? Where is there respect for others' – this time my own – peace of mind? Where is effort to diminish the faults of committed absurdities by thoughtful and tactful behaviour??? Having perpetrated stupidities, you lose your head, stake all on chance. For, if your telegrams had not found me at home, and this could very well have happened, if on the first occasion I hadn't had money deposited in Cracow, and on the second if a few days credit had not been granted me? Of what unpleasantness for yourself and expense for me would you have been the cause? Consider all this my dear fellow – and you'll admit that I am right – beat your breast (in contrition) – and promise reform.

What conclusion can be drawn from this whole recapitulation of our actions? This, that you who have committed absurdities – in view of your youth, and because it's the first time, all this should be forgiven you – while I, the victim of these absurdities, forgive with all my heart, provided *that this is the first and the last time*!! And am I in this quite innocent? Certainly, guilty, because I met your demands so promptly! And I also beat my breast and promise myself that this is the first and the last similar submissiveness on my part! And I pledge myself to keep my word! And ask you to remember this – for yourself and for me. I would at once refuse my own son after so many warnings –but you, Child of my Sister, Grandson of my Mother, once and once only do I forgive, – I save you –

so that it should be said that I was not too hard with him! May the shades of those Beings, dear to us both, continue to protect you from similar transgressions, my dear boy, *for believe me*, I shall not submit to any tenderness of heart a second time.

What practical way is there of patching up the holes made by you? Know then, that you had 500 Rhenish (Gulden), your own, deposited in the Galician Bank, and that this money has been exhausted by your demands as you can easily calculate, and, as you spent 1919 francs, i.e. more or less 1,000 Gulden, it therefore seems to me fair that you should pay for your own stupidities with your own money – and only have recourse to my pocket for the balance! I take the balance, then, upon myself! Do you find this fair? Please let me have a plain answer! In your first letter.

I do not find your proposition practical, viz. that your extraordinary disbursements of the past be covered from your allowance – for, first of all, I don't want you to deny yourself food and clothing, modest but decent in extent; secondly by reducing an allowance that's barely sufficient I would lead you back to the path of incurring debts, which I do not want and which I forbid you under pain of forgoing my blessing; I ask that you refrain from philanthropy – until you are able to practise it at your own expense.

Thus you have 1000 francs deposited to your order, i.e. for the half-year ending 1/13th April 1877. It is my desire that, if health and M. Delestang's trading circumstances permit, you remain on land as little as possible; hence you must try to get back to sea as speedily as possible. If you have to stay on land, I ask and recommend you not to take more from the Bank than for one month or at the most for two allowances of fr. 150 each and to look after this so that it suffices . . .

Immediately after reading this letter, i.e. right after your return, please write to me about your health and further plans. Please also give me details of your studies? On what did you work during this voyage? You praise your present captain. So, you have profited by him? Did he give you lessons? and what? Did you work some out yourself? and what? Did you teach yourself? Are you also working on the English language? or some other? and so on. In short, write about everything regarding your moral and physical being? Did you recover the trunk so carelessly left behind in Havre? Your things and Polish books must have been in it? I know what happened from a later letter.

. . . Well, enough of this, my boy; you have had a recapitulation of your wisdom, a *lavasse* which you have deserved – you have advice and warnings for the future! Hope that it is the first and the last time that you have caused me so much unpleasantness, here is an embrace and my blessing. May they be effective!!!

Your uncle,
T. Bobrowski
[26 October 1876]

However, if Conrad's explanation is to be believed, he then had a piece of bad luck. He was due to sail again in the *Saint-Antoine* on 31 March but contracted an anal abscess and was thus prevented from doing so.[31] He seems to have impressed Captain Escarras of the *Saint-Antoine*, who went so far as to write to tell Bobrowski how much he regretted having had to leave Conrad behind.[32] Conrad for his part had apparently decided that if he could not sail with Escarras he would stay on land, and he was soon in trouble again. We learn from a letter from Bobrowski of 9 (?) August that he had quarrelled with M. Delestang:

My dear Boy,

You have evidently forgotten the national proverb that 'the humble calf sucks two mothers'. That is why you had that incident which led to a breach with M. Delestang, simply because you lost control of yourself. I don't deny at all that, if things happened as you describe, the worthy *épicier* treated you too loftily, disregarding that he had before him a descendant of the excellent house of Nałęcz – that's agreed. I see from your relation of the talk with him that you have *la repartie facile et suffisament acérée* by virtue of which I recognise your Nałęcz blood – the quality of flying into a passion.... Unfortunately I can perceive in this whole affair no trace of that prudent commonsense of which you have the right to be proud on the distaff side, deriving from the House of Jastrzębiec, to which I have the honour of belonging (28July/8 August [sic])

Conrad had, apparently for the first time, broached the possibility of transferring to the British merchant navy, and in the same letter Bobrowski wondered how far this was practicable: 'The first question is: Can you speak English? I don't know; you have never even replied to my questions whether you are learning that language.' Bobrowski then asked about Conrad's naturalization, a problem on which he was to press Conrad persistently for the next nine years because he knew that Conrad would not be safe from the Russian tentacles, particularly with regard to military service, until he had been released from his Russian nationality and become a naturalized subject of another country. Bobrowski was not in favour of French naturalization because it would entail compulsory military service, and he asked about Swiss naturalization. In a letter a month later he returned to the problem; apparently there was some drawback to Swiss naturalization and Bobrowski suggested the United States. Then Conrad had mentioned the Japanese Consul, who liked him, although he didn't know why. Bobrowski suggested:

> Perhaps, after getting your master's certificate, you might get something in Japan through him – become a Japanese admiral. Once you've decided on a cosmopolitan career, such as yours is in the marine – it doesn't really matter where you are. You don't seem to be very attached to the French, and I can't say I'm not glad of this – I should not like you to consider France as your country. [14 September 1877]

Conrad had told his uncle that he planned to make a voyage to India, or round the world, under Captain Escarras on the return of the *Saint-Antoine*; and in the autumn he wrote asking for some extra money for this purpose. Bobrowski sent 1,000 francs out of Conrad's capital and then a further 1,000 when told that this was not enough.[33] Thus, together with his next half-yearly allowance, Conrad now had the large sum of 3,000 francs at his disposal. What happened next is described in a letter which Bobrowski wrote eighteen months later to Stephen Buszczyński, Apollo Korzeniowski's closest friend:

> I was quite sure he was somewhere in the Antipodes when, suddenly, while engaged in business at the Kiev Fair in 1878, I received a telegram reading: '*Conrad blessè envoyez argent – arrivez.*' Naturally, I could not fly off at once like a bird, so, after concluding my business and having received a reply that Conrad

was recovering, I left Kiev on 24 February [Old Style] and arrived in Marseilles on the 27th. On arrival I found that Conrad was already able to walk, and, after a previous talk with his friend Mr. Richard Fecht (a very prudent and decent young man), I visited the delinquent. This is what happened. When Captain Escarras returned, Conrad was quite certain that he would sail under him; but the *Bureau de l'Inscription* forbade this as he was an alien, aged 21 and liable to military service in his country. Moreover, it came out that Conrad had never received permission from his Consul, so the former Inspector of the Port of Marseilles was summoned to explain why he had noted on the lists that such permission had been granted. He was reprimanded and very nearly lost his post. As could be expected, this was very painful for Conrad. The whole affair became too widely known – all the efforts of the Captain and the shipowner were in vain (Monsieur Delestang, the shipowner, told me all this), and Conrad had to stay ashore, without any hope of serving as a seaman in French vessels. Before all this happened, however, another catastrophe, a financial one, overtook him. Having the 3000 francs I sent him for the voyage, he met a former Captain of his, a Monsieur Duteil [of the *Mont Blanc*], who persuaded him to participate in some affair on the coast of Spain – simply, some kind of smuggling. He invested 1000 francs and made a profit of over 400 francs; this pleased them greatly, and so he thereupon engaged all he had in a second venture – and lost all. This Monsieur Duteil consoled him with a kiss, and departed for Buenos Aires, while Conrad remained, unable to sign up as a sailor, penniless and moreover in debt. For, while speculating he had lived on credit, had ordered things necessary for the voyage, and so on. Faced by such a situation, he borrowed 800 francs from his friend, Mr. Fecht, and set off for Villa-Franca [Villefranche], where an American squadron was anchored, with the intention of entering American naval service. Nothing came of this, and wishing to repair his finances, he tried his luck in Monte Carlo where he lost the borrowed 800 francs at the gaming tables. Having so excellently managed his affairs, he returned to Marseilles, and one fine evening, he invited the aforesaid friend to tea; but, before the time fixed, he attempted to kill himself with a revolver shot. (Let this detail remain between us; for I have told everyone that he was wounded in a duel. But I do not want and should not want to keep this a secret from you.) The bullet went *durch und durch* near the heart, not injuring any important organ. Luckily he had left all his addresses on top – so that good Mr.

Fecht could immediately notify me and even my brother who, again, bombarded me in turn. That is the whole story.

I spent a fortnight in Marseilles, first studying the whole affair and then the Individual. Apart from those lost 3000 francs, I had to pay off debts for a like sum. I would not have done this for a son of mine, but, for the son of my dear Sister, I admit it, I was weak enough to act contrary to my principles. Nevertheless, I took an oath that even if I knew he would shoot himself again, he could not count on a repetition of this weakness. I was concerned, too, with national honour to some extent: so that there should be no talk of one of us Poles exploiting people's liking for himself – and undoubtedly Conrad was liked by all who had relations with him. He is lucky with people . . .

He seems to know his 'trade' well and likes it very much. I suggested that he return to his country – he flatly refused; I suggested that he return to Galicia, get naturalised and seek a career there – he refused this, too, saying that he loves his profession, does not want to change it, and will not do so. I noticed none of the vices common to seamen, though I observed him closely: he drinks virtually nothing, apart from red wine; does not gamble (he told me so himself, and Mr. Fecht also testified that he had never seen him gambling, and that unfortunate trial in Monte Carlo was based merely on a belief in beginner's luck). His manners are very good – as if he spends all his time in drawing-rooms; he is very much liked by his captains and by the seamen – I have more than once seen what cordial greetings were exchanged between him and sailors, who call him Monsieur Georges. During my stay in Marseilles, he was twice summoned to bring ships into harbour, for which service he received 100 francs in each case. I must therefore accept that he knows his profession . . .

(3)

Bobrowski's letter explains a lot, but it leaves even more unexplained; moreover it must be remembered that he was relating what Conrad and his friends had told him, which may not correspond with the facts. However, the only means of filling in the gaps is through recourse to Conrad's own writings. Conrad wrote about his life in Marseilles in a number of places: in the autobiographical *Personal Record*, in *The Mirror of the Sea*; *Memories and Impressions* which could be termed semi-autobiographical, in a novel *The Arrow of Gold*, and in a fragment of a novel, *The Sisters*. Their revelatory value varies in inverse proportion to their proclaimed autobiographical content; *A Personal Record* tells scarcely anything of interest, whereas *The Arrow of Gold* tells a lot.

From these sources a coherent narrative can be constructed. In a section of *The Mirror of the Sea*, entitled 'The *Tremolino*', Conrad relates how he and three other adventurers formed a syndicate controlling a balancelle called *Tremolino* which was to carry arms for the Carlists from the neighbourhood of Marseilles to the Gulf of Rosas. The oldest and most formidable member of the syndicate was 'J. M. K. B. . . . *Américain, Catholique et Gentilhomme*', as he styled himself: 'a North Carolinian gentleman' who 'used to declare with gallant carelessness, "I live by my sword" '.

Another member was Henry C., an Englishman with a love of literature: 'Narrow-chested, tall and short-sighted, he strode along the streets and the lanes, his long feet projecting far in advance of his body, and his white nose and gingery moustache buried in an open book: for he had the habit of reading as he walked.'[34] And the third was 'Roger P. de la S—, the most Scandinavian-looking of Provençal squires, fair, and six feet high, as became a descendant of sea-roving Northmen, authoritative, incisive, wittily scornful, with a comedy in three acts in his pocket, and in his breast a heart blighted by a hopeless passion for his beautiful cousin, married to a wealthy hide and tallow merchant'.[35] Finally there was Dominic Cervoni, the *padrone* of the *Tremolino*, and his nephew César. The syndicate revolved round Doña Rita, 'young and full of illusions', who was 'a Carlist, and of Basque blood at that, with something of a lioness in the expression of her courageous face (especially when she let her hair down), and with the volatile little soul of a sparrow dressed in fine Parisian feathers, which had the trick of coming off disconcertingly at unexpected moments'.[36]

In this account Conrad seems to have been the only

active member of the syndicate. After he and Dominic had made a number of successful gun-running voyages the *Tremolino* was ambushed by coast-guards through the treachery of César Cervoni; it had to be run on the rocks and wrecked so that the crew might escape capture. When he realized who was to blame Dominic had given César a sweeping blow which had knocked him into the sea; and as he was wearing Conrad's stolen money belt, laden with gold, César sank and was drowned. Safely on land, overcome with horror and remorse that a man bearing his name should have been guilty of such treachery, Dominic

> turned and walked away from me along the bank of the stream, flourishing a vengeful arm and repeating to himself slowly, with savage emphasis: 'Ah! *Canaille! Canaille! Canaille!*' He left me there trembling with weakness and mute with awe. Unable to make a sound, I gazed after the strangely desolate figure of that seaman carrying an oar on his shoulder up a barren, rock-strewn ravine under the dreary leaden sky of *Tremolino*'s last day. Thus, walking deliberately, with his back to the sea, Dominic vanished from my sight.*

In *The Arrow of Gold*, the gun-running is in the background and Doña Rita – Rita de Lastaola† – is at the centre. Other characters from 'The *Tremolino*' besides Rita appear in the novel; there is Dominic again, J. M. K. B., who appears with his full surname, Blunt, and a formidable mother, while Henry C. appears, physically transformed, as Mills. Rita's personality and biography are of course more fully dealt with in the novel. As in 'The *Tremolino*', she was born in the Basque country of Northern Spain. As a child she looked after goats in the hills near Tolosa, but when she was about thirteen she was sent to Paris by her uncle, a fanatical

* *The Mirror of the Sea*, pp. 170–83. This version differs from the facts at least in so far as César Cervoni's fate is concerned; he lived to serve a long career in the French merchant navy (Inscription Maritime, Bastia).

† Lastaola is the name of a pass in the Basque country near Bidassoa. According to Aubry the Carlists set up a customs post there, and it was often mentioned in the papers during the early months of 1875. *The Sea Dreamer*, p. 73.

priest, to be looked after by another uncle who was an orange-merchant. There, a rich painter named Allègre discovered her one day sitting on a stone in his garden. She became his model, and mistress, and he gradually transformed her into a sophisticated society woman. When Allègre died she became the mistress of Don Carlos, whom she had met through him. During the Carlist war she was a passionate and influential supporter of the cause and spent some time at Don Carlos's headquarters at Tolosa. Then she went to live in one of the houses in Marseilles which Allègre had left her in his will; in another she installed her sister 'Therese of the whispering lips and downcast eyes . . . with her brown, dry face, her gliding motion, and her really nun-like dress, with a black handkerchief enfolding her head tightly, with the two pointed ends hanging down her back'.* Rita is at the heart of Carlist intrigues as she is in 'The *Tremolino*', but her personality is rather different and Conrad perpetrates some of his most cloying prose to convey her beauty and power, to give her 'something of the women of all time'.[37] The young hero and narrator, M. George, is introduced to her by Captain Blunt, who has been courting her, egged on by his predatory mother. This is the impression which she makes on M. George at her first appearance:

> The white stairs, the deep crimson of the carpet, and the light blue of the dress made an effective combination of colour to set off the delicate carnation of that face, which, after the first glance given to the whole person, drew irresistibly your gaze to itself by an indefinable quality of charm beyond all analysis and made you think of remote races, of strange generations, of the faces of women sculptured on immemorial monuments and of those lying unsung in their tombs.[38]

Stripped of her romantic epithets, Rita is a capricious and neurotically fastidious woman whose behaviour thoroughly justifies M. George's exasperated accusation: 'You are afraid of living flesh and blood.' For, very soon, to

* *The Arrow of Gold*, p. 40. In *The Sisters* Rita has a sister who, in the opinion of her uncle, has a 'vocation'.

the extreme irritation of Blunt and his mother, there develops a complicated relationship between M. George and Rita; he falls in love with her and she half encourages, half repulses him:

I took her hand and was raising it naturally, without premeditation, when I felt suddenly the arm to which it belonged become insensible, passive, like a stuffed limb, and the whole woman go inanimate all over! Brusquely I dropped the hand before it reached my lips; and it was so lifeless that it fell heavily on to the divan. . . . She excused herself.

'It's only habit – or instinct – or what you like. I have had to practise that in self-defence lest I should be tempted sometimes to cut the arm off.'[39]

The conflict within Rita is shown in this scene when M. George kisses her:

With every word urging me to get away, her clasp tightened, she hugged my head closer to her breast. I submitted, knowing well that I could free myself by one more effort which it was in my power to make. But before I made it, in a sort of desperation, I pressed a long kiss into the hollow of her throat. And lo – there was no need for any effort. With a stifled cry of surprise her arms fell off me as if she had been shot. I must have been giddy, and perhaps we both were giddy, but the next thing I knew there was a good foot of space between us. . . . Something in the quality of her exclamation, something utterly unexpected, something I had never heard before, and also the way she was looking at me with a sort of incredulous, concentrated attention, disconcerted me exceedingly. . . . I became suddenly abashed and I muttered that I had better go and dismiss that poor Dominic. . . . I hurried out into the hall, shamefaced, as if I were making my escape while she wasn't looking. And yet I felt her looking fixedly at me, with a sort of stupefaction on her features – in her whole attitude – as though she had never even heard of such a thing as a kiss in her life.[40]

But the most revealing insight into Rita's character comes in the passage:

It's like taking the lids off boxes and seeing ugly toads staring at you. In every one. Every one. That's what it is having to do with men more than mere – Good morning – Good evening. And if you try to avoid meddling with their lids, some of them will take them off themselves.[41]

However, after many hesitations, Rita finally surrenders to M. George and they have several months of a blissful love affair 'in the region of the Maritime Alps, in a small house built of dry stones and embowered with roses'.[42] This idyll ends when, on one of his rare visits to Marseilles, M. George hears that Blunt has been spreading calumnies about him. He fights a duel with Blunt and is quite badly wounded 'through the left side of his breast'.[43] Rita whisks him away and nurses him back to health; but when he finally emerges from his fever she has disappeared. Mills is at his bedside to console him: '"She told me amongst other things," Mills said, "if this is any satisfaction for you to know, that till she met you she knew nothing of love."' When M. George asks Mills what will become of Rita he replies: 'She will be wasted. . . . She is a most unfortunate creature. Not even poverty could save her now. She cannot go back to her goats. Yet who can tell? She may find something in life. She may! It won't be love. She has sacrified that chance to the integrity of your life – heroically.'[44] The question is how much of all this is true. Aubry and others who knew Conrad personally have accepted it almost literally; and their assumption seemed justified by what Conrad himself had said or implied. In Curle's copy of *The Arrow of Gold* Conrad wrote that 'All the persons are authentic and the facts are as stated'. Then in a letter to Sir Sidney Colvin in August 1919 he wrote:

> The Allègre affair, I understand, was a fact, of which I make an extended version.
>
> The Rita of 'The *Tremolino*' is by no means true, except as to her actual existence. I mention her lightly, the subject of the paper being the *Tremolino* and her fate. *That* is literally true, just as the Rita of the *Arrow* is true fundamentally to the shore connections of that time.[45]

And in another letter, alluding to the mistakes in the text:

> The fact is, between you and me (and Lady Colvin of course),

that I have never been able to read *these* proofs in cold blood. Ridiculous! My dear (as D. Rita would have said) there are some of these 42-year-old episodes of which I cannot think now without a slight tightness of the chest – *un petit serrement de coeur.* What a confession![46]

Certainly Jessie Conrad believed the *Tremolino* story to be true, adding a few picturesque details which Conrad did not mention in print. She says that Conrad 'and the other smugglers had hidden for days in a low *posada*, in an underground cellar that was more like a cavern, till the authorities had given up the search'.[47] Then both in the Author's Note and elsewhere Conrad implied that *The Arrow of Gold* was based firmly on autobiographical fact; he had a scar on his left breast and allowed his family and friends to believe that this was the result of a duel. Moreover here is at least an interesting confirmation of the existence of the Blunts. In a book describing his experiences among the Carlists in 1874 while organizing ambulance work, Sir John Furley mentions a Mr Blunt:

> Soon after passing Vera we met Mr. Blunt (an American gentleman, who holds a commission in the army of Don Carlos, and whom I constantly met at St. Jean de Luz). He was with a Spaniard; and he told me he was on his way, *via* Hernani, to headquarters to fetch some papers he had left there. Having convinced them that they were going in an entirely wrong direction, I invited them to take places in our carriage, and I put them into the right path, just outside the Republican lines.[48]

Unfortunately he says no more about Blunt. Then in a book of memoirs Judith Gautier mentions a Madame Key Blunt:

> Parmi tous ces solliciteurs inconnus, qui venaient sans être présentés et sans recommandation, j'ai gardé le souvenir d'une certaine madame Key Blunt qui fut particulièrement tenace et nous tourmenta longtemps. Elle arrivait d'Amérique et avait été la femme, à ce qu'elle disait, d'un président des État-Unis, mort récemment. Il l'avait laissée avec des enfants et sans ressources: mais elle avait l'amour et, à ce qu'elle croyait, le don du theâtre, qui l'aiderait, pensait-elle, à relever sa fortune. C'était une

femme assez jolie, de taille moyenne, et toujours endeuillée de voiles de crêpe: 'Mon mari est toujours mort', répondait-elle à ceux qui lui faisaient observer que le temps du deuil était passé.*

This is evidently the same Mrs Blunt. Both Conrad and Judith Gautier show her as impecunious, unscrupulous, – in *The Arrow of Gold* she 'lives by her wits'[49] – ruthlessly persistent, and surrounded by an aura of bogusness (needless to say she had not been the wife of a president of the United States). Judith Gautier's portrait of her makes quite plausible the scene in which Mrs Blunt tries to persuade M. George to depart from the West Indies and threatens him that her son is a good shot.

But there are aspects of Conrad's version which are hard to reconcile with the known facts or are directly contradicted by them; and, if this were not sufficient warning, it is always dangerous unreservedly to accept a person's own account of his past. Few people relate events with any semblance of accuracy, even if they try to do so immediately after they have occurred; whereas Conrad's inaccuracy of memory was notorious among those who knew him and he was writing about his life in Marseilles several decades later. Moreover, in his autobiographical writings it was Conrad's aim to recreate a true impression of events rather than accurately to reproduce the facts, while in his fiction his intention was, obviously enough, artistic and not autobiographical.

The first discrepancy is in the chronology of the *Tremolino* episode.† Both in 'The *Tremolino*' paper and in *The Arrow of Gold* it is made plain that the *Tremolino* was carrying contraband for the Carlists and that the war was then at its height. In 'The *Tremolino*' there is the sentence:

* Judith Gautier, *Le Collier des Jours; le second rang du collier*, Paris, n.d., pp. 135–6. cf., *L.L.*, I, 44–5. Conrad himself drew Aubry's attention to this. There can be no question of Conrad having taken Mrs Blunt from the book rather than from life because there is no similarity between Judith Gautier's anecdote and Mrs Blunt's activities in *The Arrow of Gold*.

† Despite careful research it has been impossible to find any trace of a ship named *Tremolino*. Yet Conrad lays particular emphasis on the name and, in view of his usual practice with names, it would be surprising if he had invented it.

'The possibility of raising Catalonia in the interests of the *Rey netto*, who had just then crossed the Pyrenees, was much discussed', and a little later 'one evening . . . just after the news of a considerable Carlist success . . .' In *The Arrow of Gold* the Carlist war is an essential component of the atmosphere and of the background. It is specifically stated: 'As to the time, it is easily fixed by the events at about the middle years of the seventies, when Don Carlos de Bourbon . . . made his attempt for the throne of Spain, arms in hand, amongst the hills and gorges of Guipuzcoa,'[50] while numerous details and incidents in the book depend on the war being in full progress. The Carlist venture is only described as having 'collapsed utterly' more than a year after the events recounted at the start of the book and several months after the wrecking of the *Tremolino*. Now the Carlist war was over by the end of February 1876. Don Carlos led the remnants of his defeated army across the Spanish border into France on 28 February and although, on reaching French soil, he is supposed to have said '*Volveré Volveré!*' (I shall return! I shall return!), it is clear from the proclamation which he issued at Pau that he realized his cause was hopeless. He had said: 'Being desirous of preventing further bloodshed . . . I have given up the glorious struggle which at the moment is obviously futile,' and, as if to underline this, he departed for London, then in the following year went on a long trip to the New World.[51]

The episode of the *Tremolino* should therefore, according to Conrad's version, have happened before February 1876. Now the record of Dominic Cervoni (who played such a vital role in connection with the *Tremolino*) shows that he served as second officer on the *Saint-Antoine* without interval from 14 June 1875 to 14 October 1877; which means either that he did not take part in the episode or that it happened more than a year and a half after the war was over.* The first alternative would make nonsense of

* Aubry was wrong in saying that Bobrowski alluded in a letter of 14 October 1876 (O.S.) to Conrad's intention to join the Carlist forces (*LL.*, I, p. 40). There is no such allusion.

Conrad's assertion to Colvin that his account of the *Tremolino* was 'literally true'. The second alternative is more probable. Despite the fact that the Spanish Government felt itself secure enough to declare an amnesty for the Carlist exiles in February 1877,* Spain remained unsettled for some time; the Basques in particular were unreconciled to the rule of Alfonso XII. Arms were undoubtedly still being smuggled to these provinces,[52] and it would not be surprising or reprehensible if Conrad had added the romantic war-time trappings to a more run-of-the-mill, though still dangerous, smuggling enterprise. This certainly tallies with the account which Conrad gave to Bobrowski just after the episode had taken place. Moreover it fits in with Captain Duteil's record of service; he disembarked from the sailing-ship *Montesquieu* at Marseilles on 14 April 1877 and his record is blank until he joined the coaster, *Alcyon*, again at Marseilles, on 7 November 1878.[53] Thus the evidence suggests that the *Tremolino* incident happened some time between 14 October 1877 (the date of Dominic Cervoni's discharge) and Conrad's attempted suicide at the end of February or beginning of March 1878.

(4)

The most important discrepancy between fact and fiction is the revelation in Bobrowski's letter that Conrad did not fight a duel, but tried to kill himself.† An attempt to kill oneself

* *Gaceta*, 21 February 1877, quoted in *Le Temps*, 23 February 1877. It might be said that this was not a sign of strength, but merely of a desire to lure potential intriguers off foreign soil. However, the fact that leading Carlists such as General Mongroviejo took advantage of the amnesty shows how dead the cause now was.

† In spite of what seems to me conclusive evidence it appears that certain people are still not convinced that Conrad put a bullet through himself. Bobrowski definitely believed that he had done so on the basis of what Conrad himself had told him. (Bobrowski makes two other references to the incident besides that in his letter to Buszczyński; one in a letter to Conrad dated 8 July 1878, quoted on p. 83, and another in the Document: '1878, in February in Kiev I received . . . news that you had shot and wounded yourself', '. . . *żeś się postrzelił*').

would in all circumstances be a traumatic experience; and this would have been particularly intense in Conrad's case because, according to the Roman Catholic dogma under which he had been brought up, attempted suicide is a mortal sin. This was one of those events in a person's life whose importance must be asserted but cannot be demonstrated; of no specific occasion is it possible to say that Conrad would have acted or expressed himself differently had he not tried to kill himself, and yet his action inevitably exerted an influence throughout the rest of hs life. It is only necessary to recall how often suicide crops up in his work to realize how profoundly he must have been affected. He becomes a rival to Ibsen in that no less than nine leading or important characters kill themselves; another, Flora de Barral, is only just prevented from doing so; and three more – Jim, Razumov and Peyrol – sacrifice themselves in a way that is equivalent to an exalted form of suicide. It might be asked why Conrad kept this action so carefully secret throughout his life and adopted the story of a duel as a cover (as far as is known no one apart from Bobrowski and Buszczyński knew the true story). But, although few people would regard attempted suicide as in any way dishonourable, no one, unless he wallowed in self-pity or self-dramatization, would wish it to be known that he had tried to kill himself, and as it happened that Conrad was able to conceal his action, no elaborate explanation is required for his doing so.

Bobrowski assumes that Conrad's reason for trying to kill himself was the loss of all his money. Certainly he was in serious straits; he would have dreaded the task of explaining to his uncle how he had squandered the 3,000 francs and,

---

Why should Conrad have lied about this? Duels were still of frequent occurrence and were not considered reprehensible by Polish or French society (cf. the Hugues–Daime duel); moreover Conrad could always have lied to Bobrowski about the *cause* of the duel if there had been anything disreputable in it.

Above all, clingers to the duel version would have one accept the improbable proposition that Conrad lied to Bobrowski and that Bobrowski then proceeded to invent the truth.

moreover, he had run up debts in Marseilles to about the same amount.[54]

If Conrad's clear indication that *The Arrow of Gold* was based on autobiographical fact is to be accepted there is one conspicuous gap in Bobrowski's account of the Marseilles episode: 'Rita' is not mentioned. To dismiss the whole Rita story as fabrication would amount to charging Conrad with mythomania, and there is no justification for this. Thus, although it would be unwise to assume that Conrad stuck very close to the facts in *The Arrow of Gold*, the probability is that he was involved with a 'Rita' during his stay in Marseilles. She may have had something to do with the facility with which Conrad ran through his money and may indeed have been a contributory, or even the main, cause of his attempted suicide. Perhaps the love-affair had come to a painful end at the same time as Conrad had come to the end of his money. Perhaps Conrad had never fully intended to kill himself but wished to regain Rita with this drastic declaration of love; that would at least explain why he shot himself near the heart instead of through the mouth or forehead, as might have been expected, and why he so thoughtfully arranged that Fecht should arrive soon after he had fired the shot. but this is the merest guesswork and, whatever Rita's role, it is understandable that Conrad should have kept quiet about her to his uncle.

Rita's identity has eluded the most careful research; and it is impossible to know how closely Conrad's portrayal of the fictional Rita corresponds with the original. The main facts of her childhood and youth, including her name, Rita, given in *The Arrow of Gold,* are paralleled by those in *The Sisters,* a fragment of a novel written over twenty years before. In both she was born of peasant stock in the Basque country, has a sister, Therese, or Teresa, whose leanings towards holiness contrast with her own spirited paganism, and an uncle who is a fanatical priest. In both the priest sends her when still a child to be looked after by another uncle who is an orange merchant living in Passy. In *The Sisters* his name is Ortega, which in *The Arrow of Gold* is the name of Rita's wealthy cousin, her passionate suitor since childhood, who becomes a maniacal Carlist. It is perhaps also worth noting that in both books there is a painter's studio, the pavilion, just by the orange-merchant's house. This duplication points to a basis in fact and a letter from Conrad to Pinker when he was looking for a title for *The Arrow of Gold* – 'I have an invincible dislike for calling the novel "Doña Rita". I fancy it would be unlucky. You must allow me to be unreasonable in this instance'[55] – suggests that her name actually was Rita. Aubry says, presumably on the basis of what Conrad told him, that she had a house in the rue Sylvabelle[56] in Marseilles, but the census record of this street for 1876 provides no clue to her name.

It has been confidently asserted[57] that the original of Conrad's Rita was a certain Paula de Somogyi. The flimsiest of evidence and a deal of far-fetched inferences, some of which are easily disproved, have gone to the fabrication of this theory.

The facts of Paula's relationship with Don Carlos have inevitably been somewhat garbled, but the following seems to be what happened. On his return to Vienna in November 1877, after a tour of Eastern Europe during which he visited the Russo-Turkish battlefront, Don Carlos got a certain Madame Hannover to procure for him an attractive young chorus girl from Pest, named Paulina Horvath. He decided to make this girl his mistress and offered to support her lavishly. Perhaps with this in mind, and in view of his dwindling resources, he inveigled his Modena relations into giving him a valuable heirloom, the insignia of the Golden Fleece.* He also dubbed Paula the Baroness de Somogyi.

* The chronology is established by the date of handing over the insignia, 19 November 1877 (*El Robo del Toison; Vista pública, ante el Jurado de Milán del Proceso . . . contra el Ex-General Carlista Boët*, 2nd edition, Madrid 1880, p. 4), because the sources agree that Don Carlos acquired Paula and the insignia at the same time. Count Melgar, who was writing long after the events described, was a year out with his dates (*Veinte Años con Don Carlos*, Madrid, 1940, p. 55); and Miss Allen is wrong in assuming that the famous sale in May 1877 or Pierre Véron's article on the subject

From Vienna Don Carlos took Paula to stay with his brother at Graz; then from Graz he and his entourage went, at the end of November or beginning of December, to Venice where he was seen in public with Paula. From Venice they proceeded to Milan where, it appears, a squalid fraud was perpetrated. Don Carlos had decided that he must flog the Golden Fleece and, to make this feasible, that it must first appear to have been stolen. To carry out this ruse he enlisted his aide, General Boët, and an unwilling Paula. The first half of the scheme worked and the 'theft' seems to have been accepted. Don Carlos and his party then left Milan for Paris, arriving there shortly before Christmas. On 31 December Don Carlos left Paris for England with Paula.[58]

The episode of the stolen Golden Fleece had a farcical conclusion. At Don Carlos's suggestion General Boët had enlisted his wife and mother-in-law to try to dispose of part of the Fleece but, either because the fraud was in danger of being discovered or because Boët was double-crossing him, Don Carlos decided to accuse Boët himself of the theft and brought an action against him in Milan. Boët proclaimed to the world his version of the truth, and seldom can such dirty linen have been exposed in public. He was in fact finally acquitted.

Paula held her position of favour until the spring of 1882, when, allegedly, a crisis of conscience occasioned by the forthcoming first communion of his son, Don Jaime, caused Don Carlos regretfully to break the tie and dismiss her with a generous settlement. Five years later Paula was married off to a young baritone with a promising future, named Don Angel de Trabadelo. The marriage was apparently successful and lasted until Paula's death in about 1917.[59]

Now on the basis of chronology alone it is virtually impos-

---

in *Le Monde Illustré* of 26 May had anything to do with Paula (*The Thunder and the Sunshine*, pp. 130–31). The person concerned was a more celebrated *demi-mondaine*, Mme Cora Pearl (cf., *Figaro*, 25–6 May 1877).

sible that Paula was the 'Rita' in Conrad's life.* She arrived on the scene much too late for this and was, moreover, very much under Don Carlos's wing. It is most improbable that Conrad had the opportunity of meeting her, let alone of having an affair with her. There is no evidence of her going to Marseilles, and why should she have gone there? Don Carlos had clearly lost interest in his own cause and, besides, even he would scarcely have used as his emissary a young Hungarian chorus-girl, who knew, apart from her own language, only a little German.

Nor is there much resemblance between Paula and the fictional Rita. When 'M. George' met Rita she was a sophisticated woman of the world who wielded great influence in Carlist circles and she was the heiress of the painter, Allègre's fortune. But it is clear that Paula could have had no such influence when Conrad was in Marseilles (nor was someone of her background likely to be accepted in Legitimist circles at any time). And she was not an heiress; thus the whole point of Mrs Blunt's scheme to marry her son off to Rita, in order to nab the Allègre fortune, vanishes – and this is by far the most authentic-sounding episode in the book.

But some slight similarities between her life and Rita's suggest that Conrad had read or heard about her, probably at the time of Boët's trial. Thus Paula was allegedly of peasant stock and, like Rita, had been given her religious instruction by her uncle, a priest;[60] then there is a photograph, taken in 1880, of Paula wearing an ornamental arrow on her dress which may have suggested the title of the novel to Conrad.†

* I have not been able to trace Don Carlos's precise movements after his departure for England but it is doubtful whether he returned to France before Conrad put a bullet through himself; at least this still most newsworthy figure managed to keep himself out of the leading French newspapers during this period.

† Too much, however, should not be made of this. A piece of jewellery in the form of an arrow was after all a common enough object and Paula's arrow was very different from the 'Philistinish' ornament belonging to Rita. It may be that jewellery in the form of an arrow had assumed some

More conclusive, there is clear reference in *The Arrow of Gold* to Paula's stay in Venice with Don Carlos,[61] which suggests that Conrad had her in mind when writing the novel.

(5)

Because he could no longer sail in a French ship it was pointless for Conrad to remain in Marseilles and, as he had refused to return to Poland, it was up to him to decide what to do next. According to Bobrowski it was arranged with the help of Richard Fecht that he should join a British merchant ship because the British did not bother about the formalities which worried the French;[62] thus, on 24 April 1878, he embarked on the *Mavis*, a freighter bound for Constantinople with a cargo of coal.[63]

This turned out to be as momentous a step as his leaving Poland; but it is evident that Conrad did not recognize it as such at the time. In retrospect one is apt to find more conscious purpose directing the course of one's life than the facts warrant; and thirty-one years after joining the *Mavis* Conrad was to write: 'Already [before leaving Poland for Marseilles] the determined resolve, that "if a seaman, then an English seaman", was formulated in my head though, of course, in the Polish language.'[64] But it is clear that it was largely circumstances outside Conrad's control and unconnected with any long-term design that persuaded him to decide to embark on a British ship; and it is equally clear that he can have had little inkling that he would spend fifteen years or so sailing throughout the world as a British seaman and become a British master mariner during the course of this career.

---

traditional significance for Don Carlos's branch of the House of Bourbon. cf., Goya's portrait of the family of Carlos IV of Spain where ornamental arrows conspicuously adorn the hair of the women composing the central group (for the background to *these* arrows see Xavier de Salas, *La Familia de Carlos IV*, Barcelona, 1944). The photograph of Paula is reproduced as frontispiece to Miss Allen's *The Thunder and the Sunshine*.

The end of the French experience marked distinctly the end of a phase in Conrad's life: it seems that in leaving Marseilles he left behind him his youth. It is possible to form quite a clear picture of what he was like in character and appearance at this period. Characteristics which had already begun to emerge in Poland had blossomed during the four years abroad. Thus he had shown himself irresponsible, undisciplined, inconsiderate, sensitive, highly-strung, passionate, apparently rather susceptible to female attraction, and apparently prone to morbid depression; while his relations with Captain Escarras showed him capable of being fired to loyalty and effort. It is also evident that he had considerable personal charm. Some of these characteristics – irresponsibility, wildness and lack of consideration – were soon cast off, whereas others persisted and became more pronounced. Bobrowski made some sharp comments on Conrad's character in his letter to Buszczyński. At the start he thanked Buszczyński for his concern over Conrad,

particularly as I am acquiring the conviction that he has absolutely no thought of gratitude for all your kindnesses to him. In this matter, I find myself blameless because, as often as I called on him to maintain correspondence at least with his paternal and maternal uncle, I invariably put your respected person on an equal footing with them. . . . He has always explained to me that he does not write to his uncles because, not knowing them, he has nothing to say. He informed me however that he writes to you. It follows, hence, that he has honoured only me with his correspondence – which can be construed as feeding the hen [*sic*] that lays the golden eggs, as the fable goes.

Later in the same letter he said:

My studies of the Individual have convinced me that he is not a bad boy – only exceedingly sensitive, conceited – reserved yet excitable. In short, I found in him all the defects of the house of Nałęcz. He is able and eloquent; he has forgotten nothing of his Polish, though since leaving Cracow he spoke Polish for the first time with me . . .

After a careful study of the Individual, I have not lost hope that something may yet come of him – as we used to say: it is certain that the Nałęcz temperament, unfortunately not of the father but of his uncle [Robert], preponderates – I should like to be mistaken in this judgement.

In appearance, his face is more like that of his mother – quite handsome – while in build he resembles his father and is quite well made. In his ideas and conversation he is animated and original. We Poles, the young ones particularly, have an inborn liking for the French and the Republic; but he does not like them at all, and is for the Emperor. *De gustibus non est disputandum* – but I couldn't stand it on several occasions, and scolded him roundly. [24 March 1879]

A photograph taken in 1873 bears out Bobrowski's comment on Conrad's likeness to his mother, but it shows a dreaminess of expression and signs of indecisiveness in the rather sensuous mouth and somewhat receding chin. Another photograph, taken ten years later when Conrad was twenty-six, shows similar characteristics, although the lower part of the face is hidden by a beard. A photograph of 1896 is the first to show the determination and power that, despite all obstacles, went to make the successful seaman and then the successful novelist.

[III]

Merchant Seaman

AFTER unloading a cargo of coal at Constantinople the *Mavis* picked up a shipment of linseed destined for Lowestoft, where she docked on 18 June 1878.[1] Conrad had arrived in England, aged twenty, knowing no one and apparently no more than a few words of the language.[2]

At some point he had quarrelled with the captain of the *Mavis*; he therefore left her at Lowestoft and went off to London, where he spent most of his money.[3] His behaviour brought him another lengthy, slightly incoherent, letter from his uncle recapitulating his misdeeds:

Ponder for a moment, if you are able so to do, over what you have perpetrated this year – and ask yourself whether you could have met with such patience and forbearance even from a father as you have with me, and whether some limit should not have been reached?

You were idle for nearly a whole year – fell into debt, purposely shot yourself* – at the worst time of the year, tired out and with the most terrible rate of exchange – I hasten to you, pay, spend about 2000 roubles – to cover your needs I increase your allowance. Was all this not enough for you? And, when I make a fresh sacrifice if only to protect you from idleness and to assure you the stay on an English ship that you fancied, you leave the ship, giving me to understand that you did so because of the impossibility of paying the premium (for which they would certainly have waited, already having your 400 francs in hand), fully aware that you could not manage by yourself, knowing neither the country nor anybody there – you lose half the money you have, doing this – and write to me, as if to some school-chum, 'send me 500 francs, which you can deduct from my allowance' (from which one? Some allowance that you give yourself?): and 'advise me in these difficult circumstances'. In other words, you treat me like your banker – asking for advice so as to get money – assuming that if I give advice – which

* The Polish reads: '. . . *postrzeliłeś się rozmyślnie.*'

you may or may not follow – then I'll also give money for its realisation!!

Really, you have surpassed the limit of stupidity permitted to one of your age! You are straining the bounds of my patience! What possible advice can I give, not knowing the conditions of your profession in general or of those on the spot with me so far away here? When you chose this unfortunate profession, I told you: that I will not hasten after you to the ends of the world, and do not want to – for I do not intend nor do I want to spoil all my life because of the fantasies of a stripling.

I will help you, but I warn you that you must persevere in the decision taken, because your whole future depends on this. I will not allow you to idle away your time at my cost; you will find help in me, but not for a lazybones and spendthrift. I repeat in my letters what I told you when you set out to be a sailor, what I repeated in Marseilles; you must think for yourself and fend for yourself, for you have chosen a career which keeps you far from your natural advisers. You wanted it; did it; voluntarily chose it. Submit to the results of what you willed.

You ask for advice in 'the present difficult situation'. I will not give it for I cannot – for I did not send you where you are now. I agreed to your sailing on an English ship – but not to your staying in England, to travelling to London and wasting my money there! I can give you only one piece of advice – not a new one (you've had it a hundred times already) and it is: 'Arrange your budget within the limits of what I give you, for I will give you no more. Make no debts, for I won't pay them. Commit no stupidities, for I have no intention of making them good any more. I repeat, it's all the same to me in which marine you serve: the choice is yours. If you decide to enter the French Navy I've nothing against it – but, until you're twenty-one, do something and don't remain idle. Don't pretend to be the rich young gentleman and wait for someone to pull your chestnuts out of the fire – for that will not happen. If you can't get a ship, then be a *commis* for a time. But do something, earn something . . .

If you learn what poverty is, that will teach you to value money. If you wish to wait before signing on as a sailor in the French Navy, find some occupation while you are waiting, for unless you do so you won't get a penny from me even if you write to me that you are certain to be a vice-admiral in the British Navy one day. . . . I have no money for drones and have no intention of working so that someone else may enjoy himself at my expense. [8 July 1878]

This time Conrad did, possibly from desperation, pay attention to his uncle's warning; on 11 July, just under a month after arriving in England, he signed on with the *Skimmer of the Sea*,[4] which, belying its romantic name, was a coaster running between Lowestoft and Newcastle. From July to September he made six voyages in her. Then, towards the end of September, according to his own account many years later, he went to London with a newspaper cutting in his pocket giving the address of an obscure shipping agent. 'No explorer could have been more lonely,' he wrote; 'I did not know a single soul of all these millions that all around me peopled the mysterious distances of the streets.'[5] He recalls his visit to a 'Dickensian' office in a 'Dickensian nook of London':

> It was one o'clock in the afternoon, but the day was gloomy. By the light of a single gas-jet depending from the smoked ceiling I saw an elderly man, in a long coat of black broadcloth. He had a grey beard, a big nose, thick lips, and heavy shoulders. His curly white hair and the general character of his head recalled vaguely a burly apostle in the *barocco* style of Italian art. Standing up at a tall, shabby, slanting desk, his silver-rimmed spectacles pushed up high on his forehead, he was eating a mutton-chop, which had been just brought to him from some Dickensian eating-house round the corner.
>
> Without ceasing to eat he turned to me his florid *barocco* apostle's face with an expression of inquiry.
>
> I produced elaborately a series of vocal sounds which must have borne sufficient resemblance to the phonetics of English speech, for his face broke into a smile of comprehension almost at once. 'Oh it's you who wrote a letter to me the other day from Lowestoft about getting a ship.'[6]

After telling Conrad that it was forbidden by Act of Parliament to procure ships for sailors he apparently relented and offered to try to get him a berth as ordinary seaman on a wool clipper named the *Duke of Sutherland*, which ran between London and Sydney. Conrad embarked on 12 October 1878 and arrived back in London almost exactly a year later.[7] In *The Mirror of the Sea*[8] he describes his experiences as night-watchman when the ship was docked in

Sydney and also gives a graphic account of the behaviour of the chief mate, who at night invariably came aboard drunk when the ship was in harbour.

He did not sign on for another voyage with the *Duke of Sutherland*. Thaddeus Bobrowski's letters show that Conrad was anxious to visit his uncle, in the Ukraine or at Odessa, at this time; but Bobrowski, knowing that it was dangerous for the son of Apollo Korzeniowski to come within the clutches of the Russian Government, dissuaded him. 'I do not want you to come to Russia before you have been naturalized as an Englishman,' he wrote. Possibly Conrad found the British Merchant Navy a little uncongenial at first because he seems to have had a hankering to return to the Mediterranean. He asked his uncle to use his good offices to persuade M. Delestang to give him a testimonial as to his services while in his employment,* but without waiting for this he embarked on a steamship, the *Europa*, for a Mediterranean voyage. To judge from a letter of Bobrowski's this was an unpleasant experience:

Dear Boy,

I assure you I did not receive your letter from Patras and remained in profound ignorance of your fate until, to my surprise and disquiet, I received your last unpleasant letter of 2 February from London, only to be plunged into fresh disquiet.

I was not so much moved by the troubles you had on the *Europa*, though I realise that you must have felt them keenly, because they are inseparable from life and getting to know people. They pain you because you feel you didn't deserve them and that you are being exploited. I quite understand this and partly agree with you. But in your position, in which you have to gain everything by work and endurance, in a profession where the conditions are extremely hard, it was to be foreseen and probably now does not surprise you that such experiences would occur. . . . I am much more moved by the news that you are 'coughing and sometimes have a fever' for these are symptoms which, if prolonged, could be decisive for your

* Letter from Bobrowski, 7 September 1879. A testimonial was in fact produced, with the date 26 April 1880 and signed by Captain Escarras, commander of the *Saint-Antoine*. It has been preserved and is now in the Keating Collection at Yale.

health and even your life. I am very worried about this cough and fever. Undoubtedly the foggy London air won't help you; more probably sailing on the Mediterranean, in warm climes, would be helpful, so long as you do not overexert yourself in your duties. Weigh all for and against from the viewpoint of your health, get the opinion of a good doctor, and write to me what he finds and advises. [12 February 1880]

Conrad had arrived back in London on 30 January 1880 after a seven weeks' voyage.[9] Apparently he was without money and feeling unsettled and depressed. He was even thinking of becoming secretary to a Mr Lascalle, a Canadian businessman concerned with railways and politics. All this comes out in a letter from his Uncle Thaddeus dated 30 May 1880:

Your troubles because of that madman Captain Munro worry me not less than they do you, although I don't understand English logic since if the captain is a madman his certificate should be withdrawn. Until he is judicially proclaimed so, his certificate must remain valid. Well, we won't transform the English, so, having to do with them, we must adapt ourselves to them. I suppose that your *Europa* is now in port and that you have a testimonial from the present captain, the previous second-mate? And that you have passed your examination or will do so shortly. I wish you to pass that examination successfully and even with honours – I am sure you believe me – so please accept my warmest wishes and blessing. Frania has promised to pray for you not only in the evenings but in the mornings – and she keeps her promise.

I said what I had to say about naturalisation in my last letter. It is impossible to be a '*Vogel frei*' all your life. You must sooner or later establish your civil status and it is always well to arrange the matter calmly and not under the pressure of circumstances and necessity.

You would not be a Nałęcz, dear boy, if you didn't have constant occupation with some enterprise and if you didn't chase after ever new projects. This refers to what you wrote about Mr. Lascalle's proposal that you become his secretary and make money later in connection with railways!

Despite his uncertainties he persevered and passed his examination as Second Mate at the beginning of June,[10] which shows that he must have already gained quite a sound knowledge of English as well as having become a proficient sailor. Conrad describes this ordeal in *A Personal Record*. The examiner was

> tall, spare, with a perfectly white head and moustache, a quiet, kindly manner, and an air of benign intelligence, [who] must, I am forced to conclude, have been unfavourably impressed by something in my appearance. His old thin hands loosely clasped resting on his crossed legs, he began by an elementary question in a mild voice, and went on, went on – It lasted for hours, for hours. . . . 'This ancient person,' I said to myself, terrified, 'is so near his grave that he must have lost all notion of time. He is considering this examination in terms of eternity. It is all very well for him. His race is run. But I may find myself coming out of this room into the world of men a stranger, friendless, forgotten by my very landlady, even were I able after this endless experience to remember the way to my hired home'. . . . At last there fell a silence, and that, too, seemed to last for ages, while, bending over his desk, the examiner wrote out my pass-slip slowly with a noiseless pen. He extended the scrap of paper to me without a word, inclined his white head gravely to my parting bow.
>
> When I got out of the room I felt limply flat, like a squeezed lemon, and the door-keeper in his glass cage, where I stopped to get my hat and tip him a shilling, said:
>
> 'Well! I thought you were never coming out.'
>
> 'How long have I been in there?' I asked faintly. He pulled out his watch.
>
> 'He kept you, sir, just under three hours. I don't think this ever happened with any of the gentlemen before.'
>
> It was only when I got out of the building that I began to walk on air. And the human animal being averse from change and timid before the unknown, I said to myself that I would not mind really being examined by the same man on a future occasion.[11]

In *Chance*, too, Conrad expresses through Powell some of the feelings which he himself must have experienced at the time.[12]

He very quickly received a delighted letter of congratulations from his good-hearted uncle:

> Dear Boy and Officer,
>
> Two days ago I received the news (two letters together) of the

fortunate outcome of the examination you took. You have given me a real pleasure and my first reward by receiving that piece of ass's hide upon which so many terrible threats were written by the gentlemen of the *Board Office* should you fall into conflict with the duties of the chosen profession in which you have reached the first hierarchical step!!

I fully share your satisfaction which you can cull from two sources. Firstly, Respected Sir, you have proved to our country and to your family that you have not during four years in the world eaten bread without payment; secondly, that you have succeeded in overcoming the difficulties that arise from the language itself, from your difficult position as a foreigner without any patronage behind you – and all this was personified in Capt. Wyndham, whom may God grant long years of life that he imbued you with salutary fear! And yet, that good old captain fellow let himself be disarmed, and that kindhearted Professor Newton, who gave you courage while saying nothing of Wyndham's prejudices, and those mariners who rejoiced in your success – all seem greatly likeable to me at this juncture . . . that they took the stranger in! There are good people everywhere; it's only necessary to know how to find them and to attract them to oneself! You cannot complain of any lack of them on your way, from the first days of your life among strangers – suffice it to mention the honest Solary and Richard and those good London chaps. This imposes upon you the duty not only of gratitude to them but also of general love for people and of helping others who might need your help and whom you might encounter on your way through life. Pessimists can say what they like about the defects of the human race, but I tell you from my own experience that there are more good than bad people; it's necessary only to deal with them and approach them properly!

Well, Mister Officer, the first step is made! Now we need work and endurance, endurance and work, to make further ones and to assure your livelihood, for you'll soon be 24 – in October 1881. You still have a year to find something that would assure you a living without having to count on your Uncle. Your Uncle will always carefully follow your further fate, you can be sure, as long as you deserve this heartfelt solicitude, only that while giving you a bigger place in his heart he will give you a smaller place in his pocket, for others are coming who demand pocket-solicitude – your other uncle's children.

Many thanks for keeping me informed regarding your projects and hopes. As always, so now do I state: do as you wish, for I am blind in all matters regarding your profession – you therefore have *carte blanche* to dispose of your person as you see fit. I do not reject all your plans to become a Yankee. I stated what I think in this connection in my last letter – that I would not be in favour of giving up your maritime career to enter the service of an American politician though it would not scandalise me if you insist on acting counter to this view – but on two conditions: (1) that you bear in mind our proverb: As you make your bed, so you must lie on it, and (2) that you never forget what is due to the dignity of the nation and families to which you belong amidst the *businesses* [*sic*] of American life. [17 June 1880]

Conrad's success seems to have decided him to stick to a career as a sailor, for, a few weeks later, his uncle wrote with relief and satisfaction:

I see with pleasure that the 'Nałęcz' in you has been modified by the influence of the Bobroszczaki,* as your incomparable mother used to call her own family before she flew away to the nest of the 'Nałęcz'. This time I rejoice over the influence of my family, though I don't deny the Nałęczs a spirit of initiative and enterprise greater than that which runs in my veins. From the blending of the blood of these two excellent races in your worthy person should spring a character whose endurance and wise enterprise will cause the whole world to be astonished! [28 June 1880]

(2)

Conrad soon succeeded in getting a berth as an officer and, on 21 August 1880, embarked on the *Loch Etive*. She was, like the *Duke of Sutherland*, a wool clipper, and was bound for Sydney.[13] In *The Mirror of the Sea*[14] he gives a sketch of Captain Stuart, 'a man famous for the quick passages he had been used to make in the old *Tweed*, a ship famous the world over for her speed', and of the chief mate, who 'was very hard of hearing' and 'had the name of being the very devil of a fellow for carrying on sail on a ship'. Captain Stuart 'had a great name for sailorlike qualities – the sort of name that compelled my youthful admiration', but in

* A facetious form of the surname, meaning 'the Bobrowski family'.

middle-age had become somewhat irascible. The result was a series of violent but indeterminate altercations between him and the mate, with 'night clouds racing overhead, wind howling, royals set, and the ship rushing on in the dark, an immense white sheet of foam level with the lee rail'.

Conrad writes that during the voyage the second mate fell ill and he was given watch-keeping duties:

> I suppose it was something of a compliment for a young fellow to be trusted, apparently without any supervision, by such a commander as Captain S—; though as far as I can remember, neither the tone, nor the manner, nor yet the drift of Captain S—'s remarks addressed to myself did ever, by the most strained interpretation, imply a favourable opinion of my abilities.

In another chapter[15] of *The Mirror of the Sea* Conrad describes how, on the return voyage by the Cape Horn route, the *Loch Etive* succeeded in rescuing the crew of a wrecked Danish brig; and in 'Christmas Day at Sea'[16] he tells of an encounter with

> the first whaler I had ever seen . . . '*Alaska* – two years out from New York – east from Honolulu – two hundred and fifteen days on the cruising ground.' We passed, sailing slowly, within a hundred yards of her; and just as our steward started ringing the breakfast bell the captain and I held aloft, in good view of the figures watching us over her stern, the keg, properly headed up and containing, besides an enormous bundle of old newspapers, two boxes of figs in honour of the day. We flung it far out over the rail. Instantly our ship, sliding down the slope of a high swell, left it far behind in our wake. On board the *Alaska* a man in a fur cap flourished an arm; another, a much be-whiskered person, ran forward suddenly. I never saw anything so ready and so smart as the way that whaler, rolling desperately all the time, lowered one of her boats. . . . That Yankee whaler lost not a moment in picking up her Christmas present from the English wool clipper.

The *Loch Etive* docked at London in April 1881 and Conrad left her on the 25th.[17] Although the voyage must have been a tough assignment it seems to have offered the kind of atmosphere and activity that suited Conrad. His uncle congratulated him on his 'professional enthusiasm' in searching for another post with such alacrity, although he hoped that it would not this time take him quite as far as Australia or Cape Horn because he was very anxious to see Conrad and had arranged to take a cure at Wiesbaden in September with this in mind. None the less Conrad must not lose an opportunity of sailing, merely for his uncle's sake; a stay on land would be harmful and costly.[18] Conrad must have replied that a meeting this year would be virtually impossible because in his next letter Bobrowski philosophically expressed his disappointment.[19]

In June it appears that Conrad had a long voyage in prospect and Bobrowski again praised him, this time for the spirit of energy and enterprise which his last letter showed. He went on to thank God that Conrad was not forgetting his Polish and returned to a suggestion which he had already made, that Conrad should try sending articles to *Wędrowiec* (Wanderer) of Warsaw as his writing was 'not bad':

> It would be an exercise in your native tongue, that thread binding you to your country and countrymen, and finally a tribute to the memory of your father who wanted to and did serve his country with his pen. Think about this, brother, draw up some reminiscences of the voyage to Australia and send them as a sample to the *Wędrowiec*. Six reports from various parts of the world during the year wouldn't take up much of your time; they would bring you merit and provide you with recreation while giving pleasure to others. [28 June 1881]

As far as is known Conrad never followed up this suggestion. Nor did the voyage take place. Instead Conrad remained on land and there followed a mystifying episode. He apparently wrote a letter dated 10 August to Bobrowski telling him that he had sailed in a ship which had been wrecked and that he had thus lost all his kit; he therefore asked urgently for £10. This emerges from a letter of Bobrowski's dated 15 August:

> I received your desperate letter yesterday evening and reply to it today with the remittance you want, in accordance with the maxim: '*Bis dat qui cito dat*', or 'Twice gives he who quickly gives'. Your letter of the 10th reached me on the 14th, so I hope

that mine will reach you on the 19th and that you won't die of hunger before that time.

Thank God that you survived, that you're alive and only had a few days of illness in hospital – a desirable refuge this time – and that you emerged safely from that fatal adventure! I should have preferred, actually, that you had saved your things too together with your bones – but what's happened has happened, and we must reconcile ourselves to the fact and patch up your poverty as well as we can. Thus, I enclose the £10 you ask for, and I shall not deduct it from your October allowance. You can have it as an 'extra', as a *mariner in distress* . . .

En revenant à nos moutons, it seems to me that the shipowners of the *Anna* [*sic*] *Frost*, in negotiating for compensation for the ship, should have demanded some, too, for the things lost by their officers. It seems elementary! But perhaps this is not practised in a country where the rich manage very well, while no one thinks of the poor???

But there is a mystery here. It appears that there was only one ship registered with a name like *Anna Frost*;[20] she was the *Annie Frost* and had sailed from London on 31 July on a voyage round the world. Conrad was not on the crew's list, nor did the ship founder at this time.[21] It seems therefore that Conrad needed some money badly and decided to take his uncle for a ride. It may well be that he had planned to sail in the *Annie Frost* and that this was the prospective long voyage to which Bobrowski had alluded in an earlier letter. The episode had an uncanny sequel: the *Annie Frost* did in fact founder on this voyage, but not until just over a year later, when she was nearing home.[22]

In the same letter as he had written about the alleged *Annie Frost* disaster Conrad had apparently mentioned that he wanted to invest some money in a business venture with a Mr Sutherland; and Bobrowski, while saying that he had nothing in principle against speculations, characteristically insisted that if Conrad wished to speculate he should do it with money he had saved and not with other people's money or on credit. Nor could he refrain from warning Conrad:

As you are a 'Nałęcz' beware of risky speculations which rest on nothing but hope, for your grandfather wasted his property in speculations, and your uncle got into debt and many awkward fixes through the same cause.

It is not known what the venture was, and nothing seems to have come of it because the following year Sutherland died. Bobrowski commented: 'May Sutherland dwell in peace with God; he was a decent man and was the first to give you a helping hand in London; if he ever "shaved" you, forgive him for my sake.'

Eventually, on 19 September, Conrad found a berth, as second mate on the *Palestine*, a barque of 425 tons commanded by Captain Beard.[23] Both the ship and the captain were old and decrepit, and the fact that Conrad took the post shows that he must have been rather desperate for a job. A letter from his uncle reveals that Conrad was not at all enthusiastic about the new ship:

Dear Boy,

Thank God that you've after all found a post, and that you're on a ship! And thanks to you for letting me know all this, that you're keeping up your spirits and not losing courage! It seems to me you're not very satisfied with the post; is it because the 'barque' touches on your honour? Then, of course, £4 monthly is disrespectful – to your pocket, and finally, the captain seems to you to be merely a 'creature', and this gives me a sad picture of his intellect. Well, perhaps the last point will enable you to distinguish yourself as 'a man conscious of his craft and useful'. The die is cast! Proceed in health and return safely. *Deus te ducat, perducat, et reducat*, as our ancestors used to say when setting out with sword in hand – and I say the same, bidding you farewell on an element unknown to them, embracing and blessing you with all my heart. [23 September 1881]

Conrad describes the eventful and disastrous voyage of the *Palestine* in 'Youth', and he referred to this story as 'a feat of memory. It is a record of experience. . .'[24] He changed the name of the *Palestine* to *Judea* but kept the name of the captain, Beard, and the mate, Mahon, unaltered;[25] he also retained some at least of the captain's characteristics: 'As to the captain . . . he could just write a kind of sketchy hand'[26] is borne out by the letter of reference which Beard wrote for Conrad.[27] In general he seems to have stuck close to the known facts except in the final scene of the drama.

The ship was dogged with bad luck from the start. She sailed from London on 21 September 1881 to pick up a cargo of coal at Newcastle to take to Bangkok, but ran into a gale on the way. At Newcastle she was rammed by a steamer and delayed for three weeks. A bald account of the subsequent events is contained in the report of the Court of Inquiry which was held in Singapore after the loss of the ship:

> On the 29th November 1881 she sailed from Newcastle-upon-Tyne with a cargo of 557 tons of West Hartley coal, bound to Bang Kok, and a crew of thirteen hands all told. Arriving in the chops of the English Channel, the vessel encountered a succession of heavy gales, losing sail and springing a leak on 24 December 1881, the crew refusing to proceed, the vessel put into Falmouth. The coal was there discharged and stored under cover, with the exception of about 90 tons, and the vessel thoroughly repaired in dock.[28]

The *Palestine* remained at Falmouth for almost nine months. Conrad relates in 'Youth' how he was given leave during this time and blew three months' pay in London:

> It took me a day to get there, and pretty well another to come back – but three months' pay went, all the same. I don't know what I did with it. I went to a Music Hall, I believe, lunched, dined, and supped in a swell place in Regent Street, and was back to time, with nothing but a complete set of Byron's works and a new railway rug to show for three months' work![29]

He must have described the *Palestine*'s misfortune to his uncle, who wrote to him in January:

> Your misfortunes of the past year filled me with despair. I speak of it as a year already over, as I hope and trust fervently that your bad luck will be over with it. Fate is no doubt in part responsible, but your judgment is also to blame. This time, at least, after your accident, your cool judgment seems to have deserted you in accepting such a wretched ship as the *Palestine*. I quite understand that you made up your mind to do so to avoid being a burden to me in London, and to qualify by serving as a second officer for your final examination. But, my dear boy, you did not take into account the

mishaps and accidents which in such a case were bound to follow. However, though you fall sick or injure yourself, I shall not abandon you. But if you succeed in drowning yourself it won't profit you to arrive at the Valley of Jehoshaphat in the rank of a third or second officer! I never think I have the right to control you now you are twenty-four, but all the same I advise you not to sail in such a lamentable ship as yours. Danger is certainly part of a sailor's life, but that does not preclude you from having a sensible attachment to life, nor prevent you taking reasonable steps to preserve it. Both your Captain Beard and you strike me as desperate men, who go out of their way to see knocks and wounds, while your ship-owner is a rascal who risks the lives of ten brave men for the sake of a blackguardly profit.

Think well, my dear fellow, over what you ought to do. I shall not come down on you if you go back to London, and I shall try to help you. For, as can be imagined, I do not want, for the sake of saving three to five hundred roubles, to see you at the bottom of the sea, or ill or injured, or crippled with rheumatism for the rest of your life. So weigh the pros and cons and the chances of carrying through your project, curb your enthusiastic ambition, and do what reason dictates. [20 January 1882]

But the ship seems to have inspired an obstinate attachment in Conrad as can be seen from a letter of Bobrowski's four months later:

Dear Boy,

Inexpressible pleasure was given me by your last letter, of 11 May, full of energy, bright ideas and the desire to work, as also no less the news of your excellent health. *Mens sana in corpore sano* . . .

You insist, my dear little one; or is it that professional honour and local customs require that you sail on a miserable ship, and break your neck? Knowing nothing of either of these, I can have no voice in the matter beyond blessing you for the voyage and wishing you a safe arrival and return . . . [26 May 1882]

Although Captain Beard was in his late fifties this was his first command and he was evidently determined not to be deprived of its enjoyment. His perseverance was rewarded and the ship sailed for the last time on 17 September 1882. All went well, if very slowly, until the *Palestine* was approaching Java Head. The report of the Court of Inquiry continues the story:

> Nothing unusual occurred until noon of 11 March, when a strong smell resembling paraffin oil was perceived; at this time the vessel's position was lat. 2 36 S and long. 105 45 E Banca Strait. Next day smoke was discovered issuing from the coals on the port side of the main hatch. Water was thrown over them until the smoke abated, the boats were lowered, water placed in them. On the thirteenth some coals were thrown overboard, about four tons, and more water poured down the hold. On the fourteenth, the hatches being on but not battened down, the decks blew up fore and aft as far as the poop. The boats were then provisioned and the vessel headed for the Sumatra shore. About 3 p.m. the S.S. *Somerset* [Conrad calls her the *Somerville*] came alongside in answer to signals and about 6 p.m. she took the vessel in tow. Shortly afterwards the fire rapidly increased and the master of the *Palestine* requested the master of the *Somerset* to tow the barque on shore. This being refused, the tow-rope was slipped and about 11 p.m. the vessel was a mass of fire, and all hands got into the boats, three in number.

At this point, in order to heighten the dramatic effect of the story, Conrad seems to have departed radically from the facts. He describes how he was in charge of the smallest boat:

> I had two men with me, a bag of biscuits, a few tins of meat, and a breaker of water. I was ordered to keep close to the long-boat, that in case of bad weather we might be taken into her.
>
> And do you know what I thought? I thought I would part company as soon as I could. I wanted to have my first command all to myself. I wasn't going to sail in a squadron if there were a chance for independent cruising. I would make land by myself . . .
>
> Before sunset a thick rain-squall passed over the two boats, which were far astern, and that was the last I saw of them for a time. Next day I sat steering my cockle-shell – my first command – with nothing but water and sky around me. I did sight in the afternoon the upper sails of a ship far away, but said nothing, and my men did not notice her. You see I was afraid she might be homeward bound, and I had no mind to turn back from the portals of the East. . . . I steered many days.

I need not tell you what it is to be knocking about in an open boat. I remember nights and days of calm, when we pulled, we pulled, and the boat seemed to stand still, as if bewitched within the circle of the sea horizon. I remember the heat, the deluge of rain-squalls that kept us baling for dear life . . . and I remember sixteen hours on end with a mouth dry as a cinder and a steering-oar over the stern to keep my first command head on to a breaking sea.

But the facts appear to have been more prosaic.* The report of the Court of Inquiry recounts how:

The boats remained by the vessel until 8.30 on the fifteenth. She was still above water, but inside appeared a mass of fire. The boats arrived at Muntok at 10 p.m. on the fifteenth [in 'Youth' Marlow took as many days to get to land as Conrad in fact took hours], and the master reported the casualty to the harbour master. The officers and crew came on to Singapore in the British steamer *Sissie* arriving on 22 March.

The Court then went on to exonerate the officers and crew from any blame in the affair.

Conrad remained in Singapore for a month waiting for a chance to get back to England and at the beginning of May took a passage for Liverpool on a passenger steamer.

Thus he had had his first contact with the East. In 'Youth' he gives a gorgeously romantic evocation of the impact which the East had on him as he reached Muntok. But it is difficult to separate his actual impression from the imaginative gloss; many years later he was irritated with Curle for mentioning in the draft of an article the name of the port at which he had landed:

The paragraph you quote of the East meeting the narrator is all right in itself; whereas directly it's connected with Muntok it becomes nothing at all. Muntok is a damned hole without any

* 'Youth', pp. 34–6. Conrad was of course under no obligation to stick to the facts and there would be no point in emphasizing the discrepancies were it not that it has been generally assumed that 'Youth' was an accurate recording of the voyage of the *Palestine*. Aubry for instance wrote that the story was 'precisely in every detail the story of the barque *Palestine*' (*L.L.* I, p. 67; cf. *The Sea Dreamer*, p. 94).

beach and without any glamour. ... Therefore the paragraph, when pinned to a particular spot, must appear diminished – a fake. And yet it is true. [24 April 1922]

Subsequently he was to show that he was indeed susceptible to the spell of the East, 'impalpable and enslaving, like a charm, like a whispered promise of mysterious delight'.[30] And it may be that he would not have returned to Europe so soon if it had not been for the need to take his mate's examination.

(3)

When Conrad arrived back in England his uncle pressed him to come and visit him in Cracow and again brought up the question of naturalization.

I must admit that I should prefer to examine your countenance a little later but belonging to a free citizen of a free country than earlier, but belonging to a citizen of the world. [5 June 1883]

However, Bobrowski's doctor had recommended him to take the waters at Marienbad and so it was decided to meet there; thus naturalization lost its urgency and Conrad joined his uncle about 22 July,[31] leaving the matter still unsettled.

This was the first time that he and his guardian had met since the fortnight Bobrowski had spent in Marseilles five years ago, just after Conrad had wounded himself. Circumstances were now very different, and although Conrad's future must still have seemed somewhat obscure he could at least claim with justifiable pride that he had successfully achieved his immediate object of becoming a proficient sailor, thus rewarding his uncle's long-suffering and devoted support – a fact which Bobrowski had been quick to applaud. Conrad stayed with his uncle for a month, first at Marienbad and then at Töplitz near the frontier of Saxony. He returned to London by way of Dresden whence he wrote what was evidently a very affectionate letter to his uncle who replied:

Your letter gave me real pleasure. Everything you say I shall remember in my heart. . . . You are right in supposing that when I returned to Töplitz I was sad and depressed when in the evening I sat down at table opposite the empty chair of my admiral. . . . As for going to sea again, the sooner you do so the better . . . and I hope you will naturalise yourself at the very earliest moment, and that the 'filthy lucre' which has been put aside for it will not be used for any other purpose. [31 August 1883]

It is clear that for financial if for no other reasons Conrad was not prepared to spend the rest of his life simply as a member of the British merchant navy; and while he was staying at Marienbad he had discussed with his uncle one of his periodic business schemes. This one was more substantial than the others. Conrad had become friendly with a man named Adolf Krieger, who was in Barr, Moering & Co., a firm of shipping agents, and wanted his uncle to advance some money to buy him an interest in the business. Bobrowski agreed to put up £300, later raising it to £350, out of a fund which he had created for Conrad's benefit.[32]

For the time being, however, Conrad was determined still to remain at sea. On 10 September 1883[33] he embarked as second mate on the *Riversdale*, a sailing ship of 1,500 tons bound for the East. Nothing is known of his experiences on this voyage except that he appears not to have got on with his captain, L. B. McDonald, because he threw up his berth and left the ship at Madras on 17 April 1884,[34] while on his certificate of discharge, against 'Character for ability' is written 'Very good' in the captain's hand, whereas against 'Character for conduct' is written 'Decline'.*

From Madras Conrad went to Bombay in search of another berth. Aubry writes that Conrad told him

he was sitting with other officers of the Mercantile Marine on the verandah of the Sailors' Home in Bombay, which overlooks the port, when he saw a lovely ship, with all the graces of a yacht, come sailing into the harbour. She was the *Narcissus*, of 1,300 tons, built by a sugar refiner of Greenock nine years before. Her owner had

* Certificate of Discharge (Yale). Conrad was well out of it because the ship foundered off Madras just under two months later (Agreement and Account of Crew).

originally intended her for some undertaking in connection with the Brazilian sugar trade. This had not come off, and subsequently he had decided to employ her in the Indian Ocean and the Far East.[35]

She was commanded by Captain Archibald Duncan.[36] A few days later Conrad signed on as her second mate.

She left Bombay on 28 April and was paid off at Dunkirk on 17 October. This voyage formed the basis of that in *The Nigger of the 'Narcissus'*, although it would be absurd to expect the novel to be an exact transcript of Conrad's actual experiences; as he told Aubry in this connection:

> I do not write history, but fiction, and I am therefore entitled to choose as I please what is most suitable in regard to characters and particulars to help me in the general impression I wish to produce.

But, he continued:

> Most of the personages I have portrayed actually belonged to the crew of the real *Narcissus* including the admirable Singleton (whose real name was Sullivan) Archie, Belfast, and Donkin. I got the two Scandinavians from associations with another ship.[37]

James Wait was not the name of the 'nigger' on the *Narcissu* but, said Conrad, of another negro sailor, on the *Duke of Sutherland*.* The 'Agreement and Account of Crew' of the *Narcissus* has survived[38] and holds some clues. Below the name of Conrad Korzeniowski on the list there is that of Joseph Barron, A.B., aged thirty-five, and born at Charlton; his last ship was the *Count of Dumfries* and, being illiterate, he signed the agreement with a cross (in the novel Wait's name is described as 'all a smudge'). Barron died at sea on 24 September, just under a month before the ship docked at Dunkirk, and as he is the only member of the crew to be listed as having died during the voyage it is safe to asume that he was the 'nigger'. Another member of the crew was an A.B.

* There was no one named Wait among the crew of the *Duke of Sutherland* when Conrad sailed in her. There was, however, a Richard Knowles who may have been the original of 'Dirty Knowles'. See Agreements for these two voyages.

named Charles Dutton who also signed his name with a cross. He is the only one for whom no age was given which suggests that he was illegitimate, while both his place of birth and his last ship are entered as St Ellens. He was put in prison when the *Narcissus* called at Cape Town on the voyage out; and although Conrad himself could not have come in contact with him it may be that talk among the crew about Dutton's behaviour and character provided him with material for Donkin. Two other members of the crew correspond to characters in the book: James Craig, aged twenty-one, from Belfast, and Archibald McLean, aged twenty-three, from Scotland. There were also a number of Scandinavians among the crew, but no one named Sullivan; and so Conrad must have been mistaken about Singleton's actual name.*

Conrad related to Aubry his last memory of the dying negro:

> I remember, Conrad said, as if it had occurred but yesterday, the last occasion I saw the Nigger. That morning I was quarter officer, and about five o'clock I entered the double-bedded cabin where he was lying full length. On the lower bunk, ropes, fids and pieces of cloth had been deposited, so as not to have to take them down into the sail-room if they should be wanted at once. I asked him how he felt, but he hardly made me any answer. A little later a man brought him some coffee in a cup provided with a hook to suspend it on the edge of the bunk. At about six o'clock the officer in charge came to tell me that he was dead. We had just experienced an awful gale in the vicinity of the Needles, south of the cape, of which I have tried to give an impression in my book.†

* There was, however, a Daniel Sullivan, born in Co. Kerry, aged fifty-four, who signed his name with a cross, on the *Tilkhurst* when Conrad sailed in her.

† Notes made in June, 1924, after a conversation with Conrad at Oswalds, Bishopsbourne (*L.L.*, I, pp. 77–8). In Melville's *Redburn* a malingerer named Jackson tyrannizes over the crew and, like James Wait, finally dies at sea from tuberculosis (cf., in particular pp. 75 and 354–6 of Vol. V of the 'Standard Edition' of Melville's works, 1922). But the similarities between *Redburn* and *The Nigger of the 'Narcissus'* are almost certainly a coincidence.

This novel contains the distilled essence of Conrad's experience at sea, on sailing ships, and is of course far more important for the understanding of his life at this period than is any mere factual account of ships and voyages. But there is one peculiarity. The process of distillation has virtually eliminated all the squalid ingredients. It is true that the storms in *The Nigger* and *Typhoon* provide a tough test of endurance, but here the situation is raised to the heroic level (although many individuals do not behave heroically). However, unlike Loti, Conrad makes scarcely an allusion to the everyday discomforts and squalor to which a seaman would inevitably have been subjected: the stench below deck, the damp and the cold or the heat, the frequent periods of bad food and of apparently interminable boredom. It is as if the First World War were to be described in terms of the battles of the Somme and Passchendaele.

(4)

Conrad spent the winter of 1884 in London, where, on 3 December, he passed his First Mate's examination[39] although his examiner's reputation was 'simply execrable'. Conrad described his ordeal in *A Personal Record*.[40] To test his ingenuity and knowledge the examiner put him in an imaginary ship and invented one mishap after another from which Conrad had to extricate himself:

> That imaginary ship seemed to labour under a most comprehensive curse. It's no use enlarging on these never-ending misfortunes; suffice it to say that long before the end I would have welcomed with gratitude an opportunity to exchange into the *Flying Dutchman*.

On 24 April of the following year he embarked at Hull as second mate on the *Tilkhurst*, a sailing ship of 1,500 tons. The ship called at Penarth, near Cardiff, to collect a cargo of coal for Singapore. During the five-day stay at Penarth, Conrad carried out a commission entrusted to him by a Polish sailor named Komorowski, who had arrived at

Cardiff some time before as a stowaway on a German ship to escape conscription in Russia.* This was to repay a small sum of money which Komorowski had borrowed from another Pole named Kliszewski who had emigrated to England after the 1830 insurrection and set up as a watchmaker in Cardiff. Conrad's visit to the Kliszewskis led to a warm friendship, particularly with the son, Spiridion, a man of Conrad's age. His letters to Spiridion Kliszewski during his voyage on the *Tilkhurst* are Conrad's earliest known pieces of writing in English. Although the English is almost correct they are stilted and impersonal except for passages couched in a quaint literary jargon.† The first letter was dated Singapore, 27 September, 1885:

Dear Sir,

According to your kindly expressed wish and my promise, I hasten to acquaint you with my safe arrival here.

This globe accomplished almost half a revolution since I parted from you in the station at Cardiff: and old Father Time, always diligent in his business, has put his eraser over many men, things and memories: yet I defy him to obliterate ever from my mind and heart the recollection of the kindness you and yours have shown to a stranger, on the strength of a distant national connection . . .[41]

He wrote again from Singapore on 13 October, thanking Spiridion Kliszewski for a letter and also for a copy of the *Daily Telegraph*. He discussed the political situation and revealed how completely he had written off the possibility of a resurgence of Poland. His hatred of Russia, however, which he retained throughout his life, did not long continue to blind him to the dangers of German policy:

. . . I saw with pleasure the evidence of improved relations with

* This is related by Aubry in *Joseph Conrad; Life and Letters*, Vol. I, p. 78, but with no source. He was no doubt given the details by the Kliszewski family. Komorowski was presumably the Polish sailor to whom Conrad refers in *A Personal Record*, pp. 119–20 (his name is two letters shorter than Korzeniowski as Conrad stated).

† Mrs Danilewicz has pointed out to me that these passages clearly show the influence of Polish literary style.

Germany, the only power with whom an Anti-Russian alliance would be useful, and even possible, for Great Britain. No wonder that in this unsettled state of affairs politics, at least foreign politics, are slightly dull. Events are casting shadows, more or less distorted, shadows deep enough to suggest the lurid light of battlefields somewhere in the near future, but all those portents of great and decisive doings leave me in a state of despairing indifference: for, whatever may be the changes in the fortunes of living nations, for the dead there is no hope and no salvation. We have passed through the gates where '*lasciate ogni speranza*' is written in letters of blood and fire, and nothing remains for us but the darkness of oblivion.

In the presence of such national misfortune, personal happiness is impossible in its absolute form of general contentment and peace of heart. Yet, I agree with you that in a free and hospitable land even the most persecuted of our race may find relative peace and a certain amount of happiness, materially at least; consequently I understood and readily accepted your reference to 'Home'. When speaking, writing or thinking in English, the word 'home' always means for me the hospitable shores of Great Britain.

We are almost discharged, but our loading port is, as yet, uncertain. At any rate, I hope to be in England some time in July, when you may depend I shall gladly avail myself of your kindness and go down to Cardiff to see you all . . .[42]

On 25 November he wrote again, 'after a tedious passage' to Calcutta. Here he showed once more that he was not prepared to accept the prospect of spending the rest of his life as a merchant seaman, and that he had lost none of his earlier enterprise and adventurousness. He outlined, for Kliszewski's comments, a scheme to go in for whaling* once he had passed his last examination:

. . . And now here I must pray you take also for granted that I am brimful of the most exhaustive information upon the subject. I have read, studied, pumped professional men and imbibed knowledge upon whale fishing and sealing for the last four years. I am acquainted with the practical part of the undertaking in a

* In *The Nigger of the 'Narcissus'* Conrad mentions that Captain Allistoun, who may have been modelled on Captain Duncan, had been a master harpooner in his youth. Perhaps Conrad had also been reading Melville at this time.

thorough manner. Moreover, I have the assurance of active help from a man brought up in the trade, and although doing well where he is now, ready to return to his former pursuit (of whales). Finally I have a vessel in view, on very advantageous terms . . .[43]

He then goes on to discuss how he can raise the necessary capital of £1,500 and asks whether it would be feasible to take out a life insurance policy and use this as a security on which to borrow the sum.

. . . I boldly ask for actual mental help in carrying the matter through, should it turn out to be something more than the ravings of an unbusinesslike lunatic.

I have thought over it in all its aspects. Believe me, it is not the desire of getting much money that prompts me. It is simply the wish to work for myself. I am sick and tired of sailing about for little money and less consideration. But I love the sea: and if I could just clear my bare living in the way I suggested I should be comparatively happy.[44]

In a second letter from Calcutta the result of the General Election called forth an almost apocalyptic diatribe against 'the rush of social-democratic ideas':

By this time, you, I and the rest of the 'right thinking' have been grievously disappointed by the result of the General Election. The newly enfranchised idiots have satisfied the yearnings of Mr. Chamberlain's herd by cooking the national goose according to his recipe. The next culinary operation will be a pretty kettle of fish of an international character. Joy reigns in St. Petersburg, no doubt, and profound disgust in Berlin: the International Socialist Association are triumphant, and every disreputable ragamuffin in Europe feels that the day of universal brotherhood, despoliation and disorder is coming apace, and nurses day-dreams of well-plenished pockets amongst the ruin of all that is respectable, venerable and holy. The great British Empire went over the edge, and yet on to the inclined plane of social progress and radical reform. The downward movement is hardly perceptible yet, and the clever men who start it may flatter themselves with the progress; but they will soon find that the fate of the nation is out of their hands now! The Alpine avalanche rolls quicker and quicker as it nears the abyss – its ultimate destination! Where's the man to stop the crashing avalanche?

Where's the man to stop the rush of social-democratic ideas? The opportunity and the day have come and are gone! Believe me: gone for ever! For the sun is set and the last barrier removed. England was the only barrier to the pressure of infernal doctrines born in continental back-slums. Now, there is nothing! The destiny of this nation and of all nations is to be accomplished in darkness amidst much weeping and gnashing of teeth, to pass through robbery, equality, anarchy and misery under the iron rule of a military despotism! Such is the lesson of common sense logic.

Socialism must inevitably end in Caesarism.

Forgive me this long disquisition, but your letter – so earnest on the subject – is my excuse. I understand you perfectly. You wish to apply remedies to quell the dangerous symptoms: you evidently hope yet.

I do so no longer. Truthfully, I have ceased to hope a long time ago. We must drift!

The whole herd of idiotic humanity are moving in that direction at the bidding of unscrupulous rascals and a few sincere, but dangerous, lunatics. These things must be. It is fatality.

I live mostly in the past and the future. The present has, you easily understand, but few charms for me. I look with the serenity of despair and the indifference of contempt upon the passing events. Disestablishment, Land Reform, Universal Brotherhood are but like milestones on the road to ruin. The end will be awful, no doubt! Neither you nor I shall live to see the final crash: although we both may turn in our graves when it comes, for we both feel deeply and sincerely. Still, there is no earthly remedy for those earthly misfortunes, and from above, I fear, we may obtain consolation, but no remedy. 'All is vanity.' [19 December 1885, *L.L.*, I, pp. 84–5]

Conrad wrote a third letter from Calcutta to Spiridion Kliszewski in which he returned to his whaling scheme:

I venture to express the hope that you will kindly write to Dundee and pronounce your verdict upon my scheme. Even should all the arrangements (as I expect) strike you as foolish, yet I pray you to opine upon the insurance part as distinct from the whaling enterprise. What I should like to know is: can I reasonably expect to be able to raise a loan upon that security, should opportunity occur (to get command for instance) on moderate terms? . . .

We are leaving tomorrow and a five months' passage is before us. [6 January 1886, *L.L.*, I, 85]

The voyage back was apparently uneventful and Conrad was discharged at Dundee on 17 June.[45] He travelled to London with his commander, Captain Blake, and his wife. Conrad liked and admired Captain Blake:

> Well over fifty years of age when I knew him, short, stout, dignified, perhaps a little pompous, he was a man of a singularly well-informed mind, the least sailor-like in outward aspect, but certainly one of the best seamen whom it has been my good luck to serve under.

Apparently the friendship was mutual because Conrad relates that Captain Blake told him:

> If you happen to be in want of employment, remember that as long as I have a ship you have a ship, too.

But this turned out to have been Captain Blake's last voyage, for he was an ailing man and Conrad was only to see him once again when he visited him, convalescent but nonetheless a sick man, at his home.[46]

Conrad must have been feeling very restless and uncertain about the future because at the same time as he was asking Kliszewski's advice on his whaling project he was apparently writing to Krieger and Bobrowski about the possibility of staying in London and going into commerce, presumably with Barr, Moering.[47] The whaling came to nothing,* and by the time that he was in London Conrad had decided to sail at least once again, as master of a ship,[48] although he came up with another business suggestion, that Bobrowski should invest some money in a transport firm.[49]

In London there were two immediate tasks: naturalization, on which Bobrowski had again been pressing him, and his examination for a master's certificate. In a letter announcing his brother Casimir's death Bobrowski wrote:

> As a closing of accounts for the past I permit myself to demand from you only two things: a master's certificate and naturalisation, and I ask in the hope that you will shortly inform me that both matters have been settled successfully. [6 July 1886]

* Spiridion Kliszewski told Aubry that he had dissuaded Conrad from this venture.

A little over a month after this letter, on 19 August,[50] Conrad was at last able to tell his uncle that he was a British subject and he soon got a letter in reply, saying

> I am extremely glad that you have completed your naturalisation, and clasp my Englishman to my breast as well as my nephew. [9 September 1886]

Then three months later, on 10 November 1886,[51] he passed the examination for a master's certificate, the triumphant culmination of around ten years of enterprise and perseverance. He describes this last examination in *A Personal Record*; it was apparently far less of an ordeal than the others, his examiner being kindly, loquacious and reminiscent. Conrad also recalls his feelings on being told that he had passed:

> It was a fact, I said to myself, that I was now a British master mariner beyond a doubt. It was not that I had an exaggerated sense of that very modest achievement, with which, however, luck, opportunity, or any extraneous influence could have had nothing to do. That fact, satisfactory and obscure in itself, had for me a certain ideal significance. It was an answer to certain outspoken scepticism, and even to some not very kind aspersions. I had vindicated myself from what had been cried upon as a stupid obstinacy or a fantastic caprice.[52]

When Bobrowski heard the news he wrote ecstatically:

> Long live the '*Ordin: Master British Merchant Service*'! May he live as long as possible! May he be healthy and may every success meet him in every enterprise on sea and on land! You really delighted me with this news about the red seal on your certificate. Not being an admiral, I have no title to give orders to a newly-created Master, and I leave to his sole discretion to solve the problem: whether he is to change his O.M. into E.U. It depends on the prospects and your plans for your future career. As the humble provider of means for that enterprise, I can only be glad that my groats were not wasted but led you to the peak of your chosen profession, in which Mr. Antony [Syroczyński], the heir to the virtues of the Romans and Greeks, drew such an unfavourable horoscope, twelve years ago, for the young aspirant to Neptune's service. You are, worthy sir, twenty-nine years of age and have a

craft in your hand, and you know and understand what you have to do further. [26 November 1886]

(5)

In the same year Conrad apparently wrote a story which he called 'The Black Mate' for a competition in the magazine *Tit-Bits.* The story was not accepted and the original version does not seem to have survived. In 1908 Conrad had a story called 'The Black Mate' published in the *London Magazine* which was presumably the original story revised. In 1922 he wrote to Pinker:

> I am surprised at the length of the thing. My feeling is that there will be nothing actually disgraceful in its inclusion in my collected editions . . . but it would complicate my literary history in a sort of futile way. I don't remember whether I told you that I wrote that thing in '86 for a prize competition, started, I think, by *Tit-Bits.* It is an extraneous phenomenon. My literary life began privately in 1890 [1889 in fact] and publicly in 1895 with *Almayer's Folly,* which is regarded generally as my very first piece of writing. However, the history of the 'Black Mate', its origin etc., etc., need not be proclaimed on housetops, and *Almayer's Folly* may keep its place as my first serious work.*

Jessie Conrad denied that the magazine story of 1908 had anything to do with the original 'Black Mate' and claimed that it was she who suggested the subject. In one of George T. Keating's copies of *Tales of Hearsay*† she wrote of 'The Black Mate':

> I was amazed one day to hear him [Conrad] assuring Mr. Curle that it was the first thing he had written. My mild protest called forth such a violent excitement that I forbore to insist. . . . I gave

* 19 January 1922, *L.L.*, II, p. 264. In Richard Curle's copy of the privately printed edition of 'The Black Mate' Conrad wrote: 'My memories of this tale are confused. I have a notion that it was first written some time in the late eighties and retouched later.' This edition appeared in February 1922.

† This was the title chosen by Richard Curle for a posthumous volume containing four of Conrad's stories which had not been published in book form.

my husband the facts and matter for the tale but he received it in such a manner that my astonishment was great when I saw the 'bones' I had given clothed in the story and heard his unexpected claim that it was his first story.*

It is difficult to know which of these statements is true. On the whole Conrad's own seems most likely to be so. His account of his literary life was based on the assumption that *Almayer's Folly* was his first piece of creative writing, and it would have been pointless and inconvenient to say that 'The Black Mate' was his first literary production if it was not. An examination of *Tit-Bits* for the 1880's has produced nothing conclusive. *Tit-Bits* was constantly running competitions of one sort or another, but the only one for which Conrad could appropriately have entered a version of 'The Black Mate' was the 'SPECIAL PRIZE FOR SAILORS. . . . We will give the sum of Twenty Guineas for the best article entitled "My Experiences as a Sailor".' This competition was announced in the number of 1 May 1886.† Perhaps Conrad had told his wife the story and when later he was looking around for a subject she had fed it back to him and forgotten that he had been the original source.

In its final form it is the story of a mate who dyes his grey hair black in order to get a ship, but during the voyages his bottles of dye get broken and in his worry that his secret will be discovered he falls down the poop ladder, cutting his head. He manages to extricate himself from his predicament by playing on the superstitions of the captain who is a con-

* *A Conrad Memorial Library*, p. 365. Jessie Conrad repeated this, more graphically, to R. L. Mégroz: 'I can remember giving Conrad material for "The Black Mate". But on one of his naughty days he said that "The Black Mate" was his first work, and when I said, "No, *Almayer's Folly* was the first thing you ever did", he burst out: "If I like to say 'The Black Mate' was my first work, I shall say so!"' *Joseph Conrad's Mind and Method*, 1931, p. 88.

† *Tit-Bits*, Vol. X, no. 237, p. 33. The Christmas competition number for 1885 had one item which might have applied if Conrad had merely submitted 'The Black Mate' in the form of a brief anecdote. It was 'What is the most embarrassing position a man can be placed in?' (Vol. IX, no. 214, p. 88). Each week a 'prize Tit-Bit' was printed which usually took the form of a story, but on no set subject.

vinced spiritualist; he pretends that he has had a supernatural 'manifestation' which caused his fall and turned his hair grey. It is a trivial story, told in a breezily colloquial style, and could equally have been written light-heartedly for a rather low-grade magazine competition or as a pot-boiler to earn a few pounds.

(6)

His master's certificate entitled Conrad to a command, but he urgently needed to earn money, particularly as he could no longer rely on Bobrowski, who on the death of his brother, Casimir, had been forced to assume the responsibility for the widow and children. Therefore, on 16 February 1887, he took the post of first mate on the *Highland Forest*,[53] a sailing ship of 1,000 tons, bound for Samarang in Java and at the moment waiting at Amsterdam for an ice-bound cargo.

In *The Mirror of the Sea*[54] Conrad has a fine description of his weeks of waiting amid a bleak winter landscape of 'snow-sprinkled waste ground, [and] the visions of ships frozen in a row, appearing vaguely like corpses of black vessels in a white world, so silent, so lifeless, so soulless they seemed to be', and of his visits to a café in the town, 'an immense place, lofty and gilt, upholstered in red plush, full of electric lights, and so thoroughly warmed that even the marble tables felt tepid to the touch', where 'the waiter who brought me my cup of coffee bore, by comparison with my utter isolation, the dear aspect of an intimate friend. There, alone in a noisy crowd, I would write slowly a letter addressed to Glasgow, of which the gist would be: there is no cargo, and no prospect of any coming till late spring apparently.' He would also visit the office of the charterers where he would implore and remonstrate with the jovial but impenetrable Mr Hudig,* 'a big, swarthy Netherlander, with black moustaches and a bold glance'.

* Conrad used this name for the Dutch trader from Macassar in *Almayer's Folly* and *An Outcast of the Islands*.

At last the thaw set in and the cargo began to arrive and, as a commander had apparently not yet been appointed, Conrad was in charge of loading the ship, with consequences fateful to himself. Then 'the day after we had finished loading, on the very eve of the day of sailing', the new captain arrived: 'I first beheld him on the quay, a complete stranger to me, obviously not a Hollander, in a black bowler and a short drab overcoat, ridiculously out of tone with the winter aspect of the waste lands, bordered by the brown fronts of houses with their roofs dripping with melting snow.' He was Captain John McWhirr on whom Conrad was to base the captain of the *Nan Shan* in 'Typhoon'.*

> The sudden, spontaneous agility with which he bounded aboard right off the rail afforded me the first glimpse of his real character. Without further preliminaries than a friendly nod, he addressed me: 'You have got her pretty well in her fore and aft trim. Now, what about your weights?' I told him I had managed to keep the weight sufficiently well up, as I thought, one third of the whole being in the upper part 'above the beams', as the technical expression has it. He whistled 'Phew!' scrutinising me from head to foot. A sort of smiling vexation was visible on his ruddy face.
>
> 'Well, we shall have a lively time of it this passage, I bet,' he said.[55]

He was right. Conrad wrote: 'Neither before nor since have I felt a ship roll so abruptly, so violently, so heavily.' In consequence, he said, some of the minor spars went and a piece of one of them hit him in the back, 'and sent him sliding on his face for quite a considerable distance along the main deck. Thereupon followed various and unpleasant consequences of a physical order . . . inexplicable periods of powerlessness, sudden accesses of mysterious pain.'†

A doctor in Samarang advised him to lay up for three months and he left the *Highland Forest* on 1 July to go into

* Conrad describes Captain McWhirr's habit of remaining in seclusion in his cabin during the first few days of the voyage in another section of *The Mirror of the Sea*, pp. 5–6.

† ibid., p. 54. In the Agreement and Account of the Crew for this voyage Conrad is entered as having left the *Highland Forest* 'by mutual consent' and above this has been written in pencil, 'bad leg – L[og] p. 18'.

the Singapore hospital.* Conrad wrote to his uncle from hospital, vaguely describing his symptoms and on 20 August 1887, his uncle replied:

> I received your letter of 2/14th July yesterday, on the day of the eclipse and very appropriately because it completely eclipsed the good and tranquil thoughts I had about you. I calculated that you were now able to stand on your own legs, that I had led you to the port, and that after fourteen years of exertion and work, you were on the right road? And now, 'pas de chance', as you say! . . . You did not write to me what the actual trouble is: is it ordinary rheumatism? or sciatica? – or perhaps a paralysis? and it can be any of these! I am cudgelling my brains as to what it is!? I should like to suppose that it is a very slight ailment – but the sad experience I have gone through with regard to Persons Dear to me continually instils the thought of something worse? With old age, doubt comes! . . .
>
> The only hope is, as with many other setbacks, that this one will pass! I suppose that on your return you can apply again to the same shipowners – for it was illness that interrupted your service, in other respects quite creditable to you, as you state yourself. But that is a question for the future. My thoughts today are chiefly directed towards the recovery of your health and your return to London, and with the ardent wish that this should take place as soon as possible, I close this subject, so sad for us both.

However, unlike the previous time that he had been at a loose end in Singapore – after the abandonment of the *Palestine* – he decided not to return to Europe; instead, on 22 August, he signed on as mate with the *Vidar*.[56] This may simply have been because he was not wholly recovered and was attracted by the opportunity of an easy berth, or it may have been that he wanted to stay in the East for a time. His early writing shows a fascination with the luxuriance and

* In *Lord Jim* (pp. 11–13) there is an interesting example of the way in which Conrad would father an episode in his own life on to a fictional character. Jim was 'disabled by a falling spar at the beginning of a week of which his Scottish captain used to say afterwards, "Man! it's a pairfect meeracle to me how she lived through it!" He had to go into hospital in an Eastern port [clearly Singapore]; when he was recovered he could not immediately find a means of getting home and took a berth as chief mate of the *Patna*.' At this point the parallel ends.

decay of the East, with the 'intensity of that tropical life which wants the sunshine but works in the gloom; which seems to be all grace of colour and form, all brilliance, all smiles, but is only the blossoming of the dead; whose mystery holds the promise of joy and beauty, yet contains nothing but poison and decay'.[57] His writing shows also that his imagination was captured by the test of character to which the East, or primitive life, subjected the Westerner, with its insidious temptation to step out of the clothes, or protective armour, of conventional European morality. He was later to write of the East: 'I have known its fascination since; I have seen the mysterious shores, the still water, the lands of brown nations, where a stealthy Nemesis lies in wait, pursues, overtakes so many of the conquering race, who are proud of their wisdom, of their knowledge, of their strength.'[58] In Conrad's work Almayer, Willems and above all Kurtz (because primitive life possessed similar powers in Africa as in the East), appear as trophies of that Nemesis.

The *Vidar* was a steamship of 800 tons belonging to an Arab named Syed Mosin Bin S. Ali Jaffree, commanded by an Englishman, Captain Craig, and sailing under the Dutch flag.[59] She was based on Singapore and used to do a voyage lasting about three weeks through the Malay Archipelago. According to Captain Craig the course of the *Vidar* was through the Carimata Strait to Banjermassim on the south coast of Borneo, then to Pulo Laut, where she coaled, on to Dongala on the west coast of the Celebes, back to the east coast of Borneo at Coti Berouw and north as far as Bulungan; then she would make the return voyage in the reverse order. She would call on the native settlements up the rivers where also one or more Europeans or halfcastes might be living; traders, expatriates, derelicts, probably married to native women. There the *Vidar* would trade in rubber, cane, gutta percha and other commodities.

It was during his five or six voyages on the *Vidar* that Conrad absorbed some of the impressions from which he was to create his first two novels, *Almayer's Folly* and *An Outcast of the Islands*, as well as local colour for *The Rescue*,

Lord Jim and a number of short stories. Among the people whose names and characteristics he was to draw on, the most important was Almayer himself. So important was he that Conrad later wrote: 'If I had not got to know Almayer pretty well it is almost certain there would never have been a line of mine in print.'[60] This was paying Almayer too big a compliment because when someone is ready to write there will always be an Almayer to hand.

His real name was William Charles Olmeijer and when Conrad knew him he was living at Berouw (sometimes called Tandjong Redeb) on the Berouw river.* Captain Craig told Aubry that Olmeijer was Eurasian but, as his memory failed him on so many details, he may have been wrong. Olmeijer was married to Johanna Cornelia van Lieshout who was either Eurasian or wholly native and they had eleven children. He traded in gutta percha, rattan and rubber which he shipped through Captain Lingard, and both made and lost a fortune in rubber. He had close relations with the Dyaks, a primitive head-hunting people in the interior, for which he was mistrusted by the Dutch authorities. Apparently he did build a large house which was called The Folly by various people. He died in Surabaya in 1900 after an operation for cancer.[61]

As can be seen Conrad did not stick to the facts of Olmeijer's life but created his fictional Almayer from the impressions which he gathered from the man's character, mode of life and reputation. Some years later Conrad gave a non-fictional account of Olmeijer, whom he still called Alma-

* Captain Craig told Aubry that Olmeijer, or Almayer as he thought his real name was, and other characters in *Almayer's Folly* lived in Bulungan. Aubry accepted this for the *Life and Letters*, nor did he alter it in *Vie de Conrad* although John Gordan's fine work of scholarship, *Joseph Conrad, the Making of a Novelist*, had been out some years. There is in fact no indication in the *Vie de Conrad* that Aubry knew of Gordan's book. In the novel Conrad called the river the Pantai but twice in the manuscript of *Almayer's Folly* he referred to it as the Brow. This was corrected in typescript; but Sambir, the name of the village in the novel, is once called Brow (p. 42) and this slip got into the printed text (Gordan, op. cit., p. 36).

yer,* where he described a farcical episode of landing a pony from the *Vidar* for him. Here he ridiculed Almayer, clothed in 'flapping pyjamas of cretonne pattern (enormous flowers with yellow petals on a disagreeable blue ground) and a thin cotton singlet with short sleeves', the proud owner of a flock of 'the only geese on the East Coast'. But, as Gordan suggests, there is no reason to suppose that this Almayer was closer to Olmeijer than the fictional character who, by this time, was probably far more vivid in Conrad's imagination than the original.

In *Almayer's Folly* Conrad also used the names, and possibly the personalities of other people whom he had come across during his voyages on the *Vidar*. Tom Lingard who plays a key part in *Almayer's Folly* and *An Outcast of the Islands* and who is the hero of *The Rescue* was an important trader in the area; he owned a schooner and had business connections in Singapore. He was called Rajah Laut by the Malays, discovered a channel for ships in the Berouw River which is still, or was until recently, called the Baak van Lingard, and was married to a sister of Olmeijer. He had a nephew, Jim Lingard, whom he took as an associate on his ship and later helped to set up as a trader in Berouw.[62] Dain Maroola, Lakamba, Babalatchi and Patalolo all apparently had their counterparts, if only in name, at Berouw and at Dongala in the Celebes;[63] and Captain Craig appeared as Captain Ford in *Almayer's Folly*. Then there was a Dutchman named de Veer with a weakness for alcohol who apparently lived with Olmeijer,† and may have suggested Willems of *An Outcast of the Islands* to Conrad; but there were many such 'outcasts' knocking around the East.

Captain Craig told Aubry[64] that when he used to go

* *A Personal Record*, p. 74 ff. He quite probably had never seen the name written and thought it really was Almayer.

† Gordan, ibid., p. 53. cf., Aubry, *L.L.*, I, p. 97. Captain Craig told Aubry that Willems—he is referred to as Willems – was a Dutch sailor, once a fine, robust man, who had taken to drink and had become entirely dependent upon Almayer and the other residents in Bulungan (in fact, Berouw).

down to the cabin to talk to Conrad he usually found him writing. Conrad's correspondence at this period was apparently confined to a monthly letter to his uncle and so, if Craig's recollection was correct, it seems that he must either have been keeping a diary (it is interesting that he quotes from alleged diaries in the largely autobiographical *Shadow-Line* and *The Arrow of Gold* and that he definitely kept one when he was in the Congo); or else he may have been trying his hand at creative writing and even perhaps making the first tentative attempts at what was to become *Almayer's Folly*. It remains a mystery because no diary or piece of writing from this time has been preserved.

(7)

The easy-going routine of life on the *Vidar* had given Conrad a chance to recuperate from his ailments and his uncle wrote to him at the time of his thirtieth birthday:

> You have relieved my anxiety by your assurance that you are feeling well as regards your leg and your liver and still more that you have assured means for returning to Europe at any time as soon as you notice that a further stay in the Indies affects your health. I earnestly ask you to be careful, for at your age and in your position, and actually in every one, there is nothing more valuable than health! I suppose it is your *objectif* to wait for a suitable opportunity to return to Europe as an officer *sans bourse délier*? and at the same time amass a certain sum in dollars or guineas? – and to save what has already been gathered. Is this so? [18 December 1887]

In another letter he wrote:

> I do not demand that you give up your intentions as to staying or returning, but I nonetheless do ask for one sacrifice – a small one, but valuable for me, namely: buy yourself, Brother, some good writing paper, and use good ink when you write to me. Your paper smudges and your ink smudges so that I have to work very hard before I can read your letter; and as I re-read your letters several times usually – my eyes suffer though my heart is gratified. [13 January 1888]

On 4 January 1888 Conrad left the *Vidar* at Singapore.[65] An account of the voyages of the *Sofala* in 'The End of the Tether' corresponds closely to the voyages of the *Vidar* and as Conrad said that the story was the 'product of experience'[66] it may reproduce his mood at this time. He describes 'this monotonous huckster's round. . . . He knew its order, its sights and its sounds.'[67] Sooner or later he was bound to become bored with the repetitive, humdrum life on the *Vidar* and he possibly had some of the feelings which he attributes to the hero of *The Shadow-Line*, a story based closely on his own life; although in the story he probably somewhat idealized existence on the *Vidar* in order to heighten the effect of the decision to leave her:

One goes on. And the time, too, goes on – till one perceives ahead a shadow-line warning one that the region of early youth, too, must be left behind.

This is the period of life in which such moments of which I have spoken are likely to come. What moments? Why, the moments of boredom, of weariness, of dissatisfaction. Rash moments. I mean moments when the still young are inclined to commit rash actions, such as getting married suddenly or else throwing up a job for no reason . . .

It was in an Eastern port. She was an Eastern ship, inasmuch as then she belonged to that port. She traded among dark islands on a blue reef-scarred sea, with the Red Ensign over the taffrail and at her masthead a house-flag, also red, but with a green border and with a white crescent in it. For an Arab owned her, and a Syed at that . . .

Excellent (and picturesque) Arab owner, about whom one needed not to trouble one's head, a most excellent Scottish ship – for she was that from the keel up – excellent sea-boat, easy to keep clean, most handy in every way, and if it had not been for her internal propulsion, worthy of any man's love, I cherish to this day a profound respect for her memory. As to the kind of trade she was engaged in and the character of my shipmates, I could not have been happier if I had had the life and the men made to my order by a benevolent Enchanter.

And suddenly I left all this. I left it in that, to us, inconsequential manner in which a bird flies away from a comfortable branch. It was as though all unknowing I had heard a whisper or seen something. Well – perhaps! One day I was perfectly right and the next everything was gone – glamour, flavour, interest, contentment – everything. It was one of these moments, you know. The green sickness of late youth descended on me and carried me off. Carried me off that ship, I mean.

We were only four white men on board, with a large crew of Kalashes and two Malay petty officers. The Captain stared hard as if wondering what ailed me. But he was a sailor, and he, too, had been young at one time. Presently a smile came to lurk under his thick iron-grey moustache, and he observed that, of course, if I felt I must go he couldn't keep me by main force. And it was arranged that I should be paid off the next morning. As I was going out of the chart-room he added suddenly, in a peculiar, wistful tone, that he hoped I would find what I was so anxious to go and look for. A soft, cryptic utterance which seemed to reach deeper than any diamond-hard tool could have done. I do believe he understood my case.[68]

He goes on to describe in *The Shadow-Line* how this young ship's officer was staying at the Sailors' Home in Singapore, waiting for a passage home, when he realized from the peculiar behaviour of the chief steward and the persistent rather cryptic hints from a certain Captain Patterson[69] (Giles in the story), that something unusual was afoot. Nagged by Patterson into challenging the steward he discovered that the marine superintendent (Conrad keeps the actual name, Ellis*) was looking for someone to take over a command and had already sent for him; the steward had held back the marine superintendent's communication in the hope that the command would be offered to a perennial loafer who was staying at the Home without paying his bill. The young man went to the marine superintendent's office without delay and was given the command of the barque

* A Memorandum signed by Henry Ellis was found in Conrad's papers. Dated 19 January 1888, it states: 'This is to inform you that you are required to proceed today in the s.s. *Melita* to Bangkok and you will report your arrival to the British Consul and produce this memorandum which will show that I have engaged you to be Master of the *Otago* in accordance with the Consul's telegram on a voyage from Bangkok to Melbourne...' It is now in the Keating Collection at Yale.

Otago, at the moment at Bangkok, whose captain had died at sea.

When he arrived at Bangkok the young man (it is easier, and perhaps permissible to call him Conrad) found a deplorable situation. From Mr Born* the chief mate, he learned that the dead master had been eccentric and neglectful:

> He was a peculiar man – of about sixty-five – iron grey, hard-faced, obstinate, and uncommunicative. He used to keep the ship loafing at sea for inscrutable reasons. Would come on deck at night sometimes, take some sail off her, God only knows why or wherefore, then go below, shut himself up in his cabin, and play on the violin for hours – till daybreak perhaps. In fact, he spent most of his time day or night playing the violin. That was when the fit took him.[70]

He had other unfortunate proclivities, too. The night he died he threw his violin overboard.

Mr Born himself was obsessed by the eerie experiences which he had had with the previous master and embittered because the owners of the *Otago* had not given him the command. It was the hope of getting the command which had made him take the ship to remote Bangkok instead of Singapore. Both he and the majority of the crew were in various states of sickness because of the long wait in the unhealthy climate of Bangkok.

Although there is no confirmation of the picturesque details which Conrad relates in *The Shadow-Line*† two letters bear out the bald facts of the situation. The first is from the owners, Henry Simpson & Sons of Adelaide, and is dated 5 April 1888:

> Your favours dated Bangkok 2 and 6 February, latter with Postscript dated 7th on the eve of sailing, duly reached me [James

* In *The Shadow-Line* and in his letter to Colvin of 27 February 1917 Conrad calls him Burns. And he is misprinted Burns in *L.L.*, I, p. 106. 'Born' twice slipped into the MS (pp. 62, 145) but was corrected.

† A similar situation is described in 'Falk: a Reminiscence' (pp. 153–4), but it is impossible to know how closely the events described in this story are based on Conrad's own experience.

Simpson], and have been interesting as detailing the melancholy circumstances under which you took charge of the barque *Otago.*

The accounts which you enclosed are no doubt at all in order but I have no means of comparing them with other documents as the late Captain never favoured me with the scratch of a pen* from the time of leaving Newcastle in August last and the acting Master Mr. Born only wrote me a brief note acquainting me with his Captain's death.

And a note to Conrad from William Willis, 'Physician to H.M. Legation in Siam', dated Bangkok, February, 1888, attests:

Dear Sir,

I think it is not out of place on my part that I should state, though not asked by you to do so, to prevent any misapprehension hereafter, that the crew of the sailing ship *Otago* has suffered severely whilst in Bangkok from tropical diseases, including fever, dysentery and cholera; and I can speak of my own knowledge that you have done all in your power in the trying and responsible position of Master of the Ship to hasten the departure of your vessel from this unhealthy place and at the same time to save the lives of the men under your command.

Yours faithfully,
William Willis, M.D., F.R.C.S.E.
Physician to H.M. Legation in Siam[71]

In *The Shadow-Line* the doctor was the only man prepared to help Conrad in his plight: 'A doctor is humane by definition,' he wrote, 'but that man was so in reality. . . . He was the only human being in the world who seemed to take the slightest interest in me.'[72] He was certainly in need of help if a dovetailing of 'Falk' and *The Shadow-Line* corresponds to the facts.† Before the cargo could be loaded the

* cf., 'A letter from the owners . . complained mildly enough that they had not been favoured by a scratch of the pen for the last eighteen months.' 'Falk', *Typhoon and Other Stories*, p. 154.

† It would be absurd to treat either as exact autobiography; moreover they contradict one another in certain respects. Of the two *The Shadow-Line* is probably the closest to autobiography; Conrad wrote to J. B.

Otago's steward died of some tropical disease in the hospital and the new steward, a Chinese, made off with all Conrad's savings, £32, while Mr Born went down with fever and had to be taken to hospital. According to 'Falk', while waiting for his cargo, Conrad became involved in a strange situation between the master of a German ship whom he used to visit in the evening and the skipper of the solitary tug-boat, who was courting the German's niece in rather an eccentric manner. Here also he apparently came across the preposterous hotel keeper, with his famous *table d'hôte*, whom he gives the name of Schomberg in 'Falk' and *Victory*.[73]

When at last the *Otago* was able to sail Born implored Conrad not to leave him behind and was brought back on board on a stretcher. Conrad's bad luck had still not left him. There was not enough wind to carry the ship away from Bangkok, which Born insisted was due to the malign influence of the late captain; the crew started to go down with fever, and to crown all Conrad then discovered that the late captain had apparently sold almost all the ship's supply of quinine. Four of the five bottles were full of a white powder, but it was not quinine.

It took the *Otago* three weeks to do the 800 miles from Bangkok to Singapore. It was a nightmarish voyage and by the end all the crew except for Conrad and the cook, Ransome, who had been his mainstay throughout, had succumbed to fever. At Singapore a fresh crew was provided, except for Mr Born, and all went well for the rest of the voyage to Sydney which the *Otago* reached in early May.[74]

Conrad stayed with the *Otago* and on 7 August took her on a voyage from Sydney to Mauritius, where he arrived on 30 September[75] having persuaded the owners to allow him

---

Pinker in 1917: 'That piece of work – which is not a story really but exact autobiography' and to Sir Sidney Colvin on 27 February of the same year: 'The very speeches are (I won't say authentic – they are that absolutely), I believe, verbally accurate. And all this happened in March–April 1887' [1888, in fact].

to follow the route through the hazardous Torres Strait between North Australia and New Guinea.*

At Port Louis, in Mauritius, some at least of the events related in 'A Smile of Fortune' seem to have taken place. A local man of letters, Auguste Esnouf, who wrote under the name of Savinien Mérédac, did some research into Conrad's stay at Port Louis and unearthed a number of interesting details.[76] The charterers of the *Otago* were Messrs Langlois and Co. and at the time when Auguste Esnouf was making his inquiries Paul Langlois claimed to remember 'Captain Korzeniowski' vividly. His impressions of Conrad are the earliest that have been preserved, although it must be remembered that they were written down forty-two years later:

> Je veux vous donner sur le Capitaine Korzeniowski des impressions qui vous intéresseront, je crois, car mes souvenirs de lui sont très précis. Je l'ai beaucoup vu pendant les six ou sept semaines qu'il a passées à Port Louis et, étant son affréteur, j'ai eu avec lui des rapports presque quotidiens.
>
> D'une taille légèrement au-dessus de la moyenne, de traits énergiques et d'une extrême mobilité, passant très rapidement de la douceur à une nervosité confinant à la colère; de grands yeux noirs généralement mélancoliques et rêveurs, doux aussi en dehors des moments assez fréquents d'agacement; un menton volontaire, une bouche d'un joli dessin, gracieuse, que surmontait une moustache châtain foncé, épaisse et d'un joli tour, telle était cette physionomie agréable certes, mais surtout étrange dans son expression et que l'on oublie difficilement lorsqu'on l'a vue une fois ou deux.
>
> Ce qui, en dehors de la distinction de ses manières, frappait le plus dans le capitaine de *l'Otago*, c'était le contraste qu'il formait avec les autres patrons de navires dont, gros exportateur de sucre, je voyais une dizaine chaque jour au bureau du 'père Krumpholtz' qui fut, pendant plus de trente ans, le seul courtier en frets du pays et dont le bureau, situé au rez-de-chaussée de l'immeuble du Mauritius Fire Insurance Cy., était entre dix heurs du matin et une

* He gives an account of this voyage in 'Geography and Some Explorers', *Last Essays*, pp. 18–21. Conrad's chart of the Torres Strait has been preserved and is in the Keating Collection at Yale.

heure de l'après-midi, le rendez-vous de tous les capitaines à la recherche d'un affrètement. Et si vous pensez qu'à cette époque, avant l'envahissement de la mer par les vapeurs, il y avait toujours dans le port, pendant la saison sucrière, une quinzaine de navires, vous pouvez vous faire une idée de la nombreuse compagnie qui emplissait chaque jour l'antichambre du 'père Krumpholtz'.

Or, ces patrons de navires, généralement vêtus de toile, coiffés de casques ou de chapeaux de paille, le visage et les mains brûlés par le soleil et l'eau salée, les ongles noirs du goudron dénonciateur du métier, le language énergique et souvent grossier, n'étaient pas des modèles d'élégance et de raffinement. Au contraire de ses collègues le capitaine Korzeniowski était tojours vêtu comme un petit-maître. Je le vois encore (et justement à cause du contraste avec les autres marins, mon souvenir est précis) arrivant presque chaque jour à mon bureau vêtu d'un veston noir ou de couleur foncée, d'un gilet généralement clair et d'un pantalon 'de fantaisie', le tout bien fait et d'une grande élégance; coiffé d'un 'melon' noir ou gris placé légèrement sur le côté, toujours ganté et portant un jonc à pomme d'or.

Vous jugez, par cette description, s'il contrastait avec les autres capitaines avec lesquels il n'avait au reste que des relations de stricte politesse se limitant, la plupart du temps, à un salut. Aussi était-il très peu populaire parmi ses collègues qui l'appelaient ironiquement 'the Russian Count'. Voilà pour le physique.

Au moral: une éducation parfaite, une conversation très variée et intéressante lorsque c'était son jour d'être communicatif. Il ne l'était pas tous les jours. Celui qui devait acquérir la célébrité sous le nom de Joseph Conrad était assez souvent très taciturne et très nerveux. Ces jours-là, il avait un tic de l'épaule et des yeux et la moindre chose inattendue, la chute d'un objet sur le plancher, une porte qui bat, le faissaient sursauter. C'était ce qu'on appellerait aujourd'hui un *neurasthénique*; à cette époque on disait un *névrosé*.

On ne le voyait chez Krumpholtz, avant son affrètement, que pendant quelques minutes chaque jour; et, une fois affrété, il n'y allait plus – . Toujours à son bord, on ne le voyait jamais à *l'Hotel Oriental* où presque tous les capitaines prenaient leur *lunch* et passaient l'après-midi; c'était là qu'on les faisait appeler lorsque l'on avait besoin d'eux. Pendant son séjour à Port-Louis, je ne crois pas que le taciturne Conrad ait une seule fois fait une promenade à la campagne et encore moins, se soit mêlé à la bonne société du pays parmi laquelle sa culture, sa parfaite éducation, ses manières d'une impeccable correction, l'élégance de sa personne lui auraient certainement fait ouvrir bien des portes.

Joseph Conrad parlait indifféremment et très purement l'Anglais et le Français, mais préférait cette dernière langue qu'il maniait avec élégance; nos conversations avaient toujours lieu en français.[77]

Apparently it was not easy to secure a cargo on favourable terms and Conrad was finally forced to accept one at the lowest freight of the season. He was able to offset this a little by a shrewd piece of business: for he had a clause inserted into the agreement whereby the charterer should stand the cost of the pilot and tug in Melbourne river. Conrad was the first to hit upon this idea which subsequently became common practice.

As in 'A Smile of Fortune', Conrad's ship was held up because of lack of sacks, although the reason for this lack was not the same; there had been a fire in the warehouse of the firm which had a monopoly of the sacks that Conrad needed to protect his cargo of sugar. Contrary to Paul Langlois's assertion, Conrad seems to have found plenty to do during his wait. Two Frenchmen, Gabriel and Henri Renouf, one a captain in the French merchant navy and the other an employee of the agents of the *Otago*, had introduced him to the household of Louis Edward Schmidt, a senior official; Schmidt was married to the Renouf brothers' elder sister and, as they were orphans, they and their two other sisters lived with him. In 'A Smile of Fortune' Conrad describes 'the S— family':

. . . one of the old French families, descendants of the old colonists; all noble, all impoverished, and living a narrow domestic life in dull, dignified decay. The men, as a rule, occupy inferior posts in government offices or in business houses. The girls are almost always pretty, ignorant of the world, kind and agreeable and generally bilingual; they prattle innocently both in French and English. The emptiness of their existence passes belief.[78]

Conrad seems to have seen quite a lot of the family; and there has been preserved an 'Album de Confidences' which shows that he was persuaded to undergo the ordeal of answering a questionnaire:

1. Quel est le principal trait de votre caractère? *Laziness.*
2. Par quels moyens cherchez-vous à plaire? *By making myself scarce.*
3. Quel nom fait battre votre coeur? *Ready to beat for any name.*
4. Quel serait votre rêve de bonheur? *Never dream of it; want reality.*
5. Où habite la personne qui occupe votre pensée? *A castle in Spain.*
6. Quelle est la qualité que vous préférez chez la femme? *Beauty.*
7. Que désirerez-vous être? *Should like not to be.*
8. Quelle est votre fleur de prédilection? *Violet.*
9. Dans quel pays voudriez-vous vivre? *Do not know. Perhaps Lapland.*
10. Quelle est la couleur des yeux que vous préférez? *Grey.*
11. Quel est le don de la nature dont vous voudriez être doué? *Self-confidence.*
12. Que préférez-vous dans un bal? *Not dancing cannot tell.*
13. Quelle est votre promenade favorite? *Hate all 'promenades'.*
14. Que préférez vous, les brunes ou les blondes? *Both.*
15. Quelle est votre plus grande distraction? *Chasing wild geese.*
16. Dîtes l'état présent de votre esprit? *Calm.*
17. Que détestez-vous le plus? *False pretences.*
18. Vous-croyez vous aimé? *Decline to state.*
19. Votre devise?
20. Votre nom?

J.C.K.[79]

It is interesting that he answered the questions in English, although of course he would have conversed with the family in French. The reply 'Decline to state' to the question 'Vous-croyez vous aimé' apparently concealed a hope, because shortly before he was due to sail Conrad told one of the Renouf brothers that he wished to marry his sister Eugénie, who was then twenty-six. But Eugénie was betrothed to a pharmacist named Loumeau, whom she married the following January. For the remaining two days before the

Otago sailed Conrad did not leave the ship but sent a letter to Gabriel Renouf saying good-bye, giving his respects to the family, and announcing that he could never return to Mauritius.

It has been suggested[80] that the sentence in 'Youth' which speaks of times in life when 'you simply can do nothing, neither great nor little – not a thing in the world – not even marry an old maid'[81] may refer, less romantically, to this incident.

Conrad had found time for other activities apart from courting Eugénie Renouf. He apparently also visited the house of a stevedore named James Horatio Shaw who had a rose-garden, unique in Port Louis, and a daughter named Alice, aged nearly seventeen. In 'A Smile of Fortune', which, to some extent at least, draws on the facts of Conrad's stay in Mauritius, the young captain pays a number of visits to the house of Alfred Jacobus, a ship-chandler. Jacobus has a magnificent garden and a daughter named Alice with whom the captain flirts. How far the events described in 'A Smile of Fortune' correspond to fact is anyone's guess. Although Conrad himself said that the story was 'not the record of personal experience'[82] Jessie has claimed that it was 'largely founded on fact', adding that Conrad used to accuse her of being jealous of Alice.[83] Aubry corroborates the story's autobiographical basis, recounting:

> ... an odd question which Conrad asked me one day when I was talking to him about this story. 'Do you think', he said to me, 'that Jacobus had seen something?' [This refers to Jacobus's appearance just after the captain has embraced Alice[84]]. When I confessed that for my part I could not decide, and, in my turn, asked him the same question, he answered, 'I never knew.'[85]

At least Conrad seems to have had good reason not to return to Port Louis.

On 22 November the *Otago* sailed for Melbourne.[86] If we are to believe 'A Smile of Fortune', the *Otago* carried, as well as her official cargo of sugar, a number of sacks of potatoes which had been forced on Conrad against his will.

The 'smile of fortune' consisted in the fact that there was a potato famine in that area of Australia when the *Otago* arrived at Melbourne, and Conrad was able to make a very handsome profit out of the deal.

At Melbourne a letter from Thaddeus Bobrowski was waiting for Conrad:

> You do not tell me how long you think you are going to remain in Australia. . . . You know that I do not wish to influence you . . . but for an old man who has not long to live, time is a matter of some interest, and also to know that he may possibly see again those who are dear to him! [24 September 1888]

He then goes on to ask anxiously if Conrad cannot get his friend Krieger to discover from the Russian Embassy whether the formal release from allegiance to the Tsar is an accomplished fact. But Conrad's relations with the *Otago*'s owners were good and he seems to have been keen to stay with the ship. In February he took the *Otago* from Melbourne to Port Minlacowie in South Australia where he picked up a cargo of grain for Adelaide. At Adelaide there was another letter from his uncle giving details of his will.[87]

Again if 'A Smile of Fortune' follows the facts, the owners wanted Conrad to do another voyage to Mauritius, but the idea was too painful and, instead, he tried to persuade them to let him take the *Otago* into the China Seas.[88] On their refusal he resigned his command. But it is just as possible that Conrad had decided that anyhow he must return to Europe to see his uncle before he died. At all events, a letter, dated 2 April, from the owners, reads:

> Referring to your resignation of the command (which in another letter we have formally accepted) of our bark *Otago*, we now have much pleasure in stating that this early severance from our employ is entirely at your own desire, with a view to visiting Europe . . .

Shortly afterwards he took a passage to England by steamship.

[IV]

Congo Episode

When Conrad arrived back in London in the early summer of 1889, after an absence of more than two years, there were still difficulties in the way of visiting his uncle. The Russian official gazette, *Senatskie Wiedomosti* (No. 49, May), had at last announced his release from the status of subject of the Russian Empire, but there were formalities to be gone through before he could enter Russian territory without risk. He therefore took furnished rooms in Bessborough Gardens, on the north bank of the Thames at Vauxhall Bridge, and set about looking for a command. Several months went by and nothing satisfactory turned up. His situation corresponded to that of Marlow, the narrator of 'Heart of Darkness':

> I had then, as you remember, just returned to London after a lot of Indian Ocean, Pacific, China Seas – a regular dose of the East – six years or so, and I was loafing about, hindering you fellows in your work and invading your homes, just as though I had got a heavenly mission to civilise you. It was very fine for a time, but after a bit I did get tired of resting. Then I began to look for a ship – I should think the hardest work on earth. But the ships wouldn't even look at me.[1]

He was thirty-one years old, had very little money and no assured position; while, although it was a fine achievement for a Polish gentleman to have become a successful captain in the British Merchant Navy, it was a personal, almost quixotic, achievement with little significance for anyone but himself. With no particular occupation, he had plenty of time on his hands and was perhaps feeling restless and dissatisfied with the seeming emptiness of his existence, a state of mind which is often the prelude to creative activity.

In a process, probably unconscious, of editing his life Conrad consistently played down any impulse which he had towards writing and insisted that his becoming an author was the merest chance, whereas he unjustifiably exaggerated the element of purpose in his career at sea, attributing to deliberate choice what was largely fortuitous. Thus he said in *A Personal Record:*

> Till I began to write that novel I had written nothing but letters, and not very many of these. I never made a note of a fact, of an impression or of an anecdote in my life. The conception of a planned book was entirely outside my mental range when I sat down to write; the ambition of being an author had never turned up amongst these gracious imaginary existences one creates fondly for oneself at times in the stillness and immobility of a day-dream.[2]

There were, however, strong reasons why the idea of giving significance to life by writing should have occurred to him; his father had been a dedicated writer and Conrad, a sensitive, highly-strung boy, had during his most impressionable years lived alone with his father in a predominantly literary atmosphere. He had helped his father with his work, and the absence of the companionships and usual activities suited to a boy of his age had encouraged him to feed his imagination on avid reading and reverie.*

Life at sea must also have given him plenty of opportunity to indulge what he called his 'pensive habits (which made me sometimes dilatory in my work about the rigging)'[3] and to develop his capacity for story-telling.[4] Then it seems clear from Bobrowski's letters that Conrad had the ability to write well and enjoyed doing so. Bobrowski had wanted him to write travel articles for a Warsaw periodical,[5] and in another letter had said: 'Let us first talk about Barataria, the metaphor of which you explained not only very wittily but also in such a pure Polish style that I had real pleasure in reading the passage.'[6] If these letters of Conrad's had survived they might well have given evidence of a conscious striving towards literary style and expression; certainly this

* The testimony that he wrote plays when a boy would show at least that he was keen to emulate his father.

is the case in some of the earliest letters that have survived, those which he wrote to Marguerite Poradowska shortly after starting *Almayer's Folly*. They contain passages with the same self-consciously composed literary quality as in the book:

> La vie roule en flots amers, comme l'ocean sombre et brutal sous un ciel couvert des tristes nuages, et il ya a des jours ou il semble aux pauvres âmes embarquées pour le désésperant voyage que jamais un rayon de soleil n'a pu penétrer ce voile douleureux; que jamais il ne luira plus, qu'il n'a jamais éxisté!
>
> Il faut pardonner aux yeux que le vent âpre du malheur a rempli des larmes s'ils se refusent de voir le bleu; il faut pardonner aux lèvres qui ont gouté l'amertume de la vie si elles se refusent a prononcer les paroles d'esperance – Il faut surtout pardonner a ces âmes malheureuses qui ont élu de faire le pélérinage a pied, qui cotoient le rivage et regardent sans comprendre l'horreur de la lutte, la joie de vaincre ni le profond déséspoir des vaincus. [23–5 March 1890]

Finally there is the story which he had written for the *Tit-Bits* competition in 1886.

It is in fact far more surprising that Conrad should have become a British Master Mariner than that he should have sat down one day in the autumn of 1889 to write a novel. Nearly twenty years later he described this fateful day in his reminiscences:

> That morning I got up from my breakfast, pushing the chair back, and rang the bell violently, or perhaps I should say resolutely, or perhaps I should say eagerly, I do not know. But manifestly it must have been a special ring of the bell, a common sound made impressive, like the ringing of a bell for the raising of the curtain upon a new scene. It was an unusual thing for me to do. Generally, I dawdled over my breakfast and I seldom took the trouble to ring the bell for the table to be cleared away; but on that morning for some reason hidden in the general mysteriousness of the event I did not dawdle. And yet I was not in a hurry. I pulled the cord casually, and while the faint tinkling somewhere down in the basement went on, I charged my pipe in the usual way and I looked for the matchbox with glances distraught indeed but exhibiting, I am ready to swear, no signs of a fine frenzy. I was composed enough to

perceive after some considerable time the matchbox lying there on the mantelpiece right under my nose. And all this was beautifully and safely usual. Before I had thrown down the match my landlady's daughter appeared with her calm, pale face and an inquisitive look, in the doorway. Of late it was the landlady's daughter who answered my bell. I mention this little fact with pride, because it proves that during the thirty or forty days of my tenancy I had produced a favourable impression. For a fortnight past I had been spared the unattractive sight of the domestic slave. The girls in that Bessborough Gardens house were often changed, but whether short or long, fair or dark, they were always untidy and particularly bedraggled, as if in a sordid version of the fairy tale the ashbin cat had been changed into a maid. I was infinitely sensible of the privilege of being waited on by my landlady's daughter. She was neat if anaemic.

'Will you please clear away all this at once?' I addressed her in convulsive accents, being at the same time engaged in getting my pipe to draw. This, I admit, was an unusual request. Generally on getting up from breakfast I would sit down in the window with a book and let them clear the table when they liked; but if you think that on that morning I was in the least impatient, you are mistaken. I remember that I was perfectly calm. As a matter of fact I was not at all certain that I wanted to write, or that I meant to write, or that I had anything to write about. No, I was not impatient. I lounged between the mantelpiece and the window not even consciously waiting for the table to be cleared. It was ten to one that before my landlady's daughter was done I would pick up a book and sit down with it all the morning in a spirit of enjoyable indolence . . .

And I remember, too, the character of the day. It was an autumn day with an opaline atmosphere, a veiled, semi-opaque, lustrous day, with fiery points and flashes of red sunlight on the roofs and windows opposite, while the trees of the square with all their leaves gone were like tracings of indian ink on a sheet of tissue paper. It was one of those London days that have the charm of mysterious amenity, of fascinating softness. The effect of opaline mist was often repeated at Bessborough Gardens on account of the nearness to the river.

There is no reason why I should remember that effect more on that day than on any other day, except that I stood for a long time looking out of the window after the landlady's daughter was gone with her spoil of cups and saucers. I heard her put the tray down in the passage and finally shut the door; and still I remained smoking with my back to the room. It is very clear that I was in no haste to take the plunge into my writing life, if as plunge this first attempt may be described. My whole being was steeped deep in the indolence of a sailor away from the sea, the scene of never-ending labour and of unceasing duty. For utter surrender to indolence you cannot beat a sailor ashore when that mood is on him, the mood of absolute irresponsibility tasted to the full. It seems to me that I thought of nothing whatever, but this is an impression which is hardly to be believed at this distance of years. What I am certain of is, that I was very far from thinking of writing a story, though it is possible and even likely that I was thinking of the man Almayer.[7]

Although it is not surprising that Conrad should have started to write a novel, there is no reason to suppose that he realized the strength and persistence behind this impulse or had an inkling of the consequences of his action. He never indeed looked on the sea and writing as two mutually exclusive occupations and was never forced to make a deliberate choice between the two. The opportunity, and probably the desire, to go to sea gradually and unobtrusively faded, whereas writing increasingly absorbed him. At the moment, however, he was primarily concerned with finding a job, and this was not easy.

(2)

For the time being Conrad seems to have worked with Barr, Moering & Co.,[8] with whom he had a small sum invested. This arrangement apparently offered no long-term satisfaction and, possibly through his friend Krieger, he was put in touch with a firm of Antwerp shippers, Messrs Walford & Co., who took him on as supercargo and held out hopes of the command of a ship to the West Indies.[9] The arrangement was rather nebulous and Conrad tried another opening. Through the good offices of Barr, Moering & Co. he was put in touch with G. de Baerdemacker, a ship-broker at Ghent, who wrote on 24 September to Captain Albert Thys, Acting Manager of the Société Anonyme Belge pour le Commerce du Haut-Congo, asking whether it would be possible to find Conrad employment in the Congo:

> Ce Monsieur m'est très chaudement recommandé par des amis de Londres et possède les meilleurs certificats: son instruction générale est supérieure à celle qu'ont habituellement les marins et c'est un parfait *gentleman*.[10]

It is difficult to know what had aroused Conrad's interest in going to the Congo. It may have been chance, the job merely coming at the end of a chain of contacts, or it may have been that tropical Africa attracted him in the same way as had the East and that, like Marlow, he was prompted by a map in a Fleet Street shop-window to take steps to get there. In 'Heart of Darkness' he ascribes to Marlow a somewhat naïve version of the appeal which the Congo may have had for him:

> Now when I was a little chap I had a passion for maps. I would look for hours at South America, or Africa, or Australia, and lose myself in all the glories of exploration. At that time there were many blank spaces on the earth, and when I saw one that looked particularly inviting on a map (but they all look that) I would put my finger on it and say, When I grow up I will go there. The North Pole was one of these places, I remember. Well, I haven't been there yet, and shall not try now.The glamour's off. Other places were scattered about the Equator, and in every sort of latitude all over the two hemispheres. I have been in some of them, and – well, we won't talk about that. But there was one yet – the biggest, the most blank, so to speak – that I had a hankering after.
>
> True, by this time it was not a blank space any more. It had got filled since my boyhood with rivers and lakes and names. It had ceased to be a blank space of delightful mystery – a white patch for a boy to dream gloriously over. It had become a place of darkness. But there was in it one river especially, a mighty big river, that you could see on the map, resembling an immense snake uncoiled, with its head in the sea, its body at rest curving afar over a vast country, and its tail lost in the depths of the land. And as I looked at the map of it in a shop-window, it fascinated me as a snake would a bird – a silly little bird. Then I remembered there was a big concern, a Company for trade on that river. Dash it all! I thought to

myself, they can't trade without using some kind of craft on that lot of fresh water – steamboats! Why shouldn't I try to get charge of one? I went on along Fleet Street, but could not shake off the idea. The snake had charmed me.[11]

Conrad has elsewhere described his own love of poring over maps and repeated more than once the story of how he put his finger on the white space at the centre of the map of Africa and said, 'When I grow up I shall go there.' He has also recalled how as a child he used to delight in reading books which recounted famous travels of exploration. There had been plenty of recent events to revive that interest for, throughout 1889, the newspapers had contained frequent reports of the expeditions of Stanley and of Dr Peters in search of Emin Pasha.

For several decades central and northern Africa had been the scene of numerous daring expeditions of exploration and of intense colonial rivalry between the leading European nations, but there was no more dramatic or amazing story than that of the personal acquisition of one of the potentially richest areas by the King of almost the least powerful European nation, the enslavement of the Congo territories by Leopold II of Belgium.

In September 1876, behind a blinding smokescreen of proclaimed noble intentions and international goodwill, the Association Internationale pour l'Exploration et la Civilisation en Afrique had been formed in Brussels at the instigation of Leopold, with himself as president. He proclaimed to the delegates to the Conférence Géographique Africaine, among them some of the most illustrious explorers and geographers in the world: 'Le sujet qui nous réunit aujourd'hui est de ceux qui méritent au premier chef d'occuper les amis de l'humanité. Ouvrir à la civilisation la seule partie du globe où elle n'a pas encore pénétré, percer les ténèbres qui enveloppent des populations entières, c'est si j'ose le dire, une croisade digne de ce siècle progrès.'[12] The first aim of the Association was to establish stations across central Africa, and for this task Leopold employed Henry Morton Stanley, who had already become famous on account of his expedition in 1876–7 through the most impenetrable area of Africa from Zanzibar to the Lower Congo. Gradually the disguises of internationalism and philanthropy were dropped; by 1885, with the ironic title of Souverain de l'État Indépendant du Congo, Leopold had become the master of vast territories bordering on the second largest river in the world, possessing apparently inexhaustible resources, which he was ruthlessly exploiting to satisfy his greed for wealth and power.

But this was not yet generally known. In the same year Stanley published in good faith a massive two-volume work giving an enthusiastic account of *The Congo and the Founding of its Free State: a Story of Work and Exploration,* and it was some time before even he realized how his pioneering work was being distorted; whereas any reports of unsavoury activities in the Congo which appeared in the press were dealt with by the simple, and temporarily effective, device of blank denial.

(3)

The Société Anonyme pour le Commerce du Haut-Congo, to which Conrad had applied for a job, was nominally independent, but was controlled by Captain Albert Thys, formerly one of Leopold's most able henchmen; he has been described, some years later, as 'gigantesque et pesant, de voix forte et main lourde, il conduit une affair comme un escadron. Le secret de sa force est là: une emprise quasi physique sur les hommes'.[13] Conrad, describing an interview with him, referred to 'an impression of pale plumpness in a frock-coat'.[14] The Société had only been in existence since 10 December of the previous year and now had plans for rapid expansion. At the beginning of November, Conrad went to Brussels for an interview with Thys.[15] This must have been a success because Thys apparently promised him the command of one of the Company's river-steamers;[16] he noted on a letter from Conrad telling him that he had severed his association with Walford & Co.: 'Bon capitaine quand nous en aurons besoin pour le Haut-Congo. Demandez reseignement (à Walford [erased] .'[17]

But then there was silence. Conrad must therefore have decided to use what influence he could muster to prod Thys into action. Either he or his Uncle Thaddeus thought of a distant cousin named Alexander Poradowski who was living in Brussels, having escaped from Russian captivity after the 1863 insurrection, and whose wife, Marguerite, had useful connections with the rulers of Leopold's Congo.* On 16 January of the new year he wrote introducing himself to Alexander Poradowski:

> The purpose of this scribbling is to recall myself to a relative whose kindness – shown to me in Cracow – I have by no means forgotten. I do not ask if you will allow me to visit you, for I permit myself not to doubt this, but I should like to know with certainty that you are in Brussels and that I can, in the course of the next month, find you there.[18]

He goes on to say that he intends to visit his uncle soon and plans to return via Brussels, but if the visit has to be postponed he will at any rate be in Brussels in March to see about the position in the Congo. Alexander Poradowski quickly replied, evidently pressing Conrad to visit him, but warning him that he was in poor health and was due soon to have an operation. Conrad had by then had a letter from Bobrowski fixing a date for his visit, and so told Alexander Poradowski that he would call on him on the way to Poland instead of on the return journey because 'after your operation you will need complete rest and not visits'.[19] He arrived in Brussels on 5 February, but two days later Alexander Poradowski died, at the age of fifty-four.[20]

Despite, or perhaps because of, the harrowing situation a

* Aubry does not mention what these connections were. Charles Buls, a devoted admirer of Marguerite Poradowska (cf., Gee and Sturm 94, xiv), who visited the Congo a few years later and dedicated a book describing his travels to Thys, may have been one of them. He subsequently became burgomaster of Brussels. The geographer A. J. Wauters, who was closely connected with Leopold's Congo schemes, was evidently another (cf., Conrad's letter to Mme Poradowska of 26 September 1890).

firm bond of sympathy was quickly formed between Conrad and Marguerite Poradowska. She was in her early forties and renowned for her beauty; Jessie Conrad, who met her ten years later, wrote that 'she was, I think, the most beautiful woman I had ever seen'.[21] A photograph published in 1896 shows her as handsome but matronly. Her father, Emile Gachet, had been a distinguished scholar and she herself had taken up writing. When Conrad met her she had published two *nouvelles, Tournesol* and *Yaga; Esquisse de Moeurs Ruthènes,* which last, despite its rather amateurish quality, had appeared in the *Revue des Deux Mondes* in 1887. She went on to publish a number of other works, chiefly concerned with Ruthenian life and customs; they are of little merit, but by 1896 she had become sufficiently well known to be included in an article on *La Femme Moderne* in the *Revue Encyclopédique,* at the end of which was placed a motto in her own handwriting: *'Espérer toujours! Espérer quand même.'*[22]

Conrad always professed himself enraptured with Marguerite Poradowska's work, but this was presumably a mark of his gallantry rather than his literary taste. During the next five years they wrote to one another frequently; Marguerite Poradowska was, apart from Bobrowski, the only person of education with whom Conrad was intimate at this time and he revealed to her many of his moods and thoughts, telling her a lot about his progress and difficulties with *Almayer's Folly* and *An Outcast of the Islands.* At one point, before *Almayer's Folly* had been accepted in England, he even suggested that they should publish it in French as a collaboration.

Conrad had to leave Brussels before the funeral of Alexander Poradowski. He travelled via Warsaw and Lublin, calling, presumably at Marguerite Poradowska's request, on the Zagórski family to tell them of the death of Alexander Poradowski, who was Mrs Zagórska's brother. On 16 February he arrived at Bobrowski's estate at Kazimierowka in the province of Kiev. It was fifteen years since he had left Poland and six since he had seen his uncle. The visit must have been deeply affecting for Conrad and have given Bobrowski immense pleasure; Conrad had been met by Bobrowski's servant, who had told him that the old man had hardly slept since he had received the telegram announcing that Conrad was on his way.[23]

Conrad stayed at Kazimierowka for two months, and during his visit Bobrowski took the opportunity to hand over to him the meticulous account which he had kept of the cost of Conrad's upbringing, 'with heartfelt blessing for your future way of life'. At the end of the account Bobrowski had written: '*Thus the upbringing of Master Conrad to manly status has cost* (apart from the capital sum of 3600 roubles given him) 17,454 roubles.'[24] Conrad discussed his plans for going to the Congo with his uncle, who was strongly against the idea but forbore to try to dissuade him. He therefore continued with his efforts to bring pressure on Thys. In one of several affectionate and sympathetic letters to Marguerite Poradowska he said he was afraid that his recommendation to the Company had not been strong enough and that the affair would not go through.[25] A month later, a week before leaving Kazimierowka, he heard that Thys had written to him at his London address,[26] and wrote thanking Marguerite Poradowska profusely for having concerned herself with his African affairs.* He arrived in Brussels in the last week of April to find that there was an end to procrastination. The Company had just heard that one of its steamer captains had been killed by the Africans† and had decided to appoint Conrad in his place. He immediately set about hectic preparations for his departure, having to make

* 14 April 1890. In 'Heart of Darkness' (p. 53) which in many details follows the actual events very closely there is the passage: 'Then – would you believe it? – I tried the women. I, Charlie Marlow, set the women to work – to get a job.'

† Again 'Heart of Darkness' (pp. 53–4) sticks close to the facts. Even the name of the dead captain is barely altered, and that probably unintentionally. In the story his name was Fresleven and in reality Freisleben. Aubry, 'Joseph Conrad au Congo', loc. cit., p. 304, quoting *Mouvement Géographique*, 8 September 1889; and Rapport au Roi Souverain (Bulletin officiel de l'État Indépendant du Congo), July 1891.

two journeys between London and Brussels in the course of a few days. In 'Heart of Darkness' Conrad describes Marlow's last days in Europe, his final visit to the Company's office in the rue Brédérode, his medical inspection by the macabrely facetious doctor and his farewell to his aunt. He then went by rail from Brussels to Bordeaux, whence he sailed for Boma on the *Ville de Maceio* in the second week of May,[27] apparently taking with him what he had written of *Almayer's Folly*. In the tranquillity of the voyage he recalled the last fortnight on land in a letter to Charles Zagórski:

> Freetown, Sierra Leone
>
> It is just a month to-day since you were scandalised by my hurried departure from Lublin. From the date and address of this letter you will see that I have had to be pretty quick, and I am only just beginning to breathe a little more calmly. If you only knew the devilish haste I had to make! From London to Brussels, and back again to London! And again to Brussels! If you had only seen all the tin boxes and revolvers, the high boots and the touching farewells; just another handshake and just another pair of trousers! – and if you knew all the bottles of medicine and all the affectionate wishes I took away with me, you would understand in what a typhoon, cyclone, hurricane, earthquake – no! – in what a universal cataclysm, in what a fantastic atmosphere of mixed shopping, business and affecting scenes, I passed two whole weeks. [22 May 1890, *L.L.*, I, p. 126]

(4)

Before leaving London Conrad had written to a Polish cousin that he was departing 'for a stay of three years in the middle of Africa'.[28] But, whatever may have been his enthusiasm at the start, it appears soon to have been tempered. In a letter to Marguerite Poradowska from Tenerife he says that he is comparatively happy, but then launches into a series of typically Conradian reflections:

> On doute de l'avenir. Car enfin – je me demande – pourquoi y croirait on? Et aussi pourquoi s'attrister? – Un peu d'illusion, beaucoup des rêves, un rare eclair de bonheur puis le desillusionment,

un peu de colère et beaucoup de souffrance et puis la fin; – la paix! – Voilà le programme, et nous aurons a voir cette tragi-comedie jusqu'a la fin. Il faut en prendre son parti. [15 May 1890]

Then from Freetown, Sierra Leone, in the letter to Charles Zagórski already mentioned he wrote, a little apprehensively:

What makes me rather uneasy is the information that 60 per cent of our company's employees return to Europe before they have completed even six months' service. Fever and dysentery! There are others who are sent home in a hurry at the end of a year, so that they shouldn't die in the Congo. God forbid! It would spoil the statistics which are excellent, you see! In a word, it seems there are only 7 per cent who can do their three years' service.... Yes! But a Polish gentleman, cased in British tar! *Nous verrons!* In any case I shall console myself by remembering – faithful to our national traditions – that it is of my own free will that I have thrust myself into this business [22 May 1890, *L.L.*, I, pp. 126–27]

And at Libreville on 10 June he again wrote to Marguerite Poradowska, saying how much he would prefer to have command of one of the Company's ocean-going vessels and wondering whether this might not be possible to arrange. In 'Heart of Darkness' there is a passage based on this voyage down the coast of Africa:

Every day the coast looked the same, as though we had not moved; but we passed various places – trading places – with names like Gran' Bassam, Little Popo; names that seemed to belong to some sordid farce acted in front of a sinister back-cloth.... Once, I remember, we came upon a man-of-war anchored off the coast. There wasn't even a shed there, and she was shelling the bush. It appears the French had one of their wars going on thereabouts. Her ensign dropped limp like a rag; the muzzles of the long six-inch guns stuck out all over the low hull; the greasy, slimy swell swung her up lazily and let her down, swaying her thin masts. In the empty immensity of earth, sky, and water, there she was, incomprehensible, firing into a continent.[29]

Conrad disembarked from the *Ville de Maceio* at Boma and continued on a smaller boat to Matadi about forty miles up the Congo and the highest navigable point, where he arrived on 13 June.[30]

At this date it was an important station, with 170 European inhabitants and four factories – English, Portuguese, Dutch and French – as well as the Sanford Exploring Expedition's buildings, which had been taken over by SACHC. Work was also in progress on a railroad which was to run from Matadi to Kinshasa. At Matadi the Congo spreads out into a lake enclosed by high mountains, and from Captain Thys's description it seems to have been a gloomy spot:

> Lorsqu'on arrive à Matadi on se croirait devant un pays maudit, véritable barrière qui semble créée par la nature pour arrêter le progrès.[31]

It was a peculiar form of progress. As has been said, 'Heart of Darkness' is closely based on Conrad's own experiences, and in one of his most powerful pieces of writing he gives an impression of Matadi with the Africans organized into chain-gangs, driven to the point of exhaustion and then allowed to crawl away to the 'grove of death':[32]

> They were dying slowly – it was very clear. They were not enemies, they were not criminals, they were nothing earthly now, – nothing but black shadows of disease and starvation, lying confusedly in the greenish gloom. Brought from all the recesses of the coast in all the legality of time contracts, lost in uncongenial surroundings, fed on unfamiliar food, they sickened, became inefficient, and were then allowed to crawl away and rest.[33]

Thirty-three years after these experiences Conrad did not disguise his contemptuous indignation at the folly and greed of the Europeans taking part in what he called 'the vilest scramble for loot that ever disfigured the history of human conscience and geographical exploration'.[34] Marlow's criticism of the Roman settlers in Britain is an obvious disguise for Conrad's own opinion of the colonizers in the Congo:

> They were no colonists; their administration was merely a squeeze, and nothing more, I suspect. They were conquerors, and

for that you want only brute force – nothing to boast of, when you have it, since your strength is just an accident arising from the weakness of others. They grabbed what they could get for the sake of what was to be got. It was just robbery with violence, aggravated murder on a great scale, and men going at it blind – as is very proper for those who tackle a darkness. The conquest of the earth, which mostly means the taking it away from those who have a different complexion or slightly flatter noses than ourselves, is not a pretty thing when you look into it too much.[35]

While at Matadi Conrad started to keep a diary which has been preserved.[36] In the first entry he wrote:

Feel considerably in doubt about the future. Think just now that my life amongst the people (white) around here cannot be very comfortable. Intend avoid acquaintances as much as possible.[37]

And in the next entry:

Prominent characteristic of the social life here; people speaking ill of each other.[38]

This impression is echoed by Marlow in 'Heart of Darkness'.

The Congo had without question attracted a mixed assortment of whites. The most sinister and ruthless group consisted of those lured by the vision of immense riches, who were determined to make their packet and then get out before the climate killed them; then there were misfits, like Carlier in 'An Outpost of Progress', or men who for some reason had found it advisable to leave Europe for an area where it did not much matter if their pasts caught up with them. But there were also tough adventurers who were tempted by the magnitude and novelty of the challenge which such an enterprise presented, and ardent missionaries enticed by the number of souls available for conversion. Finally there were men, impatient with the humdrum routine of highly organized civilized life, who were constantly attracted by the unknown and felt that they could only express themselves amid the freedom of unsubdued humanity and nature; among them were Conrad himself and Roger Casement, the only man from the whole Congo episode of whom Conrad spoke with any enthusiasm. He wrote in his diary:

> Made the acquaintance of Mr Roger Casement, which I should consider as a great pleasure under any circumstances and now it becomes a positive piece of luck. Thinks, speaks well, most intelligent and very sympathetic.[39]

Some years later Conrad enlarged on this portrait in a letter to Cunninghame Graham:

> I send two letters I had from a man called Casement, premising that I knew him first in the Congo just twelve years ago. Perhaps you've heard or seen in print his name. He's a Protestant Irishman, pious too. But so was Pizarro. For the rest I can assure you that he is a limpid personality. There is a touch of the conquistador in him too; for I've seen him start off into an unspeakable wilderness swinging a crookhandled stick for all weapons, with two bulldogs, Paddy (white) and Biddy (brindle), at his heels and a Loanda boy carrying a bundle for all company. A few months afterwards it so happened that I saw him come out again, a little leaner, a little browner, with his stick, dogs and Loanda boy, and quietly serene as though he had been for a stroll in a park. Then we lost sight of each other. [26 December 1903, *L.L.*, p. 325]

It was Casement who played one of the leading parts in 1903, when British Consul at Boma, in the exposure of the appalling abuses being perpetrated in the Congo.

After just over a fortnight at Matadi – 'an eternity'* to Marlow – where he filled in some of the time packing ivory into cases,[40] Conrad and a M. Harou left on 28 June with a caravan and thirty-one carriers on a 200-mile trek to another of the Company's stations at Kinshasa on Stanley Pool.

The journey must have been an ordeal. The party travelled on what were little more than tracks through fairly open but rough, hilly country, a landscape which Conrad described at first as 'gray-yellowish (dry grass) with reddish patches (soil) and clumps of dark green vegetation scattered sparsely about',[41] and a few days later as 'a confused wil-

* 'Heart of Darkness', *Youth*, p. 68. Conrad's reference to the blasting activities at Matadi are based on fact; a railway was in the process of construction.

derness of hills, landslips on their sides showing red'.[42] There were numerous ravines carrying streams or rivers into the Congo, and at a later stage of the journey – presumably the caravan had been left behind – at least one river to be crossed by canoe. After a cold night spent battling with mosquitoes they would set out shortly after dawn when the mists were still hovering and the sky was overcast and tramp through deserted country, except for an occasional native market, the gruesome sight of the decaying corpse of an African, or the distant beating of drums. At about midday, when the temperature was becoming too hot for travel, they would stop at a camping-place which was often dirty and without an adequate supply of water; it was a relief to come upon the clean and comfortable Protestant Mission at Sutili, where they were entertained by Mrs Percy Comber.

Conrad's white co-traveller, Harou, whom he described in 'Heart of Darkness' as 'not a bad chap, but rather too fleshy and with the exasperating habit of fainting on the hot hillsides, miles away from the least bit of shade and water',[43] was constantly ill from the start. He was immensely heavy and the need to have him carried much of the way in a hammock caused frequent rows with the carriers. Although he was ill at Manyanga and several other times confessed to feeling seedy, Conrad's own health seems to have held out remarkably well.

Here are some of the more interesting or typical entries in his diary:

Thursday, 3rd July. Left at 6 a.m. after a good night's rest. Crossed a low range of hills and entered a broad valley, or rather plain, with a break in the middle. Met an officer of the State inspecting. A few minutes afterwards saw at a camp[g] place the dead body of a Backongo. Shot? Horrid smell . . .

Noticed Palma Christi – Oil Palm. Very straight, tall and thick trees in some places. Name not known to me . . .

Bird notes charming. One especially a flute-like note. Another kind of 'boom' ressembling [*sic*] the very distant baying of a hound. Saw only pigeons and a few green parroquets. Very small and not many. No birds of prey seen by me.[44]

These notes are interesting because Conrad very seldom refers to objects of natural history in his work and Richard Curle states that he 'practically never showed the slightest interest'[45] in such things.

Friday, 4th July. . . . Saw another dead body lying by the path in an attitude of meditative repose.* . . . At night when the moon rose heard shouts and drumming in distant villages. Passed a bad night.[46]

Saturday, 5th July. . . . Today fell into a muddy puddle – Beastly! The fault of the man that carried me. After camp^g went to a small stream bathed and washed clothes. Getting jolly well sick of this fun.[47]

Monday, 7th July. Left at 6 after good night's rest, on the road to Inkandu, which is some distance past Lukunga Govt. station. Route very accidented. Succession of round steep hills. At times walking along the crest of a chain of hills. Just before Lukunga our carriers took a wide sweep to the southward till the station bore N^th. Walking through long grass for 1½ hours. Crossed a river about 100 feet wide and 4 deep.

After another 1½-hour's walk through manoic plantations in good order rejoined our route to the E^d. of Lukunga sta^on, walking along an undulating plain towards the Inkandu market on a hill. Hot, thirsty and tired. At eleven arrived on the mket place. About 200 people. No water. No camp^g place. After remaining for one hour left in search of a resting place. Row with carriers. No water. At last about 1½ p.m. camped on an exposed hill side near a muddy creek. No shade. Tent on a slope. Sun heavy. Wretched.

Direction N.E. by N. – Distance 22 miles.

Night miserably cold. No sleep. Mosquitos.[48]

Tuesday, 29th. . . . On the road today passed a skeleton tied up to a post. Also white man's grave – no name – heap of stones in the form of a cross. Health good now.[49]

Thursday, 31st. . . . From 9 a.m. infernally hot day. Harou very little better. Self rather seedy. Bathed.[50]

Then, on the last day before reaching Kinshasa (when the first notebook ends):

Friday, 1st of August, 1890. . . . Harou not very well. Mosquitos

* As Richard Curle says, this is the most 'Conradesque' phrase in the diary (p. 165, note 1). It is really the only phrase in which care seems to have been taken with the expression.

– frogs – beastly! Glad to see the end of this stupid tramp. Feel rather seedy. Sun rose red. Very hot day. Wind S^{th}.[51]

The journey had lasted thirty-six days, including a halt of seventeen at Manyanga.

At Kinshasa Conrad's sense of foreboding was given tangible confirmation. The Company's steamer, *Florida*, of which he was supposed to take command had been badly damaged and was at the moment undergoing repairs.[52] However, he was not kept hanging about but was immediately attached as supernumerary to another of the Company's steamers, the *Roi des Belges*, in order to learn the river.[53] The *Roi des Belges* was about to leave for Stanley Falls with Camille Delcommune, who had just been made acting-director of SACHC in the Congo, and one of its objects was to collect the Company's agent named Georges Antoine Klein who was seriously ill.

Conrad was not mollified by this arrangement and before leaving wrote an exasperated letter to his uncle, to whom he had written at each stage of his journey. His uncle replied with a good-natured but doubtless irritating homily:

> I see from your last letter that you are sorely aggrieved with the Belgians for their ruthless exploitation of your person. You are not enamoured of the Latin race in general. But, this time, admit that nothing impelled you to put yourself into the hands of the Belgians. '*Tu l'as voulu, Georges Dandin*' – you can tell yourself, and, if you had paid attention to my ideas on this matter . . .
>
> In any case – first of all, I earnestly ask you to calm yourself and not to work yourself up – for this reacts strongly on the liver. *Ne Vs gatez pas le sang et le foie.* Then I must point out that if you break off your contract you run the risk of considerable costs, as also of the certain accusation of irresponsible action which may turn out harmful for your future career. As long as all this does not affect your health it would be advisable to persevere – I think so at least? [9 November 1890]

During the voyage on the *Roi des Belges* the captain became ill and Conrad was put temporarily in command.[54] *Mouvement Géographique*[55] singled out this voyage as having been done in particularly good time; nonetheless

Klein, like Kurtz, died on the way back. Conrad used the voyage as the basis for that described in 'Heart of Darkness' and the correspondence between the names Kurtz and Klein is obvious; in the manuscript of the story Conrad starts by writing Klein and then changes to Kurtz;[56] but it is not known how closely Kurtz is modelled on the activities and character of Klein. Conrad described 'Heart of Darkness' as 'experience pushed a little (and only very little) beyond the actual facts of the case', and this story only differs significantly from several other accounts of events in the Congo in the intensity with which the experiences are realized; there is nothing improbable in the portrait of Kurtz.

(5)

On 24 September, the day of his return to Kinshasa, Conrad wrote to Maria Tyszka that he was very busy preparing for a new expedition, on the river Kassaï, which might mean an absence of more than ten months.[57] This was the expedition of Alexandre Delcommune, Camille's elder brother, and Conrad had been designated to command the steamer when he was engaged by the Company in Brussels. But during his voyage with Camille Delcommune on the *Roi des Belges* a strong antipathy must have developed between the two men, and two days after his letter to Maria Tyszka he wrote to Marguerite Poradowska giving vent to his disillusion and grievances:

> ... Mes journées ici sont tristes. Il n'y pas a s'y tromper! Decidement je regrette d'etre venu ici. Je le regrette même amèrement ...
>
> Tout m'est antipathique ici. Les hommes et les choses; mais surtout les hommes. Et moi je leur suis antipathique aussi. A commencer par le directeur en Afrique qui a pris la peine de dire a bien de monde que je lui déplaisai souverainement jusqu'au a finir par le plus vulgaire mécanicien ils ont tous le don de m'agacer les nerfs – de sorte que je ne suis pas aussi agréable pour eux peut-être que je pourrai l'être. Le directeur est un vulgaire marchand d'ivoire a instincts sordides qui s'imagine être un commerçant

tandis qu'il n'est qu'une éspèce de boutiquier africain. Son nom est Delcommune. Il deteste les Anglais et je suis naturellement regardé comme tel ici.

He goes on to say that Delcommune has no intention of keeping the promises made in Europe and that the new boat, which he is to command, will not be ready until the following June. To cap all his health is not good; he has had fever and dysentery.

Je me sens assez faible de corps et tant soit peu demoralisé, et puis ma foi je crois que j'ai la nostalgie de la mer, l'envie de revoir ces plaines d'eau salé qui m'a si souvent bercé, qui m'a souri tant de fois sous le scintillement des rayons de soleil par une belle journée, qui bien des fois aussi m'a lancé la menace de mort a la figure dans un tourbillon d'ecume blanche fouettée par le vent sous le ciel sombre de Decembre.

Then he again returned to the possibility of getting the command of one of the Company's ocean-going vessels, asking Marguerite Poradowska to use her influence.[58]

She did in fact write to Albert Thys at the end of November,[59] but by then Conrad had taken his decision and was on the way back to Europe. When he discovered that he would not be given the command of the steamer destined to carry Alexandre Delcommune's expedition he realized that his position was intolerable and gave up. He was also ill. He wrote giving the news to his uncle who replied:

My dear boy,

Three days ago I received your letter of 19 October dated from Kinshasa, informing me of the unsuccessful outcome of your expedition to the Congo, as also of your return to Europe? . . .

In spite of your assurance: that the first sea breeze will restore you to health, I found your hand so greatly changed – which I ascribe to the weakening and exhaustion of fever and dysentery; – that I have since then given myself over to far from merry thoughts! I made no secret before you that I was absolutely against your African plan and more than once expressed myself in this spirit during your stay in my home, but, faithful to the principle 'laisser chacun être heureux ou content à sa manière', I did not attack your decisions, particularly as I was sure that you would have yielded in deference to me – but I could not have a thorough knowledge of things and relations behind my convictions while you had it. Thus, your intentions were realised – to your confusion, for neither people nor circumstances answered your expectations? [27 December 1890]

Conrad has described his last journey down the Congo in *A Personal Record*:

I got round the turn [between Kinshasa and Léopoldville] more or less alive, though I was too sick to care whether I did or not, and, always with *Almayer's Folly* amongst my diminishing baggage, I arrived at that delectable capital Boma, where before the departure of the steamer which was to take me home I had the time to wish myself dead over and over again with perfect sincerity.[60]

He probably did not realize at the time to what extent these four months in the Congo had affected his health. It had never been very strong and the Congo climate permanently undermined it so that for the rest of his life he was dogged by recurrent fever and gouty symptoms. Nor was his body alone affected. It would be absurd to attribute his long periods of despair to the Congo experience – there had been enough previous experiences to confirm an innately gloomy disposition – and his remark to Garnett that 'before the Congo I was a mere animal' is an obvious exaggeration. But 'An Outpost of Progress', for all its irony and macabre humour and 'Heart of Darkness', with its tone of outraged humanism and its consciousness of evil, show how deeply he was affected emotionally by the sight of such human baseness and degradation; moreover his Congo experience devastatingly exposed the cleavage between human pretensions and practice, a consciousness of which underlies Conrad's philosophy of life.

[V]

Seaman to Novelist

CONRAD arrived back in England some time in January 1891, and one of the first things he did was to visit Marguerite Poradowska in Brussels;[1] he may also have called on Klein's 'intended'.[2] During this visit he naturally discussed his future with his aunt and she promised to use her influence with M. Pécher, whose firm was the agent for the 'Prince' Steam Shipping Company Ltd, which operated a fleet of small vessels mostly in the African service.[3]

But the effects of the Congo were making themselves painfully felt, and on his return from Brussels he went straight to the doctor, who ordered him to bed. Although his doctor reassured him about his general state of health he must have been thoroughly unwell, as can be deduced from a letter from Bobrowski, to whom he would certainly have minimized his ailments:

> I received your last letter, of 4/16 February, on my return from Kiev, and together with you deplore the shapelessness of your legs, of which one has swollen while the other is a normal size, as also do I deplore the scarcity of hair presaging future baldness. But, in my arsenal of experience there is no help for this and we must therefore in this touchy matter pass to the next item on the agenda, and patiently await whatever the gods of hirsuteness decide. [10 March 1891]

A few days in bed did him good and he wrote to his aunt a facetious letter suggesting how she might recommend him to Pécher:

> Vous pourrez aussi ajouter que jugent a l'apparance de mon nez je ne m'enivre qu'une fois par an, que je n'ai pas l'air d'avoir un penchant vers la piraterie et que – d'après ce que Vous savez de moi – Vous ne me croyez pas capable de commettre un detournement des fonds. Je n'ai jamais passé a la police cor-

rectionelle et je suis capable de donner un coup d'oeil discret à un joli minois sans loucher. Il est vrai que je boîte, mais je suis en compagnie distinguée. Timoléon etait boîteux et il y a même un Diable qui l'est d'après ce que j'ai entendu dire. [Sunday (1 February 1891)]

He was well enough to go to Scotland in the middle of February to see about a job,[4] but shortly after his return had to go into the German Hospital in London, where he stayed for over a month.

He wrote a note to Marguerite Poradowska on 27 February in a very shaky hand: 'Malade au lit a l'hôpital. Rheumatisme de jambe gauche et neuralgie de bras droit. Merci pour Vos bontés. Aussitot possible ecrirais. Je Vous embrasse.' Then again, on 12 March, saying that his legs and stomach were in a bad condition and that he was not in a very cheerful mood. On 30 March he told his aunt that he had just got up but was still far from well, adding that Mr Knott of the 'Prince' Steam Shipping Company had, at the request of M. Pécher, been making overtures to him with regard to the command of a steamer, but that he was too ill to follow this up. He also wrote a letter to Bobrowski, who replied:

Thank the Lord that you have left your bed, but from your description, which you try to make comic, I see that you are still very enfeebled and very exhausted – and that the slightest thing may lay you prostrate again. [12 April 1891]

He was apparently in as bad a state mentally as he was physically. On 14 April he wrote to Marguerite Poradowska:

Je vois tout avec un tel decouragement – tout en noir. Mes nerfs sont tout a fait detraqués.

A fortnight later he wrote in much the same vein and said that he would probably be going to a hydropathic establishment near Geneva for a cure. This was La Roseraie at Champel, where he stayed for nearly a month, leaving England on 17 May.[5] While he was there he apparently worked at *Almayer's Folly* because he wrote in *A Personal Record:*

Geneva, or more precisely the hydropathic establishment of Champel, is rendered for ever famous by the termination of the eighth chapter in the history of Almayer's decline and fall.[6]

He returned to London in the middle of June temporarily restored in body and mind. On the return journey he called on his aunt, who had just moved to Paris.[7] The good effects of the cure were quick to wear off and this was doubtless due partly to Conrad's difficulty in finding a satisfactory job. There seem to have been several possibilities; one was connected with the Niger River, probably an offer of a command from the 'Prince' Company, which Conrad turned down because he had had enough of Africa; another was some business post in London which his friend Hope was trying to get for him.[8] On 22 June he wrote to his aunt: 'Je forme des vagues projets pour l'avenir; très vagues! Du reste, a quoi bon projeter, puisque c'est toujours l'imprévu qui arrive', but ten days later: 'Tous mes plans ont manqué, aussi je n'en fais plus.'[9]

His vacillation began to worry Bobrowski, who thought it advisable to write in a manner which recalls, though more genially, his admonitions of more than ten years ago:

My dear boy,

We write to each other nearly every week now. ... In my last letter, unasked and unquestioned by my Dear Sir, I touched slightly on certain defects in *my dear boy*, defects with which, for that matter, it is possible to live and be loved. Today, you yourself ask me to indicate those shortcomings of your character that I have observed during thirty-four years in the light of my 'cold reasoning', shortcomings that make your life difficult, as you yourself admit. You state in advance that you can't perceive them yourself and for that reason ask me to conduct this operation upon your person. If this is an oblique summons that I assure you, and even swear to it, that I haven't perceived even the slightest shortcoming in you, and that I consider you perfection without flaw – then, forgive me, brother, but I shall not say that – because I see in you an ordinary mortal, and the usual shortcomings, since who is free of them? Well then, I consider that you have always lacked endurance and steadfastness of decision, which is the result of your lack of steadfastness in your aims and desires. You lack endurance, brother, towards facts – and I suppose towards people, too? This is the gift of character inherited from your grandfather – paternal uncle – and even Father – the Nałęczs. The first two were always plunged in plans of various kinds, the most diverse, mostly of a fantastic nature – they laid them in their imagination and were even offended when anyone criticised them – considering opponents to be 'idiots'; but the facts most often gave the lie to their dreams, hence bitterness towards those who saw better. . . . Your Father, again, was an idealistic dreamer; he loved people certainly, and certainly desired their happiness – though he usually applied two measures to them – he was a very lenient judge for the poor and the weak of this world – while he judged the rich and powerful very sharply and pitilessly – hence we have an ethical cleavage. All thought very highly of themselves and suffered much after failures, suffered more intensely than could appear and could be expected. Thus, brother . . . you are subject to these inherited shortcomings – and bear their punishment. You permit yourself to be carried away by your imagination when laying plans – you become an optimist, when you encounter disappointments, contrarities discourage you – you easily fall into pessimism – and as you have too much pride you suffer by reason of disappointments more than would suffer anybody with more moderate imagination and endowed with greater endurance in activity and relations. This is what I think in this connection – and I again repeat what I said in my previous letter: these are shortcomings – but even with them one can be loved, while life will teach you a better knowledge of perspective in appraising people and facts. [30 July 1891]

These strictures must have been galling to Conrad. But were they justified? The bald facts of Conrad's life since his departure from Marseilles show a record of steady achievement, the only setback being the Congo episode. However, Bobrowski's letters to Conrad reveal the turbulence underlying this achievement, and this impression would certainly have been reinforced if Conrad's own letters had survived because he was prone to see and paint 'tout en noir'. Moreover he seems to have propounded in his letters to Bobrowski a succession of schemes most of which would have entailed a radical change of occupation – and the fact that none of them came to anything implies that they were somewhat impractical and goes some way towards justifying Bobrowski's claim that Conrad was a true Nałęcz Korzeniowski. Nor was this restlessness and discontent surprising, let alone reprehensible. A merchant seaman's life was not such as to satisfy fully a man of Conrad's temperament and capabilities.

In the letter just quoted Bobrowski warned Conrad against becoming too involved with Marguerite Poradowska:

Why do you say you are one-eyed; have you trouble with your eye? – or is this some metaphor arising from your position as Tante Margot's 'support'? Well, it seems to me that neither of you can see, that you're only flirting with each other since the death of that poor Oleś – while I, as an old sparrow friendly to you both, would advise you to give up this game, which will end in nothing wise. A patched up grannie, and if she is to convolve, it will be with Buls – who would propose to her and who has given proofs of love. For you, it would be a stone round your neck – and for her also. Leave this recreation alone and part before harm is done, if you want to be wise – if not, however, you have my *avertissement* – so that you shouldn't say later that you lacked it. I suppose that that locomotive, which found itself in Aunt's life as you say in the letter and 'a écrasé son cousin' – is really that nonsense which arose in the mind of one or both of you. 'A word is enough to a wise head' – you know the proverb of old.

Keep well my dear – please write, we can have differing views while loving each other with all our hearts.

In his next letter he returned to the same subject, dealing with Conrad's protest of innocence:

If the Prince of Benevento of 'accursed memory' was right when he said that 'speech (in this case written) was given us to conceal our thoughts', then you have coped excellently with the task, telling me on five sheets about all the young and old, beautiful and ugly, Englishwomen, whom you know and who successfully or unsuccessfully impel you to flirt, the Lord knows this alone? – only to omit the Only One with whom I suspect you of such practices, and I do not have in mind any flat-footed Englishwoman but the Margaret well known to me. [26 August 1891]

There is no evidence to support Bobrowski's suspicion at this time. Certainly the letters which Conrad was writing to Marguerite Poradowska do not read like love letters. It seems incredible that he should have been having an affair or even flirting with a woman whom he was calling 'Chère Tante' or 'Très chère Tante' and to whom he signed himself 'Votre neveu très dévoué, J. Conrad'; he also used the 'vous', not the 'tu' form of address. What happened later is another matter.

(2)

As he could not find a satisfactory job, and was merely agreeably filling in time yachting with Hope, Conrad took a temporary post with Barr, Moering, but just as he was about to start work he went down with a bout of malaria. 'Je suis comme abasourdi par ce nouveau desastre,'[10] he told his aunt. However, he quickly recovered and started work on 4 August in charge of one of the firm's warehouses. This occupation seems, if anything, to have depressed him more than his enforced idleness. He was later to describe his state at this time as having been neurasthenic;[11] a strong word for Conrad to use. He wrote to his aunt:

> Après tout je ne suis pas aussi heureux de travailler comme Vous sembler le penser. Il n'y a rien de bien rejouissant a faire un travail qui déplait . . . [26 August 1891]

The self-mockery of two further letters to Mme Poradowska does not hide his depression and dissatisfaction:

> Votre sympathie m'est très precieuse mais a Vous dire vrai je me moque pas mal du bonheur. A peine je sais ce que c'est. Je ne suis ni plus courageux ni plus indépendant que les autres; je suis peut-être plus indifferent, ce qui n'est pas une qualité, sans etre cependant une faute. . . . Si je vous laisse entrevoir quelque fois que la vie fait mal de temps en temps c'est une faiblesse a moi dont j'ai tres honte – mais il ne faut pas me prendre trop au serieux. Je supporte très bien le fardeau du monde entier sur mes epaules comme du reste le font les cinq millions des misérables dont se compose la population de cette ville. [15 September 1891]

And a month later:

Je n'ai absolument rien a Vous dire. Je vegète. Je ne pense même pas; – donc je n'existe pas (selon Descartes). Mais un autre individu (un savant) a dit: 'Sans phosphore point de pensée'. D'où il semble que c'est le phosphore qui est absent et moi je suis toujours là. Mais dans ce cas j'existerais sans penser, ce qui (selon Descartes) est impossible. – Grand Dieux! Serai-je un Polichinelle? Le Polichinelle de mon enfance, Vous savez – l'echine cassée en deux le nez par terre entre les pieds; les jambes et les bras raidement écartés, dans cette attitude de profond desespoir, so pathetiquement drôle, des jouets jétés dans un coin. Lui n'a avait pas de phosphore; je sais, car j'ai léché toute la peinture de ces joues vermeilles, embrassé, et même mordu, son nez bien des fois sans m'en trouver plus mal. C'etait un ami fidèle. Il recevait mes confidences d'un air sympathique en me regardant d'un oeil affectueux. Je dis d'un oeil dans les premiers jours de notre amitié je lui avais crevé l'autre dans un acces de folle tendresse. Du rest il n'a jamais semblé s'en aperçevoir de peur de me causer de la peine. C'était un 'gentleman'. Les autres polichinelles que j'ai connu depuis criaient quand on leur marchait sur le pied. A-t-on l'idée d'une impertinence pareille!? Après tout rien ne remplace les amitiés de notre enfance. –

Ce soir il me semble que je suis dans un coin, l'echine cassée, le nez dan la poussière. Voulez Vous avoir la bonté de ramasser le pauvre diable, le mettre tendrement dans Votre tablier, le presenter a Vos poupées, lui faire faire la dinette avec les autres. Je me vois d'ici a ce festin le nez barbouillé des confitures, les autres me regardant avec cet air d'etonnement frigide qui est naturel aux poupées bien fabriquées. J'ai été regardé comme cela bien des fois par des mannequins innombrables. Ma foi! Je leur pardonne; il y a eu un temps où j'étais chrétien! – [16 October (1891)]

He even revealed his state of mind to his uncle, from whom he usually tried to keep such worries, in letters which may have reminded Bobrowski of Apollo's plaints in the past. In one letter Bobrowski replied:

To philosophise thus on death and maintain that *en fin de compte* 'it is better to die young for after all one is bound to die sooner or later' implies feeling *profondement découragé* or being ill and perhaps both?? It is not natural at your age . . . for such a philosophy to find room in the heads of young, healthy people, and that seriously worries me, my dear. [8 October 1891]

He followed this up a month later with another letter which he started: '*My dear Boy*, – I begin as usual though I should perhaps begin with "*My dear Pessimist*" because that is the aroma which your letters have for some time been bringing.' He then goes on to discourse at length on the causes of pessimism in general and of Conrad's in particular, reaching the conclusion that Conrad's is pathological or, what he seems to mean, innate. He cites Conrad's recent African trials and his illness as having accentuated this state, and continues:

> Finally I base myself on what I believe to be an exactly observed structure of your character and mind which, in you as an individual and hereditarily, are predominantly visionary in spite of your very practical profession – or perhaps just because of it? Perhaps my supposition is wrong, but I think that the same pessimistic disposition governed you in Marseilles years ago, only against the background of your youth ...

He then tries to suggest the remedy for this ailment, and his advice is very similar to that which Stein gives to Jim in *Lord Jim*; indeed his inference of Conrad's visionary nature resembles Stein's inference of Jim's romanticism. It is no use declaiming against the structure of the world because that won't alter it; the answer is 'in the destructive element immerse', although Bobrowski would certainly not have used the word 'destructive' in this context:

> If both Individuals and Nations instead of the ideal of greatness were to establish their aim as 'duty', would the world not certainly be better than it is? And those crowds 'instinctively aiming at securing only bread', so detestable to all visionaries, have their *raison d'être*: to satisfy the material needs of life, – and are no longer detestable when a more precise examination often reveals that they illumine their existence by their work, and often even by their shortcomings, and by some higher moral idea of duty accomplished, of love for family and country, to whom they bequeath the fruit of their effort and labours by generosity or after their death ...

Perhaps you will tell me what I have said is but the words of one who has always been comfortable in the world '*qui a eu toujours chaud*' – but this is not so, you know this well; I have had my ups and downs, I have suffered over my own fate and that of my family and Nation; and just because of these sufferings, perhaps, these disappointments, I have developed in myself this calm point of view on the tasks of life, whose motto I venture to say, was, is, and will be, *Usque ad finem* [Stein in *Lord Jim* uses this same motto] the love of duty more narrowly or widely conceived, depending on circumstances and time. This comprises my practical creed which, backed up by the experience of my sixty years of life, may possibly be useful to you; don't you think so? I shall learn the results probably from your next letters. Faithful to the principle *mens sana in corpore sano*, I raise a prayer for your health, for it is certain that it is most at fault in your present spiritual mood, and I am glad of what you write in your last letter: may it continue – and pessimism will then be beaten off, I hope. [9 November 1891]

But then, to jog him out of his depression, the unexpected happened, as he had predicted in a previous letter to his aunt. On 14 November he was able to announce to her that an acquaintance of his who commanded the *Torrens* had offered him the post of first mate, which he had accepted, and that he was due to sail for Adelaide in six days.[12]

The 'wonderful *Torrens*' as Basil Lubbock called her was a clipper of 1,276 tons and one of the most famous ships of her time. Lubbock described her as 'without doubt one of the most successful ships every built, besides being one of the fastest, and for many years . . . the favourite passenger ship to Adelaide'.[13] For the first fifteen years of her life, from 1875 to 1890, under her chief owner, Captain H. R. Angel, she had a fine record of fast passages without mishap. But when he retired she was dismasted on her first voyage under her new captain, W. H. Cope, and it was said that her luck had deserted her; certainly she never quite attained her former achievement. There were naturally plenty of candidates keen to serve in such a distinguished ship, particularly in the senior posts, and it was an honour to be asked to become first mate, although Conrad was accepting a position below that to which his master's certificate entitled him.

The *Torrens* sailed from Plymouth on 25 November, and on 28 February 1892 Conrad disembarked at Port Adelaide. This, her second voyage out under Captain Cope, was uneventful, but took ninety-five days, considerably more than Captain Angel's average of seventy-four.[14]

The sea does not seem to have entirely cured Conrad's depression because, writing to Marguerite Poradowska from Adelaide, he complained of 'une espèce de torpeur intellectuelle qui m'oppresse';[15] and, the day after his return to London, he wrote that 'je vois tout en noir depuis que ma santé n'est plus bonne. C'est bête mais c'est comme cela.'[16] But he had recovered enough to write more cheerfully to his uncle, who replied:

> Your letter of 23 September which I received the day before yesterday gave me much pleasure by its gaiety and the news of your good health and I sincerely rejoice at this change of mood. [1 October 1892]

However an earlier letter from Bobrowski shows that Conrad was restless: 'I can share your feelings and understand that you long for a command.' In the same letter there is an amusingly acid comment on Marguerite Poradowska:

> Madame Marguerite has been writing me voluminous letters, so illegible that I have had to use a magnifying glass – but I reply to every one. Her enthusiasm has now cooled a little and she has not written, I think, since April. The dear woman is a *bas bleu* – I tried to persuade her that it would be better if she changed this title for Madame la Bourgmestre Buls, but she would not listen. She's as romantic as a girl of sixteen. [18 September 1892]

Conrad sailed with the *Torrens* again on 25 October, bound for Adelaide.[17] In *A Personal Record* he describes how, during this voyage, he showed the manuscript of *Almayer's Folly* to a passenger, a young man just down from Cambridge named Jacques.

When Jacques handed back the manuscript:

> 'Well, what do you say?' I asked at last. 'Is it worth finishing?' ...

'Distinctly,' he answered in his sedate veiled voice, and then coughed a little.
'Were you interested?' I inquired further, almost in a whisper.
'Very much!' . . .
'Now let me ask you one more thing: Is the story quite clear to you as it stands?'
He raised his dark, gentle eyes to my face and seemed surprised.
'Yes! Perfectly.'
This was all I was to hear from his lips concerning the merits of *Almayer's Folly*. We never spoke together of the book again.[18]

On the return voyage there were two further passengers, also just down from the University, who were to become firm friends of Conrad for the rest of his life. They were Edward Sanderson, son of the headmaster of Elstree preparatory school, and John Galsworthy. In a letter written during the voyage Galsworthy gave his impression of the man who has gained a niche in literary history as the first reader of Conrad: 'We have three unattached men – two with beards grown on the voyage out – nomine J—, H— and A—, all harmless but not interesting, J— being the least harmless and the most interesting. He was a first class classical man at Cambridge and plays chess a good deal with Ted . . .'[19]

Jacques was seriously ill with tuberculosis and died shortly after his return to England.[20]

(3)

Galsworthy was the son of a well-to-do solicitor and had been educated at Harrow, then at New College. Although he read Law and was called to the Bar he showed no inclination to take up Law as a profession but, with his father's encouragement, spent the next four years after coming down from Oxford travelling, ostensibly to learn something of business and legal affairs.

Judging from his letters, his career at Harrow and New College, and the testimony of those who knew him at the time, he showed every sign of developing into a paragon of middle-class conventionality. But during his travels there began to appear some faint yearning towards a more profound experience. In a letter to his friend Monica Sanderson he said: 'I always want to get inside beautiful things and feel more in touch with them; and somehow one can never get far enough; I wonder if you have the feeling too,'[21] – and later in the same letter: 'I do wish I had the gift of writing, I really think that is the nicest way of making money going, only it isn't really the writing so much as the thoughts that one wants; and, when you feel like a very shallow pond, with no nice cool deep pools with queer and pleasant things at the bottom, what's the good? I suppose one could cultivate writing, but one can't cultivate clear depths and quaint plants.'[22]

Whether this impulse would have come to anything unaided is impossible to know. But then in 1895 there occurred the most important event in his life: he and Ada Galsworthy, the wife of his first cousin, fell in love. The daughter of Emanuel Cooper, a Norwich doctor, Ada was a woman of beauty, intelligence, and character whose marriage to Arthur Galsworthy had very soon shown itself to be an appalling mistake.

The obstacles in the way of the two lovers achieving happiness at first seemed insuperable. The desire not to outrage John Galsworthy's father, whose views on marriage and divorce derived from the rigid conventions of the age, forced them to pursue their love in secret. There were nine years of torment, during which they had to be content with occasional snatched holidays abroad together, before John Galsworthy senior died, in December 1904. They now saw no reason why they should not live openly together, and a few weeks later were served with divorce papers. In September 1905 they were married; Galsworthy was now thirty-eight, nine months younger than Ada.

The situation in which Galsworthy had found himself had shaken his emotional and moral outlook and led him to examine the assumptions on which his life had been based. This, coupled with Ada's encouragement, no doubt provided the decisive stimulus to become a writer. In 1897, two years after he and Ada had fallen in love, a volume called *From the Four Winds*, containing ten of his short stories, appeared under the pseudonym of John Sinjohn. The edition was of 500 copies published at the author's expense by the tight-fisted Fisher Unwin. This was followed by a mediocre novel, *Jocelyn*, published with the encouragement and help of Conrad[23] in 1898, and *The Villa Rubein* in 1900. It was only with his fifth book, *The Island Pharisees*, published in 1904, that he shed his pseudonymity.

Although he was a man of strong feelings and sincerity he had neither an original nor a profound mind. He was enlightened and intensely humane and his views frequently set him at odds with society, but he was one of the least imaginative creative writers who have succeeded in being taken seriously; his range was narrowly circumscribed and he never wholly disproved Garnett's claim that he would 'always look at life as from the windows of a club'.[24] He was too much a moralist, too little an artist, and was utterly unconvincing whenever he tried to portray a complex mind, as in the case of Bosinney, Mark Lennan, Cortier, Hilary Dallison, or even 'young' Jolyon.

It is difficult to know what Conrad really thought of Galsworthy as a writer, and tempting to foist on him an opinion which one thinks he ought to have had. He was almost invariably enthusiastic in his praise of Galsworthy's work in letters to him, but this cannot be taken as the true expression of his opinion. He was himself hypersensitive to criticism and wisely chose to avoid any risk of wounding others. He wrote about Galsworthy's work with a tact guided by his feeling for the man, but on the whole his praise was too vague and generalized to carry much conviction, whereas Galsworthy on his side showed little understanding of Conrad's work.*

But there can be no doubt as to Conrad's feelings for Gals-

* cf., 'Conrad (a painter's writer) is perhaps the best specimen I can think of as a pure artist (there is practically nothing of the moralist in him) amongst moderns.' Letter to R. H. Mottram, 4 August 1906; Marrot, op. cit., p. 194.

worthy himself; Conrad clearly had a deep and lasting affection for him. In his integrity and generosity of spirit Galsworthy personified those qualities which Conrad admired most; embedded in the rock of moral certitudes, he was always there to sustain Conrad's more profound and insecure nature, and often to help him materially.

(4)

There is no mention of Conrad in Galsworthy's first letter from the *Torrens*, in which he describes Captain and Mrs Cope. But in the second he wrote:

> The first mate is a Pole called Conrad and is a capital chap, though queer to look at; he is a man of travel and experience in many parts of the world, and has a fund of yarns on which I draw freely. He has been right up the Congo and all around Malacca and Borneo and other out of the way parts, to say nothing of a little smuggling in the days of his youth. . . .*

On this voyage, too, Conrad seems to have been dogged by periods of gloom. On 3 February he wrote to Marguerite Poradowska:

> Cette même existence commence a me fatiguer tant soit peu. Ce n'est pas le mal present (car je me sens beaucoup mieux en ce moment) mais c'est l'incertitude de l'avenir, ou plutôt la certitude du 'gris uniforme' qui m'attend qui cause ce decouragement. Je sais fort bien que ce que je viens de dire – et que je ressens – manque de dignité; mais au moins le sentiment e[s]t vrai – il n'est pas morbide car j'envisage la situation sans aucune amertume. Sans doute il serait plus digne d'envisager sans souffler mot mais ma foi – on ne peut pas rester toujours perché sur les echasses de ses principes.

In another letter[25] he said that he hoped to be on the way to the Ukraine via Paris by the end of August.

When he arrived in London on 26 July 1893[26] there was a letter from his uncle again pressing him to take what might

* Letter of 23 April 1893, Marrot, op. cit., p. 88. Thirty-one years later Galsworthy elaborated these impressions in an obituary notice entitled 'Reminiscences of Conrad' which was reprinted in *Castles in Spain.*

be the last opportunity of visiting him.[27] Conrad left for the Ukraine towards the end of August and stayed with his uncle for about a month. During his visit he was apparently quite ill and was in bed for five days, nursed by his uncle, who, Conrad said, treated him like a small child. While still at Kazimierowka he received a letter from Marguerite Poradowska, who must have heard a rumour that he was about to marry her niece by marriage, Maria Ołdakowska. He replied making fun of the idea and saying that the girl was indeed to marry, but a man named Rakowski and not himself.[28]

Back in London, in rooms at 17 Gillingham Street, near Victoria Station, he was faced with the recurrent problem of finding another job.[29] The enforced idleness again plunged him into gloom,[30] but at least gave him the chance to go on working at his manuscript of *Almayer's Folly*.[31] Then he was unexpectedly offered the post of first officer on an English steamship named the *Adowa*, which had been chartered by the Franco-Canadian Transport Company to carry emigrants from France to Canada.[32]

By 6 December he was at Rouen on the *Adowa*, expecting to sail for La Rochelle in three days and thence to Halifax.[33] On 18 December he was still at Rouen. The whole undertaking had collapsed, as the Company had not carried out its contract; and the owners of the *Adowa* were being forced to make other plans. Thus the future was once more uncertain, and Conrad wondered whether it would be possible for Marguerite Poradowska to use her influence to get him a job as a Suez pilot.[34] A couple of days later he wrote again from Rouen to Marguerite Poradowska:

> C'est vrai que la vie ici n'est guère amusante mais comme je suis payé pour m'embêter! – Tout de même ça ne mène a rien et je commence a me sentir vieux. Il faudrait se caser quelque part si on a l'idée de vivre. A vrai dire je n'en vois pas la nécéssité – mais d'un autre côté je ne suis point préparé a prendre de l'arsenic ou me jeter a la mer. Donc il faut que je me case.

He goes on to say that he is taking steps – or steps are being taken for him – to get a job in the pearl fisheries off the Australian coast.[35]

The *Adowa* stayed at Rouen for another three weeks.[36] Three days before leaving Conrad wrote to Marguerite Poradowska:

Si Vous êtes une petite fille bien sage je Vous laisserai lire mon histoire d'Almayer quand je l'aurai fini.*

It appears that Conrad spent some at least of this abortive wait adding to the manuscript. *A Personal Record* opens:

Books may be written in all sorts of places. Verbal inspiration may enter the berth of a mariner on board a ship frozen fast in a river in the middle of a town; and since saints are supposed to look benignantly on humble believers, I indulge in the pleasant fantasy that the shade of old Flaubert . . . might have hovered with amused interest over the decks of a 2,000 ton steamer called the *Adowa*, on board of which, gripped by the inclement winter alongside a quay in Rouen, the tenth chapter of *Almayer's Folly* was begun.[37]

On 17 January 1894 Conrad disembarked from the *Adowa* in London, and returned to his rooms at 17 Gillingham Street. He wrote to Marguerite Poradowska[38] that he expected soon to be leaving on a long voyage; but this did not come off and, although he made repeated attempts to get to sea right up to 1898, the *Adowa* proved to be the last ship on which he was to serve as a merchant sailor. Conrad drifted unintentionally out of the British Merchant Navy just as he had drifted into it.

He had been in London a month when he heard from Poland that Thaddeus Bobrowski had died.[39] Conrad may perhaps at times have been exasperated by his uncle's delight in preaching or pointing a moral, but his lovable qualities stand out so strongly from his letters, and his devotion to Conrad was so clear, that Conrad was doubtless not exaggerating when he wrote to Marguerite Poradowska:

Ile me semble que tout est mort en moi. Il semble emporter mon ame avec lui. [18 February 1894]

* Sunday (7 January 1894). This is the first preserved mention of the existence of *Almayer's Folly*, but it is clear from the manner in which it is made that Conrad had already spoken of the book to Marguerite Poradowska; the allusion would otherwise have been unintelligible.

or some years later when he wrote that his uncle was:

> the wisest, the firmest, the most indulgent of guardians, extending over me a paternal care and affection, a moral support which I seemed to feel always near me in the most distant parts of the earth.[40]

Conrad had already been told by Bobrowski that he would receive 15,000 roubles, which Bobrowski had loaned to the Zaleski family, a year after his death.[41] He also appointed Conrad one of a committee to decide about the publication of his memoirs.[42]

Three weeks after his uncle's death Conrad wrote a depressed letter to Marguerite Poradowska:

> Je suis un peu comme un animal sauvage; je cherche a me cacher quand je souffre soit de corps soit d'esprit et en ce moment je souffre de deux. [2 March 1894]

He was again worried by his lack of a job, and asked Marguerite Poradowska whether she thought he would get an answer to his application to become a Suez Canal pilot. He probably visited her in Brussels at this time.

But the lack of a job again allowed him the opportunity to go on with *Almayer's Folly* and by the end of the month he was grappling with Chapter XI. He wrote to Marguerite Poradowska:

> Je suis en train de lutter avec Chap. XI; une lutte a mort Vous savez! Si je me laisse aller je suis perdu! . . . Je regrette chaque minute que je passe loin du papier. Je ne dis pas de la plume car j'ai ecrit fort peu, mais l'inspiration me vient en regardant le papier. Puis ce sont des echappées a perte de vue; la pensée s'en va vagabondant dans des grands espaces remplis des formes vague. Tout e[s]t chaos encore mais – lentement – les spectres se changent en chair vivante, les vapeurs flottantes se solidifient et qui sait? peut-être quelque chose naitra dans le choc des idées indistinctes.[43]

On 16 April he wrote to Marguerite Poradowska from the Sandersons at Elstree saying that Chapter XI was finished and that his health was 'comme çi comme ça'. This was probably the visit to which Mrs Reynolds, Galsworthy's sister, referred when she wrote:

I stayed there [The Schoolhouse, Elstree] often myself, and I remember that both Ted [Sanderson] and his mother ... took a hand, and considerable trouble, in editing the already amazingly excellent English of their Polish friend's 'Almayer' manuscript, and in generally screwing up Conrad's courage to the sticking-point of publication.[44]

Then, at last, on 24 April, five years (according to Conrad's reckoning) after he had written the first words, he announced to Marguerite Poradowska:

J'ai la douleur de Vous faire part de la mort de M. Kaspar Almayer qui a eu lieu ce matin a 3h.

C'est fini! Un grattement de plume ecrivant le mot de la fin et soudain toute cette compagnie des gens qui ont parlé dans mon oreille, gesticulé devant mes yeux, vécu avec moi pendant tant d'années devient une bande des fantômes qui s'eloignent, s'efface se brouillant; indistincts et palis par le soleil de cette brillante et sombre journée. –

Depuis que je me suis reveillé ce matin il me semble que j'ai enseveli une part de moi-même dans les pages qui sont là devant mes yeux. Et cependant je suis content – un peu. –

Immediately he had finished *Almayer's Folly* he started to revise it. In two letters[45] to Marguerite Poradowska he mentions particularly the first four chapters, but he worked very carefully over the whole manuscript; in fact the earlier chapters have fewer alterations than the later, although important aspects of the plot, such as the influence of Almayer's love for his daughter, were added to Chapter I.[46]

The revision completed, Conrad wrote to Marguerite Poradowska that the manuscript was 'entre les mains d'un critique assez distingué: Edmund Gosse'.[47] At this time Gosse was editing for Heinemann the 'International Library', consisting of foreign novels translated into English, and perhaps Conrad thought that a novel in English by a Pole might fit into the series:[48] or he may simply have wanted Gosse's advice and help. As he makes no other reference to this and there is no record of Gosse having seen the manuscript, the affair must remain a mystery. It is possible that Gosse advised him to send it to Fisher Unwin.

At any rate, on 12 July Conrad told Marguerite Poradowska that he had sent the manuscript to Fisher Unwin as a candidate for their 'Pseudonym Library'.* But:

> Pas de reponse encore. Elle viendra sans doute dans la forme de renvoi de ce chef d'oeuvre en vue de quoi j'ai envoyé les timbres-poste nécéssaires. –
>
> A Vous dire toute la verité je n'eprouve aucun interet au sort d'*Almayer's Folly*. – C'est fini. Du reste dans tous les cas cela ne pouvait être qu'un épisode sans conséquence dans ma vie.

It would of course be wrong to look on this as Conrad's real attitude. Many artists, particularly when they are unsure of themselves, hide their concern under a feigned indifference; and the fact that he started to write another story[49] before he heard that *Almayer's Folly* had been accepted discounts the last sentence.

While waiting for the verdict, Conrad wrote a letter to Marguerite Poradowska which gives a revealing glimpse of his state of mind and which typically reflects feelings that were to afflict him for the rest of his life.

> Sans doute Vous avez reçu ma lettre et Vous me croyez fou. Je le suis a peu de chose près. Ma maladie des nerfs me torture, me rend malheureux et paralyse action, pensée, tout! Je me demande pourquoi j'existe? C'est un état affreux. Même dans les intervalles – quand je suis censé d'être bien – je vis dans la peur du retour de ce mal tourmentant . . .
>
> Je n'ai plus le courage de rien faire. J'ai a peine celui de Vous écrire. C'est un effort; un elan hatif pour finir avant que la plume ne tombe de la main dans l'affaissement du decouragement complet. . . . Je regrette de Vous avoir dit tout çela. Jamais je n'en ai dit tant que çela a personne. Vous ferez bien d'oublier ce que Vous venez d'entendre. [Wednesday (25 July? 1894)]

Hearing nothing from Fisher Unwin, and fearing the worst, Conrad made a proposal to his aunt which, if he had

* He had chosen the pseudonym of 'Kamudi' which appears on the title-page of the typescript of *Almayer's Folly*; Gordan, op. cit., pp. 182–3.

needed to have recourse to it, would have constituted a curious start to his literary career:

Si Vous n'aviez rien dit a la *Revue* nous aurions pu peut-être faire paraître *Almayer* pas comme traduction mais comme collaboration. [Monday (30 ? July 1894)]

Marguerite Poradowska seems to have accepted the idea because Conrad wrote a few weeks later from Champel, where he had suddenly rushed off to try to recover his health, elaborating his proposal:

Puisque Vous êtes assez bonne pour Vous en occuper, parlons de cet imbécile d'Almayer. J'ai envoyé reclamer le renvoi du MS. et aussitot mon retour en Angleterre je le tiendrais a votre disposition. . . . Le nom 'Kamondi' [*sic*] en petites lettres quelque part suffira. Laissez votre nom paraitre en titre – une note explicative suffira pour dire que K. y a collaboré.* [Saturday (18? August 1894)]

In the same letter he took up Marguerite Poradowska's offer to try to get him a job, saying that his reserves were almost exhausted and that he must find a position very quickly.

Then, despite having heard nothing from Fisher Unwin – and this is particularly interesting and important because it shows how strong was Conrad's urge to write – he announced:

J'ai commencé d'ecrire – Avant hier seulement. Je vaux faire cela tout court – Disons 20 a 25 pages comme celles de la *Revue*. J'appelle ça *Deux Vagabonds* (*Two Vagabonds*) et je veux decrire a grand traits – sans ombres ni details – deux epaves humaines comme on en renco[n]tre dans les coins perdus du monde. Un homme blanc et un Malais. Vous voyez que les Malais me tiennent. Je suis voué au Borneo. Ce qui m'ennuie le plus ce que mes personnages sont si vrais. Je les connais si bien qu'ils m'entravent l'imagination. . . . Mais une catastrophe dramatique me manque. La tête est vide et même pour le commencement

* This suggestion may have been the origin of Sir Hugh Clifford's story that before writing *Almayer's Folly* Conrad had hesitated between French and English. See p. 189.

il y a du tirage! Je ne Vous dis que ça! J'ai envie de lacher tout déjà – Pensez-Vous que l'on peut faire une chose intéréssante sans la femme?!

Back at Gillingham Street he wrote to Marguerite Poradowska

Les deux Vagabonds dorment. Je ne suis pas satisfait avec moi-même – du tout. Il me manque des idées. J'ai beaucoup brulé. Ce sera a recommencer!

Je viens d'ecrire a Fisher Unwin quand au *Almayer*. Je leur demande une reponse ou le retour du MS. . . . Si je pars on tiendra le MS. a Votre disposition chez MM. Barr, Moreing. . . . Vous ecrirez que l'on Vous l'envoie quand Vous Vous sentirez l'envie de commencer. [8 September 1894]

The letter to Unwin was sent the same day:

Gentlemen,

On the 4th July 1894 there was delivered in your Pub.^g offices of Paternoster Row a typewritten work.

Title: *Almayer's Folly*; it was enclosed in brown paper wrapper addressed to J. Conrad, 17 Gillingham St., S.W. and franked, for return by parcel post, by twelve 1^d stamps. The brown paper package was put between two detached sheets of cardboard secured together by a string. One of the cardboard sheets bore your address. The boy mess.^ger produced the usual receipt slip, duly signed, but I do not remember the name or initials of the signature.

I venture now upon the liberty of asking you whether there is the slightest likelihood of the MS. (Malay life, about 64,000 words) being read at some future time? If not, it would be – probably – no worse fate than it deserves, yet, in that case I am sure you will not take it amiss if I remind you that, however worthless for the purpose of publication, it is very dear to me. A ridiculous feeling – no doubt – but not unprecedented I believe. In this instance it is intensified by the accident that I do not possess another copy, either written or typed.

I beg to apologise for taking up your time with this matter . . .[50]

On 2 October he wrote again to Marguerite Poradowska along much the same lines:

Je ne peux pas obtenir mon manuscript. J'ai réclamé deux fois et chaque foi j'ai eu la reponse que l'on s'en occupe. Je vais attendre quelque jours encore avant de demander le renvoi quand même.

Then, at last, two days later, he wrote triumphantly:

On a accepte mon Manuscrit. Je viens d'en recevoir la nouvelle. F.U. ne m'offre que £20 pour le copyright.

J'ai ecrit que j'acceptais ces conditions. . . . J'ai pris ce que l'on m'offrait car vraiment le fait même de la publication est de grande importance. Chaque semaine des douzaines des romans paraissent – et il est bien difficile de se faire imprimer. – A present il ne me manque qu'un navire pour être a peu près heureux . . .

Les Deux Vagabonds chôment. Je suis trop occupé a courir après les navires. Rien encore de ce coté là.

(5)

The first few sentences of *Almayer's Folly* should have been enough to show any publisher's reader that here was a manuscript out of the ordinary in competence and individuality:

'Kaspar! Makan!'

The well-known shrill voice startled Almayer from his dream of splendid future into the unpleasant realities of the present hour. An unpleasant voice too. He had heard it for many years, and with every year he liked it less. No matter; there would be an end to all this soon.

He shuffled uneasily, but took no further notice of the call. Leaning with both his elbows on the balustrade of the verandah, he went on looking fixedly at the great river that flowed – indifferent and [un]hurried – before his eyes. He liked to look at it about the time of sunset; perhaps because at that time the sinking sun would spread a glowing gold tinge on the waters of the Pantai, and Almayer's thoughts were often busy with gold; gold he had failed to secure; gold the others had secured – dishonestly, of course – or gold he meant to secure yet, through his own honest exertions, for himself and Nina.[51]

In fact the manuscript had finally been given to Edward Garnett; thus not only was it assured of a perceptive and sympathetic reading, but a man was brought into Conrad's life who was to have considerable influence on his early development as a novelist and to remain a close friend until Conrad died. Edward Garnett was the son of the distinguished scholar, Richard Garnett, and at the age of twenty-six was already showing that skill as publisher's reader which gained him the position of one of the most influential publishing figures of his time. According to David Garnett his father's mission 'was to discover the genius and to fight for his recognition';[52] and his 'discoveries' were to include Galsworthy, D. H. Lawrence, W. H. Davies, Hudson, as well as numerous others who disappeared from the literary scene after showing signs of brilliance or who, like H. E. Bates, are still writing with success. David Garnett also says that 'it was inconceivable to Edward that he might be completely mistaken in a literary judgement'.[53] This quality led to an intense loyalty to his protégés and, at least when he became older, to his sometimes treating them with the patronizing dogmatism that a schoolmaster might use to a promising but fractiously precocious pupil. He possessed a withering irony and, in his letters, a force of expression which could devastate a piece of writing like a hurricane. But his mind was not attuned to creativeness and he frittered away his talents in ephemeral criticism, sketches, and satire, or on plays which showed little sense of the theatre. Because of his failure to find an adequate form of self-expression and because of his resentment at the ingratitude of protégés who, as they matured, inevitably drifted away from their position of tutelage, he became increasingly soured and insisted that success was always in inverse ratio to merit. It is revealing to compare a photograph of him as a young man with one of him in middle age; the first shows him as good-looking, extremely sensitive, intelligent, and perhaps vulnerable, while the second shows the lines of the mouth fallen into an expression of embitterment. But he never apparently lost an underlying warmth of heart nor his intense concern with literature and would be ready to lavish on other people's work a care which many writers are not even prepared to give to their own.

On 8 October Conrad went to discuss terms with Unwin, apparently at his office.[54] He described to Marguerite Poradowska how he was first received by the firm's two readers, presumably W. H. Chesson and Edward Garnett, who 'm'ont complimenté avec effusion (se sont-ils moqué de moi par hasard?)', and was then conducted into the presence of Unwin, who told him that he could have a share of the profits if he wanted to bear part of the risk of publication; if not, Unwin renewed the offer of an outright payment of £20 for the copyright, which Conrad accepted after he had persuaded Unwin to allow him to keep the French translation rights:

'Nous vous payons très peu – a-t-il dit – mais considerez cher monsieur que vous êtes un inconnu et que votre livre appelle a un public très limité. Puis il y a la question du gout. Le Public le goutera-t-il? Nous risquons quelque chose aussi. Nous vous fairons paraître en un beau volume a 6 shillings et vous savez que ce qui parait chez nous reçoit toujours du critique serieuses dans les journaux littéraires. Vous êtes sure d'une longue 'notices' dans la *Saturday Review* et *l'Athenaeum* sans parler de la presse en general. . . . Ecrivez quelque chose de plus court – même genre – pour notre Pseudonym Library et si la chose convient nous serons très heureux de pouvoir vous donner un bien meilleur chèque'. [10 October, 1894]

The details of Conrad's first meeting with Garnett have become hopelessly confused by the recollections of the two men many years later. Garnett says that, living in the country, he seldom met authors, but in this case his curiosity about the author of *Almayer's Folly* had been excited and Unwin had arranged a meeting which took place at the National Liberal Club in November and not at the firm's office in October as seems evident from Conrad's letter to Marguerite Poradowska. He has given his version of what happened:

My memory is of seeing a dark-haired man, short but extremely graceful in his nervous gestures, with brilliant eyes, now narrowed and penetrating, now soft and warm, with a manner alert yet caressing, whose speech was ingratiating, guarded, and brusque by turn. I had never seen before a man so masculinely keen yet so femininely sensitive. The conversation between our host and Conrad for some time was halting and jerky. Mr. Unwin's efforts to interest his guest in some political personages, and in literary figures such as John Oliver Hobbes and S. R. Crockett, were as successful, as an attempt to thread an eyeless needle. Conrad, extremely polite, grew nervously brusque in his responses, and kept shifting his feet one over the other, so that I became fascinated in watching the flash of his pointed patent leather shoes. The climax came unexpectedly when in answer to Mr. Unwin's casual but significant reference to 'your next book', Conrad threw himself back on the broad leather lounge and in a tone that put a clear cold space between himself and his hearers, said: 'I don't expect to write again. It is likely that I shall soon be going to sea.' A silence fell. With one sharp snick he had cut the rope between us and we were left holding the loose end. I felt disappointed and cheated. Mr. Unwin expressed some deprecatory ambiguities and then, after turning his falcon-like glance down the long smoking-room, apologised for having to greet some friends in a far corner.

Left alone with Conrad, Garnett continues, words came to him in a rush as he set about trying to persuade Conrad to continue writing. He quotes an account of their conversation which Conrad had given to Mrs Bone on the last Christmas before his death:

The first time I saw Edward . . . I dare not open my mouth. I had gone to meet him to hear what he thought of *Almayer's Folly*. I saw a young man enter the room. 'That cannot be Edward so young as that,' I thought. He began to talk. Oh yes! It was Edward. I had no longer doubt. But I was too frightened to speak. But this is what I want to tell you, how he made me go on writing. If he had said to me, 'Why not go on writing?' I should have been paralysed. I could not have done it. But he said to me 'You have written one book. It is very good. *Why not write another?*' Do you see what a difference that made? Another? Yes, I would do that. I *could* do that. Many others I could not. Another I could. That is how Edward made me go on writing. That is what made me an author.[55]

Conrad had already, in his Author's Note to *An Outcast of the Islands*, given a slightly different version of this conversation and had placed it during a later meeting with Garnett. But he again emphasized that it was Garnett who was responsible for his starting his second novel and added: 'I remember that on getting home I sat down and wrote about half a page of *An Outcast of the Islands* before I slept.'[56]

The discrepancies between the various versions of the facts and the facts themselves show how easy it is for events in a person's life to become distorted and romanticized. More important still, this provides a further example of Conrad's persistent tendency to play down the strength of his impulse to write. He wished it to be thought that his process of becoming an author was due first to chance and then to the persuasion of Garnett.

It is of course possible that Conrad really did tell Unwin that he did not expect to write again; but, as he was hard at work on his next story and in his letters to Marguerite Poradowska showed himself most gratified by Unwin's request for another book, it is unlikely, at least, that he should have intended his remark to be taken seriously. It is not surprising that Garnett should in absolutely good faith have allowed Conrad to mould his memory for him; in fact a conversation along the lines described probably did take place, and there can be no doubt about the value of Garnett's encouragement at this stage. But Garnett did not play as decisive a role as Conrad claimed.

(6)

There could be no falser picture than that of a sea captain suddenly sitting down to write a yarn about a subject that happened to take his fancy, and looking on this as an isolated interlude in his seafaring life. Although *Almayer's Folly* shows signs of being the work of a novice it is certainly not that of an amateur, and its technical accomplishment clearly disproves Conrad's contention that 'the conception of a planned book was entirely outside my mental range when I sat down to write'.[57] If proof is needed, other than that contained in the novel, it is supplied by a letter which Conrad wrote to a friend, Edward Noble, who was also setting out to become a writer. His remarks are undoubtedly based on his own experience. Speaking of one of Noble's stories he says: 'All the charm, all the truth of it are thrown away by the construction – by the mechanism (so to speak) of the story which makes it appear false,' and continues:

> You have much imagination: much more than I ever will have if I live to be a hundred years old. That much is clear to me. Well, that imagination (I wish I had it) should be used to create human souls: to disclose human hearts, – and not to create events that are properly speaking *accidents* only. To accomplish it you must cultivate your poetic faculty, – you must give yourself up to emotions (no easy task). You must squeeze out of yourself every sensation, every thought, every image, – mercilessly, without reserve and without remorse: you must search the darkest corners of your heart, the most remote recesses of your brain, – you must search them for the image, for the glamour, for the right expression. And you must do it sincerely, at any cost: you must do it so that at the end of your day's work you should feel exhausted, emptied of every sensation and every thought, with a blank mind and an aching heart, with the notion that there is nothing, – nothing left in you. To me it seems that it is the only way to achieve true distinction – even to go some way towards it.
>
> It took me three years to finish the *Folly*. There was not a day I did not think of it. Not a day. [28 October 1895, *L.L.*, I, p. 183]

It seems clear that Conrad had carefully studied the craft of writing and that his masters were those who themselves excelled in technique. Conrad's early literary background has already been described and some may detect in his writing echoes of the sonorities of Hugo's style, but Hugo's prose rhythms are totally different from Conrad's and the resemblances are too vague and generalized to be of much significance. Indeed the pursuit of influences can be as pointless as the doing of a crossword puzzle unless their detection brings some new insight into the mind of the writer or reveals an actual plagiarism.

Conrad had read Marryat, Fenimore Cooper, and Dickens as a child; he apparently knew Thackeray and has said that he might have been reading Trollope on the day that he started to write *Almayer's Folly*;[58] then there was the set of

Byron which he bought during his leave from the *Palestine*[59] and the famous 'thick green-covered volume' of Shakespeare which he said he had bought with his first earnings.[60] There are no other specific details of his background in English literature at this time and it is probable that during his sea life he went through a haphazard collection of books of the sort that could be picked up in ports or borrowed on board a ship; the picture of old Singleton poring over the 'polished and so curiously insincere sentences'[61] of Bulwer Lytton's *Pelham* gives an idea of what may have come Conrad's way. But his masters were clearly not the nineteenth-century classic Anglo-Saxon novelists; their method and attitude were alien to Conrad's, as he showed in a rather disparaging reference to them.

> The national English novelist seldom regards his work – the exercise of his Art – as an achievement of active life by which he will produce certain definite effects upon the emotions of his readers, but simply as an instinctive, often unreasoned, outpouring of his own emotions. He does not go about building up his book with a precise intention and a steady mind. It never occurs to him that a book is a deed, that the writing of it is an enterprise as much as the conquest of a colony. He has no such clear conception of his craft.[62]

Among living novelists writing in English Henry James was of course the great exception, and there were Meredith and Hardy, as well as a number of minor figures. Conrad was later to show great admiration for James's work, but it is not certain how early he came to know it. In an 'Appreciation' of James written in 1905 he claimed 'some twenty years of attentive acquaintance' with his work and referred to 'one of his critical studies, published some fifteen years ago'.[63]

Conrad gave his view of the contemporary British literary scene in a letter to his cousin, Aniela Zagórska, who was evidently anxious to write an article on the subject and was also on the look-out for British authors to translate into Polish. After some contemptuous remarks about Grant Allen's *Woman Who Did*, then about Marie Corelli and Hall Caine, he continued:

Marie Corelli is *not* noticed critically by the serious reviews. She is simply ignored. Her books sell enormously. Hall Caine is a kind of male Marie Corelli.

Among the people in literature who deserve attention the first is Rudyard Kipling (his last book *The Day's Work*, novel), J. M. Barrie – a Scotsman. His last book *Sentimental Tommy* (last year). George Meredith did not publish anything this year. The last volumes of the charming translation of Turgenev came out a fortnight ago. ... George Moore has published the novel *Evelyn Innes – un succès d'estime*. He is supposed to belong to the naturalistic school and Zola is his prophet. *Tout ça, c'est très vieux jeu.* ... H. G. Wells published *The War of the Worlds* and *The Invisible Man* this year. He is a very original writer with a very individual judgment in all things and an astonishing imagination. [Christmas 1898, *L.L.*, I, p.264]

James is not mentioned, nor is Hardy; and it is not known whether Conrad ever read Hardy or Meredith. He seems to have had little interest in his British contemporaries and only to have read their books when the author was a personal friend.

Without doubt it was the French novelists of the nineteenth century whom Conrad knew best and it was to them that he went to study the craft, as indeed did the most considerable of his British contemporaries.

Conrad apparently knew Balzac's work well[64] and he told Walpole: 'One can learn something from Balzac.'[65] He may have done so. He may, for instance, have learned something of the technique of the time-shift from Balzac: for example, the switches in *Almayer's Folly* almost exactly parallel those in *Le Curé de Tours*. But this device, which is an adaptation of the classical formula for the construction of a novel, is too common for it to be possible without concrete evidence to pin down an influence. Unreliable though Hueffer is, his statement[66] that Conrad owned a copy of *Pêcheur d'Islande* which he had annotated may be true. In his life and in his writing Loti had superficial resemblances to Conrad. He was an officer in the French navy who had become a writer, delighting in the exotic, and whose novels usually had the sea as a setting. With Loti as with Conrad exile and solitude was a major theme – Ramuntcho might well have been one of Conrad's heroes – while *An Outcast of the Islands* and 'Heart of Darkness' have similarities, possibly quite fortuitous, with *Le Roman d'un Spahi.* In style too Conrad's descriptive writing at its worst reflects Loti's inflated and rhetorical phraseology with the equivalents of 'insaisissable', 'incompréhensible', 'immensité des eaux', 'soleil éternel', 'profondeurs cosmiques, vagues infinies', which are sprinkled over Loti's pages. It is curious that Henry James compared *The Nigger of the 'Narcissus'* with the work of Loti, intending this as a high compliment.[67] Heuffer also remarked that *Almayer's Folly* was written too much in the style of Daudet,[68] and it is true that Conrad had at this time great admiration for Daudet. He wrote to Marguerite Poradowska:

> Vous connaissez mon culte [pour] Daudet. Croyez-Vous que ce serait ridicule de ma part de lui envoyer mon livre – moi qui a lu tous les siens sous tous les cieux? Ce n'est pas pour qu'il le lise – simplement un acte d'hommage car après tout il est un de mes enthousiasmes de jeunesse qui a survecu – même qui a grandi.[69]

There may therefore be some grounds for Hueffer's assertion, and *Almayer's Folly*, unlike Conrad's subsequent work, does show traces of that brand of sentimental irony in which Daudet specialized. But the temperamental differences between the two writers were so great as to nullify any lasting influence. Brunetière characterized the two opposing French schools of realism as the sentimental, exemplified by Daudet, and the misanthropic, exemplified by Flaubert.[70] This definition is prejudiced, and rather crude because there was a strong element of sentimentality in Flaubert, but it points to Conrad's true literary provenance.

His masters were Flaubert and Maupassant. In an otherwise misleading and puerile little study of Conrad's work, Hugh Walpole pointed out the influence of *Madame Bovary* on his early books.[71] Conrad denied this in a letter to Walpole:

You say that I have been under the formative influence of *Madame Bovary*. In fact, I read it only after finishing *Almayer's Folly*, as I did all the other works of Flaubert, and anyhow, my Flaubert is the Flaubert of *St. Antoine* and *Education Sentimentale* and that only from the point of view of the rendering of concrete things and visual impressions. I thought him marvellous in that respect. I don't think I learned anything from him. What he did for me was to open my eyes and arouse my emulation. One can learn something from Balzac, but what could one learn from Flaubert? He compels admiration, – about the greatest service one artist can render to another. [7 June 1918, *L.L.*, II, p. 206]

But Conrad's memory had misled him. While he was in the midst of *Almayer's Folly*, in 1892, he had written to Marguerite Poradowska:

Je viens de relire *Madame Bovary* avec une admiration pleine de respect. ... En voilà un qui avait assez d'imagination pour deux realistes. Il y a peu d'auteurs qui soit aussi créatures que lui. On ne questionne jamais pour un moment ni ses personnes ni ses evenements; on douterai plutôt de sa propre existence. [6 April 1892]

Whether there was conscious or unconscious influence, there are undeniable similarities between *Madame Bovary* and *Almayer's Folly* in choice of subject and in treatment. Flaubert chose a group of people distinguished by their ordinariness and frailty, while his leading character is immersed in visions of a life totally at variance with her actual circumstances. The same is true of Almayer. Then, from being in a position like Emma Bovary's, on the elopement of his daughter Almayer comes to resemble Charles Bovary after the death of Emma; there is the same helpless grief leading to a rapid decline and an undignified death on the last page.

In method, too, Conrad meticulously applied Flaubert's pronouncement that 'l'auteur, dans son oeuvre, doit être comme Dieu dans l'univers, présent partout, et visible nulle part'.[72] The ironic detachment with which he treats Almayer and the other characters is identical with Flaubert's method in *Madame Bovary*; and like Flaubert, Conrad's intention in *Almayer's Folly* was not to arouse pity or scorn or indignation but to create a work of art. Flaubert's pupil Maupassant had said in his essay on 'Le Roman' prefacing *Pierre et Jean* that the writer should only listen to the demand 'Faites-moi quelque chose de beau', which Conrad showed that he had heeded in his declaration: 'I, who have never sought in the written word anything else but a form of the Beautiful ...'[73] This may sound a common enough aim, but it places Conrad in his tradition.

He never minimized the influence that Maupassant had on him. He told Marguerite Poradowska in 1894:

> Vous êtes trop tard avec Votre avis Madame ma Tante. J'ai peur que je ne sois trop sous l'influence de Maupassant. J'ai étudié *Pierre et Jean* – pensée, methode et tout – avec le plus profond désépoir. Ça n'a l'air de rien, mais c'est d'un compliqué comme mécanisme qui me fait m'arracher les cheveux. On a envie de pleurer de rage en lisant cela. – Enfin! – [Monday morning (29 October or 5 November (?) 1894)]

A few years later, in a letter to Garnett, he called *Bel-Ami* 'that amazing masterpiece' and added: 'The technique of that work gives to one acute pleasure. It is simply enchanting to see how it's done.'[74] And to one of his French translators he spoke of himself as being 'saturé de Maupassant'.[75]

The influence of Maupassant, specifically his essay on 'Le Roman', showed itself most clearly when Conrad came to declare his artistic aim and faith in the preface to *The Nigger of the 'Narcissus'* and, later, in the preface to *A Personal Record*.* A number of the assertions common to both writers would be expected to figure in the creeds of most self-conscious artists of the period, but the most important similarity is the prominence both give to expression and style. Maupassant quotes Boileau's 'D'un mot mis en sa place enseigna le pouvoir',[76] and Conrad echoes him with: 'Give

* Edgar Wright in a hitherto unpublished thesis has exhaustively compared the similarities (*Joseph Conrad; his expressed views about technique and the principles underlying them, with a study of their relevance to certain novels*; M.A. thesis, London University, March 1955).

me the right word and the right accent and I will move the world.'[77] And when Conrad writes: 'It is only through an unremitting never-discouraged care for the shape and ring of sentences that an approach can be made to plasticity, to colour, and that the light of magic suggestiveness may be brought to play for an evanescent instant over the commonplace surface of words: of the old, old words, worn thin, defaced by ages of careless usage',[78] he is saying much the same as Maupassant's: 'il faut discerner avec une extrême lucidité toutes les modifications de la valeur d'un mot suivant la place qu'il occupe. Ayons ... plus de phrases différentes, diversement construites, ingénieusement coupées, pleines de sonorités et de rhythmes savants. Efforçons-nous d'être des stylistes excellents ...'[79]

Conrad's words were of course written several years after he had finished *Almayer's Folly*, but the important thing is that he had studied Maupassant's theory and practice so early in his writing life. The deep impression which this had made is shown by the cropping up at a much later date of what must surely be a memory of Maupassant's essay. In 'Le Roman' is the passage: 'Quelle que soit la chose qu'on veut dire, il n'y a qu'un mot pour l'exprimer' qu'un verbe pour l'animer et qu'un adjectif pour la qualifier. Il faut donc chercher, jusqu'a ce qu'on les ait découverts, ce mot, ce verbe et cet adjectif, et ne jamais se contenter de l'à peu près.'[80] In a letter in 1910 to a novice Conrad said: 'In writing and especially in descriptive writing one must guard oneself against the "à peu près" – the horrid danger of the "near enough".'[81]

It is evident then that Conrad served his apprenticeship under Flaubert and Maupassant. It was of course no more than an apprenticeship. *Almayer's Folly*, *An Outcast of the Islands*, the short stories 'An Outpost of Progress' and 'The Idiots' and, at least in form, *The Nigger of the 'Narcissus'*, reveal the Flaubert–Maupassant influence, but with *Lord Jim* Conrad showed that he had evolved an original and personal method suited to his particular aims.

(7)

The most valid criticism of *Almayer's Folly* is that it is too self-conscious a literary creation, written according to an adopted formula. It tells the story of a man who is a pathetic failure, portraying, with flashbacks, the last stages in the collapse of his dreams of a luxurious future. Almayer has been enticed by the promises of Tom Lingard, a rich and dashing trader, to marry his Malay protégée and take charge of a river trading post. But all Lingard's plans founder and Almayer, who is an ineffectual man of mediocre talents, is left bemoaning his fate among the débris, with his wife, now a harridan, and his beautiful daughter, Nina. All his love and what remain of his hopes are now concentrated on Nina, and when she elopes with a Malay trader, the son of a rajah, Almayer's desolation is complete; he rapidly goes to pieces, takes to opium-smoking, and dies.

Almayer's Folly does show flashes of those qualities which were to distinguish Conrad's later work:

'Arrest!' laughed Almayer, discordantly. 'Ha! ha! ha! Arrest! Why, I have been trying to get out of this infernal place for twenty years, and I can't. You hear, man! I can't, and never shall! Never!'

He ended his words with a sob, and walked unsteadily down the stairs. When in the courtyard the lieutenant approached him, and took him by the arm. The sub-lieutenant and Babalatchi followed close.

'That's better, Almayer,' said the officer encouragingly. 'Where are you going to? There are only planks there. Here,' he went on, shaking him slightly, 'do we want the boats?'

'No,' answered Almayer, viciously. 'You want a grave.'

'What? Wild again! Try to talk sense.'

'Grave!' roared Almayer, struggling to get himself free. 'A hole in the ground. Don't you understand? You must be drunk. Let me go! Let go, I tell you!' . . . 'There!' he said at last. 'Are you all there? He is a dangerous man.'

He dragged at the cover with hasty violence, and the body rolled stiffly off the planks and fell at his feet in rigid helplessness.

'Cold, perfectly cold,' said Almayer, looking round with a mirthless smile. 'Sorry can do no better. And you can't hang him, either. As you observe, gentlemen,' he added gravely, 'there is no head, and hardly any neck.'[82]

This scene is convincingly alive and has the type of savagely macabre humour that is constantly cropping up in Conrad's work and is an integral part of his outlook on life. It is at the centre of 'An Outpost of Progress' and 'Falk'; it surrounds the fate of Señor Hirsch in *Nostromo* and constantly crops up in *The Secret Agent*.

There are also a few imaginative touches, such as Almayer's pathetic wiping out of Nina's footprints in order to forget her, or, when he returned to the house in despair after Nina's departure:

A few of Nina's dresses hung on wooden pegs, stiffened in a look of offended dignity at their abandonment. He remembered making the pegs himself and noticed that they were very good pegs.[83]

But such details are infrequent rocks of authenticity protruding from an ocean of impersonal prose. Almayer, for instance, only comes alive in extreme situations, when he is drunk, angry, or in despair. For the rest Conrad resorts too much to a generalized summary of events and character instead of presenting them through the action. An example is the visit of the Dutch commission to Sambir. This episode does not carry the story forward and would therefore only be justified if it contributed to the understanding of Almayer. But this is what happens:

The younger men in an access of good fellowship made their host talk, and Almayer, excited by the sight of European faces, by the sound of European voices, opened his heart before the sympathising strangers, unaware of the amusement the recital of his many misfortunes caused to those future admirals.[84]

And so on. There is no direct speech throughout the episode; but it is essential to hear Almayer recite his misfortunes in order to be able to grasp his individuality.

There are similar shortcomings in the presentation of Nina. Although her mixed blood offers ample opportunity for individual characterization, her psychology is never realized, but is summarized in such general terms that she remains the most insubstantial of types. When she is dumped unexpectedly in Sambir, her upbringing among Europeans abruptly ended, we are told merely that she 'adapted herself wonderfully to the circumstances of a half-savage and miserable life'[85] and her reactions are summed up as follows:

> It seemed to Nina that there was no change and no difference. Whether they traded in brick godowns or on the muddy river bank; whether they reached after much or little; whether they made love under the shadows of the great trees or in the shadow of the cathedral on the Singapore promenade; whether they plotted for their own ends under the protection of laws and according to the rules of Christian conduct, or whether they sought the gratification of their desires with the savage cunning and the unrestrained fierceness of natures as innocent of culture as their own immense and gloomy forests, Nina saw only the same manifestations of love and hate and of sordid greed chasing the uncertain dollar in all its multifarious and vanishing shapes.[86]

This passage, with its balanced sonorities, its banality transformed into pretentiousness, and its vague, inflated imagery, is also an example of the excessively literary and artificial style in which much of the book is written. Such writing is as different from organic expression as is a stuffed from a live peacock.*

The remainder of the characters suffer from being Malays. If Conrad was unable to get inside a European or Eurasian character it is not surprising that his Malays are romantically conventionalized because, as his friend Sir Hugh Clifford said, and he himself admitted, he knew very little about Malays.[87] No lover ever courted in such words as does Dain, nor does the presumed remoteness of Malay from European psychology warrant:

> Now he [Dain] wanted but immortality, he thought, to be the

* Mrs Danilewicz has pointed out to me how strongly the set-pieces in Conrad's early novels are influenced by Polish literary style and syntax.

equal of gods, and the creature that could open so the gates of paradise must be his – soon would be his for ever.[88]

In so far as Conrad does succeed with his Malays it is primarily the situation that brings them alive, even if a trifle cornily, as in the delightful scene where Babalatchi plays the hand-organ to Lakamba.[89]

Although in this first novel Conrad's characters are not impressive, he is at least able to envelop them in a convincing atmosphere of tropical abundance and decay. The dominant taste of today is antipathetic to pieces of self-consciously 'fine' writing incorporated in a novel for their own sake and not for their contribution to the situation; and it is hard to judge fairly Conrad's purple passages, particularly as they have been seized on by the anthologists as examples of his greatness as a writer, to the neglect of his more important qualities. Without question Conrad daubs the purple too heavily on to some of his descriptions in *Almayer's Folly* or numbs the reader with the boom of an emotive bombardment, as in

> plants shooting upward, entwined, interlaced in inextricable confusion, climbing madly and brutally over each other in the terrible silence of a desperate struggle towards the life-giving sunshine above – as if struck with sudden horror at the seething mass of corruption below, at the death and decay from which they sprang.[90]

Having fired one salvo, Conrad cannot refrain from firing another just to make sure. Thus 'interlaced in inextricable confusion' is followed by 'climbing madly and brutally over each other', and as if that were not enough we are told that it is a 'desperate struggle'; and after 'seething mass of corruption' comes 'death and decay'.

But there are also passages which are very effective of their kind:

> As he skirted in his weary march the edge of the forest he glanced now and then into its dark shade, so enticing in its deceptive appearance of coolness, so repellent with its unrelieved gloom, where lay, entombed and rotting, countless generations of trees, and

where their successors stood as if mourning, in dark green foliage, immense and helpless, awaiting their turn. Only the parasites seemed to live there in a sinuous rush upwards into the air and sunshine, feeding on the dead and the dying alike, and crowning their victims with pink and blue flowers that gleamed amongst the boughs, incongruous and cruel, like a strident and mocking note in the solemn harmony of the doomed trees.[91]

If *Almayer's Folly* has to be judged harshly against the highest standards and against Conrad's best work, this should not obscure Conrad's amazing achievement in having written such a book; not only was it a first novel but it was written in a foreign language which its author had only begun to learn at the age of twenty. Moreover Conrad can have had little opportunity to develop his English through conversation with educated people, and when he started *Almayer's Folly* he could only have come in contact with a large area of the language through books. Edward Garnett corroborates this: 'When he read aloud to me some new written MS. pages of *An Outcast of the Islands* he mispronounced so many words that I followed him with difficulty. I found then that he had never once heard these English words spoken, but had learned them all from books!'[92]

But Conrad had no wish to be regarded as a prodigy or a curiosity. He was understandably upset when it was stated in 1908 by a reviewer of *A Set of Six* that he was a man 'without country or language';[93] and he was exasperated when Sir Hugh Clifford told the story that he had hesitated between French and English. When Hugh Walpole repeated this story in his book on Conrad he was pounced upon:

I want to thank you at once for the little book and to tell you that I am profoundly touched by many things you have found it possible in your heart and conscience to say about my work. The only thing that grieves me and makes me dance with rage is the cropping up of the legend set afloat by Hugh Clifford about my hesitation between English and French as a writing language. For it is absurd. When I wrote the first words of *Almayer's Folly*, I had been already for years and years *thinking* in English. I began to think in English long before I mastered, I won't say the style (I haven't done that yet), but the mere uttered speech. Is it thinkable that anybody possessed of some effective inspiration should contemplate for a moment such a frantic thing as translating it into another tongue? And there are also other considerations: such as the sheer appeal of the language, my quickly awakened love for its prose cadences, a subtle and unforeseen accord of my emotional nature with its genius. . . . You may take it from me that if I had not known English I wouldn't have written a line for print, in my life.[94]

Conrad was particularly keen to emphasize his bond with English and made a similar, but public, protest at Clifford's story in the 'Author's Note' to *A Personal Record*. In his anxiety to make his point he almost implied a mystic union with the language:

My faculty to write in English is as natural as any other aptitude with which I might have been born. I have a strange and overpowering feeling that it had always been an inherent part of myself. English was for me neither a matter of choice nor adoption. The merest idea of choice had never entered my head. And as to adoption – well, yes, there was adoption; but it was I who was adopted by the genius of the language, which directly I came out of the stammering stage made me its own so completely that its very idioms I truly believe had a direct action on my temperament and fashioned my still plastic character. . . . If I had not written in English I would not have written at all.[95]

Whatever Conrad told Clifford,[96] who stuck to and repeated the story, it seems fairly certain that he could never seriously have hesitated between French and English. He told Walpole that he had been thinking in English 'for years and years', which may have been an exaggeration, but at least he had been living among the English for ten years and had absorbed much of the idiom of the language. It is significant that the jottings which make up his Congo notebooks are in English, and not Polish or French, although he was living among French-speaking people at the time. Moreover, when he was thinking of having *Almayer's Folly* published in French as a collaboration he was writing *An*

Outcast in English even though he seems to have contemplated trying to get it published by the *Revue des Deux Mondes*. In both cases he was relying on Marguerite Poradowska to make the translation. And although he had been taught French since a child and French rather than English had been for him the language of cultured communication it was none the less a foreign language. He spoke it fluently and, according to Valéry,[97] with a Provençal rather than a Polish accent. He also wrote French excellently but as a foreigner; in his letters his expression is idiosyncratic, and, incidentally, sprinkled with anglicisms, but lacks the deeper individuality which can only come from having lived into a language. Added to this, the setting of *Almayer's Folly* and Almayer himself had certainly been experienced in English. To have written the book in French would have necessitated translating his impressions; if his first novel had been based on his experiences in Marseilles he might conceivably have chosen to write it in French.

As has been said, the characters, above all Almayer himself, and the background of the novel were based on Conrad's experiences when he was in the *Vidar*. But there remains the more important question of why, from the many people whom he had come across, he chose Almayer (or Olmeijer) as the hero of his first novel and why he gave him the career that he did, because there is no reason to suppose that he stuck closely to the actual facts of Olmeijer's life; indeed he diverged significantly in his portrayal of Almayer's eventual fate and in giving him a solitary daughter instead of eleven children.

It is frequently asserted, and in general rightly, that a first novel will contain a greater autobiographical element than those that follow. In the case of a young man this is almost inevitable because his experience is bound to be limited. Conrad, however, was a mature and experienced man of thirty-two when he started to write *Almayer's Folly*, and there was more likelihood of the autobiographical element being diluted – or at least submerged.

But there is good reason to believe that the central situation in the novel – the relationship between Almayer, Nina, and Dain – had its counterpart in Conrad's own life. Conrad himself unconsciously revealed the autobiographical clue in a conversation with a friend. His story 'A Smile of Fortune' had cropped up and he said 'Toute ma vie, j'ai été extrêmement préoccupé par les rapports de père à fille.'[98] On the face of it this interest is surprising because there is no reason to suppose that Conrad had been affected by a relationship of this kind. Yet the father–daughter relationship occurs repeatedly in Conrad's work: there is Almayer and Nina, then Omar and Aïssa in *An Outcast of the Islands,* 'Nelson or Nielson' and Freya, de Barral and Flora, Jacobus and Alice in 'A Smile of Fortune'; and it is perhaps legitimate to add Hermann and his niece in 'Falk' because Lena is in the position of a daughter. A single motif runs through all these relationships: the father stands in the way of, and attempts to thwart, his daughter's impulse towards what she believes to be freedom and happiness.*

In contrast, there is a total absence of any significant relationship between father and son in Conrad's work, although it was his relationship with his father that dominated Conrad's youth. This situation was doubtless far too charged emotionally for Conrad to be able to represent it directly, whereas his deepest impulses could find disguised expression through a portrayal of the father–daughter relationship. Once this is understood the rest falls into place without difficulty. When he left Poland in search of freedom Conrad must have known that he was flouting the principle which had governed his father's life. Apollo Korzeniowski had dedicated himself to the service of the Polish nation and had done his utmost to instil the same principle into Conrad.

These factors have no bearing on the literary quality of *Almayer's Folly*, but they give an insight into Conrad's mind; the conflict within Nina between her father's

* The enigmatic role of Jacobus does not quite fit this description, but the fact that he had virtually kept Alice a prisoner provides the common element.

demands and the glamour offered by Dain takes on an added significance when it is seen in terms of the conflict in Conrad's mind between loyalty to his father's memory and the desire to create his own life.

[VI]

Literary Apprenticeship

The acceptance of *Almayer's Folly* by Unwin did not materially affect Conrad's immediate predicament. He could not live on Unwin's £20 for long and there could have been no possibility at this point of his deciding to concentrate on writing as a profession. He had to have a job of some sort and was trying hard to get to sea. Marguerite Poradowska had again approached M. Pécher of Antwerp, but nothing had materialized, and Conrad was also negotiating with a Liverpool firm about the command of a small barque called *Primavera*.[1]

Amid this uncertainty he was finding it hard to concentrate on his new novel:

> Voilà trois jours que je m'assois devant une page blanche – et la page est toujours blanche excépté pour un IV en tête. A vrai dire je suis mal parti. . . . Que voulez-Vous? Je ne ressens le moindre enthousiasme. C'est fatal, cela . . .
>
> Mme. M. Wood m'a volé mon titre. Elle vient de publier un livre: *The Vagabonds* et me voilà joliment embêté. Non! Si Vous saviez comme ça m'ennuie Vous auriez pitié de moi. [Monday morning (29 October or 5 November? 1894)]

then, some days later:

> Le travail ne va pas, et la santé n'est plus aussi bonne. Si je reste plus longtemps à terre, tout se gatera, helas! [Wednesday (14 or 21 November? 1894)]

and again:

> Je suis absolument embourbé. Il y a quinze jours déjà que je n'ai ecrit un seul mot. C'est bien fini il me semble. J'ai envie de bruler ce qui est là. C'est très mauvais! Trop mauvais! Ceci est ma profonde conviction et non pas un cri de stupide modestie. [Monday (26 November or 3 December? 1894)]

Nonetheless, despite continued torment and doubt, he had by the end of the year written a further four chapters. Announcing the change of the title to *An Outcast of the Islands* he said:

Et la chose elle-même est changée. Tout est changé excepté le doute. Tout – excepté la peur de ces phantômes que l'on evoque soi même et qui souvent refusent d'obeir la cervelle qui les a crées.

Enfin! Voilà le chapitre VIII terminé. Encore quatre! Quatre siècles d'agonie – quatre minutes des délices et puis la fin – la tête vide – le decouragement et le doute eternel. [27 December 1894]

In the new year he was beginning to see something of Garnett and due, no doubt, partly to his encouragement *An Outcast* was going 'son petit bonhomme de chemin au milieu des pleurs et des grincements des dents usuels'.[2] By 12 April[3] he had reached Chapter XVII, having added eight chapters since the end of December.

But his health was bad, which prevented him from going to sea,* and he was afflicted with bouts of depression 'Ah mon dieu. Comme tout est noir noir noir. Ceci est un de mes mauvais jours. Faîtes pas attention.'[4] He twice mentioned spending several days in bed and by the end of April he had decided that he must try another cure at Champel. On the thirtieth he wrote to Marguerite Poradowska: 'Vous savez quand je ne suis pas bien j'ai des accès de melancholia qui me paralysent la pensée et la volonté.'
And the following day to Garnett:

I am going to look for Willems in Switzerland. It is written. I go! today at 9 a.m....

Seriously I find I can't work. Simply can't! I am going to try what mountain air combined with active fire-hose (twice a day) will do for divine inspiration, I shall try it for about three weeks and maybe the lenient gods will allow me to finish that infernal manuscript. [1 May 1895]

* To Mme Poradowska, Saturday, 23 (?) February 1895. He mentions that he has had to put off a business trip to Newfoundland because of his health. Nothing seems to be known of this project.

The change made Conrad feel better immediately,[5] and also enabled him to write. He had only been at Champel four days when he told Marguerite Poradowska: 'Je continue a ecrire et cela n'en finit pas. Je crains les longueurs mais je ne sais pas comment leur echapper.'[6] And a few days later he wrote to Garnett:

I am working every day: – tolerably bad work. Like poor Risler the Elder's cashier 'I haf' no confidence'. . . . I dread the moment when you shall see my *Outcast* as a whole. It seems frightful bosh. I never felt like that even in the first days of my *Folly*.

Meantime I live lazily and digest satisfactorily. [12 May 1895]

He returned to Gillingham Street at the beginning of June and after a week in London wrote to Marguerite Poradowska:

Je me suis remis a ecrire fort encouragé par les *sept colonnes et demie* du *Weekly Sun* ou T. P. O'Connor m'a enterré sous une avalanche des compliments, du admirations, d'analyse, et de citations. [11 June 1895]

Conrad was referring to a review of *Almayer's Folly* and O'Connor had indeed been lavish with his enthusiasm. Each Sunday the *Weekly Sun* chose a 'Book of the Week' for a leading article and on 9 June the book was *Almayer's Folly*. O'Connor's article was headed 'A Fine New Note' and began: 'This is a book a few people have already read with rapture; by-and-bye everybody will have read it, and then the world will know that a new great writer and a new and splendid region of romance have entered into our literature.' He courageously proclaimed Conrad to be a 'writer of genius' and went on, as Conrad said, to bury him under an avalanche of compliments, admiration, and quotations – chiefly quotations. He ended by picking out the one scene which would now be acknowledged to show signs of genius, that in which Almayer covered up the traces of Nina's footsteps in the sand: '". . . He piled up small heaps of sand, *leaving behind him a line of miniature graves right down to the water*." It is only a writer of genius who could write that and many another passage in this startling, unique, splendid book.'[7]

Almayer's Folly had come out on 29 April* and with this one exception had had the sort of reception from the critics that might have been expected for a serious and rather out of the ordinary first novel. 'Promise', 'originality', and 'power' were the words that cropped up most often in the reviews, which were for the most part very favourable. The influential *Saturday Review* said that:

> Almayer's Folly is a very powerful story indeed, with effects that will certainly capture the imagination and haunt the memory of the reader ...
>
> It is a gloomy tale, but its gloom is relieved by the rare beauty of the love-story between Nina and Dain, and by such flashes of humour as Babalatchi's grinding at the hand-organ when the Rajah, his master, could not sleep. It is indeed exceedingly well imagined and well written, and it will certainly secure Mr. Conrad a high place among contemporary storytellers.[8]

The *Academy*, on the other hand, in an obviously intelligent review, was lukewarm, saying that the book was 'so much more of a promise than of a performance', but the reviewer admitted that it 'somehow leaves an impression of grasp and power'.[9] The *Speaker* appears to have summed up the dominant feeling when it said: 'The press has already given utterance to very favourable criticisms on the new story by a new writer called *Almayer's Folly*, and it only remains for us to join in the expression of the hope that this may not be the last work from the same pen.'[10] The public reacted as it usually does in such cases unless it is caught up on a wave of fashion – it virtually ignored the book's existence. The first edition had been of 2,000 copies and it was seven years before a third impression was needed.

* The novel was published under the name Joseph Conrad. No significance should be attached to Conrad's decision to drop his surname, although Poles were apparently prepared to include even this in their charge of apostasy (cf., Conrad's letter to Joseph Korzeniowski of 14 February 1901). Conrad had had enough experience of the havoc wrought with his surname during his time at sea – witness his various certificates of discharge – to appreciate the advantage of using a name that the British could pronounce; and he must have realized the needless disability that he would have suffered if he had written novels in English under the name of Korzeniowski.

The next few months were taken up primarily with finishing *An Outcast*. But there were interludes of yachting with his friend, G. F. W. Hope, and taking part in what appear to have been quite exciting business deals. He had at last been given an opportunity of indulging the Korzeniowski proclivity. He recounted his activities in a letter to Edward Sanderson. Apparently Hope's brother-in-law was in danger of being swindled out of his title-deeds to 150 claims on the Roodepoort reef by a European syndicate, and was on the brink of ruin. Conrad made three journeys to Paris and, with the help of several influential contacts, was instrumental in persuading the original shady syndicate to part with the deeds for £100 and in having another syndicate formed which paid £8,000 to Hope's brother-in-law. 'Of course I do not make anything,' Conrad wrote. 'My expenses are paid and I shall take 200 shares as acknowledgement of my services. They wanted to give me 1,000, which I declined. Yet I must say I was very smart. Nobody was more surprised than myself!'[11]

Then a Johannesburg friend, hearing of this success, asked Conrad to sell fifty claims on another reef, which he did, because 'I wanted funds for the base purpose of carrying on a wretched and useless existence'.[12]

In the same letter Conrad announced that he had sold the rights of *An Outcast* to Fisher Unwin for £50 and about 12½ per cent royalty, and a month later he announced to Garnett that he had finished the book:

> It is my painful duty to inform you of the sad death of Mr Peter Willems late of Rotterdam and Macassar who has been murdered on the 16th inst at 4 p.m. while the sun shone joyously and the barrel organ sang on the pavement the abominable Intermezzo of the ghastly Cavalleria. [17 September 1895]

He sent it to Garnett at Fisher Unwin's, who wrote strongly criticizing the ending, both in matter and execution. Conrad replied defending his conception of how the book should end but acquiescing in some of Garnett's criticisms:

As to the XXIV I feel convinced that the right course would be to destroy it, to scatter its ashes to the four winds of heaven. The only question is: can I?

I am afraid I can't! I lack the courage to set before myself the task of rewriting the thing. It is not – as you say – a matter of correction here and there – a matter of changed words – or lines – or pages. The whole conception seems to me wrong. I seem to have seen the wrong side of the situation. I was always afraid of it. – For months I have been afraid of that chapter – and now it is written – and the foreboding is realised in a dismal failure.

Nothing now can unmake my mistake. I shall try – but I shall try without faith, because all my work is produced unconsciously (so to speak) and I cannot meddle to any purpose with what is within myself. – I am sure you understand what I mean – it isn't in me to improve what has got itself written.

Still with your help I may try. All the paragraphs marked by you to that effect shall be cut out. . . . [Tuesday (24 September 1895)]

He appears to have made very little alteration to the development of events,* but may have made some adjustments of detail and presumably cut some passages. This was a fair example of how Conrad reacted to Garnett's advice during this period; the key-note seems to have been contained in his words: 'Destroy, yes. Alter, no.'

(2)

The subject of *An Outcast of the Islands* is the enslavement and eventual destruction of a white man, whose self-respect has already been undermined by a piece of dishonesty, by his passion for a Malay woman. In the course of his decline he betrays the trust that other men have put in him and the proclaimed ideals of his race. In other respects Conrad's second novel is very similar to his first. The scene is once more set in Sambir, at a time before the events described in *Almayer's Folly*, and several of the characters, including Almayer, are used again. The chief difference between the two

* The chapters were rearranged, and so it is not now absolutely clear what Garnett was referring to. It seems from Conrad's letter that what became Part 5 chapters III–IV was in question.

books is that *An Outcast* is almost twice as long, and without any justification for being so. The story is excessively slow-moving and the elaboration does not contribute to the understanding of the characters or to the development of the theme; rather, the expression, as prolific as the tropical vegetation which Conrad delighted to describe, smothers the narrative, and at times even the sense. For example:

> A shadow passed over Willems's face. He put his hand over his lips as if to keep back the words that wanted to come out in a surge of impulsive necessity, the outcome of dominant thought that rushes from the heart to the brain and must be spoken in the face of doubt, of danger, of fear, of destruction itself.
>
> 'You are beautiful', he whispered.[13]

Or,

> On Lingard's departure solitude and silence closed round Willems; the cruel solitude of one abandoned by men; the reproachful silence which surrounds an outcast ejected by his kind, the silence unbroken by the slightest whisper of hope; an immense and impenetrable silence that swallows up without echo the murmur of regret and the cry of revolt.[14]

The two books have almost identical merits and defects, although both are greater in *An Outcast*. Thus, possibly because Conrad was in his second book more self-consciously an author, his style is even more artificially literary and composed than before; he had not yet evolved a sufficiently individual style or an adequate range of expression for his more ambitious periods to sound other than hollow, without power or suggestivity. This is Willem's struggle against the fascination of Aïssa:

> And under the immobilised gesture of lofty protection in the branches outspread wide above his head, under the high branches where white birds slept wing to wing in the shelter of countless leaves, he tossed like a grain of dust in a whirlwind – sinking and rising – round and round – always near that gate. All through the languid stillness of that night he fought with the impalpable; he fought with the shadows, with the darkness, with the silence. He fought without a sound, striking futile blows, dashing from side to

side; obstinate, hopeless, and always beaten back; like a man bewitched within the invisible sweep of a magic circle.[15]

Or,

> The anger of his outraged pride, the anger of his outraged heart, had gone out in the blow; and there remained nothing but the sense of some immense infamy – of something vague, disgusting and terrible, which seemed to surround him on all sides, hover about him with shadowy and stealthy movements, like a band of assassins in the darkness of vast and unsafe places.[16]

Immediately after he had finished *An Outcast* he wrote to Garnett: 'You know what strong affection I had for the poor departed so you won't be surprised to hear that to me – since yesterday – life seems a blank.'[17] But this was a mock serious reference, although his feeling of aimlessness was doubtless real enough and is experienced by most writers when they have just finished a book. He confessed later in the 'Author's Note' that 'the story itself was never very near my heart',[18] and it is difficult to feel affection or compassion for Willems, who is contemptible without even being pitiable. Willems's worthlessness detracts from the impact of the book; his betrayal of the secret of the river to the Arab trader has not the inevitable or exclusive connection with his passion for Aïssa that it should have; one feels that he would have betrayed the secret anyhow – merely out of spite. And whether it was due to lack of sympathy or to inexperience, Conrad again showed himself unable to get inside a character in order to reproduce his mental processes; Willems remains a shadowy, conventional figure throughout and the presentation of his psychology is rudimentary. This is how he is supposed to think:

> He wondered at the wickedness of Providence that had made him what he was; that, worse still, permitted such a creature as Almayer to live. He had done his duty by going to him. Why did he not understand? All men were fools. He gave him his chance. The fellow did not see it. It was hard, very hard on himself – Willems. He wanted to take her from amongst her own people. That's why he had condescended to go to Almayer. He examined himself.

With a sinking heart he thought that really he could not – somehow – live without her. It was terrible and sweet. He remembered the first days. Her appearance, her face, her smile, her eyes, her words. A savage woman! Yet he perceived that he could think of nothing else but of the three days of their separation, of the few hours since their reunion . . .[19]

and so on.

It is perhaps unjust to demand of Conrad that he should be so far ahead of the convention of his time as to present an interior monologue with the realism of Joyce, but it is not unreasonable to demand more depth and individuality than this. Then instead of expressing his characters' thoughts he embalms them in an excessive literariness:

He would be dead. He would be stretched upon the warm moisture of the ground, feeling nothing, seeing nothing, knowing nothing; he would lie stiff, passive, rotting slowly; while over him, under him, through him – unopposed, busy, hurried – the endless and minute throngs of insects, little shining monsters of repulsive shapes, with horns, with claws, with pincers, would swarm in streams, in rushes, in eager struggle for his body; would swarm countless, persistent, ferocious and greedy – till there would remain nothing but the white gleam of bleaching bones in the long grass; in the long grass that would shoot its feathery heads between the bare and polished ribs. There would be that only left of him; nobody would miss him; no one would remember him.[20]

This is supposed to represent 'the inarticulate delirium' of Willems's thoughts. Such a passage could only have come from someone who, in his anxiety to write well, loses touch with the context; thus words and images come between him and the situation he is trying to depict.

But in other respects Conrad showed that he had gained in skill. Against his failure with Willems must be set his success in presenting Almayer, although dramatically and not through interior monologue. Almayer's conversation with the drunken Rumanian naturalist which ends the book is brilliant; and he emerges from his previous rather amorphous state in *Almayer's Folly* with a distinctive idiom and manner of speech, as in his diatribe against Willems:

'If I believed one word of what you say, I would. . . . As it is what's – the use? You know where the gun is; you may take it or leave it. Gun. Deer. Bosh! Hunt deer! Pah! it's a – gazelle you are after, my honoured guest. You want gold anklets and silk sarongs for that game – my mighty hunter . . .'[21]

and again,

'But, Almayer, don't you see – '
'Yes, I see. I see a mysterious ass.'[22]

There are, too, passages where the material background is precisely and imaginatively visualized, which give a foretaste of Conrad's achievement in *Nostromo* or *The Secret Agent*. The description of Joanna's room, for instance, contrasts with the perfunctory references to the Folly in *Almayer's Folly*:

Bits of white stuff; rags yellow, pink, blue: rags limp, brilliant and soiled, trailed on the floor, lay on the desk amongst the sombre covers of books soiled, grimy, but stiff-backed, in virtue, perhaps, of their European origin. The biggest set of bookshelves was partly hidden by a petticoat, the waistband of which was caught upon the back of a slender book pulled a little out of the row so as to make an improvised clothes peg. The folding canvas bedstead stood nearly in the middle of the room, stood anyhow, parallel to no wall, as if it had been, in the process of transportation to some remote place, dropped casually there by tired bearers. And on the tumbled blankets that lay in a disordered heap on its edge, Joanna sat almost all day with her stockingless feet upon one of the bed pillows that were somehow always kicking about the floor.[23]

In one respect *An Outcast* was a more ambitious book than *Almayer's Folly*. Although Almayer is a type and the situation which confronts him is typical there is no question of his transcending his particularity as do, for instance, Charles and Emma Bovary, who, without losing their individuality, come to symbolize aspects of human nature and the human predicament. The misfortunes of Almayer have little reference beyond himself.

Of Willems and Aïssa in *An Outcast*, on the other hand, Conrad told Garnett that

They both long to have a significance in the order of nature or of society. To me they are typical of mankind where every individual wishes to assert his power, woman by sentiment, man by achievement of some sort – mostly base. [Tuesday (24 September 1895)]

But it is the negative rather than the positive aspect of their situation which is emphasized most. In *An Outcast* Conrad touches on a universal theme which was to occupy him ceaselessly: there is a sense of solitude and isolation which hovers over the characters and at times overwhelms them. Thus, Conrad is writing of Aïssa:

Her hands slipped slowly off Lingard's shoulders and her arms fell by her side, listless, discouraged, as if to her – to her, the savage, violent, and ignorant creature – had been revealed clearly in that moment the tremendous fact of our isolation, of the loneliness impenetrable and transparent, elusive and everlasting; of the indestructible loneliness that surrounds, envelops, clothes every human soul from the cradle to the grave, and perhaps, beyond.[24]

Or, of Willems:

On Lingard's departure solitude and silence closed round Willems; the cruel solitude of one abandoned by men . . .[25]

and this theme is constantly recurring in the last pages of the book. Willems, Aïssa and the old serving-woman:

Those three human beings abandoned by all were like shipwrecked people left on an insecure and slippery ledge by the retiring tide of an angry sea – listening to its distant roar, living anguished between the menace of its return and the hopeless horror of their solitude.[26]

Only when his wife arrives with a boat does Willems have momentary visions of a 'hopeful future'[27] looking 'into liberty, into the future, into his triumph – into the great possibility of a startling revenge'.[28] This hope is quickly destroyed and the final comment comes in the drunken, deserted cry of Almayer:

'The world's a swindle! A swindle! Why should I suffer? What have I done to be treated so?'[29]

(3)

An Outcast was published in March 1896 and the critics were on the whole complimentary, although they did not receive it quite as well as they had *Almayer's Folly.* The most telling notice appeared in the *Saturday Review.* The anonymous reviewer called *An Outcast* 'perhaps the finest piece of fiction that has been published this year, as *Almayer's Folly* was one of the finest that was published in 1895'; but he had a very sharp criticism to make of the book: 'One fault it has, and a glaring fault. . . . Mr Conrad is wordy; his story is not so much told as seen intermittently through a haze of sentences. . . . He has still to learn the great half of his art, the art of leaving things unwritten.' Summing up, the reviewer expressed himself even more forcibly: '. . . and he writes despicably. He writes so as to mask and dishonour the greatness that is in him. Greatness is deliberately written . . .'[30]

Conrad described the sequel to this review in a letter to Garnett:

> I wrote to the reviewer. I did! And he wrote to me. He did! And who do you think it is? – He lives in Woking. Guess. Can't tell? I will tell you. It is H. G. Wells. May I be cremated alive like a miserable moth if I suspected it! Anyway he descended from his 'Time-Machine' to be kind as he knew how. [24 May 1896]

In his reply to Conrad Wells had said:

> I really don't see why you should think gratitude necessary when a reviewer gives you your deserts . . .
>
> If I have indeed put my finger on a weak point in your armour of technique, so that you may be able to strengthen it against your next occasion, I shall have done the best a reviewer can do. You have everything for the making of a splendid novelist except dexterity, and that is attainable by drill. [Undated (May 1896)][31]

Two years later Conrad was to tell Wells:

> For the last two years (since your review of the *Outcast* in the

Saturday Review compelled me to think seriously of many things till then unseen) I have lived on terms of close intimacy with you, referring to you many a page of my work, scrutinising many sentences by the light of your criticism. You are responsible for many sheets torn up and also for those that remained untorn . . . [6 September 1898, *L.L.*, I, p. 248]

But to Garnett Conrad had professed himself puzzled by Wells's criticism and had defended himself:

Something brings the impression off – makes its effect. What? It can be nothing but the expression – the arrangement of words, the style – Ergo: the style is not dishonourable. [24 May 1896]

And to Unwin he had been vehement:

It (the notice) is valuable – but it is fallacious on the critic's own showing. I do not defend my performance. There is nothing respectable there but the endeavour. I grant, the achievement is wretched – but not in the way the critic says – at least not altogether. But enough of this. My style may be atrocious – but it produces its effect – is as unalterable as – say – the size of my feet – and I will never disguise it in boots of Wells's (or anybody else's) making. It would be utter folly. I shall make my own boots or perish. [28 May 1896]

If Conrad's assertion to Wells was more than polite flattery *The Sisters* and even more *The Rescuer* show that Wells's criticism had at the most a delayed effect. Conrad must have begun a new novel *The Sisters* shortly after finishing *An Outcast*, and he laid it aside on the advice of Garnett after writing about ten thousand words. In a letter to Garnett in February he referred to 'my horrible inability (for the last fortnight) to write a line'[32] and a month later announced the abandonment of the novel:

As to that other kind of foolishness: my work, there you have driven home the conviction and I *shall* write the sea story – at once (twelve months). It will be on the lines indicated to you. I surrender to the infamous spirit which you have awakened within me and as I want my abasement to be very complete I am looking for a sensational title. You had better help O Gentle and Murderous

Spirit! You have killed my cherished aspiration and now must come along and help to bury the corpse decently. I suggest

THE RESCUER
A Tale of Narrow Waters

Meditate for a fortnight and by that time you will get my address and will be able to let me know what your natural aptitude for faithlessness and crime has suggested to you. [Monday (23 March 1896)]

That the 'cherished aspiration' was *The Sisters* is proved by Conrad's next letter to Garnett, in which he says, '*The Sisters* are laid aside'.[33] This fragment survived and, after Conrad's death, was published under the aegis of Hueffer. It is not known why Garnett advised him to abandon *The Sisters* but perhaps he felt that Conrad was not getting to grips with the story and was anxious to guide him back to a sphere which he really knew so that he could both develop his talent and at the same time have some likelihood of a popular success. Certainly the rarefied atmosphere which Conrad was creating in *The Sisters* was unlikely to have much general appeal. And apart from this there can be little question that Garnett's advice was wise because *The Sisters,* although not so verbose as *An Outcast*, is bizarrely stilted and lifeless; it reads like a painstaking exercise in the art of fine writing. There are sentences like 'Associating with many he communed with none'[34] or 'The western life captivated him by the amplitude of its complicated surface, horrified him by the interior jumble of its variegated littleness. It was full of endeavour, of feverish effort, of endless theories, of preconceived hates, of misplaced loves'.[35] And this is his description of bohemian Paris:

He had visited that town before, in the second year of his travels, and then had, for some months, camped in the land of Bohemia; in that strange holy land of art abandoned by its High Priests; in the land of true faith and sincere blasphemies; where, in the midst of strife for immortal truth, hollow idols sit in imbecile and hieratic poses looking with approving eyes and their tongues in their cheeks at the agitated crowds of neophytes bringing fuel to the undying blaze of the sacred fire. It is a land of dazzling clearness and of distorted shadows; a country loud with the brazen trumpetings of assertion, and eloquent with the whisper of honest hopes and high endeavours; – with the sighs of the, not less noble, failures; of not ignoble discouragements. Over it, the neophytic smoke of the sacred fire hangs thick; and the outer world looks with disapproval at the black and repulsive pall hiding the light, the faith, the sacrifices: sacrifices of youth, of burnt hearts, of many bright futures – of not a few convictions![36]

The novel concerns, on the one hand, a young Russian named Stephen who has left his home to go in search of a 'creed' and after wandering about Europe, unable to find what he is looking for, has settled in Paris; on the other, a Basque girl named Rita, who, on the death of her parents, has been sent to Paris to be looked after by her uncle, an orange-merchant. Stephen's studio is in the courtyard of the orange-merchant's house. It is justifiable to assume that these two are destined to meet and fall in love; it is also clear from the words '. . . how short his [Stephen's] life, how faint his trace on earth, was fated to be'[37] that Conrad intended the story to have a tragic ending, but the rest is guesswork, although it is quite probable that Conrad proposed to incorporate incidents which he subsequently used in *The Arrow of Gold*. There is no evidence to support Hueffer's assertion that the story was to be about incest, and as Hueffer had not even noticed the similarities between *The Sisters* and *The Arrow of Gold* his comments are not worth much.

Apart from grappling with *The Sisters*, Conrad was trying to get to sea again. He was offered the command of a sailing-ship, 'but the conditions were so unsatisfactory that I turned it down';[38] this was probably the dilapidated barque *Windermere*, which Jessie Conrad describes having visited at Grangemouth with her future husband and their friend Hope.[39] He had also persuaded Garnett to help him. Garnett quotes a reply which he received from a friend of his wife, Charles Booth, a shipowner:

I am afraid I can do nothing to help Mr. Conrad. I wish I could. He certainly can write and it seems very hard if he cannot find present living with hope of future fame in his pen. He must be a very remarkable man.

The plan of a captain taking a share of the vessel he commands with the management is I believe common, but such work lies outside of my own experience . . .[40]

It is clear from this letter that Conrad felt himself to be committed to writing but could not yet live by his pen and was anxious to ensure some sort of material security. Garnett quotes Conrad as having said during their first conversation at Gillingham Street: 'But I *won't* live in an attic: I'm past that, you understand? I *won't* live in an attic!'[41]

Moreover, an additional and very important reason for wanting security had appeared. Conrad and Jessie George had decided to marry. He announced the news to Charles Zagórski:

I inform you solemnly (as the occasion requires) that I am marrying. No one could be more surprised by this event than I. But I am by no means terrified, accustomed as I am to an adventurous life and to stumbling upon terrible dangers. For that matter I must admit that my fiancée does not appear dangerous at all. Her name is Jessie and her surname is George. She is an inconspicuous little person (if the truth must be told, she is, unfortunately, plain) who is nonetheless very dear to me. When I first met her, eighteen months ago, she was earning a living in the City as a type-writer in the office of an American firm called Calligraph. Her father died three years ago. There are ten in her family. The mother is a very decent woman (and, I have no doubt, very virtuous). But I admit that it is all the same to me as – *Vous comprenez?* – I am not marrying the whole family. The marriage will take place on the 24th instant. [10 March 1896][42]

According to Jessie she was first introduced to her future husband 'early in November 1894' by a 'mutual friend',* G. F. W. Hope,[43] and the Hopes were apparently friends of her family.[44] By the end of 1895 their relationship had

* Jessie Conrad, *Joseph Conrad as I Knew Him*, 1926, p. 101. Jessie Conrad was even more inaccurate in her recollections than most people and in her second book on Conrad, published nineteen years after the first, she places the first meeting at the end of 1893. Aubry accepts this date without giving any reasons.

become close. Jessie recalls that she had letters from Conrad while he was at Champel[45] and, on his return, he had become a frequent visitor to her mother's house.[46] It appears that they became engaged early in the new year and that Conrad insisted on a wedding in six weeks' time. The account which Jessie gives of the manner of their engagement, Conrad demanding a speedy marriage because he had not long to live, is dramatic and amusing, but Jessie doubtless let her imagination run away with her.[47]

Just over a week before the date of the wedding Conrad took Jessie down to see the Garnetts in Surrey. Garnett says that Conrad's 'ultra-nervous organization appeared to make matrimony extremely hazardous'[48] and he must have taken this eleventh-hour chance to warn him. At least this seems to be a fair deduction from a letter of Conrad's written on the eve of his marriage:

> I am very glad you wrote to me the few lines I have just received. If you spoke as a friend I listened in the same manner – listened and was only a little, a very little dismayed. If one looks at life in its true aspect then everything loses much of its unpleasant importance and the atmosphere becomes cleared of what are only unimportant mists that drift past in imposing shapes. When once the truth is grasped that one's own personality is only a ridiculous and aimless masquerade of something hopelessly unknown the attainment of serenity is not very far off. Then there remains nothing but the surrender to one's impulses, the fidelity to passing emotions which is perhaps a nearer approach to truth than any other philosophy of life. And why not? If we are 'ever becoming – never being' then I would be a fool if I tried to become this thing rather than that; for I know well that I never will be anything. I would rather grasp the solid satisfaction of my wrong-headedness and shake my fist at the idiotic mystery of Heaven.[49]

And so the marriage took place on 24 March, at the St George Register Office, Hanover Square. Conrad's old friends Hope and Krieger and Jessie's mother, Jane, were the witnesses.[50] On the face of it a match between the fastidious, aristocratic Pole and an English girl, fifteen years younger than himself, of humble birth and little education must have seemed incongruous.* But Garnett was probably justified in saying that Conrad's 'instinct proved right' or, at least, if instinct was not at work, as it seldom is in the choice of spouse, he had been lucky. Jessie seems to have been well suited to his needs. Although it is possible that Conrad was overwhelmingly in love with her, his letter to Charles Zagórski does not give this impression and, not surprisingly, there is nothing to show what prompted his desire to marry at this moment nor why his choice fell on Jessie. For the first time since leaving Poland he had spent two years on land, in one place, and there was no immediate prospect of a move. Living in a large city with few friends, perhaps none with whom he was truly intimate, it was natural that he should have felt insecure and lonely and have thought of marriage as a solution. There is still the question of why Jessie and not someone nearer his own social background; but he had had no opportunity in England of meeting educated people. It is just possible, and this is the merest conjecture, that he had wanted to marry Marguerite Poradowska and been refused. Throughout 1894 and for the first six months of 1895 Conrad had written to her approximately once a week; an affectionate letter dated 11 June 1895 has been preserved and then there is an abrupt gap until 1900, when there is a letter from Conrad to his 'Très chère et bonne'. Without question he wrote letters to Marguerite Poradowska during this period which she either destroyed or which have been withheld,† and it is not unreasonable to presume that these letters contained matter which she thought was better not revealed. It may be, therefore, that Conrad turned to Jessie on the rebound from Marguerite Poradowska.

* Jessie was born on 22 February 1873. Her parents then lived at 10 Shepherds Place, Kennington Lane (birth certificate from Somerset House). On her birth certificate her father was described as a 'warehouseman', and on the certificate of marriage between her and Conrad, as a 'bookseller'.

† cf., letter to Aniela Zagórska of 20 December 1897: 'A few days ago I had news from good-natured Margot. Her life is not very easy either. I do not know if she has written to you that we expect a baby here.' *L.L.*, I, pp. 217–18.

From a photograph taken in the year of her marriage, Jessie appears a little plump but attractive, with pertly good-humoured mouth and eyes (after an accident in 1904 she became a partial cripple and rapidly gave way to a tendency to become fat, and later photographs show her as large and placidly good-natured). She seems to have been a simple, straightforward girl, and her even temperament, good nature and competence – she was an excellent cook – provided Conrad with the emotional and material anchorage for which his mercurial nature yearned. But her mind was too undeveloped for her ever to be able to give Conrad full companionship and she could not prevent his cries of loneliness. Eighteen months after their marriage he wrote to Garnett: 'On that day [3 December] I went over the rise of forty to travel downwards – and a little more lonely than before,'[51] and he told Cunninghame Graham, 'I live so alone that often I fancy myself clinging stupidly to a derelict planet abandoned by its precious crew.'[52] Perhaps, though, no one could have freed Conrad from his sense of solitude.

(4)

After their marriage[53] they left for Brittany, where they planned to stay for several months so that Conrad could work at his new novel, *The Rescuer*, which on Garnett's advice was to aim at being a popular sea-story.[54] They took a 'small house all kitchen downstairs and all bedroom upstairs on as rocky and barren island as the heart of (right thinking) man would wish to have'[55] – that is to say, Ile Grande, near Lannion. After a week there, Conrad wrote cheerfully to Edward Sanderson:

> At last, from my new (and very first) home, I write you to say that I am quite oppressed by my sense of importance in having a house, – actually a whole house!!, – to live in. It's the first time, – since I came to years of discretion, – that such an event happened in my life.
>
> Jess is immensely amused by the kitchen (the fireplace alone is big enough for her to live in) and spends most of her time trying to

talk with the girl (who is a perfect treasure). The kitchen is the most splendid and best furnished apartment of the palace, – and the only way in or out, anyhow. So we see it pretty often. Our sticks and caps have their domicile there all together. [14 April 1896, *L.L.*, I, p.188]

He had set to work on *The Rescuer* even before leaving the hotel at Lannion for Ile Grande[56] and on 13 April he wrote to Garnett:

I am sending you MS. already – if it's only twenty-four pages. But I must let you see it. I am so afraid of myself, of my likes and dislikes, of my thoughts and of my expression, that I must fly to you for relief – or condemnation – for anything to kill doubt with, for with doubt I cannot live – at least not for long.

Is the thing tolerable? Is the thing readable? Is the damned thing altogether insupportable? Am I mindful enough of your teaching – of your expoundings of the ways of the readers? Am I blessed? Or am I condemned? Or am I totally and utterly a hopeless driveller unworthy even of a curse?

Do tell the truth. I do not mind telling you that I have become such a scoundrel that all your remarks shall be accepted by me without a kick, without a moan, without the most abject of timid whispers! I am ready to cut, slash, erase, destroy, spit, trample, jump, wipe my feet on that MS. at a word from you. Only say where, how, when I have become one of the damned and the lost – I want to get on! [Monday (13 April 1896)]

Despite these doubts he managed to add nearly fifty pages during April. But then things started to go wrong. On 24 May he wrote again to Garnett:

I have been rather ill. Lots of pain, fever, etc. etc. The left hand is useless still. This month I have done nothing to *The Rescuer* – but I have about seventy pages of the most rotten twaddle. In the intervals of squirming I wrote also a short story of Brittany. Peasant life. I do not know whether it's worth anything . . .

I've been living in a kind of trance from which I am only waking up now to a sober existence. And it appears to me that I will never write anything worth reading. But you have heard all this before.

The 'short story of Brittany' was 'The Idiots'. Conrad sent it to the magazine *Cosmopolis*, which refused it, but it was accepted by *The Savoy*. Jessie describes[57] coming across the idiots when she and Conrad were driving or walking on the mainland, and it is probable that the beginning of the story, 'We were driving along the road from Treguier to Kervanda . . .'[58] describes the first encounter as it happened. It is a savage tale of a woman who has given birth to four idiot children and stabs her husband when he tries to make love to her again; then rushing in a frenzy along the cliffs she mistakes a seaweed-gatherer, who has come in pursuit, for her dead husband and flings herself into the sea below to drown. It is a well-told and effective story, but without much importance in Conrad's work, being, as he confessed,[59] closely derivative from Maupassant. The writing is a little too artificial in places, but there are some fine touches, such as:

> The darkness came from the hills, flowed over the coast, put out the red fires of sunset, and went on to seaward pursuing the retiring tide. The wind dropped with the sun, leaving a maddened sea and a devastated sky. The heavens above the house seemed to be draped in black rags, held up here and there by pins of fire.[60]

At the end of May Garnett sent back the first chapter of *The Rescuer* with enthusiastic comments:

> Excellent, oh Conrad, Excellent. I have read every word of *The Rescuer* and think you have struck a new note . . .[61]

But, in spite of this encouragement, Conrad was finding it increasingly difficult to make any headway with the book. In a letter thanking Garnett for his comments on the first chapter, he wrote:

> And every day *The Rescuer* crawls a page forward – sometimes with cold despair – at times with hot hope. I have long fits of depression, that in a lunatic asylum would be called madness. I do not know what it is. It springs from nothing. It is ghastly. It lasts an hour or a day: and when it departs it leaves a fear. [2 June 1896]

However he persevered, dragging himself amid agonized groans through another thirty pages to reach the end of Part I. Then he wrote to Garnett:

Since I sent you that Part Ist (on the eleventh of the month) I have written one page. Just one page. I went about thinking and forgetting – sitting down before the blank page to find that I could not put one sentence together. To be able to think and unable to express is a fine torture. I am undergoing it without patience. I don't see the end of it. It's very ridiculous and very awful. Now I've got all my people together I don't know what to do with them. The progressive episodes of the story *will* not emerge from the chaos of my sensations. I feel nothing clearly. And I am frightened when I remember that I have to drag it all out of myself. Other writers have some starting point. Something to catch hold of. They start from an anecdote – from a newspaper paragraph (a book may be suggested by a casual sentence in an old almanack). They lean on dialect – or on tradition – or on history – or on the prejudice or fad of the hour; they trade upon some tie or some conviction of their time – or upon the absence of these things – which they can abuse or praise. But at any rate they know something to begin with – while I don't. I have had some impressions, some sensations – in my time: – impression and sensations of common things. And it's all faded – my very being seems faded and thin like the ghost of a blonde and sentimental woman, haunting romantic ruins pervaded by rats. I am exceedingly miserable. My task appears to me as sensible as lifting the world without that fulcrum which even that conceited ass, Archimedes, admitted to be necessary. [19 June 1896]

This of course primarily reflected a state of mind. Conrad had had experiences which would have been the envy of any novelist (as Galsworthy had discovered on the *Torrens*). But it may be that he was feeling the effect of his nomadic life, of being an expatriate and thus unable to draw on a body of experience common to his prospective readers.

He continued the struggle for another two months, and wrote to Garnett on 5 August:

There is twelve pages written and I sit before them every morning, day after day, for the last two months and cannot add a sentence, add a word! I am paralysed by doubt and have just sense enough to feel the agony but am powerless to invent a way out of it. This is sober truth. I had bad moments with the *Outcast* but never anything so ghastly, nothing half so hopeless. When I face that fatal manuscript it seems to me that I have forgotten how to think – worse! how to write. [5 August 1896]

This was the end of his first concentrated attempt at a book which was to dog him off and on for more than twenty years. On 14 August he announced his defeat: 'I wish I could tackle *The Rescuer* again. I simply *can't*!'[62]

It seems that Conrad's difficulties were increasing with each novel that he wrote; *Almayer's Folly* had apparently been a relatively easy task; the writing of *An Outcast* was beset with doubts and at times anguish, but although he was driven to Switzerland he at least managed to keep going without too many blank days; then came the abortive *Sisters* and then the losing battle with *The Rescuer*. The main reason is perhaps that with his second novel Conrad felt himself committed to being an author; therefore much more, emotionally and materially, depended on the result than during the writing of *Almayer's Folly*, when he could always console himself that little would be lost if the book turned out to be no good. Then, with *An Outcast* finished, his prospective marriage must have added still more to his awareness of how much depended on his ability to write. There was another reason, too; it seems that with each book Conrad was deliberately trying to develop that aspect of his writing which was most likely to stifle his talent. He was moving away from the specific and concrete presentation of scene or character to the generalized, literary fabrication of atmosphere.

Thus, the abandonment of *The Sisters* led to no significant change in his style, except that as the scene was set in the Malay Archipelago the first attempt at *The Rescuer* is turgid with the exoticism of *An Outcast* rather than with the aridity of *The Sisters*. Here is an example from the inflated opening set-piece:

> And the imposing solitude, the austere loneliness of the great sea becomes only a mocking pretence for the narrow waters. They claim the majestic vastness of the ocean by the deceptive emptiness of their horizons; of the horizons that hide beyond the circular blaze of sunshine the unconquerable limits of an illusive greatness.

Humanity presses from all sides upon the narrow waters desecrating with the whisper of its hopes and fears, with the cry of its strife, with the sigh of its longings, the august unconcern of a limitless space. The islets hang suspended in a great sheen of undulating azure – for the narrow, for the shallow and audacious sea fears not to borrow the fathomless serenity, the profound blueness of the sky. From land to land the islets stretch in dots of rock and verdure, like stepping-stones that are to serve for escape and for pursuit, for terror and for anger, for greed and for revenge – or for the stealthy wanderings of outcasts.[63]

This is not an isolated instance; there are many passages as bad or worse. The action of this first version of the novel is as becalmed as Mr Travers's yacht, and the fog of verbiage only very seldom lifts enough to reveal scene or character in sharp outline; it is not surprising that Conrad finally lost his bearings. But it is surprising that Garnett seems genuinely to have admired what he was shown and to have encouraged Conrad to persevere, although it is easy to be wise in retrospect.

To add still further to Conrad's difficulties there had also been a financial disaster. He had told Garnett: 'I have had a lot of worries. A man I love much had been very unfortunate in affairs and I also lose pretty well all that remained.'* The friend was Hope,[64] and Conrad had apparently put some money into the South African gold-mining venture belonging to Hope's brother-in-law; if he had still been alive Thaddeus Bobrowski would not have missed the opportunity of a sermon on the Korzeniowski weakness for speculation.

All this must have been very dismal for Jessie, who had nursed her husband through an unpleasant illness and was

* 22 July 1896. It is difficult to gather when Conrad first heard about the disaster. According to Jessie it was a fortnight before their marriage and their hopes of something being salvaged were dashed when a director of the gold mine went down on the *Drummond Castle* off Ushant (*Joseph Conrad and his Circle*, pp. 27–31). This is clearly absurd because the director would hardly have been returning with gold nuggets strapped round him. The *Drummond Castle* sank at about midnight on 17 June. There were three survivors (*The Times*, 18 June 1896).

taking very seriously her role as the wife of an author, having got hold of a typewriter to type his manuscripts for him. But the gloom was not unmitigated. The Conrads seem to have enjoyed themselves going for trips in a small sailing-boat which they had hired.[65] Moreover, although he was stuck with *The Rescuer*, Conrad was at least able to write two more short stories, 'An Outpost of Progress' and 'The Lagoon'; and he may also have written a few pages of *The Nigger of the 'Narcissus'*.* On 22 July he sent 'An Outpost of Progress' to Garnett saying, 'I send it to you first of all. It's yours. It shall be the first of a vol. ded. to you – but this story is *meant* for you. I am pleased with it. That's why you shall get it.' On the same day he wrote to Unwin describing the story:

> It is a story of the Congo. There is no love interest in it and no woman – only incidentally. The exact locality is not mentioned. All the bitterness of those days, all my puzzled wonder as to the meaning of all I saw – all my indignation at masquerading philanthropy have been with me again while I wrote. The story is simple – there is hardly any description. The most common incidents are related – the life in a lonely station on the Kassai. I have divested myself of everything but pity – and some scorn – while putting down the insignificant events that bring on the catastrophe.[66]

Subsequently he described 'An Outpost of Progress' as 'the lightest part of the loot I carried off from Central Africa'.[67] Although it may not have the scope or power of 'Heart of Darkness' (Conrad's only other story with the Congo as setting) and again shows the influence of Maupassant it has a well-handled and original subject: the rapid disintegration of two white traders, average products of the machine of civilization, when confronted with the corroding power of solitude and the unusual. Finally one of the traders blunders into shooting the other and then hangs himself.

* There is no reliable information about this. Jessie says that he began the *Nigger* on Ile Grande (*Joseph Conrad as I Knew Him*, p. 106), and the wrapper of the MS. has: 'Begun in 1896—June. Finished in 1897—February.' Apparently Conrad's first mention of it is in a letter to Unwin of 19 October 1896 in which he says, 'The story will contain 25,000 words *at least* and shall be ready very soon.' Keating Collection, Yale.

Apart from a sprinkling of general reflections the style is terse and direct and the story is told with ferociously ironical humour (there is no trace of pity), rising to a macabre climax:

> 'Run! Run to the house! I've found one of them. Run, look for the other!'
>
> He had found one of them! And even he, the man of varied and startling experience, was somewhat discomposed by the manner of this finding. He stood and fumbled in his pockets (for a knife) while he faced Kayerts, who was hanging by a leather strap from the cross. . . . His toes were only a couple of inches above the ground; his arms hung stiffly down; he seemed to be standing rigidly at attention, but with one purple cheek playfully posed on the shoulder. And, irreverently, he was putting out a swollen tongue at his Managing Director.[68]

The other, very short, story has a Malayan setting and is concerned with betrayal, remorse, and retribution, but it is slight and of little interest. Conrad told Garnett on 5 August, 'I wrote the "Outpost of Progress" with pleasure if with difficulty. The one I am writing now I hammer out of myself with difficulty but without pleasure. It is called "The Lagoon", and is very much Malay indeed.' And in another letter to Garnett he accurately described it as 'a tricky thing with the usual forests – river – stars – wind – sunrise, and so on – and lots of second hand Conradese in it'.[69] Whether this was Conrad's real opinion is another matter. He was inclined violently to disparage his work, particularly while he was still engaged on it. But, naturally enough, he was quick to respond to praise, and eighteen months later, when 'The Lagoon' was published, he wrote to Miss Watson, his friend Edward Sanderson's fianceé:

> I am right glad to know you like 'The Lagoon'. To be quite confidential I must tell you it is, of my short stories, the one I like the best myself. I did write it to please myself, – and I am truly delighted to find that I have also pleased you. [14 March 1897, *LL.*, I, p. 202]

In September the Conrads returned to England. They

spent a few days in Conrad's old Gillingham Street rooms[70] and then moved into a small villa at Stanford-le-Hope in Essex, just inland from the Thames estuary, about five miles north-east of Tilbury. They presumably chose this district in order to be near their friends, the Hopes, and because it was well placed for sailing. From Jessie's description it seems to have been a depressing house and she quotes Conrad as having called it a 'damned jerry-built rabbit hutch'.[71]

Soon after his return Conrad fell out with Unwin, his publisher. Unwin had offered him a low royalty and the small advance of £50 in two payments for the volume of short stories which he was to publish. On Garnett's advice[72] Conrad demanded higher royalties and double the advance, telling Unwin:

> As to my demands, which you might think excessive, it's just this: I can't afford to work for less than ten pence per hour and must work in a way that will give me this magnificent income. I don't like to give up anything I have taken hold of and intend to stick to scribbling till I am fairly convinced of my wisdom or my folly. I will see it out – but I do not wish to see it out at your expense. After all my work has some value but if people won't have any of it I can do one or two other things less gentlemanly (save the mark) but not a whit less honourable or useful. [19 October 1896 (Yale)]

Unwin replied with a flat refusal to raise his terms and Conrad decided to look for another publisher. As Garnett was reader to Unwin he was in a delicate position, but he had already sounded Smith Elder as to their interest, and Conrad went through some abortive negotiations with them. Garnett then turned to Sidney Pawling of Heinemann and got him interested in the novel which Conrad was working on at the moment, *The Nigger of the 'Narcissus'*. Pawling promised to consider it for publication and also to show it to W. E. Henley, editor of the *New Review* and tyrant of the literary world.[73]

This book had been coming along quite well since the Conrads' return to England and there were none of the despairing moans which accompanied his struggle with *The*

Rescuer or *An Outcast*. It was only towards the end that he showed any doubts:

My only fear is that I will droop with the end of the *Narcissus*. I am horribly dissatisfied with the ideas yet unwritten. Nothing effective suggests itself. It's ghastly. I shall, end [of] this week, send you on a good many pages – but the end is not yet. I think I could almost *pray* for inspiration if I only knew where to turn my face. [Wednesday (25 November 1896)]

But this was apparently a momentary misgiving, and four days later he was talking confidently of his 'Beloved *Nigger*'.[74] A week later he must have heard that Henley liked what he had seen of the *Nigger* and, although he had to wait six months[75] before knowing definitely that it would be serialized in the *New Review*, Henley's approval greatly encouraged him:

Now I have conquered Henley I ain't afraid of the divvle himself. I will drink to the success of *The Rescuer*. I will even get drunk to make it all safe – no morality! I feel like, in old days, when I got a ship and started off in a hurry to cram a lot of shore-going emotions into one short evening before going off into a year's slavery upon the sea. Ah! Tempi passati. There were then other prejudices to conquer. Same fate in another garb. [Monday morning (7 December 1896)]

The Nigger spun itself out longer than Conrad had expected and Christmas, with a visit to his old friends the Kliszewskis at Cardiff, came along before he had finished.[76] On 10 January he wrote to Garnett:

Nigger died on the 7th at 6 p.m.; but the ship is not home yet. Expected to arrive tonight and be paid off tomorrow. And the end! I can't eat – I dream – nightmares – and scare my wife. I wish it was over! But I think it will do! It will do! – Mind I only think – not sure. But if I didn't think so I would jump overboard.

He finally reached the end sometime before 19 January, when he wrote to Garnett that he had been in bed for two days, 'a cheap price for finishing that story'.

(5)

The Nigger of the 'Narcissus' is the culmination of Conrad's apprenticeship as a novelist; in it he showed not only that he had fully mastered the art which he had been learning from Flaubert and Maupassant but that he could accomplish something significantly unique, though according to their formal prescription. The author seldom intrudes himself into the action and comment is kept down to the minimum. He rarely goes inside the characters, but gains his effect through the minute recording of external impressions; the men's physical suffering is portrayed thus:

> Mr Baker crawled along the line of men, asking: – 'Are you all there?' and looking them over. Some blinked vacantly, others shook convulsively; Wamibo's head hung over his breast; and in painful attitudes, cut by lashings, exhausted with clutching, screwed up in corners, they breathed heavily. Their lips twitched, and at every sickening heave of the overturned ship they opened them wide as if to shout.[77]

There is a shadowy, anonymous narrator, one of the crew who occasionally reveals himself through the use of 'we' or 'us', as at the start of *Madame Bovary*, and only emerges individually as 'I' or 'me' at the end, after the crew has been paid off; this device, by indicating that the account of the voyage comes from a member of the crew, adds a sense of authenticity and immediacy to the story, but leads Conrad into a number of solecisms, such as his account of the last scene between Donkin and Jimmy or of the mental processes of various characters which the narrator could not have reported.

The style of the *Nigger* is far more flexible and the imagery, for the most part, more visually precise than that of Conrad's previous work; there are some excellent scenes of violence and action – during the storm, Captain Allistoun's humiliation of Donkin, the burial of Jimmy – as well as some fine descriptive passages. For example:

> The ship tossed about, shaken furiously, like a toy in the hand of a lunatic. Just at sunset there was a rush to shorten sail before the menace of a sombre hail cloud. The hard gust of wind came brutal like the blow of a fist. The ship relieved of her canvas in time received it pluckily: she yielded reluctantly to the violent onset; then, coming up with a stately and irresistible motion, brought her spars to windward in the teeth of the screeching squall. Out of the abysmal darkness of the black cloud overhead white hail streamed on her, rattled on the rigging, leaped in handfuls off the yards, rebounded on the deck – round and gleaming in the murky turmoil like a shower of pearls. It passed away. For a moment a livid sun shot horizontally the last rays of sinister light between the hills of steep, rolling waves. Then a wild night rushed in – stamped out in a great howl that dismal remnant of a stormy day.[78]

At times, when he is straining after the grand effect, Conrad gives way to the pretentious overwriting which marred his earlier work. The passage describing the journey of the *Narcissus* up the Channel into port is overweighted with epithets and imagery, and produces the effect of an overdressed woman:

> The lights of the earth mingled with the lights of heaven; and above the tossing lanterns of a trawling fleet a great lighthouse shone steadily like an enormous riding light burning above a vessel of fabulous dimensions. Below its steady glow, the coast, stretching away straight and black, resembled the high side of an indestructible craft riding motionless upon the immortal and unresting sea. The dark land lay alone in the midst of waters, like a mighty ship bestarred with vigilant lights . . .[79]

'Great', 'enormous', 'fabulous', 'mighty', 'indestructible', 'immortal'; this glut of grandiose epithets merely reduces the value of the words. Or another example,

> A bridge broke in two before her, as if by enchantment; big hydraulic capstans began to turn all by themselves, as though animated by a mysterious and unholy spell.[80]

What spell is not mysterious and why is this one more unholy than another?

Occasionally, too, there are incongruous traces of Conrad's earlier artificially literary style. Thus, 'At some opinion of dirty Knowles, delivered with an air of supernatural cunning, a ripple of laughter ran along, rose like a wave, burst with a startling roar.'[81] This description would suit a drawing-room or a dinner party but is absurdly inappropriate in the coarse atmosphere of the crew of the *Narcissus*. Again, 'They cursed their fate, contemned their life, and wasted their breath in deadly imprecations upon one another.'[82] The idea of anyone on the *Narcissus* 'contemning' his life is ludicrous.

Conrad's portrayal of the crew of the *Narcissus* has been compared to Flaubert's of the Carthaginian troops at the beginning of *Salammbô*, but in this case he excelled his master. He knew just what he needed for his purpose and there is no superfluous description. The major characters are presented with vivid detail. The others are hit off in a few picturesque phrases, down to the shadowy but effective Knowles and Davies. There is a magnificent portrait of Singleton:

> Old Singleton, the oldest able seaman in the ship, set [sat?] apart on the deck right under the lamps, stripped to the waist, tattooed like a cannibal chief all over his powerful chest and enormous biceps. Between the blue and red patterns his white skin gleamed like satin; his bare back was propped against the heel of the bowsprit, and he held a book at arm's length before his big, sunburnt face. With his spectacles and a venerable white beard, he resembled a learned and savage patriarch, the incarnation of barbarian wisdom serene in the blasphemous turmoil of the world. He was intensely absorbed, and as he turned the pages an expression of grave surprise would pass over his rugged features. He was reading *Pelham*. . . . Old Singleton sat unmoved in the clash of voices and cries, spelling through *Pelham* with slow labour, and lost in an absorption profound enough to resemble a trance. He breathed regularly. Every time he turned the book in his enormous and blackened hands the muscles of his big white arms rolled slightly under the smooth skin. Hidden by the white moustache, his lips, stained with tobacco juice that trickled down the long beard, moved in inward whisper. His bleared eyes gazed fixedly from behind the glitter of black-rimmed glasses.[83]

Podmore, the cook, on the other hand, is created with one

brilliantly humorous touch, 'beaming with the inward consciousness of his faith, like a conceited saint unable to forget his glorious reward',[84] as are the two Norwegians who 'sat on a chest side by side, alike and placid, resembling a pair of love-birds on a perch, and with round eyes stared innocently'.[85]

Then, once introduced, the characters are fully exploited to comment on and develop the action; for example, Singleton with his dotty theory about head winds (which is ironically and by coincidence borne out), Podmore with his raving about hell and wickedness:

> 'Look here, cook,' interrupted Mr. Baker, 'the men are perishing with cold.' 'Cold!' said the cook, mournfully; 'they will be warm enough before long.' – 'What?' asked Mr. Baker. . . . 'They are a wicked lot,' continued the cook solemnly, but in an unsteady voice, 'about as wicked as any ship's company in this sinful world! Now, I . . .'[86]

And others who, with one remark, or in the case of Wamibo and the two Norwegians with unintelligible noises, supply the spark to light up a scene.

There was one, amazingly obtuse, criticism of the *Nigger* which particularly worried Conrad. Reviewing an English translation of d'Annunzio's *Trionfo della Morte*, Arthur Symons contrasted it with the *Nigger* and *Captains Courageous*. He praised their descriptive power but complained:

> What more is there? Where is the idea of which such things as these should be but servants? Ah, there has been an oversight; everything else is there, but that, these brilliant writers have forgotten to put in. Now d'Annunzio, whether you like his idea or not, never forgets to put it in.[87]

Conrad immediately asked Cunninghame Graham and Garnett whether they thought the criticism was true and was even roused to write an article for the press in defence of Kipling and, by implication, of himself.[88]

He told a friend that he had 'tried to get through the veil of details at the essence of life'[89] and years later he defined the subject as the portrayal of 'the crew of a merchant ship, brought to the test of what I may venture to call the moral problem of conduct'.[90]

In fact, *The Nigger of the 'Narcissus'*, which was the first of Conrad's novels to have the sea as a setting, contains, more than anything else he wrote, the essence of his experience at sea and of his views on the practical conduct of life. To Conrad the sea was neither a god to be submitted to nor a devil to be overcome. The relationship of a sailor individually to the sea provided a test of character and skill; it resembled that of a lion-tamer to a lion or a bullfighter to a bull, offering exceptional opportunities for the exercise of prowess but leading to harsh, even fatal, consequences in the event of failure through loss of nerve or inefficiency. The sea also provided a test of those corporate ideals of human solidarity on which Conrad considered that society must be based in order to survive. The merchant navy, possibly more than any other sphere of life, has relied on a sense of human solidarity. Among landsmen this sense arises only in moments of crisis; in the regular services discipline deprives it of its spontaneity and therefore its virtue; but, 'discipline is not ceremonious in merchant ships, where the sense of hierarchy is weak, and where all feel themselves equal before the unconcerned immensity of the sea and the exacting appeal of the work'.[91] Although life on a merchant ship provided an excellent setting for the test of human solidarity Conrad always emphasized the universal application of this theme and vehemently defended himself against the classification of a writer of sea-tales which dogged him throughout his life. Just before his death he wrote:

> In the *Nigger* I give the psychology of a group of men and render certain aspects of nature. But the problem that faces them is not a problem of the sea, it is merely a problem that has arisen on board a ship where the conditions of complete isolation from all land entanglements make it stand out with a particular force and colouring.[92]

Again shortly before his death, Conrad described the *Nigger* as an 'effort to present a group of men held together by a common loyalty and a common perplexity in a struggle not with human enemies, but with the hostile conditions testing their faithfulness to the conditions of their own calling'.[93] But he must have forgotten how complex a book he had written because, although his description is adequate in respect of the storm, a straightforward non-human test, it ignores the far more insidious threat to human solidarity from Jimmy and Donkin. As might be expected, the need to fight the storm strengthens the bonds uniting the crew to each other and, very important, to the ship, but the reverse is true of the behaviour of Jimmy and Donkin. Although neither of them triumphs finally they succeed in cracking the solidarity of the ship.

The threat that Donkin offers is comparatively crude. He is a wholly contemptible character and Conrad pours on him his concentrated scorn:

> They all knew him! He was the man that cannot steer, that cannot splice, that dodges the work on dark nights; that, aloft, holds on frantically with both arms and legs, and swears at the wind, the sleet, the darkness; the man who curses the sea while others work. The man who is the last out and the first in when all hands are called. The man who can't do most things and won't do the rest. The pet of philanthropists and self-seeking landlubbers. The sympathetic and deserving creature that knows all about his rights, but knows nothing of courage, of endurance, and of the unexpressed faith, of the unspoken loyalty that knits together a ship's company. The independent offspring of the ignoble freedom of the slums full of disdain and hate of the austere servitude of the sea . . .[94]
>
> It was his deserved misfortune that those rags which nobody could possibly be supposed to own looked on him as if they had been stolen.[95]

The threat presented by Jimmy, the dying 'nigger', is more complex and more dangerous. He has almost persuaded the crew except, ironically, Donkin that he is dying but, because he is afraid of death, has deceived himself into thinking that he is a malingerer who is exploiting the good will of the crew into allowing him to escape duty. There is, however, a lurking doubt among the crew: 'We hated James

Wait. We could not get rid of the monstrous suspicion that this astounding black-man was shamming sick, had been malingering heartlessly in the face of our toil, of our scorn, of our patience – and now was malingering in the face of our devotion – in the face of death.'[96]

It is that which is so insidious; the crew would have known what to do if they had been certain that Jimmy was dying or that he was a fraud. But the uncertainty enabled him to blackmail them; to undermine and corrupt the spirit of the ship. 'He had found the secret of keeping for ever on the run the fundamental imbecility of mankind; he had the secret of life, that confounded dying man, and he made himself master of every moment of our existence.'[97] 'The latent egoism of tenderness to suffering appeared in the developing anxiety not to see him die.'[98] Only old Singleton, the captain, and of course Donkin were immune to this blackmail. Singleton's incorruptibility appeared shockingly callous: ' "Well, get on with your dying," he said with venerable mildness; "don't raise a blamed fuss with us over that job. We can't help you." '[99] But Jimmy held the crew in a 'weird servitude':[100]

He overshadowed the ship. Invulnerable in his promise of speedy corruption he trampled on our self-respect, he demonstrated to us daily our want of moral courage; he tainted our lives. Had we been a miserable gang of wretched immortals, unhallowed alike by hope and fear, he could not have lorded it over us with a more pitiless assertion of his sublime privilege.[101]

Jimmy was superior to Donkin because he could create a situation, whereas Donkin was merely able to take advantage of it. When the crew had a grievance Donkin could aggravate it, but only up to a certain point, because they had no illusions about Donkin and 'under extreme provocation men will be just – whether they want to be so or not'[102] – a dubious assertion. Thus 'his care for our rights, his disinterested concern for our dignity, were not discouraged by the invariable contumely of our words, by the disdain of our looks. Our contempt for him was unbounded – and we could not but listen with interest to that consummate artist.'[103]

He can exploit the orgy of self-satisfaction in which the crew indulge after the storm, and on another occasion is able to bring the men to the point of mutiny because of their resentment at Captain Allistoun's treatment of Jimmy. But when he throws a belaying pin at Captain Allistoun he is immediately disowned by the rest of the crew, because he has overstepped the tacitly accepted bounds of what is permissible. Again Donkin's isolation from the rest of the crew is ignoble and forced: 'He stood on the bad eminence of a general dislike. He was left alone; and in his isolation he could do nothing but think of the gales of the Cape of Good Hope and envy us the possession of warm clothing and waterproofs',[104] whereas Jimmy's isolation is chosen and superb: 'He cared for no one.'[105]

The men can contend with Donkin, and in the final test he is impotent, but Jimmy on the other hand has his moment of triumph, although after his death: 'A common bond was gone; the strong, effective and respectable bond of a sentimental lie. ... Like a community of banded criminals disintegrated by a touch of grace, we were profoundly scandalized with each other. Men spoke unkindly to their best chums. ...'[106] It is in fact strange that Conrad should have declared his wish to 'enshrine my old chums in a decent edifice'[107] and then put a curse on the edifice. But he was a novelist and not a hagiographer; he chose an exceptional situation in which to place his 'chums' and was too sincere an artist to idealize their behaviour, believing that the closer to truth he could come the more worthy of them he would be.

Of all his books the *Nigger* seems to have been that which gave Conrad the most pleasure, or least agony, in writing and the most satisfaction when finished. He retained a special feeling for it throughout his life, calling it 'the story by which, as a creative artist, I stand or fall, and which, at any rate, no one else could have written. A landmark in literature, I can safely say, for nothing like it has ever been done before.'[108] And although he was to go on to more ambitious and greater achievements, the *Nigger* holds a unique position in his work as a masterpiece of poetic realism. It would be hard to find a passage in any of his novels to excel the following in its insight and power of suggestion; Captain Allistoun is speaking:

> 'You've been braying in the dark about "See to-morrow morning!" Well, you see now. What do you want?' He waited, stepping quickly to and fro, giving them searching glances. What did they want? They shifted from foot to foot, they balanced their bodies; some, pushing back their caps, scratched their heads. What did they want? Jimmy was forgotten; no one thought of him, alone forward in his cabin, fighting great shadows, clinging to brazen lies, chuckling painfully over his transparent deceptions. No, not Jimmy; he was more forgotten than if he had been dead. They wanted great things. And suddenly all the simple words they knew seemed to be lost for ever in the immensity of their vague and burning desire. They knew what they wanted, but they could not find anything worth saying. They stirred on one spot, swinging, at the end of muscular arms, big tarry hands with crooked fingers. A murmur died out.[109]

(6)

A few months after finishing the *Nigger*, Conrad wrote a preface to it[110] in which he gave his conception of the aim of the artist and declared his own method. This preface is supremely important for the understanding of Conrad's intention as an artist; it is also, together with the preface to *A Personal Record*, the finest piece of non-fictional prose that he wrote, although it is slightly marred by repetitiveness.

In it Conrad achieves a subtle and satisfying fusion between the artist and the moralist. He begins by defining art as 'a single-minded attempt to render the highest kind of justice to the visible universe, by bringing to light the truth, manifold and one, underlying its every aspect'.[111] He then goes on to expound the nature of artistic communication: 'All art ... appeals primarily to the senses, and the artistic aim when expressing itself in written words must also make its appeal through the senses. ... It must strenuously aspire to the plasticity of sculpture, to the colour of painting, and to the magic suggestiveness of music – which is the art of arts.'[112] Therefore, 'My task ... is by the power of the written word to make you hear, to make you feel – it is, before all, to make you *see*.'[113] This leads to a declaration of belief identical with that of the impressionists,* although in practice Conrad was never an impressionist:

> To arrest, for the space of a breath, the hands busy about the work of the earth, and compel men entranced by the sight of distant goals to glance for a moment at the surrounding vision of form and colour, of sunshine and shadows; to make them pause for a look, for a sigh, for a smile – such is the aim, difficult and evanescent, and reserved only for a very few to achieve. But sometimes, by the deserving and the fortunate, even that task is accomplished. And when it is accomplished – behold! – all the truth of life is there: a moment of vision, a sigh, a smile – and the return to an eternal rest.[114]

The method is thus wholly sensuous, but the result achieved is also moral. If the artist succeeds in his aim he 'may perchance attain to such clearness of sincerity that at last the presented vision ... shall awaken in the hearts of the beholders that feeling of unavoidable solidarity; of the solidarity in mysterious origin, in toil, in joy, in hope, in uncertain fate, which binds men to each other and all mankind to the visible world'.[115]

* It is also very similar to that which Pater gives to Marius at one stage in his development (*Marius the Epicurean*, 3rd edition, 1892, I, pp. 167–8). Garnett had sent Conrad a copy of *Marius the Epicurean* in May 1897 and it was in August that Conrad told Garnett that he had written a preface to the *Nigger*. It is therefore quite possible that Pater's ideas influenced the preface.

[VII]

Frustration

IN March of 1897 the Conrads moved out of their little villa into an Elizabethan farmhouse called Ivy Walls,[1] just outside Stanford-le-Hope. Jessie later recalled that the first year spent in this neighbourhood was

> one of the most difficult in the whole of our married life. It was some time before it dawned upon me that he [Conrad] must be feeling the isolation from men of his own standard of intellect. The only man who was close at hand was dear Mr. Hope, and he was not always at home. Then the persistent attacks of gout interfering with the only form of recreation I knew appealed to him. Every Sunday he was well enough we would take a picnic lunch and join Mr. Hope on a boating expedition . . .
>
> I was thankful when one of those most intimate friends, John Galsworthy, Edward Garnett or E. L. Sanderson could be induced to pay us a visit, for a long week-end. The effect of their sympathetic and sustaining presence would lubricate the mental machinery, so to speak, and a good advance would be made.[2]

Shortly after finishing the *Nigger** Conrad began 'Karain', another Malay short story, which he sent off to Unwin, to whom he was bound for a volume of short stories, on 14 April.[3] He had had difficulty writing it and seems to have been a little ashamed of it once he had done so. In sending Garnett the first batch of manuscript he had said: 'If you say "Burn:" I will burn – and won't hate you. But if you say: "Correct – Alter:" I won't do it – but shall hate you henceforth and for ever:'[4] Garnett said 'Correct – Alter!' and Conrad did so. Nearly a month later he referred to 'that infernal story. I can't shake myself free of it, though I don't like it – never shall: But I can get rid of it only by finishing it

* Conrad revised the *Nigger* for a further month after reaching the end, and 'Karain' was probably begun about 19 February. cf., Conrad's letter to Garnett of that date: 'I shall try to begin that short story today.'

coûte-que-coûte.'[5] Writing to Cunninghame Graham after it had been published he called it 'magazine'ish'.[6]

In his Author's Note, written much later for the collected edition, Conrad said that he 'didn't notice then [at the time of writing] that the *motif* of the story is almost identical with the *motif* of "The Lagoon".'[7] Like 'The Lagoon' it is a story of betrayal and remorse. Karain is haunted by the spirit of the man he had killed for the sake of a woman, just as Arsat in 'The Lagoon' was obsessed by the image of the brother whom he had allowed to die in order to save the woman he loved. 'Karain', like 'The Lagoon', oozes lush romanticism, and is written in the artificial style which Conrad had begun to eliminate from his work but which lingered on in his Malayan tales. But Conrad gives 'Karain' a welcome ironical twist by allowing an English well-wisher cynically to exorcize with a Jubilee sixpenny piece the spirit which is haunting Karain.

Another *motif*, which had been hinted at in 'The Lagoon', crops up in 'Karain'. In the last sentence of 'The Lagoon', Arsat looks 'beyond the great light of a cloudless day into the darkness of a world of illusions',[8] and the narrator says of Karain: 'I thought of his wanderings, of that obscure Odyssey of revenge, of all the men that wander amongst illusions; of the illusions as restless as men; of the illusions faithful, faithless; of the illusions that give joy, that give sorrow, that give pain, that give peace; of the invincible illusions that can make life and death appear serene, inspiring, tormented, or ignoble.'[9] And at the end of the story two of the white men now in London, in the Strand, discuss whether the events which Karain described were real or illusory – they then wonder whether the tangible hurly-burly of London which surrounds them can be called any more real. Calderon's theme of 'Life is a Dream' had a persistent fascination for Conrad.

Incidentally, it was on these two Malay stories that Max Beerbohm based his witty parody of Conrad in *A Christmas Garland*.

At Garnett's suggestion Unwin sent 'Karain' to David

Meldrum, literary adviser to Blackwood's, in the hope that it would be accepted for 'Maga'. Meldrum passed it on with a warm recommendation to William Blackwood, who accepted it, and this was the start of a profitable association, for Conrad, with the house of Blackwood.[10] At the time of finishing 'Karain' it seems that Conrad was feeling happy about the way his life was developing. He told Spiridion Kliszewski: 'I feel very hopeful; more so than at any time of my life as I can remember.' But he asked Kliszewski to lend him £20 because the publication of 'An Outpost of Progress' in *Cosmopolis* had been postponed, and he also mentioned Jessie's poor health.[11] His hopeful mood did not last, because he began to have great trouble with his next story, 'The Return', as well as making no progress with *The Rescuer*, which he wanted to take up again. He wrote to Garnett:

> I am so so – horribly irritable and muddle-headed. Thinking of *Rescuer;* writing nothing; often restraining tears; never restraining curses. At times thinking the world *has* come to an end – at others convinced that it has not yet come out of chaos. But generally I feel like the impenitent thief on the cross (he is one of my early heroes) – defiant and bitter. [Friday (11 June 1897)]

and, later, more desperately, to Edward Sanderson:

> I've been ten weeks trying to write a story of about twenty pages of print. I haven't finished yet! and what I've written seems to me too contemptible for words. Not in conception perhaps, – but in execution. This state of affairs spells Ruin, – and I can't help it, – I can't. [19 July 1897, *L.L.,* I, pp. 206–7]

In the same letter he told Sanderson that Jessie was pregnant:

> There is no other news, – unless the information that there is a prospect of some kind of descendant may be looked upon in the light of something new. I am not unduly elated. Johnson says it may mend Jess's health permanently, – if it does not end her. The last he does not say in so many words, but I can see an implication through a wall of words. This attitude does not contribute to my peace of mind, – and now, when I think of it, there is nothing very

shocking in my not being able to finish a short story in three months.

It took Conrad another month to finish 'The Return',[12] and he sent it to Garnett, telling him: 'The work is vile – or else good. I don't know. I can't know. But I swear to you that I won't alter a line – a word – not a comma – for you. There! And this for the reason that I have a physical horror of that story. I simply won't look at it any more. It has embittered five months of my life. I hate it.'[13] Garnett soon sent Conrad his reactions, which seem to have been rather obtuse, and Conrad replied with a mixture of dismay and exasperation:

I don't know whether to weep or to laugh at your letter. I have already torn out several handfuls of hair. And there seems nothing else left to do.

I am hoist with my own petard. My dear fellow what I aimed at was just to produce the effect of cold water in every one of my man's speeches. I swear to you that was my intention. I wanted to produce the effect of insincerity, or artificiality. Yes! I wanted the reader to *see him think* and then to hear him speak – and shudder. The whole point of the joke is there. I wanted the truth to be first dimly seen through the fabulous untruth of that man's convictions – of his idea of life – and then to make its way out with a rush at the end. But if I have to explain that to you – to you! – then I've egregiously failed. I've tried with all my might to avoid just these trivialities of rage and distraction which you judge necessary to the truth of the picture. I counted it a virtue, and lo and behold! You say it is a sin. Well! Never more! It is evident that my fate is to be descriptive and descriptive only. There are things I *must* leave alone.

This thing however *is* . . . And the question presents itself: is it to be put away in an unhonoured grave or sent into the world? To tell you the truth I haven't the courage to alter it. It seems to me, if I do, it will become so utterly something else, something I did not mean. What strange illusions we scribblers have! Probably the thing means nothing anyhow. [Wednesday (29 September 1897)]

Garnett's opinion and Conrad's failure to place the story serially (it was long and he would not consent to a division) gradually convinced him that it was a failure. He tried to defend it and asked Garnett to get his wife, whose translations of Turgenev Conrad had much admired, to give her opinion.[14] But his final verdict seems to have been that expressed in the Author's Note to *Tales of Unrest*: 'My innermost feeling, now, is that "The Return" is a left-handed production.'[15]

Most people, with the notable exception of Hueffer, seem to have accepted Conrad's verdict, and the story has been virtually ignored. It is quite unlike any of Conrad's other stories, being a psychological drama without any important objective action. There are two characters, husband and wife, who 'skimmed over the surface of life hand in hand, in a pure and frosty atmosphere – like two skilful skaters cutting figures on thick ice for the admiration of the beholders, and disdainfully ignoring the hidden stream, the stream restless and dark; the stream of life, profound and unfrozen'.[16]

The wife suddenly finds this life unbearable and goes to another man, leaving a note for her husband. While he is contemplating his shattered assumptions the wife returns; she has realized that she has not the strength, the courage, perhaps the desire to get away – and then, she hopes that her action may have broken the ice of her husband's superficial existence. But he has not changed. She tries to get him to show genuine feeling, but he seems concerned only with her offence against propriety and with the need to preserve appearances, and is totally unaware of what has caused her action. When she realizes this she tries to leave a second time, but his power holds her back. She then knows that she has lost: she must accept life exactly as it was before she left.

However, her action has affected him. As the long scene in which he reproaches her drags on, he realizes that nothing can be the same again. The ice has in fact broken. It is revealed to him – and this is perhaps implausible – that 'there can be no life without faith and love – faith in a human heart, love of a human being',[17] and that his wife 'had in her hands an indispensable gift which nothing else on earth could give'.[18] But now it is too late; she does not understand him and cannot respond. Thus, having had his revelation, and seeing that life with her would be life without faith and love, he leaves. The last words of the story are: 'He never returned.'[19]

It is a tragedy of misunderstanding and of failure to connect. There is something strangely compulsive about the story because it seems that these two people are doomed not to make contact. They are both able to have a revelation, but it is impossible for them to share it. Conrad may not have been entirely aware of the implications of this story and it may throw an interesting sidelight on his own problems of human contacts.

The story tends in places towards ponderousness and prolixity, but it is packed with remarkably sharp insight and ironical wit. It was a brilliant idea to have looking-glasses in the room where the scene takes place which reflect the caricature and actions of the husband:

> He waved his arm once, and three exact replicas of his face, of his clothes, of his dull severity, of his solemn grief, repeated the wide gesture that in its comprehensive sweep indicated an infinity of moral sweetness . . .[20]

or,

> He caught sight of himself in the pier glass, drawn up to his full height, and with a face so white that his eyes, at the distance, resembled the black cavities in a skull. He saw himself as if about to launch imprecations, with arms uplifted above her bowed head. He was ashamed of that unseemly posture, and put his hands in his pockets hurriedly.[21]

Then Conrad has caught the absurdly inconsequential little actions which a person is apt to perform in the midst of great stress: 'For some reason he felt that he must know the time. He consulted his watch gloomily. Half-past seven.'[22] And there is fine irony in: 'She seemed touched by the emotion of his voice. Her lips quivered a little, and she made one faltering step towards him, putting out her hands in a beseeching gesture, when she perceived, just in time, that being absorbed by the tragedy of his life he had absolutely forgotten her very existence.'[23]

It is interesting to speculate how Conrad might have developed if Garnett had praised 'The Return'; because it was his condemnation of this story far more than of *The Sisters* that radically influenced the course of Conrad's writing. He held to his assertion 'Never more'. He did not again try to present characters or psychological situations primarily through dialogue – with the exception of his dramatizations of certain stories – until almost the end of his life, in *The Arrow of Gold* and the final draft of *The Rescue*.

Even before finishing 'The Return', Conrad was again thinking of *The Rescue*.* Blackwood, delighted by the acquisition of Conrad as a contributor to 'Maga', had asked him whether he had 'anything on the stocks in the form of a serial story'. Conrad had already shown what there was of *The Rescue* to Pawling, and felt committed to Heinemann's for book publication, but he thought that Blackwood might be prepared to run the story serially in 'Maga'. He therefore sent Blackwood Part I and a brief outline of the rest of the story;[24] but he could make no progress with the writing and told Garnett in October: 'I can't get on with *The Rescue*. In all these days I haven't written a line, but there hadn't been a day when I did not wish myself dead. It is too ghastly. I positively don't know what to do. Am I out to the end of my tether? Sometimes I think it must be so.'[25] Hearing nothing from Blackwood, who in fact shortly afterwards turned down the serial as he could not have the book, Conrad returned to Pawling and sent him a 'long epitome' of the story which, he said, 'has brought me to terms with myself'.[26] It does seem to have had a salutary effect, because a little later he was telling Garnett: 'I feel cheerful and have at last made a start with *The Rescue*.'[27] Although Pawling did not offer any money immediately he was so

* Conrad must have changed the title from *The Rescuer* to *The Rescue* at about this time. He headed Part II of the MS. *The Rescue* but it is not known exactly when he did this; the first dated references are in letters from Conrad to Garnett and to Blackwood of 28 August 1897. Henceforth the novel will be referred to as *The Rescue,* its final title.

encouraging that Conrad declared himself completely satisfied,[28] and was able to persevere with *The Rescue*. At the end of the year he told Garnett: 'I am writing *The Rescue*. I am writing! I am harassed with anxieties but the thing comes out!'[29] At Christmas he wrote summing up the year to Aniela Zagórska:

> In all sincerity I may add in earnest that there is in me so much of the Englishman, the sailor and the adventurer, that I do not care to write – even to my nearest and dearest relatives – when things do not go well. This is the reason for my long silence. I do not want to count the months. I prefer to ask you to forget them. We have lived another year. Autant de gagné! Therefore we must wish one another happiness – ce bonheur dont personne ne connait le premier mot – and wish it sincerely with all our hearts; try to forget that man's wishes are seldom fulfilled . . .
>
> I have worked during the whole year. I have finished two volumes [*The Nigger of the 'Narcissus'* and *Tales of Unrest*]. One came out a fortnight ago and the other is ready for the press. Voilà. And while waiting I live in a state of uncertainty. I enjoy a good reputation but no popularity. And as to money I have none, either. Triste. But things are going better at present. That I shall some day attain material success there is no reason to doubt. But that requires time and meanwhile???
>
> The worst is that my health is not good. Les nerfs, les nerfs! Uncertainty torments me. It is very foolish, no doubt – mais que voulez-vous? l'homme est bête. [20 December 1897, *L.L.*, I, p. 217]

And he confessed to Edward Sanderson:

> Life passes and it would pass like a dream were it not that the nerves are stretched like fiddle strings. Something always turns up to give a turn to the screw. Domestic life would be tolerable if – but that soon will be over [presumably an allusion to the prospective baby]. [26 December 1897, *L.L.*, I, p.218]

(2)

The appearance of 'An Outpost of Progress' in *Cosmopolis* in June and July of this year had given rise to one of the most important events in Conrad's personal life. Robert Bontine

Cunninghame Graham wrote an enthusiastic letter about it to Conrad, and this was the start of a life-long friendship between the two men. Of all Conrad's friends Cunninghame Graham was undoubtedly the closest in temperament. He was five years older than Conrad, and had had a life even more adventurous and romantic than Conrad's own. He was an aristocrat descended from King Robert II of Scotland, and was three-quarters Scot and a quarter Spanish with a dash of Italian. He had been brought up on his ancestral Scottish estates, paying occasional visits to Spain. Educated at Harrow and in Brussels, he went at the age of seventeen to try to make his fortune in the Argentine and spent most of the next eight years in various parts of South America, ranching and living among gauchos – he became one of the great horsemen of his day. Among other adventures he was impressed into a revolutionary *partido*, spent some time in a prison, and rode into war-ravaged Paraguay, where the ratio of men to women was said to be one to thirteen. He returned to Britain when he heard that his father, Major Bontine,* was dying, but as the news was premature he set out to travel in France and Spain. When he was riding in Paris his horse began to play up; he nearly knocked over a girl and dismounted to apologize. Thus he met the beautiful and intelligent eighteen-year-old Gabrielle de la Balmondière daughter of a French father and a Spanish mother. This encounter quickly led to an elopement and marriage in England. Six months later they left Britain to make their fortune in Texas.

They failed to make their fortune either in Texas or in Mexico City, where they had gone hoping to sell a load of cotton at a big profit; and he was reduced to giving fencing lessons as Professor Bontini, she to teaching French, painting, and the guitar.

On Major Bontine's death in 1883 they returned to Britain and Cunninghame Graham 'plunged' into politics as

* Under the provisions of an old family entail the eldest son had to bear the surname and arms of Bontine until the death of his father, after which he used the name Cunninghame Graham.

Liberal Member for North-West Lanarkshire, although he held the views of an extreme radical. He was an eloquent, fiery, unorthodox Member and became famed for his retort to the Speaker: 'I never withdraw!' But the highlight of his political career was the 'Bloody Sunday' demonstration in Trafalgar Square in which Hyndman, William Morris, Prince Kropotkin, Mrs Besant, Shaw, and John Burns took part. A policeman knocked him on the head with a truncheon and he spent six weeks in gaol for 'unlawful assembly, assault of the police . . . thereby endangering public peace'.

After losing his seat in Parliament he and Gabrielle went to 'prospect for gold in Spain on the strength of a passage in Pliny's description of ancient Lusitania'. They found no gold. Three years later, in 1897, shortly after first writing to Conrad, Cunninghame Graham set out to ride to the 'forbidden city' of Tarudant in the Atlas Mountains, but was arrested and turned back by a local Caid. This was his second attempt to penetrate into Islam; he had previously tried to reach Fez with William Rothenstein.[30]

As Paul Bloomfield has said, a list of those to whom he dedicated his books epitomizes the variety of his life and interests: his brother Charles, W. H. Hudson, a poacher at Gartmore (one of his Scottish estates), a President of Chile, a horse, a President of the Argentine, his friend A. F. Tschiffely and his two famous horses, Edward Garnett, the piratical Haj Mohammed es Swani el Bahri, Wilfred Scawen Blunt, and the painter Lavery.[31]

Cunninghame Graham is reported to have claimed that 'unless I do not know even a little about myself, I have always felt that my outlook on most things in life has been, and is, Spanish';[32] and he has frequently, almost inevitably, been compared to Don Quixote. This is misleading because he was neither comic nor pathetic. If his outlook really was Spanish it was that of a true *hidalgo* born out of his time. But he was perhaps more like an Elizabethan adventurer, such as Raleigh, and it was appropriate that he should have been chosen by Solomon J. Solomon to sit for a portrait of Raleigh for the House of Commons.

He was slightly built, with rather sloping shoulders, but strong and wiry. From photographs he seems to have been a flamboyantly handsome man with a thin face, sharp, rather prominent nose, striking, almost visionary eyes, a pointed beard, up-curling but not aggressive moustache, and a fine mop of reddish hair.[33] He was always very careful and conscious of his appearance; Shaw, whom he dazzled, called him a dandy, and Tschiffely mentions that he could not pass a mirror without looking at himself; he adds, charmingly, that Cunninghame Graham did this as a kindness to his friends.[34] He clearly enjoyed dressing up and assuming a role, but the important thing is that he was able to do this so convincingly, whether it was a question of becoming a gaucho, a cavalier, or Sheik Mohammed el Fasi.

He was chivalrous, fearless, generous, and had an intelligence that was exuberantly masculine rather than subtle. A militant radical in his political period, he advocated reforms which shocked his contemporaries but now have either been adopted or have so lost their power to arouse interest that they have fallen into an uncontroversial limbo: universal suffrage, abolition of the House of Lords, nationalization of land, free secular education with a free meal, Disestablishment, graduated income tax, and so on.[35] He was anti-imperialist, anti-clerical, and a champion of all those whom he considered the victims of cruelty, hardship, or injustice – especially horses and prostitutes.

It might be wondered what there could be in common between an avowed radical and a man who thought that 'Disestablishment, Land Reform, Universal Brotherhood are but like milestones on the road to ruin' and that social-democratic ideas – 'infernal doctrines born in continental back-slums' – would destroy 'all that is respectable, venerable and holy'.[36]

But these were superficial differences. When explaining to Blackwood why he wanted to dedicate a book to Cunninghame Graham, Conrad said:

I do not dedicate to C. Graham the socialist or to C. Graham the aristocrat (he is both – you know) but to one of the few men I *know* – in the full sense of the word – and knowing cannot but appreciate and respect – abstractedly [*sic*] as human beings. I do not share his political convictions or even all his ideas of art, but we have enough ideas in common to base a strong friendship upon.[37]

There was a close temperamental affinity between the two men. Their outlook was essentially aristocratic. Although Cunninghame Graham's exuberance encouraged him to lead an intensely active political life, whereas Conrad built a protective wall of fatalism round himself, both men had a deep strain of scepticism. Cunninghame Graham championed causes because he was roused to do so, not because he expected them to triumph (if he had he probably would not have bothered). Both were particularly conscious of human stupidity; it was perhaps chiefly exasperation at the obtuseness of the ruling classes that stimulated Cunninghame Graham's radicalism, and when the Labour movement became powerful he was equally scornful of its leaders.[38] Then, despite his hatred of social-democratic ideas, Conrad was a humane and just man who detested the exploitation of human beings as much as did Cunninghame Graham. It is not surprising that Conrad's depiction in 'An Outpost of Progress' of the brutishness of the European 'civilizers' in Africa should have appealed to Cunninghame Graham and have prompted him to write in congratulation. Conrad was delighted with the letter and wrote back:

You've given me a few moments of real, solid excitement. I scuttled about for the signature, – then laid the letter down. I am a prudent man. Very soon it occurred to me that you would hardly go out of your way (in the month of August) to kick an utter stranger. So, I said to myself, 'These, – no doubt, – are halfpence. Let us see.' And, behold! It was real gold, a ducat for a begger, – a treasure for the very poor! You'll ruin yourself: but (I am a white man) what does it matter to me as long as the profit is mine?

And I feel distinctly richer since this morning. I admire so much your vision and your expression that your commendation has for me a very high value, – the very highest! Believe that I appreciate fully the kind impulse that prompted you to write . . .

You did not expect such a *tuile sur la tête* as this in answer to your letter. Well! it's only five pages at the most, and life is long, – and art is so short that no one sees the miserable thing. Most of my life has been spent between sky and water and I live so alone that often I fancy myself clinging stupidly to a derelict planet abandoned by its precious crew. Your voice is not a voice in the wilderness, – it seems to come through the clean emptiness of space. If, under the circumstances, I hail back lustily I know you won't count it to me for a crime. [5 August 1897, *L.L.*, I, pp. 207–8]

Cunninghame Graham replied immediately to this, and Conrad wrote him another long letter on 9 August, in which he said: 'I am both touched and frightened by what you say about being the prophet of my inarticulate and wandering shadow.'[39] The two men were anxious to meet, but the first meeting did not take place until the end of November. Conrad wrote to Garnett: 'Cunninghame Graham writes to ask me to dine with him tonight. I shall do so for I am interested in the man. ... The chiel writes to the papers – you know.'[40]

When *The Nigger of the 'Narcissus'* came out in December[41] Cunninghame Graham wrote in admiration to Conrad. In the same letter he evidently suggested that 'Singleton with an education' was an ideal to aim at. Conrad's pessimistic conservatism was outraged at this and the issue was the start of a good-natured dispute.

Well, yes! everything is possible, and most things come to pass (when you don't want them). However I think Singleton with an education is impossible. But first of all, – what education? If it is the knowledge of how to live, my man essentially possessed it. He was in perfect accord with his life . . .

Would you seriously, of malice prepense, cultivate in that unconscious man the power to think? Then he would become conscious, – and much smaller, – and very unhappy. Now he is simple and great like an elemental force. Nothing can touch him but the curse of decay, – the eternal decree that will extinguish the sun, the stars, one by one, and in another instant shall spread a frozen darkness over the whole universe. Nothing else can touch him, – he does not think.

Would you seriously wish to tell such a man 'Know thyself!

Understand that you are nothing, less than a shadow, more insignificant than a drop of water in the ocean, more fleeting than the illusion of a dream?' Would you? [14 December 1897, *L.L.*, I, pp. 214–15]

Six days later Conrad wrote in answer to another letter from Cunninghame Graham:

Your letter reached me just when I was preparing to write to you. What I said in my incoherent missive of last week, was not for the purpose of arguing really. I did not seek controversy with you, – for this reason: I think that we do agree. If I've read you aright (and I have been reading you for some years now) you are a most hopeless idealist, – your aspirations are irrealisable. You want from men faith, honour, fidelity to truth in themselves and others. You want them to have all this, to show it every day, to make out of these words their rules of life. The respectable classes which suspect you of such pernicious longings lock you up and would just as soon have you shot, – because your personality counts and you cannot deny that you are a dangerous man. What makes you dangerous is your unwarrantable belief that your desire may be realised. This is the only point of difference between us. I do not believe. And if I desire the very same things no one cares. Consequently I am not likely to be locked up or shot. There is another difference, – this time to your manifest advantage.

There is a, – let us say, – a machine. It evolved itself (I am severely scientific) out of a chaos of scraps of iron and behold! – it knits. I am horrified at the horrible work and stand appalled. I feel it ought to embroider, – but it goes on knitting. You come and say: 'This is all right: It's only a question of the right kind of oil. Let us use this, – for instance, – celestial oil and the machine will embroider a most beautiful design in purple and gold.' Will it? Alas, no! You cannot by any special lubrication make embroidery with a knitting machine. And the most withering thought is that the infamous thing has made itself: made itself without thought, without conscience, without foresight, without eyes, without heart. It is tragic accident, – and it has happened. You can't interfere with it. The last drop of bitterness is in the suspicion that you can't even smash it. In virtue of that truth one and immortal which lurks in the force that made it spring into existence it is what it is, – and it is indestructible!

It knits us in and it knits us out. It has knitted time, space, pain, death, corruption, despair and all the illusions, – and nothing matters. I'll admit however that to look at the remoreseless process is sometimes amusing. [20 December 1897, *L.L.*, I., pp. 215–16]

A few days later Conrad summed up their relationship to Edward Sanderson:

I went up to town at the beginning of this month to dine with Cunninghame Graham on his return from the captivity amongst the Moors. We had exchanged four or five letters before. He is a most interesting man, not at all bigoted in his socialistic-republican ideas, which I treated to his face with a philosophic contempt. We got on very well. Of course, as is often the case, the groundwork of his ideas is, I may say, intensely aristocratic [this recalls Bobrowski's comments on the views of Conrad's father]. We talked in two languages. I like him, – and I verily believe he likes me. [26 December 1897, *L.L.*, I, p. 219]

And he told Garnett: 'I am in *intimate* correspondence with him. He writes to me every week once or even twice. He is struck.'[42]

A letter which Conrad wrote to Cunninghame Graham just over a year later illustrates their relationship particularly well and is also the most intimate avowal of his political belief, above all in respect of Poland, that Conrad made:

As to the peace meeting. If you want me to come I want still more to hear you. But, – I am not a peace man, not a democrat (I don't know what the word means really), and if I come, I shall go into the body of the hall. I want to hear you, – just as I want always to read you. I can't be an accomplice after or before the fact to any sort of fraternity that includes the westerners [?] whom I so dislike. The platform! Y pensez-vous? Il y aura des Russes. Impossible! I cannot admit the idea of fraternity, not so much because I believe it impracticable, but because its propaganda (the only thing really tangible about it) tends to weaken the national sentiment, the preservation of which is my concern. When I was in Poland five years ago and managed to get in contact with the youth of the University in Warsaw I preached at them and abused them for their social democratic tendencies. L'idée démocratique est un très beau phantome [*sic*], and to run after it may be fine sport, but I confess I do not see what evils it is destined to remedy. It confers distinction on Messieurs Jaurès, Liebknecht & Co. and your adhesion confers distinction upon it. International fraternity may be an object to strive for, and, in sober truth, since it has your support I will try to think it serious, but that illusion imposes by its size alone. Franchement, what would you think of an attempt to promote fraternity amongst people living in the same street, I don't even mention two neighbouring streets? Two ends of the same street.

There is already as much fraternity as there can be, – and that's very little and that very little is no good. What does fraternity mean? Abnegation, – self-sacrifice means something. Fraternity means nothing unless the Cain-Abel business. That's your true fraternity. Assez ...

Il faut un principe défini. Si l'idée nationale apporte la souffrance et son service donne la mort, ça vaut toujours mieux que de servir les ombres d'une éloquence qui est morte, justement parce qu'elle n'a pas de corps. Croyez-moi si je vous dis que ces questions-là sont pour moi très sérieuses, – beaucoup plus que pour Messieurs Jaurès, Liebknecht et Cie. Vous, – vous êtes essentiellement un frondeur. Cela vous est permis. Ce sont les nobles qui ont fait la Fronde, du reste. Moi, je regarde l'avenir du fond d'un passé très noir et je trouve que rien ne m'est permis hormis la fidélité à une cause absolument perdue, à une idée sans avenir.

Aussi, souvent, je n'y pense pas. Tout disparaît. Il ne reste que la vérité, – une ombre sinistre et fuyante dont il est impossible de fixer l'image. Je ne regrette rien, – je n'espère rien, car je m'aperçois que ni le regret ni l'espérance ne signifient rien à ma personnalité. C'est un égoisme rationel et féroce que j'exerce envers moi-même. Je me repose là-dedans. Puis, la pensée revient. La vie recommence, les regrets, les souvenirs et un désespoir plus sombre que la nuit.

Je ne sais pas pourquoi je vous dis tout cela aujourd'hui. C'est que je ne veux pas que vous me croyiez indifférent. Je ne suis pas indifférent à ce qui vous intéresse. Seulement mon interêt est ailleurs, ma pensée suit une autre route, mon coeur désire autre chose, mon âme souffre d'une autre espèce d'impuissance. Comprenez-vous? Vous qui dévouez votre enthousiasme et vos talents à la cause de l'humanité, vous comprendrez sans doute pourquoi je dois, – j'ai besoin, – de garder ma pensée intacte comme dernier hommage de fidélité à une cause qui est perdue. C'est tout ce que je puis faire. J'ai jeté ma vie à tous les vents du ciel, mais j'ai gardé ma pensée. C'est peu de chose, – c'est tout, ce n'est rien, – c'est la vie même. [8 February 1899, *L.L.*, I, pp. 268–70]

Cunninghame Graham had published little of importance when he and Conrad first met, but thenceforth they sent one another their books. Conrad always expressed admiration for what Cunninghame Graham wrote (as he did for the writing of his other friends), and of one of the stories he said: 'As to the *Saga* it confirms me in my conviction that you have a fiendish gift for showing the futility, the ghastly, jocular futility of life. Et c'est très fin, – très fin. C'est finement vu et c'est exprimé avec finesse, presque à mots couverts, avec de l'esprit dans chaque phrase.'[43]

Cunninghame Graham's approach to writing was very different from Conrad's. His style was personal, virile, and unconcerned; he was never primarily a writer, let alone an artist. Most of his work is in the borderland between fiction and non-fiction and it may be that in conversation he encouraged Conrad to try his hand in that sphere. It may not be a coincidence that soon after meeting Cunninghame Graham, Conrad started 'Youth', which was one of the stories most closely based on his own experiences, that he then went on to another which drew heavily on personal experience, 'Heart of Darkness', and that for these two as well as for *Lord Jim* he used, for the first time, Marlow, as a device to give actuality and authenticity to the events described.

(3)

Conrad also formed another important, though tragically short-lived, friendship at this time, with Stephen Crane, the brilliant young American author of *The Red Badge of Courage*, who had come to settle in England in the summer of 1897.[44] *The Red Badge* had been published in Britain at the end of 1895 and had been acclaimed by the critics; the Americans, whose initial reaction to the book had been lukewarm, were influenced by the British praise, and Crane then found himself one of the most boomed authors of the day.[45]

Serialization of Conrad's *Nigger* had started in the August number of the *New Review*. It is not surprising that Crane became very enthusiastic about the tale and was keen to meet its author. Heinemann had published *The Red Badge* and were about to publish *The Nigger*; Crane therefore got Pawling to arrange a meeting between Conrad and himself. The three men had lunch together in October or November, Conrad telling Garnett the day before: 'I *do* admire him [Crane]. I shan't have to pretend.'[46] According to Conrad the three of them sat over lunch until four o'clock, when Pawling was forced to leave the other two. Conrad and Crane then wandered, talking, through London, oblivious of time and place; they had dinner together and did not part until late in the evening.[47] What they found in common to talk about can only, for the most part, be guessed at; many years later Conrad recalled that at one point Crane made him discourse at length on Balzac and the 'Comédie Humaine'.

Although he had not had such wide or varied experience as Conrad (he was only twenty-six at the time), Crane had led a far from conventional or uneventful life. He was the son of a Methodist clergyman and his mother was the daughter of a Methodist clergyman, but a *nostalgie de la boue* and *de la guerre* asserted itself quite early. As a young man he gravitated into the world of journalism; wallowed in New York's Bowery (subsequently he proclaimed that he got his 'artistic education on the Bowery'); wrote some short stories, *Maggie, a Girl of the Streets*, then *The Red Badge of Courage*, which was published when he was a month short of twenty-four. Next year he went to Florida to report the Cuban insurrection against the Spanish. In Jacksonville he joined a tug carrying arms to the Cubans which foundered during the voyage; the experience of getting to shore in a lifeboat formed the basis of one of his most admired short stories, 'The Open Boat'. Immediately after this he dashed off to report another war, between Greece and Turkey, for the New York *Journal*. In Greece he went around with Cora Stewart, whom he had picked up in Jacksonville; she was the wife of a Briton, Captain Donald Stewart, and was also reporting the war for the *Journal*. The war quickly fizzled out and Crane and Cora came to England; they lived together until Crane died, but apparently never married because Captain Stewart refused to agree to a divorce.

After his meeting with Crane, Conrad wrote inviting him to stay at Ivy Walls and said:

> The world looks different to me now, since our long powwow. It was good. The memory of it is good. And now and then (human nature *is* a vile thing) I ask myself whether you meant half of what you said! You must forgive me. The mistrust is not of you – it is of myself. [16 November 1897][48]

He need not have doubted Crane's sincerity. Crane seems quickly to have developed a hero-worship of Conrad; James Huneker has said that Crane used to speak of him 'as if he were the B.V.M.'[49] It is clear also that Conrad became very fond of Crane.

After a visit of Crane's to Ivy Walls, Conrad wrote to Garnett: 'I had Crane here last Sunday. We talked and smoked half the night. He is strangely hopeless about himself. I like him.'[50] Although neither Conrad nor he himself fully realized it Crane had cause to be hopeless because the tuberculosis which was to kill him two-and-a-half years later was already undermining his health. During the remaining years of Crane's life the two men kept in close touch and visited each other quite frequently.

Crane admired Conrad's work, or at least *The Nigger*, as much as he did Conrad. He told his friend Harold Frederic: 'You and I and Kipling couldn't have written *The Nigger*'[51] and to another person described the book as 'a crackerjack'.[52] Conrad on the other hand was well aware of the limitations of Crane's work. He told Garnett:

> His eye is very individual and his expression satisfies me artistically. He certainly is *the* impressionist and his temperament is curiously unique. His thought is concise, connected, never very deep – yet often startling. He is *the only* impressionist and *only* an impressionist. . . . I could not explain why he disappoints me – why

my enthusiasm withers as soon as I close the book. While one reads, of course he is not to be questioned. He is the master of his reader to the very last line – then – apparently for no reason at all – he seems to let go his hold.[53]

And to Cunninghame Graham he said: 'The man sees the outside of many things and the inside of some.'[54]

As both *The Red Badge* and *The Nigger* had attempted to portray realistically the behaviour of individuals in a corporate setting it was inevitable that the two books, coming so closely one upon the other, should have been compared. For instance, W. L. Courtney wrote in the *Daily Telegraph*:

Mr Joseph Conrad has chosen Mr Stephen Crane for his example, and has determined to do for the sea and the sailor what his predecessor had done for war and warriors. The style, though a good deal better than Mr Crane's, has the same jerky and spasmodic quality; while a spirit of faithful and minute description – even to the verge of the wearisome – is common to both.[55]

This must have galled Conrad because he was undoubtedly convinced that *The Nigger* was a far more substantial piece of work than *The Red Badge*. Crane barely scratched the surface of his characters, and there is only one really great passage in *The Red Badge*: the last moments of Jim Conklin, which perhaps brings the mystery of death closer than any other piece of writing. The talents of the two men were so different that it is difficult to see in what way Crane could have influenced Conrad; but it is quite possible that Conrad's reading of *The Red Badge* gave him the impetus to undertake a similar subject.

The Nigger of the 'Narcissus' had come out in December of 1897 and been praised by almost all the critics. Conrad got most pleasure from a review in the *Pall Mall Magazine*[56] by Quiller-Couch, who also wrote to him personally in praise of the book.[57] The *Spectator* declared: 'Mr Conrad is a writer of genius; but his choice of themes, and the uncompromising nature of his methods, debar him from attaining a wide popularity.'[58] That was the trouble; he could not keep himself and his family on the reviewers' praise. In the new year he told Garnett 'that I must borrow money somewhere is very evident' and propounded to him a scheme for mortgaging *The Rescue* to Pawling.[59] He also got Cunninghame Graham to try to persuade Frank Harris to serialize it in the *Saturday Review*.[60] In a letter to Cunninghame Graham discussing the proposal he launched into a gloomy homily on the fate of mankind:

> 'Put the tongue out,' why not? One ought to really. And the machine will run on all the same. The question is whether the fatigue of the muscular exertion is worth the transient pleasure of indulged scorn. On the other hand one may ask whether scorn, love, or hate are justified in the face of such shadowy illusions . . .
>
> Life knows us not and we do not know life, – we don't know even our own thoughts. Half the words we use have no meaning whatever and of the other half each man understands each word after the fashion of his own folly and conceit. Faith is a myth and beliefs shift like mists on the shore: thoughts vanish: words, once pronounced, die: and the memory of yesterday is as shadowy as the hope of to-morrow, – only the string of my platitudes seems to have no end. As our peasants say: 'Pray, brother, forgive me for the love of God.' And we don't know what forgiveness is, nor what is love, nor where God is. Assez!

Then in a P.S. he wrote:

> This letter misses this morning's post because an infant of male persuasion arrived and made such a row that I could not hear the postman's whistle. It's a fine commentary upon this letter. But salvation lies in being illogical. Still I feel remorse. [10 p.m., 14 January 1898, *L.L.* I, pp. 223–3]

The relaxation of tension which the birth of Borys should have produced seems to have done little to dispel the depression which Conrad was feeling at this time, and, probably as a delayed result of the nervous strain, he had an attack of gout.[61]

At this point, in order to make some money, he took up writing for the press; he wrote an article on Alphonse Daudet for *Outlook*[62] and, for the *Academy*, a review[63] of a book of Malayan impressions by Hugh Clifford, the

Resident of Pahang, which called forth an appreciative letter from the author and was the start of another life-long friendship.

In February[64] the whole Conrad family went off to stay with the Cranes at Ravensbrook, near Oxted in Surrey. Jessie's description of the journey is funny enough to quote whether it is strictly true or not:

> The day arrived, and according to plan, we met Joseph Conrad at Charing Cross station, where he had preceded us. I think I was justly proud of my young son's travelling outfit, and expected his father to express his approval when he saw him. Joseph Conrad approached to within speaking distance and laid down the law in a manner that admitted of no appeal. He had taken our tickets, first class, and intended travelling in the same carriage, but – here he became most emphatic – on no account were we to give any indication that he belonged to our little party. I was rather hurt for I had not then the experience of later years. Soberly we installed ourselves in that railway carriage, and, in due course, he also entered and seated himself in a far corner, ostentatiously concealing himself behind his newspaper and completely ignoring his family. My lips quivered: then I could not forbear a smile. The baby whimpered and refused to be comforted. I caught a glance of warning directed at me from over the top of the paper. All my efforts to soothe the infant proved unavailing, and the whole carriage re-echoed with his lusty howls. The paper was flung aside and from all sides came murmurs of consternation and sympathy for him – the only man; the stranger in the carriage. No less than four other occupants, all ladies, offered suggestions as to the cause of the yells. Then the whole carriage was convulsed with suppressed merriment when my young sister turned to Joseph Conrad and, forgetting his injunction, demanded that he should reach down the case that contained the baby's bottle from the rack above his head.[65]

It is not surprising that Conrad told Garnett: 'I hate babies.'[66]

According to Jessie, Garnett came over while the Conrads were staying at Ravensbrook, and made the baby cry, peering at him through his glasses.[67] Garnett gives a description of Conrad and Crane together, based partly on this visit:

> Conrad's moods of gay tenderness could be quite seductive. On

the few occasions I saw him with Stephen Crane he was delightfully sunny, and bantered 'poor Steve' in the gentlest, most affectionate style, while the latter sat silent, Indian-like, turning enquiring eyes under his chiselled brow, now and then jumping up suddenly and confiding some new project with intensely electric feeling. At one of these sittings Crane passionately appealed to me to support his idea that Conrad should collaborate with him in a play on the theme of a ship wrecked on an island. I knew it was hopelessly unworkable this plan, but Crane's brilliant visualisation of the scenes was so strong and infectious that I had not the heart to declare my own opinion. And Conrad's sceptical answers were couched in the tenderest, most reluctant tone. I can still hear the shades of Crane's poignant friendliness in his cry 'Joseph!' and Conrad's delight in Crane's personality glowed in the shining warmth of his brown eyes.[68]

The proposal to collaborate on a play is borne out by a letter of Conrad's to Sanderson: 'Stephen Crane is worrying me to write a play with him. He won't believe me when I swear by all the gods and all the muses that I have no dramatic gift. Probably something will be attempted but I would bet nothing shall be done.'[69]

It appears that Conrad was more tempted by the idea of collaborating on a play with Crane than Garnett supposed, because there is a letter from him to Crane written with a mixture of polite humility and hope:

I am very curious to know your idea; but I feel somehow that collaborating with you would be either cheating or deceiving you. In any case disappointing you. I have no dramatic gift . . .

But I want to know! Your idea is good – I am certain. Perhaps you, yourself, don't know how good it is. I ask you as a friend's favour to let me have a sketch of it when you have the time and in a moment of inclination. I shall – if you allow me – write you *all* I think of it, about it, around it. Then you shall see how worthless I would be to you. But if by chance such was not your deliberate opinion – if you should really, honestly artistically think I could be of some use – then my dear Crane I would be only too glad to work by your side and with your lead.[70]

However, nothing direct came of this project. According to Conrad the play was to be called 'The Predecessor' and the action 'would have been frankly melodramatic'. He added that he later used 'the shadow of the primary idea' of 'The Predecessor' in a short story, 'The Planter of Malata'.[71]

Back from the Cranes, Conrad resumed his struggle with *The Rescue* and was at least temporarily relieved from his most pressing worry by the news that Pawling had sold the serial rights to McClure of New York for £250, of which £100 was to be paid on account.[72] But his distaste for the book increased and he poured out his exasperation in a letter to Garnett:

I am ashamed of myself. I ought to have written to you before, but the fact is I have not written anything at all. When I received your letter together with part II[d] of *The Rescue* I was in bed – this beastly nervous trouble. Since then I've been better but have been unable to write. I sit down religiously every morning. I sit down for eight hours every day – and the sitting down is all. In the course of that working day of eight hours I write three sentences which I erase before leaving the table in despair. There's not a single word to send you. Not one! And time passes – and McClure waits – not to speak of Eternity for which I don't care a damn. Of McClure however I am afraid.

I ask myself sometimes whether I am bewitched, whether I am the victim of an evil eye? But there is no 'jettature' in England – is there? I assure you – speaking soberly and on my word of honour – that sometimes it takes all my resolution and power of self-control to refrain from butting my head against the wall. I want to howl and foam at the mouth but I daren't do it for fear of waking the baby and alarming my wife. It's no joking matter. After such crises of despair I doze for hours still half conscious that there is that story I am unable to write. Then I wake up, try again – and at last go to bed completely done-up. So the days pass and nothing is done. At night I sleep. In the morning I get up with the horror of that powerlessness I must face through a day of vain efforts.

In these circumstances you imagine I feel not much inclination to write letters. As a matter of fact I had a great difficulty in writing the most commonplace note. I seem to have lost all *sense* of style and yet I am haunted, mercilessly haunted by the *necessity* of style. And that story I can't write weaves itself into all I see, into all I speak, into all I think, into the lines of every book I try to read. I haven't read for days. You know how bad it is when one *feels* one's liver, or lungs. Well I feel my brain. I am distinctly conscious of the contents of my head. My story is there in a fluid – in an evading shape. I can't get hold of it. It is all there – to bursting, yet I can't get hold of it no more than you can grasp a handful of water.

There! I've told you all and feel better. While I write this I am amazed to see that I can write. It looks as though the spell were broken but I hasten, I hasten lest it should in five minutes or in half an hour be laid again. [29 March (1898)]

The spell cannot have remained broken for long. Conrad presumably battled with *The Rescue* for a few more weeks without making any real progress; then perhaps the idea of using a narrator to tell his stories occurred to him as a means of overcoming his difficulties with expression. At all events he abandoned *The Rescue* and Marlow appeared on the scene.

[VIII]

Enter Marlow

THE first indication that Conrad was escaping from the impasse into which *The Rescue* had led him comes in a letter which he wrote to Garnett at the end of May or beginning of June 1898:

> I've sold (I think) the sea thing to Blackwood for £35 (13,000 words). Meldrum thinks there's no doubt – but still Blackwood must see it himself. McClure has been the pink of perfection. . . . He is anxious to have a book of short tales. I think 'Jim' (20,000) 'Youth' (13,000) 'A Seaman' (5,000) 'Dynamite' (5,000) and another story of say 15,000 would make a volume for Blackwood here and for McClure there.[1]

'Youth' appears already to have been written by then[2] and 'Jim' just to have been started;[3] 'Dynamite' was probably the story that Conrad began to write some years later and then developed into *Chance*;[4] and although he several times mentioned 'A Seaman' in letters to Blackwood this story cannot be identified.

On the title-page Conrad described 'Youth' as 'a Narrative', and it is in fact a recreation of an episode of his life at sea.[5] But it is also more than a narrative. Marlow describes the voyage of the *Judea* as one of 'those voyages that seem ordered for the illustration of life, that might stand for a symbol of existence',[6] and 'Youth' is an evocation of a mood of exhilaration, in which experience is grasped for the sake of the pleasure that it gives; it is a rhapsody on the glamour of youth and of the East. The refrain of the joy of youth constantly recurs: 'O youth! The strength of it, the faith of it, the imagination of it!'[7] 'Oh, the glamour of youth! Oh, the fire of it, more dazzling than the flames of the burning ship . . .'[8] 'Youth! All youth! The silly, charming, beautiful youth.'[9] And the East: 'Bankok! I thrilled.'[10] 'To Bankok! Magic name, blessed name. Mesopotamia wasn't a patch on it.'[11] Then the climax, when Marlow's boat is approaching land, containing the experience as well as the idea:

> And this is how I see the East. I have seen its secret places and looked into its very soul; but now I see it always from a small boat, a high outline of mountains, blue and afar in the morning; like faint mist at noon; a jagged wall of purple at sunset. I have the feel of the oar in my hand, the vision of a scorching blue sea in my eyes. And I see a bay, a wide bay, smooth as glass and polished like ice, shimmering in the dark. A red light burns far off upon the gloom of the land, and the night is soft and warm. We drag at the oars with aching arms, and suddenly a puff of wind, a puff faint and tepid and laden with strange odours of blossoms, or aromatic wood, comes out of the still night – the first sigh of the East on my face. That I can never forget. It was impalpable and enslaving, like a charm, like a whispered promise of mysterious delight.[12]

Then both refrains are taken up and united at the end:

> For me all the East is contained in that vision of my youth. It is all in that moment when I opened my young eyes on it. I came upon it from a tussle with the sea – and I was young – and I saw it looking at me. And this is all that is left of it! Only a moment; a moment of strength, of romance, of glamour – of youth! A flick of sunshine upon a strange shore, the time to remember, the time for a sigh, and – good-bye! – Night – Good-bye – ![13]

Although it is Conrad's most consistently cheerful story, even 'Youth' has a taste of ashes: 'Oh, the glamour of youth! Oh, the fire of it, more dazzling than the flames of the burning ship, throwing a magic light on the wide earth, leaping audaciously to the sky, presently to be quenched by time, more cruel, more pitiless, more bitter than the sea – and like the flames of the burning ship surrounded by an impenetrable night.'[14] Not only is 'Youth' an evocation, it is a recollection of a mood, of an attitude that cannot be recaptured; thus the narrative ends on a note of nostalgia and melancholy:

> And we all nodded at him . . . our weary eyes looking still, looking always, looking anxiously for something out of life, that while it is expected is already gone – has passed unseen, in a sigh, in a flash

– together with the youth, with the strength, with the romance of illusions.[15]

Conrad's method is to collect together a group of people: 'We were sitting round a mahogany table that reflected the bottle, the claret glasses, and our faces as we leaned on our elbows. There was a director of companies, an accountant, a lawyer, Marlow, and myself.'[16] Then: 'Marlow (at least I think that is how he spelt his name) told the story, or rather the chronicle, of a voyage.'[17] This recalls a similar technique in Turgenev's *First Love* or Gobineau's *Les Pléiades.* The story is then set forth in Marlow's words by the narrator. It is given actuality by periodic references to the setting; there is the often repeated 'pass the bottle' – 'I never saw her again – Pass the bottle'[18] – the chatty asides – 'What could you expect? She was tired – that old ship. Her youth was where mine is – where yours is – you fellows who listen to this yarn'[19] – and the deliberately casual colloquial style of 'She belonged to a man Wilmer, Wilcox – some name like that.'[20] And then at times Marlow will stand back and reflect on the action which he is describing: 'There was a completeness in it, something solid like a principle, and masterful like an instinct – a disclosure of something secret – of that hidden something, that gift of good or evil that makes racial difference, that shapes the fate of nations.'[21]

This was the first time that Conrad used the device of Marlow and, as 'Youth' was aiming at a straightforward effect, Marlow's role was simple: to give the tone of the narrative. But Conrad must have felt at ease with the style which the use of Marlow allowed him and must have realized the advantage of having a character who could both tell and comment upon the story because he again used Marlow in his next two stories, and gave him an increasingly complex role.

(2)

As Conrad had told Garnett, he was thinking of a volume of short stories for Blackwood and McClure. Thus after finishing 'Youth' he started 'Jim, a Sketch', which he envisaged as another short story,[22] but laid it aside after a few thousand words and went apprehensively back to *The Rescue*.[23] He felt morally bound to do so because of the money which McClure had already paid him, on the understanding that the book would be finished in July.[24] He managed to get some more written but without feeling that he had made any progress. He told Garnett, 'I am writing hopelessly – but still I am writing. How I feel I cannot express. Pages accumulate and the story stands still. I feel suicidal.'[25] His lack of progress was dragging him more and more deeply into a financial bog. On top of his other commitments he borrowed in August £20 from Meldrum as a sort of unofficial advance on *Jim* (to be repaid when Blackwood paid the actual advance) and said that he thought September would be quite safe for serialization of the story to begin. He wrote pathetically:

> I *never mean* to be slow. The stuff comes out at its own rate. I am always ready to put it down; nothing would induce me to lay down my pen if I *feel* a sentence – or even a word ready to my hand. The trouble is that too often – alas! – I've to wait for the sentence – for the word.
>
> What wonder then that during the long blank hours the doubt creeps into the mind and I ask myself whether I am fitted for that work. The worst is that while I am thus powerless to produce my imagination is extremely active: whole paragraphs, whole pages, whole chapters pass through my mind. Everything is there: descriptions, dialogue, reflexion – everything – everything but the belief, the conviction, the only thing needed to make me put pen to paper. I've thought out a volume in a day till I felt sick in mind and heart and gone to bed, completely done up, without having written a line. The effort I put out should give birth to Masterpieces as big As Mountains – and it brings forth a ridiculous mouse now and then.
>
> Therefore I must sell my mice as dear as I can since I must live; that's why I beg you very earnestly to arrange matters so as not to give McClure any excuse for losing My American Serial rights of *Jim*. It looks as if I were very mercenary but God knows, it is not so. I am impatient of material anxieties and they frighten me too because I feel how mysteriously independent of myself is my power

of expression. It is there – I believe – and some thought, and a little insight. All this is there; but I am not as the workmen who can take up and lay down their tools. I am, so to speak, only the agent of an unreliable master. [10 August 1898]

In view of his difficulties it is not surprising that Conrad should have made a serious attempt to get to sea again. At the beginning of the year he had written nostalgically to Cunninghame Graham:

Last night a heavy gale was blowing and I lay awake thinking that I would give ever so much (the most flattering criticism) for being at sea, the soul of some patient faithful ship standing up to it, under lower top-sails and no land anywhere within a thousand miles. Wouldn't I jump at a command, if some literary shipowner suddenly offered it to me! [31 January 1898, *L.L.*, I, p.227]

Cunninghame Graham must have volunteered to help and have given him an introduction to Sir Francis Evans of the Union Line. On 19 July he told Cunninghame Graham:

I've seen Sir Francis Evans this morning. . . . It is of course impossible to place me in the Union Line, – I said I did not even dream of such a thing but explained that I thought he might have some tramp or good collier. The Company, he said, owns no tramp or colliers, but he might hear of something of the kind and in such a case would let me know . . .

Something may come of it. In any case many thanks. Since you have begun that trouble yourself I feel less compunction in asking you to keep it up when an opportunity offers. Now some shadow of possibility to go to sea has been thus presented to me I am almost frantic with the longing to get away. Absurd![26]

Later in the month he asked Cunninghame Graham to put in a word for him to Sir Donald Currie of the Castle Line. Currie seems to have been no direct help,[27] and in September Conrad went to Glasgow, where he did a round of the shipowners. He evidently enjoyed himself there and was entertained by Glasgow literary society.* There was no

* See letter to Garnett of 29 September 1898. Also, account given by Neil Munro, in George T. Keating's *Conrad Memorial Library*, pp. 288–91. In

promise of a command although he wrote to Garnett on his return:

> I got back today. Nothing decisive happened in Glasgow, my impression however is that a command will come out of it sooner or later – most likely later, when the pressing need is past and I had found my way on shore. I do not regret having gone . . .
>
> I feel less hopeless about things and particularly about the damned thing called *The Rescue* . . . [29 September 1898]

But when he wrote to Cunninghame Graham a month later, his hopes of a command had receded:

> I had a most enjoyable trip to Glasgow. I saw Neil Munro and heaps of shipowners, and that's all I can say. The fact is from novel writing to skippering *il y a trop de tirage.* This confounded literature has ruined me entirely. There is a time in the affairs of men when the tide of folly taken at the flood sweeps them to destruction. *La mer monte, cher ami; la mer monte* and the phenomenon is not worth a thought. [9 November 1898, *L.L.*, I, p. 253]

There were no more developments and thus Conrad's last attempt to get to sea as a merchant seaman fizzled out.

It was in this autumn that the most important event in Conrad's literary career occurred. At the beginning of September the Conrads went to stay with the Garnetts at Limpsfield in Surrey. There they met Ford Hueffer* and his wife Elsie, who had recently taken a small cottage near the Garnetts and were busy practising the simple life – growing potatoes and lettuces.[28]

Hueffer was then twenty-four and had published three delightful fairy tales, a volume of poetry, a talented but

---

his *Don Roberto* (p. 331), A. F. Tschiffely, without quoting a source, says that Conrad stayed with Cunninghame Graham on this visit to Scotland and that he, wishing to preserve Conrad wholly for writing, asked the shipowners not to give him a command. But Cunninghame Graham was not even in Scotland at the time and anyhow it is most unlikely that he would have behaved so double-facedly to Conrad.

* His name on his birth certificate is Ford Hermann Hueffer, but he progressively eliminated the German elements and pre-raphaelitized his name, finishing up as Ford Madox Ford.

callow and unexceptional novel called *The Shifting of the Fire*, and a weighty biography of his maternal grandfather, Ford Madox Brown. His father, Dr Franz Hueffer, was the son of a German banker and became a distinguished musical critic, a contributor to *The Times* and *Fortnightly Review*. He had published *The Troubadours; a History of Provençal Life and Literature in the Middle Ages*, and was one of the most enthusiastic pioneers of Wagner in England.[29] Hueffer's mother was Catherine Madox Brown, daughter of the painter and sister-in-law of William Michael Rossetti. Dr Hueffer died in 1889 and his wife took the children to live with her father in St Edmund's Terrace, Regent's Park, almost next door to Mr and Mrs William Michael Rossetti.[30] Thus 'Fordy', as he was called, grew up against a background of pre-Raphaelites and other famous Victorian artists and writers; his first fairy tale, *The Brown Owl*, published when he was eighteen, has two illustrations by Madox Brown, and his second, *The Queen who Flew*, has a frontispiece by Burne-Jones.

He had also had an unconventional and cosmopolitan education, first at an advanced school called Praetoria House and later in Paris.[31]

In 1894, when he was twenty, he had eloped with and married Elsie Martindale, the seventeen-year-old daughter of Dr William Martindale, colleague of Lord Lister and compiler of the *Extra Pharmacopoeia*.

H. G. Wells, who knew Hueffer at the time of his collaboration with Conrad, describes him as:

> a long blond with a drawling manner . . . and oddly resembling George Moore the novelist in pose and person. What he is really or if he is really, nobody knows now and he least of all; he has become a great system of assumed personas and dramatised selves. His brain is an exceptionally good one and when first he came along, he had cast himself for the rôle of a very gifted scion of the Pre-Raphaelite stem, given over to artistic purposes and a little undecided between music, poetry, criticism, The Novel, Thoreau-istic horticulture and the simple appreciation of life.[32]

One of the results of the Conrads' meeting with Hueffer at

Limpsfield was the idea that they should rent from him Pent Farm, a small and old farmhouse embedded in gentle Kentish hills near Aldington. The other was Conrad's suggestion that he and Hueffer should collaborate in the writing of a novel. The Conrad-Hueffer relationship has produced more misleading and mistaken statements than any other episode in Conrad's life. The first point in question has been from whom the suggestion for collaboration came. Wells asserted that it came from Hueffer.[33] Hueffer denied this but his own version was so confused, romantic, and contradictory that it is difficult to sort out truth from fiction. In his impressions of Conrad,[34] published just after Conrad's death, and in one of his several autobiographical volumes Hueffer claimed that when he had returned to the Pent after the Limpsfield meeting a letter arrived unexpectedly from Conrad in which he asked to be allowed to collaborate in the novel that Hueffer was then writing:

> It was the novel about Aaron Smith. I must have told him the plot when he came to see me at Limpsfield. I had forgotten the fact and his letter to me making the proposition seemed to come to me out of a clear sky. I can remember to this day its aspect and how I read it in bed at the Pent with the robin that always accompanied the morning tray up the stairs, sitting on a comb on the dressing table.*

Hueffer says that he replied suggesting that Conrad had better visit him at the Pent and see what he had let himself in for. He then gives a largely apocryphal account of what happened during the visit:

* *Return to Yesterday*, 1931, p. 189. Although all Conrad's letters to Hueffer written at this time seem to have survived there is none which contains such a proposal. One dated 'Thursday' and presumably written on the Thursday before Conrad left for the Pent has a cryptic passage which might allude to collaboration:

'There are other interests – not mentioned here. No room. They are big – big – . The fact is I would be glad of a quiet half hour with you. I have a word for your ear. Hist – Mystery – Silence! "Codlins your friend – not Short"!'

But Conrad's letter to Henley indicates that the matter must have been discussed before this.

Conrad confessed to the writer that previous to suggesting a collaboration he had consulted a number of men of letters as to its advisability. He said that he had put before them his difficulties with the language, the slowness with which he wrote and the increased fluency that he might acquire in the process of going minutely into words with an acknowledged master of English.... He stated succinctly and carefully that he had said to Henley ... 'Look here. I write with such difficulty: my intimate, automatic less expressed thoughts are in Polish; when I express myself with care I do it in French. When I write I think in French and then translate the words of my thoughts into English. This is an impossible process for one desiring to make a living by writing in the English language – .' And Henley, according to Conrad on that evening, had said: 'Why don't you ask H. to collaborate with you? He is the finest stylist in the English language of to-day – ' ...

Henley obviously had said nothing of the sort. Indeed as the writer has elsewhere related, on the occasion of a verbal duel that he had later with Henley that violent mouthed personality remarked to him: 'Who the Hell are you? I never even heard your name!' or words to that effect.[35]

Conrad remained silent about the origins of the collaboration but there are two letters from him which show conclusively that it was he who made the suggestion; one to Hueffer states specifically that 'the proposal certainly came from me'[36] and one to Henley reads:

Dear Mr. Henley,

I don't know how to thank you for your letter. I don't know how to begin. I won't begin. I shall accept my good fortune 'sans phrases', but I would have answered yesterday, by return, had I not been in the midst of concocting a letter to *The Times* about the *Mohegan* affaire. Whether they will print I don't know. I have relieved my feelings by firing off three thousand words. I've never worked so fast with pen and ink before, and I wouldn't stop, feeling that if I did I would never take up the job again. The difficulty to keep swear words out of that communication was very great. There were also other difficulties. That of writing at all, is always the greatest with me.

I have meditated your letter. The line of your argument has surprised me. R.L.S. – Dumas – these are big names and I assure you it had never occurred to me they could be pronounced in connection with my plan to work with Hueffer. But you have judged proper to pronounce them and I am bound to look seriously at that aspect of the matter. When talking with Hueffer my first thought was that the man there who couldn't find a publisher had some good stuff to use and that if we worked it up together my name, probably, would get a publisher for it. On the other hand I thought that working with him would keep under the particular devil that spoils my work for me as quick as I turn it out (that's why I work so slow and break my word to publishers), and that the material being of the kind that appeals to my imagination and the man being an honest workman we could turn out something tolerable – perhaps; and if not he would be no worse off than before. It struck me the expression he cared for was in verse; he has the faculty; I have not; I reasoned that partnership in prose would not affect any chances he may have to attain distinction – of the real kind – in verse. It seemed to me that a man capable of the higher form could not care much for the lower. These considerations encouraged me in my idea. It never entered my head I could be dangerous to Hueffer in the way you point out. The affair had a material rather than an artistic aspect for me. It would give – I reflected – more time to Hueffer for tinkering at his verses; for digging, hammering, chiselling or whatever process by which that mysterious thing – a poem – is shaped out of that barren thing – inspiration. As for myself I meant to keep the right to descend into my own private little hell – whenever the spirit moved me to do that foolish thing – and produce alone from time to time – verbiage no doubt – my own – therefore very dear. This is the truth – the whole truth. Now of course all this looks otherwise. Were I a Dumas I would eat up Hueffer without compunction. Was it you who called the old man 'a natural force'? He was *that*; and a natural force need not be scrupulous. Not being *that* I must navigate cautiously at this juncture lest my battered, ill-ballasted craft should run down a boat with youth at the helm and hope at the prow – pursuing shapes – shapes. I know a man who at the end of a long talk was moved to tell me – 'You don't seem to have a conception of what Sin is.' Perhaps not! but it seems to me it would be sinful to sink Hueffer's boat which for all I know may be loaded with splendid gems or delicate roses – and all for my private ends. No. I shall not go mad and bite him – at least not without a fair warning. If I do speak at all I shall recite to him faithfully the substance of your letter – that is if he does not kick me out before we get so far. If he does he shall never know he had the high fortune to occupy your thought for an appreciable space of time. He will miss a fine chance for gratitude. I – thanks to Pawling – haven't missed mine.

And this brings me to what was in my mind all the time when writing this, for months before, not only in my mind – a poor habitation – but in me, from the crown of my head to the tips of my fingers. That I've during the last year composed, walking up and down my room (a quarter-deck habit) several letters to you need not be an alarming intelligence. I've forgotten them – and it is well. Words blow away like mist, and like mist they serve only to obscure, to make vague the real shape of one's feelings. I have let out some of these words before Edwin Pugh at one o'clock in the morning before the steps of the Mansion house and – since nothing is lost in this world – they may be knocking about yet amongst the stones. He said, I remember 'You're with me; the best – the kindest' – well 'we will let it go at that' as the Baboo in Kipling's tale of 'the finest story in the world' says. It has been a fine story to me; so fine that I have suddenly regretted the years gone by, regretted not being young when the future seems as vast as all eternity and the story could go on without end; so fine – you are to understand – that when it comes to setting it down the gods of life say nay and one can only mutter 'No doubt – but the door is shut.'

And what you say of 'Youth' is part, another line, of my 'Finest story in the world'. Yes – but the door is shut. Were I to write and talk till Doomsday you would never really know what it all means to me. You would not know because you never had just the same experience. Therein I have the advantage of you and I shall hug this incredible, amazing, fabulous precious advantage with both hands, I shall hug it as long as I can grip anything at all 'in this valley'. A chance comes once in life to all of us. Not the chance to get on; that only comes to good men. Fate is inexorably just. But Fate also is merciful and even to the poorest there comes sometimes the chance of an intimate, full, complete and pure satisfaction. That chance came to me when you accepted the *Nigger*. I've got it, I hold it, I keep it, and all the machinations of my private devil cannot rob me of it. No man, either, can do aught against it. Even you, yourself, have no power. You have given it and it is out of your hands.

This last reflexion is prompted not by impudence but by a less useful and a shade more honourable sentiment. I ask myself sometimes whether you know exactly what you have given, to whom, how much. But I love to think that if you perceive the shade of meaning within these lines you will not – perhaps – regret your gift – whatever happens tomorrow, or the day after.

Satis. Enough words. The postman will carry away this letter, the mist shall blow away and in the morning I shall discern clearly what tonight I am trying to interpet into writing – which remains. Let it remain, to show with what thundering kick the gods of life shut the door between our feeling and its expression. It is the old tale, the eternal grievance. If it were not for the illusion of the open door – sometimes – we would all be dumb, and it wouldn't matter, for no one would care to listen.

I've run on trying to tell you something and haven't told you how concerned I am at the news of your ill-health. Had I known I would have been still more appalled when Pawling told me he had sent my letter to you. I never dreamt of his doing that. I am very glad, inexpressibly glad though not a little remorseful, now I know the full extent of your generosity. If I could honestly think myself worth your trouble it is to you I would turn for advice, with perfect confidence with certain trust. And for what you have given I am honestly grateful I am faithfully and affectionately grateful.

Jph. Conrad

[18 October 1898, Pierpont Morgan Library, New York]

This letter disposes of some of Hueffer's extraordinarily garbled story, but it does corroborate his basic assertion that the proposal came from Conrad. Hueffer also made some wildly inaccurate statements about the relative fame of Conrad and himself. In *Joseph Conrad* he wrote patronizingly of Conrad at their first meeting; 'Upon the writer Conrad made no impression at all. Mr Conrad was the author of *Almayer's Folly*, a great book of a romantic fashion, but written too much in the style of Alphonse Daudet, whom the writer had outgrown at school, knowing the *Lettres de mon Moulin* at eighteen by heart. A great, new writer then. But as to great writers or artists this writer even then en avait soupé . . .'[37] This did not stop him from saying later in *Return to Yesterday*: 'In the days of which I am writing [when Conrad suggested collaboration] . . . Conrad had as yet published nothing but *Almayer's Folly* was about to appear.'[38]

In fact Conrad was a writer of considerable standing and

achievement by this time, having published *Almayer's Folly*, *An Outcast of the Islands* and *The Nigger of the 'Narcissus'*, while *Tales of Unrest* was about to appear. Hueffer, on the other hand, had done little more than show brilliant promise and it was not until seven years later, with the publication of *The Soul of London*, that he was to have any real critical or financial success for his writing,* whereas *The Good Soldier*, published in 1915, was his first considerable work of fiction.

Conrad's reasons for wanting to collaborate with Hueffer emerge fairly clearly from his letter to Henley. Undoubtedly the main reason, without which he would never have made the suggestion, was his need for money. 1898 had been a barren year, 'Youth' being the only piece of work, apart from three reviews, that he had succeeded in finishing, and he was obsessed by the problem of *The Rescue*; nor had 1897 been much better. He could not support his family on that basis and his hopes of going to sea showed no immediate likelihood of being realized. He had even had to borrow money from the ever loyal and willing Galsworthy.[39] Hueffer was subsequently to construct a mystique out of the collaboration but, although Conrad undoubtedly enjoyed it and profited from it, he clearly looked on it primarily as a material arrangement. Nonetheless, although Hueffer's nonsense about Conrad thinking in French when he wrote and then translating his thoughts into English must be discounted, there can be no doubt that Conrad was still finding it extremely difficult to express himself fluently in English and hoped to acquire fluency through the experience of literary partnership. Moreover, the hope which he expressed to Henley that working with Hueffer 'would keep under the particular devil that spoils my work for me as quick as I turn it out' suggests a great lack of confidence. At a time when he was growing out of Garnett's perhaps too rigorous tutelage he seems still to have been unable to judge the quality of his work with any certainty; he needed reassurance and support,

* His first fairy tale, however, *The Brown Owl*, reached a fourth edition. But they may well have been very small editions.

even guidance. Nor was literary collaboration such an astonishing phenomenon then as it is today; there were for instance Walter Besant and James Rice churning out novels in partnership, Israel Zangwill and Louis Cowen, who had collaborated on *The Premier and the Painter*, there was the more illustrious association between Stevenson and Lloyd Osborne; Kipling, even, had appeared as joint author of a novel with Wolcott Balestier.

Hueffer would have seemed to Conrad an excellent choice. Being younger and less distinguished he would be the junior partner; yet he was at the centre of the literary world and wrote with style and facility.

Hueffer's reasons for agreeing to collaborate are more obscure. He had no trouble in expressing himself and he was not in need of money. It is difficult to decide what he hoped to gain from the arrangement. Conrad's references in his letter to Henley to 'the man there who couldn't find a publisher' is probably one reason. For although Hueffer was a prolific writer his work was not on the whole easy to sell; Conrad later persuaded Pinker to handle Hueffer's work, but Pinker for some time had considerable difficulty in placing it.* Hueffer may also have been flattered by such a suggestion coming from an older and more illustrious writer, and then he was a generous-minded man who would certainly have been prepared to make a sacrifice for art which to him really was the most important thing in life.

Finally, the idea of collaboration must have appealed to both of them because, different though they were in temperament and character, there was much common ground between them. They were both steeped in French literature, above all Flaubert and Maupassant, intensely interested in the technique of the novel and convinced of its importance as an art. There may, too, have been an emotional bond

* Letter from Conrad to Hueffer, 5 September 1904: 'You are for him [Pinker] the man who can write anything at any time – and write it well – he means in a not ordinary way. His belief in you is by no means shaken. He admits in effect that he had failed both with the *London* and the novel. But he does not admit that he has failed finally.'

between the two of them as 'outsiders'; Conrad, a Pole, and Hueffer, half German. Hueffer tells an absurd anecdote which, literally true or not, probably gives a correct impression:

> Once we were sitting in the front row of the stalls at the Empire. ... On that night ... there was at least one clergyman with a number of women: ladies is meant – . And during applause by the audience of some *too* middle class joke one of us leaned over towards the other and said: 'Doesn't one feel lonely in this beastly country!' – Which of us it was that spoke neither remembered after: the other had been at that moment thinking so exactly the same thing.[40]

The 'good stuff' which Conrad told Henley that Hueffer had was presumably the idea, either on paper or in Hueffer's head, for a political extravaganza which was to become their first published collaboration, *The Inheritors*. Hueffer also had a partially written first draft of a novel based on the trial for piracy of an innocent man named Aaron Smith. He had called it *Seraphina*, after the heroine, and it was subsequently to be developed into *Romance* by the two men.

(3)

Immediately Conrad got back from his search for a command in Glasgow he wrote to Hueffer asking him to clinch the matter of the Pent:

> I've just got back from Glasgow and write without loss of time asking you to conclude the affair with the landlord.... This opportunity is a perfect Godsend to me. It preserves what's left of my piety and belief in a benevolent Providence and probably also my sanity. [29 September 1898]

The Conrads moved into the Pent on 26–7 October and somewhere around this time Conrad and Hueffer concluded their arrangement for collaboration.[41] The Hueffers themselves moved to a cottage at Aldington,[42] and so were quite close to the Conrads, which made collaboration easier. They seem to have set to work quickly, because Conrad wrote to Hueffer some time in November:

The acceptance of our joint work [*The Inheritors*] is assured so far as Pawling is concerned. McClure I guess is all right. We must serialise next year on both sides of the pond . . .

Have you written far Serafina (or Seraphina?). I get on dreamily with *The Rescue*, dreamily dreaming how fine it could be if the thought did not escape – if the expression did not hide underground, if the idea had a substance and words a magic power, if the invisible could be snared into a shape. And it is sad to think that even if all this came to pass – even then it could never be so fine to anybody as it is fine to me now, lurking in the blank pages in an intensity of existence without voice, without form – but without blemish. [Saturday (November 1898)]

Then, a few days later, he told Hueffer: 'Come when you like. . . . I would be very pleased to hear Serafina *read*. I would *afterwards* read it myself.'[43] And, probably as a result of the reading – according to Hueffer Conrad violently disapproved of his treatment of the story – they drew up a synopsis of the plot, announcing that 'the story of which this skeleton and many details are already worked out shall be greatly advanced if not absolutely finished in July, 1899'.[44]

Meanwhile Conrad's own work was stagnant and in almost every letter he bewailed his inability to make progress with *The Rescue*. Then, as had happened previously in the case of 'Youth', he abandoned his struggle with *The Rescue* and, in the middle of December, started 'Heart of Darkness' for *Blackwood's* 'which I must get out for the sake of the shekels'[45] he told Garnett. He was able to write it quickly and finished it in the first week of February.[46]

'Heart of Darkness', Conrad said in the Author's Note, 'is experience pushed a little (and only very little) beyond the actual facts of the case for the perfectly legitimate, I believe, purpose of bringing it home to the minds and bosoms of the readers. . . . That sombre theme had to be given a sinister resonance, a tonality of its own, a continued vibration that, I hoped, would hang in the air and dwell on the ear after the last note had been struck.'[47]

To achieve this effect Conrad again had recourse to

Marlow because, as in 'Youth', he was concerned primarily not with the events described but with their impression on a consciousness like his own. He uses a similar setting to that in 'Youth' with the same group of people, united by the 'bond of the sea':[48] the Director of Companies, the Lawyer, the Accountant, Marlow, and the narrator. They are sitting on the deck of the cruising yawl *Nellie*, and Marlow starts a reflective monologue leading into an account of his experience in the 'heart of darkness'.

But 'Heart of Darkness' aims at a far more subtle effect than 'Youth' and Marlow's role is correspondingly more complex. The narrator warns that 'we knew we were fated, before the ebb began to run, to hear about one of Marlow's inconclusive experiences', and Marlow says of the experience: 'It seemed somehow to throw a kind of light on everything about me – and into my thoughts. It was sombre enough, too – and pitiful – not extraordinary in any way – not very clear either. No, not very clear. And yet it seemed to throw a kind of light.'[49] For Marlow 'the meaning of an episode was not inside like a kernel but outside, enveloping the tale which brought it out only as a glow brings out a haze, in the likeness of one of these misty halos that sometimes are made visible by the spectral illumination of moonshine'.[50] Conrad did not live in a world of sharp emotional or intellectual distinctions, and the power and fascination of 'Heart of Darkness' rest upon the tale's moral elusiveness and ambiguity.

Conrad himself implied this in a letter to Cunninghame Graham when 'Heart of Darkness' was running serially: 'I am simply in the seventh heaven to find you like the "Heart of Darkness" so far. You bless me indeed. Mind you don't curse me by and bye for the very same thing. There are two more instalments in which the idea is so wrapped up in secondary notions that you, – even you! – may miss it.'[51] So wrapped up is it that one wonders whether Conrad was always clear as to his intention and whether one is justified in trying to unravel the story to the extent of imparting a coherent meaning to it.

In 'Youth' Conrad was dealing with simple emotions and could rely on his readers' response, but in 'Heart of Darkness' he is dealing with such complex emotions that he has several times to prick the reader's imagination into grasping the significance of the events by making Marlow doubt the possibility of giving an adequate impression of them, or of any events:

> I did not see the man in the name any more than you do. Do you see him? Do you see the story? Do you see anything? It seems to me I am trying to tell you a dream – making a vain attempt, because no relation of a dream can convey the dream sensation, that commingling of absurdity, surprise, and bewilderment in a tremor of struggling revolt, that notion of being captured by the incredible which is of the very essence of dreams. . . . No, it is impossible; it is impossible to convey the life-sensation of any given epoch of one's existence – that which makes its truth, its meaning – its subtle and penetrating essence. It is impossible. We live, as we dream – alone.[52]

And again:

> I've been telling you what we said – repeating the phrases we pronounced – but what's the good? They were common everyday words – the familiar, vague sounds exchanged on every waking day of life. But what of that? They had behind them, to my mind, the terrific suggestiveness of words heard in dreams, of phrases spoken in nightmares.[53]

Then Marlow draws the events closer to his listeners by his introductory remarks about the first Roman settlers in Britain and their venture into the heart of darkness, or else emphasizes the contrast between the experiences he is describing and the comfortable security of his listeners:

> 'Absurd!' he cried. 'This is the worst of trying to tell – . Here you all are, each moored with two good addresses, like a hulk with two anchors, a butcher round one corner, a policeman round another, excellent appetites, and temperature normal – you hear – normal from year's end to year's end. And you say, Absurd!'[54]

These devices are effective but Conrad overdoes his other more direct means of conveying an impression of the unusual or of intensity. As in most of his early work, the reader's emotions are bombarded to excess – there are too often those extra salvoes that Conrad cannot refrain from firing even though the defences are already flattened. The pages are spattered with such epithets and phrases as 'inconceivable', 'incomprehensible', 'implacable', 'inscrutable', 'inexplicable', 'irresistible', 'impenetrable', 'impalpable', 'unfathomable enigma', 'indefinable meaning'. These words become debased by their constant use, while a sentence like 'the cry of inconceivable triumph and of unspeakable pain' is almost devoid of meaning.

However, despite this straining of language, 'Heart of Darkness' is one of the finest short stories that have been written.

The manner in which Kurtz is dramatically built up before his appearance is masterly. His name crops up almost immediately Marlow arrives in Africa; the Company's chief accountant, who 'was amazing, and had a penholder behind his ear',[55] is the first to mention him: 'One day he remarked, without lifting his head, "In the interior you will no doubt meet Mr Kurtz. ... He is a very remarkable person." '[56] Thenceforth, Marlow often hears him spoken of until his interest is aroused: 'I was curious to see whether this man, who had come out equipped with moral ideas of some sort, would climb to the top after all and how he would set about his work when there.'[57] As he hears more about Kurtz he becomes increasingly excited at the prospect of meeting him, and when it is feared that the boat may not arrive at Kurtz's station before he dies Marlow has 'a sense of extreme disappointment. ... I couldn't have been more disgusted if I had travelled all this way for the sole purpose of talking with Mr Kurtz.'[58]

Kurtz had come to Africa armed, apparently, with grandiose ideals; in his paper written for the International Society for the Suppression of Savage Customs he had claimed that 'we whites' 'must necessarily appear to them (the Savages) in the nature of supernatural beings. ... By the simple exercise of our will we can exert a power for good practically unbounded'.[59] But the 'idea' which 'redeems' had gone rotten because at the foot of this pamphlet Kurtz had scrawled, 'evidently much later', 'Exterminate all the brutes'. His actual conduct was more sophisticated than this would imply because

> the wilderness had found him out early, and had taken on him a terrible vengeance for the fantastic invasion. I think it had whispered to him things about himself which he did not know, things of which he had no conception till he took counsel with his great solitude – and the whisper had proved irresistibly fascinating. It echoed loudly within him because he was hollow at the core.[60]

Conrad is not specific about Kurtz's behaviour. It appears that he had allowed himself to be deified; the natives 'adored him',[61] and he presided at 'certain midnight dances ending with unspeakable rites, which . . . were offered up to him – do you understand? – to Mr Kurtz himself'.[62] And the heads on the poles in front of his house 'showed that Mr Kurtz lacked restraint in the gratification of his various lusts'.[63]

The 'sombre theme' of the story, in part at least, is the conflict between the power of the wilderness to release 'forgotten and brutal instincts' and the capacity of a human being to resist this pressure. Thus Marlow, like Kurtz, is subjected to the test of the wilderness: 'Could we handle that dumb thing, or would it handle us?'[64] And he feels its power, particularly when confronted with the jungle humanity: 'a glimpse of rush walls, of peaked grass-roofs, a burst of yells, a whirl of black limbs, a mass of hands clapping, of feet stamping, of bodies swaying, of eyes rolling, under the droop of heavy and motionless foliage'.[65] 'It was unearthly, and the men were – No, they were not inhuman. . . . What thrilled you was just the thought of their humanity – like yours – the thought of your remote kinship with this wild and passionate uproar.'[66] But, although Marlow claimed that 'if you were man enough you would admit to yourself that there was in you just the faintest trace of a response to the terrible frankness of that noise, a dim suspicion of there being a meaning in it which you – you so remote from the night of first ages – could comprehend',[67] he was not 'found out' by the wilderness. 'You wonder I didn't go ashore for a howl and a dance?'[68] he asked. But he could resist the 'powers of darkness'[69] through his 'innate strength', his 'capacity for faithfulness';[70] 'Let the fool gape and shudder – the man knows, and can look on without a wink. But he must at least be as much of a man as these on shore. He must meet that truth with his own true stuff – with his own inborn strength. Principles won't do. . . . No; you want a deliberate belief.'[71] And, further, there was the Conradian antidote of work: 'I had no time. I had to mess about with white-lead and strips of woollen blanket helping to put bandages on those leaky steam-pipes – I tell you. I had to watch the steering, and circumvent those snags, and get the tin-pot along by hook or by crook. There was surface-truth enough in these things to save a wiser man.'[72]

Thus Marlow was proof against the direct challenge of the wilderness straightforwardly expressing the primitive, but he was also confronted with the challenge of Kurtz or rather of the wilderness expressing itself through Kurtz. To understand what is involved in this it is necessary to decide what Kurtz is intended to represent. Conrad told Elsie Hueffer: 'What I distinctly admit is the fault of having made Kurtz too symbolic or rather symbolic at all. But the story being mainly a vehicle for conveying a batch of personal impressions I gave the rein to my mental laziness and took the line of least resistance.'[73]

In his presentation of Kurtz, Conrad seems to have intended primarily to show that a person who is 'hollow at the core', who has 'something wanting in him', becomes a victim of the wilderness, or of his unconscious desires, when he is released from the social restrictions of organized society; freedom from outer restraint exposes the absence of inner restraint. And the wilderness seems to have both a literal, objective, and a symbolical, subjective connotation. Conrad is not so much concerned with the form in which these desires express themselves as with the effect their release may have on the person concerned, summed up by Kurtz in his last cry of 'the horror!'

The corrupting power of the wilderness expressed through Kurtz is infinitely more complex and subtle than that of the wilderness alone. Moreover, Marlow is driven to ally himself with Kurtz in revulsion against the moral squalor of the 'pilgrims'. He is faced with a 'choice of nightmares':[74] 'It seemed to me I had never breathed an atmosphere so vile, and I turned mentally to Kurtz for relief – positively for relief. . . . I had turned to the wilderness really, not to Mr Kurtz, who, I was ready to admit, was as good as buried. And for a moment it seemed to me as if I also were buried in a vast grave full of unspeakable secrets.'[75] But, unlike Kurtz, Marlow does not succumb and is even able to wrest Kurtz from the grasp of the wilderness when he is drawn back to it: 'I tried to break the spell – the heavy, mute spell of the wilderness – that seemed to draw him to its pitiless breast by the awakening of forgotten and brutal instincts, by the memory of gratified and monstrous passions.'*

However Marlow is radically affected by his experience of Kurtz, whose power continues after his death. Marlow says: 'It was written I should be loyal to the nightmare of my choice.'[76] He becomes Kurtz's self-appointed executor and refuses to hand over any of Kurtz's papers to the Company. He even visits Kurtz's 'intended' to give back her letters and photograph to her. His motive for this is obscure to himself and he supposes that it may have been 'unconscious loyalty'.[77] Conrad did not choose to develop Marlow's reasons for this loyalty but as Kurtz had enlarged the mind[78] of his naïve disciple, the crazy Russian trader, he had also gained Marlow's respect: he was a 'remarkable man'. Marlow was with Kurtz just before he died:

> I saw on that ivory face the expression of sombre pride, of ruthless power, of craven terror – of an intense and hopeless despair. . . .

* *Youth*, p. 144. This episode disproves Douglas Hewitt's assertion that Marlow is 'powerless when confronted by the darkness of Mr Kurtz' (*Conrad, a Reassessment*, Cambridge, 1952, pp. 26–7).

He cried in a whisper at some image, at some vision – he cried out twice, a cry that was no more than a breath –

'The horror! The horror' – –

Then Marlow himself became seriously ill:

> I was within a hair's breadth of the last opportunity for pronouncement, and I found with humiliation that probably I would have nothing to say. This is the reason why I affirm that Kurtz was a remarkable man. He had something to say. . . . He had summed up – he had judged. 'The horror!' He was a remarkable man. After all, this was the expression of some sort of belief; it had candour, it had conviction, it had a vibrating note of revolt in its whisper, it had the appalling face of a glimpsed truth. . . . I like to think my summing up would not have been a word of careless contempt. Better his cry – much better. It was an affirmation, a moral victory paid for by innumerable defeats, by abominable terrors, by abominable satisfactions. But it was a victory! That is why I have remained loyal to Kurtz to the last, and even beyond.[79]

That is the crux of the story. Just before he dies Kurtz is vindicated by a full emotional realization of his experience. For this 'supreme moment of complete knowledge'[80] is the most that can be expected from life: 'Droll thing life is,' Marlow says, '— that mysterious arrangement of merciless logic for a futile purpose The most you can hope from it is some knowledge of yourself – that comes too late – a crop of unextinguishable regrets.'[81] And he has vicariously gained this knowledge from Kurtz. When Marlow was on the brink of death, 'it is not my own extremity I remember best – a vision of greyness without form filled with physical pain, and a careless contempt for the evanescence of all things – even of this pain itself. No! It is his extremity that I seem to have lived through.'[82]

But Marlow has to pay for his knowledge because the wilderness belatedly exacts its toll. It is as if he were re-enacting the legend of The Fall. In the epilogue, where he visits Kurtz's 'intended', he supports the girl in her ideal of Kurtz, down to telling a lie for her sake; he substitutes her own name for 'the horror' as the last word that Kurtz spoke.

Marlow 'laid the ghost of his [Kurtz's] gifts at last with a lie'.[83] Earlier he had said:

> I would not have gone so far as to fight for Kurtz, but I went for him near enough to a lie. You know I hate, detest, and can't bear a lie, not because I am straighter than the rest of us, but simply because it appals me. There is a taint of death, a flavour of mortality in lies. . .[84]

In deceiving the girl Marlow has failed to render Kurtz 'that justice which was his due. . . . But I couldn't. I could not tell her. It would have been too dark – too dark altogether.'* Indeed his visit roused intense memories of Kurtz and even gives the wilderness 'a moment of triumph'[85] when he has a vision of Kurtz as he had seen him in the heart of darkness. Therefore he bowed his 'head before the faith that was in her, before that great and saving illusion that shone with an unearthly glow in the darkness, in the triumphant darkness from which I could not have defended her – from which I could not even defend myself'.[86] This brings out the radical difference in the effect that the wilderness has on Kurtz and on Marlow. Kurtz succumbs totally to the power of the wilderness and only emerges momentarily at the end to full awareness of his experience, whereas Marlow is forced to make a limited concession to the wilderness but preserves his moral being because he is not 'hollow at the core'. The irony that it was morally right for Marlow to make this concession is an essential ingredient of Conrad's view of life. In a corrupt world one is bound to commit a corrupt act.† Tragedy would have been the result of telling the truth; the 'salvation of another soul' was at stake. Marlow was in a situation for which he was not to blame, but was compelled to violate one

* *Youth*, p. 162. Marlow's statement that in lying to the girl he has failed to render Kurtz 'that justice which was his due' conflicts with his other statement that he 'went for him near enough to a lie'. The lie was told in the interest of the girl, not of Kurtz.

† cf., letter to Cunninghame Graham, 8 February 1899, *L.L.*, I, p. 269. 'L'homme est un animal méchant. . . . Le crime est une condition nécessaire de l'existence organisée. La société est essentiellement criminelle.'

of his most strongly held principles, and to acknowledge mortality in order to preserve the 'saving illusion' of another. He had gained his knowledge but lost his innocence.

It is not, however, this somewhat esoteric meaning that has gained 'Heart of Darkness' its exalted position in literature. Conrad's achievement consisted primarily in his creation of visual scene upon visual scene charged with emotive impact – from the French man-of-war shelling the coast, the grove of death, and the journey up the river, to the wresting of Kurtz from the wilderness and his death on the boat – to attain the cumulative effect of human imbecility, of evil and horror.

(4)

The move to Kent brought Conrad within a galaxy of literary figures. Besides Hueffer at Aldington, there was Henry James at Rye, Kipling at Rottingdean, then at Burwash, and Wells at Sandgate, while Stephen Crane and Cora were soon to move to a romantic part-fourteenth-century, part-Elizabethan house near Rye, called Brede Place, which had been generously handed over to them at a nominal rent. Conrad did not know Kipling; he had exchanged letters of exquisite politeness with James and was to develop 'a profound affection for him';[87] and with Crane he was on terms of intimate friendship. He had corresponded with Wells over Wells's review of *An Outcast*, and when the idea of going to the Pent was first broached had written delightedly to him: 'I am writing in a state of jubilation at the thought we are going to be nearer neighbours than I dared to hope a fortnight ago.'[88]

Once at the Pent he lost little time in going over to call on Wells – who happened not to be in. In fact the Conrads were rather unfortunate in their visits to Wells. On another unheralded visit in which Hueffer apparently took part Wells was again out:

We called yesterday by an act of inspiration, so to speak, and with the neglect of common civilities did so at 2.45 p.m., for which we were very properly punished by not finding you at home. We would have waited, but we'd left the baby in the gutter (there was a fly under him tho') and the days are too short to allow of camping in a friend's drawing-room. So we went despondently. And by the by, there was an Invisible Man (apparently of a jocose disposition) on your doorstep, because when I rang (modestly), an invisible finger kept the button down (or in, rather) and the bell jingling continuously to my extreme confusion (and the evident surprise of your girl). I wish you would keep your creations in some kind of order, confined in books or locked up in the cells of your brain, to be let out at stated times (frequently, frequently of course!) instead of letting them wander about the premises, startling visitors who mean you no harm – anyhow my nerves can't stand that kind of thing – and now I shan't come near you till next year. There! [23 December 1898, *L.L.*, I, p. 263]

Conrad and Wells remained on friendly terms for a number of years, visiting and sending each other their books as they were published. In a letter to Pinker, Conrad referred to Wells 'to whom I tell all my troubles'.[89] Without question Conrad admired Wells's mind and his science fiction such as *The Invisible Man* and *The War of the Worlds*. He told Aniela Zagórska, who wanted to translate *The Invisible Man* into Polish, that Wells was 'a very original writer with a very individualistic judgment in all things and an astonishing imagination',[90] and in a letter to Wells he proclaimed him 'the one honest thinker of the day'.[91] He dedicated *The Secret Agent* to Wells and, writing to A. H. Davray about the book, praised Wells glowingly: 'Son livre sur les États-Unis est tout-à-fait chic. Il a compris un tas de choses incompréhensibles en elles-mêmes. Voilà à quoi sert une imagination comme la sienne servie par une intelligence mordante comme un acide.'[92]

But it must have been soon after this that their friendship started to cool. The cause is not known because no correspondence between them after the publication of *The Secret Agent* seems to have been preserved. But it is not surprising that they fell out because two men more different in outlook and temperament could scarcely be conceived. Despite his imaginative gifts Wells proclaimed himself a 'journalist' and his ideals were revolutionary, while Conrad was an artist and profoundly conservative, to whom Wells's intense concern with socialism, democracy, and a world state must have been strongly antipathetic. Conrad could put up with Cunninghame Graham's reformist fervour, although thinking it misguided, because there was a deeper bond of sympathy and outlook between the two men. Conrad probably felt that nothing he valued was really threatened by Cunninghame Graham, whereas he would have found insufferable a world governed according to Wells's principles. But principles were probably less important than temperament; Conrad was fundamentally pessimistic and aristocratic in outlook, whereas Wells was optimistic and stridently plebeian. Conrad himself neatly expressed his notion of their temperamental antagonism: 'The difference between us, Wells, is fundamental. You don't care for humanity but think they are to be improved. I love humanity but know they are not!'[93]

Wells's admiration for Conrad's work seems always to have been qualified. He neither fully understood it nor sympathized with its aims; and he intensely disliked Conrad's style of expression. He liked best *The Mirror of the Sea*, one of Conrad's least profound works. It may in fact well be that they fell out over some too outspoken criticism which Wells had made of Conrad's writing. It was not in Wells's nature to disguise his opinion of the work of others (or of anything else); and Conrad was inordinately sensitive to criticism unless it was of the most tactful and deferential kind. The relationship between James and Wells* throws light on the course which that between Conrad and Wells took, although it is unlikely that the positive feelings were ever so intense. Wells never had the respect for Conrad that he had for James, whereas it is doubtful whether Conrad ever gave as much of himself to Wells as did James. The first sign of

* For an admirable exposition of this relationship see *Henry James and H. G. Wells; a Record of their Friendship, their Debate on the Art of Fiction, and their Quarrel*, edited with an Introduction by Leon Edel and Gordon N. Ray, 1958.

Wells's antagonism to Conrad appears in 1915 in the literary fantasia which he called *Boon*, where there are two vicious jabs. He says of the hero, Boon: 'Conrad he could not endure. I do him no wrong in mentioning that; it is the way with most of us . . .' And later, Boon, giving an account of the literary taste of America, says 'she'll sit never knowing she's had a Stephen Crane, adoring the European reputation, the florid mental gestures of a Conrad. You see, she can tell Conrad "writes". It shows.'[94]

In his autobiography Wells gave an account of his relations with Conrad:

At first he impressed me, as he impressed Henry James, as the strangest of creatures. He was rather short and round-shouldered with his head as it were sunken into his body. He had a dark retreating face with a very carefully trimmed and pointed beard, a trouble-wrinkled forehead and very troubled dark eyes, and the gestures of his hands and arms were from the shoulders and very Oriental indeed. He reminded people of Du Maurier's Svengali and, in the nautical trimness of his costume, of Cutliffe Hyne's Captain Kettle. He spoke English strangely. Not badly altogether; he would supplement his vocabulary – especially if he were discussing cultural or political matters – with French words; but with certain oddities. He had learnt to read English long before he spoke it [this wasn't true] and he had formed wrong sound impressions of many familiar words; he had for example acquired an incurable tendency to pronounce the last 'e' in these and those. He would say, '*Wat* shall we do with *thesa* things?' and he was always incalculable about the use of 'shall' and 'will'. When he talked of seafaring his terminology was excellent but when he turned to less familiar topics he was often at a loss for phrases . . .

He talked with me mostly of adventure and dangers, Hueffer talked criticism and style and words, and our encounter was the beginning of a long, fairly friendly but always rather strained acquaintance. Conrad with Mrs. Conrad and his small blond-haired bright-eyed boy, would come over to Sandgate, cracking a whip along the road, driving a little black pony carriage as though it was a droshky and encouraging a puzzled little Kentish pony with loud cries and endearments in Polish, to the dismay of all beholders. We never really 'got on' together. I was perhaps more unsympathetic and incomprehensible to Conrad than he was to me. I think he found me Philistine, stupid and intensely English; he was incredulous that I could take social and political issues seriously; he was always trying to penetrate below my foundations, discover my imaginative obsessions and see what I was really up to. The frequent carelessness of my writing, my scientific qualifications of statement and provisional inconclusiveness, and my indifference to intensity of effect, perplexed and irritated him. Why didn't I *write*? Why had I no care for my reputation?

'My dear Wells, what is this *Love and Mr. Lewisham about*?' he would ask. But then he would ask also, wringing his hands and wrinkling his forehead, 'What is all this about Jane Austen? What is there *in* her? What is it all *about*? . . .'

He had set himself to be a great writer, an artist in words, and to achieve all the recognition and distinction that he imagined should go with that ambition, he had gone literary with a singleness and intensity of purpose that made the kindred concentration of Henry James seem lax and large and pale . . .

I found . . . something . . . ridiculous in Conrad's *persona* of a romantic adventurous un-mercenary intensely artistic European gentleman carrying an exquisite code of unblemished honour through a universe of baseness . . .

When Conrad first met Shaw in my house, Shaw talked with his customary freedoms. 'You know, my dear fellow, your books won't *do*' – for some Shavian reason I have forgotten – and so forth.

I went out of the room and suddenly found Conrad on my heels, swift and white-faced. 'Does that man want to *insult* me?' he demanded.

The provocation to say 'Yes' and assist at the subsequent duel was very great, but I overcame it. 'It's humour,' I said, and took Conrad out into the garden to cool. One could always baffle Conrad by saying 'humour'. It was one of our damned English tricks he had never learnt to tackle.[95]

Wells then relates that Conrad at one time wanted Hueffer to challenge him to a duel, but as the story came from Hueffer it can be taken with a grain of salt.

Jessie Conrad also has an account of an uncomfortable meeting between Conrad and Shaw which may well refer to the same occasion:

It was to the Pent that H. G. Wells came, bringing G. B. Shaw, George Gissing and many other men, and not a few young ladies. I always remember a lunch that H. G. Wells partook of and one that exasperated my husband very much. He arrived with a terrible headache and would eat nothing but a slice of dry bread, washed down by a glass of quinine and water, while G. B. Shaw made a tea off Van Houten's cocoa and a dry biscuit.[96]

In a letter to Garnett, Conrad mentions that 'four or five months ago G.B.S. towed by Wells came to see me reluctantly and I nearly bit him'.[97]

(5)

Apart from visits to and from Wells the Conrads, soon after moving into the Pent, started to have friends down to stay. There was Edwin Pugh,[98] author of *Tony Drum*, Galsworthy,[99] Cunninghame Graham,[100] Hugh Clifford,[101] and others. Conrad always seems to have been very sociable and to have enjoyed conversation. His occasional complaints that entertaining interrupted his work were probably a little disingenuous. Jessie was an excellent cook, and as Conrad had high standards of hospitality it is not surprising that they never had enough money.

Besides these friends there was of course Hueffer. Conrad must have seen a certain amount of him,[102] although to begin with, as far as the collaboration went, it was Hueffer who did most of the work because, during 1899, Conrad was primarily concerned with *Lord Jim*,[103] which he had again taken up immediately after finishing 'Heart of Darkness'.

His writing was accompanied by the usual despairing groans and attacks of gout, and although he seems to have been progressing quite fast he was dissatisfied with what he wrote:

> I *feel* it bad; and, unless I am hopelessly morbid, I cannot be altogether wrong. So much I am conceited; I fancy that I know a good thing when I see it.
>
> I am weary of the difficulty of it. The game is not worth the candle; of course there is no question of throwing up the hand. It must be played out to the end but it is the other men who hold the

trumps and the prospect is not inspiriting. [To Garnett, 26 October 1899]

Conrad's difficulties with writing also affected the 'partnership'. There is a letter to Hueffer, written in November:

My dear Ford,

Your letter distressed me a little by the sign of nervous irritation and its exasperated tone. I can quite enter into your feelings. I am sorry your wife seems to think I've induced you to waste your time.

I had no idea you had any profitable work to do – For otherwise effort after expression is not wasted even if it is not paid for. What you have written now is infinitely nearer to actuality, to life, to reality than anything (in prose) you have written before. It is nearer 'creation' than the *Shifting of the Fire*. That much for the substance.

I do not want to repeat here how highly I think of the purely literary side of your work.

You know my opinion.

But beautiful lines do not make a drawing nor splashes of beautiful colour a picture. Out of discussion there may come conception however. For discussion I am ready, willing and even anxious.

If I had influence enough with the publishers I would make them publish the book in your name alone – because the *work* is all yours – I have shared only a little of your worry . . .

Whether I am worth anything to you or not, it is for you to determine. The proposal certainly came from me under a false impression of my power of work. I am much weaker than I thought I was but this does not affect you fundamentally.

Heinemann (and McClure too I fancy) are waiting for our joint book and I am not going to draw back if you will only consent to sweat long enough.

I am not going to make any sort of difficulty about it – I shall take the money if you make a point of that. I am not going to stick at that trifle.

Do come when you like. Bring only one (or at most two) chapters at a time and we shall have it out over each separately. Don't you good people think hardly of me. I've been – I am animated by the best intentions. I shall always be!

We expected you both today. Come as soon as you feel you want to.

Kindest regards,
Yours,
Jph. Conrad

To his friend Edward Sanderson, Conrad summed up his life and poured forth his fears:

Try to imagine yourself trying your hardest to save the School from downfall, annihilation, and disaster: and the thing going on and on endlessly. That's exactly how I am situated: and the worst is that the menace (in my case) does not seem to come from outside but from within: that the menace and danger or weakness are in me, in myself alone. I fear I have not the capacity and the power to go on, – to satisfy the just expectations of those who are dependent on my exertions. I fear! I fear! And sometimes I hope. But it is the fear that abides.

But even were I wrong in my fear the very fact that such a fear exists would argue that everything is not right, – would in itself be a danger and a menace. So I turn in this vicious circle and the work itself becomes like the work in a treadmill, – a thing without joy, – a punishing task . . .

I am ashamed, bitterly ashamed, to make the same eternal answer, the same eternal wail of incertitude, to your hospitable voice. I am now trying to finish a story [*Lord Jim*] which began in the Oct. No. of *Blackwood*. I am at it day after day, and I want all day, every minute of a day, to produce a beggarly tale of words or perhaps to produce nothing at all. And when that is finished (I thought it would be so on the first of this month, – but no fear!) I must go on, even go on at once and drag out of myself another 20,000 words, if the boy is to have his milk and I my beer (this is a figure of speech, – I don't drink beer, I drink weak tea, yearn after dry champagne) and if the world is not absolutely to come to an end. And after I have written and been paid, I shall have the satisfaction of knowing that I can't allow myself the relaxation of being ill more than three days under the penalty of starvation: nor the luxury of going off the hooks altogether without playing the part of a thief regarding various confiding persons, whose desire to serve me was greater than their wisdom. . . . And Oh! dear Ted, it is a fool's business to write fiction for a living. It is indeed.

It is strange. The unreality of it seems to enter one's real life, penetrate into the bones, make the very heartbeats pulsate illusions through the arteries. One's will becomes the slave of hallucinations, responds only to shadowy impulses, waits on imagination alone. A strange state, a trying experience, a kind of fiery trial of untruthfulness. And one goes through it with an exaltation as false as all the rest of it. One goes through it, – and there's nothing to show at the end. Nothing! Nothing! Nothing! [12 October 1899, *L.L.*, I, pp. 282–3]

Although there may be an element of self-dramatization in this, and although it may be the expression of a mood it seems to have been a dominant mood. The letter must have called forth an anxious and consolatory reply from Sanderson but Conrad stuck to his gloom:

I had no idea my wail had been so loud and so lamentable, and though I am sorry I have intruded with my miseries on your serious preoccupations, I congratulate myself on my lack of restraint since it has drawn from you a fraternal answer . . .

There follows a long disquisition on the Boer War, and then:

My dearest Ted, your letter did me good. It is *great* to hear you talk like this of my work. I wish I could be sure the partiality of your affection does not mislead you. Ah! my dear fellow. If you knew how ambitious I am, how my ambition checks my pen at every turn. Doubts assail me from every side. The doubt of form, – the doubt of tendency, – a mistrust of my own conceptions, – and scruples of the moral order. Ridiculous, – isn't it? [26 October 1899, *L.L.*, I, pp. 285–7]

In addition to his personal worries the Boer War seems to have strongly affected Conrad. He wrote to Cunninghame Graham:

There is an appalling fatuity in this business. If I am to believe Kipling this is a war undertaken for the cause of democracy. *C'est à crever de rire!* However, now the fun has commenced, I trust British successes will be crushing from the first, – on the same principle that if there's murder being done in the next room and you can't stop it, you wish the head of the victim to be bashed in forthwith and the whole thing over for the sake of your own feelings. [14 October 1899, *L.L.*, I, pp. 284–5]

Then, a couple of months later:

I am so utterly and radically sick of this African business that if I could take a sleeping draft on the chance of not waking till it is all over, I would let *Jim* go and take the consequences. [10 December 1899, *L.L.*, I, p. 287]

And to Garnett in the new Year:

Times are deucedly hard here. But it's no use talking. This imbecile war has just about done for me. [15 January 1900]

He clearly disapproved vehemently of Britain's conduct but when his Polish cousin Aniela Zagórska came out with some of the criticism which was so widespread on the Continent he sprang to Britain's defence:

Much might be said about the war. My feelings are very complex – as you may guess. That they – the Boers – are struggling in good faith for their independence cannot be doubted; but it is also a fact that they have no idea of liberty, which can only be found under the English flag all over the world . . .

Europe rejoices and is moved because Europe is jealous and here in England there is more real sympathy and regard for the Boers than on the whole Continent, which calls out its compassion at the top of its voice. *Quelle Bourde!* [25 December 1899, *L.L.*, I, p. 288]

In the new year Hueffer and Conrad finished *The Inheritors* and the book was accepted by Heinemann. Conrad wrote to Garnett:

I consider the acceptance of the *Inheritors* a distinct bit of luck. Jove! What a lark!

I set myself to look upon the thing as a sort of skit upon the sort of political(?!) novel, fools of the N.S. sort do write. This in my heart of hearts. And poor H. was dead in earnest! Oh Lord. How he worked! There is not a chapter I haven't made him write twice – most of them three times over.

This is collaboration if you like! Joking apart the expenditure of nervous fluid was immense. There were moments when I cursed the day I was born and dared not look up at the light of day I had to live through with this thing on my mind. H. has been as patient as no angel had ever been. I've been fiendish. I've been rude to him; if I've not called him names I've *implied* in my remarks and the course of our discussions the most opprobrious epithets. He wouldn't recognise them. 'Pon my word it was touching. And there's no doubt that in the course of that agony I have been ready to weep more than once. Yet not for him. Not for him.

You'll have to burn this letter – but I shall say no more. Some day we shall meet and then – ! [26 March 1900]

The book is an extravaganza with a political setting. The hero is an unsuccessful, or as yet unappreciated, young writer called Etchingham Granger who comes of an old English family, and resembles a socially idealized version of Hueffer himself. He meets a young woman who turns out to be one of the Fourth Dimensionists, a race of people with superior powers but devoid of emotion who will 'inherit the earth'; she has come to wreck an elaborate political scheme for the exploitation of Greenland and to ruin those connected with it, good and bad alike, thus undermining public confidence and facilitating the triumph of the Fourth Dimensionists. She succeeds in her task, because Fourth Dimensionists are irresistible if they remain emotionally void, and corrupts Etchingham Granger in the process because he has fallen in love with her and become her tool. Various people are satirized or portrayed in the book: King Leopold II of Belgium (the unscrupulous and lecherous Duc de Mersch), Balfour (treated very sympathetically as the honourable Churchill), Joseph Chamberlain (the ruthlessly ambitious Gurnard – also a Fourth Dimensionist), Northcliffe (the brilliant but unreliable Fox, a 'fallen Fourth Dimensionist), Crockett the novelist (the pompous mediocrity, Callan). There is also a sympathetic and attractive portrait of Edward Garnett as the publisher's reader, Lea, and a merciless caricature of Fisher Unwin, Conrad's and Hueffer's first publisher, in Polehampton who would seize any pretext to cheesepare his payments to authors.

Hueffer had intended *The Inheritors* as

a political work, rather allegorically backing Mr Balfour in the then Government; the villain was to be Joseph Chamberlain who had made the [Boer] war. The sub-villain was to be Leopold II,

King of the Belgians, the foul – and incidentally lecherous – beast who had created the Congo Free State. . . . For the writer . . . it had appeared to be an allegorico-realist romance: it showed the superseding of previous generations and codes by the merciless young who are always alien and without remorse.[104]

And Conrad declared in a letter to the *New York Times Saturday Review*[105] that the book was directed 'at the self-seeking, at the falsehood that had been (to quote the book) "hiding under the words that had for ages spurred men to noble deeds, to self-sacrifice and to heroism".'

Conrad's opinion of the book is clear enough from his letter to Garnett and in Wise's copy he wrote: 'The idea of this book is entirely Hueffer's, and so is most of the writing.' In Curle's copy he wrote: 'My share in this work is very small as far as actual writing goes. But it had been the cause of long and heated discussion, lasting well into many nights.' There seems to be scarcely anything of Conrad in the writing or the conception, although he doubtless made a number of suggestions; the Système Groënlandais, based as it is on the exploitation of the Congo, may well have been Conrad's idea.

The Inheritors is written in a sophisticated and at times elliptical style, perhaps a little influenced by Henry James, and is obviously the work of a clever and talented man but it is rather silly and very boring; it fails to involve the reader emotionally or intellectually. Hueffer himself claimed that he regarded it 'with an intense dislike'[106] but insisted that Conrad thought it was 'a *damn* good book'.[107]

(6)

Meanwhile *Lord Jim* continued to expand beyond Conrad's original conception of it as a short story concerned only with the pilgrim-ship episode. In September of 1899 he announced that *Jim* would be finished by the end of the month and continued to forecast its imminent completion during the next ten months.[108] He was ill for nearly three weeks at the end of January: 'Malaria, bronchitis and gout. In reality a breakdown!'[109] But he appears to have got over this quite quickly and was well enough to spend a couple of days with Wells at Sandgate in the middle of February. Then at the beginning of April he had Marguerite Poradowska to stay, and in May he made a dash to Dover to see Stephen Crane,[110] who was being moved from Brede Place to the Black Forest in a desperate attempt to save his life. The attempt was vain and Crane died at Badenweiler on 5 June. One of the last things Crane did before leaving England was to write a solicitous letter about Conrad to Sanford Bennett:

> My condition is probably known to you. . . . I have Conrad on my mind very much just now. Garnett does not think it likely that his writing will ever be popular outside the ring of men who write. He is poor and a gentleman and proud. His wife is not strong and they have a kid. If Garnett should ask you to help pull wires for a place on the Civil List for Conrad please do me that last favor. . . . I am sure you will.[111]

Not only was Conrad able to be quite active, he was also writing hard. *Jim* went on and on – a very different matter from the mental constipation from which Conrad had suffered over *The Rescue* – and, what was more, Blackwood was paying generously for copy as it arrived.* Conrad told Garnett in March: 'I am old and sick and in debt – but lately I've found I can write – *it* comes! *it* comes! – and I am young and healthy and rich.'[112] Finally, with a dramatic last spurt he finished the novel during 13 and 14 July.[113] It ran to over 140,000 words instead of the 20,000 which he had originally envisaged. Conrad described the last lap to Galsworthy:

> The end of *Lord Jim* has been pulled off with a steady drag of twenty-one hours. I sent wife and child out of the house (to London) and sat down at 9 a.m. with a desperate resolve to be done

* Several letters from 21 August 1899 to 18 July 1900. In a letter dated 18 July 1900 Blackwood calculated that, on receipt of completed copy, he would have paid Conrad £500 (£300 for the serial rights and £200 in advance of royalties).

with it. Now and then I took a walk round the house, out at one door in at the other. Ten-minute meals. A great hush. Cigarette ends growing into a mound similar to a cairn over a dead hero. Moon rose over the barn, looked in at the window and climbed out of sight. Dawn broke, brightened. I put the lamp out and went on, with the morning breeze blowing the sheets of MS. all over the room. Sun rose. I wrote the last word and went into the dining-room. Six o'clock I shared a piece of cold chicken with Escamillo (who was very miserable and in want of sympathy, having missed the child dreadfully all day). Felt very well, only sleepy; had a bath at seven and at 8.30 was on my way to London. [Friday (20 July 1900), *L.L.*, I, p. 295]

In Richard Curle's copy of *Lord Jim* Conrad wrote:

When I began this story, which some people think my best (1915) – personally I don't – I formed the resolve to cram as much character and episode into it as it could hold. This explains its great length which the story itself does not justify.[114]

Like most of Conrad's statements about his own work, this is misleading. Conrad was never primarily concerned with character and episode for their own sake, nor, for that matter, with telling a 'tale'. In fact, the action hinges on a situation similar to that portrayed in *The Nigger of the 'Narcissus'*: a threat to the solidarity of mankind. In *Lord Jim* it is an act of cowardice by Jim. The ramshackle old *Patna* is carrying a large number of pilgrims to their Holy Land. During the voyage she strikes something below the surface which holes her badly. The officers alone know of the disaster and they, except for Jim, the chief mate, decide to abandon the ship secretly, leaving the pilgrims to their fate. Jim takes no part in their frantic efforts to launch a lifeboat but stands dazed, hating their cowardly antics, resisting their attempts to make him join them, and waiting for the *Patna* to sink. However, when the others are finally in the boat and the *Patna* seems on the point of sinking Jim jumps to join them. But the *Patna* does not sink and is towed to port by a French gunboat.

Conrad raises the significance of Jim's action to a metaphysical level and in his portrayal of Jim's spiritual Odyssey explores the theme of guilt and atonement. Every character and every incident is subordinated to and intended to develop this theme. But it is so intricately worked out that it is sometimes difficult to grasp the purport of a remark or an episode. And, as in 'Heart of Darkness', one may be tempted to wonder whether even Conrad himself was always quite clear as to what he was trying to say or, in this case, whether there was not some unresolved ambiguity in his own attitude to the events described.

Conrad had attempted nothing so ambitious, complex, or profound before; and he required a correspondingly complex method to enable him to achieve his aim. What Maupassant had called the 'objective' method[115] had proved adequate for the limited aim of the *Nigger* but in *Lord Jim* he was concerned primarily with subjective states of mind and with the analysis of motives. Like Henry James he was determined to extract the full emotional and moral significance of a situation. For James

> The person capable of feeling in the given case more than another of what is to be felt for it, and so serving in the highest degree to *record* it dramatically and objectively, is the only sort of person on whom we can count not to betray, to cheapen or, as we say, give away, the value and beauty of the thing.[116]

And,

> I never see the *leading* interest of any human hazard but in a consciousness (on the part of the moved and moving creature) subject to fine intensification and wide enlargement.[117]

But Conrad was not prepared to adopt James's method because the use of an exceptional person as the central character would restrict the application of what he had to say. Moreover, James's method entailed getting inside the central character and recording his thoughts and feelings by means of interior monologue or summary; and Conrad probably realized that his attempts at this had not been very successful in *Almayer's Folly* or *An Outcast*.

He therefore chose an average person for the central character. In the Author's Note, Conrad called Jim 'a simple and sensitive character',[118] while Marlow says that 'he complicated matters by being so simple'[119] and:

> He was outwardly so typical of that good, stupid kind we like to feel marching right and left of us in life, of the kind that is not disturbed by the vagaries of intelligence and the perversions of – of nerves, let us say.[120]

Nor did his appearance really belie him. He had 'imagination', but that is not so very exceptional, and, according to Stein, he was 'romantic', again not an uncommon trait. He was one of those who instinctively react to the moral subtleties of a situation but, possessing only an average consciousness, is unable to express them.

Therefore, as an essential counterpart to Jim, Conrad used the device of Marlow. Hitherto, in 'Youth' and 'Heart of Darkness', Marlow had been used to record a situation in terms of his own sensations. His role was now, as a character in the book and as Conrad's mouthpiece, to probe, analyse, and comment on the states of mind of another. There was thus no need for the author to commit what was to Conrad the cardinal sin of breaking the illusion with the obtrusion of his own comments.

Marlow then was the chief device for developing the theme. But, in addition, Conrad used a number of characters and incidents as moral touchstones for Jim's situation. There is the apparently impeccable Brierly with his 'Let him creep twenty feet underground'[121] and his suicide; the French Lieutenant – 'What life may be worth . . . when the honour is gone . . . I can offer no opinion';[122] the happy-go-lucky Chester – 'What's all the to-do about? A bit of ass's skin',[123] and the oracular Stein with his 'He is romantic' and 'In the destructive element immerse'.[124] These phrases recur often, like musical themes, and heighten and enrich the impact of the novel by bringing a multiple point of view to bear on the events.

In the *Nigger* the threat to the solidarity of mankind and to the efficacy of the 'few very simple ideas' came from James Wait and Donkin. But by their nature these men could only be a limited threat because, being worthless scoundrels, they were outside the circle in which these ideas ruled. Jim, on the other hand, was an infinitely greater threat because he was inside the circle. The phrase 'he was one of us' is stressed by Conrad in the Author's Note[125] and constantly crops up in Marlow's narration; 'He was too much like one of us not to be dangerous.'[126] Captain Allistoun, the other officers and Singleton had been impervious to Wait's blackmail and of course to Donkin. Marlow, on the other hand, felt that Jim's action threatened to undermine his own belief in the 'solidarity of the craft'[127] and 'the sovereign power enthroned in a fixed standard of conduct'.[128] 'I would have trusted the deck to that youngster,' he said, 'on the strength of a single glance . . . and, by Jove! it wouldn't have been safe. There are depths of horror in that thought.'[129]

Despite the fact that Jim was 'one of us' his 'jump' had associated him with a group of irredeemable reprobates, the other officers who had deserted the *Patna*. But he refused to accept this association and did his utmost to distinguish himself from them. 'They all got out of it in one way or another, but it wouldn't do for me.'[130] And Marlow was delighted when the French lieutenant saw the distinction:

> 'And so that poor young man ran away along with the others,' he said with grave tranquillity. . . . And suddenly I began to admire the discrimination of the man. He had made out the point at once: he did get hold of the only thing I cared about.[131]

It was the attempt of the 'others' to link him with them that most disturbed Jim. When they were in the boat after abandoning the *Patna*:

> 'They called out to me from aft', said Jim, 'as though we had been chums together. I heard them. They were begging me to be sensible and drop that "blooming piece of wood." Why *would* I carry on so? They hadn't done me any harm – had they? There had been no harm – No harm!'[132]

Then, after the inquiry, when Marlow had got Jim a position with a friend of his, the little second engineer of the *Patna* turned up:

'He made it a kind of confidential business between us. He was most damnably mysterious whenever I came over to the mill; he would wink at me in a respectful manner – as much as to say, "We know what we know." Infernally fawning and familiar – and that sort of thing.'[133]

Finally, and most disconcerting of all, the villainous Gentleman Brown unwittingly tore the scar from Jim's wound. He knew nothing of the *Patna* episode, but, trying to justify the shooting of one of the Bugis community, he asked Jim

whether he himself – straight now – didn't understand that when 'it came to saving one's life in the dark, one didn't care who else went – three, thirty, three hundred people. . . .' He asked Jim whether he had nothing fishy in his life to remember that he was so damnably hard upon a man trying to get out of a deadly hole by the first means that came to hand. . . . There ran through the rough talk a vein of subtle reference to their common blood, an assumption of common experience; a sickening suggestion of common guilt, of secret knowledge that was like a bond of their minds and of their hearts.[134]

Throughout the book it is as if two opposing forces were battling for the possession of Jim's soul.

The crucial action itself, Jim's jump, is presented with consummate subtlety. It is shown to be disgraceful, yet, throughout, Jim retains a degree of probity, so that the jump calls up sorrow and pity rather than contempt. Then each stage in the action happens so inevitably that it is hard to blame Jim. He does not decide to jump; he discovers that he has jumped. 'I had jumped . . . it seems.'[135] And it is impossible to answer with certainty the question which Jim several times asks Marlow: 'What would you have done?'[136] 'Do you know what *you* would have done?'[137] Marlow never answers directly, but he chews over Jim's situation:

He was tempted to grip and shake the shoulder of the nearest lascar, but he didn't. Something held his arms down along his sides. He was not afraid – oh no! only he just couldn't – that's all. He was not afraid of death perhaps, but I'll tell you what, he was afraid of the emergency. His confounded imagination had evoked for him all the horrors of panic, the trampling rush, the pitiful screams, boats swamped – all the appalling incidents of a disaster at sea he had ever heard of. He might have been resigned to die but I suspect he wanted to die without added terrors, quietly, in a sort of peaceful trance. A certain readiness to perish is not so very rare, but it is seldom that you meet men whose souls, steeled in the impenetrable armour of resolution, are ready to fight a losing battle to the last, the desire of peace waxes stronger as hope declines, till at last it conquers the very desire of life. Which of us here has not observed this, or maybe experienced something of that feeling in his own person – this extreme weariness of emotions, the vanity of effort, the yearning for rest? Those striving with unreasonable forces know it well, – the shipwrecked castaways in boats, wanderers lost in a desert, men battling against the unthinking might of nature, or the stupid brutality of crowds.[138]

Yet, despite Jim's 'conviction of innate blamelessness',[139] he was to blame, and the rest of the book is taken up with his attempts to deal with his action whereby he comes to a gradual realization of its significance and to the fulfilment of his destiny. At first his attitude is totally negative. 'I wished I could die. . . . There was no going back. It was as if I had jumped into a well – into an everlasting deep hole.'[140] Then, when a Court of Inquiry is to be held, Jim decides that he must face the consequences of his action and attend instead of doing a bunk like the other officers. Nonetheless, dining with Marlow while the court is in session, he tries to exonerate himself: 'It was their doing as plainly as if they had reached up with a boat-hook and pulled me over.'[141] 'There was not the thickness of a sheet of paper between the right and wrong of this affair.'[142] 'How much more did you want?' was Marlow's pitiless comment. Since his youth Jim had dreamed of 'valorous deeds'[143] and, after an incident on a training ship when he was 'too late' for a rescue, he had consoled himself that 'when all men flinched, then – he felt sure – he alone would know how to deal with the spurious menace of wind and seas'.[144] But when the test came he was not ready: 'It is all in being ready. I wasn't; not – not then. I don't want to excuse myself; but I would like to explain . . .'[145] he pleaded.

By deciding to face the Court of Inquiry he has dissociated himself from the others who can merely decamp because, being morally atrophied, they have no problem except that of survival. But in taking the first step towards rehabilitation he outrages Captain Brierly, who is on the Court and thinks that Jim should have cleared out:

'Can't he see that wretched skipper of his has cleared out? What does he expect to happen? Nothing can save him. He's done for. . . . Why eat all that dirt?'

If he can't clear out:

'Well, then, let him creep twenty feet underground and stay there! By heavens! *I* would . . .

'This is a disgrace. We've got all kinds amongst us – some anointed scoundrels in the lot; but, hang it, we must preserve professional decency or we become no better than so many tinkers going about loose. We are trusted. Do you understand? – trusted! Frankly, I don't care a snap for all the pilgrims that ever came out of Asia, but a decent man would not have behaved like this to a full cargo of old rags in bales. We aren't an organised body of men, and the only thing that holds us together is just the name of that kind of decency. Such an affair destroys one's confidence. A man may go pretty near through his whole sea-life without any call to show a stiff upper lip. But when the call comes – Aha! – If I – '[146]

Brierly himself is the centre of an important and enigmatical episode in the book. He has been an outstandingly successful and efficient seaman, respected, envied, but disliked for his conviction of superiority. Just after the Court of Inquiry he kills himself, having left his ship in meticulous order. The reason remains unknown. Marlow says he is in a position to know that it wasn't money, drink, or women[147] and remarks to Brierly's old mate, Jones:

'You may depend on it . . . it wasn't anything that would have disturbed much either of us two.'

and Jones answers with 'amazing profundity':

'Ay, ay! neither you nor I, sir, had ever thought so much of ourselves.'[148]

The only hint Marlow can give is:

> If I understand anything of men, the matter was no doubt of the gravest import, one of those trifles that awaken ideas – start into life some thought with which a man unused to such a companionship finds it impossible to live.[149]

This rather cryptic utterance is partially explained by another passage in which Marlow says:

> Hang ideas! They are tramps, vagabonds, knocking at the back-door of your mind, each taking a little of your substance, each taking away some crumb of that belief in a few simple notions you must cling to if you want to live decently and would like to die easy![150]

Brierly's suicide stands as a comment on, and a possible alternative to, Jim's own conduct. But it is not an action of which Conrad approves and he implies that it is to be condemned because it is fundamentally egotistical.

Nor does he approve of Brierly's condemnation of Jim's decision to face the Court. Marlow says:

> I became positive in my mind that the inquiry was a severe punishment to that Jim, and that his facing it – practically of his own free will – was a redeeming feature in his abominable case.[151]

After the Court has reached the inevitable decision and cancelled Jim's certificate Marlow decides that he will try to help Jim towards rehabilitation and gets him a job with an old friend of his, away from all who know of Jim's connection with the *Patna*. But Jim takes a negative view of his action and thinks in terms of escaping from it, of living it down[152] or burying it.[153] His last words to Marlow, on leaving for his new life, are:

> 'I always thought that if a fellow could begin with a clean slate –'[154]

whereas Marlow's comment to himself is:

> A clean slate, did he say? As if the initial word of each our

destiny were not graven in imperishable characters upon the face of a rock.[155]

Marlow has in fact already formulated the crucial question:

> The idea obtrudes itself that he made so much of his disgrace while it is the guilt alone that matters.[156]

Because he concentrates on externals and is obsessed by the world's opinion of him – 'a sort of sublimated, idealized selfishness' Marlow dubs it – he does a series of 'bunks' from one job and one place to another as his past threatens to catch up with him. At last, in despair, Marlow consults his friend Stein: businessman, philosopher, entomologist, and, like Brierly, another of Conrad's touchstones. Stein diagnoses Jim's case:

> 'I understand very well. He is romantic.'

Man's failing, continues Stein, is that:

> 'He wants to be a saint, and he wants to be a devil – and every time he shuts his eyes he sees himself as a very fine fellow – so fine as he can never be – In a dream – . . .
>
> 'I tell you, my friend, it is not good for you to find you cannot make your dream come true, for the reason that you not strong enough are, or not clever enough . . .'[157]

This recalls an earlier passage, where Jim day-dreams:

> At such times his thoughts would be full of valorous deeds: he loved these dreams and the success of his imaginary achievements. They were the best parts of life, its secret truth, its hidden reality. They had a gorgeous virility, the charm of vagueness, they passed before him with a heroic tread; they carried his soul away with them and made it drunk with the divine philtre of an unbounded confidence in itself. There was nothing he could not face.[158]

Stein goes on:

> 'A man that is born falls into a dream like a man who falls into the sea. If he tries to climb out into the air as inexperienced people endeavour to do, he drowns – *nicht wahr*? – No! I tell you! The

way is to the destructive element submit yourself, and with the exertions of your hands and feet in the water make the deep, deep sea keep you up.'*

Jim is romantic and that, says Stein, is 'very bad – very bad – – Very good, too.'[159] It is a burden but it is also the quality whereby a man can know himself and exist for others. Jim must be given the opportunity to realize his romantic ideal.

Stein therefore arranges that Jim shall be sent as his representative to an isolated trading-post in Patusan, a remote district of a native-ruled state. Jim had already hinted that he needed the opportunity to redeem himself in his own eyes and in the eyes of the world,[160] and on his way to Patusan 'his opportunity sat veiled by his side like an Eastern bride waiting to be uncovered by the hand of the master'.[161]

He took full advantage of his opportunity. By his courage, integrity and understanding Jim created a peaceful and flourishing community out of the chaotic, warring elements which he found at Patusan. He had gained their trust and respect and love. He could with justice boast to Marlow: 'If you ask them who is brave – who is true – who is just – who is it they would trust with their lives? – they would say, Tuan Jim.'[162]

Marlow, who visited him at Patusan, had made up his mind that Jim 'had at last mastered his fate. He had told me he was satisfied – nearly. This is going further than most of us dare.'[163] But he had not eliminated his past. Apparently no amount of achievement could counterbalance the one action, the jump. Surrounded by his success he turned on Marlow: 'But all the same, you wouldn't like to have me aboard your own ship – hey?'[164] And Marlow could not deny it. When he was parting from Marlow Jim again understood the limits of his achievement:

> 'I have got back my confidence in myself – a good name – yet sometimes I wish – No! I shall hold what I've got. Can't expect

* *Lord Jim*, p. 214. Conrad makes these passages more obscure than they need be by using 'dream' in two different senses: first as an ideal image and then equated with life itself.

anything more.' He flung his arm out towards the sea. 'Not out there anyhow.' He stamped his foot upon the sand. 'This is my limit, bcause nothing less will do.'[165]

He realized that he could not send a message to the outside world. He shouted as Marlow was being rowed away: ' "Tell them – ," he began . . . "No – nothing," he said, and with a slight wave of his hand motioned the boat away.'[166]

Then Gentleman Brown and his blackguards arrived to threaten the world which Jim had built up.

It has been claimed that Jim was 'mentally helpless'[167] before Brown and, because of a 'paralysed identification',[168] was unable to disown him, thus bringing disaster on the community. Far from being mentally paralysed, Jim 'had for the first time to affirm his will in the face of outspoken opposition' from the Bugis. He succeeded, and Marlow summed up: 'In this simple form of assent to his will lies the whole gist of the situation; their creed, his truth; and the testimony to that faithfulness which made him in his own eyes the equal of the impeccable men who never fall out of the ranks.[169] His actions were in no way affected by Brown's innuendoes. Although he was being quixotically chivalrous in the eyes of Doramin and his Bugis community, he was by European standards right to let Brown and his men go; the offer of 'a clear road or else a clear fight'[170] expressed the conviction of an honourable, civilized man, and not mental paralysis. It was also an entirely sensible decision because he could not have foreseen that Brown would treacherously fall upon Dain Waris's party and murder them. But the appalling disaster irredeemably destroyed Jim's position with the community. 'Everything was gone, and he who had been once unfaithful to his trust had lost again all men's confidence.'[171] It is again a typical piece of Conradian irony that this time he should have been blameless.

He now had three choices before him. He could flee or fight, either of which would have been approved by his faithful retainer, Tamb 'Itam, and by his girl, Jewel. 'She cried "Fight!" into his ear. She could not understand. There was nothing to fight for. He was going to prove his power in another way and conquer the fatal destiny itself.'[172] When he had persuaded the Bugis chiefs to let Brown and his men go, Jim had pledged his life against the safety of the community, and so he chose the third course and delivered himself to Doramin knowing that Doramin would exact death as retribution for the death of his son, Dain Waris.

> Not in the wildest days of his boyish visions could he have seen the alluring shape of such an extraordinary success! For it may very well be that in the short moment of his last proud and unflinching glance, he had beheld the face of that opportunity which, like an eastern bride, had come veiled to his side.
>
> But we can see him, an obscure conqueror of fame, tearing himself out of the arms of a jealous love at the sign, at the call of his exalted egoism. He goes away from a living woman to celebrate his pitiless wedding with a shadowy ideal of conduct. Is he satisfied – quite, now, I wonder? We ought to know. He is one of us – and have I not stood up once, like an evoked ghost, to answer for his eternal constancy?[173]

Some critics have asserted that Jim's life ended in defeat but despite the reference to his 'exalted egoism' which recalls Brierly's suicide there can be little doubt that Conrad approved of Jim's action. Conrad's 'victories' and 'successes' always had a taste of ashes and death in them and it would be wrong to interpret as condemnation the comment: 'He goes away from a living woman to celebrate a pitiless wedding with a shadowy ideal of conduct.' Conrad would never have disparaged such a 'shadowy ideal of conduct', and the context with the reference to Jim's 'eternal constancy' shows clear approval. There are two other comments of Marlow's to reinforce this:

> One wonders whether this was perhaps that supreme opportunity, that last and satisfying test for which I had always suspected him to be waiting, before he could frame a message to the impeccable world.[174]

and

> I affirm he had achieved greatness.[175]

It seems, indeed, that Jim had no acceptable alternative. The girl was not for him. As Marlow had said:

> You must touch your reward with clean hands, lest it turn to dead leaves, to thorns, in your grasp.[176]

And constantly Conrad harps on Jim's fate and destiny. Marlow is commenting on the final scene:

> There is . . . a sort of profound and terrifying logic in it, as if it were our imagination alone that could set loose upon us the might of an overwhelming destiny. . . . This astounding adventure . . . comes on as an unavoidable consequence. Something of the sort had to happen[177]

It is a strange theory that destiny should be reserved only for the elect, for those with imagination, but that seems to be Conrad's contention in *Lord Jim*. Nor is it a question of a person fulfilling his destiny. Fate and destiny are forces to be mastered[178] and conquered.[179] Cowardice in the face of the crucial test was contained in Jim's destiny; and only by conquering his destiny could he atone for his offence. An act of cowardice had to be expiated with the supreme act of courage, the deliberate going to meet certain death.

(7)

Conrad drew on a variety of sources for the material of *Lord Jim*. The pilgrim-ship episode was based closely on events connected with an old steamer named the *Jeddah*,* which left Singapore in the summer of 1880 with about nine hundred and fifty pilgrims bound for Jeddah, the port of Mecca.

Off Cape Gardafui the *Jeddah* ran into rough weather. As she was in a deplorable condition her boilers started to give trouble and she was leaking badly. Either because he was

* Sir Frank Swettenham revealed this source in a letter to *The Times Literary Supplement*, 6 September 1923, occasioned by Richard Curle's 'The History of Mr Conrad's Books'. Swettenham appears to have been relying on his memory which misled him in a number of details.

convinced that she would sink or, as he told the Court of Inquiry, because he feared the hostile intentions of the pilgrims, the captain, named Clark, and his wife abandoned the ship. They were followed by other officers and members of the crew. The second mate lost his life when jumping into the boat and the second engineer was prevented from leaving the ship by the pilgrims; he was thus the only European to remain on board. Captain Clark and the other deserters were picked up and taken to Aden. Shortly after Clark had announced its 'total loss by foundering', the *Jeddah,* to his embarrassment, was towed into Aden harbour by another ship. The disreputable details of the episode came out at the Court of Inquiry and Clark was given what was thought to be the very mild sentence of three years' suspension of his certificate.

The affair was widely reported in the press in the East and in Britain; Clark's conduct roused much indignation and the Singapore Legislative Assembly even debated a motion to have him arrested and re-tried.[180] Conrad would therefore have had plenty of opportunity to hear about the incident. Moreover, a Captain Craig was sent from Singapore to take over command of the *Jeddah,*[181] and this may well have been the Craig under whom Conrad later served on the *Vidar.*

None of the crew, as far as is known, played the role which Conrad gave to Jim. According to Sir Frank Swettenham the second engineer was turned into a hero and 'taken to Singapore, where he found work in a ship chandler's store, grew fat and prospered'.

During his voyages on the *Vidar*, Conrad had come across Jim Lingard, the nephew of Tom Lingard, who, like Olmeijer, lived at Tandjong Redeb on the Berouw river and was married to an Eurasian girl.[182] There he worked as an independent trader and later in the employment of the Marquis de Thorez. His daughter said that he was much loved and respected by the natives, and known as Tuan Jim. But there is no evidence that Jim Lingard had in any way been 'under a cloud'. After some years at Tandjong Redeb he became ill and was taken to Sumatra by de Thorez.[183] Nothing seems to be known of what happened to him in Sumatra where he apparently died at the age of fifty-four around 1917.[184]

But there were, at the time of Conrad's service on the *Vidar* and earlier, a number of white men, traders or adventurers, who had established themselves in out-of-the-way places and gained influence over the local native rulers. There had been Lingard, and a man named Wyndham at the court of the Sultan of Sulu, both of whom had been in Conrad's mind during his abortive attempt at *The Rescue*. Above all there was a man who, like Jim, was far more than an adventurer or a trader: Sir James Brooke, Rajah of Sarawak, to whom Conrad pays an enthusiastic tribute in the opening pages of *The Rescue*.[185] As Gordan has shown there are some general similarities between the career of Brooke and that of Jim, in that they were both white men who became the adored masters of native states through the exercise of fine qualities, although Brooke's activities were on a much bigger scale. But there were also important differences and the analogy should not be pushed too far. A number of books dealing with the career of Brooke were available and many details in *Lord Jim* and *The Rescue* show that Conrad had read some of these at least.* He drew on them for names, minor characters, background, and local colour.

He also had recourse to other books than *Brookiana*. Wallace's *Malay Archipelago*, apparently one of his favourite books, supplied him with a number of details for *Lord Jim*, *The Rescue*, and other novels; and Stein's physical ap-

* Certainly Captain the Hon. Henry Keppel's *Expedition to Borneo of 'HMS Dido' for the Suppression of Piracy; with extracts from the Journal of James Brooke*, his *Visit to the Indian Archipelago, in 'H.M. Ship Maeander', with Portions of the Private Journal of Sir James Brooke*, and Captain Rodney Mundy's *Narrative of Events in Borneo and Celebes down to the occupation of Labuan; from the Journals of James Brooke*. Brierly's name came from Keppel's *Expedition to Borneo*, Kassim from his *Indian Archipelago* and Karain, Matherson and M'Neil from Mundy. See pp. 502–503 notes 31 and 33; Gordan, op. cit., *passim*.

pearance, his apprenticeship as a watchmaker, and his butterfly collecting are based on Wallace himself.[186] Then from Major Fred McNair's *Perak and the Malays*[187] he took the names of Doramin, Tamb 'Itam and Tunku Allang as well as the Rajah's 'You hear, my people! No more of these little games.'[188] One of the few genuine pieces of Malay lore that Conrad uses, 'Even a lizard will give a fly time to say its prayers',[189] is presumably taken from McNair's book. It is probable that Conrad used other books which have not yet been traced.

He also added to Jim's biography a few details from his own, such as Jim's disablement by a falling spar and his 'half-crown complete Shakespeare'. Moreover, in a less literal sense he probably put more of his own most intimate preoccupations into Jim's and, later, Razumov's career than into any other character. The idea of guilt or betrayal and atonement or justification dominated Conrad's life.* His leaving Poland was at the root of these feelings, although it is likely that his attempted suicide enhanced them. It is not stretching psychological probability to see in Jim's 'jump' or Razumov's 'betrayal' of Haldin a, presumably unconscious, symbolical representation of Conrad's action in leaving Poland. It is particularly revealing that Conrad uses the word 'jump' with reference to his departure from Poland: 'I verily believe mine was the only case of a boy of my nationality and antecedents taking a, so to speak, standing jump out of his racial surroundings and associations.'[190] It is easy to see a psychological parallel between Jim's efforts to vindicate himself after his desertion of the *Patna* and Conrad's own life.

* It may well be that Eliza Orzeszkowa's attack on Conrad in the debate on the 'Emigration of the Talents' influenced the theme of *Lord Jim*. See pp. 423–4.

[IX]

The Partnership

ONCE *Lord Jim* was out of the way, the Conrad family went off to Bruges, towards the end of July, 'to join the disconsolate and much enduring Hueffer'[1] with the idea of combining a holiday with some collaboration on *Seraphina*. From Bruges the whole party moved to Knocke, on the coast near Ostend. Here Borys got dysentery and nearly died:

> The whole hotel was in a commotion: Dutch, Belgians and French prowled about the corridor on the look-out for news. Women with babies of their own offered to sit up, and a painter of religious subjects, Paulus by name, rose up and declared himself ready to do likewise. Elsie Hueffer helped a bit, but poor H. did not get much collaboration out of me this time.[2]

It is not surprising that Jessie described the holiday as a 'nightmarish time'.[3] The episode gave rise to almost the only good words that Jessie had to say for Hueffer: 'At this crisis I have nothing but praise for F. M. H. He earned my gratitude and appreciation by the manner he showed his practical sympathy. He was always at hand to shift my small invalid, fetch the doctor or help with the nursing.'[4]

After this disastrous month abroad the Conrads returned to the Pent, and during the rest of the year Conrad worked at his collaboration on *Seraphina*. He also, probably in September,[5] started another story of his own, *Typhoon*, which he finished in January of the new year, 1901.[6]

In the Author's Note Conrad says that he had heard the incident on which *Typhoon* is based – the taking of a ship with a large number of coolies on board through the centre of a typhoon – 'being talked about in the East'. He adds that 'I never met anybody personally concerned in this affair.' The hero, Captain MacWhirr, 'is not an acquaintance of a few hours, or a few weeks, or a few months. He is the product of twenty years of life. My own life. Conscious invention had little to do with him.'* Some at least of his characteristics, as well as his name, were, however, drawn from the Captain McWhirr under whom Conrad served on the *Highland Forest*.

Typhoon is one of Conrad's simplest important tales, and has none of the ambiguous moral and philosophical overtones with which 'Heart of Darkness' or *Lord Jim* reverberates. He mentioned in the Author's Note that 'at its first appearance *Typhoon* ... was classed by some critics as a deliberately intended storm-piece'.[7] There is indeed plenty of straightforward portrayal of the typhoon unconnected with any human reaction to it and Conrad's pleasure in describing elemental nature for its own sake cannot be discounted. But, although *Typhoon* deals with a less complex situation than does its sailing-ship counterpart, *The Nigger of the 'Narcissus'*, its prime interest is, as Conrad said, 'not the bad weather but the extraordinary complication brought into the ship's life at a moment of exceptional stress by the human element below her deck'.[8] However, Conrad confines the scope of the tale to the hero's capacity to react, which is limited. Captain MacWhirr had 'just enough imagination to carry him through each successive day, and no more'.[9]

> He had never been given a glimpse of immeasurable strength and of immoderate wrath. ... Captain MacWhirr had sailed over the surface of the oceans as some men go skimming over the years of existence to sink gently into a placid grave, ignorant of life to the last, without ever having been made to see all it may contain of perfidy, of violence, and of terror. There are on sea and land such men thus fortunate – or thus disdained by destiny or by the sea.[10]

* *Typhoon and Other Stories*, v–vi. The Author's Note is an example of Conrad's inaccuracy with regard to chronology. He writes: 'The main characteristic of this volume consists in this, that all the stories composing it belong not only to the same period but have been written one after another in the order in which they appear in the book. The period is that which follows on my connection with *Blackwood's Magazine*. I had just finished writing "The End of the Tether" ...' But the stories are not printed in order of writing and were all written before 'The End of the Tether'.

This lack of imagination and experience, together with a contempt for anything that smacked of old-womanliness which made him ignore the advice on 'storm-strategy in Captain Wilson's book', led him to do a very stupid thing. For there is no question that he was wrong to take the *Nan-Shan* straight through the typhoon; he needlessly endangered the ship and the men on her. It is merely ironical that he should have based his action on the admirable dictum that 'you don't find everything in books' when in this case he could have found all that he needed to know in a book.

But despite his obtuse stubbornness Captain MacWhirr has qualities which enable him to emerge from his ordeal as an heroic figure. He is honest, courageous, humane, and just. These qualities enable him to deal so simply and sensibly with the coolies' mixed-up belongings by dividing them equally. In this case he was justified in saying 'you don't find everything in books'. But at the end of the story there is no suggestion that he has learned anything from his experience or been deeply affected by it. That is the important difference between him and Marlow in 'Heart of Darkness'.

Within its limitations *Typhoon* is a fine tale. Except for very occasional overwriting – for instance, the bizarrely out-of-place 'unbounded wonder was the intellectual meaning of his eye, while incredulity was seated in his whole countenance'[11] – the style is concrete and powerful and there are some intensely vizualized descriptions:

> The *Nan-Shan* was ploughing a vanishing furrow upon the circle of the sea that had the surface and the shimmer of an undulating piece of gray silk. The sun, pale and without rays, poured down leaden heat in a strangely indecisive light, and the Chinamen were lying prostrate about the decks. Their bloodless, pinched, yellow faces were like the faces of bilious invalids. Captain MacWhirr noticed two of them especially, stretched out on their backs below the bridge. As soon as they had closed their eyes they seemed dead. Three others, however, were quarrelling barbarously away forward; and one big fellow, half naked, with herculean shoulders, was hanging limply over a winch; another, sitting on the deck, his

knees up and his head dropping sideways in a girlish attitude, was plaiting his pigtail with infinite languor depicted in his whole person and in the very movement of his fingers. The smoke struggled with difficulty out of the funnel, and instead of streaming away spread itself out like an infernal sort of cloud, smelling of sulphur and raining soot all over the decks.[12]

It is a cheerful tale, perhaps Conrad's most cheerful, without a trace of the customary gloom or foreboding. He told Pinker that it was 'my first attempt at treating a subject jocularly so to speak',[13] and there is no justification here for Wells's claim that his humour was 'dismal'.[14] Conrad has from time to time unjustifiably been charged with lacking humour. Humour, except for *Galgenhumor*, is rather rare in his work but he can sometimes be delightfully funny as in the altercation over the Siamese flag between Captain MacWhirr and Jukes:

The first morning the new flag floated over the stern of the *Nan-Shan* Jukes stood looking at it bitterly from the bridge. He struggled with his feelings for a while, and then remarked, 'Queer flag for a man to sail under, sir.'

'What's the matter with the flag?' inquired Captain MacWhirr. 'Seems all right to me.' And he walked across to the end of the bridge to have a good look.

'Well, it looks queer to me,' burst out Jukes, greatly exasperated, and flung off the bridge.

Captain MacWhirr was amazed at these manners. After a while he stepped quietly into the chart-room, and opened his International Signal Code-book at the plate where the flags of all the nations are correctly figured in gaudy rows. He ran his finger over them, and when he came to Siam he contemplated with great attention the red field and the white elephant. Nothing could be more simple; but to make sure he brought the book out on the bridge for the purpose of comparing the coloured drawing with the real thing at the flag-staff astern. When next Jukes, who was carrying on the duty that day with a sort of suppressed fierceness, happened on the bridge, his commander observed:

'There's nothing amiss with that flag.'

'Isn't there?' mumbled Jukes, falling on his knees before a deck-locker and jerking therefrom viciously a spare lead-line.

'No. I looked up the book. Length twice the breadth and the

elephant exactly in the middle. I thought the people ashore would know how to make the local flag. Stands to reason. You were wrong, Jukes – '.

'Well, sir,' began Jukes, getting up excitedly, 'all I can say – ' He fumbled for the end of the coil of line with trembling hands.

'That's all right.' Captain MacWhirr soothed him, sitting heavily on a little canvas folding-stool he greatly affected. 'All you have to do is to take care they don't hoist the elephant upside-down before they get quite used to it.'

Jukes flung the new lead-line over on the fore-deck with a loud 'Here you are, bo'ss'en – don't forget to wet it thoroughly,' and turned with immense resolution towards his commander; but Captain MacWhirr spread his elbows on the bridge-rail comfortably.

'Because it would be, I suppose, understood as a signal of distress,' he went on. 'What do you think? That elephant there, I take it, stands for something in the nature of the Union Jack in the flag – '

'Does it!' yelled Jukes, so that every head on the *Nan-Shan*'s decks looked towards the bridge. Then he sighed, and with sudden resignation: 'It would certainly be a dam' distressful sight,' he said, meekly.[15]

Then there are fine comic touches of authenticity. The typhoon is at its height:

He [the boatswain] shouted also something about the smokestack being as likely to go overboard as not. Jukes thought it very possible, and imagined the fires out, the ship helpless – . The boatswain by his side kept on yelling. 'What? What is it?' Jukes cried distressfully; and the other repeated, 'What would my old woman say if she saw me now?'[16]

It is interesting to note that, as in *The Nigger of the 'Narcissus'*, the crew as a whole do not show up very well. Apart from Captain MacWhirr and Jukes, only a few others, such as the excellent Solomon Rout, the heroic helmsman, and the amiably conscientious boatswain, stand out. During the typhoon the majority of the crew cower under the bridge. 'The boatswain had been keeping up a gruff talk, but a more unreasonable lot of men, he said afterwards, he had never been with. They were snug enough there, out of harm's way, and not wanted to do anything, either; and yet they did nothing but grumble and complain peevishly like so many sick kids.'[17]

Again Conrad was not prepared to sacrifice reality. But reality set him one difficult artistic problem which he could not solve. He only described the first part of the typhoon. From the forecast that 'the worst was to come'[18] and the preparations for it Conrad skips to 'On a bright sunshiny day, with the breeze chasing her smoke far ahead, the *Nan-Shan* came into Fu-Chau.'[19] Of course it would have been artistically impossible to have described the second part of the typhoon as well. By then Conrad and the reader and, one would have thought, the *Nan-Shan* had done as much as could be expected of them. But he could perhaps have got through the typhoon without such an awkward technical crack. However, this is a minor blemish.

Typhoon was the first of Conrad's stories to be handled by J. B. Pinker, the literary agent. The appearance on the scene of literary agents was comparatively recent, but such men as A. P. Watt, Curtis Brown and Pinker were soon to establish the literary agent as an intermediary between author and publisher. Some time back Garnett seems to have suggested to Conrad that he would be wise to employ an agent and to have mentioned Watt; Conrad replied that 'it would be a great relief to have someone to do one's "dirty work" as the sailors say of any occupation they dislike'[20] but apparently did no more about it. However, when he was approached by Pinker three years later he decided to let him act for him – a decision for which he was to have good reason to be thankful in the long run, although it may have affected adversely his relations with Blackwood.

(2)

Almost immediately after he had finished *Typhoon* Conrad started another story[21] which he finished some time in May.[22] It was called 'Falk: a Reminiscence' and in Curle's copy Conrad wrote that it was '... partly biographical being an episode in the story of my first command'. It seems therefore that the story of Falk was based on fact, much though it sounds like fiction. Probably Conrad embroidered the facts considerably and he may well have drawn on local gossip about Falk. Jessie Conrad merely says that the story was 'culled from a short paragraph in a newspaper which had some relation to an episode known to Conrad many years before, while he was at sea'.[23] But the passage where the narrator of the tale describes the problems connected with the ship of which he had been sent to take command[24] is certainly based closely on Conrad's own experiences with the *Otago* in Bangkok.

Technically 'Falk' is presented in the same way as 'Youth' and 'Heart of Darkness'. A similar group of people 'all more or less connected with the sea, were dining in a small river-hostelry'.[25] The chops 'brought forcibly to one's mind the night of ages when the primeval man, evolving the first rudiments of cookery from his dim consciousness, scorched lumps of flesh at a fire of sticks in the company of other good fellows; then, gorged and happy, sat him back among the gnawed bones to tell his artless tales of experience – the tales of hunger and hunt – and of women, perhaps!'[26] And the talk is of 'wrecks, of short rations and of heroism'.[27] All this encourages one of the company to recount an episode from his life which concerns a wreck, short rations, heroism, and which shows the elemental, primeval instincts taking possession of civilized man.

Conrad thus had the material for a story with a theme similar to that of 'Heart of Darkness'. But he chose not to exploit it fully and barely touches the profound issues presented in that story. The tone is set at the start. The narrator, who is kept anonymous and is more impersonal than Marlow, says: 'This reminds me of an absurd episode in my life ...'[28] There is an underlying humorous note throughout and Falk himself, the centaur-like 'man-boat', despite his appalling secret, is treated primarily as a comic figure. Furthermore the tale ends happily.

Most of the story is taken up with Falk's persecution of the narrator, a young captain come to take over the command of a ship in an eastern port. The reason for this persecution is Falk's suspicion that the captain is his rival for the love of the niece of a homely German captain named Hermann.*

Hermann and his family, on their patriarchal old tub, the *Diana*, present an epitome of bourgeois virtues and limitations: 'There apparently no whisper of the world's iniquities had ever penetrated. . . . She [the *Diana*] was worldproof. Her venerable innocence apparently put a restraint on the roaring lusts of the sea. ... It looked as if the allied oceans had refrained from smashing these high bulwarks, unshipping the lumpy rudder, frightening the children, and generally opening this family's eyes out of sheer reticence.'[29] Hermann was thus in the same category as Captain MacWhirr but, instead of a typhoon, 'the ruthless disclosure was, in the end, left for a man to make; a man strong and elemental enough and driven to unveil some secrets of the sea by the power of a simple and elemental desire'.[30] And Hermann had none of the heroic qualities which had enabled MacWhirr gloriously to survive the test.

Falk is a man haunted by an episode in his past which he feels obliged to reveal before asking Hermann for the hand of his niece, in spite of the advice of the young captain, who has turned out not to be a rival, to say nothing about it.[31] 'I have eaten man,'[32] he declares.

Falk describes to the young captain how this happened and it is in these few pages that Conrad touches on the theme of *The Nigger*, human solidarity threatened, and shows how an elemental impulse to live may in extremity sweep aside the assumptions of civilized society. On the *Borgmester Dahl,* floating helpless in the southern seas, Falk was the man who showed most spirit and initiative; he tried to

* It is a technical curiosity of the story that Hermann's niece does not utter a word throughout although she is present during dramatic scenes involving her future. Conrad's explanation that 'whenever she happens to come under the observation of the narrator she has either no occasion or is too profoundly moved to speak' is not convincing.

inspire energy and fortitude in the rest of the crew and did his utmost to prevent one of them from killing himself, but without success. 'The bonds of discipline became relaxed'[33] and 'the apathy of utter hopelessness' overcame the men:

> The organised life of the ship had come to an end. The solidarity of the men had gone. They became indifferent to each other. It was Falk who took in hand the distribution of such food as remained. Sometimes whispers of hate were heard passing between the languid skeletons . . .[34]

Then the ship's carpenter 'spoke of the last sacrifice. There was nothing eatable left on board.'[35] 'Falk liked the big carpenter. He had been the best man of the lot, helpful and ready as long as there was anything to do, the longest hopeful, and had preserved to the last some vigour and decision of mind.'[36] But then in his desperation he tried to kill Falk with a crowbar. Falk decided that 'the best man shall survive' and armed himself with a pistol. Thus he was ready when the carpenter, who was also armed, fired point blank at him:

> He missed – and Falk, instead of attempting to seize the arm holding the weapon, opened his door unexpectedly, and with the muzzle of his revolver nearly touching the other's side, shot him dead.
>
> The best man had survived. Both of them had at the beginning just strength enough to stand on their feet, and both had displayed pitiless resolution, endurance, cunning and courage – all the qualities of classic heroism.[37]

The carpenter was eaten and Falk was now undisputed master of the ship, the only man with a gun:

> He lived! Some of the others lived, too – concealed, anxious, coming out one by one from their hiding-place at the seductive sound of a shot. And he was not selfish. They shared all alike.[38]

That was Falk's secret and it now seemed, from Hermann's indignation, that he would be thwarted in his equally strong desire to marry the girl. In the Author's Note Conrad described Falk as being 'absolutely true to my experience of certain straightforward characters combining a perfectly natural ruthlessness with a certain amount of moral delicacy. Falk obeys the law of self-preservation without the slightest misgivings as to his right, but at a crucial turn of that ruthlessly preserved life he will not condescend to dodge the truth.'[39] In fact the possibility of his actions having been morally wrong did not occur to Falk: 'Somebody had to die – but why me?'[40] he asked. That he had been forced to kill and eat men he regarded as his 'misfortune'. To Hermann, on the other hand, 'the duty of a human being was to starve'.[41] What Conrad himself thought is another matter. Hermann, the only person to protest at Falk's action, is treated as a comic figure; he is told by the captain that he is too squeamish and his scruples are revealed as very easy to overcome; he agrees to give his niece to Falk after the captain has diplomatically pointed out that he will be saving her fare home, but maintains that Falk should have kept his secret. Moreover, it is a curiosity of the story that Conrad concentrates on the effect of eating, not killing man. Yet Falk's crime was to kill the carpenter and the others, for Conrad makes it clear that this was not done in self-defence; once the carpenter was dead it would have been foolish for starving men not to eat him. It is impossible to know whether this emphasis was intentional or not. If it was intentional the implication is that Conrad wished to concentrate on the less reprehensible part of the action, or that it was a piece of deliberate irony to show Hermann's misplaced sense of outrage.

There seems no justification for Douglas Hewitt's claim that 'Falk' is one of those stories in which the narrator 'is insecure and the chief effect of the story is to undermine the values and assumptions with which he is satisfied at the beginning'.[42] The main conclusion, which Conrad expresses through the mouth of the narrator, is:

> He [Falk] wanted to live. He had always wanted to live. So we all do – but in us the instinct serves a complex conception, and in him this instinct existed alone. . . . I think I saw then the obscure beginning, the seed germinating in the soil of an unconscious need, the first shoot of that tree bearing now for a mature mankind the

flower and the fruit, the infinite gradation in shades and in flavour of our discriminating love. He was a child. He was as frank as a child, too. He was hungry for the girl, terribly hungry, as he had been terribly hungry for food.

Don't be shocked if I declare that in my belief it was the same need, the same pain, the same torture. We are in this case allowed to contemplate the foundation of all the emotions – that one joy which is to live, and the one sadness at the root of the innumerable torments.[43]

Douglas Hewitt asserts that this passage contains 'profoundly disturbing reflections on the roots of all our emotions'.[44] But does it? 'Don't be shocked ...' Evidently the narrator was not shocked; nor are these reflections disturbing, though they may *épater le bourgeois*. Falk's instincts were straightforward and healthy, if ruthless; there was no trace in him of Kurtz's corruption which had so appalled Marlow. The story does not undermine values in which Conrad believed; it shows only that there are situations in which certain values may not apply. Summarizing the story to his French translator he wrote: 'Ideé: Contraste du sentimentalisme commun avec le point de vue net d'un homme à peu près primitif ... qui considère la préservation de la vie comme la loi suprème et morale.'[45]

'Falk' was apparently considered offensive by magazine editors and was never placed serially. Conrad thought highly of it[46] and it is certainly one of his best short stories. It is well written and there are delightful descriptions of the way in which Falk expresses himself by means of his tug. For example:

He ranged close by us, passing out dead slow, without a hail. ... Abreast of Hermann's ship Falk stopped the engines; and a profound silence reigned over the rocks, the shore and the sea, for the time it took him to raise his hat aloft before the nymph of the grey print frock. I had snatched up my binoculars, and I can answer for it she didn't stir a limb, standing by the rail shapely and erect, with one of her hands grasping a rope at the height of her head, while the way of the tug carried slowly past her the lingering and profound homage of the man. There was for me an enormous significance in the scene, the sense of having witnessed a solemn declaration. . . . With a rush of black smoke belching suddenly out of the funnel, and a mad swirl of paddle-wheels provoking a burst of weird and precipitated clapping, the tug shot out of the desolate arena.[47]

Conrad seems to have been working easily at this time because he quickly went on from 'Falk' to another story. On 8 June he wrote to Pinker that 'the short story (entitled – either "A Husband" or "A Castaway") will be ready in a week'[48] and on the twentieth he told Galsworthy that he had finished it.[49]

'Amy Foster', which was the title finally chosen, is the moving story of a man from Austrian Poland who is the solitary survivor of a ship wrecked on the Kentish coast while carrying emigrants to America. He roams the countryside in search of food and shelter, but 'in his desperate endeavours to get help, and in his need to get in touch with someone'[50] he is met only with hostile incomprehension. Finally a farmer, in sheer terror of him, locks him in a wood shed. Here he receives his first act of kindness in the form of a loaf of bread from Amy Foster, the farmer's servant.

He gradually becomes tolerated by the community and marries Amy Foster. She is a dull-witted peasant girl but 'with enough imagination to fall in love'.[51] '. . . There is no kindness of heart without a certain amount of imagination. She had some. She had even more than is necessary to understand suffering and to be moved by pity.'[52] They have a child but gradually Amy becomes alienated by her husband's strangeness and resents his wish to teach the child his language. The narrator of the story, a country doctor, reflects: 'I wondered whether his difference, his strangeness, were not penetrating with repulsion that dull nature they had begun by irresistibly attracting.'[53] He becomes ill with lung trouble and during his illness Amy finds 'terror, the unreasonable terror, of that man she could not understand creeping over her'.[54] Finally, in his fever, when he calls out for water in his own language:

She jumped to her feet, snatched up the child, and stood still,

He spoke to her, and his passionate remonstrances only increased her fear of that strange man. I believe he spoke to her for a long time, entreating, wondering, pleading, ordering. ... And then a gust of rage came over him.

He sat up and called out terribly one word – some word. Then he got up as though he hadn't been ill at all, she says. And as in fevered dismay, indignation, and wonder he tried to get to her round the table, she simply opened the door and ran out with the child in her arms.[55]

The next morning the doctor finds him 'lying face down and his body in a puddle, just outside the little wicket-gate'. The doctor takes him inside, but he dies, more, the doctor suggests, from a broken heart than from exposure. He was 'cast out mysteriously by the sea to perish in the supreme disaster of loneliness and despair'.[56]

The subject of the story is stated in general terms when the doctor speaks of 'tragedies ... arising from irreconcilable differences and from that fear of the Incomprehensible that hang over all our heads'.[57] And the behaviour of the villagers towards Yanko Goorall is a horrifying picture of the degree of cruelty that fear or hatred of the strange and unknown can engender. Yanko Goorall 'remembered the pain of his wretchedness and misery, his heartbroken astonishment that it was neither seen nor understood, his dismay at finding all the men angry and all the women fierce'.[58] Then, when it might have been supposed that he had endeared himself to the community by saving a child from drowning the thought that he will marry Amy Foster arouses all their latent hostility: 'It was only when he declared his purpose to get married that I fully understood how, for a hundred futile and inappreciable reasons, how – shall I say odious? – he was to all the countryside.'[59]

There is an interesting parallel between the attitude of the villagers to Yanko Goorall and the treatment of the mysterious but kindly Gilliat in *Les Travailleurs de la Mer*. 'Gilliat habitait la paroisse de Saint-Sampson. Il n'y était pas aimé' because 'les gens des pays n'aiment pas qu'il y ait des énigmes sur les étrangers.'[60]

Apart from its considerable merit as a story 'Amy Foster' is important in that it vividly and simply illustrates one of the main themes of Conrad's work, the essential isolation and loneliness of the individual. Moreover, the tale probably draws some of its horror and power from Conrad's own experience as a foreigner in a strange country, speaking scarcely a word of the language.* It is easy to detect an autobiographical note in Conrad's description of Yanko Goorall 'feeling bitterly as he lay in his emigrant bunk his utter loneliness; for his was a highly sensitive nature',[61] or in the reflection that 'it is indeed hard upon a man to find himself a lost stranger, helpless, incomprehensible, and of a mysterious origin, in some obscure corner of the earth'.[62] And the mournful picture of the countryside of Kent presumably reflects what Conrad himself felt at times:

> With the sun hanging low on its western limit, the expanse of the grasslands framed in the counter-scarps of the rising ground took on a gorgeous and sombre aspect. A sense of penetrating sadness, like that inspired by a grave strain of music, disengaged itself from the silence of the fields. The men we met walked past, slow, unsmiling, with downcast eyes, as if the melancholy of an overburdened earth had weighted their feet, bowed their shoulders, borne down their glances.
>
> 'Yes,' said the doctor ... 'one would think the earth is under a curse, since of all her children these that cling to her the closest are uncouth in body and as leaden of gait as if their very hearts were loaded with chains.'[63]

Conrad apparently got the suggestion for the story of a castaway from Hueffer, who had mentioned in his *Cinque Ports*[64] that one of the crew of a shipwrecked German merchantman had gone round knocking at doors but had been unable to make himself understood and had eventually been found by the police asleep in a pigsty.[65] But he says no more about the man and presumably the story is largely Conrad's invention. According to Jessie Conrad, 'Amy Foster' herself was for many years in the Conrads' service.[66]

* Bertrand Russell, who knew Conrad, has cited this story as a key to Conrad's character, *Portraits from Memory and other Essays*, 1956, p. 83.

(3)

After finishing 'Amy Foster', Conrad concentrated for the rest of 1901 on *Romance*, or *Seraphina* as it was still called.[67] But this was rather a long-term project and his need for money was again pressing. Already in June he had told Pinker: 'You will have to advance something on that ['Amy Foster'] too if you don't want me to roll over on my side and give up writing altogether. It's awful. Awful.'* In July the ever-generous and willing Hueffer 'advanced' him (presumably on the basis of Conrad's share in the expected proceeds from *Seraphina*) £100 on the security of Conrad's insurance policy.[68]

By the new year his financial position was desperate. He wrote rather incoherently to Pinker.

> I am nearly going mad with worry. . . . Really all these anxieties do drive me to the verge of madness – but death would be the best thing. It would pay off all my debts and there would be no question of MS. Really if one hadn't wife and child I don't know – There are also some pressing bills. Damn. And with all this my bodily health is excellent. It is the brain only that is fagged.[69]

In the same letter Conrad described *Seraphina* and asked for another £40 advance on it. Pinker dug his heels in and wrote him a lecture instead, at which Conrad bitterly protested.[70] However, Wells came over, saw the MS. of *Seraphina* and also of another story, 'Tomorrow', which Conrad was finishing and sent Pinker a telegram asking him to advance the money. Pinker immediately did so and Conrad apologized for his earlier flare-up, admitting that Pinker's refusal had been justified.[71]

On 16 January Conrad sent 'Tomorrow' off to Pinker, describing it as ' "Conrad" adapted down to the needs of a magazine' but 'by no means a potboiler'. It is a strange,

* 7 June 1901. Another letter, of 7 November 1901, shows that during this year Conrad had recieved £240 from Pinker, but part of this was for work still unplaced; Conrad lists '*Typhoon*: £100, "Falk": £60, "Amy Foster": £40, *Seraphina* (on account my share): £40'.

haunting story about a mad old retired sea captain who is waiting for the return of his son, Harry, whom he has driven from home many years before. Captain Hagberd expects Harry to arrive 'tomorrow' and involves Bessie Carvil, the downtrodden daughter of his blind next-door neighbour, in his fantasy, telling her that she shall marry his son when he returns. She almost comes to believe this. Then Harry does turn up, in order to cadge five pounds, but Captain Hagberd refuses to believe that this is his son and still insists that he is coming 'tomorrow'. He tries to drive Harry away and then shuts himself in the house. Harry, who is a rascal and a womanizer, hears the story of his father's fantasy from Bessie and then discovers that she is the girl designed for him. But he has no intention of putting himself at his father's mercy again and leaves after smothering Bessie with passionate kisses. The old man is delighted that Harry has gone but Bessie is overwhelmed with despair:

> It was as if all the hopeful madness of the world had broken out to bring terror upon her heart, with the voice of that old man shouting of his trust in an everlasting to-morrow.[72]

It is not one of Conrad's most impressive short stories and there is something gratuitously unpleasant in a madman and a blind old tyrant being the cause of Bessie Carvil's tragedy. It has in fact a rather un-Conradian flavour and it is not surprising to discover that Hueffer apparently had a hand in it. Writing to Hueffer, Conrad remarks of Harry: '*All your* suggestion and *absolutely my* conception. It's most interesting and funny to see.'[73]

Jessie has said that Conrad never liked the story;[74] but he thought highly enough of it to realize its genuine dramatic qualities and base a one-act play on it a few years later.

When he had finished 'Tomorrow' Conrad settled down to do his share of *Romance*. This novel, under its original title of *Seraphina*, was first mentioned some time towards the end of 1898,[75] when the collaborators had optimistically hoped to have it 'greatly advanced if not absolutely finished in July, 1899'.[76] But Conrad was concentrating on his own work, while Hueffer was taken up with *The Inheritors* and afterwards his book on *The Cinque Ports.* Thus, in April 1900, Conrad could only tell Blackwood that if *The Inheritors* 'goes down well with the public we shall try our hand at an adventure story of which the skeleton is set up – with some modelling here and there already worked up'.[77] When *Romance* was being prepared for publication Hueffer had typically put the dates of writing at 1896–1903. Conrad wisely protested that this was laying themselves open to the jibes of the critics and added: 'Moreover we didn't collaborate six years at that. We began in December 1900 and finished in July 1902 really.'[78]

But there are two references to the work earlier than this which suggest that Hueffer must have been at work on a draft during 1900. In September Conrad wrote to Pinker asking him to take in hand a joint work of his and Hueffer's which 'is nearing completion', adding that he could let Pinker have fourteen chapters out of the twenty the work contained.[79] Then, probably some time in October, he told Pinker that *Seraphina* was finished and would be ready for him in a fortnight.[80]

Nothing more seems to be known of this draft, which must, except perhaps for the earlier chapters, have been very different from the final version because it almost certainly contained none of Conrad's writing. It may be that Conrad disapproved so strongly of Hueffer's treatment that the draft was never sent to Pinker.

No more is heard of *Seraphina* for some seven months, and then, in June 1901, Conrad told Pinker that it was now complete in MS.[81] A fortnight later he wrote to Galsworthy from Winchelsea, where he was staying with the Hueffers: 'Now I am here working at *Seraphina.* There are 10,000 words which I am going to write *in manu propria.* I reckon to be done on Sunday sometime.'[82] And at the beginning of July he told Pinker that he was working at Part III.[83]

An undated letter to Hueffer which Aubry assigns to 1903

but which clearly belongs to this period[84] helps to sort out the tangle. In this letter Conrad tells Hueffer that Parts I, II, and IV are being sent to Blackwood[85] and that he will write an epitome of Part III. He adds:

> I've studied p. III as a whole very earnestly. It is most important and it wants doing over. It must be given hard *reality*. The treatment as it stands is too much in the air – in places. I don't want to bother you now by going into the argument. I shall do the thing myself, but of course I would want to speak to you about it. [(June, 1901), *L.L.*, I, p. 312]

This must still have been basically Hueffer's early draft and very different from the final version (it has no Part V, for instance).

Blackwood declined the book[86] and the two collaborators seem to have set about some thorough rewriting. In November Conrad again announced that *Seraphina* was finished, 'at last', and added: 'I've put remarkable guts into that story. It goes now to Hueffer . . .'[87] But he continued to work at it into the new year, telling Meldrum: '*Seraphina* seems to hang about me like a curse. There is always something wrong turning up about that story.'[88] He was not finally rid of it until March when he wrote to Galsworthy: '*Seraphina* is finished and gone out of the house she has haunted for this year past. I do really hope it will hit the taste of the street – unless the devil's in it.'[89]

The writing of the book seems to have been divided roughly as stated in a letter from Conrad to Hueffer:

> I suppose our recollections agree. Mine, in their simplest form, are: First part yours; second part mainly yours, with a little by me, on points of seamanship and such like small matters; third part about 60% mine, with important touches by you; fourth part mine, with here and there an important sentence by you; fifth part practically all yours, including the famous sentence at which we both exclaimed 'This is genius,' (Do you remember what it is?) with perhaps half a dozen lines by me. I think that, *en gros*, this is absolutely correct. Intellectually and artistically it is of course, right through, a joint production. [10 November 1923]

Elsewhere Conrad claimed a little more for himself:

> In this book I have done my share of writing. Most of the characters (with the exception of Mrs Williams, Sebright and the seamen) were introduced by Hueffer, and developed then in my own way, with, of course, his consent and collaboration. The last part is (like the first) the work of Hueffer, except for a few paragraphs written by me. Part second is actually joint work. Parts three and four are my writing, with here and there a sentence by Hueffer.[90]

It was a strange way to write a novel. Sometimes Conrad and Hueffer would work together in the same house, planning, discussing, writing, and revising. But more often they would work apart and then all that one had written had to be sent to the other for comment and possible alteration, after which it would be sent back for final approval. Jessie gives an account of what collaboration under one roof was like:

> Sometimes the two would elect to start work as we, Mrs Hueffer and I, were retiring for the night. For hours after I had gone to bed the voices would reach me through the floor. Sometimes the tones would appear to mingle in pleasant accord, their ideas flowing easily, amused laughs and chuckles. At others sounds of wordy strife and disagreement penetrated to my ears, and raised voices came distinctly into my room. Then F. M. H., who was a very tall man, would relieve his feelings by thumping the oaken beam that crossed the ceiling below and my small son would stir in his sleep and mutter sleepily: 'Mama, dear, moo-cows down there.'
>
> The small house seemed at times full to overflowing and there were days when the two artists with their vagaries, temperaments and heated discussions made it seem rather a warm place. Still, to give F. M. H. his due, he was the least peppery of the two, being a native of a less excitable nation and his drawling voice made a sharp contrast with the quick, un-English utterances of the fellow collaborator.[91]

Both had temperamental, highly-strung natures and were quick to take offence, so that collaboration must have been far from easy at times. An undated letter from Conrad to Hueffer gives a glimpse of the sort of problems that arose:

You cannot really suppose that there is anything between us except our mutual regard and our partnership – in crime. 'Voyons, Señorita quelle folie.' Upon my word I am quite confounded by your letter which my speaking 'à coeur ouvert' to Auntie Elsie did not deserve.

I was afraid of taking a course that would seem heartless or offensive to you – especially in your low state of health; and I mistrusted my own nerves which, as you may have perceived, are and were devilishly attuned to the concert pitch of gloom and absurd irritation.

But of any irritation or of any thought about you but of the most affectionate nature I have been utterly unconscious then or now.

It is a fact I work better in your home in touch with your sympathy. Still I can do something here too. I am very grateful to you for the days I have passed in Winchelsea.

I could write much more in the strain of thanks . . .

Report; O'Brien just out of Kemp's room. – Another two hours work'll push the story along.[92]

Hueffer must have suffered a lot from Conrad's dilatoriness and frequently gloomy state of mind as other letters show. For instance:

Don't think evil of me. I am doing my damnedest. I have been interrupted; I have been upset too; and generally I am not allowed to forget how impossible my position daily is becoming. . . . Ah! for three days peace of mind. If I had that I would move mountains. Three days only![93]

A further problem was that Jessie disliked Hueffer and his wife. Very naturally she resented the supercilious disdain with which Hueffer seems to have treated her and she was probably rather jealous of Conrad's relationship with Elsie who was an intelligent and educated woman. Jessie describes an incident during the collaboration which gives a revealing picture of all four of them:

He [Conrad] stalked through the dining-room with the terse request that I should at once prepare him a dose of gout medicine. He then announced to all and sundry his intention of retiring to the next room and trying to rest. He wished to be alone there, too, and in a tone tantamount to a command he added: 'And keep those two children quiet, and out of this, where they can't disturb me.'

Totally disregarding his guests, who looked, as they must have felt, uncomfortable, he closed one door after the other with considerable violence behind him.

This first experience of their host as anything but the acme of politeness and courtesy was received in silence, except for the rather sarcastic suggestion from F. M. H. that we, my sister and I, should take Christina with my boy with us for a walk.

He then walked slowly to the window-seat and seated himself, a gloomy silhouette, his drooping bulldog pipe at an even more depressed angle than usual. His wife flung herself on the couch the other side of the room. When we returned nearly two hours later they had not changed their position. F. M. H. still sat on the window-seat, a book in his hand and many more on the floor at his feet, together with both the lady's shoes.

Just then Joseph Conrad appeared refreshed after his nap, and quite ready to make himself agreeable, both his irritation and the threatened gout forgotten . . .

He greeted F. M. H. with jocular friendliness and the wife with a show of ceremonious politeness that might have been taken as an apology for his lack of good manners a little while ago. He stopped short at the sight of the miscellaneous collection on the floor, and turned to me with a pained expression and rebuked me rather severely for not leaving the room tidy for my guests before going for my walk. 'I am very surprised and displeased,' he finished up, as he held open the door with a return of his rather grand manner, inviting the couple with a courtly gesture to precede him into the other room. I gasped, and turned away to hide a smile. Once again my sense of humour threatened to overcome me. I marvelled at his want of understanding, but by that time I had ceased to be upset at trifles that certainly had their humorous side. This attitude on the part of F. M. H. was typical of both him and his wife for the whole of that close acquaintance. Sometimes I boiled inwardly and my sense of justice was outraged, still I prided myself upon my complete self-control, and did not lose my temper.[94]

In contrast, a letter which Conrad wrote to Hueffer, apparently in connection with a party to celebrate the birthdays of Borys and Christina, gives a charming picture of the relationship, as well as showing how unreservedly Conrad could enter into the life of those around him:

Jessie directs me to tell you that you are to come right in (in overcoats) at the *front door* and walk into the parlour where there will be tea laid out (I hope not on the floor but answer for nothing).

At 3.40 the Young Lady having had barely time to smooth her plumes shall proceed (attended by the Lady Regent – the Lord Regent is at liberty to swoon for fifty minutes) shall proceed – I say – to the Baronial Kitchen (where the feast is to be engulfed) to receive the guests with the Young Cavalier.

Then she takes her armchair
at the
High End

Engulfing by the young princes, princesses of the name of Hopkins, Mills, etc. etc. begins.

The Dames Graham and Gates would have come over at two to help. They preside at the flow of tea.

The Lady Regent, the Chatelaine and the Chatelain assisted by the Maid of Honour, Nelly, strut about more or less effectively. But it is *distinctly understood* that the Lady Regent is *not to tire herself out in any way*. What is wanted mostly of her is to shed extra radiance on the glory of her daughter.

Engulfing Stops
in the
Natural Course of things.
then
The Young Lady
arises from her armchair.

And proceeding up the table on *her* right pulls a cracker with every feaster on that side. The Young Cavalier performs the same rite on *his* right side.

Feasters don caps out of Crackers
A Bell rings cheerfully!
(it is then five of the clock)

And the open door reveals Tree which has been lighted up by the efforts of the Lord Regent (now recovered from the Swoon) and the Chatelain.

Inspection of Same – Feast
for the eyes and Flow of Soul.
A Bell rings imperatively!
All sit down.

Whereupon the distribution of presents begins by the Young Lady and Cavalier assisted by the Nomenclators exclaiming in loud tones, Snippers (armed with scissors) harvesting the boughs of the tree with dexterous snips, Burden Bearers carrying large packages with ease etc. etc.

5.45 p.m.
Feasters depart in batches per
Hired Wagonette
with
The Young Lady & Cavalier
speeding the parting guests at the door.
'The Rest is Silence'[95]

(4)

Romance is the only considerable product of the 'partnership'; but in relation to Conrad's main work it is of small importance. Hueffer was always anxious to magnify the significance of the collaboration and Conrad was careful not to belittle their joint work to him. Conrad does in fact seem to have got some satisfaction from working at *Romance*, because he told Garnett: 'Strangely enough it is yet my share of *Romance* . . . that fills me with the least dismay'.[96] It was doubtless a relief to be able to give himself to an aesthetic exercise which called up none of the agonizing struggle of his own work simply because it was on a more superficial level. In a letter to the Polish writer, K. Waliszewski, he showed that he did not value the book highly:

Je regard *Romance* comme une chose sans aucune importance: J'ai collaboré pendant qu'il m'était impossible de faire autre chose. Il était facile de raconter quelques événements sans me préoccuper autrement du sujet. L'idée que nous avions était purement esthètique: rendre quelques scènes, quelques situations, d'une façon convenable. Puis il ne nous déplaisait pas de montrer que nous pouvions faire quelque chose dans le genre fort en vogue avec le public en ce moment-ci. . . . Mais on soignait la technique tout de même. Avouez que c'est bien écrit. Flaubert . . . s'est bien mis à faire une féerie.[97]

Conrad might more aptly have come closer home and mentioned Stevenson. It seems fair to say that in conception and spirit the book owes little to Conrad. The subject was originally Hueffer's and it is easy to see why the romantic adventures of the aristocratic young John Kemp would have appealed to him. But for anything of importance that he wrote Conrad needed a moral pivot, a problem of conduct, at the centre and in *Romance* there is none. In a letter to Pinker Conrad tried to describe the intention. He spoke of 'the Romantic feeling being the basis of the book which is NOT a boy's story . . . the aim being to present the scenes and events and people *strictly realistically* in a glamour of *Romance* . . . a serious attempt at *interesting, animated Romance* with no more psychology than comes naturally into the action'.[98] In the book there is an attempt to state a serious theme:

> How often the activity of our life is the least real part of it! Life, looked upon as a whole, presents itself to my fancy as a pursuit with open arms of a winged and magnificent dream, hovering just over our heads and casting its glory upon our hopes.[99]

But the treatment of the story cannot sustain such an elevated image. It is more in keeping with the callow idea of 'romance': 'I had not had a very happy life, and I had lived shut in on myself, thinking of the wide world beyond my reach, that seemed to hold out infinite possibilities of romance, of adventure, of love, perhaps, and stores of gold.'[100] This cheapening of the effect is particularly blatant in the first and last Parts of the book. 'Romance' is constantly cropping up and the tone is set by a paragraph of pretentious philosophizing, obviously from the hand of Hueffer:

> Journeying in search of romance – and that, after all, is our business in this world – is much like trying to catch the horizon. It lies a little distance before us, and a little distance behind – about, as far as the eye can carry. One discovers that one has passed through it just as one passed what is today our horizon. One looks back and says, 'Why, there it is.' One looks forward and says the same. It lies either in the old days when we used to, or in the new days when we shall. I look back upon those days of mine, and little things remain, come back to me, assume an atmosphere, take significance, go to the making of a *temps jadis*. Probably, when I

look back upon what is the dull, arid waste of today, it will be much the same.[101]

The last paragraph of the book is on the same level, and was claimed by Hueffer as his:

> And, looking back, we see Romance – that subtle thing that is mirage – that is life. It is the goodness of the years we have lived through, of the old time when we did this or that, when we dwelt here or there. Looking back, it seems a wonderful enough thing that I who am this, and she who is that, commencing so far away a life that, after such sufferings borne together and apart, ended so tranquilly there in a world so stable – that she and I should have passed through so much, good chance and evil chance, sad hours and joyful, all lived down and swept away into the little heap of dust that is life. That, too, is Romance![102]

Then the characters are all, except for those on board the *Lion*, typical figures of romantic adventure, and John Kemp is a particularly conventional and doltish hero. Seraphina herself is wholly delightful. But, although she is a girl of spirit, she is constantly presented enshrouded with a romantic aura – 'the girl with the lizard, the girl with the dagger'[103] – and there is little attempt to develop her into a realistic character. Some of the other characters are picturesque but without depth or interest: the romantic Carlos Riego with his sepulchral cough, his faithful retainer Tomas Castro, who executes a little dance before darting in to kill with the blade of his forearm, the ludicrous, mournful, singing pirate leader, Manuel-del-Popolo, and the villainous O'Brien with his obsessional hatred of the English. The chief interest of the book is in the atmosphere created and the excitement of the story told. But the action frequently becomes unreal or melodramatic and at the end, during the trial, is at times merely absurd, such as when Kemp forgets to ask his father to find out about the *Lion*, which is the one thing that is supposed to obsess him, or when in his excitement he pierces his hand on the spikes of the rail and remains unaware of having done so.

Although Part Four, which was almost wholly by Conrad,

contains most of the best scenes and the best writing, it would be unfair to assume that Hueffer was responsible for all the defects of the book. There are numerous weak passages in the parts which Conrad supposedly wrote, and he showed in his own work that he could stoop to melodrama, while *Chance* is hung on a thread just as inadequate as *Romance*.

None the less direct collaboration with Hueffer certainly did not bring out Conrad's best. Henry James's reported comment may be an exaggeration: 'To me this is like a bad dream which one relates at breakfast! Their traditions and their gifts are so dissimilar. Collaboration between them is to me inconceivable.'[104] But there is something unsatisfactory and impersonal about this novel and it has its chief interest as a literary curiosity. Nor is it easy to imagine a really satisfactory work of imagination coming from the minds of two people.

Apart from the worthless fragment *The Nature of a Crime*, Conrad and Hueffer did not collaborate officially again, although they had ambitious plans which clearly show that Conrad took the idea of collaboration seriously and had high hopes of it. In the same letter to Waliszewski in which he dismissed *Romance* he outlined the plot of another joint novel:

> H. et moi nous avons voulu nous faire la main en vue d'un roman sérieux que nous voulons écrire un jour. Il s'agirait d'un tableau comme pivot de l'action d'un peintre vieux et célèbre et des intrigues basses et perverses dans l'entourage d'un grand homme qui a eu son succès, mais qui – justement parce qu'il était un artiste suprême, – est resté incompris. On peut 'faire grand' dans un sujet comme celà, dire ce que l'on pense sur l'art qui plane et sur le matérialisme qui rampe dans la vie . . .[105]

(5)

After finishing *Romance*, Conrad started on 'The End of the Tether'. He had been staying with the Hueffers and had evidently discussed this story with them, because he wrote to

Elsie in March: 'I am in an hour or so going to begin my Blackwood stuff – "The End of the Song" [*sic*] – as Ford has suggested and advised.'[106] But it did not go well. He wrote to Hueffer a little later: 'The cause of my silence is as usual the worry about stuff that won't get itself written. Vous connaissez celá – I miss collaboration in a most ridiculous manner – I hope you don't intend dropping me altogether.'[107] And a couple of months later he was complaining that the story was 'all behind. I am tired – I am tired of sitting on the knees of the unpropitious Gods.'[108]

Then, as he was coming to the end of the second instalment of the story, there was a disaster. On 24 June he wrote to Hueffer:

> Last night the lamp exploded here and before I could run back into the room the whole round table was in a blaze – Books, cigarettes, MS. alas! The whole second part of 'End of the Tether' ready to go to Edinburgh. The whole! The fire ran in streams and Jess and I threw blankets and danced around on them; the blaze in the window was remarked in Postling, then all was over but the horrid stink . . .
>
> This morning looking at the pile of charred paper MS and typed copy – my head swam; it seemed to me the earth was turning backwards. I must buckle to, the MS. was due to-day in Edinburgh. I have wired to Blackwoods.
>
> It is a disaster but the text is fairly fresh in my mind yet. The thing simply *has* to be done. [24 June 1902]

Thenceforth it was a race against time culminating in a hectic spurt which he described to Garnett:

> When the book arrived I had been up two nights trying to finish my Blackwood story to time. It was a matter of life and death as it were for otherwise I would have missed an instalment. . . . I had three hours' sleep for two nights and for the third no sleep at all going to bed as I am in a state. I may describe it as frenetic idiocy. [17 October 1902]

Hueffer claims that he gave Conrad quite a lot of help with this story and he may well have done so. He says that the Conrads took a cottage opposite him in Winchelsea so that both men could cooperate and he gives a dramatic, probably too dramatic, account of the last stage:

> At two in the morning the mare . . . was saddled by the writer [i.e. Hueffer] and the stable-boy. The stable-boy was to ride to the junction with the manuscript and catch the six in the morning mail train. The soup kept hot; the writers wrote. By three the writer had done all that he could in his room. He went across the road to where Conrad was still at it. Conrad said: 'For God's sake – another half-hour: just finishing – ' At four the writer looked over Conrad's shoulder. He was writing: 'The blow had come, softened by the spaces of the earth, by the years of absence.' The writer said: 'You must finish now' –

And so on until finally:

> The writer shouted: it had come to him as an inspiration: 'In the name of God, don't you know you can write those two paragraphs into the proofs when you get them back? – '
>
> That was what life was like with us.[109]

And so 'Maga' had its instalment on time. 'The End of the Tether' is the story of a courageous and honourable man who is destroyed by a compromise with his conscience combined with some exceptionally bad luck. Now sixty-seven years old, Captain Whalley had the well-earned reputation of being a fine sailor and a man of the utmost integrity:

> With age he had put on flesh a little, had increased his girth like an old tree presenting no symptoms of decay; and even the opulent, lustrous ripple of white hairs upon his chest seemed an attribute of unquenchable vitality and vigour.
>
> Once rather proud of his great bodily strength, and even of his personal appearance, conscious of his worth, and firm in his rectitude, there had remained to him, like the heritage of departed prosperity, the tranquil bearing of a man who had proved himself fit in every sort of way for the life of his choice.[110]

His philosophy matched his character. He 'believed a disposition for good existed in every man'[111] and 'his mind seemed steeped in the serenity of boundless trust in a higher power'.[112] The first blow to his philosophy came with the loss of all his savings through the failure of his bank. He was left only with his barque, the *Fair Maid*, which he was soon forced to sell in order to help his daughter, on whom he doted. Then, for the sake of his daughter, he compromised his integrity for the first time: with the remainder of the money from the sale of the *Fair Maid* he bought a share in the old steamboat, *Sofala*. It was an unwise action because Massy, the owner of the boat, had an unsavoury reputation; moreover, although 'he had never *said* anything misleading',[113] he knew that Massy thought he was a rich man and might be prepared to put more money into the partnership; and 'he had never before allowed anybody to remain under any sort of false impression as to himself',[114] but 'I wanted to keep up my importance – because there was poor Ivy away there – my daughter'.[115] He 'felt himself corrupt to the marrow of his bones'.[116] He had disliked Massy but he stilled his foreboding with the thought that 'men were not evil, after all.... No. On the whole, men were not bad – they were only silly or unhappy.'[117]

All might yet have been well if Captain Whalley had not been dealt a second blow: he started to go blind. Again he compromised with his conscience and in order not to forfeit his £500 in the *Sofala* hid his ailment from everyone. As captain of the *Sofala* he had betrayed his trust, 'walking in his darkness to the very verge of a crime',[118] because he was responsible for the 'certitude of the ship's position on which may depend a man's good fame and the peace of his conscience'[119] and the lives of other men. In fact Whalley's blindness enabled Massy to deflect the *Sofala*'s compass needle and wreck the ship in order to collect the insurance money. When this disaster happened Whalley realized he had lost all that he valued: 'He had nothing of his own – even his own past of honour, of truth, of just pride, was gone. All his spotless life had fallen into the abyss.'[120] Therefore, although 'the idea of suicide was revolting to the vigour of his manhood', he deliberately went down with the boat whose fate his deception had made possible.[121] Although Whalley was in a large measure responsible for his own destruction, Conrad's conclusion is that a man is defenceless if he is not aware of the evil surrounding him. Whalley 'had drifted into it [his falsehood] from paternal love, from incredulity, from boundless trust in divine justice meted out to men's feelings on this earth'.[122] It will be seen that the same incomprehension of evil brings about the destruction of Heyst in *Victory*.

Although it loses some of its power through being rather long drawn out, 'The End of the Tether' is a moving, well-told story and Conrad effectively builds up the suspense by the hints he drops as to Whalley's disability. Thus, the reader has guessed some time before he is told but is kept on tenterhooks whether Whalley will be exposed. The writing is consistently good; Conrad has an amazing knack of immediately striking in a couple of sentences the desired physical atmosphere as well as foreshadowing the kernel of the plot. The story begins:

> For a long time after the course of the steamer *Sofala* had been altered for the land, the low swampy coast had retained its appearance of a mere smudge of darkness beyond a belt of glitter. The sunrays fell violently upon the calm sea – seemed to shatter themselves upon an adamantine surface into sparkling dust, into a dazzling vapour of light that blinded the eye and wearied the brain with its unsteady brightness.[123]

(6)

Although *Blackwood's* published two of the pieces that were subsequently included in *The Mirror of the Sea*, 'The End of the Tether' can be taken as marking the end of Conrad's association with 'Maga'. This association was the closest that Conrad came in his early career as an author to being launched as a popular writer. That the attempt failed is not surprising. *Blackwood's* was a conservative, traditionalist magazine that liked to give its readers good fare in masculine story-telling. William Blackwood was keen to enlist Conrad to serve this purpose and the misconception of Conrad's art underlying the attempt emerges comically from their correspondence. Blackwood wanted Conrad to write something 'on the lines say of Mr Irving's paper entitled "Tiger Majesty" '[124] and was sure that people would want more of Lingard,[125] whereas Conrad was talking of his aim in *The Rescue* being primarily aesthetic.[126] And, although Blackwood disguised his feelings to Conrad and even insisted that Conrad must not restrict himself in the ending of *Lord Jim*,[127] it is easy to detect his horror at the seemingly interminable convolutions of a story which he had expected to be another good yarn. Then he was doubtless aghast at Conrad's unpredictability in the production of copy – it would inevitably arrive late, a promised short story would turn into a long novel or would not materialize at all. But he was determined to uphold the humane traditions of his house and, however incomprehensible he may have found Conrad's difficulties with expression, he proclaimed: 'I have always looked upon the writing of fiction as something not to be bound altogether by time or space', although he could not forbear to add the rider, 'notwithstanding my old friend Anthony Trollope who went to a desk as a shoemaker goes to his last'.[128]

Blackwood took an interest in his authors personally as well as in their work; becoming a contributor to 'Maga' was like marrying into a large family, and Blackwood delighted in introducing a new author to other contributors. But he did much more than this. In his relations with Conrad, undoubtedly pricked on by his righthand man, Meldrum, he showed the utmost humanity and generosity in word and deed; both men were always ready with encouragement when Conrad was oppressed and with financial help when he hinted that this would be welcome. Thus not only were Conrad's material problems eased during this crucial period when he was battling to establish himself, but he was able to feel that real value was placed on himself and what he had to offer. However Conrad's inability to keep to even the most flexible timetable and his perpetual need for money must constantly have strained the goodwill of Blackwood and Meldrum. The climax came when Conrad, in desperate straits, propounded a scheme whereby Blackwood's should grant him a loan of £300 plus an advance of £50 in return for the copyrights of *Lord Jim* and 'Youth' together with the security of an insurance policy of £400 with guaranteed premiums.[129] In the early days Blackwood doubtless would have been ready to oblige, but experience had shown what a bad risk Conrad was and he regretfully turned down the proposal. Unfortunately during their discussion Blackwood had let drop that Conrad had been a loss to the firm. This wounded Conrad deeply and called forth an impassioned assertion of his 'value':

Directly on my return I sit down to thank you for your very kind and patient hearing. That the occasion was painful to me (it is always painful to be 'asking') makes your friendly attitude the more valuable: and to say this is the primary object of my letter. But there is something more.

I admit that after leaving you I remained for some time under the impression of my 'worthlessness'; but I beg to assure you that I've never fostered any illusions as to my value. You may believe me implicitly when I say that I never work in a self-satisfied elation, which to my mind is no better than a state of inebriety unworthy of a man who means to achieve something. That – labouring against an anxious tomorrow, under the stress of an uncertain future, I have been at times consoled, re-assured and uplifted by a finished page – I'll not deny. This however is not intoxication: it is the Grace of God that will not pass by even an unsuccessful novelist. For the rest I am conscious of having pursued with pain and labour a calm conception of a definite ideal in a perfect soberness of spirit.

That strong sense of sober endeavour and of calm conception has helped me to shake off the painful impression I had, notwithstanding your kindness, carried away from our interview. I don't – in the remotest degree – mean to imply that you wished to crush me. Nothing's further from my thought; but you are aware, I hope, that your words carry a considerable weight with me; and now I have no longer the buoyancy of youth to bear me up through the deep hours of depression. I have nothing but a faith – a little against the world – in my reasoned conviction.

I've rejected the idea of worthlessness and I'll tell you, dear Mr Blackwood, on what ground mainly. It is this: – that, given my talent (which appeals to such widely different personalities as

W. H. Henley and Bernard Shaw – H. G. Wells and professor Trgö Tirn of the Finland University – to Maurice Greiffenhagen a painter and to the skipper of a Persian Gulf steamer who wrote to the papers of my *Typhoon* – to the Editor of the *Pall Mall Magazine* – to a charming old lady in Winchester) given my talent, the fundamental and permanent failure could be only the outcome of an inherent worthlessness of character. Now my character is formed: it has been tried by experience. I have looked upon the worst life can do – and I am sure of myself, even against the demoralising effect of straitened circumstances.

I know exactly what I am doing. Mr George Blackwood's incidental remark in his last letter that the story ['The End of the Tether'] is not fairly begun yet is in a measure correct but, on a large view, beside the point. For, the writing is as good as I can make it (first duty), and in the light of the final incident, the whole story in all its descriptive detail shall fall into its place – acquire its value and its significance. This is my method based on deliberate conviction. I've never departed from it . . .

And however unfavourably it may affect the business in hand I must confess that I shall not depart from my method. I am at need prepared to explain on what grounds I think it a true method. All my endeavours shall be directed to understand it better, to develop its great possibilities, to acquire greater skill in the handling – to mastery in short. You may wonder why I am telling you all this.

First because I am sure of your sympathy. I hope that this letter will find its place in that memoir which one or two of my young faithfuls have promised to offer to my *manes*. It would be good for people to know that in the 20th century in the age of Besants, Authors' Clubs and literary agents there existed a publisher to whom not an altogether contemptible author could write safely in that strain. Next because I want to make good my contention that I am not writing 'in the air'. It is not the haphazard business of a mere temperament. There is in it as much intelligent action guided by a deliberate view of the effect to be attained as in any business enterprise. Therefore I am emboldened to say that ultimate and irretrievable failure is *not* to be my lot. I know that it is not necessary to say to you but I may just as well point out that I must not by any means be taken for a gifted loafer intent on living upon credulous publishers. Pardon this remark – but in a time when Sherlock Holmes looms so big I may be excused my little bit of self-assertion.

I am long in my development. What of that? Is not Thackeray's pennyworth of mediocre fact drowned in an ocean of twaddle? And yet he lives. And Sir Walter, himself, was not the writer of concise anecdotes I fancy. And G. Elliot [*sic*] – is she as swift as the present public (incapable of fixing its attention for five consecutive minutes) requires us to be at the cost of all honesty, of all truth, and even the most elementary conception of art? But these are great names. I don't compare myself with them. I am *modern*, and I would rather recall Wagner the musician and Rodin the sculptor who both had to starve a little in their day – and Whistler the painter who made Ruskin the critic foam at the mouth with scorn and indignation. They too have arrived. They had to suffer for being 'new'. And I too hope to find my place in the rear of my betters. But still – my place. My work shall not be an utter failure because it has the solid basis of a definite intention – first: and next because it is not an endless analysis of affected sentiments but in its essence it is action (strange as this affirmation may sound at the present time) nothing but action – action observed, felt and interpreted with an absolute truth to my sensations (which are the basis of art in literature) – action of human beings that will bleed to a prick, and are moving in a visible world.

This is my creed. Time will show. And this you may say is my over-weening conceit. Well, no. I know well enough that I know nothing. I should like to think that some of my casual critics are in the possession of that piece of information about themselves. Starting from that knowledge one may learn to look on with some attention – at least. But enough of that.

Believe me, dear Mr Blackwood in all trust and confidence yours Jph Conrad. [31 May 1902]

Although Conrad remained on friendly terms with Blackwood and with Meldrum, he was forced to look elsewhere for immediate support and the intimate connection was broken. From the personal point of view it was sad but, even if material necessity* had not forced the issue, an estrangement was perhaps inevitable. Conrad's talent was not suited to the pages of 'Maga' and he would soon have been in the

* Thanks to the efforts of his friends, which resulted in a grant of £300 from the Royal Literary Fund in July 1902 he was enabled to pay some of his most pressing debts. He received a further grant of £200 from the same source in April 1908. (Information supplied by the kindness of Mr John Broadbent, Secretary to the Royal Literary Fund).

position either of making concessions to his medium or of having his work rejected.*

* Mr Oliver Warner has pointed out to me that both the character of Marlow and the colloquial style of presentation associated with him fitted 'Maga' well; he suggests that 'Maga' may indeed have influenced Conrad in the creation of Marlow, which is quite probable. The trouble came when Conrad developed Marlow, and his art, beyond the limitations of 'Maga'.

[X]

Achievement without Success, I

AFTER finishing 'The End of the Tether', Conrad took Jessie to London for 'a week of what to rustics of our sort was a Whirl – (with a capital W)'[1] where they saw something of the Galsworthys.

Back at work again Conrad made yet another attempt to tackle *The Rescue*,[2] but with as little success as before. In desperation he sent it off to Hueffer's 'friendly hands for the only real work of Rescue that will ever be found in its text'.[3] It is not known what, if anything, Hueffer did to it.

At the same time he started work on another story, telling Hueffer: 'I believe it will end in something silly and saleable as "Youth" seems to be in a measure.'[4] He had previously told Galsworthy that with his 'head full of a story, I have not been able to write a single word – except the title, which shall be, I think: *Nostromo*: the story belonging to the "Karain" class of tales...'[5] His original conception of this novel thus seems to have been totally different from its final form.

1903 was to be a year of worry and bad health, but also of some achievement. In February Conrad told Ernest Dawson that he had been 'rather seedy and somehow very wretched'.[6] He was of course still very worried about money and in March he wrote to Hueffer:

> I just only begin to pick up. I had two days in bed. As it was to be expected I found myself in a hole on my return with a stiff letter from Watson [his banker] – d'un ton très rogue – indeed.
>
> However, it's no use. He must put up with me up to that point. I've no doubt he will take good care I don't go beyond.
>
> Damn! Anyhow if I can finish *N*. in three months I am saved for a time. And if then I can finish *Rescue* by December next I am saved altogether. The question is – Can I make the effort – is it in me?

But he went on:

> I have begun to write at a good rate enough for a sick man and I shall improve on that no doubt. [23 March 1903]

On 26 May he told Elsie Hueffer that 'despair of ever accomplishing anything good has dulled my nerves and I plod on drearily and caring but very little'. He persevered and in August was able to tell Pinker that he had written about 42,000 words of *Nostromo*.[7] He continued:

> I have never worked so hard before – with so much anxiety. But the result is good. You know I take no credit to myself for what I do – and so I may judge my own performance. There is no mistake about this. You may take up a strong position when you offer it here. It is a very genuine Conrad. At the same time it is more of a Novel pure and simple than anything I've done since *Almayer's Folly* . . .
>
> But it's a miserable life anyhow. Have you sent anything to Watson this month? I daren't draw a cheque. But I felt too sick of everything to write you before. Moreover, my salvation is to shut eyes and ears to everything – or else I couldn't write a line. And yet sometimes I can't forget – I remember the tradesmen, and all the horrors descend upon me. Damn! Try to help me out to the end of this and then we will see how we stand. [22 August 1903, *L.L.*,I, p. 316]

He also wrote to Galsworthy:

> Dearest Jack,
>
> The book is, this moment, half done [it turned out to be no more than a quarter] and I feel half dead and wholly imbecile.
>
> If you want to do your part by a man, for whom you have done so much already, then do not fail to come down here the first day you can spare.
>
> To work in the conditions which are, I suppose, the outcome of my character mainly, is belittling – it is demoralising. I fight against demoralisation, of which fight I bear the brunt and my friends bear the cost. All this is very beautiful and inspiriting to think about, and elevating and encouraging and – I can't think of any more pretty words . . .
>
> I didn't write to you because, upon my word, I am ashamed to write to anybody. I feel myself strangely growing into a sort of

outcast. A mental and moral outcast. I hear of nothing – I think of nothing – I reflect upon nothing – I cut myself off – and with all that I can just only keep going, or rather keep on lagging from one wretched story to another – and always deeper in the mire.

We are so glad to hear your father is really better. Remember us all round, pray, as kindly as you know.

And do come. The prospect of your going abroad fills me with dread. Why? Nerves?

Don't you think I ought to apologise for this silly letter? I do! I do! [22 August 1903, *L.L.*, I, p. 317]

He continued to plod on but then had a relapse. At the end of November he wrote once more to Galsworthy:

I've been ill again. Just got down, shaky, weak, dispirited.

No work done. No spring left to grapple with it. Everything looks black, but I suppose that will wear off, and anyhow, I am trying to keep despair under. Nevertheless I feel myself losing my footing in deep waters. They are lapping about my lips.

My dear fellow it is not so much the frequency of these gout attacks, but I feel so beastly ill between, ill in body and mind. It has never been so before. Impossible to write – while the brain riots in incoherent images. It is sometimes quite alarming. [30 November 1903, *L.L.*, I, p. 322]

To crown the year he wrote to Miss Capes in December:

My mind struggles with a strange sort of torpor, struggles desperately while the sands are running out. That is the most terrifying thought of all. They are running out – and there is nothing done; nothing of what one desires to do. [26 December 1903, Keating Collection]

And to Meldrum:

It has been a most disastrous year for my work. If I had written each page with my blood I could not feel more exhausted at the end of this twelvemonth. [26 December 1903]

It might be thought that Conrad was exaggerating his disorders. He was certainly no stoic, but these letters reflected his state of mind as is shown by a letter which William Rothenstein wrote to Gosse eighteen months later. 'Of course he is terribly hysterical – indeed last year I feared for his reason;' and, after referring to Conrad's 'morbid excitable mind', Rothenstein added, 'I am terribly sorry for him, but it is very hard at times to be patient – natures like his demand as a right, if one once gives affection, a very great deal of one's time and energy.'[8] How far his ills were psychologically induced is another matter. As Jessie pointed out, Conrad almost invariably went down with gout after a period of stress or a crisis, which suggests a psychological element. However there are not adequate grounds for doubting a physical basis, and Conrad's bad teeth (he was apparently very loth to visit the dentist) indicate a possible cause of his gout.

The new year started with a misfortune which did not seem serious at first but which affected the rest of Conrad and Jessie's life. In January Conrad took Jessie to London to consult a doctor because he was worried about her heart.[9] He was reassured on this, but as Jessie was coming out of John Barker's after doing some shopping she 'slipped the cartilage of both knees at once and fell on the pavement, hurting very badly the knee already damaged by an accident I had at the age of sixteen'.[10] The result of this accident was that Jessie remained a partial cripple for the rest of her life, despite a number of operations.

On top of this came a further disaster. Conrad's bankers, Watson and Co., failed. He thus 'lost a good friend for he did back me up through all these years',[11] as he told Wells, and was faced with the necessity to pay off his overdraft. In the same letter he told Wells that he had 'started a series of sea sketches and have sent out Pinker on the hunt to place them. This must save me. I've discovered that I can dictate that sort of bosh without effort at the rate of 3,000 words in four hours. Fact. The only thing now is to sell it to a paper and then make a book of the rubbish. Hang! So in the day *Nostromo* and, from 11 to 1 a.m., dictation.'[12] The sea sketches were the beginning of *The Mirror of the Sea*.

He also said that, on Sidney Colvin's advice, he had started to write a play in one act, based on the short story 'To-morrow'. He called the play *One Day More*. Although

Conrad never apparently showed much interest in the theatre, disparaged it as a medium of expression – proclaiming his 'ineradicable mistrust of the theatre as the destroyer of all suggestiveness'[13] – and frequently inveighed against actors, he had some years earlier confessed his desire, like so many novelists and poets, to write a play. In a letter to Cunninghame Graham he had said:

> I haven't seen a play for years, but I have read this one [*Admiral Guinea,* by Henley and Stevenson]. And that's all I can say about it. I have no notion of a play. No play grips me on the stage or off. Each of them seems to me an amazing freak of folly. They are all unbelievable and as disillusioning as a bang on the head. I greatly desire to write a play myself. It is my dark and secret ambition. And yet I can't conceive how a sane man can sit down deliberately to write a play and not go mad before he has done. The actors appear to me like a lot of *wrong-headed* lunatics pretending to be sane. Their malice is stitched with white threads. They are disguised and ugly. To look at them breeds in my melancholy soul thoughts of murder and suicide, – such is my anger and my loathing of their transparent pretences. There is a taint of subtle corruption in their blank voices, in their blinking eyes, in the grimacing faces, in the false light, in the false passion, in the words that have been learned by heart. [6 December 1897, *L.L.,* I, p. 213]

It is not known why Conrad felt this astonishing hostility towards actors or on what he based it. He confessed in the letter that he had not seen a play 'for years' and so he presumably had little or no experience of the English theatre. In a letter to Garnett he shows that he knew the work of Scribe and Sardou[14] and he may well have frequented the theatre while he was based on Marseilles.*

This was not a solitary outburst and he seems to have persisted in his dislike of actors and acting throughout his life;

* It is possible that in Marseilles Conrad had had a painful experience over someone connected with the stage; 'Rita' may have been an actress or a rival for her favours may have been an actor. The sentence, 'To look at them [actors] breeds in my melancholy soul thoughts of murder and suicide' may be more significant than at first appears. But this is all very tenuous.

more than ten years later he told Garnett: 'Though I detest the stage I have a theatrical imagination – that's why perhaps I detest the stage – that is the actors who mostly, poor souls, have no imagination.'[15] And four years before he died he wrote to Curle:

> The Movie is just a silly stunt for silly people – but the theatre is more compromising since it is capable of falsifying the very soul of one's work, both on the imaginative and on the intellectual side – besides having some sort of inferior poetics of its own which is bound to play havoc with that imponderable quality of creative literary expression, which depends on one's individuality.[16]

Despite this prejudice he persisted in his ambition to write a successful play.

(2)

Although there was no longer any specific collaboration, Hueffer was still very close to Conrad, both in his personal life and in his work. He had helped Conrad with *One Day More* by extracting all the dialogue from 'To-morrow'.[17] It is clear that he also gave considerable help to Conrad with six of the 'sketches' which were subsequently collected together as *The Mirror of the Sea.* In a letter to Hueffer Conrad wrote:

> I saw Pinker the other day. No word yet from Harvey as to sketches. Halkett offered to take *six* at 5 guineas per thousand. Halkett really is a last resource and I told Pinker not to throw the thing away in haste.
>
> But still Halkett's proposal means 90 guineas of which (I told Pinker again) I must have 30 when – and if – the affair is concluded, pour votre Seigneurie.
>
> As to the book form (which Harvey already is ready to take) a small calculation will fix our proportions; for I suppose we cannot now finish the whole together. Can we? [29 May 1904]

Hueffer gives an account of how he helped Conrad:

> *The Mirror of the Sea* and *A Personal Record* were mostly written by my hand from Conrad's dictation. Whilst he was dictating

them, I would recall incidents to him – I mean incidents of his past life which he had told me but which did not come freely back to his mind because at the time he was mentally ill, in desperate need of money, and, above all, sceptical as to the merits of the reminiscential form which I had suggested to him. The fact is I could make Conrad write at periods when his despair and fatigue were such that in no other way would it have been possible to him. He would be lying on the sofa or pacing the room, railing at life and literature as practised in England, and I would get a writing pad and pencil and, whilst he was still raving, would interject: 'Now then, what was it you were saying about coming up the Channel and nearly running over a fishing boat that suddenly appeared under your bows?' and gradually there would come 'Landfalls and Departures'.[18]

Even Jessie concedes Hueffer's help in this case, saying:

F. M. H. has made the most fantastic claims with regard to my husband's various plots, yet *The Mirror of the Sea* owes a great deal to his ready and patient assistance – not perhaps to the actual writing, but that book would never have come into being if Joseph Conrad had had no intelligent person with whom to talk over these intimate reminiscences.[19]

Their intimacy during this period was such that when Conrad was asked for a story by the Northern Newspaper Syndicate he wrote to Hueffer: 'I was going to fling it [the letter] into the paper basket. Still – if you have something written that you do *not* care for *in the least* send it on. I'll put in a few of my jargon phrases and send it on. As I remarked – nothing matters – and we are intimate enough to say anything to each other. You may as well have this modest cheque. If the thing shocks you tear the sweet note up.'[20] Hueffer also claims to have helped with *Nostromo*, but it is difficult to discover how far he did so. Certainly Conrad seems to have been prepared to call on Hueffer if necessary because, in the early stages of *Nostromo*, he wrote to him: 'I do not doubt of your assistance in my efforts. You must run down and see me soon.'[21] And he told Pinker: 'If people want to begin printing (serial) say in Sept[er] you may let them safely – for you know that, at the very worst, H. stands in the background (quite confidentially you understand). But there's no reason to anticipate anything of the kind. If I am to break down it will be after this infernal thing is finished.[22] Moreover, Hueffer sold to Keating fifteen pages of manuscript of the *Nostromo* text written in his own hand. This fragment comes early in Part II,[23] and Hueffer would have had to have known the story very well indeed to have written the passage himself; he may have done so, but it is more likely that he took it down from Conrad's dictation.

The first five papers of *The Mirror of the Sea*, a little more of *Nostromo*, and three articles for the *Daily Mail* were all written while the Conrads were still in London after Jessie's accident.* The Conrads' rooms in Gordon Place were very close to the Hueffers, and during this period the two families apparently shared household expenses, the Conrads usually going to have their meals with the Hueffers although Jessie says that she 'never felt at home and welcome there'.[24] There was an influenza epidemic raging at the time and both households were prostrated, including Conrad. Hueffer tells how, his German cook having been taken off in an ambulance with influenza, he did the cooking himself without Conrad being aware of the change as long as he imitated Johanna's plain German cooking. Then one day he decided to do a *civet de lièvre à la Parisienne*:

> Conrad inspected it as he always did, carefully and with his monocle screwed into his eye. He rubbed his hands and with enthusiasm unfolded his napkin. When, with head on one side and a look of pleased anticipation, he had tasted it, he started slightly. He said:
>
> 'My dear faller. – The admirable Johanna has of course surpassed herself. – But – eh – my gout! – *Une telle succulence, mon cher.* – Tebb [his doctor] says the greatest abstinence. – ' He added that – if there remained a little of the admirable saddle of lamb of the night before – a small slice, cold, with a leaf of salad. –

* Letters to Pinker of Wednesday 2 March [1904] and Monday, rather later. The *Daily Mail* articles were subsequently incorporated in *The Mirror of the Sea* as 'Overdue and Missing' and 'The Grip of the Land'. From the two letters to Pinker it appears that Conrad had originally thought of these articles as separate from the *Mirror* papers.

> I went down wearily into the kitchen, put the remains of lamb on the dumbwaiter, washed a lettuce and beat up some dressing. – I imitated Johanna from then on.[25]

The Conrads returned to the Pent some time in March and both of them retired to bed.[26] Jessie was laid up for a month with her knee.

For the next five months Conrad worked hard at *Nostromo,* which he finished on 30 August [27] amid the usual dramatic circumstances:

> Phoo! I am weary. For more than a month I have been sitting up till three a.m. – ending with a solid 36 hours, (in the middle of which I had to wire for the dentist and have a tooth drawn!! . . .) It broke!! . . . !! Till at 11.30 *I* broke down just after raising my eyes to the clock.
>
> Then I don't know; two blank hours during which I must have got out and sat down – (not fallen) on the concrete outside the door.
>
> That's how I found myself; and crawling in again noted the time; considerably after one.
>
> But I've finished. There's no elation. No relief even. Nothing. Moreover I've yet a good fortnight's work for the book form. . . . I am weary! weary.[28]

(3)

In the Author's Note to *Nostromo,* Conrad mentioned that 'after finishing the last story of the *Typhoon* volume it seemed somehow that there was nothing more in the world to write about'.[29] All his substantial work had hitherto been based on his own experience or on hearsay within a context which he knew well and he presumably felt that he had now exhausted this source. He therefore began to search further afield and, during the period of his greatest achievement, his novels were to range over areas of which he had had virtually no personal experience.

In the same Author's Note he continued: 'This so strangely negative but disturbing mood lasted some little time; and then, as with many of my longer stories, the first hint for *Nostromo* came to me in the shape of a vagrant anecdote completely destitute of valuable details;'[30] this was the story of a man having stolen single-handed a lighter full of silver on the Tierra Firma seaboard during a revolution. Conrad says that he had first heard the story in 1875 or '76 when he was in the Gulf of Mexico and that he had later discovered an account of the exploit in the memoirs of a seaman which he had picked up outside a second-hand bookshop. The book to which Conrad was evidently alluding has recently been tracked down; it is *On Many Seas: the Life and Exploits of a Yankee Sailor*, by Frederick Benton Williams, edited by his Friend William Stone Booth.* Frederick Benton Williams is the pseudonym of Herbert Elliot Hamblen and *On Many Seas* is an account of his youthful adventures as a seaman from 1864 to 1878. In Chapter XXXII Hamblen describes his association with a 'swarthy, piratical-looking fellow' named Nicolo who told him one night how he had been entrusted with a lighter full of silver during a revolution; Nicolo had killed the two other members of the crew, then scuttled the lighter near the shore and had since been growing rich slowly.† Conrad used a few details from this story, but transformed the character of Nicolo which was that of an 'unmitigated rascal'[31] into that of Nostromo. It appears most likely that Nicolo's exploit had never occurred but, somewhere along the line, had been invented;[32] in view of this and of Conrad's tendency to disguise his indebtedness to books, his claim to have heard the anecdote himself in the Gulf of Mexico must be treated with circumspection.

In the Author's Note he goes on facetiously to say that his principal authority for the history of Costaguana is Don José

* London and New York, 1897. This discovery was made by Mr John Halverson and Professor Ian Watt of the University of California. An article by them on the subject is due to appear in *The Review of English Studies* and I am greatly indebted to the authors for their generosity in allowing me to quote from their typescript.

† 'I must git reesh slow, don' you see?' *On Many Seas*, p. 289. cf., *Nostromo*, viii and p. 503.

Avellanos's fictitious *History of Fifty Years of Misrule*. And, until recently, it had been generally assumed that, apart from a few details picked up here and there,* the whole South American background to the novel was the product of Conrad's imagination. The remarks of two of his closest friends are typical. Galsworthy wrote that *Nostromo* was Conrad's 'most sheer piece of creation. For by his own confession, very much of his work was based intimately on his own adventures and experiences; and *Nostromo* creates a continent which he had only glimpsed.'[33] While Richard Curle has said: 'His [Conrad's] power of visualisation was immense. For example, he built up the whole atmosphere of *Nostromo*, which breathes the very spirit of South America, from a few days upon the coast.'[34] Conrad had told Curle:

> As to *Nostromo*. If I ever mentioned twelve hours it must relate to Puerto Cabello where I was ashore about that time. In La Guayra, as I went up the hill and had a distant view of Caracas, I must have been two and a half to three days. It's such a long time ago! And there were a few hours in a few other places on that dreary coast of Venezuela. [22 July 1923]

When he was grappling with the novel, Conrad complained to Cunninghame Graham: 'I am dying over that cursed *Nostromo* thing. All my memories of Central America seem to slip away. I just had a glimpse twenty-five years ago – a short glance. That is not enough pour bâtir un roman dessus. And yet one must live.'[35] Perhaps Cunninghame Graham then advised that Conrad should turn to books to supplement his memories and suggested some titles or perhaps Conrad had already decided to fill in the gaps and stimulate his imagination with some reading about South America. At all events it is clear that at some point he carefully studied George Frederick Masterman's *Seven*

* Conrad confessed to Cunninghame Graham that he had stolen the dentist anecdote from him and was 'compunctious' about the use he had made of Ex. Sr. Don Perez Triana's personality (presumably in the character of Don José Avellanos). Letters to Cunninghame Graham of 7 and 31 October 1904, *L.L.*, I, pp. 337–8.

Eventful Years in Paraguay,[36] Edward B. Eastwick's *Venezuela,*[37] probably one or more of Sir Clements Markham's books on South America,[38] and possibly some others. From Masterman, Conrad took most of the names of his characters, including Gould, Decoud, Corbelàn, Mitchell (Michell in Masterman), Fidanza (Nostromo's surname), Barrios and Monygham. Masterman was a doctor and Conrad based his account of Dr Monygham's torture and confession on that of Masterman himself;[39] the character and career of the tyrannical dictator, Francisco Solano Lopez, supplied Conrad with material on which to draw for the Montero brothers[40] and for the ruthless Guzman Bento.* There are also a number of other small details. From Eastwick, Conrad took some more names; there are names of geographical features like Mt Higuerota and of people, like Sotillo, General Guzman Blanco, whom Conrad turned into Guzman Bento, while the reigning beauty of Valencia is Antonia Ribera. Her surname is used for that of the benevolent President of Costaguana and although Conrad said that Antonia Avellanos was modelled on his first love[41] there is a very close correspondence between her character and appearance and that of Antonia Ribera. Eastwick's Antonia was, like Conrad's, emancipated and Europeanized; her opening remark to Eastwick was 'Caballero, are you married?' to which he, taken aback but hopeful, replied: 'Sometimes'.[42] 'The other young ladies of Sulaco stood in awe of' the 'character and accomplishments' of Antonia Avellanos. 'She was reputed to be terribly learned and serious.'[43] Eastwick found that Antonia Ribera 'talked like a bookworm, like a politician, like a diplomatist, like a savant'.[44] In appearance Antonia Avellanos was a 'tall, grave girl, with a self-possessed manner, a wide, white forehead, a wealth of

* Masterman, op. cit., p. 39 ff. and p. 84; *Nostromo, passim,* particularly p. 137 ff. It may be thought that these claims are inadequately based but curious little details, such as the fact that both Lopez and Guzman Bento had lost their lower teeth, add up to substantial evidence.

The fate of Guzman Bento's body after his death seems to be based on the history of another tyrant, Dr Francia (*Nostromo,* p. 47 and Masterman, pp. 31–2).

rich brown hair, and blue eyes',[45] while Eastwick said of the other Antonia: 'her eyes were dark blue, her hair a rich brown, her nose Grecian, her eyebrows arched'.[46]

Eastwick describes Puerto Cabello in some detail and Conrad evidently used this to revive his own memories in order to base the topography of the port of Sulaco on that of Puerto Cabello. The latter is situated in the Golfo Triste, which became the Golfo Placido in *Nostromo* and is protected by a spit of land, like the peninsula of Azuera, on which was situated an unused lighthouse. Opposite the spit are the reefs of Punta Brava, which became the cape of Punta Mala. It is 'protected from all winds, on the east, north, and south' by the land and from the west by a group of islands as well as the mainland. 'In short, there is perhaps no harbour in the world where the sea is at all times so calm as at Puerto Cabello.'[47] The customs houses at Sulaco and Puerto Cabello are similarly situated, and for some of the topography of the town of Sulaco Conrad draws on Eastwick's description of the inland town of Valencia. It is fascinating how even the most insignificant detail would be picked up and used by Conrad. At one point, at a reception, when Eastwick was presented with a yellow flower there was much delight at his exclamation of 'Viva la Amarilla' because yellow was, unknown to him, the colour of the political party in power; in *Nostromo* the most exclusive club of Sulaco is called the Amarilla.[48]

Through the reading of these books, written at first hand by intelligent, observant men, Conrad was able to immerse himself in the authentic atmosphere of the South America of the middle of the nineteenth century. The points of view of the authors, particularly that of Eastwick, would have been sympathetic to Conrad. For instance:

> Those who think that the overthrow of a bad government implies the inauguration of a better will do well to ponder over these remarks, and the more they reflect upon them and study the history of the events to which they refer, the less will be their sympathy with the revolutionary principles which are spreading so rapidly in Europe.[49]

But although this knowledge of Conrad's sources invalidates the assumption that he created Costaguana out of his head it in no way detracts from the far more important aspects of his achievement. There is no question of plagiarism because these books only supplied the raw material with which he built the edifice. A comparison between the sources and what Conrad made of them serves above all to underline the transmuting power of his imagination. For instance, there are mundane allusions in Eastwick to the uncompleted railroad from Puerto Cabello to San Felipe; from this hint Conrad creates the scene of the inauguration of that 'progressive and patriotic undertaking', the National Central Railway, with all its philosophical overtones,[50] the description of the trains passing old Viola's house,[51] and Nostromo's magnificent dash to the construction camp on an engine.[52] Equally interesting are the modifications which Conrad added to Eastwick's topographical descriptions; Douglas Hewitt has stressed the significance of Conrad's emphasis on the isolation, the inaccessibility of Sulaco[53] and there is no parallel to this in Eastwick or Masterman. In fact all the important elements of *Nostromo* are to be found either not at all in Conrad's sources (although the possibility of an undiscovered source cannot be ruled out) or else in the merest embryo.

(4)

Nostromo is Conrad's most ambitious feat of imagination and is worthy of comparison with the most ambitious of all great novels, *War and Peace*. Hitherto Conrad had written primarily about men in communion with themselves, and in relation to one another or within the restricted society of a ship's crew, although it is true that 'Heart of Darkness' contains an implied criticism of colonialism and commercial exploitation of backward peoples and wider issues are broached in the Patusan section of *Lord Jim*. In *Nostromo* he maintained his concern with the individual and with personal relations but extended his range to include public as well as private life. He chose a far larger canvas than he had used before or was to use again; it is as large as that of any great novel except *War and Peace*. On it he placed not only the lives and fates of an array of characters but the physical and political composition of a whole country, creating it with the most meticulous though selective detail. The account of Mrs Gould's travels through the Occidental Province is an example of the care with which be built up the visual background to the events:

> She saw them on the road carrying loads, lonely figures upon the plain, toiling under great straw hats, with their white clothing flapping about their limbs in the wind; she remembered the villages by some group of Indian women at the fountain impressed upon her memory, by the face of some young Indian girl with a melancholy and sensual profile, raising an earthenware vessel of cool water at the door of a dark hut with a wooden porch cumbered with great brown jars. The solid wooden wheels of an ox-cart, halted with its shafts in the dust, showed the strokes of the axe; and a party of charcoal carriers, with each man's load resting above his head on the top of the low mud wall, slept stretched in a row within the strip of shade.[54]

The frequent allusions to light show the extent to which Conrad must have projected himself visually into Costaguana, while the topographical description of the surroundings of Sulaco, shut off from the sea by the vast Golfo Placido and dominated by the Cordillera, where 'the white head of Higuerota rises majestically upon the blue',[55] has such precision that it remains imprinted photographically upon the mind throughout the book.*

Conrad allows himself an assortment of devices to develop his subject. There is no narrator as there was in his previous long novel, *Lord Jim*. Instead most of the book is written anonymously and directly in the third person, although the anonymity is occasionally broken by phrases like 'those of us

* Edward Crankshaw, *Joseph Conrad; some Aspects of the Art of the Novel*, 1936, pp. 178–90, has pointed out the economy with which the details are chosen to set the scene and atmosphere in chapters I–II.

whom business or curiosity took to Sulaco ... can remember'[56] or '... as I am told'.[57] Then on one important occasion Conrad uses the garrulous and portentious Captain Mitchell to relate the events and on another Decoud describes them in a long letter to his sister.

Without a narrator to perform the task of analysis and comment Conrad uses the characters to comment on each other and to reflect events. The sardonic Dr Monygham and the sceptical Decoud are particularly exploited in this way, and Captain Mitchell is used to impart unconsciously an ironic tone. Although they can often be taken as reflecting the author's view Dr Monygham and Decoud are characters in their own right; they reveal themselves as well as others by their comments and it is always necessary to take the commentator's own character into account when assessing the comment. Conrad does not, however, rely on this method alone, but frequently intervenes with impersonal judgements and reflections.

It is perhaps the lack of a narrator which exposes the weakness of Conrad's characterization, because far more is demanded of the characters than when Marlow is there as Master of Ceremonies. It is evident that most of the characters, in particular the leading ones, exist for what they represent rather than for what they are. Although they play important roles in the development of the themes and are in that respect vivid and real, their psychology is on the whole crude, blurred, or even unconvincing. It is with the minor, picturesque characters such as Sotillo, General Montero, and Mitchell that Conrad succeeds best.

For instance, magnificent figure though Nostromo is, his psychology is rudimentary. He is summed up in a few words and the comments upon him of the other characters, as well as those of the author, tend to be repetitive. So do his own actions and words. Conrad himself does not seem to have been satisfied with him. He agreed with Cunninghame Graham's criticism, although it must be admitted that he would not have been likely to dispute the point in this context:

I don't defend Nostromo himself. Fact is he does not take my fancy either. As to his conduct generally and with women in particular, I only wish to say that he is not a Spaniard or S. American. I tried to differentiate him even to the point of mounting him upon a mare, which I believe is not or *was not* the proper thing to do in Argentine: though in Chile there was never much of that nonsense. But truly N. is nothing at all, – a fiction, embodied vanity of the sailor kind, – a romantic mouthpiece of the 'people' which (I mean 'the people') frequently experience the very feelings to which he gives utterance. I do not defend him as a creation. [31 October 1904, *L.L.*, I, p. 338]

Nostromo might be looked on as an exception, but Gould too, on whom depends so much of the effect of the book, is far from clear. His thoughts, feelings, and actions as well as the opinions of other characters on him accumulate into a pile of separate entities but never coalesce into a vital organism.

Apart from this weakness of characterization and from the melodrama of the last two chapters presented in appropriately magazinish language the book is almost without blemish. The writing is otherwise on a consistently high level and perhaps Conrad's greatest sustained achievement; it has none of the purple passages or philosophical effusions that sometimes mar his work. He shows a wonderful versatility of style and mood ranging from deep seriousness and irony to scenes of superb comedy such as those between Sotillo and Mitchell.

The complexity of intention expressed through such a diversity of character and incident demanded an exceptionally intricate structure if the peaks of significance were not to be submerged by the flood of detail. Aside from the epilogue, the events take place in a period of a little over eighteen months, although there are numerous references to the past, particularly to the tyranny of Guzman Bento, in the biographical flashbacks of the important characters. Conrad deliberately flouts chronological narration in *Nostromo* and it is here that the 'unconventional grouping and perspective ... wherein', he claimed, 'almost all my "art" consists'[58] is most in evidence. He uses the device of the time-shift to gain an effect of irony. Thus, in Part I, the day of President Ribiera's subsequent flight across the mountains is described before the festivities in Sulaco at which he inaugurates a new era for Costaguana 'emerging after this last struggle, he hoped, into a period of peace and material prosperity'.[59] The irony is pointed at the end of the ceremony:

> As the mail-boat headed through the pass, the badly timed reports announced the end of Don Vincente Ribiera's first official visit to Sulaco, and for Captain Mitchell the end of another 'historic occasion'. Next time when the 'Hope of honest men' was to come that way, a year and a half later, it was unofficially, over the mountain tracks, fleeing after a defeat on a lame mule, to be only just saved by Nostromo from an ignominious death at the hands of a mob. It was a very different event . . .[60]

Part II is again concerned with events leading up to Ribiera's flight and it is not for almost another hundred pages that we are abreast of the day of his escape. Thenceforth the time-shifts are largely mechanical and dictated by the need to follow the various threads of the plot until we come to the most important of all chronological breaks: just when the book seems to be building up to an exciting climax[61] Conrad jumps to a time some years later and makes Captain Mitchell, in the role of unofficial guide to the sights of Sulaco, tell the story of the dramatic events which led to the defeat of the Monteros and the establishment of the Occidental Republic. Then the thread is picked up again.

Apart from showing that Conrad had no intention of writing an exciting tale of action, the effect of these time-shifts is almost to abolish time in *Nostromo*. In fact it seems to have been Conrad's aim to approach the simultaneity of visual experience which a painting offers. The elimination of progression from one event to another also has the effect of implying that nothing is ever achieved. By the end of the book we are virtually back where we started; it looks as if the future of Costaguana will be very similar to her past.

Unlike some great works, *Nostromo* is not a book whose

subject can be summed up in a sentence. Conrad wrote in Curle's copy that it had been his 'ambition to render the spirit of an epoch in the history of South America'. And in this he succeeded, creating a world compounded of tragedy and farce, brutality, pathos, idealism, and venality. But his claim was too modest because the life described in Costaguana transcends a particular epoch or continent and contains an element of the universal. It is thus not too much to claim that *Nostromo* is an investigation of the motives of human behaviour, in which idealism is set against scepticism, illusion against disillusion, and responsibility against irresponsibility. Every category of human activity which Conrad considered important, except the arts (it is significant that religion is only dealt with in its temporal aspect) is portrayed and analysed.

Because of the title as well as the prominent part that Nostromo plays, it would be natural to assume that the book is concerned primarily with the fate of Nostromo. But although Nostromo is constantly alluded to – it is in this indirect manner that Conrad first builds up his reputation as he did that of Kurtz in 'Heart of Darkness' – he is barely concerned with the most important issues of the book and Conrad has specifically stated that he was not intended to be the hero.

In a letter to Ernst Bendz, a Swedish professor who had written a study of Conrad's work, he said:

> I will take the liberty to point out that Nostromo has never been intended for the hero of the Tale of the Seaboard. Silver is the pivot of the moral and material events, affecting the lives of everybody in the tale. [7 March 1923, *L.L.*, II, p. 296]

Even this statement needs modifying because although the silver is the thread which binds the book together it has only a superficial or formal connection with some of the most important moral events. In its crudest aspect, the desire for gain, the silver only influences the lives of Nostromo and of one other character, Major Sotillo, who is killed during his frantic search for the sunken lighter. But even in the case of Nostromo the theft of the silver is more the effect than the cause of his downfall. The theme of the corruptive power of riches is broached in the first chapter, in the story of the two gringos hunting the forbidden treasure on Azuera ('The poor, associating by an obscure instinct of consolation the ideas of evil and wealth ...'[62]), and that story is frequently alluded to throughout the book, serving the same purpose as the recurring phrases in *Lord Jim*. This theme is worked out in the fate of Nostromo.

From the start Nostromo is presented as dependable and resourceful. Whenever there is a job to be done it is Nostromo who is sent for; Captain Mitchell, the pompous and stupid representative of the O.S.N., has developed a mania for 'lending' his illustrious Capataz de Cargadores. But above all Nostromo is 'incorruptible'; this is insisted on again and again. He has built up his reputation for resourcefulness and incorruptibility until, as Decoud says, he is 'the next great man of Sulaco after Don Carlos Gould'.[63] And it is his reputation alone about which he seems to care. In Decoud's words: 'The only thing he seems to care for ... is to be well spoken of. ... He does not seem to make any difference between speaking and thinking.'[64] And again: 'He is more naïve than shrewd, more masterful than crafty, more generous with his personality than the people who make use of him are with their money. ... It is curious to have met a man for whom the value of life seems to consist in personal prestige.'[65]

Nostromo does indeed possess these qualities but they are, as Decoud says, the expression only of 'his enormous vanity, that first form of egoism which can take on the aspect of every virtue.'[66] Dr Monygham also penetrates to the springs of Nostromo's conduct: 'I believe him capable of anything – even of the most absurd fidelity.'* Nostromo has been impelled by vanity to win his reputation and if this is

* *Nostromo*, p. 319. There is a discrepancy between Dr Monygham's attitude expressed in this conversation with the chief engineer and later (p. 432) when he is made to appear unperceptive and rather simple-minded.

endangered his reliability, fidelity, and incorruptibility are also endangered. It is only those such as Don Pepe, a sort of South American Singleton, mounting guard over the mine, General Barrios in his raddled way and, one should add, Captain Mitchell, whose incorruptibility and fidelity can be relied on because in their case these qualities derive from a belief, from their concept of service, and are not merely an expression of their egoism.

Nostromo resents being entrusted with the removal of the silver from Sulaco because he realizes that his reputation is at stake and is afraid that he may fail.[67] Similarly, he cannot tolerate being taken for granted by the 'hombres finos' because it belittles his reputation. That is why he proclaims that he is determined to make the removal of the silver 'the most famous and desperate affair of my life'.[68]

Thus when he has partially failed in his mission he begins to disintegrate and 'the confused and intimate impressions of universal dissolution which beset a subjective nature at any strong check to its ruling passion had a bitterness approaching that of death itself. ... The facts of his situation he could appreciate like a man with a distinct experience of the country. ... He was as if sobered after a long bout of intoxication. His fidelity had been taken advantage of.'[69] He imagines the world on which his reputation depends collapsing and himself a hunted man. 'He had been betrayed!'[70]

Returning to the Great Isabel, where he has left Decoud with the hidden silver,

> He descended the ridge and found himself in the open solitude, between the harbour and the town. Its spaciousness, extended indefinitely by an effect of obscurity, rendered more sensible his profound isolation. His pace became slower. No one waited for him; no one thought of him; no one expected or wished his return. 'Betrayed! Betrayed!' he muttered to himself. No one cared.[71]

Although Nostromo's imagination has run away with him and his world, though threatened, has not collapsed, the spell has been broken and he persists in the feeling that he has been exploited and must henceforth look after his own interests. He can no longer rely on his reputation. It is at this point, after his created world has begun to crumble, that the silver takes hold of him:

> 'There is something in a treasure that fastens upon a man's mind. He will pray and blaspheme and still persevere, and will curse the day he ever heard of it, and will let his last hour come upon him unawares, still believing that he missed it only by a foot. He will see it every time he closes his eyes. He will never forget it till he is dead – and even then – Doctor, did you ever hear of the miserable gringos on Azuera, that cannot die? Ha! Ha! Sailors like myself. There is no getting away from a treasure that once fastens upon your mind.'[72]

Thus, although he goes on to transcend even his own past achievement and saves the Occidental Province in his great ride to Cayta, his thoughts remain with the silver. And when he realizes that, with the death of Decoud, he is the only person who knows that the silver has not been sunk in the lighter, he decides not to disclose its whereabouts but to use it to enrich himself. And at this moment the San Tomé mine 'appeared to him hateful and immense, lording it by its vast wealth over the valour, the toil, the fidelity of the poor, over war and peace, over the labours of the town, the sea, and the Campo'.[73] Thenceforth Nostromo is corrupted:

> A transgression, a crime, entering a man's existence, eats it up like a malignant growth, consumes it like a fever. Nostromo had lost his peace; the genuineness of all his qualities was destroyed. He felt it himself, and often cursed the silver of San Tomé. His courage, his magnificence, his leisure, his work, everything was as before, only everything was a sham. But the treasure was real. He clung to it with a more tenacious, mental grip. But he hated the feel of the ingots. Sometimes, after putting away a couple of them in his cabin – the fruit of a secret night expedition to the Great Isabel – he would look fixedly at his fingers, as if surprised they had left no stain on his skin.[74]

Retribution comes in the end. When Nostromo is dying, shot in error by his devoted admirer, Old Viola, he tells Mrs

Gould with literal and symbolical truth, 'The silver has killed me.'[75]

Silver is both the symbol and the embodiment of those 'material interests' which are transforming Sulaco, capital of the isolated Occidental Province and once 'an inviolable sanctuary from the temptations of a trading world' protected by 'the prevailing calms of its vast gulf'.[76]

The power of the San Tomé mine or, in effect, of Charles Gould who controls it, dominates the Occidental Province of Costaguana and even extends to the rest of the country, because Gould has used the wealth of the mine to finance a revolution which brought to power Don Vincente Ribiera, 'a man of culture and of unblemished character, invested with a mandate of reform by the best elements of the State'.[77]

Gould has not achieved this dominant position through the desire for enrichment or for power. Although the San Tomé mine has brought nothing but misfortune to his family, on the death of his father Gould is determined to accept its challenge: 'The mine had been the cause of an absurd moral disaster; its working must be made a serious and moral success.'[78] But 'after all his [Gould's father's] misery I simply could not have touched it for money alone'[79] and throughout the book there is no mention of Gould becoming rich or being interested in that aspect of the situation. As for power, Gould has always shunned it. He was no 'political intriguer'[80] and had supported Ribiera primarily in order to assure the unhampered working of the mine. 'He had persuaded himself that, apart from higher considerations, the backing up of Don José's hopes of reform was good business.'[81] Thus when the Ribiera regime is in danger and General Barrios's counter-stroke is planned, he holds himself aloof:

> Charles Gould was not present at the anxious and patriotic send-off. It was not his part to see the soldiers embark. It was neither his part, nor his inclination, nor his policy. His part, his inclination, and his policy were united in one endeavour to keep unchecked the flow of treasure he had started singlehanded from the re-opened scar in the flank of the mountain.[82]

The successful working of the mine is sufficient justification in itself and his satisfaction is gained through the essentially Conradian formula of the idealization of action:

> It hurt Charles Gould to feel that never more, by no effort of will, would he be able to think of his father in the same way he used to think of him when the poor man was alive. His breathing image was no longer in his power. This consideration, closely affecting his own identity, filled his breast with a mournful and angry desire for action. In this his instinct was unerring. Action is consolatory. It is the enemy of thought and the friend of flattering illusions. Only in the conduct of our action can we find the sense of mastery over the Fates.[83]

As the chief engineer says later: 'Upon my word, doctor, things seem to be worth nothing by what they are in themselves. I begin to believe that the only solid thing about them is the spiritual value which everyone discovers in his own form of activity.'[84]

Gould finds a philosophy to express this belief:

> What is wanted here is law, good faith, order, security. Any one can declaim about these things, but I pin my faith to material interests. Only let the material interests once get a firm footing, and they are bound to impose the conditions on which alone they can continue to exist. That's how your money-making is justified here in the face of lawlessness and disorder. It is justified because the security which it demands must be shared with an oppressed people. A better justice will come afterwards.[85]

But Gould's belief in the value of action does not save him, as it did Marlow in 'Heart of Darkness'; it ends by enslaving him.

Mrs Gould, on the other hand, distrusts material interests and progress from the start. In her conversation with the chairman of the railway board she looks back wistfully to the past. The chairman is speaking:

> '... What an out-of-the-way place Sulaco is! – and for a harbour, too! Astonishing!'
>
> 'Ah, but we are very proud of it. It used to be historically import-

ant. The highest ecclesiastical court, for two viceroyalties, sat here in the olden time,' she instructed him with animation . . .

and the chairman replies:

'We can't give you your ecclesiastical court back again; but you shall have more steamers, a railway, a telegraph-cable – a future in the great world which is worth infinitely more than any amount of ecclesiastical past. You shall be brought in touch with something greater than two viceroyalties . . .'[86]

But she none the less follows her husband in attaching a spiritual value to the mine. Her original impulse of enthusiasm is personal and derives from her devotion to Gould[87] and her desire for adventure. But she soon idealizes the meaning of the mine:

. . . She had laid her unmercenary hands, with an eagerness that made them tremble, upon the first silver ingot turned out still warm from the mould; and by her imaginative estimate of its power she endowed that lump of metal with a justificative conception, as though it were not a mere fact, but something far-reaching and impalpable, like the true expression of an emotion or the emergence of a principle.[88]

Thus, in different ways, for both the Goulds 'each passing of the escort under the balconies of the Casa Gould was like another victory gained in the conquest of peace for Sulaco'.[89]

The Goulds, then, are idealists, although at opposite ends of the scale; he has become the victim of his ideal to the point of obsession whereas she has sunk her personality in the ideal of service. Around the Goulds there revolve the conflicting forces of idealism, scepticism, and brazen self-interest. Among the idealists there is Holroyd, the great power in San Francisco who is financing the mine. He has 'the temperament of a Puritan and an insatiable imagination of conquest'.[90] He 'attached a strangely idealistic meaning to concrete facts' and combines a 'lavish patronage of "the purer forms of Christianity" '[91] with ruthless exploitation of material interests. There is Mrs Gould's protégé, Giorgio

Viola, the old Garibaldino, with his 'worship and service of liberty'.[92]

> The spirt of self-forgetfulness, the simple devotion to a vast humanitarian idea which inspired the thought and stress of that revolutionary time, had left its mark upon Giorgio in a sort of austere contempt for all personal advantage.[93]

There are Don José Avellanos and his daughter Antonia with their profound love of their country. Don José sees in Gould's power the means whereby his ideals may be realized. He 'was ruined in every way, but a man possessed of passion is not a bankrupt in life. Don José Avellanos desired passionately for his country: peace, prosperity, and . . . "an honourable place in the comity of civilized nations".'[94] Then, standing apart in his fanaticism, there is Antonia's uncle, Father Corbelàn, with his demands for the restitution of the confiscated church lands.

Self-interest is embodied in the crude lust for power of the Monteros, the squalid demagoguery of Gamacho and Fuentes, the equally crude desire for wealth on the part of Sotillo, and of the unfortunate Señor Hirsch, and, in disguised form, in Nostromo's conduct.

Dr Monygham and Decoud, on the other hand, are both self-proclaimed sceptics. Dr Monygham's scepticism, or cynicism, has been forced on him, having its roots in a physical defeat when he had succumbed to atrocious torture during the tyranny of Guzman Bento; he had therefore lost faith in himself and others. This event placed him in the same situation as Jim and Razumov. He feels cut off from social communion with others and because of his uncouth behaviour is distrusted by them. He is sustained only by his devotion to Mrs Gould, which is 'like a store of unlawful wealth'.[95] Decoud's scepticism, on the other hand, is a mental attitude; he 'recognised no other virtue than intelligence'[96] and 'had pushed the habit of universal raillery to a point where it blinded him to the genuine impulses of his own nature'.[97] He feels bound to explain away such impulses, or relate them to self-interest. Later he is able, like Dr

Monygham, to attribute all his actions to one passion, his love for Antonia. 'I have no patriotic illusions,' he says: 'I have only the supreme illusion of a lover.'[98] He is confronted with Antonio's 'belief in the cause'[99] and with her accusation that he never sees 'the aim'.[100]

To Mrs Gould, Decoud ruthlessly analyses Gould's character:

> 'Don't you see, he's such an idealist. . . . It's a wonderful thing to say with the sight of the San Tomé mine, the greatest fact in the whole of South America, perhaps, before our very eyes. But look even at that, he has idealised this fact to a point – . . . Are you aware to what point he has idealised the existence, the worth, the meaning of the San Tomé mine? Are you aware of it?' . . .
>
> 'What do you know?' she asked in a feeble voice.
>
> 'Nothing,' answered Decoud, firmly. 'But, then, don't you see, he's an Englishman?'
>
> 'Well, what of that?' asked Mrs. Gould.
>
> 'Simply that he cannot act or exist without idealising every simple feeling, desire, or achievement. He could not believe his own motives if he did not make them first a part of some fairy tale. The earth is not quite good enough for him, I fear. Do you excuse my frankness? Besides, whether you excuse it or not, it is part of the truth of things which hurts the – what do you call them? – the Anglo-Saxon susceptibilities, and at the present moment I don't feel as if I could treat seriously either his conception of things or – if you allow me to say so – or yet yours.'[101]

In Decoud's mind there is only one step from idealism to sentimentalism. He claims that both Gould and Holroyd are sentimentalists.[102] He tells Mrs Gould that her husband is a 'sentimentalist, after the amazing manner of your people'[103] and expounding his scheme for the Occidental Republic he says: 'I think he [Gould] can be drawn into it, like all idealists, when he once sees a sentimental basis for his action.'[104]

It is Decoud who sees that Gould's idealization of the mine has become an obsession. He speaks of 'this "Imperium in Imperio", this wealth-producing thing, to which his [Gould's] sentimentalism attaches a strange idea of justice. Unless I am much mistaken in the man, it must remain inviolate or perish by an act of his will alone. A passion has crept into his cold and idealistic life.'[105]

Gould has eventually reversed the order of values. Instead of the mine being justified by its service to 'law, good faith, order, security',[106] these ideals have become subordinated to the importance of the mine. He has become a monomaniac who can only think of the mine as identified with himself and plans to blow it up rather than let it fall into the hands of another. Decoud realizes that the mine represents a tragedy in the personal relations of the Goulds, for Mrs Gould 'has discovered that he [Gould] lives for the mine rather than for her'.[107] It is Mrs Gould's 'mission to save him from the effects of that cold and overmastering passion which she dreads more than if it were an infatuation for another woman'.[108] She has found that her husband is becoming gradually estranged from her:

> Mrs. Gould continued along the corridor away from her husband's room. The fate of the San Tomé mine was lying heavy upon her heart. It was a long time now since she had begun to fear it. It had been an idea. She had watched it with misgivings turning into a fetish, and now the fetish had grown into a monstrous and crushing weight. It was as if the inspiration of their early years had left her heart to turn into a wall of silver-bricks, erected by the silent work of evil spirits, between her and her husband. He seemed to dwell alone within a circumvallation of precious metal, leaving her outside with her school, her hospital, the sick mothers and the feeble old men, mere insignificant vestiges of the initial inspiration.[109]

She sees that 'the mine had got hold of Charles Gould with a grip as deadly as ever it had laid upon his father',[110] or, it might be added, as deadly as that which bound the ghosts of the two gringos to the treasure on Azuera. 'She saw clearly the San Tomé mine possessing, consuming, burning up the life of the last of the Costaguana Goulds.'[111] She only once tries to break down the wall and regain the intimacy of their early days together.[112] Otherwise she accepts her isolation fatalistically, but confesses at Nostromo's deathbed: 'I, too, have hated the idea of that silver from the bottom of my heart.'[113] Even she herself has been tainted by the silver because, persuaded by Decoud, 'for the first and last time of her life she had concealed the truth from her husband about that very silver. She had been corrupted by her fears at that time, and had never forgiven herself.'[114]

The silver, or the mine, happens to have been the cause of the tragedy, but the real cause is in Gould's obsessive character. He could have dedicated himself to something unconnected with wealth, with the same tragic consequences because:

> A man haunted by a fixed idea is insane. He is dangerous even if that idea is an idea of justice; for may he not bring the heaven down pitilessly upon a loved head?[115]

To Decoud it seemed that 'every conviction, as soon as it became effective, turned into that form of dementia the gods send upon those they wish to destroy'.[116] But his scepticism leads him to a fate even more tragic than that of the Goulds. For when he is put to the ultimate test he fails. Alone on the Great Isabel his sense of his own personality disintegrates, as does that of Nostromo in similar circumstances. 'He had recognised no other virtue than intelligence, and had erected passions into duties. Both his intelligence and his passion were swallowed up easily in this great unbroken solitude of waiting without faith.'[117] Finally he can stand it no longer and shoots himself:

> He died from solitude, the enemy known but to few on this earth, and whom only the simplest of us are fit to withstand. The brilliant Costaguanero of the boulevards had died from solitude and want of faith in himself and others.[118]

Thus idealism and scepticism, faith and want of faith, both seem to lead to disaster. *Nostromo* is an intensely pessimistic book; it is perhaps the most impressive monument to futility ever created. Apart from Captain Mitchell with his comfortable old age secured by his seventeen shares in the San Tomé mine, no one achieves satisfaction; and Mitchell is certainly among those, like MacWhirr and Hermann, who have been 'disdained by destiny or by the sea'.

The fate of the individuals with whom *Nostromo* has been particularly concerned and of Costaguana as a whole are equally hopeless. Antonia Avellanos and Linda Viola both have the men they love taken away by death. Mrs Gould virtually loses her husband to the mine and is in the end disillusioned: 'She resembled a good fairy, weary with a long career of well-doing, touched by the withering suspicion of the uselessness of her labours, the powerlessness of her magic.'[119] She is engulfed by 'an immense desolation, the dread of her own continued life'.[120] Don José Avellanos dies 'vanquished in a lifelong struggle with the powers of moral darkness, whose stagnant depths breed monstrous crimes and monstrous illusions'.[121] Decoud dies 'a victim of the disillusioned weariness which is the retribution meted out to intellectual audacity'[122] just as Nostromo is the 'victim of the disenchanted vanity which is the reward of audacious action'.[123] This is the most deeply pessimistic judgement of all, because the 'audacity' has produced the two most constructive actions in the book. It is due to Decoud that the Occidental Republic is proclaimed and to Nostromo's ride to Cayta that it is established.

The country as a whole comes off no better. In an article on Anatole France written just after finishing *Nostromo* Conrad said: 'Political institutions, whether contrived by the wisdom of the few or the ignorance of the many, are incapable of securing the happiness of mankind.'[124] It is not surprising therefore that no section of the community seems to offer any hope for a permanently better future. The Democrats naturally get short shrift from Conrad, who goes out of his way to make their leaders, Gamacho and Fuentes, thoroughly disreputable and unscrupulous. Don Juste Lopez, the conservative champion of parliamentary institutions, is made to appear pathetic and craven in his readiness to propitiate the villainous Pedrito Montero 'in order to save the form at least of parliamentary institutions';[125] Conrad cannot even resist making him ridiculous by having half his beard blown off. Similarly, Ribiera, the 'hope of honest men', flees ignominiously from the Monteros; and it is significant that he is a particularly poor physical specimen, 'obese to the point of infirmity', 'almost a cripple'.[126] And at the end the fanatical Father Corbelàn is threatening the overthrow of the material interests which have made the Occidental Republic secure, justifying Dr Monygham's verdict of 'incorrigible' on the Costaguaneros.[127]

Then although at the end of the book justice and order have temporarily triumphed and Sulaco is 'growing rich swiftly',[128] material interests, which dominate the Occidental Republic, have their own form of tyranny. This has been foreshadowed from the start and is expressed in one of those sentences whose full significance only becomes apparent later:

> The sparse row of telegraph poles strode obliquely clear of the town, bearing a single, almost invisible wire far into the great campo – like a slender, vibrating feeler of that progress waiting outside for a moment of peace to enter and twine itself about the weary heart of the land.[129]

Thus when Mrs Gould asks: 'Will there never be any peace?' Dr Monygham prophesies:

> 'There is no peace and no rest in the development of material interests. They have their law, and their justice. But it is founded on expediency, and is inhuman; it is without rectitude, without the continuity and the force that can be found only in a moral principle. Mrs Gould, the time approaches when all that the Gould Concession stands for shall weigh as heavily upon the people as the barbarism, cruelty, and misrule of a few years back.'[130]

Mrs Gould cannot deny this, and her vision of the future is as black as Dr Monygham's because, although in the development of the San Tomé mine her husband had achieved a 'colossal and lasting success',[131]

> there was something inherent in the necessities of successful action which carried with it the moral degradation of the idea. She saw the San Tomé mountain hanging over the Campo, over the whole

land, feared, hated, wealthy; more soulless than any tyrant, more pitiless and autocratic than the worst Government; ready to crush innumerable lives in the expansion of its greatness.[132]

So much for Gould's hope of the mine becoming 'that little rift in the darkness'[133] which his father had despaired of seeing.

The future of Costaguana is as ominous as its past has been gory. Dr Monygham does 'not believe in the reform of Costaguana',[134] and this seems to be the conclusion implicit in the novel. To seek out a hopeful interpretation Robert Penn Warren, who has written perhaps the most perceptive essay on *Nostromo* and incidentally on Conrad, is forced to search beyond the limits of the book. But perhaps the most apt implied comment on the world of *Nostromo* is contained in 'Autocracy and War', an essay which Conrad wrote a few months after finishing the novel. After saying that, in a world dominated by industrialism and commercialism, there can only be an uneasy peace based on fear, he continues: 'The true peace of the world ... will be built on less perishable foundations than those of material interests. But it must be confessed that the architectural aspect of the universal city remains as yet inconceivable – that the very ground for its erection has not been cleared of the jungle.'[135] A few paragraphs later he probes deeper:

> The intellectual stage of mankind being as yet in its infancy, and States, like most individuals, having but a feeble and imperfect consciousness of the worth and force of the inner life, the need of making their existence manifest to themselves is determined in the direction of physical activity. The idea of ceasing to grow in territory, in strength, in wealth, in influence – in anything but wisdom and self-knowledge is odious to them as the omen of the end. Action, in which is to be found the illusion of a mastered destiny, can alone satisfy our uneasy vanity and lay to rest the haunting fear of the future — a sentiment concealed, indeed, but proving its existence by the force it has, when invoked, to stir the passions of a nation. It will be long before we have learned that in the great darkness before us there is nothing that we need fear.[136]

In *Nostromo* Conrad portrayed the world as he saw it, not as he hoped it might become; nor does he allow any trace of a hope to appear without exposing the illusion on which it is based. It is clear that he regarded the dominance of material interests and the 'feeble and imperfect consciousness of the worth and force of the inner life' as a condition of humanity and not peculiar to Costaguana.

Costaguana is, however, primarily a prototype of a politically inexperienced nation and it is tempting to see an analogy between it and Poland. It is likely that Conrad was able to express some of his feelings about Poland consciously or unconsciously using the disguise of Costaguana. He might well have been thinking of Russian-dominated Poland when he referred to the 'political immaturity of the people ... the indolence of the upper classes and the mental darkness of the lower',[137] or when Gould complains: 'The words one knows so well have a nightmarish meaning in this country. Liberty, democracy, patriotism, government – all of them have a flavour of folly and murder,'[138] or when 'The cruel futility of things stood unveiled in the levity and sufferings of that incorrigible people; the cruel futility of lives and of deaths thrown away in the vain endeavour to attain an enduring solution of the problem.'[139] So, too, when Decoud says: ' "We are a wonderful people, but it has always been our fate to be" – he did not say "robbed", but added, after a pause – "exploited!" '[140] And his analysis of the predicament of Costaguana fits closely to that of Poland:

> 'There is a curse of futility upon our character: Don Quixote and Sancho Panza, chivalry and materialism, high-sounding sentiments and a supine morality, violent efforts for an idea and a sullen acquiescence in every form of corruption. We convulsed a continent for our independence only to become the passive prey of a democratic parody, the helpless victims of scoundrels and cut-throats . . .'[141]

There is little doubt that Conrad had strongly ambivalent feelings towards Polish aspirations which were closely bound up with his attitude towards his father. He had seen at first hand one of the tragic consequences of the political agitation which culminated in the 1863 rising; the exile and disillusionment of his father and the premature death of his mother. In fact the situation between Mr and Mrs Gould is analogous to that between Conrad's parents if political action is substituted for material interests; it is particularly emphasized when Conrad says that Gould is haunted by a fixed idea, and 'a man haunted by a fixed idea is insane. He is dangerous even if that idea is an idea of justice; for may he not bring the heaven down pitilessly upon a loved head?'[142] or when Decoud, speaking of Mrs Gould, points to 'some subtle wrong ... that sentimental unfaithfulness which surrenders her happiness, her life, to the seduction of an idea'.[143]

As a result of his experiences, and above all because he had left Poland, Conrad, while retaining a deep attachment to the country, refused to take her political aspirations seriously; for if he admitted that there was a genuine chance that Poland might regain her freedom he would have felt bound to remain and participate in the struggle. In the Author's Note to *Nostromo* he says that Antonia Avellanos is modelled on his 'first love' and adds: 'I was not the only one in love with her; but it was I who had to hear oftenest her scathing criticism of my levities – very much like poor Decoud – or stand the brunt of her austere, unanswerable invective.'[144] Although this must be treated circumspectly in view of Eastwick's Antonia Ribera it is not too far-fetched to see Conrad's own dilemma reflected in Decoud's attitude. Decoud at first, like Mrs Gould, finds it hard to take the affairs of Costaguana seriously; they smack of *opéra bouffe*. But he cannot withhold his sympathy for long: 'He was moved in spite of himself by that note of passion and sorrow unknown on the more refined stage of European politics',[145] and: 'To contemplate revolutions from the distance of the Parisian boulevards was quite another matter. Here on the spot it was not possible to dismiss their tragic comedy with the expression, "Quelle Farce!" ... "I suppose I am more of a Costaguanero than I would have believed possible," he thought to himself.'[146] In several of his utterances, and even of his actions, he shows signs of a passionate concern for his country's fate akin to that of Don José and Antonia Avellanos.

When Conrad condemns Decoud's attitude to life, or at least his pose of scepticism, he is perhaps recalling his own situation in Marseilles:

> He imagined himself Parisian to the tips of his fingers. But far from being that he was in danger of remaining a sort of nondescript dilettante all his life. He had pushed the habit of universal raillery to a point where it blinded him to the genuine impulses of his own nature.[147]

When Decoud says: 'What is a conviction? a particular view of our personal advantage either practical or emotional',[148] he is the witty, cynical boulevardier but when 'it seemed to him that every conviction, as soon as it became effective, turned into that form of dementia the gods send upon those they wish to destroy',[149] he is expressing the view of the mature Conrad. The statement that Decoud 'had no faith in anything except the truth of his own sensations' expresses in negative form what was the cornerstone of Conrad's own outlook,[150] and when Father Corbelàn calls Decoud 'neither the son of his own country nor of any other',[151] he designates Conrad's own predicament.

[XI]

Achievement without Success, II

A FEW weeks after *Nostromo* was finished, in October of 1904, the Conrads went to London to prepare for an operation on Jessie's knee.[1] They took a flat at 99b Addison Road. 'It was typical of Joseph Conrad with his inherent extravagance of everything', wrote Jessie, 'that the night before I left the flat in Addison Road to go into the Nursing Home, we had thirty guests for a kind of impromptu supper. I remember Mr and Mrs E. V. Lucas, A. J. Dawson ... Henry Tonks, Augustus John, among many others.'[2]

While in London Conrad turned out some incidental pieces in order to earn some money: an article on Henry James,[3] two more of his sea 'sketches',[4] and an embryo version of 'Gaspar Ruiz' for the *Strand Magazine*.[5] He was, as usual, very short of money and the cost of Jessie's operation was going to be an additional burden. But the Conrads had decided that they must have a rest and, despite their lack of money, had arranged to go to Capri as soon as Jessie was well enough. Pinker probably put up some of the money, no doubt fearing that Conrad would have a nervous breakdown if he did not get away, and it may be that other friends helped too.

They set off on 14 January.[6] It was an eventful journey. According to Jessie it started badly, as Conrad could not find his favourite glasses and had to leave without them, whereas Jessie herself forgot part of her false teeth. Then Conrad apparently took a dislike to the nurse who was to look after Jessie. Finally, Jessie, still being almost immobile, had to be carried in a chair. Boarding the ship at Dover one of the carriers

> got his hand stuck firmly between the chair and the rail of the gangway. No doubt it pinched horribly and my fortitude was severely tried while I sat poised aloft, in a frail chair without arms

even, on the top of the rail, watching the swirling waters between the ship and the quay, and listening to the howls of dismay from the onlookers, who expected every moment to see me tipped into the water.[7]

In Rome she was left hanging on to the door of the railway carriage when the chair was by mistake taken away from underneath her. In Naples the Conrads were held up for five days because it was too rough to land Jessie.[8] Finally:

My landing was accomplished in a truly marvellous manner. A number of Italian seamen appeared and amid loud, unintelligible chatter, I was hoisted over the side of the vessel and passed by willing hands down the gangway into the small boat lying alongside. I simply shut my eyes and let myself go. Still in the wooden chair, I was landed on the 'Granda Marina', without a pause as it seemed to me. Poor Joseph Conrad was loud in praise of the feat performed by the seamen – after it was all over. 'It took a sailor to do things properly.' The dear man seemed to have forgotten his agitation during the process.[9]

The journey certainly seems to have taken its toll of Conrad's nerves and purse because he wrote to Galsworthy on arrival:

... The delay of all these days in the hotel has utterly ruined me. In fact to be able to get over to Capri, I had to leave a 150 frcs. unpaid on my bill and am beginning life here in charge of a party of four with 30 frcs. in my pocket ...

The nervous irritation of these days in Naples prevented me from doing anything. I got 1000 words of a political article written (and that's all) during the voyage. Here the outlook is very promising; the rooms good, the terrace on the south side. Through the good Canonico we have fallen into the hands of priests. There were three of them waiting on the Marina Grande for our arrival, which took place on a moonlight evening about seven. The whole population surged and yelled round poor Jessie's chair, while we waited on the quay for the large carriage which was ordered but did not turn up in time. I think we will be very comfortable here. But the whole expedition is a mad thing really, for it rests upon what I am not certain of – my power to produce some sixty thousand words in four months. I feel sick with apprehension at times. [21 January 1905, *L.L.*, II, p. 9]

The expedition was not a success as far as writing was concerned. To start with, the nurse got seriously ill and instead of looking after Jessie had to be looked after by her. Conrad complained to Pinker:

> I, who now if ever wanted peace to concentrate my thoughts after all the anxieties in London, could not achieve it (as you may guess) in these lodgings. I have worked but badly – there's no use disguising the truth – I've been in a state of exasperation with the eternal something cropping up to distract my mind. . . . Of course you may say that I ought to disregard all the complications and peg away with my eyes shut to domestic affairs. I know some men are capable of that sort of thing; and with an organised household one could perhaps abstract oneself for six hours per day. It's another matter with me. You understand that my wife was pretty helpless and required some attention; the child too. For me to have to lay down my pen ten times in the course of the day is fatal. I wish there had been something of a hack-writer in my composition. [5 February 1905, *L.L.*, II, p. 11]

Conrad himself then caught influenza and bronchitis and suffered from insomnia and nerves.[10] But even after these troubles were over he found that he could not work well. Near the end of the four months he told Hueffer: 'This climate, what between Tramontana and Sirocco, has half killed me in a not unpleasant langourous, melting way. I am sunk in a vaguely uneasy dream of visions, of innumerable tales that float in an atmosphere of voluptuously aching bones.'[11]

In consequence he only succeeded in writing a long political article which he called 'Autocracy and War' and a little of a story which he was to lay aside for some years and was eventually to develop into *Chance*.[12] He also did some reading for a projected 'Mediterranean novel' in the library of a Dr Cerio; the subject was to be the struggle for Capri in 1808 between the French and the British.[13]

'Autocracy and War' is Conrad's most important piece of

political writing and he evidently set much store by it, hoping that it would cause something of a sensation.[14] It was prompted immediately by the Russo-Japanese war, but it may well be that *Nostromo* had stimulated Conrad to think particularly about political subjects. He took this opportunity to make a withering indictment of Russia. He contrasted the two armies. The Japanese 'has for its base a reasoned conviction; it has behind it the profound belief in the right of a logical necessity to be appeased at the cost of so much blood and treasure. And in that belief, whether well or ill founded, that army stands on the high ground of conscious assent, shouldering deliberately the burden of a long-tried faithfulness.' Whereas the Russian army, 'torn out from a miserable quietude resembling death itself, hurled across space, amazed, without starting-point of its own, or knowledge of the aim, can feel nothing but a horror-stricken consciousness of having mysteriously become the plaything of a black and merciless fate'.[15] He saw this war as the first step in the destruction of the Russian myth. But:

> Above it all – unaccountably persistent – the decrepit, old, hundred years old, spectre of Russia's might still faces Europe from across the teeming graves of Russian people. This dreaded and strange apparition, bristling with bayonets, armed with chains, hung over with holy images; that something not of this world, partaking of a ravenous ghoul, of a blind Djinn grown up from a cloud, and of the Old Man of the Sea, still faces us with its old stupidity, with its strange mystical arrogance, stamping its shadowy feet upon the gravestone of autocracy, already cracked beyond repair by the torpedoes of Togo and the guns of Oyama, already heaving in the blood-soaked ground with the first stirrings of a resurrection . . .[16]

The Russian autocracy is condemned absolutely:

> Spectral it lived and spectral it disappears without leaving a memory of a single generous deed, of a single service rendered – even involuntarily – to the polity of nations. Other despotisms there have been, but none whose origin was so grimly fantastic in its baseness, and the beginning of whose end was so gruesomely ignoble. . . . An attentive survey of Russia's literature, of her

Church, of her administration and the cross-currents of her thought, must end in the verdict that the Russia of today has not the right to give her voice on a single question touching the future of humanity, because from the very inception of her being the brutal destruction of dignity, of truth, of rectitude, of all that is faithful in human nature has been made the imperative condition of her existence.[17]

His close knowledge of Russia, and, no doubt too, a temperamental predisposition led him to a grim prediction of her future which was far more accurate than the optimistic hopes of the liberal Garnett and his friends:

As her boasted military force that, corrupt in its origin, has ever struck no other but faltering blows, so her soul, kept benumbed by her temporal and spiritual master with the poison of tyranny and superstition, will find itself on awakening possessed of no language, a monstrous full-grown child having first to learn the ways of living thought and articulate speech. It is safe to say tyranny, assuming a thousand protean shapes, will remain clinging to her struggles for a long time before her blind multitudes succeed at last in trampling her out of existence under their millions of bare feet.[18]

To Conrad, as a Pole, Germany, or rather Prussia, 'which has been the evil counsellor of Russia on all the questions of her Polish problem',[19] was scarcely less hateful than Russia. But whereas Russia was an object of contempt, Germany was a sinister menace. Germany, with 'a people trained to the worship of force',[20] is 'a powerful and voracious organization, full of unscrupulous self-confidence, whose appetite for aggrandisement will only be limited by the power of helping itself to the severed members of its friends and neighbours'.[21] The article ends with the prophetic warning ' "Le Prussianisme – voilà l'ennemi".'[22]

(2)

As Conrad was accomplishing so little during his stay on Capri he was again getting very short of money and there came a point when Pinker felt that he could advance no more.[23] But then there was a piece of good news. For some time William Rothenstein had been organizing support to get Conrad a grant of money from a confidential official fund; Gosse and others had taken the matter up and in March Rothenstein was able to write to Conrad that the Prime Minister, Balfour, had obtained the King's consent to a grant. This grant, of £500, was the occasion of a small rumpus. When Conrad heard that Henry Newbolt was to be a sort of trustee he took this as an aspersion on his character, implying that he was an irresponsible bohemian. He wrote an indignant letter to Gosse who was of course much put out by this apparent ingratitude and had in turn to be mollified by Rothenstein.[24]

Galsworthy and Ada came to Capri while the Conrads were there and Conrad also made a number of new friends, the most important of whom were Norman Douglas and a compatriot named Count Szembek. Douglas was just beginning his writing career and Conrad enthusiastically took him up, asking Pinker to try to place a couple of his pieces in magazines.[25]

The Conrads got back to England on 17 May,[26] having apparently met Marguerite Poradowska in Marseilles on the journey.[27] *One Day More* was to be performed by the Stage Society in a month's time, which involved a certain amount of work and a lot of worry. At the end of June Conrad gave Galsworthy a 'résumé' of his activities since his return from Capri: 'Gout. Tinkering at the play. Worry. Two *Mirror* papers. Touch of gout. Rehearsals of the play, with going up to London for the purpose (which is a game not worth the candle). Loss of time. Some experience (which may or may not be of use).'[28]

The play was performed on Sunday 25 June and the two following days; the Conrads went to the last performance. Conrad summed up the affair to Galsworthy:

> As to the success of my thing, I can't say anything. I've heard that some papers praised it and some ran it down. On Tuesday when we went (like the imbeciles we are) there was some clapping

but obviously the very smart audience did *not* catch on. And no wonder! On the other hand the celebrated 'man of the hour', G. B. Shaw, was ecstatic and enthusiastic. 'Dramatist!', says he. With three plays of his own running simultaneously at the height of the season he's entitled to speak. Of course, I don't think I am a dramatist. But I believe I've three or even five acts somewhere in me. At any rate the reception of the play was not such as to encourage me to sacrifice six months to the stage. Besides I haven't the six months to throw away.

In the end: loss of time. A thorough unsettling of the writing mood. Added weariness. [30 June 1905, *L.L.*, II, p. 21]

Although the same objections could be made to the play as to the story it is a neat and, within its limitations, effective piece of theatre.

The episode seems to have heightened Conrad's ambivalence towards the theatre. Twelve years later, when he was helping Macdonald Hastings with a dramatization of *Victory*, he wrote to Christopher Sandeman:

I have a secret horror of all actors and (not so much) of actresses since they murdered for me a one-act play I wrote once (off my own bat) and had some illusions about it. [(End of April 1917), *L.L.*, II, p. 191]

The next few months were uneventful. There were visits from a few close friends, such as the Galsworthys and the Hopes;[29] and Conrad saw a certain amount of Hueffer, who, he told Wells, 'is a sort of lifelong habit – of which I am not ashamed, because he is a much better fellow than the world gives him credit for'.[30] There was also, according to Jessie, a visit from a figure from Conrad's past, Roger Casement.[31] Conrad's health was not good at this time and he told Douglas in October that he had not had 'more than three weeks of decent health in the whole time since I left Capri'.[32] Then to complete the usual catalogue of woes Borys went down with scarlet fever while the Conrads were visiting London in November.[33] However, as if to make up for the unproductiveness of the rest of 1905, Conrad managed to end the year with a spurt of work. He finished two more pieces for *The Mirror of the Sea*[34] and seems to have developed 'Gaspar Ruiz' into its final form.* Then he wrote three other short stories, 'The Brute', 'An Anarchist' and 'The Informer';† and he also continued to work on *Chance.*

'Gaspar Ruiz' is set in Chile during her war of independence and is a by-product of Conrad's reading for *Nostromo.* He found the 'seed' for the story in Captain Basil Hall's book, *Extracts from a Journal, written on the Coasts of Chili, Peru, and Mexico.*[35] He again captured the atmosphere of a warring South American state, but it is a slight, melodramatic story and, even apart from the enormous physique of Gaspar Ruiz himself, emotions and actions give the impression of having been blown up to more than life-size. Gaspar Ruiz is a simple, humane man of the people who is unjustly sentenced to death as a deserter by the republicans. He escapes and is looked after by an aristocratic royalist girl with an implacable desire for revenge on the republicans. Having saved the life of a republican general in an earthquake he is pardoned and rises to a position of responsibility. Then, enraged by the machinations of the civil governor of the province of which he is 'military guardian', he leads a rising against the republicans. Urged on by the girl, who has become his wife and borne him a child, he successfully holds out against the government. But his wife and child are finally captured through treachery and he is killed trying to rescue them; his back is broken when he has

* The *Strand Magazine* had asked Conrad for a short story in the autumn of 1904 (Conrad to Hueffer, 15 October 1904). He had written what seems to have been the first part of 'Gaspar Ruiz' (see p. 380) and had promised two further instalments; but the *Strand* must have turned down the first instalment and so Conrad temporarily laid the story aside.

† 'Yes, I wrote the Anarchist story and now I am writing another of the sort . . .' (Conrad to Galsworthy, 29 December 1905.) Conrad told Pinker that 'The Informer' was ready in a letter dated 1 January [1906]; cf., also, to Galsworthy, 11 January 1906. The MS. of 'The Informer' is dated 11.1.06 (Quinn, 1848). I can find no record of the writing of 'The Brute' but it had certainly been written by 21 February 1906 (Conrad to Pinker of that date) and was probably written before 'An Anarchist'.

a cannon fired from it in place of the gun-carriage which has been lost over the precipice. Before he dies, the girl, who until now seems only to have been using Gaspar Ruiz as an instrument of revenge, declares her love for him and when he is dead throws herself to her death in an abyss.

The story is told by an old officer of the republican army, but the presentation is as slipshod as the characterization is crude; whenever Conrad needs to give some information which the narrator could not know he drops him and takes over himself.

'The Brute' is a short story about an unpredictable ship which had the reputation of killing a man every voyage. Conrad says that he first heard about the ship from Captain Blake, under whom he served as Second Officer on the *Tilkhurst* in 1884.[36] The 'brute' is eventually run on the rocks because the Officer of the Watch was occupied with a woman passenger; this was the fate of another ship which Conrad grafted on to the story of the brute.[37] It is a slight story, little more than a pot-boiler.

The two other products of this winter's work are, however, more substantial. 'An Anarchist' is a savage, almost mad story about a man who becomes a victim of society in rather the same way as does Anatole France's Crainquebille. 'The principal truth discoverable in the views of Paul the engineer was that a little thing may bring about the undoing of a man.'[38] He is a decent, hard-working man who gets drunk when celebrating one day and is arrested for causing a disturbance and shouting anarchist slogans. At his trial:

> Whatever chance he had was done away with by a young socialist lawyer who volunteered to undertake his defence. In vain he assured him that he was no anarchist; that he was a quiet, respectable mechanic, only too anxious to work ten hours per day at his trade. He was represented at the trial as the victim of society and his drunken shoutings as the expression of infinite suffering. The young lawyer had his way to make, and this case was just what he wanted for a start. The speech for the defence was pronounced magnificent.[39]

He received the maximum sentence for a first offence.

When he comes out his old employer refuses to take him back and he falls into the hands of a group of anarchists who terrorize and exploit him. He is involved in a bank robbery and is sentenced to the penal colony at Cayenne. During a convicts' revolt he and two of the anarchists with whom he has been associated escape in a boat. He has managed to get hold of a pistol and he forces the two men to row to the point of exhaustion. 'It made me smile. Ah! They loved their life these two, in this evil world of theirs, just as I used to love my life, too, before they spoiled it for me with their phrases.[40]

Eventually he sees a sail on the horizon:

I remembered their lies, their promises, their menaces, and all my days of misery. Why could they not have left me alone after I came out of prison? I looked at them and thought that while they lived I could never be free. Never. Neither I nor others like me with warm hearts and weak heads. For I know I have not a strong head, monsieur. A black rage came upon me – the rage of extreme intoxication – but not against the injustice of society. Oh, no!

'I must be free!' I cried, furiously.

'*Vive la liberté!*' yells that ruffian Mafile. '*Mort aux bourgeois* who send us to Cayenne! They shall soon know that we are free.'

The sky, the sea, the whole horizon, seemed to turn red, blood red all round the boat. My temples were beating so loud that I wondered they did not hear. How is it that they did not? How is it they did not understand?

I heard Simon ask, 'Have we not pulled far enough out now?'

'Yes. Far enough,' I said. I was sorry for him; it was the other I hated. He hauled in his oar with a loud sigh, and as he was raising his hand to wipe his forehead with the air of a man who has done his work, I pulled the trigger of my revolver and shot him like this off the knee, right through the heart.

He tumbled down, with his head hanging over the side of the boat. I did not give him a second glance. The other cried out piercingly. Only one shriek of horror. Then all was still.

He slipped off the thwart on to his knees and raised his clasped hands before his face in an attitude of supplication. 'Mercy,' he whispered, faintly. 'Mercy for me! – comrade.'

'Ah, comrade,' I said, in a low tone. 'Yes, comrade, of course. Well, then, shout *Vive l'anarchie.*'

He flung up his arms, his face up to the sky and his mouth wide open in a great yell of despair. '*Vive l'anarchie! Vive* –'

He collapsed all in a heap, with a bullet through his head.[41]

The story is told by a lepidopterist who finds the 'anarchist', after his escape, being exploited by the callous manager of a cattle estate whose steam-launch he is working. Despite the man's blood-curdling past he is portrayed as a desolate, sympathetic figure. In his isolation from all around him he is a little like Yanko Goorall of 'Amy Foster'. He is enveloped in an aura of mystery; thus although he is French the manager insists that he comes from Barcelona and he is called Anarchisto de Barcelone 'as if it were his christian name and surname'.[42] The lepidopterist's conclusion is that

he was much more of an anarchist than he confessed to me or to himself; and that, the special features of his case apart, he was very much like many other anarchists. Warm heart and weak head – that is the word of the riddle; and it is a fact that the bitterest contradictions and the deadliest conflicts of the world are carried on in every individual breast capable of feeling and passion.[43]

'The Informer' is also a savage story concerned with anarchism, but not of the warm-hearted type. The story is told at one remove; the narrator relates what he has been told by Mr X, the anarchist, for whom he shows a strong distaste. It is by revealing the cynicism of Mr X who is also an 'enlightened connoisseur of bronzes and china'[44] and a luxurious liver, that Conrad expresses his own antipathy towards anarchism. The use of Mr X greatly enriches the texture of the story, as when the girl's misguided belief in the 'informer' Sevrin is portrayed through Mr X's own callous contempt for her behaviour. Through him Conrad also condemns those of the bourgeoisie who foster the anarchists:

'Don't you know yet,' he [Mr X] said, 'that an idle and selfish class loves to see mischief being made, even if it is made at its own expense? Its own life being all a matter of pose and gesture, it is unable to realise the power and the danger of a real movement and of words that have no sham meaning. It is all fun and sentiment. ... The demagogue carries the amateurs of emotion with him. Amateurism in this, that, and the other thing is a delightfully easy way of killing time, and feeding one's own vanity – the silly vanity of being abreast with the ideas of the day after tomorrow.'[45]

It is significant of Conrad's contempt for anarchism that in both "The Informer' and *The Secret Agent* the central character is a police agent, a traitor to his professed cause. In this story Sevrin is an informer 'from conviction':[46]

A vague but ardent humanitarianism had urged him in his first youth into the bitterest extremity of negation and revolt. Afterwards his optimism flinched. He doubted and became lost. You have heard of converted atheists. These turn often into dangerous fanatics, but the soul remains the same. ... The fact is, he was not enough of an optimist. You must be a savage, tyrannical, pitiless, thick-and-thin optimist, like Horne, for instance, to make a good social rebel of the extreme type.[47]

But Sevrin is not a convincing character. His loss of faith should have led him to despair, not to fanaticism. To become a fanatic he should have acquired another faith, but Conrad does not provide him with one; to be merely a fanatical informer is too negative. Despite its incidental interest this is not a well worked out or satisfying story.

Conrad had been 'abominably ill'[48] in December and in the new year, 1906, he and Jessie decided to go to Montpellier to escape the rest of the English winter. Conrad's first task in Montpellier was to prepare the 'sea sketches', which he had written during the last two years, for publication in book form as *The Mirror of the Sea.*

From the beginning Conrad had planned to make a book out of these sketches or essays, and he described his aim in a letter to Colonel Harvey of Harper's. They were to compose 'a volume of sea sketches, something in the spirit of Turgeniev's *Sportsman's Sketches*, but concerned with ships and the sea with a distinct autobiographical and anecdotal note running through what is mainly meant for a record of remembered feelings'.[49] But when he started to write these sketches he does not seem to have looked on them as of much importance, telling Wells: 'I've discovered that I can dictate that sort of bosh without effort at the rate of 3,000 words in four hours.'[50] When, however, he wrote the Author's Note to *The Mirror of the Sea* he called the book 'a very intimate revelation' and said: 'I have attempted here to lay bare with the unreserve of a last hour's confession the terms of my relation with the sea.'[51] The correct assessment of the book is perhaps somewhere between these two judgements and it had been admired most by those, such as Wells and Galsworthy, who liked or understood Conrad's work least.

As was perhaps inevitable from the manner of its composition, *The Mirror of the Sea* is an uneven book containing some fine things like 'Initiation' or, a very different type of sketch, 'The *Tremolino*', and also some bad, inflated writing like much of 'Rulers of East and West' or 'Overdue and Missing'. It lacks unity of approach or design – for instance 'The Heroic Age', an essay on Nelson, seems only to have been tagged on at the end because it happened to have been written for the centenary of Trafalgar – and the book is certainly far from being the 'very intimate revelation' which Conrad claimed. Some of the pieces are no more than impersonal and general essays, a form of writing in which Conrad was weakest. There would be no point in mentioning these defects if *The Mirror of the Sea* had not been exalted by some into one of Conrad's most important books. The writing, which has been admired, is often muddled, overstrained, and excessively metaphorical. For instance, the two similes blur this description:

> a white mast, slender like a stalk of straw and crossed by a yard like a knitting needle, flying the signals of flag and balloon, watches over a set of heavy dock-gates.[52]

or,

> What had become of the dazzling hoard of royal jewels exhibited at every close of day? Gone, disappeared, extinguished, carried off

without leaving a single gold band or the flash of a single sunbeam in the evening sky.[53]

Jewels cannot be extinguished, nor can they leave flashes of sunbeams in the sky.

Then 'Rulers of East and West' is burdened with the most elaborate and inconsistent anthropomorphism, much of which merely obscures or belittles the effect, as when Conrad speaks of the west wind as a king 'playing his royal game of quoits with hurricanes, tossing them over from the continent of republics to the continent of kingdoms....'[54]

Conrad was always at his best when he could find a concrete framework for what he had to say, and it is his portraits of the merchant navy seamen whom he knew, of scenes like those in Sydney harbour or frozen Amsterdam, or of a piece of action like the *Tremolino* episode which stand out as the finest parts of the book.

(3)

Conrad was soon feeling refreshed by the move to Montpellier and on 13 February he wrote a cheerful letter to Pinker telling him that the air was 'splendid' and describing a carnival with masked revellers and political riots. A week later he sent Pinker the first thirteen pages of *The Secret Agent*, at this stage called 'Verloc' which he envisaged as a short story.[55] He said that he was doing much of his writing under a sunny wall in the gardens of Peyron.

After he had dealt with *The Mirror of the Sea*, Conrad concentrated on *The Secret Agent* for the rest of the time that he was at Montpellier, although he had to break off to write a review of Galsworthy's *Man of Property*.[56] As usual he felt that he was working too slowly and wrote to Galsworthy towards the end of the visit:

As to myself, my dear Jack, I have always that feeling of loafing at my work, as if powerless in an exhaustion of thought and will. Not enough, not enough! And yet perhaps those days without a line, nay, without a word, the hard, atrocious, agonising days are simply part of my *method* of work, a decreed necessity of my production. . . . I doubt not only my talent (I was never so sure of that) but my character. Is it indolence, – which in my case would be nothing short of baseness, – or what? No man has a right to go on as I am doing without producing manifest masterpieces. [9 April 1906, *L.L.*, II, p. 33]

When the Conrads got back to England the Hueffers lent them their house in Winchelsea for a fortnight. This was not a success. Hueffer came down for both week-ends and Jessie's dislike of his bohemianism was brought to a climax by a series of incidents:

The next day I was cooking the lunch when he appeared with a Panama hat he had washed, and to my amazement opened the oven door and placed that hat on a sheet of paper above my joint. It was a real Panama, but his washing had been strictly confined to the outside only, there was too much grease inside the lining for my liking – even had I not had our meat beneath, and I would have liked above everything to have put it on the fire. I removed it to a chair as close to the fire as possible, and resolutely closed the oven, voicing my displeasure in as few words as possible.

My next surprise was a request put forward by my husband that I should, on a Sunday morning, out of the blue, so to speak, provide a new black ribbon and put it on the hat. But even this fantastic request was possible as it happened that I had some few yards of black ribbon I had been giving the maid to tie her collar with. I dutifully sewed it on the hat.

The next morning before F. M. H. started to go to the station, which he did after nearly making me break the rule I had set for a guest under the same roof as myself – although it was somewhat difficult to fix who was host and who was the guest under the circumstances. He had entered the dining-room for his breakfast after Joseph Conrad had left the room. The first thing that caught his eye was a small cut in the tablecloth. 'Look at that, Elsie will be furious.' I paused in the act of pouring out his coffee and said indifferently: 'I don't suppose she will ever see it.' F. M. H. jumped to his feet with surprising energy, and almost forgot to drawl: 'Not see it, what do you mean? It's the first thing she will see. I must say that when I lent the house I expected ordinary care – '. I rose quickly to my feet and hastily turned another corner of the cloth towards him, saying slowly and distinctly: 'I said she most probably would not see it. You see my name is on the corner. I brought my own linen, and I shall take it home with me. Are you satisfied?'

He uttered a short vexed laugh and stalked out of the house, or rather had started to do so when I recalled him with the remark: 'Oh, by the way, be kind enough to look at the date of the laundry book you gave me last night. You will see the last entry is three weeks before I came into the house, and that week's laundry is entered in the name of Hyde. Moreover, I put away the first day I came into the place everything of yours in the shape of linen *without using it* and we have been using our own.'

I could cheerfully have devoured my husband who entered the room at that moment and caught something of the last remark. 'Pay the laundry bill, of course, my dear fellow.' F. M. H. gave me a supercilious glance and a condescending 'Good morning'. But I took care to forget to settle the account which was distinctly not mine . . .

The host-guest had only left the house an hour or so when the young maid appeared at the kitchen door with a miscellaneous collection of masculine garments crumpled out of all recognition in her arms, and asked what was she to do with them. Some she had found on the bed occupied by F. M. H. and some beneath. They turned out to be my husband's robes of ceremony. Frock-coat and striped grey trousers. I was puzzled for it was my pride to keep my husband's wardrobe in proper condition for instant wear. I had carefully pressed and ironed the crease myself and had also laid them flat in the drawer when we had taken temporary possession of that house. I made my difficult way upstairs, and such was my disgust I could not forbear calling Joseph Conrad and drawing his attention to the wanton treatment of his dress suit and other garments. It was quite plain to see what had happened. F. M. H. had not found the curtains thick enough in the room he had occupied to keep out the early morning light, and had hung one of the blankets over the window. Then not finding himself warm enough in bed, had removed the suits from the drawer to pile on the bed. It was an effective eye-opener to the owner. For once he could not blame me for this calm appropriation and misuse of his wardrobe, because there had been too little clothes on a guest's bed. F. M. H. was in his own place and any responsibility for the dearth of covering was his own, not mine.[57]

Jessie's nerves were probably on edge because she was reaching the end of her pregnancy with her second child.

The Galsworthys lent the Conrads their London house in Addison Road when the child was due and it was there, on 2 August 1906, that John Conrad was born.[58]

Throughout the summer and autumn Conrad continued to work at *The Secret Agent*, which he finished early in November.[59]

(4)

The Secret Agent is held by some to be one of Conrad's greatest achievements. Although it is in many ways a fine piece of work and is superlatively expressed it has some rather serious flaws and lacks the power and range of *Under Western Eyes, Nostromo, Lord Jim* or *Victory.*

In the Author's Note Conrad says that the story had two separate sources. He recounts how he was discussing anarchism with a friend, apparently Hueffer,[60] when one of them mentioned the attempt to blow up Greenwich Observatory: 'a bloodstained inanity of so fatuous a kind that it was impossible to fathom its origin by any reasonable or even unreasonable process of thought'. The friend 'remarked in his characteristically casual and omniscient manner: "Oh, that fellow was half an idiot. His sister committed suicide afterwards." '[61] This gave Conrad the kernel round which he was able to build a plausible story. The other source was, he says, a book of recollections by an assistant commissioner of police in which the author – 'I believe his name was Anderson'[62] – reproduced a short dialogue between the Home Secretary and himself after some unexpected anarchist outrage. At one point the Home Secretary said: ' "All that's very well. But your idea of secrecy over there seems to consist of keeping the Home Secretary in the dark." '[63]

This, Conrad wrote, was 'the tiniest little drop of the right kind, precipitating the process of crystallisation'.[64] From this 'Winnie Verloc's story'[65] grew. But like most of Conrad's accounts of the origins of a story this is misleading. It is clear that he first conceived of *The Secret Agent* as a short story with Verloc at the centre and it is only in the last third of the book that Winnie emerges at all fully, while the centre of interest does not shift to her until after she has killed Verloc.

The only similarity between the actual Greenwich Bomb Outrage which took place on 15 February 1894[66] and the use which Conrad made of it is that neither Conrad's Stevie nor the actual perpetrator, Martial Bourdin, damaged the Observatory but were themselves blown up, and they resembled each other physically. Stevie is slight and fair[67] while Martial Bourdin was described as a 'remarkably short man, 5 ft. 1 in. by measurement, well-nourished and proportioned, but inadequately developed'; his hair and moustache were 'silky and fair'.[68] The physical resemblance was probably a coincidence, although Conrad may have come upon an account of the outrage in some book, or details from contemporary reports may have lingered in his mind.

As seems to have been invariably the case when he was not relying on personal knowledge, Conrad did some background reading for the novel. An Assistant Commissioner of Police named Robert Anderson, who had been engaged on Secret Service work, had published a book called *Sidelights on the Home Rule Movement* just as Conrad was starting his novel. It contained a certain amount about the use of police agents to foil the Fenian plots; the author also quotes Sir William Harcourt's remark which caught Conrad's fancy: 'Anderson's idea of secrecy is not to tell the Secretary of State.'[69]

Conrad told Cunninghame Graham that 'Mr Vladmir was suggested to me by that scoundrel General Seliwertsow whom Padlewski shot (in Paris) in the nineties', adding: 'Perhaps you will remember, as there were peculiar circumstances in that case.'[70] The outstanding feature of the Seliwertsow, or Seliwerstow, case was its obscurity. The General, who seems to have had a most unsavoury character, had at one time been head of the notorious Third Section of the Russian police, but had been living in Paris for some years, allegedly as a Russian agent. After mortally wounding him in his hotel room Padlewski disappeared; there were the wildest rumours as to his whereabouts and it was suggested that the French police were most unanxious to have him traced.[71] Conrad no doubt had recourse to other background material, but this has not yet come to light.

Several times Conrad described *The Secret Agent* as an attempt to treat a melodramatic theme ironically and certainly there is plenty of melodrama; a particularly gory death, murder and suicide within a framework of anarchist activities, foreign embassy plotting and police investigation. But, as always with Conrad, the interest is in the treatment and not in the facts themselves.

In the Author's Note he says it was his 'earnest belief that ironic treatment alone would enable me to say all I felt I would have to say in scorn as well as in pity',[72] and in *The Secret Agent* more than any of his other novels the effect is gained through the diversity of ironic treatment.

First, the predominantly ironic tone is set by the author's assumed emotional detachment from the action, expressed through the dry, at times sardonic, manner of telling the tale. This is particularly evident in the scenes which are potentially the most dramatic. Thus when Winnie Verloc pushes Ossipon, 'the robust anarchist', into the room where her murdered husband is 'reposing quietly on the sofa':

> The true sense of the scene he was beholding came to Ossipon through the contemplation of the hat. It seemed an extraordinary thing, an ominous object, a sign. Black, and rim upward, it lay on the floor before the couch as if prepared to receive the contributions of pence from people who would come presently to behold Mr Verloc in the fullness of his domestic ease reposing on a sofa. From the hat the eyes of the robust anarchist wandered to the displaced table, gazed at the broken dish for a time, received a kind of optical shock from observing a white gleam under the imperfectly closed eyelids of the man on the couch. Mr Verloc did not seem so much asleep now as lying down with a bent head and looking insistently at his left breast. And when Comrade Ossipon had made out the handle of the knife he turned away from the glazed door and retched violently.[73]

Such passages go towards justifying Douglas Hewitt's characterization of the book as 'more nearly a comedy than any other novel of Conrad'.[74] There is underlying comedy in the last scene between the Verlocs and even macabre humour in Conrad's treatment of Stevie's gory death, as when the police constable repeatedly and self-satisfiedly insists that the body 'is all there' – 'I don't think I missed a single piece as big as a postage stamp'[75] – or when Chief Inspector Heat peers at Stevie's remains on the table 'with a calm face and the slightly anxious attention of an indigent customer bending over what may be called the by-products of a butcher's shop with a view to an inexpensive Sunday dinner',[76] or in Winnie Verloc's image of 'a park – smashed branches, torn leaves, gravel, bits of brotherly flesh and bone, all spouting up together in the manner of a firework. . . . Mrs Verloc closed her eyes desperately, throwing upon that vision the night of her eyelids, where after a rainlike fall of mangled limbs the decapitated head of Stevie lingered suspended alone, and fading out slowly like the last star of a pyrotechnic display.'[77]

Conrad also uses the time-shift to achieve an ironical effect as he did in *Nostromo*. After setting the scene of the novel (pp. 3–60) he goes straight to the Greenwich Park explosion, which is discussed by Ossipon and the Professor on the basis of the newspaper report. Then after the reader has realized that Stevie was the victim of the explosion* Conrad goes back to events which take place before Verloc and Stevie set out for Greenwich Park. Thus the reader is aware of the poignant irony in Winnie Verloc's comments on the relationship between her husband and Stevie. She congratulates herself on Verloc's growing affection for Stevie and thinks with pride that they 'might be father and son'.[78] To Winnie this bond has seemed the culmination of her seven years' effort to ensure Stevie's security. She has forced the two together and, with assertions such as 'You could do anything with that boy, Adolf. . . . He would go through fire

* The description (pp. 88–9) of the victim as having been slight and fair presumably discloses to the reader that it was Stevie.

for you,'[79] has inadvertently suggested the answer to Verloc's problem. The reader knows what Stevie has actually done for Verloc.

In the great scene of the book, that between Winnie and Verloc which leads up to the stabbing, the irony is gained through the reader's knowledge of the situation in contrast with Verloc's total unawareness.

The reader knows that Winnie is obsessed with Stevie's welfare to the exclusion of everything else, and that she married Verloc only because he was willing to take over Stevie along 'with the furniture'.[80] He knows Winnie's reaction to the news of Stevie's death: her 'moral nature had been subjected to a shock of which, in the physical order, the most violent earthquake of history could only be a faint and languid rendering'.[81] He thus experiences the full ironical impact of Verloc's fumbling attempts to console Winnie which culminate in the magnificent 'Do be reasonable Winnie. What would it have been if you had lost me?'[82] Verloc's pathetically inadequate advice is to have 'a good cry'.[83]

Not only is Verloc emotionally obtuse but he is unaware of the enormity of his using Stevie for such a task. He even imagines that he is showing restraint and magnanimity in not reproaching Winnie for bringing the police down on them; after all it was she who had put Stevie's address in the coat. His attitude expresses that 'moral nihilism'[84] which Conrad had earlier attributed to him:

> 'By heavens! You know that I hunted high and low. I ran the risk of giving myself away to find somebody for that accursed job. And I tell you again I couldn't find anyone crazy enough or hungry enough. What do you take me for – a murderer, or what? The boy is gone. Do you think I wanted him to blow himself up? . . . I don't blame you. But just try to understand that it was a pure accident; as much an accident as if he had been run over by a bus while crossing the street.'
>
> His generosity was not infinite, because he was a human being – and not a monster, as Mrs Verloc believed him to be.[85]

It is a triumph of subtlety that Verloc remains a far from

unpleasant human being throughout, so much so that the reader is constantly on the verge of accepting his point of view, and sympathizes with him sitting in the parlour of the Cheshire Cheese thinking over the best way to break the news. Of course it is easy enough to make a villain appear pleasant, but Conrad never blurs the moral issue and the impact of Verloc's crime is all the greater because Conrad shows how easily it happened.

The Verlocs remain at cross-purposes to the end:

> 'Come here,' he said in a peculiar tone, which might have been the tone of brutality, but was intimately known to Mrs Verloc as the note of wooing.
>
> She started forward at once . . .[86]

But she was coming to kill him, not to answer his call, and Mr Verloc dies 'in the muttered sound of the word "Don't" by way of protest'.[87]

Conrad told Cunninghame Graham: 'I don't think that I've been satirizing the revolutionary world. All these people are not revolutionaries – they are shams;'[88] and some years later he insisted to another correspondent: 'I hope you have seen that the purpose of the book was *not* to attack any doctrine, or even the men holding that doctrine.'[89] But if it wasn't Conrad's main purpose to satirize anarchism and anarchists he leaves no doubt as to his contempt for them and treats them throughout with scornful irony, untouched by pity. In his Author's Note he speaks of 'the criminal futility of the whole thing, doctrine, action, mentality . . . the contemptible aspect of the half-crazy pose as of a brazen cheat exploiting the poignant miseries and passionate credulities of a mankind always so tragically eager for self-destruction'.[90] Then in the novel he describes Karl Yundt, the most repellent of the anarchists, as 'an insolent and venomous evoker of sinister impulses which lurk in the blind envy and exasperated vanity of ignorance, in the suffering and misery of poverty, in all the hopeful and noble illusions of righteous anger, pity, and revolt'.[91]

It is true that Karl Yundt, Michaelis and Ossipon are

shams, for there is no accord between their words and their actions; Yundt, for instance, 'had never in his life raised personally as much as his little finger against the social edifice'.[92] But Conrad so hated revolutionary views and activity that he found it almost impossible to allow revolutionaries any sincerity. At the best his sincere revolutionaries are victims of an illusion, like Haldin and Sophia Antonovna in *Under Western Eyes*; at the worst their creed is based, like the Professor's, on 'ambition' and 'vengeful bitterness'.[93] Indeed, Conrad says that 'the way of even the most justifiable revolutions is prepared by personal impulses disguised into creeds'.[94] But the anarchists in *The Secret Agent* are not very convincing; or rather they are slight, two-dimensional characters, and Conrad gives less care to their presentation than he does to that of Chief Inspector Heat or the Assistant Commissioner. Yundt is a caricature, Michaelis is a harmless absurdity, and Ossipon is a rogue portrayed with a few vigorous strokes which tend to be repeated at each of his appearances. The Professor comes in a slightly different category, in that he is a genuine nihilist and there is some attempt to present his views. He is the embodiment of all that is anti-social and destructive. His single-minded ruthlessness and his incorruptibility raise him above the others, so that he is Chief Inspector Heat's only formidable opponent; Heat knows that the Professor always carries a bomb on him which he will not hesitate to explode if he is molested by the police. But, although it is a tribute to his pre-eminence among the anarchists that he is given the last paragraph of the book, even he is no more than a stock figure.

As a corollary to the moral repulsiveness of the anarchists Conrad emphasizes their physical defects. Karl Yundt is

> old and bald. ... An extraordinary expression of underhand malevolence survived in his extinguished eyes. When he rose painfully the thrusting forward of a skinny groping hand deformed by gouty swellings suggested the effort of a moribund murderer summoning all his remaining strength for a last stab. He leaned on a thick stick, which trembled under his other hand. ... His worn-out passion,

resembling in its impotent fierceness the excitement of a senile sensualist, was badly served by a dried throat and toothless gums which seemed to catch the tip of his tongue.[95]

Michaelis's repulsive corpulence is constantly mentioned. His voice

wheezed as if deadened and oppressed by the layer of fat on his chest. He had come out of a highly hygienic prison round like a tub, with an enormous stomach and distended cheeks of a pale, semi-transparent complexion, as though for fifteen years the servants of an outraged society had made a point of stuffing him with fattening foods in a damp and lightless cellar.[96]

Ossipon is always ironically referred to as 'the robust anarchist', because, although he has a good physique, he is particularly feeble when action is demanded. But he has 'a flattened nose and prominent mouth cast in the rough mould of the negro type',[97] a mark of degeneracy to Conrad, and there is obvious irony in Ossipon's dubbing Stevie a degenerate on the basis of Lombroso's theories. The 'Professor' is a puny, unhealthy man, an 'unwholesome-looking little moral agent of destruction':[98] 'The lamentable inferiority of the whole physique was made ludicrous by the supremely self-confident bearing of the individual.'[99]

Verloc himself is supremely well presented; he makes a stronger physical impact on the reader than any of Conrad's characters. His appearance and habits are a counterpart to his moral indolence. 'He had an air of having wallowed, fully dressed, all day on an unmade bed.'[100] The Chancelier d'Ambassade tells him, 'You are very corpulent,'[101] and Mr Vladimir asks him: 'What do you mean by getting out of condition like this?'[102] 'I'll tell you what I think is the matter,' he goes on. 'You are a lazy fellow.'

In fact the whole book could be regarded as a homily on sloth. 'With the insight of a kindred temperament', Mr Verloc pronounces the anarchists – Yundt, Michaelis and Ossipon – 'a lazy lot' and Conrad generalizes:

Mr Verloc, temperamentally identical with his associates, drew fine distinctions in his mind on the strength of insignificant differences. He drew them with a certain complacency, because the instinct of conventional respectability was strong within him, being only overcome by his dislike of all kinds of recognised labour – a temperamental defect which he shared with a large proportion of revolutionary reformers of a given social state. For obviously one does not revolt against the advantages and opportunities of that state, but against the price which must be paid for the same in the coin of accepted morality, self-restraint, and toil. The majority of revolutionists are the enemies of discipline and fatigue mostly.[103]

The Verlocs' relationship is conditioned by their indolence: 'Their accord was perfect, but it was not precise. It was a tacit accord, congenial to Mrs Verloc's incuriosity and to Mr Verloc's habits of mind, which were indolent and secret. They refrained from going to the bottom of facts and motives.'[104] Winnie Verloc's conviction that 'things did not stand being looked into'[105] is constantly reiterated. 'Mrs Verloc wasted no portion of this transient life in seeking for fundamental information. This is a sort of economy having all the appearances and some of the advantages of prudence. Obviously it may be good for one not to know too much. And such a view accords very well with constitutional indolence.'[106] Without this indolence the Verlocs could hardly have remained together, but with it they are able to live insulated from each other, like two wires in an electric flex; the breaking of the insulation brings immediate disaster.

Thus Mrs Verloc deliberately ignores her husband's nefarious activities on which their life is built, while Mr Verloc remains unaware that his wife has married him solely for the sake of Stevie's welfare, complacent in 'the idealistic belief in being loved for himself'.[107] For Mrs Verloc has a ruthless streak which enables her to carry out her thoroughly reprehensible deception of Mr Verloc, but also sets her above most of the rest of the characters, inasmuch as she is able to sacrifice herself totally for another person – a quality which she shares with her mother. It seems that Conrad did not intend Mrs Verloc to be very strongly condemned for her treatment of Mr Verloc. He speaks of 'this woman, capable of a bargain the mere suspicion of which would have been infinitely shocking to Mr Verloc's idea of love',[108] – and, one should add, to that of most people – but emphasizes that she loyally carried out her unspoken bargain and was a model wife. He commends her 'exalted faithfulness of purpose, even unto murder'[109] and describes the Verlocs' life as 'an existence created by Mrs Verloc's genius; an existence foreign to all grace and charm, without beauty and almost without decency, but admirable in the continuity of feeling and tenacity of purpose'.[110]

It seems that Conrad intended her to be a sort of feminine counterpart of MacWhirr, but she does not emerge as a very sympathetic or admirable character, and it is only when she becomes the victim of the despicable Ossipon that she arouses pity or concern. It is this that reduces the impact of the book because, although it contains the seeds of a conflict between the altruism or capacity for self-sacrifice of Winnie and her mother on the one side and of the ruthless self-centredness of Verloc and the anarchists on the other, the two women are essentially minor characters. Winnie's mother plays only an insignificant part, and Winnie herself is on such a low mental level that one wonders whether there was ever an element of choice, therefore of virtue, in her self-sacrifice or whether it was merely as instinctive as an animal's defence of its offspring; certainly her terror of death at the end is closer to the reaction of an animal scenting blood in a slaughterhouse than to that of a human being. Thus although there is pathos in the book there is no tragedy because there is no sense of waste, no suggestion that the characters were made for better things: Winnie and Stevie might have had a less gruesome fate, certainly, but not a nobler. The final effect is of negation and squalor.

There are other aspects of the book which have barely been mentioned. There is Mr Vladimir, First Secretary of the foreign Embassy (the Russian, of course), whose instructions to Verloc to carry out the bomb outrage on Greenwich Observatory, in order to frighten the British police into rounding up all the known anarchists, set the events of the story in motion. In Mr Vladimir, with his contempt for Western legality, Conrad expresses something of his dislike of Russians and Russian methods. Mr Vladimir is famous for his witticisms, a favourite of society drawing-rooms and a member of an exclusive club, but his civilized manners are only a veneer on innate savagery:

> 'Aha! You dare be impudent,' Mr Vladimir began, with an amazingly guttural intonation not only utterly un-English, but absolutely un-European, and startling even to Mr Verloc's experience of cosmopolitan slums.[111]

And,

> The features of Mr Vladimir, so well known in the best society by their humorous urbanity, beamed with cynical self-satisfaction, which would have astonished the intelligent women his wit entertained so exquisitely. 'Yes,' he continued, with a contemptuous smile, 'the blowing up of the first meridian is bound to raise a howl of execration.'[112]

Contrasted with this method of dealing with anarchism is that of the British police, for whom Vladimir at first has an 'immense contempt',[113] although, 'descended from generations victimized by the instruments of an arbitrary power, he was racially, nationally, and individually afraid of the police. It was an inherited weakness, altogether independent of his judgement, of his reason, of his experience. He was born to it.'[114]

There is a conflict between the aims and approach of the two police officers dealing with the bomb outrage. On one side there is Chief Inspector Heat, the reliable 'old departmental hand'[115] whose rise to prominence has been due to his successful handling of thieves and who 'could understand the mind of a burglar, because, as a matter of fact, the mind and the instincts of a burglar are of the same kind as the mind and the instincts of a police officer. Both recognize the same conventions, and have a working knowledge of each other's methods and of the routine of their respective trades.'[116] Confronted with an anarchist, Heat 'gave a thought of regret to the world of thieves – sane, without morbid ideals, working by routine, respectful of constituted authorities, free from all taint of hate and despair'.[117] – 'Catching thieves ... had that quality of seriousness belonging to every form of open sport where the best man wins under perfectly comprehensible rules. There were no rules for dealing with anarchists.'[118] Heat had therefore devised his own method, which was to use Verloc as a private source of information about anarchist activities in the hope thereby of forestalling any violent action. When he discovers that Verloc was connected with the Greenwich bomb explosion he withholds his knowledge from his superior, the Assistant Commissioner, because he does not want his source of information to be endangered. Instead he wants to make a scapegoat of the ticket-of-leave ex-convict, Michaelis, although he is almost certain that Michaelis is innocent, because he 'did logically believe that incarceration was the proper fate for every declared enemy of the law'.[119] The Assistant Commissioner, on the other hand, is repelled by Heat's hole-in-the-corner methods and is determined to destroy the squalid system of embassy spies and double agents; moreover he has strong reasons for not wanting Michaelis to be touched, because Michaelis has been taken up by an elderly rich woman who was 'one of the most influential and distinguished connections of the Assistant Commissioner's wife',[120] and he knows that he will never be forgiven by the woman or by his wife if any harm comes to Michaelis. Thus when the Assistant Commissioner has managed to wheedle the culprit's name out of Heat and when he discovers that Verloc is also an embassy spy he is determined to teach the foreign power a lesson, even though it means destroying Heat's source of information. He tells the Home Secretary:

> 'The existence of secret agents should not be tolerated, as tending to augment the positive dangers of the evil against which they are used. That the spy will fabricate his information is a mere commonplace. But in the sphere of political and revolutionary action, relying partly on violence, the professional spy has every

facility to fabricate the very facts themselves, and will spread the double evil of emulation in one direction, and of panic, hasty legislation, unreflecting hate, in the other.'[121]

In fact Heat is intent, unknowingly, on fulfilling Mr Vladimir's hopes, whereas the Assistant Commissioner is determined to thwart them. As he tells the Home Secretary: 'For him [Heat] the plain duty is to fasten the guilt upon as many prominent anarchists as he can ... whereas I, he would say, am bent upon vindicating their innocence.'[122] Thus, although Heat and the Assistant Commissioner are both genuinely acting as they think right, their conduct coincides with their personal interests.

The wrangle between Heat and the Assistant Commissioner is extremely well done; the one an 'old police hand'[123] and the other new to his job, just back from a tropical colony whose freedom he loved, chained to an office desk, which he hates. Conrad takes great care to make them both rounded and convincing characters. But if the book is to be looked on as 'Winnie Verloc's story' or as Verloc's, or, more correctly, if the theme is thought of in general terms such as an attempt 'to hold up the worthlessness of certain individuals and the baseness of some others',[124] the scenes between Heat and the Assistant Commissioner and still more between the Assistant Commissioner and the Home Secretary seem to contribute little to the central interest.* Moreover, it is very hard to decide what the central interest is; for, although the ironical treatment provides a unity of mood, the book lacks, unlike most of Conrad's work, a unifying theme, and when it is carefully examined falls apart into a succession of only superficially related scenes; in fact the 'crystallization' of which Conrad speaks in the Author's Note never occurs.

* F. R. Leavis, who has written the most stimulating analysis of *The Secret Agent,* maintains the opposite. *The Great Tradition,* 1948, pp. 216 ff.

(5)

After he had finished *The Secret Agent*, Conrad, feeling 'horribly seedy and depressed',[125] again decided to escape the English winter by going to Montpellier. Before leaving he was able to dash off a story, 'Il Conde', which he apparently finished on 4 December.[126] It is an excellently told but very short and unimportant story about an elderly and intensely civilized Count living in Naples who is the victim of an outrage by an aristocratic young member of a *Camorra*. The young man stops him in a public place and, threatening him with a knife, demands his money. The Count has left his pocket-book at his hotel and genuinely believes that he has no money to hand over. When the young man has gone he remembers that he has a twenty-five-franc piece tucked away as a reserve. Very much shaken by the incident he goes into a restaurant, but when he is paying his bill he sees the young man again, who comes up and insults him:

> 'Ah! So you had some gold on you – you old liar – you old *birba* – you *furfante*! But you are not done with me yet.'[127]

The Count decides that he must leave Southern Italy, although he is convinced that his health cannot stand any other climate.

> He was not afraid of what could be done to him. His delicate conception of his dignity was defiled by a degrading experience. He couldn't stand that.[128]

This story was apparently based on an experience which happened to the Count Szembek, of whom Conrad had seen quite a lot when he was in Capri.*

* *A Set of Six*, vii and Jessie Conrad, *Joseph Conrad as I Knew Him*, p. 127. 'Il Conde' has been the victim of one of the most astonishing pieces of interpretative criticism that I have come across, in an article by John Howard Wills in *Modern Fiction Studies*, Vol. I, No. 1, February 1955, pp. 22–5. Mr Wills is one of a number of literary critics who appear to have assumed the mantle of the alchemists or dabblers in the occult; to them literary texts are arcana offering knowledge to those who can find the

The Conrad family left for Montpellier on 16 December, meeting Marguerite Poradowska in Paris on the way.[129] All went well at the start; the weather was 'cold, calm, dry, brilliant',[130] and Conrad rested except for revising the French translations of some of the *Tales of Unrest*. During January of 1907 he must have worked hard. He wrote a lot of 'The Duel' and seems again to have tried to grapple with *Chance*.[131] He also began to take Spanish lessons as a 'mental stimulant',[132] and did some reading about Napoleon in search of a subject for the perennial 'Mediterranean novel'.[133]

Then troubles began. At the end of January it was discovered that Borys had adenoids and the following month he caught measles, after which he developed what seemed to be bronchitis. The doctor then suspected tuberculosis, saying that both lungs were threatened. Both parents were intensely worried and Conrad wrote to Galsworthy on 5 March:

> The doctor imparted to me his fears yesterday. The most terrific part of it was that for the last month, even before he sickened for measles, I myself had a notion of something of the kind – a sort of gnawing fear which I kept from Jessie of course. . . . I had no other ground but the expression of his face, which struck me one evening as he sat opposite me. We were having a game of dominoes and I had the greatest difficulty to finish the hundred. Then I went out and walked about the streets for hours. I managed to quiet myself, but the impression remained. It turns out now that poor Jessie on her side had the same fears – and observed the same discretion. . . . For the last ten days he has got dreadfully thin. We can't get him to eat more than a few mouthfuls and that only he will do for his mother's sake. . . . The change in his character is also astonishing. But this won't bear being written about.

---

key. Mr Wills discovers more esoteric significance in this essentially simple and slight story than many people would find in the whole of Conrad. 'Il Conde' was the last story in *A Set of Six*, the other five being 'Gaspar Ruiz', 'The Informer', 'The Brute', 'An Anarchist', and 'The Duel'. As Conrad told his publisher, 'they are not studies – they touch no problem. They are just stories in which I've tried my best to be *simply entertaining*.' (Letter to Sir Algernon Methuen, 26 January 1908, *L.L.*, II, p. 66.)

An analysis would have been made already but we can't get him to expectorate as yet, tho' he is trying his hardest in order to please me. This is the tenth night I haven't slept. I don't mean to say I have had no sleep for all that time; but I hang about his room all night listening and watching. I simply can't go to bed. Then in the afternoon I throw myself down on the sofa and sleep from sheer weariness. For four days I haven't written anything. Jessie is wholly admirable, sharing herself between the two boys with the utmost serenity. [*L.L.*, II, pp. 43–4]

The agony must have been increased by the knowledge that both Conrad's parents had died of tuberculosis, but a week later[134] Conrad was able to tell Pinker that the analysis was favourable, although he had been advised by the doctor to take Borys to Geneva instead of returning to England. Conrad had decided on the hydropathic establishment at Champel, to which he had been in the 1890's, hoping that he too might benefit from taking a cure. He was of course worried about the expense and went into detailed calculations for Pinker. Meanwhile he continued to work at *Chance* and 'The Duel', which last he finished on 11 April.[135] It is a delightful tale of how one of Napoleon's officers, Feraud, a fiery little Gascon, compels another, a cautious and gentle Picardian named d'Hubert, to fight a succession of duels with him because he imagines himself insulted. The quarrel lasts for sixteen years, during Napoleon's domination of Europe and after. No one except the antagonists knows its trivial cause, and when d'Hubert finally reveals it, one of the characters comments: 'If that's the tale the fellow made up for his wife, and during the honeymoon, too, you may depend on it that no one will ever know now the secret of this affair'.[136] It is an excellently told story, gently humorous and ironical, but touches no very deep emotions and Conrad was claiming rather a lot to describe it as an attempt to 'capture ... the Spirit of the Epoch'.[137]

He also mentions that he 'had heard in my boyhood a good deal of the great Napoleonic legend. I had a genuine feeling that I would find myself at home in it.'[138] Napoleon had a fascination for Conrad, and doubtless his imagination had first been stirred by the glamour surrounding his Uncle Nicholas, whose tales of the Retreat from Moscow particularly impressed him; there is a fine passage on the episode in 'The Duel', and Conrad returned to the subject in a later tale, 'The Warrior's Soul'. Like those of most Poles, his feelings about Napoleon seem to have been ambivalent. Thus in 'Autocracy and War' he lashed out at him:

> The degradation of the ideas of freedom and justice at the root of the French Revolution is made manifest in the person of its heir; a personality without law or faith, whom it has been the fashion to represent as an eagle, but who was, in truth, more like a sort of vulture preying upon the body of a Europe which did, indeed, for some dozen of years, very much resemble a corpse. The subtle and manifold influence for evil of the Napoleonic episode as a school of violence, as a sower of national hatreds, as the direct provocator of obscurantism and reaction, of political tyranny and injustice, cannot well be exaggerated.[139]

But he was also captivated by the magnificence of the Napoleonic legend, and in 'The Duel' wrote of 'the triumphant return from Elba, a historical fact as marvellous and incredible as the exploits of some mythological demi-god'.[140] Conrad saturated himself in the history and memoirs of the period with the prime aim of preparing the background for his Napoleonic novel, but his reading went far beyond this limited purpose, and his library contained more books connected with this subject than with any other.[141] It was no doubt during his reading about Napoleon at Montpellier that he had come upon an account in a periodical or a book of the story which he used for 'The Duel'. J. DeLancey Ferguson[142] has discovered a version of the story, allegedly based on fact, in *Harper's Magazine* for September, 1858, and it is clear, from the similarity between the events and details in this version and 'The Duel', that Conrad either consciously followed it or, more likely, an earlier French version on which the *Harper's* story was based. The *Harper's* version has no pretensions to literary merit.

Shortly before leaving for Geneva Conrad wrote

despairingly to Galsworthy, telling him that he had gout and adding, 'the state of worry in which I am living, – and writing, – is simply indescribable. It's a constant breaking strain.'[143] But worse was to come; the baby came out with whooping-cough just before they started. Nonetheless they did not postpone the journey. Conrad wrote a heartrending letter to Pinker from the Hotel de la Poste at Geneva:

> Here I am stranded again with baby at its last gasp with whooping-cough. It began in Montpellier. We started by medical advice, counting on the change of climate to check the disease, but it has developed on the road in the most alarming manner. The poor little devil has melted down to half his size. Since yesterday morning he has had a coughing fit every quarter of an hour or so and will not eat anything. We'll have to resort to artificial feeding very soon. Of course La Roseraie Hotel won't take us now. We stick here isolated at the end of a corridor. Really I haven't got my share of the commonest sort of luck. I suppose *Chance* will have to pay for all this. But if you think I ought to come home I will do so as soon as baby can travel, and will let my cure go to the devil. Borys of course has whooping-cough too, but very mildly. Still, it isn't good for him. My dear Pinker, I feel that all this is almost too much for me. [18 May 1907, *L.L.*, II, p. 48]

Three weeks later he followed this up with a rather hysterical letter to Galsworthy (Borys had by then developed rheumatism in both his ankles):[144]

> ... All this is ghastly. I seem to move, talk, write in a sort of quiet nightmare that goes on and on. I wouldn't wish my worst enemy this experience ...
>
> From the sound next door (we have three rooms) I know that the pain has roused Borys from his feverish doze. I won't go to him. It's no use. Presently I shall give him his salicylate, take his temperature and shall then go to elaborate a little more the conversation of Mr Verloc with his wife. It is very important that the conversation of Mr Verloc with his wife should be elaborated, – made more effective, don't you know, – more *true* to the situation and character of these people.
>
> By Jove! I've got to hold myself with both hands not to burst into a laugh which would scare wife, baby and the other invalid, – let

alone the lady whose room is on the other side of the corridor! [6 June 1907, *L.L.*, II, pp. 51–2]

Nonetheless, despite these appalling troubles, Conrad was able to do some very important and extensive revision of *The Secret Agent* for book form, writing in almost 30,000 words.[145] This was no doubt largely due to Jessie's ability to deal with the situation. Conrad told Rothenstein that 'Jessie has been simply heroic in the awful Montpellier adventure, never giving a sign of anxiety not only before the boy, but even out of his sight; always calm, serene, equable, going from one to the other and apparently never tired though cruelly crippled by her leg.'[146] As Jessie has been subjected to so much disparagement it is perhaps worth mentioning that there could have been few people temperamentally better equipped than her to cope with such a situation; her efficiency and equability may well have saved Conrad from a nervous breakdown, then and at other times.

Gradually the troubles subsided, and by the middle of August the Conrads were back at the Pent, but looking for another house.[147] They finally found one called Someries, in Bedfordshire, on the Luton Hoo estate, and moved there in September.[148] Conrad seems to have struggled on with *Chance* during most of the rest of the year, but when he found that he could make little progress he started another story which he called *Razumov* and which was to become *Under Western Eyes*.[149]

During the autumn he also wrote, out of friendship for Edward Garnett, an attack on the censorship of plays which was published in slightly emasculated form in the *Daily Mail*.[150] It is a splendid piece of scathing derision. Of the Censor Conrad says: 'He has power. He can kill thought, and incidentally truth, and incidentally beauty, providing they seek to live in a dramatic form. He can do it, without seeing, without understanding, without feeling anything; out of mere stupid suspicion, as an irresponsible Roman Caesar could kill a senator.'[151] And his final paragraph is:

> Frankly, is it not time to knock the improper object off its shelf? It has stood too long there. Hatched in Pekin (I should say) by some Board of Respectable Rites, the little caravan monster has come to us by way of Moscow – I suppose. It is outlandish. It is not venerable. It does not belong here. Is it not time to knock it off its dark shelf with some implement appropriate to its worth and status? With an old broom handle for instance.[152]

But only recently has legislation realized Conrad's proposal.

[XII]

Achievement without Success, III

1908 was Conrad's fiftieth year, and it did not start well. In a listless letter to Marguerite Poradowska sending her the new year's greetings, he wrote: 'Moi je suis fatigué et attristé. Le travail m'est très difficile et les affaires en general ne marchent pas'.[1] He had reason to be depressed. Although in the judgement of today he had already achieved enough to set him among the greatest novelists of all nations and his last two novels had shown his powers at their height, the situation appeared very different at the time. Thus whereas his early work had been duly recognized and *The Nigger of the 'Narcissus'*, followed by *Lord Jim*, had carried him to the crest of critical acclaim, his two latest novels had had a mixed reception. The critical reaction to *Nostromo*, which he knew to be his most ambitious book and which had cost him so much effort, must have been particularly galling. In the reviews he was treated with a respect which acknowledged his position as one of the leading novelists of the day, and there was much praise for the book, the ever-loyal Garnett above all doing his best to point out its quality;[2] but there was much wistful harking back to the earlier tales, while in places, such as *The Times Literary Supplement*,[3] where it was reasonable to expect some measure of understanding and appreciation, *Nostromo* was handled with fatuous obtuseness.

The reaction to *The Secret Agent* had been similar and there were a number of complaints that Conrad's method, particularly his use of the time-shift, put his work above the head of the average reader. This was the most worrying aspect; the sales of both books had been mediocre, and Conrad was increasingly becoming a novelist of the élite without popular appeal. Several years back Henry James had already concluded that Conrad's work was 'of the sort greeted more by the expert and the critic than (as people say), by the man in the street',[4] and the reviewer of *The Secret Agent* in the *Athenaeum* stressed the same point:

> The subtlety of his mental processes, the keenness of his artistic senses, have placed him further away from the great reading public – if infinitely nearer to the select few who have trained faculties of literary appreciation – than many a writer of far less worth.[5]

Conrad was, understandably, becoming obsessed by his failure to establish himself as a 'selling' author, confessing to Galsworthy:

> Ah my dear, you don't know what an inspiration-killing anxiety it is to think: is it saleable? There's nothing more cruel than to be caught between one's impulse, one's act, and that question, which for me simply is a question of life and death. There are moments when the unholy [?] fear sweeps my head clear of every thought. It is agonising – no less. And – you know – that pressure grows from day to day instead of getting less. [6 January 1908, *L.L.*, II, p. 65]

In the same letter he looked back on his financial achievement during the twelve years of his writing career. He worked out that he had written eleven novels (volumes, to be precise) and had lived at an average rate of £650 a year. If, he said, each book had brought him in £1,000 he would have had £5,000 in hand, but as it was he owed Pinker £1,572 and had other debts as well.

A further ground for depression was Someries. Conrad seems to have disliked the house and area from the start. He wrote to Elsie Hueffer: 'You have no idea of the soul corroding bleakness of earth and sky here when the east wind blows.'[6] The climate affected his health and he told Galsworthy: 'I've known not a single moment of bodily ease since we got into this new house.'[7] As a result of all these physical and mental afflictions he went down with an attack of gout.[8]

But after he had recovered from his illness he became more cheerful, and as he did most of the writing of *Under Western Eyes* during 1908 it can be considered a good year so far as work was concerned. The second version of 'The Black Mate' also made its appearance, in the *London Magazine* for April. The year was otherwise uneventful. In August Conrad was still complaining about Someries, telling Galsworthy that he would like to spend a few weeks in Kent,[9] and at the end of August the family went to stay for a month in the village of Aldington, near the Hueffers.[10] It was probably then that Conrad first met Arthur Marwood, who was living close by, and was a friend of Hueffer's.[11] In retrospect Marwood appears a slightly mysterious figure; not because he was in fact mysterious but because all that has been preserved of him are a few rather slight reminiscences by friends and some articles on economic subjects. The comments of his friends or acquaintances[12] agree in their expression of extreme admiration for his character, his profound intelligence, and his encyclopaedic knowledge. Conrad undoubtedly had a very great respect for Marwood and saw a lot of him in the following years. At one period, at least, the two men met regularly once a week.[13] Marwood had apparently been a sick man for most of his life and he died in 1916 when he was forty-seven. He came from a well-to-do Yorkshire family, and Hueffer regarded him as the ideal English gentleman, using him as the model for Christopher Tietjens in that series of novels.[14]

Hueffer and Conrad had resumed their intimacy, and it was on Hueffer's suggestion that Conrad started, probably when he was at Aldington, to write his reminiscences for the *English Review*, which was to be started in a new form in December under the editorship of Hueffer. When the first number was being prepared for press, to Jessie's dismay, Hueffer arrived at Someries with all the copy and several assistants. According to Jessie:

> Lights blazed from every room downstairs – no expense was spared. To have some four or five strangers quartered on one without more notice than an hour or so was not exactly comfortable. Only the baby and the maids slept that night. Orders, directions, or suggestions were shouted from room to room. It was an uproar all night, and the next day the house was in a chaos. My monthly stock

of provisions were soon devoured, and the great trouble was that we had to use lamps and candles . . .[15]

Conrad, too, recalled that night in a letter to Hueffer, to be printed in the *transatlantic review.*

You arrived one evening with your amiable myrmidons and parcels of copy. I shall never forget the cold of that night, the black grates, the guttering candles, the dimmed lamps – and the desperate stillness of that house, where women and children were innocently sleeping, when you sought me out at 2 a.m. in my dismal study to make me concentrate suddenly on a two page notice of the *Ile des Pingouins.* A marvellously successful instance of editorial tyranny! I suppose you were justified. The Number One of the *E.R.* could not have come out with two blank pages in it. It would have been too sensational. I have forgiven you long ago.[16]

Thus the first number of this distinguished review appeared with two contributions from Conrad. Other contributors were Hardy with the poem 'A Sunday Morning Tragedy', Henry James with 'The Jolly Corner', Wells with an instalment of *Tono-Bungay,* Galsworthy, Hudson, Cunninghame Graham, W. H. Davies, and Marwood with the first part of 'A Complete Actuarial Scheme for Insuring John Doe against all the Vicissitudes of Life'.

It was lavish fare, a hundred-and-ninety-two pages for half-a-crown. Hueffer was a remarkable editor with a flare for discovering new talent as well as mustering the old, but he was a most incompetent business man. The *Review* lost heavily from the start and after a few months financial control was taken out of Hueffer's hands, although he was allowed to stay on as editor.[17]

Conrad's reminiscences had been running for seven months when they became the cause, or the occasion, of a quarrel between Hueffer and himself. An attack of gout had prevented Conrad from writing the instalment for July[18] and, to his great annoyance, Hueffer had printed a dramatic note in the July number saying:

We regret that owing to the serious illness of Mr Joseph Conrad we are compelled to postpone the publication of the next instalment of his Reminiscences.[19]

But, for reasons that remain obscure, Conrad decided not to contribute any further reminiscences. This must have called forth an indignant outburst from Hueffer, whose resentment was probably aggravated by his own insecure position as editor. He no doubt felt that he particularly needed the support of his friends at this moment. But only Conrad's reply has been preserved. He starts with the formal 'Dear Hueffer' instead of his usual 'My dear Hueffer', 'My dear Ford', or some other affectionate term of address, and continues:

If you think I have discredited you and the *Review,* why then it must be even so. And as far as the Editor of the *E.R.* is concerned, we will let it go at that, with the proviso that I don't want to hear anything more about it.

But as writing to a man with a fine sense of form and a complete understanding, for years, of the way in which my literary intentions work themselves out, I wish to protest against the words, – *Ragged condition.*

It is so little *ragged* to my feeling, and in point of literary fact, that in the book (if the book ever appears) the *whole* of the contribution to the *E.R.* as it stands now without the addition of a single word shall form the Part First.

It expresses perfectly my purpose of treating the literary life and the sea life on parallel lines, with a running reference to my early years. It treats of the inception of my first book and of my first contact (psychologically and de facto) with the sea. It begins practically with the first words of appreciation of my writing I ever heard and ends with the first words ever addressed to me personally in the English tongue. And actually the very phrase ending the seventh instalment is to my mind an excellent terminal, a perfect pause carrying out the spirit of the work . . .

It is another instalment which would make the thing *ragged.* It would have to begin another period and another phase. On a dispassionate view I see it so clearly that nothing on earth would induce me to spoil the thing as it now stands by an irrelevant single instalment. I will say no more, except to add that my contributions were for a *person* not for an *editor.* The *E.R.*, I hear, is no longer your property and there is, I believe, another circumstance which for a purely personal reason (exceptionally personal, I mean) makes me unwilling to contribute anything more to the *E.R.* This reason has, of course, nothing to do with you, you understand. It is not a critical reason. A pure matter of feeling. If I have discredited the *R.*, well, I must bear the disgrace. [31 July 1909, *L.L.*, II, pp. 101–2]

Conrad's 'purely personal reason' apparently did have something to do with the change in ownership. He had acquired an intense dislike for Dr David Soskice, Hueffer's brother-in-law, who had been called in to try to save the *Review* financially, and he wrote to Galsworthy: 'I hear Ford is enraged with me for not giving him more of my Reminiscences. He says I made a fool of him. I don't see how that can be. A Russian has got hold of the *E.R.* and I cannot contribute any more.'[20] It must remain in doubt whether this was the real reason or whether, as seems more likely, Conrad was merely seizing a pretext to cut himself off from Hueffer, whose behaviour in the affair had exasperated him.

Conrad let himself go on the subject in a letter to Pinker: 'I am made responsible for the failure of a negotiation with McClure for the sale of the *E.R.*,' he said; and he had heard that Hueffer was going about saying he had 'called Conrad out'. He went on:

His conduct is *impossible*. ... He's a megalomaniac who imagines that he is managing the Universe and that everybody treats him with the blackest ingratitude. A fierce and exasperated vanity is hidden under his calm manner which misleads people. ... I do not hesitate to say that there are cases, not quite as bad, under medical treatment. ...

Generally he is behaving like a spoilt kid – and not a nice kid either. [Wednesday (probably July 1909)]

Conrad's quarrel with Hueffer seems to have produced an estrangement which was never fully healed. But before the break the two men collaborated on a worthless trifle entitled *The Nature of a Crime*,* which appeared in the April and

* There appears to be no reference to the composition of this piece of work; it may have been written much earlier and then laid aside.

May numbers of the *English Review* under the pseudonym of Baron Ignatz von Aschendrof. No trace of Conrad's influence is apparent either in the writing or in the conception, except that the story of Nicholas Bobrowski's stepfather filching his stepson's inheritance which Conrad told in his reminiscences may have suggested the plot. However, about four hundred words of the manuscript in Conrad's handwriting have survived,[21] which proves that he had some connection with the story.

The design of the reminiscences was essentially discursive and time was deliberately banished, but Conrad handled his material with consummate adroitness and there is no impression of scrappiness. Nonetheless Hueffer was justified in claiming that the seventh instalment provided a weak ending to the series. However, Conrad more than stood by the intention expressed in his letter; he never added anything to his reminiscences and they were printed in book form virtually without alteration, although this was due more to chance than design. It is clear from a letter to E. V. Lucas[22] that he wanted to continue them, and he was possibly dissuaded from doing so by Pinker, who had failed to place them serially in America and seems never to have been particularly enthusiastic about them.[23]

In the 'Familiar Preface' to *A Personal Record** which is a very fine piece of writing, almost equal to the preface to *The Nigger of the 'Narcissus'*, Conrad described the intention of the book:

> They [the reminiscences] have their hope and aim. The hope that from the reading of these pages there may emerge at last the vision of a personality; the man behind the books so fundamentally dissimilar as, for instance, *Almayer's Folly* and *The Secret Agent*, and yet a coherent, justifiable personality both in its origin and in its action. This is the hope. The immediate aim, closely associated with the hope, is to give the record of personal memories by presenting faithfully the feelings and sensations connected with the

* The reminiscences were first published in book form in 1912 with the title *Some Reminiscences*, but the book will throughout be referred to by its final title.

writing of my first book and with my first contact with the sea.[24]

The decision to leave Poland and the decision – although he would protest at the implication of so conscious a mental process – to write were the two most important events in Conrad's life. They were also two events about which he was particularly sensitive because they were bound up with his personal honour. Although honour and dishonour, in their particular aspects of fidelity and betrayal, were constantly recurring themes throughout Conrad's work, it is clear from *Under Western Eyes* and 'The Secret Sharer' that he was specially concerned with them at this time. It is thus not surprising to find that much of *A Personal Record* reads like an *apologia pro vita sua*. When he comes to deal with his going to sea, Conrad brings into the open certain charges which had been made or which he sensed:

> Alas! I have the conviction that there are men of unstained rectitude who are ready to murmur scornfully the word desertion. Thus the taste of innocent adventure may be made bitter to the palate. The part of the inexplicable should be allowed for in appraising the conduct of men in a world where no explanation is final. No charge of faithlessness ought to be lightly uttered.[25]

In the next paragraph he adds that 'it would take too long to explain the intimate alliance of contradictions in human nature which makes love itself wear at times the desperate shape of betrayal'.[26] Then he returns to the subject much later when he says: 'I have been charged with the want of patriotism, the want of sense, and the want of heart too [for going to sea],'[27] and confesses: 'I catch myself in hours of solitude and retrospect meeting arguments and charges made thirty-five years ago by voices now for ever still.'[28]

If it seems far-fetched to link Conrad's start of a career as an author with the idea of desertion or betrayal, it is only necessary to refer to a discussion on the 'Emigration of the Talents', which took place in Poland in 1899, to realize that many Poles considered the decision to become a writer in English, for the English, was more important and final than the decision to go to sea; sailors usually come home in the end, writers seldom. The subject of the discussion was whether people of ability, opposed to mere manual workers, had the moral right to emigrate from Poland. Eliza Orzeszkowa, a popular novelist, maintained that such people should stay in Poland, participating in the nation's sufferings and sustaining it through the application of their talents. They should not adopt the materialistic attitude that it pays better to work in other countries. She goes on to single out Conrad and accuse him, ironically in view of his actual material position, of writing in English merely because he is so well paid for this. She apparently either sent him the article or wrote to him about it. An interesting sidelight is thrown on the matter in a report by a Pole, W. Chwalewik, based on a conversation with Conrad's early Polish friends living in England. Spiridion Kliszewski expressed the hope that Conrad would devote his talent as a writer to extolling the fame of Poland. Conrad was shocked; raising both arms, he exclaimed: 'Ah, mon ami, que voulez-vouz? I should lose my public . . .' Apparently the Kliszewskis were rather disgusted by this attitude and their relations with Conrad cooled off.[29]

It seems that Conrad was not able to rid himself of a sense of guilt, at least until, by becoming a famous writer, he could qualify for the position of a national hero. Aniela Zagórska has related how on his visit to Poland in 1914 he still had a sense of guilt and a fear of being slighted by other Poles.[30] She also showed how deeply Conrad had been affected by Eliza Orzeszkowa's attack; it still rankled. When Aniela Zagórska innocently suggested that Conrad should read Mrs Orzeszkowa's novel *Nad Niemnem,* she was greeted with the outburst: 'Don't bring me anything by that shrew – You don't know about it, but she once wrote me a letter – '[31]

Elsewhere Karola Zagórska has repeated a conversation between Conrad and herself in which he asked whether she would forgive him because his sons could not speak Polish; on her reassuring him he said: 'Thank you for not having a grudge against me for this.'[32]

Against this background it is easier to understand why Conrad should have played down any element of deliberate intention in his decision to begin writing *Almayer's Folly.* It also explains why he should have been so anxious to emphasize that it was Garnett who persuaded him to undertake *An Outcast of the Islands,* because his starting of a second novel was the most decisive step along the path towards becoming a professional author.

It is equally natural that he should have exaggerated the element of choice in his career as a sailor and emphasized the positive aspect of his decision in order to answer the charge that his real reason was to escape from Poland.

When he started to write the reminiscences, Conrad told Pinker that it was his 'ambition' to 'make Polish life enter English literature', and this may partly explain why the most vivid and detailed portrait that emerges is of his uncle Nicolas Bobrowski rather than of Conrad himself. But although the reminiscences are woven round the two most important events in his life, it was never the intention of a man so reticent about himself in public as Conrad to reveal much of himself; Henry James's autobiographical volumes are examples of blatant self-exposure compared with *A Personal Record.* In his objective re-creation of scenes from his past it is as if Conrad were carrying on a long reminiscent monologue in front of a smouldering camp-fire which from time to time flares up to illuminate a part of the speaker. And it is Conrad's public face that is displayed; there is no analysis, no probing below the surface.

(2)

By the end of 1908 the Conrads had had enough of Someries and decided definitely to move back to Kent. They had found a cottage in Aldington, of which they were to have half, and seem to have made the move early in March.[33] But the change did not improve Conrad's health, and he was in and out of bed for the first seven months of the year.[34] Thus he seems to have seen scarcely any of his friends, and went to London only once, in order to see Galsworthy's play, *Strife*, in March.[35] But Conrad had one visit that had important repercussions on his work; it was from a Captain Marris who lived in Penang and was married to a Malayan girl. He described the visit to Pinker:

> It was like the raising of a lot of dead – dead to me, because most of them live out there and even read my books and wonder who [the] devil has been around taking notes. My visitor told me that Joshua Lingard made the guess: 'It must have been the fellow who was mate in the *Vidar* with Craig'. That's me right enough. And the best of it is that all these men of 22 years ago feel kindly to the Chronicler of their lives and adventures. They shall have some more of the stories they like. [Monday (October 1909), *L.L.*, II, p. 103]

Conrad kept his word. This visit no doubt stirred his memory and prompted him to write the three stories set, broadly speaking, in the Indian Ocean: 'The Secret Sharer', 'A Smile of Fortune', and 'Freya of the Seven Isles'. They were published together as *'Twixt Land and Sea; Tales* and dedicated to Captain Marris.

Conrad wrote 'The Secret Sharer' some time during the end of November and early December[36] – exceptionally quick for him. It is undoubtedly one of his best short stories, but certain critics, notably Albert Guerard and Douglas Hewitt, have claimed for it a position as a key story in Conrad's work and attributed to it a significance which I do not believe that it can hold. It is intensely dramatic but, on the psychological and moral level, rather slight.

The story is based on an incident which happened on board the *Cutty Sark* in 1880.[37] The *Cutty Sark* had put in to Singapore on 18 September, three days after the chief officer of the *Jeddah* (the *Patna* in *Lord Jim*) had arrived there.* In Conrad's adaptation of the *Cutty Sark* incident,

* *Singapore Daily Times*, 18 September 1880. Another ship in Singapore was the *Bates Family* which had been totally dismasted and had the whole deck smashed up. She may have been Conrad's model for the *Apse Family* in 'The Brute'.

Leggatt, the mate of the *Sephora*, kills a disobedient member of the crew during a storm and is put under arrest by his captain. But he escapes and swims to another ship of which the narrator of the story is captain. The captain is a young, comparatively inexperienced man who has just been given his first command – here Conrad seems to draw on his own experiences on the *Otago* – 'a stranger to the ship' and 'somewhat of a stranger to myself'.[38] He had taken the anchor watch himself and thus spots Leggatt in the water, clinging to a rope ladder; without calling anyone, for 'a mysterious communication was established already between us two',[39] he lets Leggatt come on board and fetches some clothes for him.

> In a moment he had concealed his damp body in a sleeping-suit of the same grey-stripe pattern as the one I was wearing and followed me like my double on the poop.[40]

When the captain has heard Leggatt's story he decides that he must hide him in his cabin. He does this at great risk and strain to himself and at the cost of becoming somewhat estranged from the rest of the crew because of the precautionary antics he has to go through to prevent Leggatt being discovered.

After some eventful days which include a visit from the captain of the *Sephora* he is able to come in close to shore and allow Leggatt to escape.

Constantly throughout the story it is emphasized that the young captain regards Leggatt as his double, and in a letter to Pinker Conrad suggested for titles of the story 'The Second Self', 'The Secret Self', 'The Other Self'[41] (these three phrases, without the definite article of course, occur in the text); he also suggested 'The Secret Sharer', but wondered whether it might not be too enigmatic. The point of this, apart from heightening the dramatic effect, and the point of the story, is to suggest that the fates of these two men were interchangeable, that it was quite possible for an ordinary, decent, conscientious person to kill someone or to commit some action which would make him 'a fugitive and vagabond on the earth'.[42] Thus Leggatt takes his place alongside Jim and Razumov. There is no suggestion of a transcendental relationship between Leggatt and the captain or of the 'double' being a psychological manifestation of an aspect of the original as there is in Poe's vulgar, trashy 'Richard Wilson' or Dostoevsky's obscure nightmare, 'The Double'.

But that is the way in which Guerard interprets the story. For him the 'hero' is the young captain: 'The real moral dilemma is *his*, not Leggatt's.'[43] He, and Marlow in 'Heart of Darkness', 'must recognize their own potential criminality and test their own resources, must travel through Kurtz and Leggatt, before they will be capable of manhood ... and moral survival'.[44] The story will bear this interpretation, as long as it is realized that such was no part of the author's conscious intention. However, Guerard goes on to assert that Leggatt is not merely an 'other self', he is a 'lower self', 'the embodiment of a more instinctive, more primitive, less rational self'.* I believe that this misses the whole point. Leggatt is not a symbol of the unconscious but a man on precisely the same level as the young captain; their selves are interchangeable (the epithet 'secret' might imply the opposite but its context and the whole tone of the story show that the word was intended in its literal sense: Leggatt was 'secret' because he had to be kept secret or hidden). Guerard's interpretation makes nonsense of the last sentence of the story, in which Leggatt departs, 'a free man, a proud swimmer striking out for a new destiny'. This is no way for a symbol of the unconscious to behave; Guerard's answer is that Leggatt is both a symbol and a 'man of flesh and blood'.[45] He continues: 'By seeing his own dilemmas and difficulties in Leggatt, the captain has turned this man into symbol and spirit.... But at the end, emerging from his self-examination, the captain can see Leggatt as a separate and real human being.'[46] But there is no indication in the story, explicit or implicit, that the captain sees any of his dilemma

* Curiously, R. W. Stallmann (*Accent*, IX, 1949, pp. 131–44), one of the alchemical critics, has decided that Leggatt is a manifestation of the captain's superior self.

or difficulties in Leggatt or that he performs any self-examination. Nor is there any 'moral dilemma'.

Guerard's interpretation is based partly on what I believe is a mistaken assessment of the narrator's, or Conrad's, attitude to Leggatt's action. He claims that, for Conrad, 'a crime on shipboard . . . was simply and irrevocably a crime'.[47] But there is no suggestion that Conrad or the captain-narrator condemns Leggatt's action; quite the contrary. At the start the captain says that he knew Leggatt was 'no homicidal ruffian';[48] and when the foolish mate comments on the event as 'A very horrible affair. . . . Beats all these tales about murders in Yankee ships,' the captain snaps back: 'I don't think it beats them. I don't think it resembles them in the least.'[49] His own opinion is summed up: 'It was all very simple. The same strung-up force which had given twenty-four men a chance, at least, for their lives, had, in a sort of recoil, crushed an unworthy mutinous existence.'[50]

In this connection it is interesting to see that Conrad softened the crime, if it can be called a crime, which took place on the *Cutty Sark* and also softened the character of the mate. The mate of the *Cutty Sark* was apparently a despotic character with a sinister reputation.[51] An order which he gave to an incompetent Negro named John Francis was twice disobeyed, and when he went forward to deal with Francis the insubordinate seaman attacked him with a capstan bar; after a struggle the mate got hold of the bar and brought it down on Francis's head so heavily that he never regained consciousness and died three days later. None the less the captain of the *Cutty Sark*, who was by no means a hard man, is supposed to have said that it served Francis right, and he helped the mate to escape from the law. When the mate was eventually captured and tried, he was acquitted of murder and the judge, 'with great pain', sentenced him to seven years for manslaughter.[52]

Leggatt was, however, clearly an exemplary sailor, and his provocation was greater; it was in the middle of a storm when the fate of the ship was at stake and the captain had lost his nerve. Leggatt was in the process of performing an action, which probably saved the ship, when one of the sailors was insubordinate; Leggatt 'felled him like an ox. He up and at me. We closed just as an awful sea made for the ship. All hands saw it coming and took to the rigging, but I had him by the throat, and went on shaking him like a rat, the men above us yelling, "Look out: look out!" Then a crash as if the sky had fallen on my head.'[53] Although Leggatt says, 'It's clear that I meant business, because I was holding him by the throat still when they picked us up,'[54] his action was far less deliberate than that of the mate of the *Cutty Sark*.

The object of this digression is to show that Conrad had no wish to condemn Leggatt but considered him an honourable man who had done something that other honourable men might equally well have done under similar circumstances. He was in fact 'simply knocked over' when a reviewer described Leggatt as 'a murderous ruffian',[55] and certainly had no intention that he should be a symbol of the dark impulses of human nature.

Although his interpretation is not so extreme, Hewitt also regards Leggatt as a symbol, 'an embodiment of his [the captain's] original feeling of being a "stranger" to himself, of that fear that there are parts of himself which he has not yet brought into the light of day', and this 'strangeness' is finally exorcized with the departure of Leggatt.'[56] But this is again reading a meaning into the story which the text neither explicitly nor implicitly warrants; and despite the young captain's initial feeling of 'strangeness', the passage at the end where he says 'Nothing! no one in the world should stand now between us, throwing a shadow on the way of silent knowledge and mute affection, the perfect communion of a seaman with his first command'[57] can be countered by a similar passage, before Leggatt turns up, where the captain is alone in 'quiet communion' with the ship, his 'hand resting lightly on my ship's rail as if on the shoulder of a trusted friend'.[58]

Although I do not believe that Conrad intended 'The Secret Sharer' to be interpreted symbolically, it is easy to discover an unconscious symbolism which has no direct literary relevance but is important psychologically and autobiographically. Conrad had just left off writing his reminiscences for the *English Review*, in which he had been particularly concerned to justify his action in leaving Poland and to answer charges of desertion. It is tempting to identify Conrad with Leggatt and to see the implicit justification of Leggatt's action as a justification of Conrad's own, which metaphorically had made him too 'a fugitive and a vagabond on the earth, with no brand of the curse on his sane forehead to stay a slaying hand – too proud to explain'.[59] It seems that in the twelve months which saw the completion of the reminiscences, the writing of 'The Secret Sharer' and the finishing of *Under Western Eyes*, Conrad finally succeeded in coming to terms with his sense of guilt with regard to Poland. It is thus that the last sentence of 'The Secret Sharer' acquires an added significance as an expression of Conrad's desire to be:

> a free man, a proud swimmer striking out for a new destiny.[60]

(3)

Chiefly because of his bad health, 'The Secret Sharer', the reminiscences, 'The Black Mate' and a short article for the *Daily Mail*[61] were all that Conrad had been able to complete during the last two years. *Under Western Eyes* was still not finished, and thus although by November Conrad was working well – 'The tone of my mind is better than it has been for years – and the old power may come back yet'[62] – he was not able to stave off a financial crisis. The burden of supporting Conrad had fallen primarily upon Pinker, who had made various arrangements, such as standing security for a loan, to help him. But Pinker was now becoming restless. Conrad told his friend, Perceval Gibbon, that Pinker had written saying 'he hopes to have MS sent regularly, that I've given him nothing to sell for two years and threatening to stop short if he don't get end of *Razumov* in a fortnight.... You imagine how charming it is to be following the psychology of Mr Razumov under these conditions. It's like working in Hell.'[63] Conrad had asked Pinker for some money on account of 'The Secret Sharer', but Pinker had dug in his heels and demanded more copy of *Razumov*. Conrad then made a desperate plea to Pinker and asked him whether he meant to 'slam the door'. He poured himself out to Galsworthy:

I have been nearly out of my mind ever since. If he says *yes* – that was what he meant I wonder if I can restrain myself from throwing the MS. in the fire. It is outrageous. Does he think I am the sort of man who wouldn't finish the story in a week if he could? Do you? Why? For what reason? Is it my habit to lie about drunk for days instead of working? I reckon he knows well enough I don't. It's a contemptuous playing with my worry. If he had said – No. I will stick to the lot – I would have been hurt. But this gratuitous ignoring of my sincerity in spirit and also in fact is almost more than I can bear. I who can hardly bear to look at the kids, who without you could not have held [?] the boy at school even – I wouldn't finish the book in a week if I could – unless a bribe of six pounds is dangled before me! – I sit twelve hours at the table, sleep six, and worry the rest of the time, feeling the age creeping on and looking at those I love. For two years I haven't seen a picture heard a note of music, hadn't a moment of ease in human intercourse – not really. – And he talks of *regular supplies of manuscript* to a man who in these conditions (taking all the time together, ill and well) sends him MS. at the rate of 7,600 words a month; and he actually writes as if I were a swindler from whom nothing can be got unless he's pinched. Is it a swindle to write a long novel? He had better get some of his clerks to write stuff he can sell. But sixteen months for a long novel nearly done and some 57,000 words of other work is not so bad – even for a man with his mind at ease, with his spirits kept up by prosperity, with his inspiration buoyed by hope. There is nothing of that for me! I don't complain, dear Jack. I only state it as an argument – for when people appraise me later on with severity I wish you to be able to say: – I knew him – he was not so bad. By Jove all the moral tortures are not in prison-life. I assure you I feel sometimes as if I could drop everything and beat at the door – you understand. The thing is that, so far, I don't. But I feel now that if he stops the miserable pound a day I *must* throw the MS. in the fire. – And indeed why not. It's nothing – it's a mere swindle – it's no good to me. . . . I am at the present moment unable to write a line. One must secure a certain detachment which is beyond me. I can hardly sit still. If it wasn't for dear Jess – well I don't know. [22 December 1909]

However he managed to finish the book by the end of the year.[64]

In *Under Western Eyes* Conrad returned to the theme which he had handled in *Lord Jim*, that of guilt and atonement, worked out in the fate of Razumov, which is of course the same theme as that of the mis-titled *Crime and Punishment*. He had a strong antipathy to Dostoevsky. When Edward Garnett sent him his wife's translation of *The Brothers Karamazov*, Conrad wrote back praising the translation but saying of the book:

It's terrifically bad and impressive and exasperating. Moreover, I don't know what Dostoevsky stands for or reveals, but I do know that he is too Russian for me. It sounds to me like some fierce mouthings from prehistoric ages.[65]

And on another occasion he referred to Dostoevsky as 'the grimacing, haunted creature'.[66] It seems almost as if *Under Western Eyes* were a challenge to Dostoevsky on his own ground. The book is 'an attempt to render ... the psychology of Russia',[67] but set in a Western European perspective. To achieve this Conrad uses a similar method to that of *Lord Jim*; the events are registered through the 'western eyes' of the elderly teacher of languages, and it is his comments, like those of Marlow, that draw out the moral significance.

As well as being the story of the fate of an individual, *Under Western Eyes* is a terrible indictment of Russia; the Russian autocracy dominates the book and controls the destiny of every character in it. In the Author's Note Conrad wrote:

The ferocity and imbecility of an autocratic rule rejecting all legality and in fact basing itself upon complete moral anarchism provokes the no less imbecile and atrocious answer of a purely Utopian revolutionism encompassing destruction by the first means to hand, in the strange conviction that a fundamental change of hearts must follow the downfall of any given human institutions. These people are unable to see that all they can effect is merely a change of names. The oppressors and the oppressed are all Russians together; and the world is brought once more face to face with the saying that the tiger cannot change his stripes nor the leopard his spots.[68]

This contention underlies the whole book and is constantly reflected in the comments of the teacher of languages. Above all, he stresses his incomprehension of the Russian character and the difference between Russia and the rest of Europe – at one point he calls the book 'a Russian story for Western ears, which, as I have observed already, are not attuned to certain tones of cynicism and cruelty, of moral negation, and even of moral distress already silenced at our end of Europe'.[69] Again, when Haldin has arrived in Razumov's rooms after killing Mr de P – the teacher of languages comments:

> It is unthinkable that any young Englishman should find himself in Razumov's situation. This being so it would be a vain enterprise to imagine what he would think. The only safe surmise to make is that he would not think as Mr Razumov thought at this crisis of his fate. He would not have an hereditary and personal knowledge of the means by which a historical autocracy represses ideas, guards its power, and defends its existence.[70]

Of course this is only a rhetorical device to emphasize the chasm between East and West. There is a very successful attempt to present what Razamov thought, then and at other times; indeed, the characters in *Under Western Eyes* are more subtly and convincingly developed than those in any other of Conrad's novels. Razumov himself is the most considerable character that Conrad created; his thoughts, words, and actions reveal depths of personality which show that Conrad succeeded in identifying himself imaginatively with him. The only exception is his lamentably uncharacteristic, Dostoevskyeyan apologia[71] in which he raves about 'evil', gloats over his abasement of 'madcap' Kostia, and talks of stealing Natalia Haldin's soul from her (there has been no suggestion in what has gone before that this was his design).

Of the other characters, Natalia Haldin is Conrad's most effective portrait of a woman. She is a noble, intensely idealistic girl, an identical type to Antonia Avellanos, but Conrad develops her character more fully and gives her greater warmth. She has a mystical belief in the superior destiny of Russia: 'We Russians shall find some better form of national freedom than an artificial conflict of parties.'[72] And: 'There are nations that have made their bargain with fate. . . . We need not envy them.'[73]

Then, the anarchists in *The Secret Agent* are mere puppets compared with the revolutionary Peter Ivanovitch and Sophia Antonovna.

Peter Ivanovitch has been physically a victim of autocracy, having been 'imprisoned in fortresses, beaten within an inch of his life, and condemned to work in mines, with common criminals'.[74] It is one of the most significant aspects of the books that despite Peter Ivanovitch's undeniably heroic behaviour Conrad does not present him as a hero, but recounts his experiences in Siberia ironically and gives him a most unsavoury character. In Geneva, Peter Ivanovitch is living off an elderly woman who is 'avaricious, greedy, and unscrupulous',[75] and believes that she has been robbed by her late husband's family. The ménage exists in an atmosphere of squalid farce, and there is a very funny scene when Mme de S— works herself into a state of hysteria over her supposed wrongs:

> '*Voleurs! Voleurs! Vol –* '
>
> 'No power on earth can rob you of your genius,' shouted Peter Ivanovitch in an overpowering bass, but without stirring, without a gesture of any kind. A profound silence fell.[76]

In public Peter Ivanovitch proclaims grandiloquent ideals, but in private life he is a petty tyrant, mercilessly bullying the inoffensive, self-sacrificing secretary and *dame de compagnie*, Tekla.

In contrast to Peter Ivanovitch, two other revolutionaries, Sophia Antonovna and Viktor Haldin, are genuine idealists with noble characters, but their tragedy is that they are Russians, because all Russians are 'under a curse',[77] victims of autocracy 'in their submission or in their revolt'.[78] Their optimism is based on an illusion, and in incidentals they are gullible. Thus, although Ziemianitch is a notoriously worthless person whose drunkenness leads to Haldin's arrest, Haldin looks on him as a 'bright Russian soul'[79] and asserts: 'It's extraordinary what a sense of the necessity of freedom there is in that man.'[80] Sophia Antonovna who proclaims, ' I don't think, young man. I just simply believe,'[81] is taken in by the repellent Nikita and the hypocritical Peter Ivanovitch; the last, superbly ironical, sentence of the book is her 'Peter Ivanovitch is an inspired man.'[82]

But to Conrad their illusion is fundamental. The teacher of languages, speaking with Conrad's voice, proclaims to Natalia Haldin:

> In a real revolution – not a simple dynastic change or a mere reform of institutions – in a real revolution the best characters do not come to the front. A violent revolution falls into the hands of narrow-minded fanatics and of tyrannical hypocrites at first. Afterwards comes the turn of all the pretentious intellectual failures of the time. Such are the chiefs and the leaders. You will notice that I have left out the mere rogues. The scrupulous and the just, the noble, humane and devoted natures; the unselfish and the intelligent may begin a movement – but it passes away from them. They are not the leaders of a revolution. They are its victims: the victims of disgust, of disenchantment – often of remorse. Hopes grotesquely betrayed, ideals caricatured – that is the definition of revolutionary success. There have been in every revolution hearts broken by such successes.[83]

Conrad's insistence that revolutionaries are also victims and that revolt is as hopeless as submission again reveals his extreme pessimism and, as in *Nostromo*, his conviction of the ultimate futility of all political action. Thus Haldin's murder of Mr de P—, which precipitates the events of the novel, typifies both the inverted morality to which a noble character can be driven by autocracy and the utter uselessness of such an act of protest. No good can come of it because the supply of de P—s is inexhaustible; it is 'characteristic of the moral corruption of an oppressed society where the noblest aspirations of humanity, the desire of freedom, an ardent patriotism, the love of justice, the sense of pity, and even the fidelity of simple minds are prostituted to the lusts of hate and fear, the inseparable companions of an uneasy despotism'.[84]

In submission to autocracy it is perhaps possible for coarse fanatics like General T— to get by, but a humane, intelligent, relatively enlightened man like Councillor Mikulin, although he is a loyal servant of autocracy, is always in danger. For autocracy is so crass that it will not allow intelligent submission, but 'devours its friends and servants as well'[85] as its enemies.

This was Razumov's tragedy. He was a decent, hard-working, even admirable, student whose 'main concern was with his work, his studies, and with his own future'.[86] All he wanted was to be left unmolested so that he could concentrate on creating the foundations of an honourable life. But all his hopes for the future were destoyed when Haldin arrived to take refuge in Razumov's rooms after killing Mr de P—. Ironically, had Razumov approved of Haldin's action he could almost certainly have saved his own future and Haldin's life. As he disapproved he gave Haldin up to the authorities, and thereby found himself irretrievably embroiled with the workings of autocracy.

Razumov's condemnation of Haldin is perfectly sincere and valid. Haldin's action was opposed to all that Razumov believed in. Razumov's philosophy, which he jots down under contrasting heads, would have Conrad's own approval:

History not Theory
Patriotism not Internationalism
Evolution not Revolution

Direction not Destruction
Unity not Disruption[87]

He, as well as the teacher of languages, is often Conrad's mouthpiece and uses arguments which Conrad himself might have used:

Haldin means disruption. . . . What is he with his indignation, with his talk of bondage – with his talk of God's justice? All that means disruption. Better that thousands should suffer than that a people should become a disintegrated mass, helpless like dust in the wind. Obscurantism is better than the light of incendiary torches. The seed germinates in the night. Out of the dark soil springs the perfect plant. But a volcanic eruption is sterile, the ruin of the fertile ground.[88]

Or,

Visionaries work everlasting evil on earth. Their Utopians inspire in the mass of mediocre minds a disgust of reality and a contempt for the secular logic of human development.[89]

His bitterness against Haldin, 'this man who had robbed me of my hard-working, purposeful existence',[90] is justified:

I, too, had my guiding idea; and remember that, amongst us, it is more difficult to lead a life of toil and self-denial than to go out in the street and kill from conviction.[91]

So is his claim that to give up Haldin is no betrayal:

I shall give him up . . .
Betray. A great word. What is betrayal? They talk of a man betraying his country, his friends, his sweetheart. There must be a moral bond first. All a man can betray is his conscience. And how is my conscience engaged here; by what bond of common faith, of common conviction, am I obliged to let that fanatical idiot drag me down with him?[92]

This is incontrovertible. And yet why does Razumov's mind jump from the words 'give up' to 'betray'? He could convince himself intellectually, but not emotionally. If an ordinary murderer throws himself on a person's mercy he may hope for a sympathetic response prompted by humaneness or sentimentality, but he cannot expect approval of his action. Haldin, however, was a high-minded idealist who had murdered a ruthless tyrant and could reasonably expect approval, yet Razumov was handing him over to a brutal autocracy. It is not surprising that Razumov was in mental torment. For although he certainly could not be blamed for his disapproval and had no obligation to help Haldin, he need not have given him up. His self-justification is a little specious, and there is the suspicion that cowardice, fear for his future, was at the bottom of his action; the honourable course would have been to tell Haldin to go away immediately even if at some risk to himself, although, as this alternative never crops up, we must assume either that it did not occur to Conrad or that he wished deliberately to exclude it from consideration.

There is a similarity between Razumov's action and Jim's jump from the pilgrim ship. They were both acts of cowardice committed in exceptional circumstances by unexceptional people with average moral sensibility. Other ordinary people might also have behaved in the same way. This is what separates them from Raskolnikov. Dostoevsky's writing is often tinged with abnormality, showing marks of the author's own abnormality, and Raskolnikov's planning and carrying out of the murder of the old pawnbrokeress is definitely abnormal. Many people may have fantasies such as Raskolnikov's, but it is Dostoevsky's genius alone that is able to make Raskolnikov translate his fantasies into action without seeming a monster.

Razumov's action in giving up Haldin committed him inevitably to further actions because he 'had his being in the willed, in the determined future – in that future menaced by the lawlessness of autocracy – for autocracy knows no law – and the lawlessness of revolution'.[93] This fact is brought home to him in his interview with Councillor Mikulin after Haldin has been executed. For insight and dramatic effect it is one of Conrad's finest scenes; Razumov reaches such a pitch of nervous exasperation that he scarcely knows what he is saying:

'... I protest against this comedy of persecution. The whole affair is becoming too comical altogether for my taste. A comedy of errors, phantoms, and suspicions. It's positively indecent – '

Councillor Mikulin turned an attentive ear.

'Did you say phantoms?' he murmured.

'I could walk over dozens of them.' Razumov, with an impatient wave of his hand, went on headlong, 'But, really, I must claim the right to be done once for all with that man. And in order to accomplish this I shall take the liberty – '

Razumov on his side of the table bowed slightly to the seated bureaucrat.

'– To retire – simply to retire,' he finished with great resolution ...

An unhurried voice said –

'Kirylo Sidorovitch.'

Razumov at the door turned his head.

'To retire,' he repeated.

'Where to?' asked Councillor Mikulin softly.[94]

This scene ends Part I. The rest of the novel, except for a short retrospect, is set in Geneva, that 'serious-minded town of dreary hotels, tendering the same indifferent hospitality to tourists of all nations and to international conspirators of every shade';[95] 'the very perfection of mediocrity attained at last after centuries of toil and culture'.[96] Razumov has come to the city as an agent of the Russian Government to report on the plottings of the revolutionaries, and they have accepted him enthusiastically in the belief that he was Haldin's partner in the killing of Mr de P—.

He had tried to resume his student's life as if nothing had happened, but it was impossible:

Everything abandoned him – hope, courage, belief in himself, trust in men. His heart had, as it were, suddenly emptied itself. It was no use struggling on. Rest, work, solitude, and the frankness of intercourse with his kind were alike forbidden to him. Everything was gone.[97]

Therefore he succumbed to Mikulin's blandishments.

In Part I the teacher of languages has told the story as set down in Razumov's diary. Henceforth, although he still has occasional recourse to the diary, the teacher of languages takes part in the action and relates the events as he himself has experienced them or as they are reported to him by other characters. The tempo of the rest of the novel is also different from that of Part I, where the tension is sustained with the help of dramatic external events. Henceforth the interest is concentrated on Razumov's tormented mind, on the mental torture which he is forced to undergo in the process of working out his fate and achieving final atonement. (It is worth noting the similarity in structure, as well as in theme, between *Under Western Eyes* and *Lord Jim*: the first part centres on the vital 'act', and the rest, set in a different place with a variety of new characters, is devoted to the consequences of this act.)

Razumov's straightforward, honest character is singularly ill-adapted to the role of informer. He cannot disguise his embitterment and enforced cynicism, which express themselves in apparently boorish behaviour. However, the Russian colony is, with the notable exception of Nikita, predisposed in his favour and consistently misinterprets his behaviour. Razumov finds his false position unpleasant enough in his relations with the revolutionaries, but the presence of Haldin's mother and sister in Geneva makes the situation wholly odious. Both look to Razumov for information about the fate of Haldin and for some solace in their grief: but that is what he cannot give. Natalia Haldin has worshipped her brother, and the only person that he mentioned in his letters was Razumov, speaking of his 'unstained, lofty, and solitary existence'.[98] Razumov at first avoids the Haldins, but eventually meets Natalia. She describes their meeting to the teacher of languages; when she had mentioned the name of Victor Haldin 'You should have seen his face. He positively reeled. He leaned against the wall of the terrace. Their friendship must have been the very brotherhood of souls!'[99]

After this Razumov again avoids Natalia for a time, but

then they start seeing each other regularly and Razumov finds that he is falling in love with her. Finally the situation becomes intolerable to him, and at the moment when his position among the revolutionaries is most secure he confesses to Natalia the part which he has played in the death of Haldin.* At the same time he exposes the extent of his loneliness:

> 'Do you know why I came to you? It is simply because there is no one anywhere in the whole great world I could go to. Do you understand what I say? Not one to go to. Do you conceive the desolation of the thought – no one – to – go – to?'[100]

This constantly recurring theme in Conrad's work has been touched on at the start of the novel. Razumov is a bastard and is not overtly acknowledged by his father, whom he knows as a remote, almost inaccessible aristocrat. 'He was as lonely in the world as a man swimming in the deep sea. The word Razumov was the mere label of a solitary individuality. There were no Razumovs belonging to him anywhere.'[101]

At the crucial point, when he is deciding what to do about Haldin:

> Razumov longed desperately for a word of advice, for moral support. Who knows what true loneliness is – not the conventional word, but the naked terror? To the lonely themselves it wears a mask. The most miserable outcast hugs some memory or some illusion. Now and then a fatal conjunction of events may lift the veil for an instant. For an instant only. No human being could bear a steady view of moral solitude without going mad.[102]

And again, when Mikulin is trying to persuade him to go to Geneva as an agent:

> The obscure, unrelated young student Razumov, in the moment of great moral loneliness, was allowed to feel that he was an object of interest to a small group of people of high position.[103]

* In his original, much less subtle, conception of the story Conrad had intended to create a somewhat melodramatic situation by making Razumov marry Natalia Haldin and have a child by her; he was to be driven to confess mainly because of the resemblance of the child to Victor Haldin. Letter to Galsworthy of 6 January 1908, *L.L.*, II, p. 65.

Before he confesses Razumov asks Natalia whether she believes in the 'efficacy of remorse', and she replies with a firm 'Yes'.[104] Through his confession Razumov feels that he has atoned for his action of giving up Haldin and expresses his conviction through a magnificent piece of verbal ambiguity; on the way back to his lodgings he is drenched by a shower and the owner of the house remarks:

> 'You've got very wet.'
> 'Yes, I am washed clean,' muttered Razumov . . .[105]

But he has still not completed his task. After writing his *apologia*, designed for Natalia Haldin, 'he sat down with the watch before him. He could have gone out at once, but the hour had not struck yet. The hour would be midnight. There was no reason for that choice except that the facts and the words of a certain evening in his past were timing his conduct in the present.'[106] He had decided that he must also confess his role to the revolutionaries. Again there is a close parallel with Jim going to meet his doom at the hands of Doramin.

He finds them in conclave. Their reaction is one of horror, and with some demur they allow the loathsome brute Nikita, terrorist killer, and undisclosed police agent, to deafen him by breaking his eardrums. Then, wandering about the streets afterwards, he is run into by a tram which he does not hear coming, and badly injured. He will be an invalid for the rest of his life; he returns to Russia and is looked after by Tekla, who has dedicated herself to him, just as Sonia dedicated herself to Raskolnikov and followed him to Siberia.

Thus there is a parallel between the course of events in *Under Western Eyes* and in *Crime and Punishment*. Razumov and Raskolnikov commit an act, cowardly or criminal, which causes them mental agony and isolates them by destroying the possibility of normal relations with other human beings, and their torment finally drives them to confess. But their confessions emphasize above all the difference between the two authors. Raskolnikov's confession is the beginning of a process which leads to full repentance and to spiritual regeneration, whereas Razumov's confession is a culmination and is conclusive; Raskolnikov finds his god, but for Razumov, as for Conrad, there is no god. Thus while Sonia is midwife to Raskolnikov's rebirth there is no suggestion that Tekla in any way influenced Razumov spiritually. After Razumov's confession Conrad virtually withdraws his interest from him.

The aim, tone, and form of the two books are absolutely opposed. *Under Western Eyes* is an indictment; its mood is fatalistic, and Conrad's compassion is controlled by a predominantly ironical approach. *Crime and Punishment* is an assertion of ultimate human goodness and the mercy of God, ending on a note of hope and faith, while Dostoevsky's compassion and other emotions constantly spill over in their abundance. On one hand there is carefully organized structure and on the other disordered exuberance; and ultimately it is a matter of temperament and belief which of the two books is judged the greater.

In *Under Western Eyes* there are verbal echoes of *Crime and Punishment*. It may perhaps be fanciful to suggest that they are deliberate, but the fact remains that some of the most dramatic phrases of *Under Western Eyes* have their less dramatic counterpart in Dostoevsky's novel. Thus Razumov's 'Do you conceive the desolation of the thought – no one – to – go – to?'[107] recalls Marmeladov's 'Do you understand, sir, do you understand what it means when you have absolutely nowhere to turn?'[108] Razumov calls Natalia Haldin a 'predestined victim'[109] just as Raskolnikov calls Sonia Marmeladov an 'eternal victim'.[110] Natalia Haldin says: 'It is impossible to be more unhappy,'[111] and Sonia says to Raskolnikov: 'There is no one – no one in the whole world now so unhappy as you.'[112] Then Razumov's 'It was myself, after all, whom I have betrayed'[113] recalls Raskolnikov's 'I murdered myself, not her!'[114]

As usual, Conrad dropped a few not very revealing hints about the background of *Under Western Eyes*. He said that he had been 'induced to write this novel by something told me by a man whom I met in Geneva many years ago (Razumov's fate) and by the rubbishy character of stories about Russian revolutionists published in magazines'.[115] In the Author's Note, on the other hand, he wrote that the course of the action and 'the various figures playing their part in the story . . . owe their existence to no special experience but to the general knowledge of the condition of Russia . . .'[116] Conrad had had plenty of opportunity to gather information about the Russian revolutionary movement from the Garnett family, who were friendly with several distinguished refugees, including Prince Peter Kropotkin and Felix Volkovsky. The Garnetts had also known well S. M. Kravchinsky, called Stepniak, who had fled from Russia after killing the chief of police, General Mesentzev; Stepniak had eventually settled in England, but in 1895 was knocked down and killed when crossing a railway track; according to David Garnett he had not heard the engine approaching because he had the capacity to make himself deaf at will, and this may have given Conrad the idea for Razumov's accident.[117]

Conrad must also have followed the frequent newspaper reports of the appalling conditions in Russia which led to periodical assassinations or attempted assassinations. It is easy enough to identify Father Zosim with Father Gapon, General T— with the notorious General Trepov, or Mr de P— with the even more infamous Minister of the Interior, de Plehve; and in fact Conrad told Galsworthy[118] that Haldin's crime was supposed to be based on the murder of de Plehve, who was blown to bits in his carriage in 1904 by a man named Sasonov – like Haldin, a student of Moscow University.[119] Sasonov was arrested on the spot, and so there is no parallel between his fate and that of Haldin.

Another matter connected with Russia which was fully reported in the press was the discovery that a certain Evno Asev was a double agent: he had for many years been an important agent of the Russian police who had manged to insinuate himself into the inner councils of the revolutionaries, but had at the same time double-crossed his employers and had failed to warn them about terroristic activities in which he was involved.

Lopuhin, the comparatively liberal head of the Police Department, had been shocked by the Government's apparent adoption of the role of *agent provocateur* of political unrest and in a conversation on a train journey had disclosed that Azev was a police agent to a journalist named Burtsev, who was closely connected with the revolutionaries. The Russian Government was appalled that its dirty linen should be washed so publicly but could not prevent the matter being debated in the Duma; however, it had its revenge on Lopuhin who was sentenced to Siberia.[120]

Councillor Mikulin is based at least in part on Lopuhin and is given the same fate; moreover, as Conrad does not seem at first to have intended to make Razumov a police agent,[121] the revelations connected with Azev may have prompted him to develop the plot along these lines, although he had already shown in *The Secret Agent* how much he knew about such police practices. The famous conversation on the train between Lopuhin and Burtsev crops up when Conrad makes Mikulin meet Peter Ivanovitch in a railway carriage and hint to him that Nikita is a police agent.

It is not known what else in the way of press reports, magazine stories and books* Conrad drew on, or whether other events or characters have a source. Peter Ivanovitch gives the impression of having been, in part at least, modelled on an actual person, and it may be that Conrad was to some extent having a dig at Tolstoy: there is the same contrast between proclaimed ideals and a squalid home life; and an allusion in a cancelled passage[122] to Peter Ivanovitch as author of 'The Resurrection of Yegor' and the 'thrice famous Pfennig Cantata' suggests that Conrad at least had Tolstoy in mind. Then some facets of Peter Ivanovitch, such as his

* There were a number of books available which described Russian revolutionary activities and conditions in Russia; for example Stepniak's *Underground Russia* and *Russia under the Tzars*, Herzen's *Le Monde Russe*, Bourdon's *La Russie Libre*, Perris's *Russia in Revolution*, Father Gapon's *The Story of My Life* and Zilliacus's *The Russian Revolutionary Movement*.

sentimental feminism, may be a guying of Kropotkin. But whether or not there are specific prototypes, Conrad's characters had their parallels among contemporary revolutionaries and those of a past generation.

Conrad apparently took the last batch of manuscript of *Under Western Eyes* up to Pinker in London to be typed and had a blazing row with him. He returned to the country with the symptoms of an acute attack of gout, but it was soon plain that he was suffering from a complete breakdown in health, no doubt the culmination of a long period of emotional strain.[123] Jessie wrote to Meldrum:

> Poor Conrad is very ill and Dr Hackney says it will be a long time before he is fit for anything requiring mental exertion. ... There is the MS. complete but uncorrected and his fierce refusal to let even I touch it. It lays on a table at the foot of his bed and he lives mixed up in the scenes and holds converse with the characters.
>
> I have been up with him night and day since Sunday week and he, who is usually so depressed by illness, maintains he is not ill, and accuses the Doctor and I of trying to put him into an asylum. [6 February 1910]

Conrad was laid up for three months.[124] After his illness he told Clifford: 'It seems I have been very ill. At the time I did not believe it, but now I begin to think that I must have been. And what's more, I begin to see the horrible nervous tension of the last two years (of which even my wife knows nothing) had to end in something of this sort.'[125] And he wrote to Norman Douglas more than a month later: 'I am all of a shake yet; I feel like a man returned from hell and look upon the very world of the living with dread.'[126]

It had particularly rankled with Conrad that Pinker had told him during their row on the eve of his illness to speak English if he could.[127] Thus, when Conrad was recovering, one of the first things he did was to write Pinker a formal letter beginning 'Dear Sir' instead of the usual 'My dear Pinker', and ending 'Yours faithfully':

> As it can't have escaped your recollection that the last time we met you told me that I 'did not speak English to you' I have asked

Robert Garnett [Edward's brother and solicitor] to be my mouthpiece – at any rate till my speech improves sufficiently to be acceptable. [23 May 1910]

The estrangement lasted for nearly two years, and although Conrad's letters to Pinker gradually became warmer he was still addressing him as 'Dear Sir' in March 1912.[128]

(4)

In June 1910 the Conrads moved from their cramped rooms in Aldington to Capel House, an isolated farmhouse near Ashford. The choice was a success: 'Yes, this place is all right. I can work here. We are surrounded by woods and the soil is clay, but the house is sympathetic.'[129] Thus, although Conrad's convalescence was slow – he was still complaining of 'strange fits of giddiness'[130] at the end of October – he managed, during the last six months of the year, to write a long short story, 'A Smile of Fortune', and two short stories, 'Prince Roman' and 'The Partner'.[131] He also did a series of three reviews for the *Daily Mail*.[132]

'The Partner' was an obvious pot-boiler about the successful wrecking of a ship in order to gain the insurance, which, however, produced as a by-product the murder of the innocent Captain. It was apparently based on fact.[133]

According to Jessie, 'Prince Roman' had originally been intended to form part of Conrad's reminiscences;[134] and in fact it is very close in form to the Polish sections of *A Personal Record*, being based partly on Conrad's own recollection of meeting, when a small boy, Prince Roman Sanguszko and partly on his Uncle Thaddeus's account in his memoirs.[135] This in no way detracts from the effectiveness of the story. It is a moving tribute to the ideals of honour, service, and patriotism of a Polish aristocrat; qualities which Conrad admired, above all, when they were untainted by 'vulgar refinement'.[136] It is interesting to note that Conrad, who sometimes showed signs of the anti-Jewish prejudice so widespread among Eastern Europeans, brings in a very friendly portrait of a Jewish innkeeper who is also 'a

Polish patriot'.[137] The story is written with a vibrant sincerity and is an indication of how very firmly Conrad had remained a Pole throughout his wanderings.

'A Smile of Fortune' is a haunting, though not entirely successful, story, elements of which were drawn from Conrad's visit to Mauritius with his first command, the *Otago*. It concerns a young Captain who becomes progressively ensnared by a persistent ship's chandler named Jacobus. The Captain is eventually lured into visiting Jacobus's house, where he meets his farouche bastard daughter, Alice. She has been forced to lead the life of a recluse, and the Captain is almost the first person from the outside world whom she has met. After strong initial resistance she falls for him, while he succumbs to her peculiar spell, although never wholly losing his heart. Jacobus hopes to palm off Alice on the Captain, but he also wants to sell him a cargo of potatoes, and it is sometimes not quite clear whether he is using Alice as a bait for the potatoes or the reverse.

Eventually the Captain takes the potatoes and leaves the girl, who has shown the strength of her feelings with a clumsy kiss, but at the cost of a sense of corruption – 'The Pearl of the Ocean [Mauritius] had in a few short hours grown odious to me.'[138] His acceptance of the unwanted potatoes was in fact a sign of his corruption; he realized that his behaviour towards Alice had made him morally helpless in the face of Jacobus's pressure. On arrival at Melbourne the Captain finds that there is a potato famine in the country, and the deal thus turns out to have been exceptionally profitable; hence the title.

The owners want the Captain to do the voyage again, but he cannot face the thought of returning to Mauritius, and is thus forced to resign his command. 'How could I go back to fan that fatal spark with my cold breath? No, no, that unexpected kiss had to be paid for at its full price.'[139]

Whether Conrad regarded the story as rather a pot-boiler or whether his literary return to the East revived his early exoticism, sentences like 'the abode of obscure desires, of extravagant hopes, of unimaginable terrors'[140] recall *An Outcast of the Islands*, while there is something magazinish about some of the descriptions, particularly of Alice, such as 'But where was the mysterious and provoking sensation which was like the perfume of her flower-like youth?'[141] or in phrases psychologically improbable in their context like 'callous with greed'[142] and 'the demon of lucre had taken possession of me'.[143]

Conrad was surprised, as indeed he might have been, when a reviewer called Alice a 'sensual animal' and said that he had 'tried to make her pathetic'.[144] In this he succeeded; on the other hand, it is doubtful whether he realized how reprehensible he had made the conduct of the Captain appear. There is something very distasteful about the way in which the Captain goads and, rather lubriciously, flirts with Alice; by arousing her feelings he may well have done irreparable harm to her. Thus, although he does in the end pay for his behaviour, this is fortuitous because he might have avoided doing so if the owners had agreed to his suggestion that he should take the ship into the China seas; nor is the resignation of a command the 'full price' for such an action.

This was a productive period, and certainly Conrad needed to make up for much lost time. Soon after finishing 'The Partner' he started another story, 'Freya of the Seven Isles', which he finished at the end of February 1911.[145] It contains the essence of Conrad's romanticism, as important an aspect of his outlook and art as was his moral preoccupation; although in an age in which so much literary criticism is concerned primarily with moral content this is apt to be overlooked. Jasper Allen is a romantic hero placed, unlike the hero of *Romance*, in a psychologically mature perspective; the psychology of *Romance* is immature because romanticism is disguised as realism; whereas, for Conrad, uninfluenced by Hueffer, the inevitable consequence of the confrontation of romance and reality was tragedy. Conrad was told by one reader that he 'had no right to write such an abominable thing which, he said, had gratuitously and intolerably harrowed his feelings'.[146] He might have replied in the same way as he replied to a critic of a similar story, 'The Planter of Malata'. 'I should like to ask him what he imagines the, so to speak, lifelong embrace of Felicia Moorsom and Geoffrey Renouard could have been like? Could it have been at all? Would it have been credible? No!'[147] What would the lifelong embrace of Freya and Jasper Allen have been like? To Conrad it was inconceivable that a Freya should become a housewife. One did not marry such people; one married Jessies.

Although there are occasional lapses into facetiousness or heartiness – presumably a concession to the magazine reader – the presentation matches the conception: the style is frankly romantic and the story throbs with movement and passion, becoming at times operatic in form; it is significant that Freya's piano-playing has an important part in the action, also that she plays Wagner.

Of Freya Conrad wrote: 'I will not compare her eyes to violets, because the real shade of their colour was peculiar, not so dark and more lustrous;'[148] and her 'wealth of hair was so glossy that when the screens of the west verandah were down, making a pleasant twilight there . . . it seemed to give out a golden light of its own'.[149] Jasper Allen was like 'a flashing sword-blade perpetually leaping out of the scabbard',[150] and his brig:

> glided, all white, round dark, frowning headlands, stole out, silent like a ghost, from behind points of land stretching out all black in the moonlight; or lay hove-to, like a sleeping sea-bird, under the shadow of some nameless mountain waiting for a signal. She would be glimpsed suddenly on misty, squally days dashing disdainfully aside the short aggressive waves of the Java Sea; or be seen far, far away, a tiny dazzling white speck flying across the brooding purple masses of thunderclouds piled up on the horizon.[151]

There is a tableau when the four chief characters are together:

> the charmingly fresh and resolute Freya, the innocently round-eyed old Nielson, Jasper, Keen, long-limbed, lean faced .. . all three tall,

fair, and blue-eyed in varied shades, and amongst them the swarthy, arrogant, black-haired Dutchman, shorter nearly by a head, and so much thicker than any of them that he seemed to have been a creature capable of inflating itself, a grotesque specimen of mankind from some other planet.[152]

Then there is a magnificent operatic scene in which Freya is on the verandah looking out through old Nielsen's long-glass towards Jasper on his brig, knowing that Heemskirk is behind her watching through a crack in the door:

Directly Freya had made out Jasper on deck with his own long-glass directed to the bungalow, she laid hers down and raised both her beautiful white arms above her head. In that attitude of supreme cry she stood still, glowing with the consciousness of Jasper's adoration going out to her figure held in the field of his glass away there, and warned, too, by the feeling of evil passion, the burning, covetous eyes of the other, fastened on her back. In the fervour of her love, in the caprice of her mind, and with that mysterious knowledge of masculine nature women seem to be born to, she thought:

'You are looking on – you will – you must! Then you shall see something.'

She brought both her hands to her lips, then flung them out, sending a kiss over the sea, as if she wanted to throw her heart along with it on the deck of the brig. Her face was rosy, her eyes shone. Her repeated, passionate gesture seemed to fling kisses by the hundred again and again and again, while the slowly ascending sun brought the glory of colour to the world, turning the islets green, the sea blue, the brig below her white – dazzlingly white in the spread of her wings – with the red ensign streaming like a tiny flame from the peak. And each time she murmured with a rising inflexion: 'Take this – and this – and this – ' till suddenly her arms fell. She had seen the ensign dipped in response, and next moment the point below hid the hull of the brig from her view.[153]

Such emotions are not compatible with the world of everyday affairs. Thus when Heemskirk triumphs by deliberately wrecking the brig it is as if a dream had ended. Both Jasper and Freya collapse; Freya literally dies of love and Jasper is visibly withering away. It is irrelevant to protest that this would not have happened; that Freya would in fact have taken the first boat to Macassar, told Jasper to pull himself together, married him and lived happily with him on another brig. For they are not realistic characters, they are heroes of romance.

The story, insofar as it concerned the wrecking of the brig by the commander of a Dutch gunboat and the character of the owner of the brig, was based on fact. Conrad told Garnett that Captain Marris, his visitor from Malaya, had said, 'You ought to write the story of the *Costa Rica.* There's a good many of us left yet who remember Sutton.'[154] Freya herself was largely invention, although Sutton was about to go home to marry a girl and used to talk about her to 'everybody and anybody'. It is interesting that the weakness in the story from the realistic point of view, Freya's failure to do anything positive about the situation, was invented.

This story was the cause of curious upheaval involving Garnett. Scribners had turned it down because 'its *overpowering* gloom makes is impossible for serialization'.[155] Pinker had therefore sent it to Garnett, who was then reader for the *Century* magazine. Garnett apparently told Pinker that he had seen the story 'years ago', whereupon Conrad wrote to Pinker indignantly denouncing Garnett's '*thundering lie*',[156] asserting that not a line was written before 26 December 1910 and citing Gibbon and Marwood as witnesses. But the row apparently blew over, and the two remained on friendly terms, although a few months later Conrad was irritated by Garnett's comments on *Under Western Eyes*, which had just been published. He wrote:

> I don't understand your picturesque allusions to packing spinach into the saucepan and the hell broth that's supposed to be the result of that culinary operation. There's just about as much or as little hatred in this book as in the *Outcast of the Islands* for instance.... You are so russianised, my dear, that you don't know the truth when you see it – unless it smells of cabbage soup when it at once secures your profoundest respect. I suppose one must make allowances for your position of Russian Embassador to the Republic of Letters ...

And anyhow if hatred there were it would be too big a thing to be put into a 6/- novel. This too might have occurred to you, if you had condescended to look beyond the literary horizon where all things sacred and profane are turned into copy. [20 October 1911, pp. 248–50]

[XIII]

Success and the War

AFTER finishing 'Freya' Conrad had a relapse for nearly two months.[1] He was then able to take advantage of a good turn that Hugh Clifford had done him some months earlier. Towards the end of 1909, in Ceylon, Clifford had met Gordon Bennett, proprietor of the *New York Herald*, and had apparently 'fired into him' the whole of Conrad's prose. As a result, in the summer of 1910, the *Herald* approached Conrad with a view to serializing a novel. However he was so bound up with a short story and, generally, in such a curious frame of mind that nothing came of these negotiations.[2] But an offer from a paper of mass circulation was not something that Conrad could afford to ignore and so he now decided to concentrate on *Chance* for the *Herald*; this was the story at which he had been tinkering for the last six years.

The agreement with the *Herald* was one of several straws in the wind. Galsworthy and others had managed to get a Civil List Pension of £100 for him,[3] while an American lawyer, John Quinn, who was a great admirer of Conrad's work and a collector, had written to ask Conrad whether he might buy some of his manuscripts;[4] Conrad agreed, and this proved a useful additional source of income, although the prices paid were not very high – for instance, £80 for *The Nigger of the 'Narcissus'*, £15 for the first draft of 'Youth', and £5 apiece for the corrected typed copies of *Almayer* and *Chance*.[5] Finally, Pinker had agreed to pay him £4 per thousand words of *Chance* (£3 on delivery and £1 deferred till completion).[6]

He managed to send in copy steadily and even told Garnett that he was 'pelting along',[7] an astonishing phrase for him to be able to use. There were of course interruptions; the most dramatic was when Norman Douglas became very seriously ill while staying with the Conrads, and was even expected to die.[8] Conrad also took his elder son, Borys, to the nautical school-ship, *H.M.S. Worcester*, and he gives a rather touching account in a letter to Galsworthy:

> Poor Mons. B. looked to me a very small and lonely figure on that enormous deck, in that big crowd, where he didn't know a single soul. It is an immense change for him. Yes. He did look a small boy. I couldn't make up my mind to leave him and at last I made rather a bolt of it. I can't get him out of my eyes ... [23 September 1911, *L.L.*, II, p. 135]

Then the family had to leave the house for a couple of days while the drains were being attended to; they went to the seaside where Conrad caught a cold.[9] However, despite inevitable periods of feeling unwell Conrad managed to keep going and finished the book in March of the new year, 1912.[10]

He was pleased with what he had achieved in *Chance* and told Pinker: 'It's the biggest piece of work I've done since *Lord Jim*. As to what *it is* I am very confident. As to what will happen to it when launched – I am much less confident. And it's a pity. One doesn't do a trick like that twice.'[11] At last his apprehension was needless.

In Britain and America *Chance* was the turning-point in Conrad's financial fortunes as a writer. The *New York Herald*'s serialization, which began on 21 January 1912, seems to have had a tonic effect. The new favourable atmosphere even affected the fate of *'Twixt Land and Sea*, which came out in 1912 and was a financial success; it certainly encouraged Doubleday, prodded by the enthusiasm and initiative of Alfred Knopf, a young newcomer to the firm, to put the full weight of his promotion behind the book.[12] He was handsomely rewarded, because Conrad suddenly became a best seller.

Much the same happened in Britain, although on a rather less dramatic scale. Methuen's, the British publishers, do not seem to have pushed the novel particularly, but in the first two years after publication they sold 13,200 copies, against 4,112 of *Under Western Eyes*, his previous novel, in the corresponding period.[13]

The question is why this happened. Presumably the main reason was the serialization in the *Herald*, because it set the ball rolling; and this was, appropriately enough, to some extent due to 'chance'. However, other factors must have been involved for the book to become a best seller on both sides of the Atlantic. It often happens in the career of a little-read but much-praised author that his reputation gradually ripens, book by book, until, like a fruit, it is ready to be sold to the public. This happened with Meredith in the case of *Diana of the Crossways*, and it has happened recently with Cozzens in the case of *By Love Possessed*. And this, to a large extent, was what happened with *Chance*. Conrad had almost always been reviewed respectfully and often enthusiastically. *Under Western Eyes* was, for instance, very well reviewed, and it is possible to collect just as impressive 'quotes' for it as for *Chance*. W. L. Courtney wrote in the *Daily Telegraph* that *Under Western Eyes* was 'a piece of work which we think will endure, because the impression which it leaves bites as deep as Turgenieff's *Father and Sons* or the great novel of Dostoieffsky'.[14] The *Pall Mall Gazette* hailed it as 'entitled to rank with the best work that Mr Joseph Conrad has given us'.[15] And even as 'popular' a paper as the *Daily Mail* gave the book a good review.[16]

It was not what the reviewers said but the amount of space in which they said it that distinguished the reception of *Chance* from that of *Under Western Eyes*. Thus Sidney Colvin gave *Chance* a long and enthusiastic review in the *Observer*.[17] The novel provided the occasion for the leading review in *The Times Literary Supplement* to present a somewhat lush panorama of Conrad's work.[18] And it gained the place of honour, with a lot of space, in most of the leading national dailies.

The novel whereby an author becomes fashionable is of course not necessarily the best that he has written – it may be the worst. But it must have certain characteristics. *Lord Jim*, for instance, might well have become a best seller had it been published in place of *Chance*, whereas it would have probably been impossible to have turned *Under Western Eyes* into a best seller in Britain or America at that time; its subject was too sombre and too remote.

Thus, *Chance* had certain qualities that made it well adapted for popularity. For a start the sea figured largely enough in it to enable the reviewers and the public with relief to fit Conrad back into his niche of a writer of sea tales. Apparently quite forgetting what he had said about *Under Western Eyes*, Courtney wrote that *Chance* was more successful because Conrad was more at home with the sea as background.[19] Then the book is packed with general reflections on life and on women (the subject of the role of woman was particularly topical in view of the suffragette agitation). As Conrad said: 'It's the sort of stuff that *may* have a chance with the public. All of it about a girl and with a steady run of references to women in general all along.... It ought to go down.'[20]

Moreover, *Chance* was, to a greater extent than Conrad's other novels, decked out to catch popularity. The title, a popular philosophical catchword, was far less forbidding than most of Conrad's titles; *Chance* was the first, and last, of his novels to have chapter headings; and Edward Garnett has suggested that the figure of the girl on the jacket helped considerably to sell the book.[21]

No doubt the failure of his last three major achievements to sell had driven Conrad to desperation, so that he rewrote the ending to make it 'nicer' – 'I am thinking of the public,'[22] he said. Both his beliefs and financial reasons would have influenced him to make this concession; there are no grounds for questioning his assertion that 'What I always feared most was drifting unconsciously into the position of a writer for a limited coterie; a position which would have been odious to me as throwing a doubt on the soundness of my belief in the solidarity of all mankind in simple ideas and in sincere emotions.'[23]

Although *Chance* was Conrad's first immediately successful novel it has now become his most controversial, and it has both its strong advocates and its strong critics. F. R.

Leavis includes it among Conrad's major works, alongside *Nostromo*, *The Secret Agent*, *Under Western Eyes* and *Victory*,[24] while Edward Crankshaw persuasively champions it in his brilliant analysis of Conrad's technique.[25] However, other critics, such as Douglas Hewitt[26] and Oliver Warner,[27] consider *Chance* to be Conrad's big failure.

Whatever its qualities it is certainly one of Conrad's most imperfect novels. The first section has only the most superficial relevance to the rest of the book; and this is not surprising because it really belonged to another story about a dynamite ship 'something like "Youth" – but not at all like it',[28] which he had called 'Explosives'.[29]

Then, Conrad used a method which he had frequently used before, but here he at times used it very clumsily. As in 'Youth', 'Heart of Darkness', and most of *Lord Jim* Marlow tells the story to the anonymous author of the book who from time to time interrupts him with a comment or a criticism; in *Chance* the interruptions are usually protests at Marlow's rather heavy outbursts of misogyny and to this extent Marlow is a character in the book, and not necessarily Conrad's mouthpiece. Marlow himself has several sources of his knowledge: there are the two Fynes, Powell, and, at the end, Flora; these, in their turn, at times relate what they have been told. Thus there are passages in which events are relayed to the reader through four consciousnesses.

However, there are only rare occasions when anything is gained from this cumbersome method of presentation, when an added subtlety and depth is achieved through the simultaneous concentration of more than one consciousness on an event. For instance, the comparatively naïve comments of Fyne or Powell successfully act as raw material for Marlow's refining irony and perspicacity.

When this succeeds the result is intensely satisfying. But even then Conrad achieves no more than he had achieved through the far simpler, directly ironical, method of presentation in *The Secret Agent*, whereas the multiplication of consciousnesses too often results in what Henry James called 'the successive members of a cue from one to the other of which the sense and the interest of the subject have to be passed on together, in the manner of the buckets of water for the improvised extinction of a fire, before reaching our apprehension: all with whatever result, to this apprehension, of a quantity to be allowed for as spilt by the way'.*

Moreover, although, as Edward Crankshaw has shown, Conrad weaves Marlow into the plot with such skill that his becoming the confidant of successive characters never strains credibility, there are many occasions when authenticity totally breaks down. An author can be allowed plenty of licence as to plausibility, but he has failed when he produces an impossibility. Thus Conrad flagrantly violates his self-imposed method when he makes Marlow describe events about which he could never have known.† For instance, the final drama in Hove, where the Governess and Charley are preparing to decamp, is supposed to have been related by Flora to Mrs Fyne, who passes it on to Marlow; but events are described, such as various scenes between the Governess and Charley, which Flora could not have witnessed or known of. Furthermore, there are scenes where Flora is present but which Marlow describes as if she were the object of observation instead of the observer. She is the original narrator and yet

> With suddenly enlarged pupils and a movement as instinctive almost as the bounding of a startled fawn, she [Flora] jumped up.[30]

or,

> She [the Governess] would have gone on regardless of the enormous eyes, of the open mouth of the girl who sat up suddenly with the wild staring expression of being choked by invisible fingers on her throat, and yet horribly pale.[31]

* 'The New Novel' (1914), *Notes on Novelists, with Some Other Notes*, 1914, p. 278. Conrad was later to describe James's criticism of his art in this essay, as 'the *only time a* criticism affected me painfully' (letter to John Quinn, 24 May 1916).

† Conrad is far from being alone, even among illustrious writers, in committing such solecisms. Samuel Butler, in *The Way of All Flesh*, was for instance an equally bad offender.

This would not jar so if we were not frequently reminded of the alleged source of our knowledge with such phrases as 'she told Mrs Fyne'[32] or 'its the very expression she used later on to Mrs Fyne'.[33]

The cumbersome technique of *Chance* raises in an acute form the question why Conrad repeatedly resorted to the device of Marlow or of a narrator. The usefulness of having a narrator has been emphasized and is obvious enough. He can perform the task of analysis and comment without the illusion being destroyed through the obtrusion of the author. He can more easily impart to the events a quality of reality and authenticity than can be conveyed by impersonal narration; for instance, Conrad defended his use of the teacher of languages in *Under Western Eyes* by his 'desire to produce the effect of actuality'.[34] He can present a character, thus avoiding the need for the author to get inside his characters and use interior monologue or to develop them solely through what they say and do; Edward Crankshaw has maintained, with justification, that this was his main reason for using a narrator, contending that Conrad was unable successfully to present a character from the inside. Crankshaw takes Garnett sharply to task for suggesting that Conrad used a narrator because it 'saved trouble'; but Garnett had been closer to Conrad's struggle with his craft than anyone except Hueffer and his opinion demands respect. In fact, Garnett and Crankshaw's contentions are not mutually exclusive; both could be right up to a point. It is undeniable that for the purpose of presentation and comment a narrator does save a lot of trouble – on the assumption that it is impermissible for the author himself to intervene. Moreover, Conrad evidently found himself linguistically much more at ease within a narrator's colloquial idiom than when he was writing impersonal prose. It is significant that the book with which he seems to have had most difficulty was *Nostromo* where, for the most part, he was without a narrator; but even in *Nostromo* he had occasional recourse to Captain Mitchell.

Crankshaw's contention that a narrator created far more

difficulties than he solved would be more valid if Conrad had not so often ignored or shirked the technical problems which a narrator presents.

In *Lord Jim* Marlow's role, apart from that of narrator, was to comment, to elucidate and, occasionally, to philosophize, but his remarks were always closely related to the action of the novel. In *Chance*, on the other hand, although his role is supposedly the same, he only very rarely says something that deepens our understanding of the events described. His comment on de Barral's leaving prison is one example:

> Prisons are wonderful contrivances. Open – shut. Very neat. Shut – open. And out comes some sort of corpse, to wander awfully in a world in which it has no possible connections and carrying with it the appalling tainted atmosphere of its silent abode.[35]

And his stricture on the inconclusive relationship between Anthony and Flora is another:

> If two beings thrown together, mutually attracted, resist the necessity, fail in understanding and voluntarily stop short of the – the embrace, in the noblest meaning of the word, then they are committing a sin against life, the call of which is simple. Perhaps sacred. And the punishment of it is an invasion of complexity, a tormenting, forcibly tortuous involution of feeling.[36]

But for the most part he pours forth a flood of rhetorical and superficial generalizations. The subject of the book, 'chance', gives plenty of scope for pseudo-philosophizing:

> And if you ask me how, wherefore, for what reason? I will answer you: Why, by chance! By the merest chance, as things do happen, lucky and unlucky, terrible or tender, important or unimportant; and even things which are neither, things so completely neutral in character that you would wonder why they do happen at all if you didn't know that they, too, carry in their insignificance the seeds of further incalculable chances.[37]

The majority of Marlow's reflections, however, concern women, or rather Woman:

> Man, we know, cannot live by bread alone, but hang me if I

don't believe that some women could live by love alone. If there be a flame in human beings fed by varied ingredients earthly and spiritual which tinge it in different hues, then I seem to see the colour of theirs. It is azure – What the devil are you laughing at? . . . You say I don't know women. Maybe. It's just as well not to come too close to the shrine. But I have a clear notion of *woman*. In all of them, termagant, flirt, crank, washerwoman, bluestocking, outcast and even in the ordinary fool of the ordinary commerce there is something left, if only a spark. And when there is a spark there can always be a flame –.[38]

But Marlow's views on women are generally sardonic, and verging on misogyny.

As to honour – you know – it's a very fine mediaeval inheritance which women never got hold of. It wasn't theirs. Since it may be laid as a general principle that women always get what they want, we must suppose they didn't want it. In addition they are devoid of decency. I mean masculine decency. . . . 'Sensation at any cost', is their secret device. All the virtues are not enough for them; they want also all the crimes for their own. And why? Because in such completeness there is power – the kind of thrill they love most.[39]

Although he also has the 'straightforward' male's awe of the mystery of woman:

. . . the part falling to women's share being all 'influence' has an air of occult and mysterious action, something not altogether trustworthy like all natural forces which, for us, work in the dark because of our imperfect comprehension.[40]

Or,

Flora de Barral was not exceptionally intelligent but she was thoroughly feminine. She would be passive (and that does not mean inanimate) in the circumstances, where the mere fact of being a woman was enough to give her an occult and supreme significance.[41]

The role of woman is so chewed over that it might be regarded as a subsidiary theme of the novel. The lesbian* and

* Conrad never states that she is lesbian, although she is given all the lesbian's most distinctive characteristics. Whether he intended her to be taken for a lesbian is difficult to say.

feminist Mrs Fyne resents the subordinate position of women and demands that they should compete with men as if they themselves were men. When Flora elopes with Anthony she arouses Mrs Fyne's extreme animosity because she has behaved like a woman. Marlow however objects that 'this is not only reasonable and natural, but it is her only chance. A woman against the world has no resources but in herself. Her only means of action is to be what *she* is.'[42] And at another point he sums up what are undoubtedly Conrad's own views on women's predicament:

> As to women, they know that the clamour for opportunities for them to become something which they cannot be is as reasonable as if mankind at large started asking for opportunities of winning immortality in this world, in which death is the very condition of life.[43]

Although *Chance* is the title of the novel, the workings of chance cannot be said to constitute its theme. The action is neither more nor less influenced by chance, or coincidence, than is that of the average novel or the average life; in fact the idea of 'chance' seems to have been superficially grafted on to the action and the frequent emphasis on its influence tends to cheapen the effect of the book. The aptest comment is the quotation on the title-page, which Marwood found for Conrad in Sir Thomas Browne: 'Those that hold that all things are governed by fortune had not erred, had they not persisted there.'[44]

The main theme is once again emotional isolation. Because of the peculiarities of her father's life, and then because of the stigma attached to her through his imprisonment, Flora has been brought up deprived of the usual human bonds. Added to this, the last cruel words of the diabolical Governess deprive her of all sense of her value as a person. Thus, when Anthony declares his love for her she can only reply, 'Nobody would love me. ... Nobody could.'[45] Even when she is Anthony's wife and on board the *Ferndale*, albeit with her father in tow, she is 'under a cloud. ... That sort of darkness which attends a woman for whom there is no clear place in the world hung over her,'[46] while later Marlow speaks of 'that solitude, that moral loneliness, which had made all her life intolerable'.[47]

The corollary of this sense of isolation and inferiority is the difficulty of any contact between herself and others, above all between herself and her husband. With the Goulds in *Nostromo*, Conrad showed he believed that even a relatively normal married couple would passively accept emotional estrangement. But the case of Flora and Anthony was far from normal; Flora's past prevented her from believing that Anthony could ever love her while her behaviour to him and his extreme sensitivity kept him from making the gesture to which she could have responded. Anthony's reticence is compounded of vanity as well as chivalry, and it is clear that Conrad does not regard him as wholly blameless for the false situation, for the failure to 'connect', or to consummate the marriage. Indeed, Flora's appeal to Anthony is very similar to Dounia's appeal to Peter Luzhin in *Crime and Punishment*. Marlow says of Anthony:

> 'The very marks and stamp of this ill-usage of which he was so certain seemed to add to the inexplicable attraction he felt for her person. It was not pity alone, I take it. It was something more spontaneous, perverse and exciting. It gave him the feeling that if only he could get hold of her, no woman would belong to him so completely as this woman.'[48]

But the similarity ends there. Luzhin had a tyrannical nature and wished to dominate Dounia, whereas Anthony's impulse expressed itself in magnanimity. The tragedy was that Anthony scrupulously refrained from asserting his 'rights':

> If Anthony's love had been as egoistic as love generally is, it would have been greater than the egoism of his vanity – or of his generosity, if you like – and all this could not have happened.[49]

It was only when he decided he had failed and 'let her off' her compact that Flora was able to show that she did not want to be let off.

From the manner in which Conrad presents Flora and Anthony, as well as from the titles to the two parts of the novel – 'The Damsel' and 'The Knight' – it is clear that he looked on them, partly at least, as romantic characters, like Freya and Jasper Allen. It might have been expected, therefore, that they would be overwhelmed by tragedy at the moment of the realization of their happiness. Perhaps this had been Conrad's original intention. As it is he compromises curiously between the demands of popular taste and his own inclination. He makes de Barral's attempt to poison Anthony fail and de Barral himself commit suicide (Flora imagines that he has died a natural death). He cannot allow Flora and Anthony to live happily ever after, but he does, rather perfunctorily, give them six years of marriage;[50] then he gratuitously kills Anthony in a collision and the book is neatly rounded off with the disclosure of Powell's frequent visits to Flora in a lonely creek on the Thames estuary and Marlow's prodding them into marriage.

Of all Conrad's novels *Chance* is perhaps the least dependent on a source in his experience* or in his reading. Powell's acquisition of his second-mate's certificate and his difficulties in finding an officer's berth, described in the first chapter of *Chance*, were based on Conrad's own experiences, and Aubry has also suggested that certain scenes on board the *Ferndale* were drawn from the situation on the *Riversdale*; but nothing is known about Conrad's voyage with this ship except that he quarrelled with the Captain and threw up his berth. Except for Franklin, the mate, one of the most delightful and successful characters in the book, and probably Captain Anthony himself, it does not seem that any of the other characters have specific prototypes, although the Fynes are so precisely observed that they may have. Nor does the story itself seem to be based directly on any source, which may account for the book's air of un-

* Devotees of psychological symbolism might, however, care to think about the following: the lonely, isolated Flora, whose father has been in prison, is Conrad; like Conrad, Flora rebels against the life mapped out for her by her guardians and escapes into the arms of Captain Anthony (for Conrad, it is the British Merchant Navy); but in attaining her freedom her father has to be sacrificed (with Conrad it is his father's ideals).

reality. De Barral, the great financier, was a new departure for Conrad. There had of course been several confidence tricksters on the grand scale during the last two decades whose downfall had been dramatic, and Conrad may have had one or more in mind when portraying de Barral. The most notorious of them were Jabez Balfour and Whitaker Wright. Balfour, creator of the Liberator Permanent Benefit Society, was sentenced to fourteen years for fraud in 1895;[51] and Whitaker Wright, architect of the London and Globe Empire, which collapsed at the end of 1900, was sentenced to seven years for fraud in 1904, but committed suicide in the precincts of the Court on hearing the sentence.[52]

Marlow's analysis of de Barral's character and his success puts forward an interesting and plausible theory of that type of man, particularly in his insistence on de Barral's lack of imagination and intelligence, and on his gullibility.[53] But when it comes to the dramatic presentation of de Barral, Conrad fails. For although de Barral's eerie and enigmatic conversations with Powell on the *Ferndale* are effective, he is too shadowy a figure for it to be possible to judge whether anything he does or says is in character or not. The characterization and action are, in general, almost completely lacking in subtlety and the climax is crudely melodramatic, which makes *Chance* the least profound and least satisfying of Conrad's major novels.

(2)

No doubt the steady flow of copy for *Chance* and Pinker's cheques of £3 a thousand words helped to ease relations between the two men. Thus when he had finished *Chance* Conrad must have thought that this would be an auspicious time to end his two-year-old quarrel with Pinker. He went up to London to deliver the last batch of copy and invited Pinker to lunch. Pinker was 'very decent' and the quarrel seems to have been made up; a few days later Conrad wrote to 'My dear Pinker': 'I've carried from our meeting the impression that there is now no misunderstanding between us.'[54] As well as restoring an old friendship Conrad started a new one; this was with a young man named Richard Curle, who had written an appreciation of Conrad's work, particularly *Nostromo*, for a magazine called *Rhythm*.[55] Curle had shown the article to Edward Garnett, and Garnett had passed it on to Conrad, who was pleased with it and anxious to meet its author. According to Curle they first met at the Mont Blanc, a restaurant in Soho where literary men such as Garnett, W. H. Hudson, and Conrad, when he was in London, used to meet for lunch one day a week.[56] This was followed by a visit to Conrad in the country;[57] then came discussions about a book on Conrad's work which Curle was keen to write and Conrad was keen to have written.[58] Thus a friendship was begun which became perhaps the most intimate of Conrad's relationships in his later years.

Another acquaintance Conrad made in 1912 was Joseph Retinger,[59] a Polish patriot of an adventurous disposition; he, too, was to play quite an important part in Conrad's later life.

After he had finished *Chance*, Conrad was as usual prostrated, this time for a fortnight.[60] Then, early in May, he started what he intended to be a short story and also again began reading for his long-planned Mediterranean novel. But the short story grew persistently, developing into the long novel to which he eventually gave the title of *Victory*; the Mediterranean novel was thus once more shelved.[61] Apart from work at the novel he wrote an article on the sinking of the *Titanic*, in its scorching irony reminiscent of his article on 'The Censor of Plays'.

Then at the end of the year he wrote a very un-typical potboiler called the 'Inn of Two Witches'.[62] This is a spooky tale, set in Northern Spain in the time of the Peninsular War. A British naval officer goes in search of his henchman and, while spending the night at an isolated inn, just escapes being murdered by suffocation in a four-poster bed with a false, movable canopy, a fate which has already overtaken his henchman. It is a story more suitable for boys than for adults. In the Author's Note, Conrad mentions that a reviewer had asked whether he had ever come across a tale called 'A Very Strange Bed' in *Household Words*.[63] He says that he did not know the story; but the beds are exactly the same, although the stories are quite different, and it is probable that both writers had come upon the same original account of such a bed.

Although he was able to work quite steadily, Conrad does not seem to have been in very good health during the latter part of this year. He told Pinker at the end of September that his depression was 'awful – awful',[64] and a month later he told Curle: 'I am not very well now and don't come downstairs, though not actually laid up.'[65]

The same state of affairs continued throughout the following year.

Material worries had by no means vanished because, although a lot more money was coming in, much of it had to go towards reducing debts. Conrad's health was again poor, particularly at the end of the summer. At the beginning of August he told Arthur Symons that he had 'been in bed for a week with an abominable attack of gout', and added: 'The worst is that I haven't done any work for a month. No inspiration; a sort of languid feeling all over, and a sensation as if my brain had turned to yeast. Horrid. I must! must!! stick to my desk....'[66] Then, at the beginning of September, he told Pinker that he felt 'absolutely rotten yet',[67] and a week later: 'I am gone so stale all over that I can't trust myself to do what I most desperately mean to do.'[68]

It was in this month that he first met Bertrand Russell, who came down to visit Conrad at Capel.[69] The two men evidently made a profound impression on each other; Russell has described the meeting:

> We talked with continually increasing intimacy. We seemed to sink through layer after layer of what was superficial, till gradually both reached the central fire. It was an experience unlike any other that I have known. We looked into each other's eyes, half appalled and half intoxicated to find ourselves together in such a region. The emotion was as intense as passionate love, and at the same time all-embracing. I came away bewildered, and hardly able to find my way among ordinary affairs.[70]

Later in the month Conrad visited Russell at Cambridge,[71] and during the following years they wrote to each other a number of times. As a mark of friendship and respect, Russell named his son, born in November 1921, John Conrad, wishing Conrad 'to be as nearly his godfather as was possible without a formal ceremony'.[72]

Conrad also saw a certain amount of Perceval Gibbon. They contemplated writing a play together,[73] but nothing came of the project, and there seem to have been few of his friends with whom Conrad did not at some time contemplate writing a play.

Despite his indifferent health, Conrad managed to get through a certain amount of work. In the early part of the year most of his time was taken up with the revision of *Chance*. But once *Chance* was out of the way he plodded on with *Victory* and then ended the year with a flourish in the form of two longish stories, 'Because of the Dollars' and 'The Planter of Malata'.[74] 'Because of the Dollars' tells the story which Conrad had originally set out to tell in what became *Victory*. It is an exciting tale, set in the Malay Archipelago, about a group of rogues who try to rob a humane and kindly ship's Captain, named Davidson, of his cargo of dollars. He is warned by the rather worthless but inoffensive and courageous woman who lives with one of the rogues, and thus foils the plot. But the ringleader, a villainous man without hands, whose prototype Conrad had seen in Sydney in 1879,[75] realizes who has betrayed them and kills the woman. Davidson can never free himself from remorse at the thought that the woman had sacrificed herself for him. It is a good, authentic story, based on personal knowledge, which vividly captures the disreputable element of life in the Eastern seas.

'The Planter of Malata' is a far more substantial and interesting piece of work and is linked with 'Freya of the Seven Isles' in its extreme romanticism. It describes how a young woman, Felicia Moorsom, comes out East to a 'great colonial city'[76] with her father and aunt, in search of a man whom she feels she has wronged. She had been engaged to him when he was suspected of some serious dishonesty and forced to decamp; subsequently it was discovered that he was innocent, and Felicia Moorsom, who had believed in his guilt, decided that she must find him and make redress by marrying him. In the colonial city she meets an enigmatic and out-of-the-ordinary young man, named Geoffrey Renouard, who has a reputation for great enterprise and owns an experimental silk farm on one of the islands. Renouard finds himself rapidly falling in love with Miss Moorsom while she, although remaining loyal to her quest, shows that she is not entirely indifferent to him. The climax comes when Renouard discovers that the man for whom she is looking was his assistant on the island; and Renouard alone knows that the man has just died. He cannot bear the thought that this is the end of Felicia Moorsom's search and that she will now return home; therefore, instead of revealing his knowledge he goes through the farce of taking the Moorsoms to his island ostensibly to meet the man. On the island he reveals the truth to Felicia Moorsom, adding that the man's last words were to curse her; at the same time he makes her a passionate declaration of love, but is rebuffed. Then, as the Moorsoms are leaving the island, he tells Felicia that he will haunt her; and when they have gone he commits suicide by setting out 'calmly to swim beyond the confines of life – with a steady stroke – his eyes fixed on a star!'[77]

The final episode on the island is intensely dramatic and would indeed be melodramatic if Conrad had not succeeded superbly in maintaining conviction. Geoffrey Renouard and Felicia Moorsom have the grandeur, tinged with morbidity, of Webster's characters and there is the same grandiloquent memorability in their language. 'I stand for truth here',[78] proclaims Miss Moorsom; and 'As to giving myself up to anything less than the shaping of a man's destiny – if I thought I could do it I would abhor myself;' while Renouard asserts: 'And yet, Felicia, a woman like you and a man like me do not often come together on this earth.'[79] But although the whole episode is consistently strong, it must be admitted that the imagery is sometimes not very striking or fresh. This is Renouard's declaration of love:

> At a sign from you I would climb up to the seventh heaven to bring you down to earth for my own – and if I saw you steeped to the lips in vice, in crime, in mud, I would go after you, take you to my arms – wear you for an incomparable jewel on my breast. And that's love – true love – the gift and the curse of the gods. There is no other.[80]

It is not surprising that Conrad modestly protests in the Author's Note that 'the task of the translator of passions into speech may be pronounced "too difficult".'[81]

The story has biographical interest as well as literary distinction. Miss Moorsom is a sketch of the unawakened or frigid woman who deals in counterfeit emotions, a forerunner of Rita de Lastaola and Mrs Travers. Professor Moorsom describes his daughter's world:

> There thoughts, sentiments, opinions, feelings, actions too, are nothing but agitation in empty space – to amuse life – a sort of superior debauchery, exciting and fatiguing, meaning nothing, leading nowhere. She is the creature of that circle. And I ask myself if she is obeying the uneasiness of an instinct seeking its satisfaction, or is it a revulsion of feeling, or is she merely deceiving her own heart by this dangerous trifling with romantic images. And everything is possible – except sincerity, such as only stark, struggling humanity can know. No woman can stand that mode of life in which women rule, and remain a perfectly genuine, simple human being.[82]

This sounds very like a portrayal of 'Rita's' world as it may have appeared to the young Conrad in Marseilles; and it may not be too fanciful to suggest that Conrad, after being encouraged by Rita, had taken part in a scene similar to that in which Renouard declares his love to Miss Moorsom, the 'beautiful sphinx'. She recoils slightly 'for she was not fit to hear it – not even a little – not even one single time in her life. It was revolting to her . . .' and she rebuffs him with: 'Assez! J'ai horreur de tout celà,'[83] which recalls Rita's fastidiousness. Perhaps Conrad too had felt bitterly with regard to Rita that he 'had nothing to offer to her vanity',[84] and it may even be significant that Renouard then commits suicide.

(3)

Despite bad health Conrad worked hard at *Victory* for the first half of 1914 and had finished it by the end of June.[85] *Victory* has the same intensely romantic tone as *Chance*, 'Freya of the Seven Isles', and 'The Planter of Malata'; moreover it presents, basically, a similar theme to that of *Chance* in similar terms: emotional isolation and the difficulty of contact between human beings are embodied in the damsel in distress and the chivalrous but excessively reticent knight. But there is no repetition, because Heyst's reticence has a very different cause to Captain Anthony's. Heyst's disillusioned and cynical father had imposed on him a superficial indifference towards life. This was their last conversation:

> 'You still believe in something, then? . . . You believe in flesh and blood, perhaps? A full and equable contempt would soon do away with that, too. But since you have not attained to it, I advise you to cultivate that form of contempt which is called pity . . .'
>
> 'What is one to do, then?' sighed the young man, regarding his father, rigid in the high-backed chair.
>
> 'Look on – make no sound,' were the last words of the man who had spent his life in blowing blasts upon a terrible trumpet which had filled heaven and earth with ruins, while mankind went on its way unheeding.[86]

As a result:

> Heyst was not conscious of either friends or of enemies. It was the very essence of his life to be a solitary achievement, accomplished not by hermit-like withdrawal with its silence and immobility, but by a system of restless wandering, by the detachment of an impermanent dweller amongst changing scenes. In this scheme he had perceived the means of passing through life without suffering and almost without a single care in the world – invulnerable because elusive.[87]

Heyst may indeed intellectually have 'perceived the means', but he had to contend with his 'heart' as well as his 'mind', and *Victory* is the story of how life gradually and ruthlessly strips off his defensive armour, leaving him with the final revelation of the inadequacy of his attitude. For there are dangerous chinks in the armour; just as the other sceptic, Decoud, finds himself, to his surprise, being forced to feel for the agonies of Costaguana, so Heyst is unable to withhold his sympathies when humanity, in the form of Morrison, demands them. When Morrison has poured out his tale of woe: 'The Swede was as much distressed as Morrison; for he understood the other's feelings perfectly. No decent feeling was ever scorned by Heyst.'[88] That starts the break-up of his attitude of detachment. He helps Morrison, not, as Lena suggests, 'for fun', but because 'I suppose the sight of this particular distress was disagreeable to me.'[89] He then finds that he has 'in a moment of inadvertence, created for myself a tie';[90] and 'he who forms a tie is lost. The germ of corruption has entered into his soul.'[91] He becomes involved in Morrison's Tropical Belt Coal Company chiefly in order not to hurt Morrison's feelings. When Morrison dies and the Tropical Belt project ends in fiasco, Heyst feels confirmed in his scepticism. He says to Davidson:

> I suppose I have done a certain amount of harm, since I allowed myself to be tempted into action. It seemed innocent enough, but all action is bound to be harmful. It is devilish. That is why this world is evil upon the whole. But I have done with it! I shall never lift a little finger again.[92]

But he does. Far more than Jim or Razumov, Heyst is portrayed as a passive instrument of fate. After their 'acts' Jim and Razumov both struggle successfully to master their destiny and the battle takes place within themselves; Heyst, on the other hand, seems right up to the climax to be at the mercy of forces outside himself or over which he has no control. Indeed, at one point, Mr Jones dramatically proclaims to Heyst: 'I am a sort of fate.'[93]

Thus although Heyst has been blameless in his dealings with Morrison he becomes a prey to remorse as well as being the victim of the grossest calumnies on the part of Schomberg. His island loses its enchantment and the solitude which he had embraced turns into loneliness.[94] He therefore visits civilization and exposes himself to a second call on his humanity. Confronted with Lena, the damsel in distress, he, in 'the fullness of his heart',[95] whisks her off to supposed safety on his island. But although Heyst is capable of such impulsive action or, more accurately perhaps, is a victim of impulsiveness, and although he gives the impression of being a man of very strong feelings, he is incapable of breaking through his self-imposed detachment. He cannot respond to Lena's frequent attempts to pierce his reserve, and the climax comes when she implores him to 'try' to love her: 'All his defences were broken now. Life had him fairly by the throat.'[96] But whereas Captain Anthony was only too painfully conscious of the imperfections of his relationship with Flora, Heyst, who is, incidentally, 'living with' Lena, is unaware of any shortcomings. He complains: 'I don't even understand what I have done or left undone to distress you like this.' However, despite this obtuseness, Lena is gradually having an effect, for Heyst finds that 'all his cherished negations were falling off him one by one'.[97]

The arrival of the weird trio, 'plain Mr Jones', his 'secretary', Ricardo, and the Caliban-like* creature, Pedro, in search of Heyst's supposed hoard of treasure provides Lena with the opportunity 'to give herself up to him more completely, by some act of absolute sacrifice',[98] to prove her love to Heyst and also her value to him; for hitherto she has believed that her very existence is a figment of Heyst's imagination: 'It seems to me, somehow, that if you were to stop thinking of me I shouldn't be in the world at all!'[99] The supreme task which she sets herself is to wrest Ricardo's knife from him and thus remove the threat to Heyst's life. She succeeds, but is mortally wounded by a bullet fired by Mr Jones and intended for Ricardo. This does not destroy

* *Victory* has several, presumably fortuitous, echoes of *The Tempest*.

her sense of triumph; she tells Heyst that she thanks God 'for having been able to do it – for giving you to me in that way ... all my own at last!'[100] She believes that she has finally won him and, as she dies, imagines that he is

> ready to lift her up in his firm arms and take her into the sanctuary of his innermost heart – for ever! The flush of rapture flooding her whole being broke out in a smile of innocent, girlish happiness; and with that divine radiance on her lips she breathed her last, triumphant, seeking for his glance in the shades of death.[101]

But her 'victory', though absolutely real to her, has no objective reality. At the last moment Heyst still could not commit himself; he could not respond to Lena's cry: 'I've saved you! Why don't you take me into your arms and carry me out of this lonely place?' Instead:

> Heyst bent low over her, cursing his fastidious soul, which even at that moment kept the true cry of love from his lips in its infernal mistrust of all life.*

The most he can do is utter the admonitory lament in the epilogue: 'Woe to the man whose heart has not learned while young to hope, to love – and to put its trust in life!'[102] This indeed is a confession of the failure of his philosophy of detachment, but he cannot profit from his discovered wisdom and performs the conclusive act of renunciation of life by killing himself. Nor, although 'fire purifies everything',[103] could this be described like Jim's death or Razumov's confession as an act of triumphant atonement; it was an act of total despair.

F. R. Leavis has said that the climax in *Victory* lacks the 'finer inevitability' of that in *Nostromo* (and, he might have added, in *Lord Jim* or *Under Western Eyes*):

> It is possible to reflect, on the one hand, that Heyst had shocking bad luck in the coincidence of Jones and Ricardo with Schomberg; and, on the other, that the antithesis of lust in Ricardo and woman-loathing in Jones on which the *dénouement* depends has no irresistible significance in relation to Conrad's main theme.[104]

* *Victory*, p. 406. Despite this F. R. Leavis (*The Great Tradition*, p. 202) claims that 'the "victory" is a victory over scepticism, a victory of life'.

But this is to apply the canons of realism to an essentially non-realistic book. It is true that Heyst's destruction is brought about, superficially, by melodramatic coincidence, as incidentally is Nostromo's, but there is an underlying psychological inevitability which throughout the book builds up to the final overwhelming sense of doom.

Heyst is perhaps the most interesting, and certainly the most complex, character that Conrad created. He comes closest to Henry James's postulate of a consciousness fine enough to record the events and on which 'we can count not to betray, to cheapen or, as we say, give away, the value and beauty of the thing'.[105] And although the subtlety of Heyst's consciousness is by no means fully exploited in the action, it does give *Victory* a depth of suggestion that places it among Conrad's best novels. But Heyst is the only three-dimensional character in the book. Lena has no dimensions at all; she is a shadow, the least convincing of any of Conrad's important women. She reacts merely as the situation demands and there is never any individuality in her words or her actions. Schomberg, within his limitations, is wholly convincing, although he would have been better without the narrator's rather heavy comments on his behaviour; his dealings with Mr Jones and Ricardo are delightfully amusing as are such remarks as 'By heavens, they are desperadoes!'[106] Mr Jones, Ricardo and Pedro are figures of melodrama; as Lena is the flawless heroine, so they are villains without a redeeming quality. At times they become mere abstractions: 'Here they are before you – evil intelligence, instinctive savagery, arm in arm. The brute force is at the back.'[107] This is reminiscent of Hugo, or Balzac at his worst, as in *La Dernière Incarnation de Vautrin*: 'Ces deux hommes, le CRIME et la JUSTICE, se regardèrent.'[108] There is little attempt to present them other than two-dimensionally and there is no sign of that bond uniting them with the rest of humanity which makes even the worst excesses of Dostoevsky's characters so disturbing. One is inclined to agree with Heyst's designation of Mr Jones as a 'morbid, senseless sort of bandit'.[109] Even the imagery which Conrad uses to characterize them is obvious and repetitive; thus Mr Jones is almost invariably described in sepulchral-spectral terms whereas Ricardo is feline or feral.

But in spite of this the trio have about them a certain glamour and even a ghoulish charm. Moreover, like so many of Dickens's characters, they have a quality, underlined by caricature, which makes them more vivid than life. The scenes in which they participate are intensely visualized, while their, and Schomberg's, behaviour is magnified. Thus at one point Schomberg 'ground his teeth so audibly that the other two looked at him in wonder. The momentary convulsion of his florid physiognomy seemed to strike them dumb.'[110] (Even Heyst gnashes his teeth).[111] While at another Mr Jones forgets himself 'to the point of executing a dance of rage in the middle of the floor'.[112]

It may have been a feeling that these characters had too tenuous a connection with reality which prompted Conrad to mention in the Author's Note, at much greater length than usual, their originals, fleetingly glimpsed though they were. He says that he came upon Mr Jones in a little hotel in St Thomas, in the West Indies,

> where we found him one hot afternoon extended on three chairs, all alone in the loud buzzing of flies to which his immobility and his cadaverous aspect gave a most gruesome significance. Our invasion must have displeased him because he got off the chairs brusquely and walked out, leaving with me an indelibly weird impression of his thin shanks. One of the men with me said that the fellow was the most desperate gambler he had ever come across.[113]

Conrad had met 'Ricardo' on a voyage in the Gulf of Mexico, seen 'Pedro' for a brief moment in a hut in some unspecified place and studied 'Lena' in a café in Montpellier. He says little about Heyst, but it may be that he and Falk, different in character though they are, had the same original; they were both Scandinavians, were both in strong disfavour with Schomberg and were both linked with a girl called Lena.

There is also a curious literary source which has been

pointed out by Katherine Haynes Gatch.[114] There can be little doubt that in choosing the name Axel for the hero of *Victory*, Conrad had consciously in mind Villiers de l'Isle Adam's *Axël;* the fact that Conrad had originally called his hero Augustus Berg only reinforces the link because this is very close to Axël's title, Comte d'Auërsperg (or d'Auersburg as it sometimes appears). How far Conrad intended the parallel to go is a moot point; and some of the similarities which Miss Gatch has ingeniously discovered are tenuous.

Probably Conrad had recently read or re-read Villiers de l'Isle Adam's drama – there are resemblances in tone between this and the Geoffrey Renouard–Felicia Moorsom relationship in 'The Planter of Malata' – was stimulated by it and decided that it provided a useful framework for his novel. Thus both Axels have chosen to lead a solitary existence, Axël d'Auërsperg in his remote Black Forest castle and Axel Heyst on his island; both have or have had their mentor preaching a form of renunciation of life, although for very different reasons; both are thought to possess hidden treasure and both are visited by someone from the outside world in search of the treasure. Commandeur Kaspar proclaims:

> Je m'appelle *la vie réelle*.[115]

and Mr Jones announces:

> I am the world itself, come to pay you a visit.[116]

The other intrusion into the solitude of Axël d'Auërsperg is Sara de Maupers, while it is Lena who has broken through Heyst's defences; both Sara and Lena try to persuade the men they love to enter life and both fail, though for different reasons. Sara and Axël drink poison and die in an embrace, because Axël is convinced that they have already in their imagination attained the height of experience: 'L'avenir? – Sara, crois en cette parole: nous venons de l'épuiser. Toutes les réalités, demain, que seraient-elles, en comparaison des mirages que nous venons de vivre?'[117] Lena dies in Heyst's arms convinced of her 'victory' and then Heyst, renouncing life, kills himself.

The two works end on opposing notes, *Axël* on a note of ecstasy, with Sara's affirmation:

> Maintenant, puisque l'infini seul n'est pas un mensonge, enlevons-nous, oublieux des autres paroles humaines, en notre même Infini![118]

and *Victory* on a note of despair. The last word of the novel is, aptly, Davidson's 'Nothing!'

It seems clear from comparison of the two works that Conrad did not intend deliberately to call attention to the parallel or to add any significance to *Victory* by adapting the framework of *Axël.* He needed it to stimulate his own creative process, and no more.

(4)

Thanks to the success of *Chance*, Pinker was able to sell the serial rights of *Victory* for the hefty sum of £1,000 and obtain the very satisfactory advance of £850 on the book rights.[119] Conrad was therefore in a relatively comfortable financial position; and so when his Polish friend, Joseph Retinger, produced an invitation for the whole Conrad family to stay with his wife's parents near Cracow, a town intimately associated with Conrad's past, he felt able to accept. It was a big event: Conrad had not visited Poland for twenty-one years and for his family it was the first visit ever. Moreover he was now returning to Poland as a distinguished man; he had at last reached the position of being a successful as well as an important writer. His visit was therefore in the nature of a triumphal homecoming. In this connection, the thoughts on 'going home' which Marlow expresses in *Lord Jim* are particularly relevant:

> We wander in our thousands over the face of the earth, the illustrious and the obscure, earning beyond the seas our fame, our money, or only a crust of bread; but it seems to me that for each of us going home must be like going to render an account. We return

to face our superiors, our kindred, our friends – those whom we obey, and those whom we love; but even they who have neither, the most free, lonely, irresponsible and bereft of ties, – even those for whom home holds no dear face, no familiar voice, – even they have to meet the spirit that dwells within the land, under its sky, in its air, in its valleys, and on its rises, in its fields, in its waters and its trees – a mute friend, judge, and inspirer. Say what you like, to get its joy, to breathe its peace, to face its truth, one must return with a clear consciousness. . . . You must touch your reward with clean hands, lest it turn to dead leaves, to thorns, in your grasp. I think it is the lonely, without a fireside or an affection they may call their own, those who return not to a dwelling but to the land itself, to meet its disembodied, eternal, and unchangeable spirit – it is those who understand best its severity, its saving power, the grace of its secular right to our fidelity, to our obedience. Yes! few of us understand, but we feel it though, and I say *all* without exception, because those who do not feel do not count. Each blade of grass has its spot on earth whence it draws its life, its strength; and so is man rooted to the land from which he draws his faith together with his life.[120]

The Conrads and the Retingers left Harwich for Hamburg on 25 July 1914.[121] It could scarcely have been a more inauspicious moment; the Austrian Archduke Ferdinand and his wife had been murdered by a Serbian in Sarajevo on 28 June, and on 23 July Austria-Hungary had delivered an ultimatum to Serbia. Few people, however, foresaw where these events would lead. In 'Poland Revisited',[122] written shortly after the trip, Conrad gives a moving account of the family's arrival in Cracow and of his nocturnal walk with Borys, into the Market Square, to look at the familiar landmarks, St Mary's Church and the Florian Gate. It was here that Conrad had lived and been to school during the last years of his father's life; and it was here that he had followed his father's funeral cortège. Conrad took Borys to visit the University and in the Jagellon Library he was shown by the librarian who by an odd coincidence had the same name as himself, Joseph Korzeniowski, manuscripts and letters written by his father which he had imagined to have been lost.

But the present quickly obtruded itself on this communion with the past. On 28 July Austria-Hungary had declared war on Serbia; then on 1 August Germany declared war on Russia and on the following day invaded France. Four years later Conrad described a scene which took place in the hotel among his fellow-countrymen at this time:*

> What produced the greatest impression on my mind was a gathering at night in the coffee-room of my hotel of a few men of mark whom I was asked to join. It was about one o'clock in the morning. The shutters were up. For some reason or other the electric light was not switched on, and the big room was lit up only by a few tall candles, just enough for us to see each other's faces by. I saw in those faces the awful desolation of men whose country, torn in three, found itself engaged in the contest with no will of its own and not even the power to assert itself at the cost of life. All the past was gone, and there was no future, whatever happened; no road which did not seem to lead to moral annihilation.

It was natural enough that Conrad's first sympathies should have been with Austria.[123] Britain was not yet in the war and it was not certain whether she would come in, or on which side, whereas Austria was the least oppressive of the three powers ruling over Polish territory and, moreover, was fighting against Russia, which for Conrad, as for most Poles, was the prime enemy; indeed the Polish Legion was soon to win distinction on the side of Austria. Thus when Conrad eventually arrived home, Britain by then being in the war, he still hoped that a reasonable peace settlement could quickly be reached between her and Austria-Hungary.[124] Before leaving Poland he had put on paper his thoughts about the outcome of the war. He envisaged a limited German victory but with Britain still retaining control of the sea. At the ensuing peace conference he hoped that Britain would support the Austro-Hungarian interests as a counter-

* 'First News', *Notes on Life and Letters*, p. 178. As might be expected Conrad's attempt to recall how his own activities fitted in with world events was confused. For instance, he set his arrival in Cracow on 1 August and wrote of Austrian mobilization as having been announced the following day whereas it was in fact announced on 31 July.

balance to the power of Germany. He of course had no opinion of Russia, assuming that she would be totally defeated and thinking that she might well become in the future an ally of Germany.[125]

But at the moment the prospect of getting home was bleak. The peaceful old university city had been transformed into a jostling military depot. No one knew what would happen next, and a journey across Europe would be hazardous; moreover Jessie was very lame and John Conrad had a temperature. Conrad therefore decided not to risk the journey and took the family to stay with Mrs Charles Zagórska, a relation by marriage, who lived in a villa at Zakopané, a resort in the Carpathians, a hundred or so kilometres from Cracow.

In Zakopané the Conrads were cut off from Britain except through the American embassy in Vienna, and had soon run out of money. Finally, in early October, Conrad decided that they must try to get home; Austria had been at war with Britain since 12 August and even the easygoing Austrians were not likely to allow British nationals freedom of movement indefinitely. The Conrads left Cracow by train for Vienna, where they had to break the journey for five days while Conrad grappled with an attack of gout. Then, with the help of the American ambassador, Frederic C. Penfield, they reached Milan on 20 October.[126] From there Conrad cabled Pinker for money and, when it arrived, set off with the family for Genoa. They left Genoa on 25 October on a Dutch mail-boat and arrived in England on 3 November.[127] Back at Capel, Conrad immediately went to bed for ten days with severe gout.

When he had recovered he wrote to the Galsworthys describing the journey:

> I was really too ill to write before. You must know that I started on our journey from Austria with an already gouty knee. It was a propitious moment which I dared not miss; the great rush of German and Austrian re-inforcing troops was over for a time and the Russians were falling back after their first advance. So we started suddenly, at one in the morning, on 7 October in a snow-

storm in an open conveyance of sorts to drive thirty miles to a small railway station where there was a chance of finding something better than a horse-truck to travel in with *ma petite famille*. From there to Cracow, some fifty miles, we sat eighteen hours in a train smelling of disinfectants and resounding with groans. In Cracow we spent untold hours sitting in the restaurant by the railway station, waiting for room in some train bound to Vienna. All the time I suffered exquisite tortures – Ada will understand. We managed to get away at last and our journey to Vienna was at comparatively lightning speed: twenty-six hours for a distance which in normal conditions is done in five hours and a half. But in Vienna I had to go to bed for five days. Directly I could put foot to the ground again we made a fresh start, making for Italy, which we entered through Cormons, the better Pontebba route being closed.

Borys was very good, showing himself vigorous and active in looking after his crippled parents and his small brother. Jessie went through it all with her usual serenity. During the sea-passage from Genoa to Gravesend (in a Dutch mailboat) I managed to hobble about the decks but felt beastly ill all the time. In London I felt even worse. On reaching home I just rolled into bed and remained there till yesterday, in a good deal of pain but mostly suffering from a sort of sick-apathy which I am trying now to shake off. [15 November 1914, *L.L.*, II, p. 163]

(5)

The war years were, for the most part, a drab and unpleasant period for Conrad. He was of course too old and unfit to take an active part, which was undoubtedly galling for a man of his temperament; while from early 1916 until the end of the war he went through the agony of having Borys at the front in France. He also found it hard to work and his feelings were probably summed up in a letter to Mrs Wedgwood: 'It seems almost criminal levity to talk at this time of books, stories, publication. This war attends my uneasy pillow like a nightmare. I feel oppressed even in my sleep and the moment of waking brings no relief, on the contrary.'[128] Thus, as he no longer had to write to live – his income for 1917 was over £2,000, although he published no new book that year[129] – he produced very little during the war.

In early 1915 he started *The Shadow-Line*,[130] which he did not finish until the end of the year,[131] although it was only about 40,000 words long. As far as the events are concerned it is a piece of fictionalized autobiography – he described it to Pinker as 'not a story really but exact autobiography'[132] – recounting his experience with his 'first command', which he had originally chosen as the title. Amid the world upheaval this was the only type of writing that he felt inclined to; he told Colvin a couple of years later: 'I discovered that this was what I could write in my then moral and intellectual condition; tho' even *that* cost me an effort which I remember with a shudder. To sit down and invent fairy tales was impossible then.'[133]

The story contains none of the emotional and moral ambiguities with which Conrad was usually concerned. The subject is the test of character presented to a man by the command of his first ship, and the young captain is given the simplified extrovert emotions which a war-time atmosphere demands (it would be quite wrong to suppose that they corresponded with Conrad's own at the time of taking over the *Otago*):

> I discovered how much of a seaman I was, in heart, in mind, and, as it were, physically – a man exclusively of sea and ships; the sea the only world that counted, and the ships the test of manliness, of temperament, of courage and fidelity – and of love.[134]

In mood and intention *The Shadow-Line* comes somewhere between 'Youth' and *Typhoon*. The simple virtues, to which Conrad attached such importance, are extolled – Ransome is a most moving embodiment of fidelity to an ideal of conduct – and the test which confronts the young captain is in psychological terms straightforward; the only problem is whether he will have the strength of mind and body to triumph. He does so, and *The Shadow-Line* is, with *Typhoon*, the most unalloyedly positive of Conrad's stories. It is also one of the very few stories to carry what amounts to an explicit, unambiguous moral or message (*Victory* is the other obvious example). Captain Giles sums up at the end:

> 'A man should stand up to his bad luck, to his mistakes, to his conscience, and all that sort of thing. Why – what else would you have to fight against? . . . You will learn soon how not to be faint-hearted. A man has got to learn everything – and that's what so many of those youngsters don't understand.'[135]

It is an outstandingly well-told tale in crisp, vivid prose, although the seemingly inevitable 'inconceivable terror' and 'inexpressible mystery'[136] have to make their appearance. The tension and eeriness are excellently maintained without resorting to the supernatural; Conrad was understandably exasperated when 'that donkey Lynd' reviewed it as a 'GHOST STORY'.[137] It is only in Burns's mind that the supernatural plays a part, although the young captain catches himself almost succumbing to Burns's delusions. Burns himself is a brilliantly portrayed character and provides some fine comic relief when he cuts his flaming red beard or appears on deck straight from his sickbed:

> Yet, all of a sudden, I fell clean over something, landing full length on my hands and face.
>
> It was something big and alive. Not a dog – more like a sheep, rather. But there were no animals in the ship. How could an animal – ? It was an added and fantastic horror which I could not resist . . .
>
> I could see It – that Thing! The darkness, of which so much had just turned into water, had thinned down a little. There It was! But I did not hit upon the notion of Mr Burns issuing out of the companion on all fours till he attempted to stand up, and even then the idea of a bear crossed my mind first.
>
> He growled like one when I seized him round the body. He had buttoned himself up into an enormous winter overcoat of some woolly material, the weight of which was too much for his reduced state.[138]

Burns's demand, too, that the crew should laugh is splendidly macabre:

> Mr Burns cut his derisive screeching dead short and turned upon them fiercely, yelling:
>
> 'Aha! Dog-gone ye! You've found your tongues – have ye? I

thought you were dumb. Well then – laugh! Laugh – I tell you. Now then – all together. One, two, three – laugh!'[139]

The following year Conrad wrote only two short stories, 'The Warrior's Soul'[140] and 'The Tale',[141] both rather war-time products. The first is a story of the Retreat from Moscow, the hint for which Conrad had found in Philippe de Ségur's *Memoirs*.[142] A Russian officer is the narrator and he tells of the peace-time rivalry in Paris between a sophisticated French officer and a young Russian, named Tomassov, who is on the staff of his country's envoy, for the favours of a beautiful *dame d'esprit*. It was on the eve of Napoleon's war with Russia, and the French officer at the desire of the woman gallantly warns Tomassov that Napoleon intends to arrest the Russian envoy and his staff; this warning enables them to escape to Russia in time and Tomassov tells the officer in gratitude: 'You may command my life.'[143] Then, during the Retreat from Moscow, Tomassov takes the officer prisoner without at first recognizing him because his face was 'frost-bitten . . . full of sores . . . framed in bits of mangy fur'.[144] The officer makes himself known and begs Tomassov to fulfil his debt of honour and kill him because his suffering during the Retreat has taken away all faith and courage. Tomassov, whose nickname is 'humane', could scarcely have a more appalling demand made of him. But after great hesitation he shoots the French officer; it is 'one warrior's soul paying its debt a hundredfold to another warrior's soul by releasing it from a fate worse than death – the loss of all faith and courage'.[145] It is a dramatic story and far from negligible – Cunninghame Graham placed it beside Hudson's 'El Ombú' and 'Wandering Willie's Tale'[146] – although, as Conrad himself confessed, 'it isn't really *done*'.[147] As in 'The Duel', however, Conrad shows how the events of that period fired his imagination. He describes the retreating column of the remnants of the *Grande Armée*:

'A crawling, stumbling, starved, half-demented mob. It issued from the forest a mile away and its head was lost in the murk of the fields. We rode into it at a trot, which was the most we could get out of our horses, and we stuck in that human mass as if in a moving bog. There was no resistance. I heard a few shots, half a dozen perhaps. Their very senses seemed frozen within them. I had time for a good look while riding at the head of my squadron. Well, I assure you, there were men walking on the outer edge so lost to everything but their misery that they never turned their heads to look at our charge. Soldiers!'[148]

In 'The Tale' Conrad turned to a contemporary subject, The Great War. 'The Tale' is almost an exact antithesis to *The Shadow-Line*, with 'The Warrior's Soul' standing midway between; it is as if Conrad had found that the further from the war his subject was the simpler and more straightforward the treatment must be, and the closer he came to the present moment the more complex. The issue in 'The Tale' is exceptionally ambiguous: it is known that neutral merchantmen are feeding German submarines with fuel, and the commanding officer of a British ship (who tells the 'tale') comes upon a floating fuel container, and then a suspicious neutral merchant ship whose captain claims to have lost his bearings in the fog. The commanding officer first suspects then becomes emotionally convinced that the neutral ship has been guilty of this particularly despicable form of commerce, involving 'the murderous stealthiness of methods and the atrocious callousness of complicities that seemed to taint the very source of men's deep emotions and noblest activities'.[149] When he boards the merchantman and talks to the captain, the commanding officer becomes convinced that his suspicions were correct. He can find no tangible evidence of nefarious activities, but 'the air of the chart-room was thick with guilt and falsehood braving the discovery, defying simple right, common decency, all humanity of feeling, every scruple of conduct ...'[150] and there was an 'atmosphere of murderous complicity ... denser, more impenetrable, more acrid than the fog outside'.[151] Because of his emotional certitude and because there is no evidence to convict the ship the commanding officer, whose 'passion for truth, his horror of deceit, his humanity'[152] is asserted in the story, decides to put to the test the captain's claim that he is lost. He insists that the captain shall set a course which will run him on some rocks. The captain does so and the ship sinks with all hands. Thus the captain had spoken the truth to that extent; he was lost. But this did not prove that he was otherwise innocent; and the commanding officer concludes: 'I don't know whether I have done stern retribution – or murder.... I shall never know.'[153]

These two stories added up to less than fifteen thousand words; and, as he told Garnett, Conrad was finding 'work, properly speaking, impossible'.[154] Then he must have been feeling somewhat isolated from the rest of the world and its preoccupations; his very close friend, Arthur Marwood, died in May, which affected him deeply, while other friends were involved in activities connected with the war. No doubt, therefore, he welcomed diversions. One occurred in the form of a 'yum-yum'[155] young woman from Arizona called Jane Anderson, although vaguely married to Deems Taylor. She was an enterprising journalist with the ability to captivate the famous, who also managed to get to France to see something of the war. Here she met Borys, and Conrad caustically commented to Pinker: 'If he must meet a "Jane" it's better he should meet her at nineteen than at twenty-four.'[156] On her return from France she spent some time with the Conrads, convalescing from her experiences. She also stayed with Jessie at Deal while Conrad was away on an Admiralty assignment. It is clear from Jessie's garbled account,[157] part of which seems to have been clumsily cut, that Conrad himself fell for her and the episode ended in a minor storm.

Lord Northcliffe had had a part in Jane Anderson's introduction, and at this period the Conrads saw quite a bit of him. Conrad seems to have been attracted by him, but to have thought him astonishingly obtuse,[158] whereas Jessie was won by his talk about his mother.[159]

Conrad had also been making determined efforts to take some active part in the war which culminated in a scheme, sponsored by the Admiralty, to visit certain British ports and observe the various naval activities. Thus in September he went off to Lowestoft and joined the minesweeper *Brigadier* on one of her patrols. Also, without telling Jessie, he made a flight from the Royal Naval Air Station at Yarmouth,[160] which was an action of some daring for a man of his age and state of health at this stage of aeronautical development. Then, at the beginning of October, he was sent to Granton Harbour near Edinburgh. There, in vile weather, he went in a vessel engaged in mending torpedo-net defences. He wrote to Jessie: 'Before long the ship was fairly washed away and blown off from her station. . . . Her captain, a lieut., said to me, "I don't think we can do any good work today." I said: "For God's sake, let's get out of this." And we got out accordingly. I was never so pleased in all my sea-life to get into shelter as I was on Friday at about 5 p.m.'[161] Then he joined a 'Q' Boat, H.M.S. *Ready*, commanded by a Captain Sutherland and, while on board, sent a staccato letter to Pinker:

8th Nov. 1916, at sea
By patrol boat

Dear Friend,

All well.
Been practice-firing in sight of coast.
Weather improved.
Health good.
Hopes of bagging Fritz high.
Have dropped a line to Jessie.
Don't expect to hear from me for ten days.

Ever yours,

P.S. Give my love to Eric [Pinker's son] when you write. [*L.L.*, II, p. 179]

Back at Capel again Conrad still could not settle down to work. He told Dent, his publisher: 'It isn't so much the war itself, as the course it has taken which is the cause of that unsatisfactory state.'[162] Moreover, for the first half of the new year he was almost continuously laid up with gout.[163] Thus, apart from writing a short preface for a book of Garnett's on Turgenev, he did little more than show strong interest in a dramatization of *Victory* by a man named Macdonald Hastings, which had been prompted by H. B Irving. Conrad's ambitions were in fact once more turning to the stage; he considered dramatizing other novels such as *Under Western Eyes* and planned to collaborate with Hastings on an original play, about a faked old master.[164] Then, in August, he began a new story in which he saw dramatic possibilities. He told Pinker that he wanted to 'launch out single-handed on the stage' and continued:

> The subject is in that very story I am writing now. Of course I am keeping the story within the limitations of magazine fiction. And it's rather a nuisance to have perceived its dramatic possibilities of which the greater part must be kept out, as much too good for the *Metropolitan Magazine*. And the play won't be easy. To put a *femme galante* (not exactly in that character but as an ardent Royalist) and her peasant sister, very hard-headed, very religious and very mercenary, on the stage will not be an easy matter.[165]

This was the story which became *The Arrow of Gold*. He had originally planned that it should take the form of 'Selected Passages from Letters'[166] to a woman whom the hero had known thirty-five years ago when they were both 'not only very young but I may say youthful' and with whom he subsequently realized that he had been in love.[167]

In November the Conrads had to go to London for nearly three months so that Jessie's knee could be given treatment.[168] In spite of gout Conrad was able to link up with old friends like Galsworthy and Garnett as well as making new acquaintances.[169] He also managed to work at *The Arrow of Gold* in the mornings, apparently for the most part by dictation: 'with groans and imprecations.... You can imagine what sort of stuff that is. No colour, no relief, no tonality, the thinnest possible squeaky bubble. And when I've finished with it, I shall go out and sell it in a market place for twenty times the money I had for the *Nigger*, thirty times the money I had for the *Mirror of the Sea*.'[170] He made good progress and had finished the novel on 4 June 1918.[171]

For its subject and setting Conrad drew on his youthful experiences when he was based on Marseilles during the middle eighteen-seventies. He called *The Arrow of Gold* a 'study of a woman'[172] and a young man's 'initiation ... into the life of passion'.[173] But he takes up a position of prostrate adoration before Rita de Lastaola, which makes any form of 'study' impossible. He envelops her in a cocoon of sleazily romantic imagery. Her face is like 'some ideal conception of art', her smile 'inscrutable' or 'mysterious', her eyes 'enigmatic' and 'inherited from the dawn of ages', her voice 'seductive' and of course she is pervaded with the scent of violets. She had 'that something secret and obscure which is in all women. Not the gross immobility of a Sphinx proposing roadside riddles but the finer immobility, almost sacred, of a fateful figure seated at the very source of the passions that have moved men from the dawn of ages.'[174] With repetitive and cliché-ridden portentousness he tries to give Rita 'something of the women of all time', but almost wholly fails to give her any individuality at all. She was 'afraid of living flesh and blood'[175] and it is living flesh and blood that she lacks.

The young man, M. George, is a callow youth, drawn on conventional lines, whose reactions and behaviour are too banal to rouse interest. And of the other characters Therèse is good as far as she goes, Blunt is a stock romantic figure – 'He paused. His dark eyes flashed fatally, away from us, in the direction of the shy dummy; and then he went on with cultivated cynicism'[176] – and Mills only justifies his existence with his wise words at the end of the book.

Perhaps Conrad was too closely involved with the events to enable him to judge the quality of presentation. Certainly the construction of the novel seems to have been adversely affected by the amount of material which he had to draw on; he told Eric Pinker that there were 'many facts in her [Rita's] story which are merely indicated in the book (and some that are not in it at all) which could be used for the purposes of the action'[177] of a proposed play. This may account for the various loose ends; Conrad does not seem to have given enough care to deciding what was relevant to his purpose and there are passages such as the journalist's visit to Rita, M. George's audience with de Villarel, and all the references to the mysterious Azzolati, which contribute nothing to the development or understanding of the action.

Writing of *The Arrow of Gold*, Conrad told Colvin that he had 'never been able to read *these* proofs in cold blood. . . . There are some of these 42-year-old episodes of which I cannot think now without a slight tightness of the chest – *un petit serrement de coeur.*'[178] But, surprisingly, the book almost totally fails to convey genuine emotion. Except for two excellent scenes, one between George and Rita[179] where Rita temporarily takes on some individuality and the other when Ortega is trying to get into Rita's room[180] which is a masterpiece of macabre humour, the tone of the book is thoroughly synthetic.

This failure of imagination could be put down to declining powers, but, in view of the quality of the writing in *The Rover*, it was more probably due to a lack of concentrated care. Conrad wrote or dictated *The Arrow of God* quite quickly and was perhaps ready to accept the first words that occurred to him, instead of searching for the *mot juste*. Then in an attempt to cover this weakness he resorted to set pieces, or lapsed into overwriting and melodrama (many of the 'heightening' adjectives and rhetorical sentences were written into typescript). *The Arrow of Gold* contains one of the worst passages in Conrad:

> Woman and the sea revealed themselves to me together, as it were: two mistresses of life's values. The illimitable greatness of the one, the unfathomable seduction of the other working their immemorial spells from generation to generation fell upon my heart at last; a common fortune, an unforgettable memory of the sea's formless might and of the sovereign charm in that woman's form wherein there seemed to beat the pulse of divinity rather than blood.[181]

The frequent straining after effect produces passages like:

With closed eyes I imagined her to be lost in thought, removed, by an incredible meditation while I clung to her, to an immense distance from the earth. The distance must have been immense because the silence was so perfect, the feeling as if of eternal stillness. I had a distinct impression of being in contact with an infinity that had the slightest possible rise and fall, was pervaded by a warm, delicate scent of violets and through which came a hand from somewhere to rest lightly on my head. Presently my ear caught the faint and regular pulsation of her heart, firm and quick, infinitely touching in its persistent mystery, disclosing itself into my very ear – and my felicity became complete.[182]

Then there are times when he surrenders all attempt at adequate expression as in the phrase: 'an infinity of pangs too complex for analysis'.[183] While a sense that the presentation is becoming a little jaded may account for such plunges into melodrama as:

A dreadful order seemed to lurk in the darkest shadows of life. The madness of that Carlist with the soul of a Jacobin, the vile fears of Baron H., that excellent organiser of supplies, the contact of their two ferocious stupidities, and at last, by a remote disaster at sea, my love brought into direct contact with the situation: all that was enough to make one shudder – not at the chance, but at the design.[184]

But it is not enough to disguise the failure to express genuine feeling.

(6)

As soon as *The Arrow of Gold* was finished the Conrads had to move to London for several weeks so that Jessie's knee could be operated on; and while in London Conrad himself was ill, first with 'flu then with gout.[185] Although the operation was considered a success Jessie continued to feel a lot of pain and the Conrads again went to London in October so that Jessie could have further treatment. Borys Conrad was given compassionate leave to be at hand during Jessie's operation;[186] then, back at the front, he was gassed and shell-shocked during the Second Army's advance in October, and was in hospital in Le Havre when the Armistice was signed.[187]

Although Conrad was of course greatly relieved that the war was over he was apprehensive about the future. On Armistice Day he wrote to Walpole:

> I cannot confess to an easy mind. Great and very blind forces are set free catastrophically all over the world. This only I know, that if we are called upon to restore order in Europe (as it may well be) then we shall be safe, at home too. To me the call is already manifest, – but it may be declined on idealistic or political grounds. [11 November 1918, *L.L.*, II, p. 211]

As a conservative European, Conrad distrusted President Wilson's idealistic policies and feared that 'the full price' would have to be paid for the United States' entry into the war. 'There is an awful sense of unreality,' he said, 'in all this babel of League of Nations and Reconstruction and production of Commodities and Industrial arrangements, while Fisher prattles solemnly about education and Conciliation Boards are being set up to bring about a union of hearts while the bare conciliation of interests is obviously impossible. It is like people laying out a tennis court on a ground that is already moving under their feet.' He was outraged by the invitation to the Bolsheviks to send delegates to the Peace Conference:

> One asks oneself whether this is idealism, stupidity or hypocrisy? I do not know who are the individuals immediately responsible, but I hope they will get bitten. The whole paltry transaction of conciliating mere crime for fear of obscure political consequences makes one sick. In a class contest there is no room for conciliation. The attacked class cannot save itself by throwing honesty, dignity and convictions overboard. The issue is simply life and death, and if anything can save the situation it is only ruthless courage. And even then I am not certain. One may just as well defy an earthquake.[188]

About Poland Conrad claimed to have no illusions. She would 'have to pay the price of some pretty ugly compromise'. Here at least he was wrong and his prophecy was not fulfilled until after the Second World War. It is not surprising that Conrad should have been pessimistic about Poland's future because although a free Poland was a declared war aim of all the leading Allies, the Poles had too often been the victims of power politics not to be sceptical of promises. However, when the Bolshevik armies invaded Poland, reaching the outskirts of Warsaw, and were then crushingly defeated by the Poles, the Allies realized the danger of the new Russia and the advantages of a strong Poland. Thus Polish independence was temporarily assured.

As a British subject Conrad always insisted that his loyalties were primarily to Britain and although united to Poland by the strongest of bonds he was loath to proclaim his views on the Polish question publicly. However, his friend Joseph Retinger, who was intensely active in the struggle for Polish independence, had persuaded him in 1916 to write a 'Note on the Polish Problem', not for publication but to be shown to various political leaders. This 'Note' asserted the value of 'Polonism' as an 'advanced outpost of Western civilization'[189] and suggested that Poland should become an Anglo-French protectorate. Then in April 1919, again urged by Retinger, Conrad wrote an article for the *Fortnightly*,[190] based on a pamphlet of Retinger's, which was a vigorous eulogy of Poland and condemnation of the cynical treatment meted out to her by all other nations. Later, when the Poles were fighting the Bolsheviks, he enthusiastically supported them in public and in private.

[XIV]

Last Years

DESPITE the domestic and political upheavals Conrad was now able to work and in the autumn of 1918 once more took up *The Rescue*.[1] Although he had periodically tried to get to grips with it he had not been able to make any appreciable headway since he had laid it aside in 1899. But, prodded perhaps by the sense that his life was nearing its end – 'after sixty, one begins to count the days'[2] – he made a determined effort to finish the book; as he subsequently said: 'It struck me then that my time was running out and I wanted the deck cleared before going below.'[3] He told Pinker in July that he was reading the manuscript for the twentieth time at least and that he must try to catch on to the old style as much as possible.[4] Then in September he referred to 'the mood for *The Rescue*, which I have been cultivating most earnestly for the last six weeks and have in a measure attained now'.[5] This time he succeeded and on 25 May 1919, twenty-three years after he had begun the novel, 'the last words of *The Rescue* were written'.[6] But even then the task was far from complete. *The Rescue* had started to appear serially in *Land and Water* on 30 January; thus, with an imposed time-limit, Conrad had not been able fully to revise the text as he sent it in and was forced, after a pause, to spend a further three months extensively correcting the *Land and Water* text for book publication.[7]

When he sold the original manuscript of *The Rescue* to Thomas J. Wise, the collector, Conrad suggested that this and the final text 'side by side may form a literary curiosity showing the modifications of my judgement, of my taste, and also of my style during the twenty years covering almost the whole writing period of my life'.[8] This is true, although it should be borne in mind that Conrad's literary development is not represented by a constantly ascending graph but by one that curves off towards the end of his life; thus the first draft of *The Rescue* is closer to the romantically nostalgic mood of his later years than it is to that of his middle period when his powers were at their height. This may partly explain why he could make no headway with *The Rescue* for so many years and then was finally able to finish it.

A few examples will show the lines along which he worked. For a start an introductory set-piece of portentously inflated atmosphere is almost entirely scrapped and a far more factual and concrete one substituted. Then the frequent passages of excessive flocculence are drastically sheared. There are two examples of this on the first page after the introduction. The printed text has:

> As far as the eye could reach there was nothing but an impressive immobility.[9]

In the manuscript the sentence read (the words that do not appear in the printed text are in italics):

> As far as the eye could reach there was nothing but an *op*pressive immobility, *an immobility so perfect as to become something distinct and appaling* [*sic*], *something incomprehensible and solid ringed in by the hard glitter of a cloudless horizon.*[10]

Then the printed text has the sentence:

> To the south and east the double islands watched silently the double ship that seemed fixed amongst them forever, a hopeless captive of the calm, a helpless prisoner of the shallow sea.[11]

In its original form it read:

> To the south and east the double islands watched silently the double ship that seemed fixed amongst them forever, a hopeless captive of the calm, *as if destined forever to remain within sight of their dark-green slopes – of their sombre and rocky shores: a hopeless captive of the calm in the wicked silence of burning days and of nights heavy-scented and poisonous that carry the perfumed breath of tropical lands to the angry and* helpless prisoner of *a narrow sea.*[12]

It is perhaps worth adding an admittedly extreme example which even a parodist might envy:

Everything was as it had been perhaps but the world was not the same. It had changed, like the blue serenity of the sea is changed by the impalpable touch of a fiery sunset into a purple plain of menacing aspect, into a brooding place for a mighty force, when a spirit of sorrow, passion and violence is felt ascending from the unruffled quietude of the waves, the indefinable truth of the sea, the immaterial emanation of its tenebrous soul. Thus with the vain sound of words, with the restless sensations, with the bewilderment of men, with the haphazard succession of events. They remained what they had ever been – the visible surface of life *lying* open in the sun to the conquering tread of an unfettered will. Yesterday they could have been discerned clearly, mastered and despised; but now another power had come into the world, and had cast over them all the wavering gloom of a dark and inscrutable purpose.[13]

Even after the passage had been heavily cut it still obscures rather than illuminates. In fact Conrad was not as ruthless as he might have been and the first half of *The Rescue* has much more purple than the second.[14]

However, Conrad largely overcame the difficulties of completing a novel laid aside so long before and produced a work of considerable merit. Indeed it is noteworthy how close Conrad stuck to his original conception of the story which he had outlined to Blackwood in 1897. The setting and the tone of the book are unashamedly romantic. There is the Shore of Refuge with the discordant groups of Malayans who had promised to help Lingard pay his debt of honour to the fugitive Rajah Hassim and restore him and his sister Immada to their country: Belarab, ruler of the Shore, man of peace, 'with his glamour of asceticism and melancholy together with a reputation for severity'.[15] Daman, 'the supreme chief of sea-robbers, with a vengeful heart and the eyes of a gazelle'; Sentot, 'the sour fanatic with the big turban'; Tengga, 'fat, good-tempered, crafty, but ready to spill blood on his ambitious way and already bold enough to flaunt a yellow state umbrella at the very gate of Belarab's stockade';[16] and of course the touching Hassim and Immada whose 'high birth, . . . warlike story, . . . wanderings, adventures and prospects had given them a glamour of their own'.[17] They are a magnificent group although, and this is not intended to be a sneer, they probably have a greater impact on the imagination of a boy than of an adult. Indeed Conrad had originally told Garnett: 'I want to make it [*The Rescue*] a kind of glorified book for boys – you know.'[18] Lingard himself, with his fine red beard, his 'eyes, as if glowing with the light of a hidden fire',[19] his manly simplicity, his strength and chivalry, has a touch of Captain Justice in the *Modern Boy*. But although a legitimately romantic figure he is presented in a wholly adult manner and is involved in an adult situation.

More, perhaps, than in any of his other novels Conrad relies, at least in the last two parts, on what is implied rather than what is explicitly stated. Once again he emphasizes that it is his intention to create a psychological and not a 'what-happens-next?' interest by breaking the time-sequence, at the beginning of Part V and on page 430;* but the first of these is clumsy compared with his manipulation of time in the earlier novels. Then an atmosphere of unreality is deliberately created through the characters' frequent reference to the dream-like quality of their experience, or, more revealingly, in Mrs Travers's assertion at one point in the action:

> 'It seemed to me that I was walking on a splendid stage in a scene from an opera, in a gorgeous show fit to make an audience hold its breath. You can't possibly guess how unreal all this seemed, and how artificial I felt myself. An opera you know . . .'

She and Lingard continue with a discussion of opera and Lingard, who has only been to one in his life, says 'I assure you that of the few shows I have seen that one was the most real to me.'[20]

* There are other time-shifts earlier in the book but they are caused by the need to pick up threads of the narrative and are not artificially created for a deliberate effect.

Unlike *Romance, The Rescue* has a firm moral pivot. The interest of the action hinges on the conflict in Lingard's mind between his pledge to Hassim and his obligation to save the lives of the people from the stranded yacht; an unenviable predicament becomes hopelessly vitiated when Lingard finds himself falling in love with Mrs Travers, the wife of the owner of the yacht. She is one of Conrad's few convincing female portraits. She is a woman of spirit and independence who has been forced to adopt a conventional, artificial veneer through being married to a self-important bore (Mr Travers would have been an excellent minor character if Conrad had not at moments unconsciously lapsed into caricature but there are nonetheless some brilliant touches). In her 'primitive', 'pagan' nature of which Mr Travers complains she recalls Rita in *The Arrow of Gold* and she is described in similar terms:

> She is a representative woman and yet one of those of whom there are but very few at any time in the world. Not that they are very rare but that there is but little room on top. They are the iridescent gleams on a hard and dark surface. . . . It is for such women that people toil on the ground and underground and artists of all sorts invoke their inspiration.[21]

Like Rita she is at first emotionally unawakened and when she meets Lingard she recognizes in him 'something real at last'.[22]

In their rapidly growing attraction towards each other Mrs Travers is held back by convention and background while Lingard finds that her power over him is paralysing his capacity to think or act and leading him to betray Hassim. A series of unforeseen events and mischances brings on the climax and, although Lingard is not directly responsible for the blowing up of the *Emma* which causes the death of Hassim and Immada, he rightly feels that his indecision has been the most important factor in the final tragedy.

Thus although he succeeds in rescuing the people of the yacht he 'seemed to have lost his soul in the attempt'.[23] He is 'a prey forever to infinite remorse and endless regrets'.[24] Mrs Travers, too, realizes her responsibility, above all for not giving Lingard the ring entrusted to her which was Hassim's final appeal, although Lingard in his magnanimity insists that if she had given him the ring 'it would have been just the same'[25] because he was 'dumb, deaf, and robbed of all courage'.[26] She is determined, for her part, that 'the uttermost farthing'[27] of retribution shall be paid and, before the yacht sails, goes at Lingard's request to meet him at night on the sandbank, with her husband's knowledge. She has felt Lingard's 'capacity for passion'[28] and even wonders whether she will ever go back to the yacht. But Lingard makes no attempt to retain her because 'now the world is dead'.[29] It is a melancholy but a moving book. Its mood of defeatism and world-weariness is even more pronounced than that of *Victory*, which does at least contain a positive admonition. Although there are similarities between Lingard and Heyst, 'a man of the last hour',[30] who finds himself unable to cope with fate or the world, Heyst conveys an awareness of missed opportunity, whereas Lingard only shows himself conscious of failing powers, helplessly buffeted by the onslaught of events which he can no longer control; once the master of his fate he has become a victim.

The sources of *The Rescue* have been touched on in connection with *Lord Jim*. There are a number of passages in *The Rescue* which show that Conrad used Keppel's *Expedition to Borneo* and Mundy's *Borneo and Celebes* to supply himself with background, local colour, and some details of the plot.[31] Above all Hassim and Immada with their faithful retainer, Jaffir, are obviously based upon the story of Muda Hassim, Bedrudin, their sister, and the slave Japar. Both brothers had been set upon by their enemies and had defended themselves gallantly. When Muda Hassim was cornered he shot himself after trying to blow himself up in a boat. Bedrudin's end was similar; when he was surrounded by his enemies he gave his signet ring to Japar to take to Rajah Brooke, whose present it had been, then blew up himself and his sister in his house.[32] When Conrad took up *The*

Rescue for the second time he went back to *Brookiana* in order to recapture the atmosphere, and read at least one more recent addition to the corpus.[33]

Apart from *Brookiana*, Conrad drew on the many stories which were current when he was in the East. He gave a glimpse of this wealth of material in a letter to Blackwood, outlining of the scope of the novel:

> I shall tell of some events I've seen, and also relate things I've heard. One or two men I've known – about others I've been told many interminable tales. The French brig *Amitié* was in 1866 stranded on the coast and attacked by some vagabonds belonging to a certain Haji Saman. I had the story from the captain of the brig. In 1848 an Englishman called Wyndham had been living for many years with the Sultan of Sulu and was the general purveyor of arms and gunpowder. In 1850 or '51 he financed a very lively row in Celebes. He is mentioned in Dutch official documents as a great nuisance – which he, no doubt, was. I've heard several versions of his end (occurred in the sixties) all very lamentable. [6 September 1897]

He goes on to describe Lingard himself (who has been dealt with in connection with *Almayer's Folly*). Captain Tom Lingard of *The Rescue* and his splendid old ghost, Jörgenson, are no doubt composite figures; and Conrad refers in the introductory pages to the 'adventurers' on whom they were based. Wyndham whose career may well have contributed to that of 'Lord Jim' makes a brief appearance under his own name in the first draft of *The Rescue* and crops up in two books by Spenser St John, one of Rajah Brooke's lieutenants. He is described as 'a short broad-shouldered fellow' who had been an officer under Cochrane; 'his had been a life of adventure; and if rumour did not belie him, all was fish that came to his net'.[34]

(2)

For the rest of 1919, after finishing *The Rescue*, Conrad was only able to do odds and ends of work: a number of Author's Notes for the collected edition of his works which

Heinemann and Doubleday were going to publish, and a short piece on Stephen Crane[35] for the *London Mercury*. Then some time in the autumn he started to work on a dramatization of *The Secret Agent* but had to drop this temporarily at the beginning of December in order to revise *The Rescue*.[36]

The Conrads had been forced to leave Capel House in March and had temporarily taken a furnished house near Wye called Spring Grove.[37] Conrad disliked the place and this was no doubt one of the reasons that prevented him from writing. In October the Conrads moved into Oswalds, a handsome, medium-sized Georgian house at Bishopsbourne, a few miles south-east of Canterbury, where they remained until Conrad died. Jessie had had great trouble from her knee throughout the year and the surgeon, Sir Robert Jones, decided that she must have another operation. It took place in Liverpool, Sir Robert's base, at the beginning of December and the Conrads were home again before the end of the year.[38] But it was not a success; Jessie had to have two more operations in the spring[39] and was laid up for most of 1920. But she was well enough for Conrad to be able to take her to Deal at the beginning of September for a three weeks' holiday, although she had more trouble with her knee when she got back.[40] Conrad's references to Jessie at this time are almost always prefixed by 'poor'.

The Conrads were at least partially relieved of one problem. They were now comparatively rich, debts to Pinker and others had been at last paid off, and both *The Arrow of Gold* and *The Rescue* had made substantial sums, the first earning £1,200 and the second £3,000 in serial rights alone,[41] while the British and American collected editions of his works were in the offing. Moreover Pinker's sale of film rights in the books had brought in about £4,000 (Conrad even wrote a film scenario of 'Gaspar Ruiz' in collaboration with Pinker).[42] But Jessie's leg was demanding enormous expenditure and the extra money was allowing Conrad to give way a little more to his innate extravagance. He told Curle:

'I am spending more than I ought to – and I am constitutionally unable to put on the brake, unless in such a manner as to smash everything.'[43] Thus he was never to be entirely free of worry about money; at the end of 1922 he was even considering living part of the year in France to escape being taxed so heavily.[44] The Conrads were leading quite a full social life with visits from old and new friends, among them Wise, 'holding us spellbound by the flow of his utterance', and Hugh Walpole who had been seeing a lot of Conrad in recent years and had written a short appreciative study of his work.

The year 1920 was again a thin one for work. At the beginning of the year Conrad had worked intensively on the revision of *The Rescue*, which he finished in bed.[45] He then returned to the *Secret Agent* play, which he had finished by the end of March,[46] dramatized 'Because of the Dollars'[47] and finished the rest of the Author's Notes for the collected edition.[48] In April he told Galsworthy: 'I am less crippled now, but I feel shaky and mentally tired – and truly there is little reason for the last. It isn't toil. I don't toil now. I wonder how much longer I'll be able to spin.'[49] And he wrote to Curle in May, that 'I can get no prose of any kind out of myself.'[50] Thus, although he was working on the background for the long-mooted Napoleonic novel in the British Museum in June,'[51] he could make little headway with the actual writing and his plaint to Rothenstein at the end of the year, that 'I have done nothing for more than a year,'[52] was broadly true. To Garnett he wrote: 'I have done nothing – can do nothing – don't want to do anything. One lives too long. Yet cutting one's throat would be too scandalous besides being unfair to other parties. Xmas greetings.'[53]

Neither Jessie nor Conrad was well and they decided to go to Corsica in the new year for three months 'in search of "climate" '.[54] They left on 23 January, travelling by car, accompanied as far as Rouen by Borys and from Rouen to Lyons by Aubry, Conrad's future biographer.[55] They stayed at the Grand Hotel in Ajaccio, where they were joined by Pinker, his wife and daughter. But as seems to have been invariably the case with the Conrads' holidays abroad this one did not fulfil their hopes. The weather was bad at first – 'Cold. Wet. Horrors'[56] – and Conrad disliked the hotel. He wrote to Aubry that he was feeling 'nerveux, exaspéré, ennuyé. . . . Nous n'avons pas fait d'excursions – Il fait assez froid dans l'après-midi. – l'hôtel est détestable. Les Corses sont charmants (je veux dire le peuple), mais les montagnes me donnent sur les nerfs avec leurs chemins qui tournent, tournent en corniche indéfiniment. – On a envie de hurler.'[57] And a month later to Garnett: 'I am neither the better nor the worse for being here – in health, that is. I would perhaps [have] done some work if I had stayed at home. But God only knows! Head empty. Feelings as of dead – except the feeling of my unalterable affection for you.'[58]

Miss Hallowes, Conrad's secretary, came out to join the party at the hotel because Conrad planned to work at his Napoleonic novel, which he was to call *Suspense*. But although he did some background reading about Napoleon on Elba, he did very little writing. All that he is known to have achieved is a short note to an anthology of Hugh Walpole's prose.[59] The Conrads returned to Britain at the beginning of April.

During the rest of 1921 Conrad continued to work at *Suspense* but was several times held up by bad health. Then, on 9 December, he told Pinker that he had written 5,500 words of a short story. But this, like *The Secret Agent* previously, seems to have run away with him because it became a full-length novel, *The Rover*, which, again despite several bouts of illness, he had finished by the end of June of the following year.[60]

The Rover is the last novel that Conrad completed, and although it does not aim at the profundity or range of his major works it is a worthy swan song. It is concerned primarily with the simple, 'masculine' virtues of duty, honour, and sacrifice in their civic context of patriotism; it only touches on more complex issues in the case of Arlette's experience and these are not followed up. The central figure, partly based once more on Dominic Cervoni, is named Peyrol; he is an elderly master gunner in the French Navy and an ex-member of the Brotherhood of the Coast, a piratical organization operating in the Indian Ocean. His life 'in the opinion of any ordinary person might have been regarded as full of marvellous incidents (only he himself had never marvelled at them)';[61] and now he has withdrawn with his booty to an isolated farmhouse-inn on the coast near Toulon, where his 'instinct of rest had found its home at last'.[62] But there is a strange set-up at the farm. It is owned by a beautiful girl, Arlette, with white cheeks, coral lips, black eyes, and raven-black hair, whose royalist parents were murdered by sansculottes in the revolutionary blood-bath and who herself took part in the orgy of killing, first unwillingly then, to her horror, willingly. From this she was extricated by one of the sansculottes, Citizen Scevola Bron, who took her back to her parents' inn, where he has since remained with her and her old aunt Catherine.

Scevola, who recalls Ortega in *The Arrow of Gold* with his combination of hysterical savagery and pathetic ineffectuality, is portrayed with all Conrad's scorn for the scum of a revolution. He is a 'creature of the universal blood-lust of the time',[63] is nicknamed a 'drinker of blood',[64] and was implicated in the murder of Arlette's parents; it is repeatedly asserted that he is a 'poor creature', and he used to be the 'butt of all the girls'.[65] Answering Garnett's pained protest at this apparent guying of the revolutionary spirit Conrad said: 'To me Scevola is not revolutionary, he is, to be frank about it, a pathological case more than anything else.'[66] He confessed that he had had a 'momentary vision' of a 'formidable' Scevola, a worthy antagonist of Peyrol, but that he deliberately shut his eyes to it. Thus the contrast between the two men is implied. Peyrol is:

> the only man who had nothing to do with the Revolution – who had not even seen it at work. The sincere lawlessness of the ex-Brother of the Coast was refreshing. That one was neither a hypocrite nor a fool. When he robbed or killed it was not in the name

of the sacred revolutionary principles or for the love of humanity.[67]

But it is not developed.

The situation at the farm is further complicated by the visits of a lieutenant in the French Navy, named Réal, who is later entrusted with the important task of arranging that bogus dispatches should fall into the hands of the British blockading fleet in order to mislead its admiral as to the intentions of the French fleet in Toulon. On a previous visit to the farm he has realized with horror that he is in love with Arlette, the girl who in her aunt's opinion is 'fit for no man's arms',[68] and she with him. 'Honour, decency, every principle forbade him to trifle with the feelings of a poor creature with her mind darkened by a very terrifying, atrocious and, as it were, guilty experience.'[69] He decides that the way out is to allow himself to be killed or captured by the British while carrying the despatches in Peyrol's tartane.

But Réal has had to confide his plan to Peyrol in order to get hold of the tartane, and the old sea-bandit has privately decided to do the task himself. His patriotic instincts have been aroused;[70] moreover Réal would leave behind him a broken-hearted Arlette whereas he would be missed by no one – although there are hints of a more than flirtatious relationship with Catherine and a more than avuncular attitude towards Arlette, while the village cripple and the simple-minded Michel have both been revivified by his kindness. Thus just before Réal is due to sail Peyrol gets rid of him and takes out the tartane himself. He solves the problem of Michel by taking him on the tartane and, by a piece of luck, also manages to take Scevola along too, as a captive, thus ridding the world of a worthless piece of human dross. The ruse succeeds and Peyrol, as he has intended, is killed during the capture of the tartane by the British. By his heroic action Peyrol has deceived Admiral Nelson (who comes into the last pages of the book) and has enabled Réal and Arlette to consummate their love:

It was as though the rover of the wide seas had left them to themselves on a sudden impulse of scorn, of magnanimity, of a passion weary of itself. However come by, Réal was ready to clasp for ever to his breast that woman touched by the red hand of the Revolution; for she, whose little feet had run ankle-deep through the terrors of death, had brought to him the sense of triumphant life.[71]

John Lehmann has suggested a fascinating parallel between Peyrol and the other wanderer, Odysseus, who returned at last to Ithaca;[72] and this, whether intended or not, enriches the evocative power of the book. Undoubtedly there are symbolical overtones to the figure of Peyrol, the man of action, of courage and loyalty, who has come home to enjoy his last days in peace, but who is ready to answer an unexpected call of patriotism and self-sacrifice without complaint, although he is 'not sick of life'.[73]

Peyrol's fate is beautifully expressed in the lines from Spenser which Conrad chose for the title-page:

> Sleep after toyle, port after stormie seas,
> Ease after warre, death after life, does greatly please.

The writing shows no decline in power. The landscape of Escampobar is portrayed with Cézanne-like strokes:

> There were leaning pines on the skyline, and in the pass itself dull silvery green patches of olive orchards below a long yellow wall backed by dark cypresses, and the red roofs of buildings which seemed to belong to a farm.[74]

and Conrad, who never overburdened his stories with detail, describes aspects of the Provençal background which he loved, with delightful minuteness. The well of the farm is not merely a well but is 'encircled by a low wall of stones and topped by an arch of wrought iron on which a wild fig-tree had twined a slender offshoot'.[75] The church which Arlette visits is described with equal care:

> She pushed open the little gate with the broken latch. The humble building of rough stones, from between which much mortar had crumbled out, looked as though it had been sinking slowly into the ground. The beds of the plot in front were choked with weeds, because the abbé had no taste for gardening.[76]

Finally, in contrast, the book ends with a sweep of serene dignity:

> The blue level of the Mediterranean, the charmer and the deceiver of audacious men, kept the secret of its fascination – hugged to its calm breast the victims of all the wars, calamities and tempests of history, under the marvellous purity of the sunset sky. A few rosy clouds floated high up over the Esterel range. The breath of the evening breeze came to cool the heated rocks of Escampobar; and the mulberry tree, the only big tree on the head of the peninsula, standing like a sentinel at the gate of the yard, sighed faintly in a shudder of all its leaves, as if regretting the Brother of the Coast, the man of dark deeds, but of large heart, who often at noonday would lie down to sleep under its shade.[77]

The subject and mood of *The Rover* do, however, suggest a writer who is reaching the end of his life. As Aubry pointed out, this was the first time in all Conrad's works that the principal character is a sailor 'who longs for rest, who no longer wishes to sail'.[78]

Conrad had probably come upon the suggestion for the framework of the plot of *The Rover* in his reading for *Suspense*. He mentions in a note in Wise's copy that 'the first notion of this story originated in the reading of Napoleon's dispatch to the admiral commanding in Toulon in 1804'; and it is of course a historical fact that the Toulon fleet gave Nelson the slip.

With *The Rover* finished he was still unable to make much progress with the big novel. There are frequent references to it in his correspondendence during the next two years and, according to Curle, he was optimistically discussing its development the day before he died.[79] But these references are usually to his inability to come to grips with it.

The last two years of Conrad's life were rather melancholy. He was constantly feeling ill, physically and mentally, and death was creating gaps among his friends and acquaintances. W. H. Hudson died in August 1918 and Northcliffe in August 1922, on which Conrad commented to

Garnett: '... Strangest still to think that I had been more intimate with Northcliffe than with Hudson. Funny world this.'[80] But what had affected him much more was Pinker's death in New York on the night of 8 February. He wrote to Doubleday a few days after Pinker died:

> I need not tell you how profoundly I feel the loss of J. B. Pinker, my friend of twenty years' standing, whose devotion to my interests and whose affection borne towards myself and all belonging to me were the greatest moral and material support through nearly all my writing life.
>
> During the years of the war our intimacy had become very close. For the last two years he was very frequently staying in our house and I learned more and more to appreciate in him qualities which were not perhaps obvious to the world, which looked upon him mainly as a successful man. [19 February 1922, *L.L.*, II, p. 266]

Some years before, Conrad had emphasized to Quinn the strong bond between the two men:

> Those books owe their existence to Mr Pinker as much as to me. For fifteen years of my writing life he has seen me through periods of unproductiveness, through illnesses, through all sorts of troubles. ... The fact remains that Pinker was the only man who backed his opinion with his money, and that in no grudging manner, to say the least of it. [15 July 1916]

Pinker was not a man of outstanding intellect and seems to have had no literary appreciation. But literary appreciation is often a handicap among publishers and agents and he had the qualities common to the most successful men in this sphere: a flair for sensing talent before it is generally recognized, coupled with the courage to back his judgement financially. Thus, at his death he was one of the most important figures on the business side of the literary world, who had handled the work of the leading novelists in Britain, among them Henry James, Galsworthy, Crane, Compton Mackenzie, and Arnold Bennett.

Conrad naturally let Eric Pinker continue to handle his literary affairs. The toughest immediate task for him was to negotiate the performance of Conrad's dramatization of *The Secret Agent*. After various delays and vicissitudes the play was taken on by J. Harry Benrimo and performed on 2 November at the Ambassadors Theatre with Miriam Lewes as Winnie Verloc, H. St Barbe West as Mr Verloc, and Russell Thorndike as Ossipon.

This was Conrad's second attempt at the stage, his first having been *One Day More*, which was performed without much success in 1905. The first night of a play is apt to be a much greater ordeal for the author than the publication date of a novel; the test is harsher and more concentrated and the verdict may be immediately lethal. Thus, despite his literary fame, Conrad showed himself subject to the misgivings and concern of an untried author; in a long letter to Eric Pinker protesting against the idea of putting on the play in July and August he wrote: 'My fear is that the play may sink unhonoured and unsung, which morally speaking would be a great disaster for me,'[81] and, when this scheme had been dropped: 'I discover in myself, rather to my surprise, an extreme interest in the production.'[82] In fact he was in a sanguine mood, generally, about the stage and again brought up the possibility of creating plays out of *The Arrow of Gold* and *Under Western Eyes*.[83] When the date of the first night was getting close he confessed to Aubry 'une extraordinaire irritation dont je souffre à propos de cette maudite pièce',[84] and although he attended several rehearsals, including the dress rehearsal, he decided that he could not face the first night. Jessie therefore went alone, but he came to London with her, having agreed to an interview in an hotel with a young admirer named Mégroz while the performance was on. Mégroz has recorded Conrad's 'intense excitement' and how 'from time to time he would leave the smoke-room where we sat and inquire at the office for a message, presumably a message from the Ambassadors Theatre'.[85]

The play was not well received by the critics or the public and was taken off on 11 November. *The Times*, which praised the acting, politely summed up, perhaps, the general verdict: 'Mr Conrad is a great novelist, but not yet a great dramatist.'[86] It is a bad play and shows that Conrad had little sense of the stage, although he would doubtless have written a much better play if he had been without the straitjacket of the novel. He seems to have tried to work in as much of the novel as possible; the result is a bewildering number of minor characters who confuse the action and do not leave enough room for the development of the major characters or of the central situation: the relationship between Mr Verloc, Winnie, and Stevie. The ironical approach which gave some unity to the novel is absent and the play therefore falls into fragments, while the rivalry between Heat and the Assistant Commissioner is fully portrayed and appears even more irrelevant here than it did in the novel. Even the dialogue is not always as convincing as that in the book and is at times clumsy or uncolloquial.

(3)

For some time F. N. Doubleday, Conrad's American publisher, had been pressing him to visit the United States and Conrad had eventually accepted an invitation to come and stay with him in the spring at his house on Oyster Bay, Long Island. Little of interest happened between the performance of *The Secret Agent* and Conrad's trip to the United States. He did some work on *Suspense* and wrote a long introduction to Thomas Beer's life of Stephen Crane. But his health was far from good. He told Eric Pinker in early April that 'the only thing I couldn't stand would be "pace". I must go slow',[87] and confessed to Sir Robert Jones two days before leaving: 'As to this voyage, I start on it without enthusiasm, not because I doubt getting a good reception in the U.S. and probably deriving a certain benefit materially from the visit, but simply because I do not feel quite fit for it – in myself.'[88]

He sailed from Glasgow on the *Tuscania* on 21 April. Her captain was David Bone, a brother of Muirhead Bone, the artist, who was also a passenger and whose cabin communicated with Conrad's. Conrad knew them both; he was thus among friends and was frequently entertained by the captain during the voyage. He clearly enjoyed his position as a distinguished passenger and experienced seaman and in a letter written on board was able to boast to Jessie: 'Water smooth. Wind east. Ship making only 11 knots since 7 o'clock as the starboard engine has been stopped on account of some small trouble. I know but the passengers don't.'[89] Although a gouty wrist and lumbago made him feel seedy he managed, before arriving at New York, to write an article for the *Evening News* which was entitled 'My Hotel in Mid-Atlantic';[90] here he expressed the contempt of a man who had served for many years under sail for an 'unpleasantly unsteady imitation of a Ritz Hotel'.[91]

Conrad was now at the height of his reputation and one of the most famous living authors in Britain and the United States. His visit was thus an important event, and he described his arrival to Jessie, or rather:

> I will not attempt to describe to you my landing, because it is indescribable. To be aimed at by forty cameras held by forty men that look as if they came on in droves[?] is a nerve-shattering experience. Even Doubleday looked exhausted after we had escaped from that mob – and the other mob of journalists.
>
> Then a Polish deputation, – men and women (some of these quite pretty) – rushed me on the wharf and thrust enormous nosegays into my hands. Eric nobly carried two of them. Mrs Doubleday took charge of another. I went along like a man in a dream and took refuge in Doubleday's car. [4 May 1923, *L.L.*, II, p. 307]

He had been inundated with invitations, offers of help and appeals from friends and admirers, but he was determined to keep the visit as private as possible. He refused to lecture, partly because, due to an ailment, his voice was liable to give out and partly because he was not anxious for the general public to know what a strong foreign accent he had.[92] He was, however, persuaded to give a talk and a reading from *Victory* to a gathering of about two hundred people at the house of Mrs Curtiss James, a fashionable hostess. He described the evening in a letter to Jessie:

> I may tell you at once that it was a most brilliant affair, and I would have given anything for you to have been there and seen all that crowd and all that splendour, the very top of the basket of the fashionable and literary circles. All last week there was desperate fighting and plotting in the N. York society to get invitations. I had the lucky inspiration to refuse to accept any payment; and, my dear, I had a perfect success. I gave a talk and pieces of reading out of *Victory*. After the applause from the audience, which stood up when I appeared, had ceased I had a moment of positive anguish. Then I took out the watch you had given me and laid it on the table, made one mighty effort and began to speak. That watch was the greatest comfort to me. Something of you. I timed myself by it all along. I began at 9.45 and ended exactly at 11. There was a most attentive silence, some laughs and at the end, when I read the chapter of Lena's death, audible snuffling. Then handshaking with 200 people. It was a great experience. [11 May 1923, *L.L.*, II, p. 309]

Although he kept clear of public engagements Conrad was heavily entertained to lunches and dinners and met a wide variety of people, among them Colonel House and Paderewski. In his state of health it must have been a strain and he wrote to Borys:

> I have seen a good many 'smart' and important people, of whom Colonel House was the most interesting and Mrs Curtis[s] James the most 'smart'. . . . All this is not unpleasant but it is not exactly enjoyable . . . not from any fault in the people, but simply because I have lost my power of enjoyment in strange surroundings and in novel conditions. [6 May 1923]

During the last half of his visit Conrad did a tour of Boston and New England. He sailed on 2 June on the *Majestic*; the Doubledays, with that immense generosity of spirit which is characteristic of Americans, came to England on the same boat, apparently with the main purpose of looking after him during the voyage.

When Conrad arrived in England he was met by a domestic bombshell: Borys was married. He had married secretly just before Conrad left for America. Jessie had been told and had then been faced with the unpleasant problem of whether or not to tell Conrad; she had decided, doubtless very wisely, not to jeopardize the whole trip and to keep her knowledge to herself. She has described Conrad's violent reaction when she broke the news:

> I had the habit of calling him 'boy' when I wished to be extra friendly. 'Boy dear – Borys is married.' – Joseph Conrad started up in bed, gripping my arm with cruel force. 'Why do you tell me that, why don't you keep such news to yourself?'

Then after an interval:

> 'I suppose you are certain of what you have told me?'
>
> Somewhat surprised I answered at once, 'Quite', and proceeded to explain the means I had taken to verify the news directly he had started for Glasgow. He interrupted me with scant ceremony. 'I don't want to know anything more about it. It is done, and I have been treated like a blamed fool, dam'.'[93]

Conrad was evidently deeply wounded, but he was a very devoted father and a generous-minded man. A couple of days after hearing the news he was arranging with Eric Pinker for an allowance to be paid to Borys:

> Marrying is not a crime and one cannot cast out one's son for that. . . . I . . . am not anxious to see his wife but I want to recognise his married status in some way or else it would be a complete break. [11 June 1923]

Nor was it long before Borys was asked to bring his wife to visit Oswalds.[94]

For the rest of 1923, and indeed up to the time that he died, Conrad was fighting against almost perpetual bad health. He managed to write a couple of articles, one for *Blue Peter* on the *Torrens,* the other for the *Daily Mail* entitled 'Christmas Day at Sea'[95] and a five thousand word preface for J. A. Hammerton's *Countries of the World;*[96] but although he told Eric Pinker in July that he had 'plunged into *Suspense*'[97] he was soon complaining that the novel was making no headway[98] and it is clear that he did not feel fit enough to tackle it seriously.

In October a figure from the past cropped up. Hueffer had become editor of a new literary periodical the *transatlantic review*, which had just been set up in Paris with the backing of John Quinn and Stella Bowen, Hueffer's mistress, and was asking contributors to the old *English Review* to produce something for the new venture. Among them he wrote to Conrad, from whom he had been virtually estranged since 1909, although he had at infrequent intervals written to Conrad on one pretext or another and received a civil reply. Conrad decided not to contribute an article, but wrote to Hueffer recalling the days of the *English Review*:

> The mere fact that it was the occasion of you putting on me that gentle but persistent pressure which extracted from the depths of my then despondency the stuff of the *Personal Record* would be enough to make its memory dear ...

and went on:

> Unlike the Serpent (which is wise) you will die in your original skin. So I have no doubt that the *Review* will be truly Fordian – at all costs. [13 October 1923, Yale]

Hueffer asked Conrad if he might quote this letter in the *transatlantic review*, and Conrad expanded it for him with a passage recalling the hectic editing of the first number of the *English Review* at Someries.[99]

Then a month later Hueffer produced another request. He had unearthed from the *English Review* a piece of collaboration between himself and Conrad, entitled *The Nature of a Crime* and printed under the pseudonym of Ignatz von Aschendrof, which he wanted to reprint in the *transatlantic review*. Conrad gave his permission grudgingly:

> *The Nature of a Crime.* I forgot all about it so completely that I mistrusted your statement till I turned up the old *E.R.*s. ... If you think it advisable to dig up this affair, well, I don't see how I can object. I looked at it and it seemed to me somewhat amateurish; which is strange, because that is not *our* failing separately or together. [10 November 1923, Yale]

Hueffer then wanted to publish this piece in book form and persuaded Conrad to write a preface to it. But he resisted Hueffer's attempt to use the negotiations over *The Nature of a Crime* as a pretext to renew the former intimacy. He described to Eric Pinker an 'interview' with Hueffer:

> We met as if we had seen each other every day for the last ten years. . . . As we talked pleasantly of old times I was asking myself, in my cynical way, when would the kink come . . . [4 February 1924]

Then three days later he said that Hueffer 'wants to be friendly in personal relations with me. In fact, *entre nous*, too friendly, but as to that I will say nothing more here.'[100] Hueffer himself must have been in a curious state of mind. Conrad describes him as 'suffering from the idea that everybody in the world has insulted him'[101] and later, when the agreement for *The Nature of a Crime* was being drawn up:

> *This stipulation* . . . is inserted in order to conciliate the swelled-headed creature who seems to imagine that he will sweep all Europe and devastate Great Britain with an eventual collected edition of his own works. I humour that strange illusion being anxious to have the matter settled. [1 May 1924]

(4)

In November there took place the sensational sale of John Quinn's collection of manuscripts and books at the Anderson Galleries in New York. By far the most important section of the collection was the manuscripts of Conrad's work which Quinn had been buying off him for the last thirteen years. The fact that Conrad's fame was now at its height coupled with the publicity gained from his recent visit to the United States convinced Quinn that now was the moment to sell; it must also be added in fairness to him that he probably realized that he had not long to live. The Conrad items fetched phenomenal prices; the highest sum paid was $8,100 for the complete manuscript of *Victory*, perhaps because this book had been chosen by Conrad for his reading at Mrs Curtiss James's; then came *Under Western Eyes* with $6,900, *Chance* with $6,600, and *Almayer's Folly* with $5,300. But perhaps more remarkable than these outstanding prices for what were after all outstanding collector's items were the prices paid for smaller items; the manuscript of a mediocre story like 'The Informer' fetched $1,700, of the *Titanic* article $425, while a totally unimportant four-page manuscript of an article 'My Best Story and Why I Think So' fetched $300.[102] There is no question that these were peak prices; items bought by dealers were not easy to dispose of and some remained in their hands for many years.

Conrad commented sardonically on the sale to Doubleday:

> All of you who went must have had a tense sort of evening at that sale. Was the atmosphere vibrating with excitement, or, on the contrary, still with awe? Did any of the bidders faint? Did the auctioneer's head swell visibly? Did Quinn enjoy his triumph lying low like Brer Rabbit, or did he enjoy his glory in public and give graciously his hand to kiss to the multitude of inferior collectors who never, never, never, dreamt of such a coup? Well, it is a wonderful adventure to happen to a still living (or at any rate half-alive) author.
>
> The reverberation in the press here was very great indeed; and the result is that lots of people, who never heard of me before, now know my name, and thousands of others, who could not have read through a page of mine without falling into convulsions, are proclaiming me a very great author. And there are a good many also whom nothing will persuade that the whole thing was not a put-up job and that I haven't got my share of the plunder. [20 November 1923, *L.L.*, II, p. 324]

He told Aubry that he reckoned Quinn had made 1,000 per cent on what he had paid him for the manuscripts.[103] But there is no justification for criticizing Quinn on this point. Conrad was not a popular author when Quinn started to buy his manuscripts and there was apparently no rival collector to push up the prices, whereas now there were several very rich and avid ones; therefore, although it is impossible to judge precisely, Quinn's prices may have been fair. Quinn had, however, apparently promised Conrad to keep the manuscripts together as a collection[104] and it is a pity that he did not do so.

Conrad had described himself as 'half-alive' in his letter to Doubleday, and, although he had been well enough in September to take John to Le Havre to fix him up with a French family in order to learn the language,[105] he was soon ill again and in November was so bad that his heart showed signs of being affected.[106] On 20 December he told Bennett: 'I have had a beastly time of it for the last month. Too much pain to think, too much pain to read – and almost to care. However, that is over apparently'[107] – and in the new year: '*Entre nous* I feel as if I were fighting my Verdun battle with my old enemy. It isn't that the symptoms are unusually severe, but it goes on and on. . . . I begin to wonder whether I have sufficient reserves.'[108]

1924 brought little respite, although in February he was able to do some work on *Suspense* and wrote a preface for a volume of his *Shorter Tales*.[109] Towards the end of March he told Elbridge Adams that 'all this year – up to three weeks ago – I have not been well at all. Now I am better and am doing some work, slowly.'[110] At the same time he was sitting to Epstein, who had come down to stay at a nearby pub to do a bust of him at Muirhead Bone's instigation. Epstein was a great admirer of Conrad who proved a 'good sitter', and the result was a powerful piece of work, in a different class from the various other portraits of him, although its qualities are on the surface emphasizing, perhaps inadvertently, the sea captain at the expense of the writer. Conrad himself, who had been reluctant to sit, was delighted and told Adams: 'It is really a magnificent piece of work. . . . It is nice to be passed to posterity in this monumental and impressive rendering.'[111] But although the visit was such a success, Epstein has, in his autobiography, drawn a gloomy picture of Conrad's condition at the time:

He was crippled with rheumatism, crotchety, nervous, and ill. He said to me, 'I am finished'. There was pathos in his pulling out of a drawer his last manuscript to show me that he was still at work. There was no triumph in his manner, however, and he said that he did not know whether he would ever finish it. 'I am played out', he said, 'played out.'[112]

Conrad struck the same note to Gide at the end of May: 'Voilà bientôt quatre ans que je n'ai fait rien qui vaille. Je me demande si c'est la fin? Peut-être.'[113]

A few days before this letter he had declined a knighthood offered him by Ramsay MacDonald.[114] There is no evidence for the calumny that he refused this because it was offered by a Socialist prime minister. It seems more probable that, like Galsworthy, he thought it inappropriate for an artist to accept such honours and that he was influenced by Galsworthy's own refusal of a knighthood a few years previously.

Conrad was not only having to worry about his own health; Jessie's leg had again been causing her a lot of pain and another operation was decided on, this time in a nursing-home in Canterbury on 13 June.[115] While Jessie was away Conrad was again ill and on 4 July he wrote to Ernest Dawson: 'I feel (and probably look) horribly limp and my spirits stand at about zero. . . . I begin to feel like a cornered rat.'[116]

Jessie was allowed out of the nursing-home on 24 July but had to remain in bed at home.[117] Curle arrived for the week-end on the night of Friday 1 August and found Conrad already in bed but cheerful and apparently well, although he had had a heart attack a few days previously. The following morning he discussed with Curle the unfinished *Suspense* and an article which he was writing on legends, and Curle reports him as saying: 'My mind seems clearer than it has been for months and I shall soon get hold of my work again.'[118] Later in the morning he and Curle set out in the car to look at a house which he was thinking of taking, but during the drive he had another heart attack and had to return before he was able to show Curle the house. Back at Oswalds he went to bed and suffered continued spasms of pain. The doctor suspected nothing serious; that evening the

Borys Conrad family and John Conrad arrived for a Bank Holiday visit which had already been arranged. Conrad had a bad night, but seemed a little better in the early morning, and Jessie, who was in the next room, remembered him having called out to her at about six: 'You Jess, I am better this morning. I can always get a rise out of you.'[119] At eight-thirty he was dead.[120]

The funeral took place on 7 August at St Thomas's Roman Catholic Church in Canterbury, when the city was festooned with gaiety for the Cricket Week. Old friends, as well as members of the family, came to the final leave-taking; there were Aubry, the Cliffords, Curle, the Dawson brothers, Garnett, Cunninghame Graham, the Wedgwoods; and there was Count Edward Raczyński, representing the Polish Minister.[121]

On his tombstone was inscribed:

Joseph Teador [*sic*] Conrad
Korzeniowski
Born December 3rd 1857
Died August 3rd 1924

and the lines from Spenser which he had chosen as epigraph to *The Rover*:

Sleep after toyle, port after stormie seas,
Ease after warre, death after life, does greatly please.

(5)

At his death Conrad had written about eighty thousand words of *Suspense*. He had been planning a novel connected with Napoleon since 1904 or earlier and had read extensively about the period of Napoleon's exile on Elba. It was finally the *Memoirs* of the Comtesse de Boigne that gave him the base of the plot;[122] early in her *Memoirs* the Comtesse remarks that 'the character of Sir John Legard would be an admirable subject for a novel'[123] and this may have alerted Conrad's mind, but it was the Comtesse herself whose fascinating life provided the main thread of the plot while Sir John played only a minor role in the novel.

Adelaide, or Adèle, d'Osmond (d'Armand in *Suspense*) had been brought by her parents to stay in Yorkshire with Sir John Legard (Sir Charles Latham), who had offered to take in the family when they became refugees from the French Revolution. The characters of the child Adèle and of her father are followed closely in *Suspense*, as are the characters of Sir John and Lady Legard and the history of their marriage.[124] After a time Adèle d'Osmond was introduced at a music party in London to General de Boigne, an upstart Frenchman who had made his fortune in the service of Mahratta princes. Adèle was then sixteen and although General de Boigne was almost three times her age he asked for her hand in marriage. Because her parents were nearly destitute she consented, but committed the appalling blunder of telling the General that she 'did not care for him in the least, and probably never should' but that if he would secure her parents' future independence her gratitude would be so great that she would marry him without reluctance.[125] Again Conrad followed the *Memoirs* almost literally, giving the name of Count Hélion de Montevesso to Adèle's husband.

It was on this base that Conrad started to build the novel which was undoubtedly to be on the grand scale because the main lines of the plot have barely begun to emerge after eighty thousand words. Conrad gives Sir Charles Latham a son, Cosmo, and the novel opens with the young man's arrival in Genoa during the period of Napoleon's exile to Elba. He has been enjoined by Sir Charles to call on his old friend the Marquis d'Armand, who is Louis XVIII's Ambassador to the King of Sardinia and at the moment living in Genoa (this again corresponds with the Marquis d'Osmond's career). Cosmo calls on the Marquis, who is living with his daughter Adèle and her husband and a strange girl who is evidently Count Hélion's natural daughter (in fact the Comte and Countesse de Boigne were living apart and Adéle was alone with her father). Cosmo is strongly affected by

Adèle and Conrad clearly shows that he intends him to fall in love with her.[126]

The plot has another thread intertwined; Genoa is seething with rumours and conspiracies connected with Napoleon and, exploring the harbour on his first evening in the city, Cosmo comes upon a sailor, named Attilio, who is engaged in smuggling dispatches to Elba. He also becomes involved with a Dr Martel, based closely on the Dr Marshall of the Comtesse de Boigne's *Memoirs*, who is acting as an agent of the French Government.[127] The novel breaks off at the point where Cosmo has again become entangled with Attilio and his fellow-conspirators and finds himself sailing off with them on a felucca bound for Elba.

The Comtesse de Boigne's *Memoirs* give no help as to how the novel might have developed and the only indication that Conrad gave of his intentions was to tell Hueffer that it was to end with Napoleon's departure from Elba.[128]

In its unfinished state *Suspense* can only be judged tentatively because Conrad may well have decided to cut much of this first version; certainly the action develops with excessive slowness. Although the writing is by no means bad – it is far better than in *The Arrow of Gold* – *Suspense* has only to be compared with *Nostromo*, which it could have resembled, for it to be revealed as the work of a man whose mind had to proceed on crutches (the almost literal incorporation of passages from the Comtesse de Boigne's *Memoirs* is a sign of this). And in fact *Suspense* stands much closer to *Romance* than to Conrad's important work.

(6)

Chronological treatment of the whole of a writer's creative effort has the advantage of bringing out the individual differences between each work at the same time as showing the development of the writer's art; above all it acts as a brake on the temptation to impose an artificial pattern of phases or periods through convenient selection and suppression. There have been such attempts to impose a pattern on Conrad's work, of which Paul Wiley's, though ingenious, is the most fantastic and Douglas Hewitt's the most fruitful; but even Hewitt has, I believe, underrated Conrad's later novels in the interests of his theory.

The disadvantage of the chronological method is that the unity of a writer's work is liable to be buried by a mass of superficial differences in detail. In his preface to *A Personal Record* Conrad hoped that there might emerge from the book 'the vision of a personality; the man behind the books so fundamentally dissimilar as, for instance, *Almayer's Folly* and *The Secret Agent*'[129] or, he might have added, as *Nostromo* and *Chance, The Nigger of the 'Narcissus'* and *Victory, Lord Jim* and *The Rover, Under Western Eyes* and *The Arrow of Gold*. It is only necessary to enumerate the leading characters from these books to be struck by the variety and range of experience which Conrad covered. Yet, different though these characters are from each other, they are all strung on the thread of Conrad's personality and any of them would look uncomfortably out of place if transferred to a novel by another writer. What then is the quality that unites them?

It may first be necessary to clear away a possible misconception. Conrad was not among the great creators of character; he could not vie with nineteenth-century masters such as Balzac, Dickens, Tolstoy, Dostoevsky, George Eliot, or even Turgenev. But he was not primarily interested in character, and certainly never for its own sake. Protesting, towards the end of his life, that, after twenty-two years of work, he had 'not been very well understood', Conrad wrote:

> I have been called a writer of the sea, of the tropics, a descriptive writer, a romantic writer – and also a realist. But as a matter of fact all my concern has been with the 'ideal' value of things, events and people. That and nothing else. The humorous, the pathetic, the passionate, the sentimental *aspects* came in of themselves – *mais en vérité c'est les valeurs idéales des faits et gestes humains qui se sont imposés à mon activité artistique.*
>
> Whatever dramatic and narrative gifts I may have are always,

instinctively, used with that object – to get at, to bring forth *les valeurs idéales.*[130]

In other words the significance of the characters lies in what they reveal within the context of a certain predicament, not in what they are. But Conrad did not deal in abstractions and it is here that his other important pronouncement on the principle of his art comes in: 'My task which I am trying to achieve is, by the power of the written word to make you hear, to make you feel – it is, before all, to make you *see.*'[131] Conrad was not an intellectual, and in his books there is remarkably little analysis when one considers how much he said about life; his imagination, when most effective, expressed itself visually or dramatically. The essence of his art lies in the construction of a setting where a complex state of mind can be presented with the fullest emotional and dramatic effect. Thus there is the voyage of the *Patna* leading to Jim's symbolical 'jump', Decoud's experience in the Golfo Placido leading to his suicide, the events leading up to Mikulin's 'Where to?' or Razumov's 'I am washed clean'. Sometimes a whole story or novel seems to build up visually to one sentence, like Kurtz's 'The horror!' or dramatically as in Heyst's 'Ah, Davidson, woe to the man whose heart has not learned while young to hope, to love – and to put its trust in life!' It is, then, the situations which the various characters express, more than any qualities which they have in common, that are important.

Although there are certain recurring themes in Conrad's work, such as that of the vital test of character, that of betrayal and retribution or, another aspect of the same theme, guilt and atonement, it is clear that no rigid pattern can be detected in the diverse situations which the novels present. However, Conrad's view of the world does impose certain common elements on these situations.

Thus his conception of life was predominantly catastrophic. His only stories that can be said to have a 'happy' ending are 'Youth', *Typhoon*, 'Falk', 'The Duel', 'The Secret Sharer', *Chance* and *The Shadow-Line.* These represent a small proportion of Conrad's work; the only full-length novel among them is *Chance*, and the 'happiness' of its ending is far from unalloyed, because the coming together of Captain Anthony and Flora involves the death of Flora's father and, moreover, Conrad has seen fit to kill off Anthony after only six years of marriage; whereas 'Youth' and *The Shadow-Line*, being in a large measure episodes from Conrad's past, come in a special category. All the other stories end in disaster or tragedy for the main characters; in fact Conrad exhibits an almost perverse fertility of imagination in devising misfortunes for them. In Conrad's world 'evil' is too powerful for rewards and punishments to be administered with justice; catastrophe comes upon the guilty, the relatively innocent and the innocent alike. The fates of Almayer, Willems, Nostromo, Verloc, for instance, can be said to be consonant with their defects of character; on the other hand, although Decoud, Winnie Verloc, Razumov, and Heyst are not without blemish, it would require a peculiar sense of nemesis to maintain that the misfortunes which overwhelmed them were deserved; whereas Freya and Jasper Allen were by usual standards wholly innocent.

Tragedy or misfortune is implicit in the destiny of these characters. Certain of them – Winnie Verloc, Razumov, Flora de Barral, Heyst – become the victims of situations or events that make the ensuing disaster inevitable, and there is virtually no suggestion that any character has the power to avoid misfortune. It is true that Razumov might not have given up Haldin or that Jim might not have jumped, but these two acts above all convey a sense of inevitability. The Russian autocracy, 'like a malignant Zeus', presides from the start over Razumov's fate and it is implicit in the novel that whatever he had done would lead to disaster; while, at the vital moment, Jim is the victim of an unconscious impulse: 'I had jumped . . . it seems.'

However, not all these characters are ultimately the puppets of fate. After the crucial event it is in the power of some of them to redeem themselves. Willems is given the opportunity, only to take the course to certain catastrophe; and when Lena is dying Heyst has the chance to make the final affirmation, 'the true cry of love', and fails. Jim and Razumov, on the other hand, finally embrace their opportunity and the climax to their lives is a triumphant atonement.

Although such a diversity of characters meets catastrophe in such a diversity of situations there is one invariable element that is either the cause of the misfortune or else an essential ingredient of the tragedy: the emotional and moral isolation of the individual. This is the theme that unites all Conrad's major work. It appears in a variety of forms. There is the isolation imposed by an act in a person's past: with Willems it is the discovery of his dishonesty, with Jim his momentary cowardice, Falk has 'eaten man', Dr Monygham has given way to torture, Razumov has given up Haldin and consented to become a police agent; the 'anarchist' has shouted 'Vive l'anarchie!'; Leggatt has killed a man, de Barral has been imprisoned as a swindler, and Arlette has taken part in a blood-orgy. All these are cut off from normal communion with the rest of humanity by a stigma, although in the case of the first four the isolation is to a large degree self-imposed; society is either unaware of the stigma or ready to overlook it. Then there is the isolation imposed by circumstances: Almayer at his trading station; Carlier and Kayerts at theirs; Wait guarding his mortal secret among the crew of the *Narcissus*; Yanko Goorall, a castaway in a strange country; Captain Whalley, grappling with blindness; Nostromo and Decoud, both compelled to face their inner selves by their isolation on the Golfo Placido; the young captain in 'The Secret Sharer' is isolated by the arrival of Leggat, Flora de Barral by her father's criminality, and Lena in *Victory* is a waif.

In each case tragedy or misfortune is the consequence of isolation, although certain of the characters surmount their misfortune and become united with humanity.

Then it is significant that it is the two intellectuals among Conrad's characters, Kurtz and Heyst, who become isolated by a deliberate decision. Kurtz has not specifically chosen isolation, but his solitary existence among the Africans has led to the severance of his bonds with civilization, while Heyst has directly chosen to cut himself off from humanity. Both pay the penalty for their presumptuous flouting of the solidarity of mankind: Kurtz is shown to be 'hollow at the core' and dies in full realization of the horror of existence and Heyst brings retribution on Lena and himself.

Even when isolation is neither imposed nor chosen it appears almost as a necessary condition of existence: in the failure to penetrate the minds of others, as when Haldin's misunderstanding of Razumov brings tragedy to a number of lives; or in an inability of two people to communicate, which brings tragedy to Yanko Goorall and Amy Foster, to Alvan Hervey and his wife, the Goulds, the captain and Alice Jacobus and to Heyst and Lena; in the case of Captain Anthony and Flora this inability is only overcome at the cost of an attempted murder and of suicide, whereas although isolation from each other is the condition of the Verlocs' artificial existence it is this very isolation that makes their tragedy possible.

If one discounts Marlow and the other narrators, which one is justified in doing because they perform the special function either of relating an episode from Conrad's past or of presenting a story and do not come wholly within Conrad's fictional world; and if one excludes Falk as something of a fluke, the only leading character who triumphs and whose triumph does not involve tragedy is MacWhirr. He alone survives the test. MacWhirr's virtues and limitations are those of the untutored, 'natural' man; he is the antithesis of the ideal towards which Western civilization is striving in that his mind is intellectually and emotionally undeveloped. He is therefore safe; he has remained united with the solid, unthinking mass of humanity. To Conrad the development of the individual carries with it the seeds of disaster because it brings awareness of personal insignificance and isolation:

> What makes mankind tragic is not that they are the victims of nature, it is that they are conscious of it. To be part of the animal kingdom under the conditions of this earth is very well – but as

soon as you know of your slavery, the pain, the anger, the strife – the tragedy begins.[132]

Hence Conrad's diatribe against Cunninghame Graham's apparent suggestion that an educated Singleton was a desirable ideal.[133] Yet education, the development of the mind, progress towards self-awareness, are inherent in human evolution. Thus, although Conrad hoped in his work to 'awaken ... that feeling of unavoidable solidarity',[134] he proclaimed in fact that isolation, with its tragic consequences, is inevitable.

The isolation of the individual is a perennial theme, although it has become particularly prominent in the last years of the nineteenth and during the twentieth century. Some of the greatest works of modern times have had this theme at their centre; but to no artist has isolation seemed so starkly to be a necessary condition of existence as it did to Conrad, perhaps because he, more fully than others, had throughout his life experienced solitude, 'the enemy known but to few on this earth, and whom only the simplest of us are fit to withstand'.

It is not too bold to claim that Conrad has presented more dramatically and profoundly than any other artist the anguished conflict between man's innate isolation and his yearning for human solidarity.

(7)

When reviewing Aubry's *Joseph Conrad; Life and Letters* Hueffer asked:

Which was Conrad? The bothered, battered person who wrote innumerable, woeful, tactful, timid letters that are here connected by a string of properly noncommital prose, or the amazing being that I remember? With a spoken word or two he could create a whole world and give to himself the aspect of a returned Sir Francis Drake emerging from the territory of the Anthropophagi and the darkness of the Land of Fire.[135]

When a biographer has not known his subject personally

he must inevitably remain at one remove from him; a truism which is nonetheless often forgotten, or deliberately disguised. Thus only the barest and least significant facts can be definitely asserted; for the rest such a biographer must depend on what his subject has said about himself or on the unsatisfactory, because incomplete and in the most important respects unverifiable, evidence of others. It is therefore impossible for the present biographer to reproduce a personality whose exceptional magnetism Conrad's friends have stressed. (It can be said on the other side that such a biographer is a freer agent and can produce a rounder portrait. One who has known his subject personally is liable to reproduce his individual impression which does not necessarily accord with that of others.)

The available evidence agrees only that Conrad possessed an exquisitely and elaborately courteous manner overlying a highly strung, excitable temperament and that there emanated from him a ceaseless flow of energy. Curle has spoken of his 'passionate vitality'. His eyes, deep-set and shining within drooped lids, had the sort of light in them of eyes that glow in the dark; his movements were unceasing, like the reflections of an inner excitement; his lined face had a mobility that momentarily took on the passing humours of his thought,[136] and Galsworthy said: 'I think I never saw Conrad quite in repose. His hands, his feet, his knees, his lips – sensitive, expressive, and ironical – something was always in motion. ...'[137] This energy would constantly be expressed as warmth of feeling, a capacity for sympathetic identification with others. However, it cannot have been very easy to remain a friend of a man so touchy, so quick to take offence; and there is no question that Conrad could be perverse, unreasonable, irascible. Some important or, equally, trivial event could snap the tension and produce a frenzy. Such outbursts, however, were usually like a tropical storm, violent but short and followed by brilliance or calm, although Curle mentions that, after a serious paroxysm, Conrad 'would sometimes smoulder for hours. It was very curious. He seemed like a man coming slowly back to life out of some hideous nightmare, and I am sure that he underwent at such times a kind of mental suffocation.'[138] This tendency of Conrad's was of course aggravated by the frequent nerve-flaying attacks of gout. Walpole noted that towards the end of his life he was 'in many ways like a child about his various diseases, groaning and even crying aloud', and he would burst into 'sudden rages about such nothings as the butter being salt, and then . . . [be] suddenly very quiet and sweet', and that, when he lost his temper he 'chattered and screamed like a monkey'.[139]

Inevitably some relationships cracked under this strain, but the tributes and examples of longstanding friends stand out all the more impressively. His friendship with Cunninghame Graham, Curle, Galsworthy, Garnett, and others proclaims Conrad's power to give, inspire, and retain deep affection; and there was the friendship with Pinker which, to the credit of both men, survived some particularly violent buffetings.

There have been a number of tributes to Conrad's powers of conversation, to his capacity vividly to create a scene out of his own or another's past. Among others, Cunninghame Graham described him as a 'brilliant conversationalist' and 'formidable in argument'.[140] But there was no Boswell to record his talk and not one sentence has been preserved of which it can definitely be asserted that this is exactly what Conrad said. There have indeed been attempts to reproduce something of his manner of speech but they tend to be contradictory or to bear a strong mark of their origin. Thus it appears certain that in speaking English he retained a strong foreign accent throughout his life[141] (Paul Valéry described it as 'horrible'[142] and Conrad himself referred to it in connection with his American visit), yet Garnett has said that as early as November 1894 his accent seemed 'only slight'.[143] Wells's impression of Conrad's manner of talking is probably accurate as far as it goes; then there is Hueffer with his insistence that Conrad prefaced his remarks with 'My dear faller', and Jessie, who reproduces a few, no doubt authentic, mannerisms.

But, while the manner can only be so inadequately recreated, the matter is almost entirely lost and has largely to be guessed at. During his literary apprenticeship Conrad presumably talked a lot about his work with Garnett; and probably literature was the main topic of conversation with Hueffer because the minds of the two men were utterly different and a devotion to the craft was all that they had in common. Throughout his life Conrad seems to have been ready to take infinite trouble with the work of others when he felt that they really wanted it; Galsworthy's early books were the subject of long letters and conversations, Conrad gave detailed advice to Clifford, Douglas, and Edward Noble, while he told E. L. Grant Watson that a manuscript of his had had 'seven readings – not all by me alone, however. . . . During the last week I went twice to see him [Marwood] exclusively with the purpose of talking you over, MS. in hand.' This produced thirty-one pages of notes.[144] On the whole, however, Conrad was too wise not to know that whatever they may say to the contrary most writers resent criticism and he confined himself to harmless or enthusiastic clichés about the works of his friends.

Moreover, he did not rate very highly the literary work of his closest friends and they, with the exception perhaps of Hueffer, had little understanding of his own work. It was, not surprisingly, their personalities rather than their writings which attracted Conrad to people; this was clearly true of Galsworthy and Walpole but was also true of Cunninghame Graham and Crane. The people with whom Conrad became most intimate, and after his marriage they were without exception men, or, to a lesser extent, the wives of these men, were either, like Galsworthy and Pinker, distinguished by a firm, masculine grasp of everyday experience or else, like Cunninghame Graham and Crane, they resembled him in having had their wayward minds tempered by an unusual diversity of experience.

Conrad was particularly aware of how much could not be said and was repelled by specious generalization. In his novels he would repeatedly point to the inexpressible, but in conversation he seems to have preferred to concentrate on the specific or the concrete. He liked, for instance, to talk about technical questions connected with the sea and to discuss history; it is typical that the subject of a conversation of his with Valéry should have been a comparison between the fighting qualities of the French and British navies. Nor, according to Curle, was he above taking an interest in local gossip.

Although all the recorded moments of good humour and gaiety have been seized on, the picture of Conrad that emerges may appear lop-sided because it is the constantly reiterated confessions of gloom and ill-health that have been preserved in his letters. However, he had another side. Walpole speaks of 'times of enchanting boyish gaiety and jokes';[145] Galsworthy says that 'he had an almost ferocious enjoyment of the absurd',[146] which is confirmed by a number of passages in the novels; and Curle has described his moods of fantastic gaiety at breakfast: 'It was like a bubbling stream of nonsense, in which each extravagance led to another and in which the ludicrous aspect of things held complete sway. The very food upon the table would be the subject of whimsical discourse, and he would discuss the dishes with far-fetched imagery.'[147] But Curle, who was closer to Conrad than any other friend during the last few years of his life, shrewdly adds: 'And yet to me there was, now and again, something almost painful about these wild bouts of fun. It was as if they had been consciously fomented as a momentary anodyne of forgetfulness.'[148]

Compulsive gaiety is frequently associated with a tendency towards morbid depression; and overwhelming evidence points to a strong depressive element in Conrad's nature. If it is possible to inherit a temperamental quality it is easy to show that Conrad could have inherited this quality from his father. If not, his childhood would certainly have accentuated any such tendency; there was the deprivation of his mother's love at an early age, then the influence of his disillusioned, broken father who, though solicitous of Conrad's wellbeing, showed all too plainly that his mind was obsessed primarily with the memory of his dead wife. Apollo's final despairing surrender must have had a profoundly disturbing effect on his son's own self-esteem. To this may be added the bruising experience of an unhappy love-affair and the sense of guilt which his departure from Poland engendered.

It is clear from Thaddeus Bobrowski's strictures that as early as the Marseilles days Conrad suffered from moods of depression; and this culminated in his attempted suicide. When Conrad went to Mauritius in 1888 he struck Paul Langlois as neurasthenic; and then, a few years later, came the Congo episode with its undermining of Conrad's always delicate health. Thenceforth he was never for any length of time free of some physical ailment, which without question influenced and at times controlled his state of mind.

Mental and physical factors therefore combined to enhance a fundamental pessimism. On a more philosophical level this expressed itself in the conviction of an inexorable destiny, a 'deep-seated sense of fatality governing this man-inhabited world'.[149] It is significant that the novels which seem to have the most intimate relation to Conrad's personal predicament, *Lord Jim* and *Under Western Eyes*, convey most strongly a sense of inevitability; above all the action of Jim and Razumov in finally going out to fulfil a destiny which brings redemption and at the same time death (although with Razumov this is not immediate) seems to provide a symbolical resolution of his own problem.

To Conrad the forces controlling the universe were impersonal. There is no evidence that has been preserved from Conrad's life and none in his work of belief in a deity; when he touches on religion in his novels it is either in its temporal aspect as in the case of Father Corbelàn or as a primitive superstition as in Therese. Although he was born and brought up a Roman Catholic, and his father was an almost mystical believer, he rejected Christianity. It was 'distasteful' to him: 'I am not blind to its services but the absurd oriental fable from which it starts irritates me. Great, improving, softening, compassionate it may be but it has lent itself with amazing facility to cruel distortion and is the only religion which, with its impossible standards, has brought an infinity of anguish to innumerable souls – on this earth.'[150] And on another occasion he said: 'It's strange how I always, from the age of fourteen, disliked the Christian religion, its doctrines, ceremonies and festivals.'[151]

His pessimistic fatalism involved an extreme scepticism as to the possible improvement of mankind. He was far more conscious of man's violent, primeval origins than of his progress. He was convinced of man's depravity – in a secular sense: 'L'homme est un animal méchant. Sa méchanceté doit être organisée. Le crime est une condition nécessaire de l'existence organisée. La société est essentiellement criminelle, – ou elle n'existerait pas. C'est l'égoïsme qui sauve tout, – absolument tout, – tout ce que nous abhorrons, tout ce que nous aimons.'[152]

Bertrand Russell has said of Conrad: 'I felt, though I do not know whether he would have accepted such an image, that he thought of civilized and morally tolerable human life as a dangerous walk on a thin crust of barely cooled lava which at any moment might break and let the unwary sink into fiery depths.'[153] The aptness of this image is borne out by a number of passages in Conrad's work. Thus Marlow in 'Heart of Darkness' speaks of a 'remote kinship with this wild and passionate uproar' of the savages; the primitive nature of Falk's instincts is emphasized, and when Winnie Verloc stabbed her husband: 'Into that plunging blow ... [she] had put all the inheritance of her immemorial and obscure descent, the simple ferocity of the age of caverns ...' And then Gentleman Brown's massacre of Dain Waris's party was 'a demonstration of some obscure and awful attribute of our nature which, I am afraid, is not so very far under the surface as we like to think'.

Above all, Conrad rejected any formulas or schemes for the betterment of the human condition. Political institutions, he said, 'whether contrived by the wisdom of the few or the ignorance of the many, are incapable of securing the happiness of mankind'.[154] And he wrote to Cunninghame

Graham: 'International fraternity may be an object to strive for ... but that illusion imposes by its size alone. *Franchement*, what would you think of an attempt to promote fraternity amongst people living in the same street, I don't even mention two neighbouring streets.'[155]

A conviction of fatality governing human actions is liable to produce a sense of unreality and it may be that this expressed itself in Conrad's frequent emphasis on the illusory nature of so much experience and on the dream-like quality of life. There is Stein's oft-quoted: 'A man that is born falls into a dream like a man who falls into the sea. . . . To follow the dream, and again to follow the dream – and so – *ewig – usque ad finem* –,' and Decoud's: 'All this is life, must be life, since it is so much like a dream.' Marlow is faced by a 'choice of nightmares' and 'remained to dream the nightmare out to the end', while the characters in *The Rescue* have the sense of experiencing a dream. Conrad echoes this himself when he says in a letter: 'In that town [Cracow] one September day in the year 1874 I got into the train (Vienna Express) as a man gets into a dream – and here is the dream going on still, only one is conscious that the moment of awakening is drawing close,'[156] and in another: 'I felt more than ever how much *la vida es sueño*,'[157] or when writing about Stephen Crane: 'Indeed life is but a dream.'[158]

It would not be difficult for someone possessing this sense of unreality and fatality to persuade himself of the logical justification of contracting out of the human struggle; and Conrad once drew this deduction in a letter to Cunninghame Graham:

The attitude of cold unconcern is the only reasonable one. Of course reason is hateful, – but why? Because it demonstrates (to those who have the courage) that we, living, are out of life, – utterly out of it. The mysteries of a universe made of drops of fire and clods of mud do not concern us in the least. The fate of a humanity condemned ultimately to perish from cold is not worth troubling about. If you take it to heart it becomes an unendurable tragedy. If you believe in improvement you must weep, for the attained perfection must end in cold, darkness and silence. In a dispassionate view the ardour for reform, improvement, for virtue, for knowledge and even for beauty is only a vain sticking up for appearances, as though one were anxious about the cut of one's clothes in a community of blind men.[159]

This might be temporarily convincing, but ultimately Conrad was deeply and perhaps inevitably involved. As a postscript to this same letter, by an ironical coincidence which he himself pointed out, he was able to announce the most tangible commitment to the continuity of human life that can be made, the birth of a son.

Necessarily committed to life as the adult Conrad presumably accepted himself to be, he was bound to search for a belief and a manner of life which would make tolerable the burden of emotional pessimism. The merchant navy, up to a point, provided both. It offered that sense of belonging, of solidarity which Conrad needed to grasp and it demanded constant immersion in practical detail; as Marlow said in 'Heart of Darkness', 'I went to work the next day. . . . In that way only it seemed to me I could keep my hold on the redeeming facts of life.'

An increasing awareness among modern students of Conrad of his pessimism, his scepticism, and his consciousness of evil has led to a discounting of his proclaimed belief in the simple, practical virtues. But there is only an apparent contradiction between these two aspects of his outlook. His assertion that 'those who read me know my conviction that the world, the temporal world, rests on a few very simple ideas; so simple that they must be as old as the hills. It rests notably, among others, on the idea of Fidelity'[160] can be accepted with only a slight gloss. Belief in the 'few very simple ideas' is necessary to the efficient functioning of the merchant navy; it was also, to Conrad, a condition of the survival of the individual and of humanity. This belief implied no denial of the existence of powerful destructive forces; on the contrary, it was necessary as an armour against them.

However, the 'few very simple ideas' and the philosophy of work were not wholly efficacious. 'Action is consolatory.

It is the enemy of thought and the friend of flattering illusions. Only in the conduct of our action can we find the sense of mastery over the Fates.' And, 'Action, in which is to be found the illusion of a mastered destiny. . . .'[161] To anyone who could think this, the life of simple dogma and physical action as offered by the merchant navy was a far from adequate form of self-justification. It was thus fortunate for Conrad that he eventually became aware of a creative impulse because the artist's bid for immortality is the form of activity least susceptible to the undermining power of scepticism.

He brought to his activity as a writer the belief in ideals similar to those that were essential to a successful merchant seaman: the belief in professional competence, in the need for a sense of 'solidarity that knits together the loneliness of innumerable hearts',[162] in fidelity which expressed itself as insistence on the necessity for sincerity or 'a conscientious regard for the truth of my own sensations',[163] and a single-minded devotion to the task in hand. It was in speaking of the role of the artist that Conrad made the most positive declaration to be found in any of his writing: 'I would require from him [the artist] many acts of faith of which the first would be the cherishing of an undying hope; and hope, it will not be contested, implies all the piety of effort and renunciation. It is the God-sent form of trust in the magic force and inspiration belonging to the life of this earth. . . . To be hopeful in an artistic sense it is not necessary to think that the world is good. It is enough to believe that there is no impossibility of its being made so.'[164]

Although writing may have seemed the ideal solution to Conrad's predicament, in practice it produced only a precarious equilibrium. He could never free himself of an apparently chronic insecurity or of doubt; insecurity because, far from uniting him to the rest of humanity, his work left him isolated amid incomprehension, and doubt of his own powers, which induced constant bouts of *'les stérilités des écrivains nerveux'*.[165] He could not escape the fear that activity of whatever sort can only weave an illusion of triumph; hence his distrust of thought, which can destroy the illusion – thought disintegrates, corrupts, undermines belief. Few writers can have suffered more from mental, physical, and material difficulties and there is justification in his claim that 'no man paid more for his lines than I have'.[166] Conrad's achievement is an assertion of the indomitability of the human spirit, but it is useless to look for consolation in his work. It concedes no hope; the fate of those undisdained by destiny and who are not MacWhirrs is tragic, and triumph inevitably brings death. But, if not consolation, his work does provide exhilaration; thirty years of dedicated effort had as their reward the presentation of depths of experience which few artists have been able to excel.

Bibliography I

Alphabetical List of Conrad's Collected Writings*

(Compiled with the help of Lohf and Sheehy's *Joseph Conrad at Mid-century*).

Title	Title of volume in Uniform Edition (if part of a volume)	First serialization or first appearance in Britain and U.S.A.	Date of publication in book under Conrad's authorship†
Almayer's Folly; a Story of an Eastern River			1895
'Alphonse Daudet'	*Notes on Life and Letters*	*Outlook*, 9 April 1898	1921
'Amy Foster'	*Typhoon; and Other Stories*	*Illustrated London News*, 14, 21, 28 Dec. 1901	1903
'An Anarchist'	*A Set of Six*	*Harper's Magazine*, Aug. 1906	1908
'Anatole France'			
(i) *Crainquebille*	*Notes on Life and Letters*	*Speaker*, 16 July 1904	1921
(ii) *L'Ile des Pingouins*	*Notes on Life and Letters*	*English Review*, Dec. 1908	1921
The Arrow of Gold; a Story between Two Notes		*Lloyd's Magazine*, Dec. 1918–Feb. 1920	1919
'The Ascending Effort'	*Notes on Life and Letters*	*Daily Mail*, 30 July 1910	1921
'Autocracy and War'	*Notes on Life and Letters*	*Fortnightly Review*, July 1905 *North American Review*, July 1905	1921

* The collections of Conrad's prefaces and notes on his books are not included; nor are the various printings of individual plays.

† The date of the first trade edition is given; printings to secure copyright or private printings are ignored.

Title	Title of volume in Uniform Edition (if part of a volume)	First serialization or first appearance in Britain and U.S.A.	Date of publication in book under Conrad's authorship
'Because of the Dollars'	*Within the Tides*	*Metropolitan Magazine* (N.Y.), Sept. 1914	1915
'The Black Mate'	*Tales of Hearsay*	*London Magazine*, April 1908	1925
'Books'	*Notes on Life and Letters*	*Speaker*, 15 July 1905 *Living Age*, 19 Aug. 1905	1921
'The Brute'	*A Set of Six*	*Daily Chronicle*, 5 Dec. 1906 *McClure's Magazine*, Nov. 1907	1908
'The Censor of Plays'	*Notes on Life and Letters*	*Daily Mail*, 12 Oct. 1907	1921
'Certain Aspects of the Admirable Inquiry into the Loss of the *Titanic*'	*Notes on Life and Letters*	*English Review*, July 1912	1921
Chance; a Tale in Two Parts		*New York Herald*, 21 Jan.–30 June 1912	1913
'The Character of the Foe'	*The Mirror of the Sea*	*Pall Mall Magazine*, March 1905 *Reader Magazine*, April 1905	1906
'Christmas Day at Sea'	*Last Essays*	*Daily Mail*, 24 Dec. 1923 *Delineator*, Dec. 1923	1926
'Cobwebs and Gossamer'	*The Mirror of the Sea*	*Harper's Weekly*, 10 June 1905	1906
'Confidence'	*Notes on Life and Letters*	*Daily Mail*, 30 June 1919	1921
'The Congo Diary'	*Last Essays*	*Blue Peter*, Oct. 1925 *Yale Review*, Jan. 1926	1926
'Cookery'	*Last Essays*	Preface to Jessie Conrad's *A Handbook of Cookery for a Small House*, 1923 *Delineator*, Aug. 1922	1926

Title	Title of volume in Uniform Edition (if part of a volume)	First serialization or first appearance in Britain and U.S.A.	Date of publication in book under Conrad's authorship
'The Crime of Partition'	*Notes on Life and Letters*	*Fortnightly Review*, 1 May 1919 *Collier's Weekly* (N.Y.), 14 June 1919	1921
'The Dover Patrol'	*Last Essays*	*The Times*, 27 July 1921	1926
'The Duel'	*A Set of Six*	*Pall Mall Magazine*, Jan.–May 1908 *Forum*, July–Oct. 1908	1908
'Emblems of Hope'	*The Mirror of the Sea*	*Pall Mall Magazine*, Feb. 1905 *Reader Magazine*, March 1905	1906
'The End of the Tether'	*Youth*	*Blackwood's Magazine*, July–Dec. 1902	1902
'The Faithful River'	*The Mirror of the Sea*	*World Today*, Dec. 1904	1906
'Falk; a Reminiscence'	*Typhoon and Other Stories*		1903
'The Fine Art'	*The Mirror of the Sea*	*Pall Mall Magazine*, April 1905	1906
'First News'	*Notes on Life and Letters*	*Reveille*, Aug. 1918	1921
'Flight'	*Notes on Life and Letters*	*Fledgling*, June 1917	1921
'Freya of the Seven Isles'	*'Twixt Land and Sea*	*Metropolitan Magazine* (N.Y.), April 1912 *London Magazine*, July 1912	1912
'A Friendly Place'	*Notes on Life and Letters*	*Daily Mail*, 10 Dec. 1912	1921
'The Future of Constantinople'	*Last Essays*	*The Times*, 7 Nov. 1912	1926
'Gaspar Ruiz'	*A Set of Six*	*Pall Mall Magazine*, July–Oct. 1906 *Saturday Evening Post*, 28 July–18 Aug. 1906	1908

Title	Title of volume in Uniform Edition (if part of a volume)	First serialization or first appearance in Britain and U.S.A.	Date of publication in book under Conrad's authorship
'Geography and Some Explorers'	*Last Essays*	*Countries of the World*, Feb. 1924 *National Geographic Magazine*, March 1924	1926
'A Glance at Two Books'	*Last Essays*	*T.P.'s and Cassell's Weekly*, 1 Aug, 1925 *Living Age*, 5 Sept. 1925 *Forum*, Aug. 1925	1926
'The Grip of the Land'	*The Mirror of the Sea*	*Daily Mail*, 2 Dec. 1904	1906
'Guy de Maupassant'	*Notes on Life and Letters*	Introduction to Maupassant's *Yvette and Other Stories*, translated by Ada Galsworthy, 1914	1921
'A Happy Wanderer'	*Notes on Life and Letters*	*Daily Mail*, 23 July 1910	1921
'Heart of Darkness'	*Youth*	*Blackwood's Magazine*, Feb.–April 1899 *Living Age*, 18 June–4 Aug. 1900	1902
'Henry James'	*Notes on Life and Letters*	*North American Review*, Jan. 1905	1921
'The Heroic Age'	*The Mirror of the Sea*	*Standard*, 21 Oct. 1905	1906
'His War Book'	*Last Essays*	Preface to Stephen Crane's *The Red Badge of Courage*, 1925	1926
'The Idiots'	*Tales of Unrest*	*Savoy*, Oct. 1896	1898
'Il Conde'	*A Set of Six*	*Cassell's Magazine*, Aug. 1908 *Hampton's Magazine*, Feb. 1909	1908
'In Captivity'	*The Mirror of the Sea*	*Blackwood's Magazine*, Sept. 1905	1906

Title	Title of volume in Uniform Edition (if part of a volume)	First serialization or first appearance in Britain and U.S.A.	Date of publication in book under Conrad's authorship
'The Informer'	*A Set of Six*	*Harper's Magazine*, Dec. 1906	1908
The Inheritors; an Extravagant Story (with F. M. Hueffer)			1901
'Initiation'	*The Mirror of the Sea*	*Blackwood's Magazine*, Jan. 1906	1906
'The Inn of Two Witches'	*Within the Tides*	*Pall Mall Magazine*, March 1913 *Metropolitan Magazine* (N. Y.), May 1913	1915
'John Galsworthy'	*Last Essays*	*Outlook*, 31 March 1906	1926
'Karain; a Memory'	*Tales of Unrest*	*Blackwood's Magazine*, Nov. 1897 *Living Age*, 18–25 Dec. 1897	1898
'The Lagoon'	*Tales of Unrest*	*Cornhill Magazine*, Jan. 1897	1898
'Landfalls and Departures'	*The Mirror of the Sea*	*Pall Mall Magazine*, Jan. 1905 *Reader Magazine*, Feb. 1905	1906
Last Essays			1926
'Legends'	*Last Essays*	*Daily Mail*, 15 Aug. 1924	1926
'The Life Beyond'	*Notes on Life and Letters*	*Daily Mail*, 16 July 1910	1921
Lord Jim; a Tale		*Blackwood's Magazine*, Oct. 1899–Nov. 1900	1900
'The Loss of the *Dalgonar*'	*Last Essays*	*London Mercury*, Dec. 1921	1926
'Memorandum on the Scheme for fitting out a Sailing Ship'	*Last Essays*		1926
The Mirror of the Sea; Memories and Impressions		See separate parts	1906

Title	Title of volume in Uniform Edition (if part of a volume)	First serialization or first appearance in Britain and U.S.A.	Date of publication in book under Conrad's authorship
The Nature of a Crime (with F. M. Hueffer)		*English Review*, April–May 1909	1924
The Nigger of the 'Narcissus'; a Tale of the Forecastle		*New Review*, Aug.–Dec. 1897	1898
Nostromo; a Tale of the Seaboard		*T.P.'s Weekly*, 29 Jan.–7 Oct. 1904	1904
'A Note on the Polish Problem'	*Notes on Life and Letters*		1921
Notes on Life and Letters			1921
'The Nursery of the Craft'	*The Mirror of the Sea*		1906
'An Observer in Malay'	*Notes on Life and Letters*	*Academy*, 23 April 1898	1921
'Ocean Travel'	*Last Essays*	*Evening News*, 15 May 1923	1926
An Outcast of the Islands			1896
'An Outpost of Progress'	*Tales of Unrest*	*Cosmopolis*, June–July 1897	1898
'Outside Literature'	*Last Essays*	*Manchester Guardian Literary Supplement for 1922*, 4 Dec. 1922 *Bookman* (N.Y.), Feb. 1923	1926
'Overdue and Missing'	*The Mirror of the Sea*	*Daily Mail*, 8 March and 16 Nov. 1904	1906
'The Partner'	*Within the Tides*	*Harper's Magazine* Nov. 1911	1915
*A Personal Record**		*English Review*, Dec. 1908–June 1909	1912
'The Planter of Malata'	*Within the Tides*	*Metropolitan Magazine* (N.Y.), June–July 1914	1915

* First published as *Some Reminiscences.*

Title	Title of volume in Uniform Edition (if part of a volume)	First serialization or first appearance in Britain and U.S.A.	Date of publication in book under Conrad's authorship
'Poland Revisited'	*Notes on Life and Letters*	*Daily News*, 29, 31 March, 6, 9 April 1915 *The Book of the Homeless*, N. Y., 1916	1921
'Preface to *The Shorter Tales of Joseph Conrad*'	*Last Essays*	*The Shorter Tales of Joseph Conrad*, 1924	1926
'Prince Roman'	*Tales of Hearsay*	*Oxford and Cambridge Review*, Oct. 1911 *Metropolitan Magazine* (N.Y.), Jan. 1912	1925
'Protection of Ocean Liners'	*Notes on Life and Letters*	*Illustrated London News*, 6 June 1914	1921
The Rescue; a Romance of the Shallows		*Land and Water*, 30 Jan.–31 July 1919 *Romance* (N.Y.), Nov. 1919–May 1920	1920
'The Return'	*Tales of Unrest*		1898
Romance; a Novel (with F. M. Hueffer)			1903
The Rover		*Pictorial Review*, Sept.–Dec. 1923	1923
'Rulers of East and West'	*The Mirror of the Sea*	*Pall Mall Magazine*, May–June 1905 *Reader Magazine*, Aug. 1907	1906
The Secret Agent; a Simple Tale		*Ridgeway's; a Militant Weekly for God and Country*, 6 Oct. 1906–12 Jan. 1907	1907
'The Secret Sharer'	*'Twixt Land and Sea*	*Harper's Magazine*, Aug.–Sept. 1910	1912
A Set of Six			1908

Title	Title of volume in Uniform Edition (if part of a volume)	First serialization or first appearance in Britain and U.S.A.	Date of publication in book under Conrad's authorship
The Shadow-Line; a Confession		*English Review*, Sept. 1916–March 1917 *Metropolitan Magazine* (N.Y.), Oct. 1916	1917
The Sisters			1928
'A Smile of Fortune'	*'Twixt Land and Sea*	*London Magazine*, Feb. 1911	1912
'Some Reflections on the Loss of the *Titanic*'	*Notes on Life and Letters*	*English Review*, May 1912	1921
'Stephen Crane; a Preface to Thomas Beer's *Stephen Crane*'	*Last Essays*	Thomas Beer's *Stephen Crane; a Study in American Letters*, N.Y., 1923	1926
'Stephen Crane; a Note without Dates'	*Notes on Life and Letters*	*London Mercury*, Dec. 1919 *Bookman* (N.Y.), Feb 1920	1921
Suspense; a Napoleonic Novel		*Saturday Review of Literature*, 27 June–12 Aug. 1925	1925
'The Tale'	*Tales of Hearsay*	*Strand Magazine*, Oct 1917	1925
Tales of Unrest			1898
Tales of Hearsay			1925
'Tales of the Sea'	*Notes on Life and Letters*	*Outlook*, 4 June 1898	1921
Three Plays; Laughing Anne; One Day More; and *The Secret Agent*			1934
'Tomorrow'	*Typhoon; and Other Stories*	*Pall Mall Magazine*, Aug. 1902	1903
'The *Torrens*; a Personal Tribute'	*Last Essays*	*Blue Peter*, Oct. 1923 *Collier's Weekly*, 27 Oct. 1923	1926
'Tradition'	*Notes on Life and Letters*	*Daily Mail*, 8 March 1918	1921

Title	Title of volume in Uniform Edition (if part of a volume)	First serialization or first appearance in Britain and U.S.A.	Date of publication in book under Conrad's authorship
'Travel'	*Last Essays*	Richard Curle's *Into the East; Notes on Burma and Malaya*, 1923	1926
'The *Tremolino*'	*The Mirror of the Sea*		1906
'Turgenev'	*Notes on Life and Letters*	Introduction to Edward Garnett's *Turgenev; a Study*, 1917	1921
'Twixt Land and Sea; Tales			1912
Typhoon	*Typhoon; and Other Stories*	*Pall Mall Magazine*, Jan.–March 1902 *Critic* (N.Y.), Feb.–May 1902	1902
Typhoon; and Other Stories			1903
Under Western Eyes; a Novel		*English Review*, Dec. 1910–Oct. 1911 *North American Review*, Dec. 1910–Oct. 1911	1911
'The Unlighted Coast'	*Last Essays*	*The Times*, 18 Aug. 1925	1926
Victory; an Island Tale		*Munsey's Magazine* (N.Y.), Feb. 1915 *Star*, 24 Aug.–9 Nov. 1915	1915
'The Warrior's Soul'	*Tales of Hearsay*	*Land and Water*, 29 March 1917	1925
'The Weight of the Burden'	*The Mirror of the Sea*	*Harper's Weekly*, 17 June 1905	1906
'Well Done!'	*Notes on Life and Letters*	*Daily Chronicle*, 22–4 Aug. 1918 *Living Age*, Oct. 1918	1921
Within the Tides; Tales			1915

Title	Title of volume in Uniform Edition (if part of a volume)	First serialization or first appearance in Britain and U.S.A.	Date of publication in book under Conrad's authorship
'Youth'	*Youth, a Narrative; and Two Other Stories*	*Blackwood's Magazine*, Sept. 1898 *Outlook* (N.Y.), 1 Oct. 1898	1902
Youth, a Narrative; and Two Other Stories			1902

Bibliography II

In the numbered references to each chapter I have tried to give the sources of all facts and information on which the book has been based. The full bibliographical reference is only given the first time a work is mentioned; for convenience, therefore, a list of the principal books quoted is given below. Readers are referred to Kenneth A. Lohf and Eugene P. Sheehy's excellent bibliography, *Joseph Conrad at Mid-Century; Editions and Studies, 1895–1955*, University of Minnesota Press, 1957, for substantially complete details of writings by and about Conrad.

Unless otherwise stated, the place of publication of the editions quoted is London if the title of the book is in English and Paris if it is in French.

ALLEN J. *The Thunder and the Sunshine; a Biography of Joseph Conrad*, New York, 1958.

AUBRY, G. J. *Joseph Conrad; Life and Letters*, 2 Vols., 1927.

The Sea Dreamer; a Definitive Biography of Joseph Conrad, translated by Helen Sebba, 1957. (This is a translation of the author's *Vie de Conrad*, 1947.)

Joseph Conrad; Lettres Françaises, avec une Introduction et des Notes, [1930].

BENNETT, A. *The Journals of Arnold Bennett*, 3 Vols., 1932.

BERRYMAN, J. *Stephen Crane*, 1950.

BLACKBURN, W. *Joseph Conrad; Letters to William Blackwood and David S. Meldrum*, edited with an introduction, Duke University Press, 1958; and Cambridge University Press, 1959

BOBROWSKI, T. *Pamiętniki*, 2 Vols., Lwów, 1900.

BUSZCZYŃSKI, S. *Malo znany poeta*, Cracow, 1870.

CLIFFORD, H. *A Talk on Joseph Conrad and his Work*, Colombo, 1927.

CONRAD, JESSIE *Joseph Conrad and his Circle*, 1935.

Joseph Conrad as I Knew Him, 1926.

CRANKSHAW, E. *Joseph Conrad; some Aspects of the Art of the Novel*, 1936.

CURLE, R. *Conrad to a Friend; 150 Selected Letters from Joseph Conrad*

to Richard Curle, edited with an Introduction and Notes, 1928.
The Last Twelve Years of Joseph Conrad, 1928.
Caravansary and Conversation, 1937.

ESTREICHER, K. *Bibliografia Polska, XIX. Stólecia*, Vols. II and V, Cracow, 1874 and 1880.

FORD, F. M., see Hueffer.

GALSWORTHY, J. *Castles in Spain and Other Screeds*, 1927

GARNETT, D. *The Golden Echo*, 1953.

GARNETT, E. *Letters from Conrad, 1895 to 1924*, edited with Introduction and Notes, 1928.

GEE, J. A. and P. J. STURM *Letters of Joseph Conrad to Marguerite Poradowska, 1890–1920*, translated from the French and edited with an Introduction, Notes and Appendices, Yale University Press, 1940.

GOLDRING, D. *The Last Pre-Raphaelite; a Record of the Life and Writings of Ford Madox Ford*, 1948.

GORDAN, J. D. *Joseph Conrad; the Making of a Novelist*, Harvard University Press, 1940.

HART-DAVIS, R. *Hugh Walpole; a Biography*, 1952.

HEWITT, D. *Conrad; a Reassessment*, Cambridge, 1952.

HUEFFER, F. M. *Joseph Conrad: A Personal Remembrance*, 1924.
Return to Yesterday, 1931

KEATING, G. T. *A Conrad Memorial Library; the Collection of George T. Keating*, Garden City, N.Y., 1929.

LEAVIS, F. R. *The Great Tradition; George Eliot, Henry James, Joseph Conrad*, 1948.

MARROT, H. V. *The Life and Letters of John Galsworthy*, 1935

MÉGROZ, R. L. *A Talk with Joseph Conrad; and a Criticism of his Mind and Method*, 1926.

MORF, G. *The Polish Heritage of Joseph Conrad*, [1930].

QUINN, J. *The Library of John Quinn*, 5 Parts, Anderson Galleries, New York, 1923–4.

ROTHENSTEIN, W. *Men and Memories*, 2 Vols., 1931–2.

SYMONS, A. *Notes on Joseph Conrad; with some Unpublished Letters*, 1925.

TABORSKI, R. *Apollo Korzeniowski; ostatni dramatopisarz romantyczny*, Wroclaw, 1957.

TSCHIFFELY, A. F. *Don Roberto; being the Account of the Life and Works of R. B. Cunninghame Graham, 1852–1936*, 1937.

UJEJSKI, J. *Joseph Conrad*, traduit par Pierre Duméril, 1939. (French translation of *O Konradzie Korzeniowskim*, Warsaw, 1936.)

Wells, H. G. *Experiment in Autobiography; Discoveries and Conclusions of a Very Ordinary Brain (since 1866)*, 2 Vols., 1934.

Wise, T. J. *A Bibliography of the Writings of Joseph Conrad (1895–1921)*, 2nd edition, 1921.

A Conrad Library; a Catologue of Printed Books, Manuscripts and Autograph Letters by Joseph Conrad, collected by Thomas James Wise, 1928.

Notes

CHAPTER I: POLISH YEARS

1. Information taken from a document in the handwriting of Thaddeus Bobrowski which is now in the Jagellon Library, Cracow. In it Bobrowski noted the sums of money which he had paid to Conrad together with bits of information that might be useful. Henceforth it will be referred to as the Bobrowski Document.

2. Thaddeus Bobrowski, *Pamiętniki*, Lwów, 1900, I, p. 363.

3. Bobrowski, op. cit., I, p. 363.

4. Letter to Garnett, 20 January 1900; *Letters from Conrad, 1895 to 1924*, edited with Introduction and Notes by Edward Garnett, (1928), p. 166.

5. Bobrowski, op. cit., I, p. 364.

6. Roman Taborski, *Apollo Korzeniowski; ostatni dramatopisarz romantyczny*, Wrocław, 1957, p. 12.

7. Bobrowski, op. cit., I, p. 361.

8. ibid., pp. 361–2.

9. ibid., I, pp. 15–16 and II, pp. 1–2.

10. ibid., I, pp. 358–9 and II, pp. 19–20.

11. ibid., II, pp. 17–19 and pp. 446–59.

12. ibid., I, p. 362.

13. ibid., II, p. 66.

14. Bobrowski, op. cit., II, p. 67, and Bobrowski Document. There is doubt about the date. In his memoirs Bobrowski gives 26 April (o.s.) and in the Document 28 April (o.s.).

15. 20 January 1900.

16. pp. 23–4.

17. Bobrowski, op. cit., II, p. 14; cf., *A Personal Record*, pp. 28–9.

18. Several of his poems dating from this time were signed as written in Nieruszek (the name of the wood).

19. Bobrowski, op. cit., II, p. 85 and Document.

20. Estreicher, *Bibliografia Polska*.

21. Stephen Buszczyński, *Mało znany poeta*, Cracow, 1870, p. 32; letters to Casimir Kaszewski of 20 January and 9 July 1860 (Jagellon Library).

22. Taborski, op. cit., p. 72.

23. Bobrowski, op. cit., I, p. 362.

24. ibid., II, pp. 49–51.

25. Roman Taborski, 'Nie drukowane wiersze Apolla Korzeniowskiego o buncie chłopskim na Ukrainie', *Pamiętnik Literacki*, XLVI, No. 1, Warsaw-Wrocław, 1955, pp. 276–90.

26. Buszczyński, op. cit., pp. 15–17.

27. *The Cambridge History of Poland*, Vol. II, *from Augustus II to Pilsudski*, Cambridge University Press, 1941, p. 366.

28. Bobrowski, op. cit., II, p. 55.

29. *Cambridge History of Poland*, Vol. II, pp. 367–8.

30. op. cit., pp. 371–4.

31. Bobrowski, op. cit., II, p. 440, and Document; Taborski,

'Polityczna i literacka działalność Apolla Korzeniowskiego w. r. 1861', *Pamiętnik Literacki*, XLVI, No. 4, Warsaw-Wrocław, 1955, p. 527 ff. There is confusion as to the title of this periodical. In the Document Bobrowski calls it *Dwutygodnik* (Fortnightly), whereas in his memoirs he calls it *Slowo* (Word), a monthly. Basing himself on *Tygodnik Illustrowany*, a contemporary source, Taborski calls it *Swiat* (World), a fortnightly, but mentions that another source, *Biblioteka Warszawska*, called it *Dwutygodnik*. It appears that an existing journal, *Swiat*, was to be transformed into a new journal, *Dwutygodnik*.

32. 20 July 1861, in the Korzeniowski Dossier in the National Archives of Ancient Documents. Quoted by Aubry, *The Sea Dreamer; a Definitive Biography of Joseph Conrad*, 1957, p. 24.

33. Danilowski, *Notatki*, 1908, pp. 53–5. Quoted by Gustav Morf, *The Polish Heritage of Joseph Conrad*, [1930], p. 28.

34. Kręcki, *Zbior Materjałow do Historji Powstania 1863*, 1916, I, pp. 5–8, quoted by Morf, op. cit., pp. 28–9. Also W. Przyborowski, *Historia Dwóch Lat, 1861–2*, Cracow, 1894, Vol. III, pp. 27–30 (quoted by Taborski, ibid., p. 529).

35. Przyborowski, ibid.; Taborski, ibid., p. 529.

36. ibid.; Taborski, ibid., p. 531.

37. Taborski, *Apollo Korzeniowski*, p. 110.

38. Taborski, 'Polityczna i literacka działalność Apolla Korzeniowskiego w. r. 1861', loc. cit., 536; Buszcyński, op. cit., p. 37.

39. Aubry, op. cit., p. 25, presumably quoting the Korzeniowski dossier containing the court records.

40. Record of Permanent Investigation Commission and Aubry, op. cit., pp. 25–6.

41. Buszczyński, op. cit., pp. 37–8.

42. Letter to John and Gabriela Zagórski, Vologda, 27 June 1862 (*Tygodnik Illustrowany*, No. 4, 1920); Bobrowski, op. cit., II, pp. 440–1. The rest of the account of the journey into exile is drawn from this passage in the Memoirs.

43. *L.L.*, I, p. 8.

44. *Cambridge History of Poland*, II, pp. 378–83.

45. Bobrowski, op. cit., II, pp. 449–52 and pp. 462–4.

46. ibid., II, p. 441, and Document.

47. ibid., p. 442. cf., *A Personal Record*, pp. 63–7.

48. *A Personal Record*, pp. 64–5.

49. Bobrowski Document.

50. ibid.

51. *A Personal Record*, p. 72.

52. loc. cit.

53. *Les Travailleurs de la Mer*, Nelson, Paris, Vol. I, pp. 100–101.

54. 18 September 1865.

55. Apollo Korzeniowski to Kaszewski, 1 February 1866.

56. *A Personal Record*, p. 70.

57. ibid., pp. 70–71; 'Tales of the Sea', *Notes on Life and Letters*, 57 and letter to David Garnett, 22 December (1902).

58. 1 February 1866.

59. Stanislas Czosnowski, 'Conradiana', *Epoka*, 1929, no. 136, reporting the memories of Zygmunt Radziczynski, whose family were friends of the Bobrowskis and

who knew Conrad at this time.

60. 'Prince Roman', *Tales of Hearsay*, pp. 34–5.

61. Apollo to Kaszewski, 22 November 1866.

62. Bobrowski Document; cf., Apollo's letter of 22 November 1866 to Kaszewski.

63. To Kaszewski, undated, Jagellon Library MS. 3057 K. p.54.

64. Issued by the Ministry of Home Affairs 2 December (o.s.) 1867. Jagellon Library MS. 6391.

65. Bobrowski Document and letters to Stephen Buszczyński of 20 April and 10 May 1868.

66. Letter to Kaszewski, 14 October 1868.

67. do., 24 December 1868.

68. Czosnowski, ibid.

69. Thaddeus Garczyński, maternal grandson of Ambrose Syroczyński. I owe this anecdote to Mr Zdzisław Najder.

70. Letter to Buszczyński, 7 February 1869.

71. do., 19 January, 7 and 17 February 1869.

72. Czosnowski, ibid.

73. *Notes on Life and Letters*, pp. 167–8.

74. Extract from register of deaths, no. 298, in the parish church of All Saints, Cracow.

75. Letter to (?) Casimir Kaszewski, 12 June 1869, Jagellon Library, 30577.

76. Letter to Garnett, 20 January 1900.

77. *My Past and Thoughts: the Memoirs of Alexander Herzen*, translated by Constance Garnett, Chatto and Windus, 1925, Vol. IV, p. 209.

78. The appointment was confirmed by the Imperial and Royal Court of Justice (Urban and Civil Division) Cracow on 2 August 1870. Jagellon Library, MS. 6391.

79. Bobrowski Document and Mrs Bobrowska to Buszczyński, 12 June 1869.

80. Bobrowski Document.

81. cf., Aubry, *The Sea Dreamer*, pp. 46–7.

82. cf., 'Geography and Some Explorers', *Last Essays*, p. 12.

83. According to Thaddeus Garczyński he was a 'dullard' (Najder).

84. Letter to Kaszewski, 12 June 1869.

85. Letter to Kaszewski, 24 December 1868.

86. Czosnowski, ibid.

87. Bobrowski Document.

88. *A Personal Record*, pp. 37–44.

89. Bobrowski Document.

90. Information supplied by Thaddeus Garczyński (Najder).

91. *Nostromo*, xiv.

92. See pp. 295–6.

93. Letter to Janina Taube (Baroness de Brunnow), 24 March 1908, *Lettres Françaises*, p. 93.

94. 9 August 1897, *Lettres Françaises*, p. 31.

95. 2 October 1897, ibid., pp. 31–3.

96. MS. entitled 'R.L.', pp. 1–3 (Yale).

97. *Nostromo*, xiv; MS. of 'R.L.', p. 4.

98. Thaddeus Garczyński (Najder).

99. Bobrowski Document.

100. *A Personal Record*, p. 70 and p. 72.

101. 'Tales of the Sea', *Notes on Life and Letters*, pp. 53–7, and letter to David Garnett, 22 December (1902).

102. Letter to Aubry, 14 May 1923, *Lettres Françaises*, p. 184.

103. 'Geography and Some Explorers', *Last Essays*, pp. 11–12.

104. ibid., p. 14 and p. 16.

105. ibid., p. 12. Originally published as 'The Romance of Travel'.

106. ibid., p. 16.

107. Bobrowski Document.

108. John D. Gordan, *Joseph Conrad, the Making of a Novelist*, Harvard University Press, 1940, pp. 8–9.

109. See p. 482.

110. *A Personal Record*, p. 122.

111. ibid., p. 121.

112. Twórczość, November 1956, p. 149.

CHAPTER II: FRENCH EXPERIENCE

1. Letter from Bobrowski to Conrad of 26 October 1876.

2. Bobrowski document, *passim*.

3. *A Personal Record*, p. 122.

4. ibid., pp. 123–4.

5. Information supplied by Mlle Forget of the Archives du Port, IIIe Région Maritime, Toulon.

6. *The Mirror of the Sea*, pp. 152–3.

7. Archives du Port, IIIe Région Maritime, Toulon.

8. Information supplied by the Administration of the Inscription Maritime of Le Havre.

9. *L.L.*, I, p. 33.

10. Report of Captain Duteil in *Journal du Havre*, 23 December 1875.

11. Bobrowski Document.

12. Aubry states (*L.L.*, I, p. 33) that he had this detail from Conrad himself.

13. See *The Mirror of the Sea*, p. 160, and *The Arrow of Gold*, pp. 242–4.

14. *A Personal Record*, pp. 124–6.

15. *The Sea Dreamer*, p. 63. Aubry presumably had this information from Conrad. cf., also Conrad's reference to his 'bohemian set (one poet, at least, emerged out of it later)', *The Arrow of Gold*, p. 5.

16. *Larousse du XXe Siècle*, III, 1086; *Encyclopaedia Britannica; Figaro*, 4 December 1877 and 22–3 February 1878.

17. *L.L.*, I, p. 35.

18. Bobrowski Document.

19. Archives du Port, IIIe Région Maritime, Toulon.

20. Born 22 May 1834 at Luri (Inscription Maritime of Bastia).

21. pp. 162–3.

22. *The Mirror of the Sea*, p. 163.

23. *The Arrow of Gold*, p. 106.

24. *Nostromo*, xii.

25. Born 18 January 1858 at Luri (Inscription Maritime of Bastia).

26. *The Arrow of Gold*, p. 8.

27. 22 July 1923, *Conrad to a Friend; 150 Selected Letters from Joseph Conrad to Richard Curle*, 1928, p. 197.

28. *Victory*, xii.

29. ibid., xiv.

30. Archives du Port, IIIe Région Maritime, Toulon.

31. Bobrowski to Buszczyński, 24 March 1879. Conrad was listed among the crew for this voyage but against his name are the words: 'embarquement nul'. Archives du Port, IIIe Région Maritime, Toulon.

32. Bobrowski to Buszczyński, 24 March 1879.
33. Bobrowski Document.
34. *The Mirror of the Sea*, p. 158.
35. ibid., p. 158.
36. ibid., p. 160.
37. *The Arrow of Gold*, p. 28, etc.
38. ibid., p. 66.
39. ibid., p. 93.
40. ibid., pp. 224–5.
41. ibid., p. 100.
42. ibid., p. 338.
43. ibid., p. 346.
44. ibid., pp. 349–50.
45. *L.L.*, II, p. 224. cf. another letter to Colvin of 9 August, *L.L.*, II, p. 224.
46. Wednesday 1919, *L.L.*, II, p. 229.
47. *Joseph Conrad as I Knew Him*, 1926, pp. 121–2.
48. *Among the Carlists*, 1876, p. 161.
49. *The Arrow of Gold*, p. 65.
50. ibid., p. 4.
51. General Edward Kirkpatrick de Closeburn, *Souvenirs de la denière Guerre Carliste (1872–6)*, (1909), p. 369 ff.; and Conde de Rodezno, *Carlos VII, Duque de Madrid*, 2nd Edition, Bilbao, 1932, pp. 218–20.
52. cf., for example the report in *Le Temps* for 10 January 1877.
53. Record of service supplied by Inscription Maritime of Bordeaux.
54. Bobrowski to Buszczyński, 24 March 1879. Also, Bobrowski Document.
55. 22 August 1918.
56. *The Sea Dreamer*, p. 74.
57. Jerry Allen, *The Thunder and the Sunshine; a Biography of Joseph Conrad*; New York, 1958, *passim.*
58. The details of Don Carlos's movements, of his acquisition of Paula and of the Golden Fleece, and of the Boët affair have been taken from *El Robo del Toison* (a record of Boët's trial), from Luis Carreras, *Boët, el Toison de Oro . . .*, Barcelona, [1881], and from newspapers of the time, in particular *Le Temps*, 15 November 1877, *Figaro*, 31 December 1877 and 1 January 1878, and *République Française*, p. 14, 24 April, 1, 16 May 1879.
59. *Veinte Años con Don Carlos; Memorias de su Secretario el Conde de Melgar*, Madrid, 1940, pp. 56–64.
60. ibid., p. 57.
61. *The Arrow of Gold*, pp. 57–8.
62. Bobrowski to Buszczyński, 24 March 1879.
63. *L.L.*, I, p. 47.
64. *A Personal Record*, 122. cf., 'Well Done', *Notes on Life and Letters*, 182.

CHAPTER III: MERCHANT SEAMAN

1. *L.L.*, I, p. 47.
2. cf., letter to Joseph de Smet, 23 January 1911, *L.L.*, II, p. 124.
3. Bobrowski Document.
4. Agreement and Account of Crew.
5. 'Poland Revisited', *Notes on Life and Letters*, pp. 150–51.
6. *Notes on Life and Letters*, pp. 152–3.
7. 19 October 1879. Agreement and Account of Crew.
8. *The Mirror of the Sea*, p. 122 ff.
9. Certificate of Discharge (Yale). He embarked on 12 December 1879.

10. 1 June 1880. Certificate No. 08361. General Register and Record Office of Shipping and Seamen.

11. *A Personal Record*, pp. 112–14.

12. *Chance*, p. 4 ff.

13. Agreement and Account of Crew.

14. pp. 38–45.

15. 'Initiation', p. 137 ff.

16. *Last Essays*, p. 31 ff. He misdates the event by a year.

17. Certificate of Discharge (Yale).

18. Letter from Bobrowski, 13 May 1881.

19. do., 30 May 1881.

20. cf., *Lloyd's Register of British and Foreign Shipping* for 1 July 1881 to 30 June 1882 and 1 July 1882 to 30 June 1883.

21. Agreement and Account of Crew for this voyage (General Register and Record Office of Shipping and Seamen). Moreover, on the Agreement for the *Palestine* Conrad gave the *Loch Etive* as the last ship on which he had served.

22. loc. cit. and Lloyd's Records. She was abandoned sinking on 3 or 4 September, latitude 43 N., longitude 27 W., and was seen to founder three minutes afterwards.

23. Agreement and Account of Crew.

24. *Youth*, xi.

25. cf., Agreement and Account of Crew.

26. *Youth*, p. 5.

27. Preserved at Yale.

28. 'Report of a Marine Court of Enquiry held at the Police Court, in Singapore, on the second day of April 1883...' (Attached to *Palestine* Agreement, Public Record Office.)

29. *Youth*, p. 16.

30. ibid., p. 37.

31. Bobrowski to Conrad, 24 June 1883.

32. Bobrowski to Conrad, 31 August 1883 and Document.

33. Agreement and Account of Crew.

34. Agreement and Account of Crew.

35. *L.L.*, I, pp. 76–7.

36. Certificate of Discharge (Yale).

37. *L.L.*, I, p. 77.

38. It is, at the time of writing, on loan to the National Maritime Museum from the Registrar General of Shipping and Seamen.

39. Certificate No. 08361. General Register and Record Office of Shipping and Seamen.

40. pp. 114–16.

41. *L.L.*, I, pp. 79–80.

42. ibid., pp. 80–81.

43. ibid., p. 82.

44. ibid., p. 83.

45. Agreement and Account of Crew.

46. *The Mirror of the Sea*, pp. 9–13.

47. Letter from Bobrowski, 5 April 1886.

48. do., 20 July 1886.

49. do., 9 and 26 November 1886.

50. His Naturalization papers are in the Keating Collection at Yale.

51. No. 08361. Certificate dated 11 November 1886 (Keating Collection).

52. *A Personal Record*, p. 120.

53. Agreement and Account of Crew.

54. *The Mirror of the Sea*, p. 48 ff.
55. 'The Weight of the Burden', *The Mirror of the Sea*, pp. 52–3.
56. Certificate of Discharge (Yale).
57. *An Outcast of the Islands*, p. 70.
58. *Youth*, pp. 41–2.
59. Information about the *Vidar* was given to Aubry in 1924 by Captain Craig, then aged seventy; *L.L.*, I, p. 94 ff.
60. *A Personal Record*, p. 87.
61. Gordan, op. cit., p. 36 ff.; Gray and Haverschmidt.
62. Gordan, ibid., pp. 44–5.
63. Gordan, ibid., pp. 46–9. Two bills of lading (Yale).
64. *L.L.*, I, p. 98.
65. Certificate of Discharge (Yale).
66. *Youth*, xii.
67. 'The End of the Tether', *Youth*, p. 166.
68. *The Shadow-Line*, pp. 3–6.
69. Named in a letter to Colvin, p. 27 February 1917. *L.L.*, II, 182.
70. *The Shadow-Line*, p. 58.
71. Keating Collection, Yale.
72. *The Shadow-Line*, p. 66.
73. 'Falk', *passim*.
74. Letter from Bobrowski, 24 September 1888.
75. Savinien Mérédac [Auguste Esnouf] 'Joseph Conrad et Nous', *Essor*, 15 February 1931.
76. Published in *Essor*, 15 February 1931, and *Radical*, 7 August 1931.
77. Extracts from a letter from Paul Langlois, 2 February 1931, to Savinien Mérédac, quoted in the article by the latter in *Essor* of 15 February 1931.
78. 'A Smile of Fortune', *'Twixt Land and Sea; Tales*, pp. 34–5.
79. *Radical*, 7 August 1931.
80. P. J. Barnwell, in *Dictionary of Mauritian Biography*, No. 4, April 1942, pp. 109–10.
81. *Youth*, 4. cf. P. J. Barnwell, loc. cit.
82. *'Twixt Land and Sea*, ix.
83. *Joseph Conrad as I Knew Him*, p. 139.
84. 'A Smile of Fortune', *'Twixt Land and Sea*, p. 71.
85. *L.L.*, I, p. 113.
86. Savienien Mérédac, *Essor*, 15 February 1931.
87. 3 January 1889.
88. 'A Smile of Fortune', *'Twixt Land and Sea*, pp. 85–6.

CHAPTER IV: CONGO EPISODE

1. 'Heart of Darkness', *Youth, a Narrative; and Two Other Stories*, pp. 51–2.
2. *A Personal Record*, p. 68.
3. *The Mirror of the Sea*, p. 122.
4. cf. Galsworthy's letter of 23 April 1893, H. V. Marrot, *The Life and Letters of John Galsworthy*, 1935, p. 88.
5. See p. 92.
6. 13 June 1885.
7. *A Personal Record*, pp. 69–70 and pp. 73–4.
8. Three letters from Conrad to Alexander Poradowski during January 1890 are written on that firm's paper.
9. cf. Conrad's letter to Albert Thys, 4 November 1889, *Lettres Françaises*, 25.
10. 24 September 1889. Quoted by Aubry in 'Joseph Conrad au

Congo', *Mercure de France*, 15 October 1925, Vol. 183, pp. 296–7.

11. 'Heart of Darkness', *Youth*, pp. 52–3.

12. Professor Jean Bruhat quoting the Compte Rendu of the sessions of 12, 13, 14 September 1876 of the Conférence Géographique Africaine à Bruxelles in *Les Politiques d'Expansion Imperialiste*, 1949, p. 78.

13. Pierre Mille, *Au Congo Belge*, 1899, p. 12.

14. 'Heart of Darkness', *Youth*, p. 56.

15. Letters from Messrs Barr, Moering to Thys of 31 October 1889 (Aubry, 'Joseph Conrad au Congo', loc. cit., p. 297) and from Conrad to Thys of 28 November 1889, *Lettres Françaises*, pp. 26–7.

16. Letter to Thys, 28 November 1889, *Lettres Françaises*, p. 27.

17. Letter of 4 November 1889 (Yale).

18. *Letters of Joseph Conrad to Marguerite Poradowska, 1890–1920*, translated from the French and edited ... by John A. Gee and Paul J. Sturm, Yale University Press, New Haven, 1940, pp. 123–4.

19. 20 January 1890, ibid., p. 124.

20. Conrad to Mme Poradowska, 4 February 1890 and ibid., xv. cf., Conrad to Thys, 11 April 1890, *Lettres Françaises*, p. 29.

21. *Joseph Conrad and His Circle*, 1935, p. 70.

22. Vol. VI, no. 169, p. 882.

23. Conrad to Mme Poradowska, 11 and 14 (but see Gee and Sturm) February 1890. Bobrowski Document.

24. Bobrowski Document.

25. 10 March 1890.

26. Letter to Thys, 11 April 1890, *Lettres Françaises*, p. 29.

27. Extract from files of SACHC communicated to Aubry and quoted by him in 'Joseph Conrad au Congo', loc. cit., p. 305.

28. To Mrs Tyszka, née Bobrowska, 2 May 1890.

29. 'Heart of Darkness', *Youth*, pp. 61–2.

30. Conrad to Mme Poradowska, 10–12 June 1890, and 'The Congo Diary', *Last Essays*, p. 161.

31. Albert Thys, *Au Congo et au Kassaï*, nouvelle édition, Bruxelles, 1888, p. 7 (quoted by Aubry, *Vie de Conrad*, [1947], p. 158).

32. 'Heart of Darkness', *Youth*, p. 70.

33. ibid., p. 66.

34. 'Geography and Some Explorers', *Last Essays*, p. 17.

35. 'Heart of Darkness', *Youth*, p. 50.

36. He kept it in two cheap little notebooks which are now at Harvard. The interesting parts of the text have been edited by Richard Curle and printed at the end of *Last Essays*.

37. 'The Congo Diary', *Last Essays*, p. 161.

38. ibid., p. 162.

39. ibid., p. 161.

40. ibid., p. 161.

41. ibid., pp. 163–4.

42. ibid., p. 167.

43. 'Heart of Darkness', *Youth*, p. 71.

44. 'The Congo Diary', *Last Essays*, pp. 163–4.

45. ibid., p. 164, Note 2.

46. ibid., p. 165.

47. ibid., p. 165.

48. ibid., p. 166.

49. ibid., p. 169.

50. ibid., p. 170.

51. ibid., p. 171.

52. *Mouvement Geographique*, 21 September 1890 (Aubry, 'Joseph Conrad au Congo', loc. cit., p. 323).

53. Conrad's second notebook is headed 'Up-river book. Commenced 3 August 1890 – *s.s. Roi des Belges*.' It is full of navigational aids and sketches.

54. Letter to Conrad from Camille Delcommune, 6 September 1890 (Yale).

55. Aubry, 'Joseph Conrad au Congo', loc, cit., p. 326.

56. MS. pp. 55, 56, 59 (Yale).

57. Aubry, 'Joseph Conrad au Congo', loc. cit., p. 330 and p. 333.

58. To Mme Poradowska, 26 September 1890.

59. 29 November 1890, *L.L.*, I, pp. 139–40.

60. *A Personal Record*, p. 14.

CHAPTER V: SEAMAN TO NOVELIST

1. Draft letter from Mme Poradowska to Conrad of 4 February 1891. Gee & Sturm, op. cit., p. 136.

2. cf., 'Heart of Darkness', *Youth*, 155 ff.

3. Draft letter from Mme Poradowska to Conrad of 4 February 1891. Gee & Sturm, op. cit., p. 136 and p. 19 Note 4.

4. Letter to Mme Poradowska, 17 February 1891.

5. According to a letter to Mme Poradowska of 10 May. He was actually at La Roseraie from 21 May to 14 June (Aubry, *L.L.*, I, p. 145).

6. *A Personal Record*, p. 14.

7. Letter to Mme Poradowska, 10 June 1891.

8. Letter from Bobrowski, 27 June 1891.

9. 2 July 1891.

10. 30 July 1891.

11. 'The *Torrens:* A Personal Tribute', *Last Essays*, p. 24.

12. Letter to Mme Poradowska, 14 November 1891.

13. Basil Lubbock, *The Colonial Clippers*, 2nd edition, Glasgow 1921, p. 157.

14. ibid., p. 162.

15. 6 April 1892.

16. 4 September 1892. Certificate of discharge dated 3 September 1892.

17. Certificate of Discharge (Yale).

18. *A Personal Record*, pp. 15–18.

19. 8 April 1893, Marrot, op. cit., p. 85. I have not been able to track down the original of this letter but it seems safe to identify J— with Jacques.

20. 19 November 1893 (Death Certificate supplied by Somerset House).

21. Letter of 8 September 1894; Marrot, op. cit., p. 95.

22. ibid., p. 97.

23. Letter from Conrad to Galsworthy, Sunday (16 January 1898), *L.L.*, I, pp. 223–4.

24. In a report of *Jocelyn* quoted in a letter from Galsworthy to Garnett, 18 September 1910; Marrot, op. cit., p. 296. The facts

relating to Galsworthy have been taken from Marrot.

25. 17 May 1893. The dates of his visit to his uncle can only be vaguely deduced from his letters to Marguerite Poradowska of 17 May, 14 September and 5 November 1893.

26. Discharge Certificate (Yale).

27. 22 May 1893.

28. 14 September 1893.

29. cf., Letter to Mme Poradowska, 5 November 1893. He had lived at this address in the autumn of 1891; cf., letters to Mme Poradowska of 15 and 30 September, etc., 1891.

30. cf., Letters to Mme Poradowska, 5 and 26 November 1893.

31. See *A Personal Record*, pp. 9–10, although he says that he was then living in 'furnished apartments in a Pimlico square'.

32. See *A Personal Record*, pp. 6–11, and letter to Mme Poradowska, 26 November 1893.

33. Letter to Mme Poradowska, 6 December 1893.

34. Letter to Mme Poradowska, 18 December 1893.

35. do., 20 December 1893.

36. cf., do., 9 January 1894.

37. *A Personal Record*, p. 3.

38. 20 January 1894.

39. *Polski Slownik Biograficzny*, II, p. 163, gives the date as 29 January 1894 (Gee and Sturm, op. cit., p. 63 Note 1). Reckoning by the Gregorian calendar this would be 10 February. cf., Letter to Mme Poradowska 18 February 1894.

40. *A Personal Record*, p. 31.

41. Letter from Bobrowski to Conrad, 3 January 1889, and from Stanislas Zaleski to Conrad dated 25 February (o.s.) 1894.

42. Copy of Bobrowski's note of 19 March 1887. National library of Warsaw, MS, 2889.

43. Dated 29 March or 5 April 1894 by Gee and Sturm, op. cit., p. 64.

44. M. E. Reynolds, *Memories of John Galsworthy*, 1936, p. 26.

45. Late April (?), Gee and Sturm no. 60; and 2 May 1894.

46. See Gordan op. cit., pp. 112–29, for an interesting comparison of the various states of the text.

47. Letter to Mme Poradowska, 17 May (?) 1894.

48. F. Whyte, *William Heinemann; a Memoir*, p. 61 ff. See Gee and Sturm, op. cit., p. 69 Note 2.

49. Letter to Mme Poradowska, 18(?) August 1894.

50. New York Public Library (Berg Collection).

51. *Almayer's Folly*, p. 3.

52. *The Golden Echo*, 1953, p. 3.

53. ibid., p. 4.

54. Letter to Unwin 8 October 1894; Gordan, op. cit., p. 186 Note 67.

55. Garnett, *Letters from Conrad*, vi–viii.

56. *An Outcast of the Islands*, viii.

57. *A Personal Record*, p. 68.

58. ibid., p. 73.

59. *Youth*, p. 16.

60. R. L. Mégroz, *A Talk with Joseph Conrad*, 1926, p. 40.

61. *The Nigger of the 'Narcissus'*, p. 7.

62. 'A Glance at Two Books', *Last Essays*, p. 132.

63. *Notes on Life and Letters*, p. 12 and 16.

64. cf., 'Stephen Crane; a Preface to Thomas Beer's *Stephen Crane*', *Last Essays*, pp. 105–6.

Also, letter to Galsworthy of 9 April 1906, *L.L.*, II, p. 33.

65. 7 June 1918, *L.L.*, II, p. 206.

66. *Joseph Conrad; a Personal Remembrance*, 1924, p. 94.

67. Letter to Gosse, 26 June 1902 (British Museum).

68. F. M. Hueffer, ibid., p. 16.

69. 23(?) February 1895.

70. *Le Roman Naturaliste*, nouvelle édition, 1892, p. 8.

71. *Joseph Conrad*, (1916), p. 77.

72. Flaubert to Louise Collet, *Œuvres Complètes, Correspondance*, nouvelle édition augmentée, III, 1927, pp. 61–2.

73. *Pierre et Jean*, Œuvres Complètes, 1919, p. ix and *A Personal Record*, xix.

74. Saturday (May 1898).

75. Letter to A. H. Davray, 22 August 1903, *Lettres Françaises*, pp. 51–2.

76. Maupassant, ibid., xxv.

77. *A Personal Record*, xiv.

78. *The Nigger of the 'Narcissus'* ix.

79. Maupassant, ibid., xxv.

80. ibid., xxiv–v.

81. To Mrs E. L. Sanderson, Sunday (September 1910), *L.L.*, II, p. 118.

82. *Almayer's Folly*, pp. 142–3.

83. ibid., p. 198.

84. ibid., p. 35.

85. ibid., p. 31.

86. ibid., p. 43.

87. Sir Hugh Clifford, *A Talk on Joseph Conrad and his Work*, English Association (Ceylon Branch), February 1927, p. 4. cf., Conrad's letter to Clifford, 17 May 1898, *L.L.*, I, p. 237 and *A Personal Record*, vi.

88. *Almayer's Folly*, pp. 72–3.

89. ibid., pp. 88–9.

90. ibid., p. 71.

91. ibid., pp. 166–7.

92. *Letters from Conrad*, xix.

93. Letter to Garnett, 21 August 1908; and to Galsworthy (about the same date), *L.L.*, II, p. 70.

94. Letter to Hugh Walpole, 7 June 1918, *L.L.*, II, p. 206.

95. *A Personal Record*, vii–viii.

96. Clifford, op. cit., p. 13.

97. Paul Valéry, 'Sujet d'une Conversation avec Conrad' in *Homage à Joseph Conrad; La Nouvelle Revue Française*, Tome XXIII, 1 December 1924, p. 663.

98. H. R. Lenormand, 'Note sur un Séjour de Conrad en Corse', *Hommage à Joseph Conrad; La Nouvelle Revue Française*, Tome XXIII, 1 December 1924, p. 668.

CHAPTER VI: LITERARY APPRENTICESHIP

1. Letters to Mme Poradowska, p. 10, 23 October and Monday morning (29 October or 5 November, 1894).

2. Letter to Mme Poradowska, p. 23 (?) February 1895.

3. do., 12 April 1895.

4. do., 23(?) February 1895.

5. do., 2 May 1895.

6. do., 6 May 1895.

7. *The Weekly Sun*, 9 June 1895, pp. 1–2.

8. 15 June 1895; Vol. 79, p. 797.

9. 15 June 1895; Vol. 47, p. 502.

10. 29 June 1895; Vol. 11, pp. 722–3. John D. Gordan gives a detailed summary of the British and American press reception of *Almayer's Folly* in his *Joseph Conrad; the Making of a Novelist*, p. 271 ff.

11. Letter to Sanderson, 24 August 1895, *L.L.*, I, pp. 176–9.

12. ibid.

13. *An Outcast of the Islands*, p. 71.

14. ibid., p. 327. This passage was quoted by H. G. Wells in his review of the book in the *Saturday Review*, LXXXI, 16 May 1896, pp. 509–10.

15. ibid., p. 157.

16. ibid., p. 265.

17. 17 September 1895.

18. *An Outcast of the Islands*, ix.

19. ibid., p. 127.

20. ibid., pp. 331–2.

21. ibid., p. 62.

22. ibid., p. 93.

23. ibid., p. 301.

24. ibid., p. 250.

25. ibid., p. 327.

26. *An Outcast of the Islands*, p. 328.

27. ibid., p. 356.

28. ibid., p. 347.

29. ibid., p. 367.

30. *Saturday Review*, LXXXI, 16 May 1896, pp. 509–10.

31. *Twenty Letters to Joseph Conrad*, edited by G. Jean-Aubry, 1926.

32. Saturday (22 February 1896).

33. 9 April 1896.

34. *The Sisters*, with an Introduction by Ford Madox Ford, New York, 1928, p. 23.

35. ibid., p. 21.

36. ibid., p. 45.

37. ibid., p. 23.

38. Letter to Charles Zagórski, 10 March 1896, *L.L.*, I, p. 185.

39. Jessie Conrad, *Joseph Conrad and His Circle*, pp. 18–19.

40. *Letters from Conrad*, xxi.

41. ibid., xiii.

42. cf., *L.L.*, I, p. 185 (with omissions).

43. *Joseph Conrad and His Circle*, pp. 9–10.

44. Letter from Mrs G. F. W. Hope to James T. Babb, 7 March 1928 (Yale).

45. *Joseph Conrad as I Knew Him*, p. 104. She misdates this visit to Champel, saying that it was in December 1895 when it was in May (see p. 157).

46. ibid., p. 102.

47. ibid., pp. 104–5, and *Joseph Conrad and His Circle*, pp. 12–15.

48. *Letters from Conrad*, xxii.

49. Monday (dated 23 March by Garnett): cf., Jessie Conrad, *Joseph Conrad and His Circle*, p. 17.

50. Marriage certificate (Somerset House).

51. Tuesday (7 December 1897).

52. 5 August 1897, *L.L.*, I, p. 208.

53. The same evening according to *Joseph Conrad as I Knew Him* (p. 25), the next day according to *Joseph Conrad and His Circle* (p. 19).

54. See *supra*, p. 207.

55. 9 April 1896.

56. Letter to Mrs Sanderson (Edward Sanderson's mother), 6 April 1896, *L.L.*, I, pp. 187–8.

57. *Joseph Conrad as I Knew Him*, p. 38 and p. 108. *Joseph Conrad and His Circle*, p. 37.

58. 'The Idiots', *Tales of Unrest*, p. 56.

59. *Tales of Unrest*, vii.

60. 'The Idiots', *Tales of Unrest*, p. 72.

61. 26 May 1896. *Letters from Conrad*, xxiii.

62. 14 August 1896.

63. MS., p. 2, Ashley Library, British Museum.

64. The name is erased in the letter.

65. *Joseph Conrad as I Knew Him*, pp. 31–7 and *Joseph Conrad and His Circle*, 25 ff.

66. Yale. cf., *A Conrad Memorial Library; the Collection of George T. Keating*, New York, 1929, pp. 61–2.

67. *Tales of Unrest*, vii.

68. 'An Outpost of Progress', *Tales of Unrest*, p. 117.

69. 14 August 1896.

70. Jessie Conrad, *Joseph Conrad and His Circle*, p. 42. Letter to Garnett with this address, dated by him September 1896.

71. *Joseph Conrad and His Circle*, p. 44.

72. Letters to Garnett, 16 October and Sunday (25 October) 1896.

73. Letters to Garnett between 16 October and 7 December 1896; and to Sanderson, 21 November 1896, *L.L.*, I, pp. 196–7.

74. Letter to Garnett, Sunday (29 November 1896).

75. His first mention that the *Nigger* was to be serialized in the *New Review* comes in a letter to Garnett of 2 June 1897.

76. Letter to Garnett, 19 December 1896.

77. *The Nigger of the 'Narcissus'*, pp. 60–61.

78. ibid., p. 53.

79. ibid., p. 162.

80. ibid., p. 164.

81. ibid., p. 33.

82. ibid., p. 93.

83. ibid., pp. 6–7.

84. ibid., p. 32.

85. ibid., p. 9.

86. ibid., p. 80.

87. *Saturday Review*, LXXXV (1898), 145–6. Symons modified his view later; see *Notes on Joseph Conrad*, 1925, p. 26.

88. Letters to Cunninghame Graham, 31 January 1898, to Garnett, Wednesday (2 February 1898), and to Sanderson, 3 February 1898; the article was called 'Concerning a Certain Criticism' and was sent to *Outlook* but not printed.

89. Letter to Miss Watson, 27 January 1897, *L.L.*, I, p. 200.

90. 'Stephen Crane; a Preface to Thomas Beer's *Stephen Crane*', *Last Essays*, p. 95.

91. *The Nigger of the 'Narcissus'*, p. 16.

92. To Henry Canby, 7 April 1924, *L.L.*, II, p. 342.

93. 'Stephen Crane; a Preface to Thomas Beer's *Stephen Crane*', *Last Essays*, p. 94.

94. *The Nigger of the 'Narcissus'*, pp. 10–11.

95. ibid., p. 10.

96. ibid., pp. 72–3.

97. ibid., p. 37.

98. ibid., p. 138.

99. ibid., p. 42.

100. *The Nigger of the 'Narcissus'*, p. 43.

101. ibid., p. 47.

102. ibid., p. 40.

103. ibid., p. 100.

104. ibid., p. 40.

105. ibid., p. 149.

106. ibid., pp. 155–6.

107. Letter to Garnett, Sunday (25 October 1896).

108. Letter to John Quinn, quoted in *The Library of John Quinn, Part I, (A–C)*, Anderson Galleries, New York, 1923, p. 170. He expressed a similar opinion in his note 'To My Readers in

America' in a new edition of the book and also in Curle's copy.

109. *The Nigger of the 'Narcissus'*, pp. 133–4.

110. Letter to Garnett, Tuesday (24 August 1897).

111. *The Nigger of the 'Narcissus'*, vii.

112. ibid., ix.

113. ibid., x.

114. ibid., xii.

115. ibid., x.

CHAPTER VII: FRUSTRATION

1. Apparently 13 March. 'We shift camp at 7 a.m. tomorrow.' Letter to Garnett, 12 March (1897).

2. *Joseph Conrad and His Circle*, pp. 50–51.

3. Letter to Garnett, 14 April 1897.

4. 28 February 1897.

5. Letter to Garnett, Wednesday (24 March 1897).

6. Thursday (April 1898). *L.L.*, I, p. 234.

7. *Tales of Unrest*, vii.

8. 'The Lagoon', ibid., p. 204.

9. 'Karain', ibid., p. 40.

10. Conrad to Garnett, 18 July 1897; Meldrum to Blackwood, 6 May 1897, *Joseph Conrad; Letters to William Blackwood and David S. Meldrum*, edited by William Blackburn, Durham, N.C., 1958, p. 3.

11. Letter to Spiridion Kliszewski, 5 April 1897, New York Public Library.

12. MS. dated 24 September 1897, and letter to Garnett of same day.

13. 27 September 1897.

14. 8 October 1897.

15. *Tales of Unrest*, viii.

16. 'The Return', *Tales of Unrest*, p. 123.

17. ibid., p. 177.

18. ibid., p. 176.

19. ibid., p. 186.

20. ibid., p. 156.

21. ibid., p. 158.

22. ibid., pp. 150–51.

23. ibid., p. 153.

24. Blackwood to Conrad, 26 August 1897, and Conrad to Blackwood of 28 August and 6 September 1897. Also, Conrad to Garnett, 2 June 1897.

25. Monday evening (11 October 1897).

26. Letter to Garnett (14 October 1897).

27. Tuesday (26 October 1897).

28. Letter to Garnett, 5 November 1897.

29. 23 December 1897.

30. See William Rothenstein's *Men and Memories*, I, 1931, pp. 215–24.

31. This sketch of Cunninghame Graham is based on A. F. Tschiffely's biography, *Don Roberto*, 1937, and Paul Bloomfield's brilliant portrait in his introduction to *The Essential R. B. Cunninghame Graham*, 1952.

32. Tschiffely, *Don Roberto*, p. 412.

33. cf., Paul Bloomfield's description of Sly's cartoon of him, op. cit., p. 13.

34. *Don Roberto*, p. 419.

35. ibid., pp. 181–2.

36. Letter to Spiridion Kliszewski, 19 December 1885, *L.L.*, I, p. 84.

37. To Blackwood, 12 February 1899.

38. cf., *Don Roberto*, p. 260.

39. *L.L.*, I, p. 209.

40. 26 November (1897).

41. 2 December 1897. T. J. Wise, *A Bibliography of the Writings of Joseph Conrad* (1895–1921), 2nd edition, 1921.

42. 6 January 1898.

43. Letter of 7 January 1898, *L.L.*, I, p. 220.

44. John Berryman, *Stephen Crane*, 1950, p. 185.

45. ibid., p. 121 and pp. 125–7.

46. (14 October 1897).

47. 'Stephen Crane: a Preface to Thomas Beer's *Stephen Crane*', *Last Essays*, pp. 100–106.

48. *Bookman* (New York), LXIX, No. 3, May 1929, p. 230.

49. Berryman, op. cit., p. 201.

50. 5 December 1897.

51. Berryman, op. cit., p. 205.

52. ibid., p. 200.

53. 5 December 1897.

54. 7 January 1898, *L.L.*, I, p. 220.

55. *Daily Telegraph*, 8 December 1897.

56. XIV (1898), pp. 428–9.

57. 20 December 1897. Keating, op. cit., p. 39.

58. LXXIX (1897), p. 940.

59. 7 January 1898.

60. Letter to Garnett, 6 January 1898.

61. Letter to Cunninghame Graham, 31 January 1898, *L.L.*, I, p. 225.

62. 9 April 1898. Letters to Garnett, Wednesday (2 February) and Sanderson, 3 February 1898, *L.L.*, I, pp. 227–8.

63. 'An Observer in Malaya', review of *Studies in Brown Humanity; Academy*, 23 April 1898. He also wrote a piece on Kipling (see Chapter VI Note 88); and one on the novels of Fenimore Cooper and Marryat which appeared in *Outlook* for June 1898 with the title 'Tales of the Sea'.

64. Letters to Garnett, Wednesday (2 February) and to Cora Crane, 25 January 1898.

65. *Joseph Conrad and His Circle*, pp. 57–8.

66. Letter of Wednesday (2 February 1898).

67. *Joseph Conrad and His Circle*, p. 58. Jessie may have confused this visit to the Cranes with a visit that the Conrads made to the Garnetts later in the year. She says that they met Hueffer for the first time at the Cranes but from Hueffer's account (*Return to Yesterday*, pp. 52–5) it seems more likely that the first meeting took place during the visit to the Garnetts.

68. *Letters from Conrad*, xv–xvi.

69. 3 February 1898, *L.L.*, I, p. 228.

70. Undated, *Bookman* (New York), LXIX, No. 3. May 1929, p. 232.

71. 'Stephen Crane', *Last Essays*, pp. 115–16, and p. 118. Crane's short play 'The Blood of the Martyr' and a story 'The Clan of No-Name' were also apparently by-products. Berryman, op. cit., pp. 206–7.

72. Letter to Cunninghame Graham, 5 March 1898, *L.L.*, I, p. 230, and to Garnett (June 1898).

CHAPTER VIII: ENTER MARLOW

1. Saturday, *Letters from Conrad*, p. 130. The chronology here is confused because the crucial letters have incomplete dates. Blackburn, op. cit., p. 22, deduces that the date of the letter to Garnett is 4 June 1898 on the basis of Conrad's letter to Mrs E. L. Sanderson, dated 3 June 1898 (a Friday), announcing the finish of a short story, presumably 'Youth' – 'When your letter arrived I was finishing a short story. . . . Half an hour ago I've written the last word' – and of his letter to Meldrum, dated Friday, announcing the despatch of the end of 'Youth'. However, this reasoning is not conclusive, as there is no certainty that Conrad wrote to Mrs Sanderson on the same day as he sent the end of 'Youth' to Meldrum and, moreover, there is nothing in his letter to Garnett to indicate that it was written the day after he had finished 'Youth'. If Blackburn's date for the letter to Garnett is accepted it must be assumed that Meldrum had already seen an earlier draft of 'Youth' before Conrad wrote to Mrs Sanderson; otherwise there would have been no time for Meldrum to read the story or give his opinion to Conrad.

2. It seems clear from the letter that Meldrum had seen at least some of the story, and the figure 13,000 implies that the whole story was already written, but cf., Gordan, op. cit., p. 259 and p. 264, for another interpretation.

3. See p. 260.

4. See p. 459.

5. See pp. 94 ff.

6. *Youth*, pp. 3–4.

7. ibid., p. 12.

8. ibid., p. 30.

9. ibid., p. 34.

10. ibid., pp. 5–6.

11. ibid., p. 15.

12. ibid., p. 37.

13. ibid., p. 42.

14. ibid., p. 30.

15. ibid., p. 42.

16. ibid., p. 3.

17. ibid., p. 3.

18. ibid., p. 10.

19. ibid., p. 17.

20. ibid., p. 5.

21. ibid., pp. 28–9.

22. Letter to Garnett, Saturday (May 1898) and to Blackwood, 11 June 1898.

23. Letter to Garnett, Tuesday (May 1898) and to Meldrum, 4 June 1898. This first attempt at what was to become *Lord Jim* runs to twenty-seven pages of a small crown octavo notebook now at Harvard. Five lines of *The Rescue* follow immediately afterwards.

24. Letter to E. L. Sanderson, 15 June 1898, *L.L.*, I, p. 240.

25. 3 August 1898.

26. *L.L.*, I, p. 241. cf., letter of 3 August 1898, *L.L.*, I, p. 244; also, letter to Garnett of Saturday (August 1898): 'He [Cunninghame Graham] got it into his head to get me the command of a steamer or ship and swears he will do it.'

27. Letters to Cunninghame Graham of Saturday and 3 August 1898, *L.L.*, I, p. 244.

28. Letters to Mrs E. L. Sanderson of 31 August and H. G. Wells of 6 September 1898; *L.L.*, I, p. 248. F. M. Ford (Hueffer), *Joseph Conrad; a Personal Remembrance*, pp. 15–17 and *Return to Yesterday*, pp. 52–5. See Chapter VI note 67 for the possibility that Conrad and Hueffer had met earlier in the year.

29. Obituary notice in *The Times*, 21 January 1889; Douglas Goldring, *The Last Pre-Raphaelite*, 1948, pp. 21–3.

30. Goldring, op. cit., p. 21 and p. 33.

31. Goldring, op. cit., pp. 31–3 and pp. 51–2.

32. *Experiment in Autobiography*, 1934, II, p. 617.

33. *English Review*, XXXI, No. 141, August 1920, p. 178.

34. *Joseph Conrad, a Personal Remembrance*, p. 12 ff.

35. *Joseph Conrad, a Personal Remembrance*, pp. 36–7. In *Return to Yesterday* (p. 66) the passage in inverted commas is supposed to have been written by Conrad in a letter, and not spoken.

36. Sunday, (November 1899).

37. *Joseph Conrad, a Personal Remembrance*, p. 16.

38. *Return to Yesterday*, p. 186.

39. Letter to Galsworthy, 28 October 1898. *L.L.*, I, p. 252.

40. *Joseph Conrad, a Personal Remembrance*, pp. 239–40.

41. Letter to Hueffer, Thursday (13 or 20 October 1898); to Henley, 18 October 1898 (Pierpont Morgan Library), quoted *supra*, pp. 265–8. And letter to Galsworthy, 28 October 1898, *L.L.*, I, pp. 252–3: 'I concluded arrangement for collaboration with Hueffer. He was pleased. I think it's all right. Details when we meet.'

42. Goldring, op. cit., p. 68.

43. 17 October 1898.

44. Keating Collection, *A Conrad Memorial Library*, pp. 131–3.

45. (18 December 1898). cf., Letter to Blackwood 31 December 1898.

46. Meldrum to Blackwood, 6 February 1899; Conrad to Meldrum, Wednesday (8 February 1899).

47. *Youth, a Narrative; and Two Other Stories*, xi.

48. ibid., p. 45.

49. ibid., p. 51.

50. ibid., p. 48.

51. 8 February 1899, *L.L.*, I, p. 268.

52. *Youth*, p. 82.

53. ibid., p. 144.

54. ibid., p. 114.

55. ibid., p. 67.

56. ibid., p. 69.

57. ibid., p. 88.

58. ibid., p. 113.

59. ibid., p. 118.

60. ibid., p. 131.

61. ibid., p. 128.

62. ibid., p. 118.

63. ibid., p. 131.

64. ibid., p. 81.

65. ibid., p. 96.

66. ibid., p. 96.

67. ibid., p. 96.

68. ibid., p. 97.

69. ibid., pp. 116–17.

70. ibid., p. 116.

71. ibid., p. 97.

72. ibid., p. 97.

73. 3 December 1902.

74. *Youth*, p. 138.

75. ibid., p. 138.

76. ibid., p. 141.

77. *Youth*, p. 155.
78. ibid., p. 125.
79. ibid., p. 149 and p. 151.
80. ibid., p. 149.
81. ibid., p. 150.
82. ibid., p. 151.
83. ibid., p. 115.
84. ibid., p. 82.
85. ibid., p. 156.
86. ibid., p. 159.
87. Letter to John Quinn, 24 May 1916 (typed copy in New York Public Library).
88. 11 September 1898, *L.L.*, I, p. 249.
89. 23 March 1902.
90. Christmas 1898, *L.L.*, I, p. 264.
91. 25 April 1905, apropos of Wells's *A Modern Utopia*, *L.L.*, II, p. 16.
92. 8 November 1906. *Lettres Françaises*, p. 78.
93. Quoted by Hugh Walpole in his diary for 23 January 1918. Rupert Hart-Davis, *Hugh Walpole, a Biography*, 1952, p. 168.
94. *Boon, The Mind of the Race, The Wild Asses of the Devil*, and *The Last Trump; being a First Selection from the Literary Remains of George Boon, Appropriate to the Times*, 1915, p. 134 and pp. 144–5.
95. Wells, *Experiment in Autobiography*, II, pp. 615–22.
96. *Joseph Conrad and His Circle*, p. 75.
97. Thursday (August 1902).
98. Letter to Wells, Friday (end of November 1898). *L.L.*, I, p. 256.
99. Letter to Mrs Cunninghame Graham, 24 February 1899, *Lettres Françaises*, p. 37.
100. Letter to Aniela Zagórska, 18 December 1898, *L.L.*, I, p. 262.
101. Letter to Clifford, 9 October 1899, *L.L.*, I, p. 281.
102. Visits from Hueffer are mentioned in a letter to Garnett, Good Friday (1899), and to Galsworthy, 2 September 1899. *L.L.*, I, p. 279.
103. Letter to Garnett (June 1899); to Meldrum, 6 and 31 July 1899.
104. *Joseph Conrad, a Personal Remembrance*, pp. 133–4.
105. 24 August 1901, p. 603. Quoted by Frank MacShane, p. 51 of a hitherto unpublished thesis on Hueffer.
106. *Joseph Conrad, a Personal Remembrance*, p. 118.
107. ibid., p. 143.
108. Letter to Galsworthy, 2 September 1899, *L.L.*, I, p. 279; letter to Garnett, 26 October 1899, and several letters to Blackwood.
109. Letter to Cunninghame Graham, 13 February 1900, *L.L.*, I, p. 293; also to Blackwood, 12 February 1900.
110. Letter to Hueffer, 17 February, to Mme Poradowska, 16 April and to Galsworthy, Thursday (7 May 1900), *L.L.*, I, p. 294.
111. Berryman, op. cit., p. 259.
112. 26 March 1900.
113. Meldrum to Blackwood 14 July 1900.
114. T. J. Wise, *A Conrad Library, a Catalogue of Printed Books, Manuscripts and Autograph Letters by Joseph Conrad*, 1928, p. 6.
115. Essay on 'Le Roman', *Pierre et Jean*, xvi ff.
116. Preface to *The Princess Casamassima*, New York Edition, 1913, xii–xiii.
117. ibid., xii.

118. *Lord Jim*, viii.
119. ibid., p. 94.
120. ibid., p. 44.
121. ibid., p. 66.
122. ibid., p. 148.
123. ibid., p. 161.
124. ibid., p. 212 and p. 214.
125. ibid., ix.
126. ibid., p. 106.
127. ibid., p. 131.
128. ibid., p. 50.
129. ibid., p. 45.
130. ibid., p. 79.
131. ibid., p. 145.
132. ibid., p. 123.
133. ibid., p. 190.
134. ibid., pp. 386–7.
135. ibid., p. 111.
136. ibid., p. 106.
137. ibid., p. 81.
138. ibid., pp. 87–8.
139. ibid., p. 79.
140. ibid., p. 111.
141. ibid., p. 123.
142. ibid., p. 130.
143. ibid., p. 20.
144. ibid., p. 9.
145. ibid., p. 81.
146. ibid., pp. 66–8.
147. ibid., p. 59.
148. ibid., p. 65.
149. ibid., pp. 58–9.
150. ibid., p. 43.
151. ibid., p. 68.
152. ibid., p. 133.
153. ibid., p. 191.
154. ibid., p. 185.
155. ibid., p. 186.
156. ibid., p. 177.
157. ibid., pp. 212–13.
158. ibid., p. 20.
159. ibid., p. 216.
160. ibid., p. 179.
161. ibid., pp. 243–4. cf., ibid., p. 416, when the same image is used for the final atonement.
162. ibid., p. 305.
163. ibid., p. 324.
164. ibid., p. 306.
165. ibid., p. 333.
166. ibid., p. 335.
167. Douglas Hewitt, *Conrad, a Reassessment*, Cambridge, 1952, p. 33.
168. Albert J. Guerard, in *Conrad the Novelist*, Harvard and Oxford University Press, 1958, p. 145 and p. 149 speaks of Jim's 'crippling identification' and 'paralyzed identification' with Brown.
169. *Lord Jim*, pp. 391–3.
170. ibid., p. 388.
171. ibid., p. 409.
172. ibid., p. 410.
173. ibid., p. 416.
174. ibid., p. 339.
175. ibid., p. 225.
176. ibid., p. 222.
177. ibid., pp. 342–3.
178. ibid., p. 324 and p. 341.
179. ibid., p. 410.
180. For details see the *Singapore Daily Times* of 12 August 1880, et seq.
181. *Singapore Daily Times*, 23 August 1880.
182. According to Mrs Oehlers, Jim Lingard's daughter, in an interview with Dr Reed, 13 April 1951. According to Mr Cools, who lived in Berouw, she was half-Malayan, half-Chinese (Gordan, op. cit., p. 58).
183. Mrs Oehlers, loc. cit.
184. It is worth noting that Richard Curle states that 'Patusan was imagined to be situated on the south coast of north-west Sumatra' in an article, 'Joseph Conrad in the East', which Conrad checked, and revised extensively in his own

hand. Most of the typescript of the article, with Conrad's corrections and comments, is in the Keating Collection; cf., *A Conrad Memorial Library*, p. 418. Mr Haverschmidt says that there was a Kampong Patusan at Sambaliung (letter to Dr Reed of 30 July 1951); while there was a Patusan up the Sakarran River where Brooke wiped out a pirate's nest in 1844 (Mundy's *Borneo and Celebes*, I, p. 376 and p. p. 379 and Keppel's *Expedition to Borneo*, II, p. 79 ff.; quoted by Gordan, op. cit., p. 66).

185. *The Rescue*, pp. 3–4.

186. See Florence Clemens, 'Conrad's Favourite Bedside Book', *South Atlantic Quarterly*, Vol. XXXVIII, 1939, pp. 305–15.

187. pp. 284, 289 and 448.

188. *Lord Jim*, p. 250, and *Last Essays*, p. 91.

189. *The Rescue*, p. 174 and cf., p. 446.

190. *A Personal Record*, p. 121.

CHAPTER IX: THE PARTNERSHIP

1. Letter to Galsworthy, Friday (20 July 1900), *L.L.*, I, pp. 295–6.

2. do., 11 August 1900, *L.L.*, I, pp. 296.

3. *Joseph Conrad and His Circle*, p. 71.

4. ibid., p. 71.

5. Letter to Meldrum, 3 October and to Pinker, 8 October 1900.

6. Letter to Pinker, 15 January 1901. Date on MS. 'Midnight, 10th–11th Jany. 1901'.

7. *Typhoon and Other Stories*, vi.

8. ibid., v.

9. ibid., p. 4.

10. ibid., pp. 18–19.

11. ibid., p. 34.

12. ibid., pp. 20–21.

13. Letter to Pinker, Monday (between 8 October and 25 November 1900).

14. Referring specifically to *The Nigger of the 'Narcissus'*; *Experiment in Autobiography*, II, p. 617.

15. *Typhoon*, pp. 10–11.

16. ibid., p. 61.

17. ibid., p. 54.

18. ibid., p. 84.

19. ibid., p. 91.

20. Letter to Garnett, 27 October 1896.

21. Letter to Pinker, 23 January 1901: 'The second story progresses having taken a start since last Monday.'

22. MS. dated 'Winchelsea, May, 1901', cf., Letter to Hueffer, 28 April 1901: 'I am finishing "Falk" story but with me such a statement may mean anything' – also to Blackwood of 24 May in which he says that he has been in Winchelsea for a fortnight finishing a story for Heinemann.

23. *Joseph Conrad as I Knew Him*, p. 118. cf., Conrad's note in the Keating copy (*A Conrad Memorial Library*, p. 115, item 46).

24. 'Falk', *Typhoon and Other Stories*, pp. 153–6.

25. ibid., p. 145.

26. ibid., pp. 145–6.

27. *Typhoon*, p. 146.

28. ibid., p. 147.

29. ibid., p. 156.

30. ibid., p. 156.

31. ibid., p. 206.

32. ibid., p. 218.

33. ibid., p. 228.
34. ibid., p. 231.
35. ibid., p. 232.
36. ibid., p. 232.
37. ibid., p. 234.
38. ibid., p. 235.
39. ibid., p. viii.
40. ibid., p. 219.
41. ibid., p. 221.
42. op. cit., p. 44.
43. 'Falk', *Typhoon and Other Stories*, pp. 223–4.
44. Hewitt, op. cit., p. 42.
45. Letter to Davray, 2 April 1902, *Lettres Françaises*, p. 45.
46. Letter to Cunninghame Graham, 2 May 1903, *L.L.*, I, p. 314.
47. 'Falk', *Typhoon and Other Stories*, pp. 208–9.
48. Gordan Collection.
49. *L.L.*, I, p. 300.
50. 'Amy Foster', *Typhoon and Other Stories*, p. 119.
51. ibid., p. 107.
52. ibid., p. 109.
53. ibid., p. 137–8.
54. ibid., p. 139.
55. ibid., p. 140.
56. ibid., p. 142.
57. ibid., pp. 107–8.
58. ibid., p. 124.
59. ibid., p. 134.
60. Edition Nelson, I, p. 94 and p. 103.
61. 'Amy Foster', *Typhoon and Other Stories*, p. 118.
62. ibid., p. 113.
63. ibid., pp. 110–111.
64. Edinburgh and London, 1900, p. 163.
65. Yanko Goorall hid in Hammond's pig-pound. *Typhoon and Other Stories*, p. 118.
66. *Joseph Conrad as I Knew Him*, p. 118.
67. Letter to Galsworthy, 20 June 1901, *L.L.*, I, p. 300. Also various letters to Pinker.
68. Letter to Hueffer, 19 July 1901.
69. 6 January 1902.
70. 8 January 1902.
71. Letters to Pinker p. 6, 8 January and Sunday evening, undated, probably 12 January 1902.
72. 'Tomorrow', *Typhoon and Other Stories*, p. 277.
73. Undated.
74. *Joseph Conrad as I Knew Him*, p. 119.
75. See p. 272.
76. From a synopsis, partly typewritten and partly in Conrad's hand, in the Keating Collection; *Conrad Memorial Library*, item 56, pp. 131–3.
77. 12 April 1900.
78. Letter to Hueffer, undated.
79. 19 September 1900. The final version ran to thirty-four chapters.
80. Undated, between 19 September and 25 November 1900.
81. Letter to Pinker, 7 June 1901.
82. 20 June 1901. *L.L.*, I, p. 300.
83. Letter to Pinker, 3 July 1901.
84. Tuesday, *L.L.*, I, p. 312. Conrad's letter to Blackwood of 4 July 1901 in which he says that he has asked Pinker to send Blackwood Parts I, II and IV of *Seraphina* fixes the date of this letter to Hueffer as the end of June or beginning of July.
85. Conrad wrote to Pinker on 8 June that Blackwood had asked to see *Seraphina*.
86. Blackwood to Conrad, 15 August 1901.

87. Letter to Pinker, 7 November 1901.

88. 7 January 1902.

89. 10 March 1902.

90. Conrad's note in Curle's copy.

91. *Joseph Conrad and His Circle*, p. 66.

92. Undated.

93. Thursday.

94. *Joseph Conrad and His Circle*, pp. 67–8.

95. Undated.

96. 10 June 1902.

97. 8 November 1903, *Lettres Françaises*, p. 54.

98. 6 January 1902.

99. *Romance*, p. 335.

100. ibid., p. 5.

101. ibid., pp. 62–3.

102. ibid., p. 541.

103. ibid., p. 158.

104. Related by David Garnett in *The Golden Echo* (1953, p. 64). James is supposed to have said this at tea with Garnett's aunt, Olivia, and Elsie Hueffer, just after the writing of *The Inheritors*.

105. *Lettres Françaises*, pp. 54–5.

106. Monday (March or early April 1902). Letter to Davray, 10 April 1902, *Lettres Françaises*, p. 48.

107. 15 April 1902.

108. 19 June 1902.

109. *Joseph Conrad; a Personal Remembrance*, pp. 243–4.

110. 'The End of the Tether', *Youth, a Narrative and Two Other Stories*, p. 187.

111. ibid., p. 289.

112. ibid., p. 293.

113. *Youth*, p. 214.

114. ibid., p. 214.

115. ibid., p. 300.

116. ibid., p. 214.

117. ibid., p. 215.

118. ibid., p. 333.

119. ibid., p. 250.

120. ibid., p. 319.

121. ibid., p. 324.

122. loc. cit.

123. ibid., p. 165.

124. 28 October 1897.

125. loc. cit.

126. 'I aim at stimulating vision in the reader' (to Blackwood 6 September 1897); cf., '... *The Rescue* where I aim at purely aesthetic ... effects' (to Meldrum, 10 August 1898).

127. Blackwood to Conrad, 24 April 1900.

128. Blackwood to Conrad, 8 September 1898.

129. To Meldrum, 31 May 1902.

CHAPTER X: ACHIEVEMENT WITHOUT SUCCESS, I

1. Letter to Elsie Hueffer, 4 November 1902.

2. Letter to Pinker, 26 November 1902.

3. Letter to Hueffer, 2 January 1903.

4. loc. cit.

5. Thursday, *L.L.*, I, p. 308.

6. 3 February 1903 (Yale).

7. Letter to Pinker, 22 August 1904, *L.L.*, I, p. 315.

8. 20 May 1905 (Yale).

9. Letter to Mme Poradowska, 15 December 1904.

10. *Joseph Conrad as I Knew Him*, p. 51.

11. Letter to Wells, 7 February 1904, *L.L.*, I, p. 326.

12. ibid., pp. 326–7.

13. Letter to Galsworthy, 28 March 1911, *L.L.*, II, p. 128.

14. Sunday (12 March 1911).

15. 17 April 1909.

16. 18 August 1920.

17. Letter to Colvin, 28 April 1905, *L.L.*, II, p. 17.

18. *Return to Yesterday*, pp. 194–5.

19. *Joseph Conrad and His Circle*, p. 87.

20. 19 July 1904.

21. 23 March 1903.

22. 22 August 1903, *L.L.*, I, p. 316.

23. The MS pages are numbered 588–603 (590 is missing). They start at 'The *Porvenir* must have a long and confident article . . .' (p. 175 of the printed text) and run to 'She did not answer. She seemed tired and they . . .' (p. 185).

24. *Joseph Conrad and His Circle*, pp. 86–7.

25. *Return to Yesterday*, pp. 286–7.

26. Letter to Pinker, 29 March 1904.

27. Letter to Galsworthy, 1 September 1904, *L.L.*, I, p. 333.

28. Letter to Hueffer, 5 September 1904.

29. *Nostromo*, vii.

30. ibid., vii.

31. ibid., viii.

32. cf., Halverson and Watt, 'The Original Nostromo; Conrad's Source'.

33. In *Conrad Memorial Library*, p. 138.

34. *The Last Twelve Years of Joseph Conrad*, 1928, p. 38.

35. 8 July 1903, *L.L.*, I, p. 315.

36. The full title is *Seven Eventful Years in Paraguay; a Narrative of Personal Experience amongst the Paraguayans*, 1869.

37. Full title: *Venezuela: or, Sketches of Life in a South American Republic*, second edition, 1868. This book was in Conrad's library sold at Hodgson's the auctioneers on 13 March 1925. Masterman's book may also have been in the library which was not catalogued in full. The credit for first discovering these two sources belongs as far as I know to Mr Edgar Wright, who examined them in his thesis. cf., also, another, independent discovery: Ivo Vidan, 'One Source of Conrad's *Nostromo*', *Review of English Studies*, New Series, vii, No. 27, July 1956 (this relates to Masterman only).

38. *The War between Peru and Chile, 1879–82*, for instance, seems to have supplied some names, such as Camacho (Gamacho in *Nostromo*) and Fuentes, Montero, Avellano[s] and *Porvenir*.

39. Masterman, op. cit., pp. 256–9; cf., *Nostromo*, pp. 371–5.

40. Masterman, op. cit., p. 39 ff. and p. 84; cf., *Nostromo, passim*, particularly pp. 38–9 and p. 385 ff.

41. *Nostromo*, xiii–xiv.

42. Eastwick, op. cit., pp. 186–7.

43. *Nostromo*, p. 140.

44. Eastwick, op. cit., p. 187.

45. *Nostromo*, p. 140.

46. Eastwick, loc. cit.

47. Eastwick, op. cit., p. 139 and pp. 141–2; cf., *Nostromo*, pp. 3–8.

48. Eastwick, op. cit., p. 76; cf., *Nostromo*, p. 474.

49. Eastwick, op. cit., p. 319.

50. *Nostromo*, pp. 34–8 *et al.*

51. ibid., p. 26.

52. ibid., pp. 482–3.

53. Hewitt, op. cit., pp. 9–10.

54. *Nostromo*, p. 89.

55. ibid., p. 6.

56. ibid., p. 95.

57. loc. cit.
58. Letter to Curle, 14 July 1923.
59. *Nostromo*, p. 119.
60. ibid., p. 130.
61. ibid., Chapter X, pp. 473–89.
62. ibid., p. 4.
63. ibid., p. 185.
64. ibid., p. 246.
65. ibid., p. 248.
66. ibid., p. 300.
67. ibid., p. 275.
68. ibid., p. 265.
69. ibid., p. 417.
70. ibid., p. 418.
71. ibid., p. 422.
72. ibid., p. 460.
73. ibid., p. 503.
74. ibid., pp. 523–4.
75. ibid., p. 559.
76. ibid., p. 3.
77. ibid., p. 117.
78. ibid., p. 66.
79. ibid., p. 74.
80. ibid., p. 142.
81. ibid., p. 365.
82. ibid., p. 148.
83. ibid., p. 226.
84. ibid., p. 318.
85. ibid., p. 84.
86. ibid., pp. 35–6.
87. ibid., p. 74.
88. ibid., p. 107.
89. ibid., p. 115.
90. ibid., p. 76.
91. ibid., p. 219 and p. 80.
92. ibid., p. 29.
93. ibid., p. 31.
94. ibid., p. 140.
95. ibid., p. 504.
96. ibid., p. 498.
97. ibid., p. 153.
98. ibid., p. 189.
99. ibid., p. 176.
100. ibid., p. 177.
101. ibid., pp. 214–15.
102. ibid., pp. 218–19.
103. ibid., p. 218.
104. ibid., p. 216.
105. ibid., pp. 244–5.
106. ibid., p. 84.
107. ibid., p. 245.
108. ibid., p. 245.
109. ibid., pp. 221–2.
110. ibid., p. 400.
111. ibid., p. 522.
112. ibid., p. 207–9.
113. ibid., p. 560.
114. ibid., p. 557.
115. ibid., p. 379.
116. ibid., p. 200.
117. ibid., p. 498.
118. ibid., p. 496.
119. ibid., p. 520.
120. ibid., p. 522.
121. ibid., p. 362.
122. ibid., p. 501.
123. ibid., p. 501.
124. *Notes on Life and Letters*, p. 33.
125. *Nostromo*, p. 355.
126. ibid., p. 119.
127. ibid., p. 510.
128. ibid., p. 504.
129. ibid., p. 166.
130. ibid., p. 511.
131. ibid., p. 521.
132. ibid., p. 521.
133. ibid., p. 84.
134. ibid., p. 370.
135. 'Autocracy and War', *Notes on Life and Letters*, p. 107.
136. ibid., pp. 108–9.
137. *Nostromo*, p. 387.
138. ibid., p. 408.
139. ibid., p. 364.
140. ibid., p. 174.
141. ibid., p. 171.
142. ibid., p. 379.
143. ibid., p. 245 (cf., *Lord Jim*, p. 416: 'He goes away from a

living woman to celebrate his pitiless wedding with a shadowy ideal of conduct').

144. *Nostromo*, xiv.

145. ibid., p. 156.

146. ibid., p. 176.

147. ibid., p. 153.

148. ibid., p. 189.

149. ibid., p. 200.

150. ibid., p. 229; cf., *Typhoon*, vii.

151. ibid., p. 198.

CHAPTER XI: ACHIEVEMENT WITHOUT SUCCESS, II

1. Letter to Cunninghame Graham, 7 October 1904, *L.L.*, I, p. 337.

2. *Joseph Conrad and His Circle*, p. 89.

3. Letter to Hueffer, 15 October 1904.

4. 'London's River', which became 'The Faithful River' in *The Mirror of the Sea*, and 'Tallness of the Spars', which became 'Cobwebs and Gossamer'. Letters to Pinker, 31 October 1904 (Gordan) and 5 February 1905 (*L.L.*, II, p. 11); and to Hueffer, 22 November 1904.

5. Letters to Pinker, 18 October and 8 November 1904, etc.; to Hueffer, 22 November 1904. The *Strand* presumably turned the story down, as it did not appear there.

6. Letter to Davray, 14 January 1905. *Lettres Françaises*, p. 68. This letter seems to put it beyond doubt that they left on the 15th. However a letter to Wells dated 13 January 2 a.m. and to Galsworthy of 14 January imply that they left on the 14th.

7. *Joseph Conrad and His Circle*, p. 92.

8. Letter to Galsworthy, 21 January 1905, *L.L.*, II, p. 9.

9. *Joseph Conrad and His Circle*, p. 95.

10. Letter to Pinker, 23 February 1905, *L.L.*, II, pp. 12–13.

11. 9 May 1905, *L.L.*, II, p. 19.

12. Various letters to Pinker and Galsworthy. Letters to Pinker, 23 February, 12 and 22 April and 12 May 1905; to Galsworthy, 8 May 1905; *L.L.*, II, p. 18.

13. Letter to Pinker, 23 February 1905, *L.L.*, II, p. 13.

14. To Galsworthy, 30 June and to Ada Galsworthy, 2 November 1905, *L.L.*, II, p. 21 and p. 28.

15. 'Autocracy and War', *Notes on Life and Letters*, pp. 87–8.

16. ibid., p. 89.

17. ibid., p. 92 and p. 99.

18. ibid., pp. 102–3.

19. *Notes on Life and Letters*, p. 95.

20. ibid., p. 112.

21. ibid., p. 104.

22. ibid., p. 114.

23. Letter to Pinker, 24 April 1905 and various other letters to Pinker.

24. Letters to Gosse, 23 March and 11 April 1905, *L.L.*, II, pp. 14–15; and 19 May 1905 (Yale). Also, Rothenstein to Gosse, 20 May 1905 (Yale) and Rothenstein, *Men and Memories*, II, 1932, p. 61.

25. Letter to Pinker, 6 May 1905.

26. Letter to Count Szembek, 21 May 1905, *Lettres Françaises*, p. 73.

27. Letter to Galsworthy, 8 May 1905, *L.L.*, II, p. 19. Jessie Con-

rad, *Joseph Conrad and His Circle*, p. 103.

28. 30 June 1905, *L.L.*, II, pp. 20–21.

29. Letter to Pinker, 6 October 1905.

30. Letter to 20 October 1905, *L.L.*, II, p. 25.

31. *Joseph Conrad and His Circle*, p. 103.

32. 18 October 1905, *L.L.*, II, p. 24.

33. Letter to Wells, 28 November 1905, ibid., p. 28.

34. 'The Inland Sea', which became 'The Nursery of the Craft' and 'The Tremolino'; and 'Palmam qui Meruit Ferat, 1805–1905', which became 'The Heroic Age'. Letters to Wells, 20 October 1905, *L.L.*, II, p. 25; to Pinker 20 September and 6 October 1905.

35. *A Set of Six*, viii. The 'seed', including the name, Gaspar Ruiz, can be found in the account of the activities of the pirate Benavides in Chapter VIII of the third edition, Edinburgh, 1824, pp. 321 ff.

36. ibid., ix.

37. loc. cit.

38. 'An Anarchist', *A Set of Six*, p. 144.

39. ibid., pp. 147–8.

40. ibid., p. 158.

41. ibid., pp. 158–9.

42. ibid., p. 143.

43. ibid., pp. 160–61.

44. ibid., p. 74.

45. 'The Informer', *A Set of Six*, p. 78.

46. ibid., p. 97.

47. ibid., pp. 100–101.

48. Letter to Galsworthy, 26 December 1905, *L.L.*, II, p. 29.

49. 15 April 1904 (Yale).

50. Letter to Wells, 7 February 1904, *L.L.*, I, p. 327.

51. *The Mirror of the Sea*, ix.

52. ibid., p. 106.

53. ibid., p. 95.

54. ibid., p. 100.

55. Letter to Pinker, 21 February 1906.

56. Letter to Pinker, undated (probably March 1906).

57. *Joseph Conrad and His Circle*, pp. 113–16.

58. Birth Certificate (Somerset House).

59. Letter to Davray 8 November 1906, *Lettres Françaises*, p. 78; and to Garnett of the same date.

60. The 'friend's' identity is based on Hueffer's own assertion, but there is no reason to doubt it.

61. *The Secret Agent*, ix–x. Hueffer gives a different version of what he actually said in *Joseph Conrad: a Personal Remembrance*, pp. 230–31.

62. *The Secret Agent*, xi.

63. ibid., xi.

64. ibid., xi.

65. ibid., xv. In a letter to a certain Ambrose J. Barker who had sent him a pamphlet entitled *The Greenwich Mystery*, published in Sheffield in 1897, Conrad said that the novel was 'in intention, the history of Winnie Verloc'. *L.L.*, II, p. 322.

66. *The Times*, 16 February 1894.

67. *The Secret Agent*, pp. 8, 10 and 88–9.

68. *The Times*, 17 February 1894.

69. *Sidelights on the Home Rule Movement*, 1906, p. 89. Conrad's library contained Anderson's autobiographical *The Lighter Side of my*

Official Life and may also have contained the other book.

70. 7 October 1907, *L.L.*, II, p. 60.

71. *The Times*, 19 November 1890 *et seq*. There may well be more relevant details connected with this case but I have not been able to discover them.

72. *The Secret Agent*, xiii.

73. ibid., pp. 284–5.

74. Douglas Hewitt, op. cit., p. 85.

75. *The Secret Agent*, pp. 87–90.

76. ibid., p. 88.

77. ibid., p. 260.

78. ibid., p. 187.

79. ibid., p. 184.

80. ibid., p. 10.

81. ibid., p. 255.

82. ibid., p. 234.

83. ibid., p. 241.

84. ibid., pp. 12–13.

85. ibid., pp. 256–7.

86. ibid., p. 262.

87. ibid., p. 263.

88. 7 October 1907, *L.L.*, II, p. 60.

89. 1 September 1923, *L.L.*, II, p. 322.

90. *The Secret Agent*, ix.

91. ibid., p. 48.

92. ibid., p. 48.

93. ibid., p. 81.

94. ibid., p. 81.

95. ibid., pp. 42–3.

96. ibid., p. 41.

97. ibid., p. 44.

98. ibid., p. 83.

99. ibid., p. 62.

100. ibid., p. 4.

101. ibid., p. 18.

102. ibid., p. 21.

103. ibid., p. 53.

104. ibid., p. 245, also p. 237.

105. ibid., p. 178 *et al.*

106. ibid., p. 169.

107. ibid., p. 288.

108. ibid., p. 259.

109. ibid., p. 298.

110. ibid., p. 244.

111. ibid., pp. 24–5.

112. ibid., p. 35.

113. ibid., p. 224.

114. ibid., p. 224.

115. ibid., p. 140.

116. ibid., p. 92.

117. ibid., pp. 92–3.

118. ibid., p. 97.

119. ibid., p. 114.

120. ibid., p. 104.

121. ibid., p. 139.

122. ibid., p. 142.

123. ibid., p. 140.

124. Letter from Conrad to Ambrose J. Barker, *L.L.*, II, p. 322.

125. Letter to Garnett, 20 November 1906.

126. Conrad has put this date at the end of the manuscript, *The Library of John Quinn*, Lot 1847, p. 183.

127. 'Il Conde', *A Set of Six*, p. 288.

128. loc. cit.

129. Letter to Davray, 5 December 1906, *Lettres Françaises*, p. 80, and to Mme Poradowska, 7 December 1906.

130. Letter to Cunninghame Graham, 31 December 1906, *L.L.*, II, p. 40.

131. Letter to Pinker, 25 January 1907, ibid., II, p. 41.

132. do., 15 January 1907.

133. do., 25 January 1907, *L.L.*, II, p. 42.

134. 13 March 1907, ibid., p. 45.

135. Letter to Pinker, 13 April 1907.

136. 'The Duel', *A Set of Six*, p. 265.

137. *A Set of Six*, xi.

138. ibid., x.

139. *Notes on Life and Letters*, p. 86.

140. 'The Duel', *A Set of Six*, p. 220.

141. See Hodgson's sale catalogue of 13 March 1925.

142. *Modern Language Notes*, L (1935), pp. 385–90.

143. 6 May 1907, *L.L.*, II, p. 47.

144. Letter to Rothenstein, 28 May 1907, ibid., p. 50.

145. Letter to Pinker, 30 July 1907, ibid., p. 54.

146. 28 May 1907, ibid., pp. 50–51.

147. Letter to Harriet Capes, 13 August 1907 (Yale).

148. do., 10 September 1907 (Yale).

149. Letters to Pinker, 30 December 1907 (Gordan) and to Galsworthy, 6 January 1908, *L.L.*, II, pp. 64–5.

150. 12 October 1907.

151. 'The Censor of Plays', *Notes on Life and Letters*, pp. 78–9.

152. ibid., p. 80.

CHAPTER XII: ACHIEVEMENT WITHOUT SUCCESS, III

1. 1 January 1908.

2. *Speaker*, 12 November 1904, New Series, XI, pp. 138–9.

3. 21 October 1904, p. 320.

4. Letter to Gosse as member of the Committee of the Royal Literary Fund, of 26 June 1902 (Ashley Library, British Museum).

5. No. 4170, 28 September 1907, p. 361.

6. 1 January 1908.

7. 6 January 1908, *L.L.*, II, p. 64.

8. loc. cit.

9. Sunday night (probably end of August 1908), *L.L.*, II, p. 70.

10. Letters to Symons, 29 August 1908, ibid., p. 84; and to Garnett, 28 August 1908.

11. cf., letters to Elsie Hueffer of 12 and 18 December 1908.

12. For instance, Richard Curle in *Caravansary and Conversation*, 1937, p. 275; Archibald Marshall, *Out and About: Random Reminiscences*, 1933, p. 275.

13. Letter to Galsworthy, 15 February 1911.

14. cf., Hueffer's *Return to Yesterday*, pp. 372–6.

15. *Joseph Conrad and His Circle*, p. 131.

16. 23 October 1923, *L.L.*, II, p. 323.

17. Douglas Goldring, op. cit., p. 150.

18. Letter to Galsworthy, 13 July 1909; *L.L.*, II, pp. 100–101; and to Garnett, 19 July 1909.

19. *English Review*, I, July 1909, p. 824.

20. 7 September 1909.

21. This fragment has been incorrectly catalogued in Keating's *Conrad Memorial Library*. It appears as item 304, 'Marriage: a fragment of an unpublished manuscript of Conrad'. The fragment, less the last few sentences, constitutes part of pp. 69–70 of the book.

22. 23 June 1909, *L.L.*, II, p. 100.

23. Letter to Galsworthy, 30 April 1909. ibid., p. 97.

24. *A Personal Record*, xxiii.

25. *A Personal Record*, p. 35.

26. ibid., p. 36.

27. ibid., p. 110.

28. ibid., p. 121.

29. W. Chwalewik, 'Joseph Conrad in Cardiff', *Ruch Literacki*, VII, No. 8, 1932.

30. 'Some Memories of Conrad', *Wiadomości Literackie*, No. 51, 1929.

31. Joseph Ujejski, *Joseph Conrad*, traduit par Pierre Duméril, 1939, p. 18. cf., Aniela Zagórska's article 'Some Memories of Conrad' in *Wiadomości Literackie*, No. 51, 1929.

32. 'At Konrad Korzeniowski's Home', *Kultura*, No. 2, 1932.

33. cf., Letter to Davray from Aldington of 10 March 1909, *Lettres Françaises*, p. 97.

34. Letter to Gibbon, 19 December 1909 (Berg Collection).

35. Letter to Galsworthy, 29 March 1909, *L.L.*, II, p. 96.

36. Letter to Galsworthy, 14 December 1909, to Gibbon, 19 December 1909 (Berg Collection) and to Pinker, Wednesday.

37. *'Twixt Land and Sea*, viii. For an account of the incident see Basil Lubbock, *The Log of the 'Cutty Sark'*, third edition, Glasgow, 1928, pp. 183–202 and pp. 410–12.

38. 'The Secret Sharer', *'Twixt Land and Sea*, p. 93.

39. ibid., p. 99.

40. ibid., p. 100.

41. Undated (December 1909).

42. *'Twixt Land and Sea*, p. 142.

43. Introduction, p. 10, to *Heart of Darkness* and *The Secret Sharer*, Signet Books, 1950.

44. ibid., p. 9.

45. ibid., p. 11.

46. ibid., p. 12.

47. ibid., p. 10.

48. 'The Secret Sharer', *'Twixt Land and Sea*, p. 102.

49. *'Twixt Land and Sea*, p. 122.

50. ibid., pp. 124–5.

51. Basil Lubbock, *The Log of the 'Cutty Sark'*, pp. 182–3.

52. Basil Lubbock, ibid., pp. 410–11.

53. 'The Secret Sharer', *'Twixt Land and Sea*, p. 102.

54. loc. cit.

55. Monday (1913), *L.L.*, II, p. 143.

56. Douglas Hewitt, op. cit., pp. 73–6.

57. 'The Secret Sharer', *'Twixt Land and Sea*, p. 143.

58. ibid., p. 92.

59. ibid., p. 142.

60. ibid., p. 143.

61. Letter to Pinker, Monday (October 1909), *L.L.*, II, p. 102.

62. To Galsworthy, 10 November 1909; cf., letter of Friday early December 1909).

63. 19 December 1909 (Berg Collection).

64. The typescript is dated 'End. 22 Jan. 1910 J.C.' (Keating Collection).

65. 27 May 1912.

66. (2 May 1917).

67. *Under Western Eyes*, vii.

68. ibid., x.

69. ibid., pp. 163–4.

70. ibid., p. 25.

71. ibid., pp. 358–62.

72. ibid., p. 106.

73. ibid., p. 114.

74. ibid., p. 120.

75. *Under Western Eyes*, p. 161.
76. ibid., p. 217.
77. ibid., p. 194.
78. ibid., p. 109; cf., also, p. 347.
79. ibid., p. 30.
80. ibid., p. 56.
81. ibid., p. 245.
82. ibid., p. 382.
83. ibid., pp. 134–5.
84. ibid., p. 7.
85. ibid., p. 306.
86. ibid., p. 10.
87. ibid., p. 66.
88. ibid., p. 34.
89. ibid., p. 95.
90. ibid., p. 358.
91. ibid., p. 358.
92. ibid., pp. 37–8.
93. ibid., p. 77.
94. ibid., p. 99.
95. ibid., p. 357.
96. ibid., p. 203.
97. ibid., p. 303.
98. ibid., p. 135.
99. ibid., p. 172.
100. ibid., pp. 353–4.
101. ibid., p. 10.
102. ibid., p. 39.
103. ibid., pp. 307–8.
104. ibid., p. 352.
105. ibid., p. 357.
106. ibid., p. 362.
107. ibid., p. 354.
108. *Crime and Punishment*, translated by Constance Garnett, Heinemann, 1914, p. 14.
109. *Under Western Eyes*, p. 349.
110. *Crime and Punishment*, p. 41.
111. *Under Western Eyes*, p. 356.
112. *Crime and Punishment*, p. 372.
113. *Under Western Eyes*, p. 361, also cf., p. 341.
114. *Crime and Punishment*, p. 379.
115. Note in Curle's copy.
116. *Under Western Eyes*, viii.
117. David Garnett, *The Golden Echo*, pp. 10–20 and *passim*; cf., also Arkady Shiryaev, *S. M. Stepniak-Krawtschinski, eine Politisch-biographische Skizze*, Zurich, 1896.
118. 6 January 1908, *L.L.*, II, p. 65.
119. cf., *The Times*, 29 July 1904 ff.
120. cf. *The Times*, 16 January 1909 ff., particularly 15 April. cf., 'The Russian Spy System; the Azeff Scandals in Russia', by D. S., *English Review*, I, March 1909, pp. 816–32.
121. cf., letter to Galsworthy, 6 January 1908, *L.L.*, II, pp. 64–5.
122. Typescript, p. 591.
123. Jessie Conrad, *Joseph Conrad as I Knew Him*, p. 135 ff., and *Joseph Conrad and His Circle*, p. 140 ff.
124. Letter to Davray, 3 May 1910, *Lettres Françaises*, p. 100.
125. 19 May 1910, *L.L.*, II, p. 109.
126. 28 June 1910, *L.L.*, II, p. 113.
127. Jessie Conrad, *Joseph Conrad and His Circle*, p. 141.
128. cf., letter of 11 March 1912.
129. Letter to Sanderson, 2 September 1910, *L.L.*, II, p. 115.
130. Letter to Galsworthy, 27 October 1910, *L.L.*, II, p. 119.
131. Letters to Galsworthy, 17 May and to Sanderson, 2 September 1910, *L.L.*, II, p. 115; to Pinker, 1 October and 10 December 1910.
132. 'A Happy Wanderer' (*Quiet Days in Spain*, by C. Bogue Luffmann), 'The Life Beyond' (*Existence After Death Implied by Science*, by Jaspar B. Hunt) and 'The Ascending Effort' (book of the same title by George Bourne);

they have been reprinted in *Notes on Life and Letters*.

133. *Within the Tides*, xi.

134. Inscription in Keating's copy of *Tales of Hearsay; A Conrad Memorial Library*, p. 365.

135. Vol. II, pp. 372–4.

136. 'Prince Roman', *Tales of Hearsay*, p. 30.

137. *Tales of Hearsay*, p. 39.

138. 'A Smile of Fortune', *'Twixt Land and Sea*, p. 81.

139. ibid., p. 87.

140. ibid., p. 66.

141. ibid., p. 77.

142. ibid., p. 84.

143. ibid., p. 85.

144. Letter to Galsworthy, Monday (1913), *L.L.*, II, p. 144.

145. Letter to Pinker, 28 February 1911.

146. *'Twixt Land and Sea*, ix–x.

147. *Within the Tides*, x.

148. 'Freya of the Seven Isles', *'Twixt Land and Sea*, p. 149.

149. ibid., p. 150.

150. ibid., p. 158.

151. ibid., p. 171.

152. ibid., pp. 164–5.

153. ibid., pp. 204–5.

154. 4 August 1911.

155. Letter to Garnett, 29 July 1911.

156. Letter to Pinker, 9 August 1911.

CHAPTER XIII: SUCCESS AND THE WAR

1. Letter to Galsworthy, Sunday (May 1911), *L.L.*, II, p. 129.

2. Letter to Galsworthy, 8 September 1910 (*L.L.*, II, pp. 118–19) and 25 September 1910. Various letters to Pinker during August and September 1910.

3. Granted 9 August 1910; *The Times*, 7 July 1911.

4. The first of Conrad's letters to Quinn printed in the typescript in the New York Public Library is dated 24 August 1911.

5. Letters to Quinn, 8 December 1912, 16 March and 17 July 1913.

6. Letter to Pinker, undated.

7. Letter to Garnett, 18 July 1911.

8. Letters to Galsworthy, Friday 11 a.m. (August 1911), *L.L.*, II, p. 133; and to Elsie Hueffer, 24 August 1911.

9. Letter to Pinker, 19 June 1911.

10. 'On the 25th at 3 a.m.' Letter to Galsworthy, 29 (possibly 27) March 1912, *L.L.*, II, p. 138.

11. 2 June 1913, *L.L.*, II, p. 146.

12. Alfred Knopf has told the story in 'Joseph Conrad, a Footnote to Publishing History', *The Atlantic Monthly*, February 1958, pp. 63–7.

13. Figures supplied by the kindness of Messrs Methuen & Co. Ltd.

14. 25 October 1911.

15. 11 October 1911.

16. 13 October 1911.

17. 18 January 1914.

18. 15 January 1914.

19. *Daily Telegraph*, 21 January 1914.

20. To Pinker, received 8 or 6 April 1913. At about this time Pinker's office adopted the practice of stamping letters with their date of arrival.

21. *Letters from Conrad*, xx.

22. To Pinker (? March 1912).

23. *Chance*, viii–ix.

24. *The Great Tradition*, pp. 222–5.

25. *Joseph Conrad; some Aspects of the Art of the Novel*, 1936, primarily pp. 122–33.

26. op. cit., pp. 89–102.

27. *Joseph Conrad*, 1915, pp. 158–63.

28. Letter to Galsworthy, 8 May 1905, *L.L.*, II, p. 18.

29. Letters to Pinker, 12 April, 22 April and 12 May 1905; erased title to MS. of *Chance*.

30. *Chance*, p. 116.

31. ibid., p. 122.

32. ibid., p. 116.

33. ibid., p. 118.

34. *Under Western Eyes*, ix.

35. *Chance*, p. 245.

36. ibid., pp. 426–7.

37. ibid., pp. 99–100.

38. ibid., p. 353.

39. ibid., p. 63.

40. ibid., p. 327.

41. ibid., p. 310.

42. ibid., p. 188.

43. ibid., pp. 281–2.

44. Letter to Pinker, Wednesday (rec'd 20 June 1913).

45. *Chance*, p. 225.

46. ibid., p. 281.

47. ibid., p. 428.

48. ibid., p. 224.

49. ibid., p. 331.

50. ibid., p. 437.

51. He published an autobiographical book, after his release from prison in 1906, entitled *My Prison Life*, 1907.

52. These facts have been taken from Aylmer Vallance's entertaining *Very Private Enterprise, an Anatomy of Fraud and High Finance*, 1955.

53. *Chance*, pp. 68–87.

54. Letter to Galsworthy, 29 (possibly 27) March 1912, *L.L.*,II, p. 138 and to Pinker, Wednesday (about the same date).

55. It appeared November 1912.

56. *Conrad to a Friend*, p. 3.

57. ibid., Wednesday (December 1912), p. 5.

58. ibid., p. 8 ff.

59. Letter to Bennett, 17 November 1912, *L.L.*, II, p. 142.

60. Letter to André Gide, 14 April 1912, *Lettres Françaises*, p. 117.

61. Letters to Pinker, 23 January, Monday evening (early May), Saturday (rec'd 13 May), Thursday (rec'd 31 May), 12 September and undated (rec'd 5 December).

62. do., Tuesday evening (rec'd 18 December), 31 May and 27 February 1913.

63. *Within the Tides*, xi. The story in *Household Words* was actually called 'A Terribly Strange Bed' and appeared on 24 April 1852, pp. 129–37.

64. Thursday night (rec'd 1 October 1912).

65. 6 November 1912.

66. Saturday (2 August 1913), *L.L.*, II, p. 149.

67. Tuesday (rec'd 4 September 1913).

68. Tuesday evening (rec'd 12 September 1913).

69. Letters from Conrad to Russell of 4 and 13 September 1913.

70. *Portraits from Memory*, p. 84.

71. Letter to Pinker, 20 (?) September 1913 (rec'd 1 October, therefore date probably 30 September).

72. *Portraits from Memory*, p. 84.

73. Letter to Pinker, Monday 2 a.m. (rec'd 5 May 1913).

74. Both were finished by 8 January 1914 (letter to Gide, *Lettres Françaises*, p. 131). The MS. of 'The Planter' is dated 14 December 1913 (Keating Collection).

75. 'Because of the Dollars', *Within the Tides*, p. 186. Conrad's letter to Editor of Sydney *Bulletin* (23 March 1916), *L.L.*, II, p. 171.

76. 'The Planter of Malata', *Within the Tides*, p. 3.

77. ibid., p. 85.

78. ibid., p. 47.

79. ibid., pp. 75–6.

80. ibid., p. 78.

81. *Within the Tides*, xi.

82. 'The Planter of Malata', *Within the Tides*, p. 41.

83. ibid., p. 78.

84. ibid., p. 80.

85. Letter to Pinker, 1 July 1914 and others, undated, and to Galsworthy, 25 July 1914, *L.L.*, II, p. 156. These sources are presumably more likely to be correct than Conrad's statement in the 'Note to the First Edition' that the last word was written on 29 May.

86. *Victory*, pp. 174–5.

87. ibid., p. 90.

88. ibid., p. 18.

89. ibid., p. 199.

90. ibid., p. 199.

91. ibid., p. 199, p. 200.

92. ibid., p. 54.

93. ibid., p. 379.

94. ibid., p. 66.

95. ibid., p. 83.

96. ibid., p. 221.

97. ibid., p. 222.

98. ibid., p. 201.

99. ibid., p. 187.

100. ibid., p. 404.

101. ibid., p. 407.

102. ibid., p. 410.

103. ibid., p. 410.

104. *The Great Tradition*, p. 208.

105. Preface to *The Princess Casamassima*, New York Edition, xii–xiii.

106. *Victory*, p. 107.

107. ibid., p. 329.

108. *Œuvres Complètes*, XVI, . . . *Splendeurs et Misères des Courtisanes;* IV, La Dernière Incarnation de Vautrin; Paris, Conard, 1913, p. 253.

109. *Victory*, p. 388.

110. ibid., p. 102.

111. ibid., p. 360.

112. ibid., p. 389.

113. ibid., xii.

114. 'Conrad's Axel', *Studies in Philology*, XLVIII (1951), pp. 98–106.

115. Villiers de l'Isle Adam, *Axël*, II, § 3, Scene x.

116. *Victory*, p. 379.

117. Villiers de l'Isle Adam, op. cit., IV, § 2.

118. loc. cit.

119. Letter to Galsworthy, 5 May 1914, *L.L.*, II, p. 154.

120. *Lord Jim*, pp. 221–2.

121. Letter to Galsworthy, 25 July 1914, *L.L.*, II, p. 157.

122. *Notes on Life and Letters*, pp. 141–73.

123. cf., Conrad's confession of sympathy for the Austrian dynasty in an interview with Marjan Dabrowski; *Tygodnik Illustrowany*, 16 April 1914, quoted by Ujejski, op. cit., p. 42.

124. See Arnold Bennett's Journal for 4 November 1914; *The Journals of Arnold Bennett*, Vol. II, 1932, p. 108.

125. He left this document with

Dr Theodor Kosch, a Cracow lawyer. It was published for the first time in 1934 in the Easter number of *Czas*. Ujejski, op. cit., p. 43.

126. Telegram of 20 October 1914 to Pinker from Milan.

127. Letter of 24 October 1914 to S. Zajączkowski; Jessie Conrad, *Joseph Conrad as I Knew Him*, p. 90.

128. 28 January 1915, *L.L.*, II, p. 168.

129. Letter to Pinker, 15 November 1918.

130. do., 3 February 1915.

131. Letter to Curle, 18 December 1915.

132. Sunday (early 1917).

133. 27 February (1917), *L.L.*, II, p. 182.

134. *The Shadow-Line; A Confession*, p. 40.

135. ibid., pp. 131–2.

136. ibid., p. 108.

137. Letter to Pinker, Wednesday, (1917).

138. *The Shadow-Line*, p. 115.

139. ibid., p. 120.

140. Finished about 30 March 1916; letter to Pinker of this date.

141. Mentioned in letter to Pinker 31 October 1916.

142. Letter to Colvin, 2 April 1917 (Yale).

143. 'The Warrior's Soul', *Tales of Hearsay*, p. 15.

144. ibid., p. 21.

145. ibid., p. 26.

146. *Tales of Hearsay*, xiii.

147. Letter to Colvin, 2 April 1917.

148. 'The Warrior's Soul', *Tales of Hearsay*, pp. 3–4.

149. 'The Tale', *Tales of Hearsay*, p. 67.

150. ibid., p. 78.

151. ibid., p. 79.

152. ibid., p. 81.

153. ibid., p. 80.

154. Thursday (13 April 1916); cf., also letter of 23 July 1916.

155. Letter to Curle, 20 August 1916.

156. Tuesday (1917).

157. *Joseph Conrad and His Circle*, pp. 204–8.

158. cf., letter to Pinker (? late 1916).

159. Jessie Conrad, ibid., p. 166 and letters to Pinker, 4 July and Curle 20 August 1916.

160. Letter to Pinker, Royal Hotel, Lowestoft, 15 September 1916.

161. Sunday morning (early November 1916), *L.L.*, II, p. 177.

162. 4 December 1916, *L.L.*, II, p. 180.

163. Letter to Cunninghame Graham, 3 January 1917, *L.L.*, II, p. 181 and to Garnett (2 May 1917).

164. Letters to Pinker, undated and Sunday (?1917). It was to be set in Italy. The outline of a play, concerning artists and set in Italy, that comes after the pages of 'Jim' in Mrs Bobrowska's commonplace-book may be connected with this scheme.

165. Letters to Pinker, 15 August 1917 and Thursday (a little later).

166. do., undated.

167. Cancelled opening, MS. pp. 1–2 (Yale).

168. Letter to Pinker, Norfolk Hotel, 26 November and to Colvin 30 November 1917.

169. cf., Galsworthy diary for 14 and 27 November 1917. Marrot, op. cit., p. 433.

170. Letter to the Sandersons, 31 December 1917, *L.L.*, II, p. 198.

171. Letter to Pinker, 4 June 1918. The 'Two Notes' were not yet written, which may account for the discrepancy between this date and that which he gave to Curle, 9 October 1918.

172. Letter to S. A. Everitt, 18 February 1918.

173. *The Arrow of Gold*, ix.

174. ibid., p. 146.

175. ibid., p. 334.

176. ibid., p. 58.

177. 8 October 1922, *L.L.*, II, p. 276.

178. Letter to Colvin, Wednesday (1919), *L.L.*, II, p. 229.

179. *The Arrow of Gold*, p. 196 ff.

180. ibid., p. 313 ff.

181. ibid., p. 88. F. R. Leavis has singled out this passage for criticism, *The Great Tradition*, p. 182.

182. ibid., p. 219.

183. ibid., p. 141.

184. ibid., p. 283.

185. Letter to Curle, 9 October 1918, and to Pinker 16 July 1918.

186. Letter to Curle, 9 October 1918.

187. Letter to Colvin, 21 October 1918 (Univ. Virginia) and 11 November 1918, *L.L.*, II, p. 211.

188. Letter to Clifford, 25 January 1919, *L.L.*, II, p. 217.

189. 'A Note on the Polish Problem' *Notes on Life and Letters*, p. 138.

190. Letter to Pinker, 11 Apri 1919.

CHAPTER XIV: LAST YEARS

1. Letters to Pinker, 25 September 1918 (*L.L.*, II, p. 208) *et al.* and to Curle, 9 October 1918.

2. Letter to Curle, 9 October 1918.

3. Letter to Admiral Goodenough, 25 September 1920, *L.L.*, II, p. 249; cf., letter to Garnett, 7 July 1919.

4. 5 July (1918).

5. Letter to Pinker, 25 September 1918, *L.L.*, II, p. 208.

6. Letter to Walpole, 30 May 1919, *L.L.*, II, p. 222; to Pinker, 25 May 1919, *et al.*

7. This occupied him during December 1919 and the first two months of 1920. Letter to Garnett, 8 December 1919, and to Curle, 19 January and 26 February 1920. The first proofs, set up from the *Land and Water* text and revised for book form, are in the Keating Collection at Yale.

8. 2 October 1918, *L.L.*, II, p. 209.

9. *The Rescue*, p. 5.

10. MS. p. 5, the Ashley Library the British Museum.

11. *The Rescue*, p. 5.

12. MS. pp. 5–6.

13. *The Rescue*, p. 210 and MS. pp. 411–12.

14. The MS. runs to p. 247 of the printed text.

15. *The Rescue*, p. 281.

16. ibid., p. 367.

17. ibid., p. 330.

18. 8 October 1897.

19. *The Rescue*, pp. 9–10.

20. ibid., pp. 300–301.

21. ibid., p. 411.

22. *The Rescue*, p. 132.

23. ibid., p. 453.

24. ibid., p. 448.

25. ibid., p. 465.

26. ibid., p. 450.

27. ibid., p. 456.

28. ibid., p. 461.

29. ibid., p. 463.

30. *Victory*, p. 359.

31. cf., particularly Keppel's *Borneo*, I, p. 107 ff. and Mundy's *Borneo and Celebes*, I, pp. 30–175. Gordan, 'The Rajah Brooke and Joseph Conrad', *Studies in Philology*, XXXV, Chapel Hill, 1938, pp. 622–3.

32. S. St John's *The Life of Sir James Brooke, Rajah of Sarawak, from his Personal Papers and Correspondence*, Edinburgh, 1879, pp. 108–11. Mundy, op. cit., II, pp. 129–34 (the names are differently spelt by the various authorities). cf., *The Rescue*, pp. 81–2 and p. 442 ff.

33. This was the Ranee Margaret Alice de Windt Brooke's *My Life in Sarawak*, 1913; he took the idea for Mrs Travers's mosquito house (*The Rescue*, p. 277) from a photograph opposite p. 136. Conrad had written to tell this to the Ranee and she passed on the information to John D. Gordan who published a note on it: *Studies in Philology*, xxxvi (1940), pp. 130–32.

34. op. cit., p. 150. cf., also the same author's *Life in the Forests of the Far East*, Vol. II, 1862, pp. 185–218. In view of Conrad's precision with dates in his letter to Blackwood I suspect that he had recently been reading about Wyndham somewhere, but Sir John's books do not supply the necessary information and I have not been able to trace another source. Haji Saman was a piratical chief who was subdued by Brooke with the help of Sir Thomas Cochrane in 1846. St John, *Sir James Brooke*, pp. 113–17, and Mundy, op. cit., II, p. 213 ff.

35. Letter to Pinker, 15 October 1919.

36. Letter to Colvin, 15 October 1919 (Duke University); to Garnett, 8 December 1919.

37. Letter to Pinker, 26 March 1919.

38. Letters to Pinker, 22 November and 29 December 1919.

39. Letter to Gardiner, 5 May 1920.

40. Letters to Aubry, 31 August (*Lettres Françaises*, p. 159) and to Curle, 9 October 1920.

41. Letter to Curle, 8 December 1922.

42. Letter to Pinker, 17 June 1919, to Curle, 18–23 August 1920 and to Wise, 1 November 1920, *L.L.*, II, p. 146. The MS. is in the Keating Collection at Yale.

43. 18–23 August 1920.

44. Letter to Curle, 8 December 1922.

45. do., 26 February 1920.

46. Letters to Aubry, 17 March, *Lettres Françaises*, p. 153, and to Eric Pinker, 27 March 1920.

47. Letter to Aubry, 10 December 1920, *Lettres Françaises*, p. 162.

48. Letter to Curle, 9 October 1920 (when he had finished the last one).

49. 4 April 1920.

50. To Curle, 15 May 1920.

51. Letter to Aubry, 14 June 1920, *L.L.*, II, p. 240.

52. 17 December 1920, ibid., p. 251.

53. 16 December 1920.

54. Letter to Sandeman, 17 January 1921, *L.L.*, II, p. 253.

55. Letter to Curle, 22 January 1921; Aubry, *The Sea Dreamer*, p. 291.

56. Letter to Eric Pinker, 5 February 1921, *L.L.*, II, p. 254 and to Aubry, 23 February 1921, *Lettres Françaises*, p. 164.

57. 23 February 1921, *Lettres Françaises*, p. 164.

58. 18 March 1921.

59. Aubry, *The Sea Dreamer*, p. 292.

60. Letter to Eric Pinker, 27 June 1922.

61. *The Rover*, p. 1.

62. ibid., p. 31.

63. ibid., p. 48.

64. ibid., p. 20, p. 41.

65. ibid., p. 92.

66. 4 December 1923.

67. *The Rover*, p. 209.

68. ibid., p. 221.

69. ibid., pp. 208–9.

70. ibid., pp. 117–19.

71. ibid., p. 260.

72. 'On Re-reading *The Rover*', *The Open Night*, pp. 54–62.

73. *The Rover*, p. 116.

74. ibid., p. 17.

75. ibid., p. 82.

76. ibid., p. 147.

77. ibid., p. 286.

78. In Keating's *A Conrad Memorial Library*, p. 331, '*The Rover*', quoting an earlier article in the *Revue de Paris*.

79. *The Last Twelve Years of Joseph Conrad*, pp. 225–6.

80. 22 August 1922.

81. 30 June 1922, *L.L.*, II, p. 272.

82. 12 October 1922.

83. 8 October 1922, *L.L.*, II, p. 276.

84. 27 October 1922, *Lettres Françaises*, p. 178.

85. R. L. Mégroz, *A Talk with Joseph Conrad*, p. 31.

86. *The Times*, 3 November 1922.

87. 9 April 1923, *L.L.*, II, p. 303.

88. 19 April 1923, ibid., II, p. 304.

89. 22 April 1923, ibid., II, p. 305.

90. Appeared 15 May 1923. Reprinted as 'Ocean Travel' in *Last Essays*.

91. 'Ocean Travel', *Last Essays*, p. 36.

92. Letter to Elbridge L. Adams, 20 November 1922, *L.L.*, II, p. 283.

93. *Joseph Conrad and His Circle*, pp. 255–6.

94. Letter to Eric Pinker, 18 July 1923.

95. The first, entitled '*The Torrens*: a Personal Tribute', appeared in *Blue Peter* for October 1923; and the second appeared in the *Daily Mail* on 24 December 1923. Both were reprinted in *Last Essays*.

96. 'The Romance of Travel' in *Countries of the World*, February 1924. Reprinted in *Last Essays* as 'Geography and Some Explorers'. Letters to Curle of 2 November 1923 ff.

97. 9 July 1923.

98. To Aubry, 5 August 1923, *Lettres Françaises*, p. 186.

99. 23 October 1923, *L.L.*, II, p. 323.

100. To Eric Pinker, 7 February 1924.

101. do., 17 February 1924.

102. *The Library of John Quinn;* List of Prices.

103. Letter of 20 November 1923, *Lettres Françaises*, p. 192.

104. Letter to Garnett, 21 November 1923.

105. Letter to Aubry, 1 September 1923, *Lettres Françaises*, p. 188, and to Curle, 20 September 1923.

106. Letter to Curle, 12 November 1923.

107. *L.L.*, II, p. 330.

108. 2 January 1924, ibid., p. 331.

109. Letters to Curle, 1 February 1924, *et al.*, and undated (May 1924).

110. 26 March 1924; *L.L.*, II, p. 341.

111. loc. cit.

112. *Let There Be Sculpture; an Autobiography*, 1940, p. 91.

113. 30 May 1924, *Lettres Françaises*, p. 200.

114. Letter of 26 May 1924 from Ramsay MacDonald (Yale).

115. Letter to Doubleday, 2 June 1924, *L.L.*, II, p. 344.

116. Yale.

117. Letter to Curle, 22 July 1924.

118. *The Last Twelve Years of Joseph Conrad*, p. 226 and *Conrad to a Friend*, pp. 241–2.

119. *Joseph Conrad and His Circle*, p. 276, and Curle, *The Last Twelve Years of Joseph Conrad*, p. 232.

120. Curle, loc. cit.

121. *Kent Herald*, 13 August 1924.

122. This was first pointed out by Miss Mildred Atkinson in a letter to *The Times Literary Supplement* of 25 February 1926. Subsequently Miss M. H. Wood wrote a detailed note on the subject in *Modern Language Notes*, L (1935), pp. 390–94.

123. *Memoirs of the Comtesse de Boigne* (1781–1814), edited from the Original MS. by M. Charles Nicoullaud, 1907, I, p. 89. The at times literal similarity between passages in this edition and in *Suspense* make it probable that Conrad used the translation and not the French original.

124. *Memoirs*, I, pp. 89–90, 95 and 100. *Suspense*, pp. 19–23 and 129. In each case only the main references are given.

125. *Memoirs*, I, pp. 111–12.

126. *Suspense*, pp. 188–9 and 195.

127. *Memoirs*, II, p. 27. *Suspense*, p. 61.

128. Letter to Hueffer, 15 December 1921, Keating, *A Conrad Memorial Library*, p. 358.

129. *A Personal Record*, xxiii.

130. Letter to Colvin (apropos *The Shadow-Line*), 1 (?) March 1917, *L.L.*, II, p. 185.

131. *The Nigger of the 'Narcissus'*, x.

132. Letter to Cunninghame Graham, 31 January 1898, *L.L.*, I, p. 226.

133. cf., pp. 244–5.

134. *The Nigger of the 'Narcissus'*, x.

135. *New York Tribune*, 18 September 1927, quoted in Keating, *A Conrad Memorial Library*, p. 268.

136. *The Last Twelve Years of Joseph Conrad*, p. 34.

137. 'Reminiscences of Conrad', *Castles in Spain & Other Screeds*, 1927, p. 87.

138. *The Last Twelve Years of Joseph Conrad*, p. 32.

139. Journal for 1918, 1921 (autumn) and 1928 quoted by Rupert Hart-Davis in *Hugh Walpole*, pp. 176, 215 and 286.

140. Preface to Conrad's *Tales of Hearsay*, p. ix.

141. Curle, *The Last Twelve Years of Joseph Conrad*, p. 61; Bertrand Russell, op. cit., p. 81.

142. 'Sujet d'une Conversation avec Conrad', *Hommage à Joseph Conrad, La Nouvelle Revue Française*, Tome XXIII, 1 December 1924, p. 663.

143. *Letters from Conrad*, xix. Cunninghame Graham asserted that Conrad's foreign accent actually did become more pronounced towards the end of his life, which would explain the discrepancy. His theory was that as we become older 'the speech that we learned at our mother's knee subconsciously reasserts itself'. Preface to Conrad's *Tales of Hearsay*, p. ix.

144. Letter of 2 September 1913, quoted by E. L. Grant Watson in *But to What Purpose. The Autobiography of a Contemporary*, 1946, pp. 148–51.

145. Quoted from his journal by Rupert Hart-Davis in *Hugh Walpole*, p. 377.

146. *Castles in Spain & Other Screeds*, p. 84.

147. *The Last Twelve Years of Joseph Conrad*, pp. 52–3.

148. loc. cit.

149. Letter to Russell, 23 October 1922, quoted in *Portraits from Memory*, p. 85.

150. Letter to Garnett, 23 February (1914).

151. Letter to Garnett, 22 December 1902.

152. Letter to Cunninghame Graham, 8 February 1899, *L.L.*, I, p. 269.

153. *Portraits from Memory*, p. 82.

154. 'Anatole France', *Notes on Life and Letters*, p. 33.

155. *L.L.*, I, p. 269.

156. To Miss Capes, 22 July 1914, *L.L.*, II, p. 155.

157. To Christopher Sandeman, 21 November 1922, ibid., II, p. 286.

158. 'Stephen Crane: a Preface to Thomas Beer's *Stephen Crane*', *Last Essays*, p. 93. In his preface to *The Shorter Tales of Joseph Conrad*, *Last Essays*, p. 142, he mentions Calderon as the source of the tag. Whether he had ever read Calderon's play, *La Vida es Sueño*, is not known. Its theme is the relation between dream and reality but there is no proof that the play influenced him and he may equally well have picked the title-phrase up from a calendar.

159. 14 January 1898, *L.L.*, I, p. 222.

160. *A Personal Record*, xxi.

161. *Nostromo*, p. 66, and 'Autocracy and War', *Notes on Life and Letters*, p. 109.

162. *The Nigger of the 'Narcissus'*, viii.

163. *Typhoon*, vii.

164. 'Books' *Notes on Life and Letters*, pp. 8–9.

165. Letter to Gosse, 23 March 1905, *L.L.*, II, p. 14.

166. Letter to Arthur Symons, Monday (August 1908), *L.L.*, II, p. 73.

Index

NOTE: *Conrad's writings are indexed under the entry for Conrad himself.*

MORE ABOUT PENGUINS, PELICANS AND PUFFINS

For further information about books available from Penguins please write to Dept EP, Penguin Books Ltd, Harmondsworth, Middlesex UB7 ODA.

In the U.S.A.: For a complete list of books available from Penguins in the United States write to Dept DG, Penguin Books, 299 Murray Hill Parkway, East Rutherford, New Jersey 07073.

In Canada: For a complete list of books available from Penguins in Canada write to Penguin Books Canada Limited, 2801 John Street, Markham, Ontario L3R 1B4.

In Australia: For a complete list of books available from Penguins in Australia write to the Marketing Department, Penguin Books Australia Ltd, P.O. Box 257, Ringwood, Victoria 3134.

In New Zealand: For a complete list of books available from Penguins in New Zealand write to the Marketing Department, Penguin Books (N.Z.) Ltd, Private Bag, Takapuna, Auckland 9.

In India: For a complete list of books available from Penguins in India write to Penguin Overseas Ltd, 706 Eros Apartments, 56 Nehru Place, New Delhi 110019.

JOSEPH CONRAD

'Conrad is among the very greatest novelists in the language – or any language' – F. R. Leavis in *The Great Tradition.*

Books by Conrad available in Penguins:

LORD JIM

The novel by which Conrad is most often remembered by perhaps a majority of readers, and the first considerable novel he wrote.

THE SECRET AGENT: *A Simple Tale*

Based on anarchist and terrorist activities in London, this novel has been described by Dr Leavis as 'indubitably a classic and a masterpiece'.

VICTORY: *An Island Tale*

In his critical biography of the author, Jocelyn Baines places this tragic story of the Malay Archipelago 'among Conrad's best novels'.

THE NIGGER OF THE NARCISSUS, TYPHOON
and Other Stories

Conrad's first sea novel, together with 'Typhoon', 'Falk', 'Amy Foster', and 'Tomorrow'.

NOSTROMO: *A Tale of the Seaboard*

His story of revolution in South America, which Arnold Bennett regarded 'as one of the greatest novels of any age'.

UNDER WESTERN EYES

An atmosphere of ominous suspense hangs over this story of revolutionaries, set in Switzerland and Russia.